CUREPEDIA

For Jayne

CUREPEDIA

An A–Z of
THE CURE

Simon Price

DEYST.

An Imprint of WILLIAM MORROW

ALSO BY SIMON PRICE

Everything (A Book About Manic Street Preachers)

 DEYST.

HarperCollins books may be purchased for educational,
business, or sales promotional use. For information, please
email the Special Markets Department at SPsales
@harpercollins.com.

First published in Great Britain in 2023 by White Rabbit,
an imprint of The Orion Publishing Group Ltd.

FIRST U.S. EDITION

Endpaper artwork © 2023 by Andy Vella

Library of Congress Cataloging-in-Publication Data has
been applied for.

ISBN 978-0-06-306864-3

23 24 25 26 27 LBC 5 4 3 2 1

Foreword

Putting into words what The Cure mean to me isn't easy. I'm sure like everyone reading this, their music has played a huge and profound part in my life. They were the first band whose music really captivated me. They were the first band I ever saw live, and *Disintegration* was the first record I ever bought. I've fallen in love with many, many bands and artists in my life as a music fan, but my love for The Cure, unlike some of them, has never wavered. Their music first touched me at a time in my life when I was absolutely open to the expansive romanticism and the depth of feeling contained in their records. Through them, I discovered other wonderful musicians, poets and authors; they were a gateway to a world far bigger than the one I knew, and I'm eternally grateful for that.

One of the many things I love about The Cure is the amount of music they've made, and the mountains of trivia pertaining to every aspect of the band. As a teenage music fan, falling in love with music for the first time, finding out everything I could about the band was an essential part of the process. This was especially challenging (and fun!) In a pre-internet age. This book was made for me and the countless others like me. The Cure are easy to fall in love with and hard to forget.

The first thing that comes to mind when I think of The Cure is romance. The romance of taking the pure essence of what music must have meant to a young Robert Smith, reinterpreting it through his own lens and creating an unparalleled and continuing body of work. Their music covers every emotion from joy to despair, from hope to tragedy – sometimes even in the same song. They mirrored my burgeoning teenage romanticism. Robert's lyrics hit me hard then, and they still do. In fact, as I grew up, rather than seeming like something from my adolescence, their music just affected me in different ways. In my thirties and forties, I would find songs that meant something very specific to me as a teenager meaning something completely different later in life. It's something very special and something unique to The Cure.

The task of putting into words everything about them and what they mean seems unfathomably challenging to me, so massive kudos to Simon for undertaking and completing it so wonderfully with this book. As a band that has been going for such an unbroken length of time – staying remarkably busy, playing thousands and thousands of concerts and releasing so much music – the sheer volume of information about them and their songs must have been daunting. Simon has managed to cover every aspect of The Cure, from the foundational and the obscure, to the trivial, with great aplomb, good humour and meticulous detail.

As a music fan, I can't think of a band with such a broad and rich catalogue. As a musician, they have been a constant inspiration and beyond supportive both to my band, Mogwai, and our label mates and friends The Twilight Sad. Robert truly champions other musicians and we have really felt that over the years; he goes above and beyond in ways both seen and unseen, and unlike so many other artists from his generation, he has never let us down. He is progressive and kind in a world where divisiveness and cruelty seem to be the paths taken by many.

The Cure are extraordinary live. There is no other band on the planet that plays shows like them. Now into their fifth decade, still playing close to three hours or beyond, changing the setlist every night and right now, with what I believe is their strongest ever line up, they are on imperious form. I've been lucky enough to tour with The Cure as well as see them dozens of other times. I was fourteen when I first saw them on the 1989 Prayer Tour, and it was a life changing gig (though I think that in some way or another every time I see them). A single concert featuring 'One Hundred Years' ('It doesn't matter if we all die') and 'Friday I'm In Love' ('It's such a gorgeous sight/to see you eat in the middle of the night') shouldn't make sense, but it does. Gloriously. The Cure are great musicians, but use their craft to add to the songs, not to show off. Their punk roots at play, I'm sure.

Those punk roots were also at play in early 2023, when Robert took on the grotesque corporate live industry by making Ticketmaster return funds to over-charged fans and put a halt to their grim new tactic of basically acting as their own ticket touts to rip off ticket buyers. On their current tour, the band are playing many songs from their as yet unreleased album, *Songs For A Lost World*, and it has all the makings of one of their best. Particularly Robert tackling the grief of losing his brother head on in the song 'I Can Never Say Goodbye' – the pain and emotion so clear to see. It can't be easy, but it feels like he needed to do it. Singing with tears in his eyes before leading huge arenas in a dance party to 'Close To Me' and 'The Walk.' A huge contrast musically and, in many ways, a contradiction. A punk rock band that plays for three hours.

In many ways, that's what The Cure are: a non-stop glorious contradiction. They've always done their own thing despite whatever else is going on in the music world. They have found themselves with No.1 records and playing stadiums, then getting less attention and playing far less grand venues, only now to find themselves as popular as ever again. In fact, probably bigger, more relevant and more beloved than ever.

And beloved is what they are. Watching people watch them is almost as gratifying as watching them themselves. They mean so much to so many people. The Cure's songs are the shared stories of people's lives, and seeing them live, you can see that. Their songs have soundtracked our lives as well as Roberts. The highs and the lows are shared. The Cure don't belong just to Robert, Simon, Roger, Jason, Reeves and Perry. Or the myriad of people that have contributed to the band over the years. They belong to all of us.

I'm sure that there is more of The Cure's story yet to come, but for now this is a perfect summary of the story so far.

Enjoy.

Stuart Braithwaite, June 2023

Introduction

It turns out that writing a book about The Cure means writing a book about *everything*.

Partly, that's just how I write. I'm able to (or unable *not* to) come up with the most elaborate sociological theory about the most frivolous and disposable of pop songs. Pop does not exist in a vacuum: it is affected by – and, in turn affects – the world around it. Context is everything, and it's rarely as simple as 'music is just music'. Pop is a product of the prevailing currents of sexuality, gender, ethnicity, religion, politics, morality, aesthetics, the arts, the media, fashion, work, economics, education: all the things that make up a culture.

It helps, though, if the band in question are as culturally rich as The Cure. Their words, music, videos and artwork are deeply infused with allusions, references and echoes (some of them not even deliberate). In the course of working on this book, I have found myself disappearing down research rabbit-holes into such arcane and diverse topics as the impact of Comet Shoemaker–Levy 9 on Jupiter, the history of the Shetlands town of Uyea, what family of animals armadillos belong to, prostitution in Amsterdam, the Mythopoetic men's movement, the tenth Duke of Northumberland, the Glencoe Massacre, the Nanjing Massacre, outbreaks of Tarantism in mediaeval Italy, magical thinking in children, the Indian self-proclaimed deity Meher Baba, the dissolution of the monasteries, Turkana Boy and the practice of 'dry-pack' in Victorian asylums. (That's one of the reasons why it's taken me so long.)

When I first heard The Cure, as a child, I already perceived that there was something else going on behind the sound itself. I vividly recall lying in the grass on the school playing fields and hearing 'A Forest' on BBC Radio 1's Top 40 countdown on my radio-cassette recorder. It wasn't for me, yet. But something about it stuck with me. 'The Walk' on *Top of the Pops* was my real entry point, and by the time of *The Head On The Door* and *Standing On A Beach*, I was fully on board. The Cure were my gateway drug into alternative music, holding my hand and leading the way. I loved them. I pretended not to, for a while, partly because it seemed too on-the-nose for a goth-looking guy like me to be into The Cure, and partly to annoy Robert Smith-besotted girlfriends. But you've got to get over yourself, sometimes.

One of the bittersweet things about being a music critic, as I have been for most of my adult life, reviewing records week in, week out, is that you rarely get to live with any one artist's music for as long as you would like. From about 1990 onwards, whenever a new Cure album has come along, I've listened, enjoyed and appreciated them, but bade them farewell in the sad knowledge that my job requires me to move onto the next thing. One of the pleasures of writing this book has been in reacquainting myself with those newer records. It's also been wonderful to have a legitimate excuse to obsess over some of my favourite songs ('Just Like Heaven' and 'One Hundred Years' being the top two, for very different reasons) and write whole essays about what makes them tick.

Robert Smith, as I've said in this book, *means* something. (Exactly what he means, of course, is subtly different from what he *intended* to mean: in pop, meaning is in the mind of the receiver, the perceiver.) If you look at his face, even his silhouette, or even simply the words 'The Cure' (especially in that classic dropped-C logo), your mind is instantly flooded with associations. The word 'iconic' is over-used, but Robert Smith is genuinely an icon. Some of this book has been devoted to examining the dynamics of that. Mostly, though, it's about The Cure's body of work, and what it gives to us, emotionally and intellectually. The Cure can swell your heart, The Cure can make you dance, but The Cure are also brain-food.

I would never claim to be an expert on The Cure. The fans know more than I ever will. Much of the deepest knowledge in this book will already have slipped from my memory by the time the book is printed. But, even though this book contains facts, *so* many facts, the facts themselves are not the point. What I've aimed to do is to cross-reference, contextualise, analyse, and provide perspective. To draw unseen connections, and find parallels that are not immediately apparent. (And also, fingers crossed, to entertain.)

I hope, at the very least, that *Curepedia* gives you something to think about. Because that's what The Cure have done for me.

Simon Price, 2023

* Note on highlighting: when a word or phrase is **highlighted in bold**, it signifies that there is another *Curepedia* entry on that subject. (The only exception is Robert Smith, because almost every entry is about him anyway.)

A

A is for . . .

A Forest

If you go down to the woods today . . .

The forest exerts a powerful hold over the Western imagination, from childhood onwards. It is a zone of mystery and menace, where ungovernable forces are freely at play. In Brothers Grimm fairy tales such as *Little Red Riding Hood* and *Hansel and Gretel*, it is a place where terrible things happen to children. In Slavic mythology, the forest is the realm of Baba Yaga, the cannibalistic witch. In the 1939 film of *The Wizard of Oz*, the haunted forest – heralded by a sign reading 'I'd Turn Back If I Were You' – is where, in a disturbing scene, Dorothy is captured by the Wicked Witch's winged monkey minions.

In New Jersey folklore, the Pine Barrens are home to a winged, hooved, wyvern-like entity called the Jersey Devil. 'Pine Barrens' is also the name of a classic *Sopranos* episode in which mobsters Christopher Moltisanti and Paulie 'Walnuts' Gualtieri find themselves lost in a snowy forest, convinced that they are being hunted by the man they came there to bury. In Robert Frost's 1922 poem 'Stopping by Woods on a Snowy Evening', wherein – at least according to noted poetry analyst Meadow Soprano in another episode of that show – the slowly whitening forest represents death.

There are counter-examples. In Alan Moore's *Swamp Thing*, the combined Parliament of Trees is a benign – though vengeful – power; an idea inspired by the sacred tree Yggdrasil from Norse myth. In Tolkien's *The Lord of the Rings*, the forest of Lothlórien is an earthly paradise. In A.A. Milne's *Winnie-the-Pooh*, Hundred Acre Wood is a mostly idyllic realm of fun and adventure. In C.S. Lewis' *Chronicles of Narnia*, the Wood Between the Worlds is a magical place where the powers of the White Witch are weakened. In *Snow White*, the forest is ultimately a place of refuge from evil (even though, in an unsettling scene in Disney's 1937 adaptation of the Grimm tale, the heroine is intimidated by owls and bats, and grabbed at by creepers, branches and roots.) In Toni Morrison's *Beloved*, fugitive slave Sethe, heavily pregnant and near death, is rescued by a young white girl called Amy, a guardian angel figure who nurtures her back to health and delivers her baby.

But these are outliers. In horror and horror-adjacent film, the forest is chiefly a place where city folk have unspeakable violence inflicted upon them. In *Deliverance*, a man is raped at gunpoint by rednecks. In Sam Raimi's *The Evil Dead*, a woman is literally raped by a tree.

In Shakespeare's *A Midsummer Night's Dream*, the forest is a realm of deception and trickery where nothing is as it seems, and all manner of bizarre events occur, including Titania, queen of the fairies, having sex with a man with the head of a donkey.

In Dante's *Inferno*, the journey to hell begins in a shadowy forest, the *selva oscura*, which serves as a metaphor for straying from the path of salvation. (Incidentally, Dante's *Inferno* has been turned into a symphony by the American composer Robert W. Smith, who is just six months older than Crawley's Robert Smith.)

Even in the popular 1930s children's song 'The Teddy Bears' Picnic', the minor chord beginning of each verse contains dire warnings that 'you'd better go in disguise', 'you'd better not go alone' and that (it's) 'safer to stay at home'.

All of this shared cultural memory plays into 'A Forest' by The Cure, and informed the listener's understanding of it when they first pulled the record out of its sleeve – a creepy inverted black and white photo of woodland, taken from a low angle – and placed the needle into the groove.

'A Forest' is, in many ways, the definitive Cure song. As egregious and overused as the word has become, 'A Forest' is undeniably an iconic single. And Robert Smith had the generosity and foresight to give it a title which places it at the top of any alphabetical list of Cure singles (and, at least until 1992 B-side 'A Foolish Arrangement', of Cure songs), making it the perfect way to start this book.

Released on 28 March 1980, with 'Another Journey by Train' on the B-side (described by Robert as 'a pisstake – a way of disassociating ourselves from the previous Cure sound'), and produced by **Mike Hedges** with Robert Smith, it was the lead single from their second album *Seventeen Seconds*, and took more time to record than any other song on that album. The effort more than paid off. Despite manager Chris Parry's belief that 'A Forest' had the potential to become a hit if only it were more 'radio friendly', Smith stayed true to his own vision for the song, and it became a hit anyway, spending eight weeks on the British charts, peaking at No.31.

It's uniquely important as the song with which The Cure found their direction; the beginning of their **gothic** rock phase. Smith, in haunted, dread-infused tones, recounts a tale of being lured 'into the trees' by a spectral apparition of a girl who, we learn in the denouement, 'was never there', leaving the singer 'lost in a forest, all alone'.

On the full-length album version, **Matthieu Hartley**'s four ominous keyboard notes herald a recurring eight-note guitar motif from Smith, creating an atmospheric Am-C-F-Dm chord progression which, aside from the bridge, continues throughout the song. It's underpinned by a bassline which, **Simon Gallup** has said, was influenced by the style of Jean-Jacques Burnel of The Stranglers and which, at the end, echoes Hartley's four-note intro to provide a sense of closure and completion. Each instrument, especially Smith's guitar, is flanged to within an inch of its life. Mike Hedges once estimated that five separate flanger effects were used on 'A Forest'. And **Lol Tolhurst**'s drum pattern has an odd shuffle to its gait, as if the forest-dwelling entity that the song's protagonist so fears has a limp, and is trailing one leg through the twigs and leaves, slouching, like W.B. Yeats' rough beast, towards Bethlehem to be born. 'This is a Cure trademark,' Tolhurst tweeted during a Tim's Twitter Listening Party about *Seventeen Seconds*, 'the metronomic beat that is simultaneously rushing forward and standing still.' He added 'We were trying to get towards that motorik ideal of Can's Jaki Liebezeit, "You must play monotonous"! I wanted the drums to be like a mantra.'

'A Forest' was the first time I ever heard The Cure – fleetingly, on a Sunday evening chart rundown on Radio 1 in the spring of 1980. In that, I wasn't alone. 'A Forest' received more airplay than previous Cure singles, and by sneaking into the Top 40, and onto *Top of the Pops*, it was many British teenagers' introduction to the band. (Teenagers who weren't quite at the age for reading the *NME* or listening to **John Peel** under their bedsheets late at night.)

That *Top of the Pops* appearance (see **TV, The Cure Appear On**) was the band's first sighting on British television, and only their second in all. The clip was cut together with footage of actual forests by director Dave Hiller to create the song's basic and highly literal video.

Its live debut is likely to have been 17 November 1979 at the London School of Economics, the first official date of the Future Pastimes tour (following a warm-up in Liverpool), when they played eight new tracks. However, the show on 12 December 1979 at the Melkweg, Amsterdam (see **Red Light District**) is the first confirmed sighting of 'A Forest' on a setlist by Cure archivists, performed twice: once mid-set, and once as their final encore.

Arguably, the song wasn't originally called 'A Forest'. It had a slow and complex genesis in the public eye. As late as 8 December 1979, when The Cure played Théâtre de l'Empire in Paris for their first-ever television appearance on a show called *Chorus*, it is (mis)labelled in the on-screen captions as 'At Night', though its lyrics bear only the vaguest resemblance to the song 'At Night' which later appeared on *Seventeen Seconds* (besides the actual words 'at night') and none whatsoever to those of 'A Forest' as we know it. It consisted of curt, disjointed phrases ('speed or sleep', 'crack down chest'), and barked solitary words ('curl', 'sound'), as if improvised rather than written.

In the footage, Robert plays a more intricate guitar intro than on the minimalist recorded version of 'A Forest' (but one that he has often reprised in the live version since), Hartley's keyboards are dirtier and more distorted, and Tolhurst's drums are more traditional and four-to-the-floor.

One of the most enjoyable facets of 'A Forest' when performed live is its ever-expanding length. It's almost become a running joke between band and audience. According to devoted fan Marion Little, '**Fans** love to count the number of times Robert says 'again' in 'A Forest'. They're also always looking out for any extended version of 'A Forest' played.' By the time of **The Cure In Orange** in 1987, it had reached nine minutes sixteen seconds. At the start of the *Wish* tour in 1992, on which it was the closing song most nights, it had expanded to fourteen minutes, with Robert singing the original lyrics (as opposed to the canonical ones). By the time they played the Kilburn National Ballroom on that tour, it was seventeen minutes, according to a review in *Cure News*, and the rendition in the Long Beach Arena was said to have lasted twenty minutes (though that is possibly an exaggeration). The billowing outro was a long-standing feature by that point, as Simon Gallup recalled in *Ten Imaginary Years*. '"A Forest" was one that just used to go on . . . and on . . . The drums would stop, Robert would carry on playing guitar and I was never sure when he was gonna stop so I'd just carry on after him.' Impatient crowds will often clap rhythmically during the song's intro, increasing in speed, forcing the band to hold their nerve and start in their own sweet time. 'A Forest' is a song that must not be rushed.

On at least one occasion, the band have used the length of 'A Forest' as a tactical weapon. By the time The Cure took the stage at Belgium's Rock Werchter festival in 1981, the day's schedule was running late, and headliner Robert Palmer's road crew attempted to force The Cure offstage after only thirty minutes. The Cure retaliated by closing with one of the most famous performances of 'A Forest' in the band's history. A myth has grown up around Werchter that they played a fifteen-minute version to spite Palmer, but surviving footage shows that it was 'only' nine minutes long.

Robert, in a fetching white headband and heavy eyeliner, announces 'This is the final song because we're not allowed to play any more, because everybody wants to see Robert Palmer.' His performance is one of defiant aggression. Just when it seems to be ending, it starts up again and Smith improvises some extra lyrics in the coda, including 'parting is such sweet sorrow' from *Romeo and Juliet* and the self-aware words 'It's such a long end . . .' Simon Gallup screams 'Fuck Robert Palmer and fuck rock and roll!' before storming off. Hilariously, they leave the Belgian crowd chanting 'We want more!'. (Meanwhile, off camera, Palmer's crew are getting their revenge by throwing The Cure's equipment off the back of the stage.)

Its length isn't the only form of mutation the song has undertaken. For example, at Glasgow Barrowlands in 1984, Robert appeared to forget the lyrics and improvised instead. And in the late 1990s, including at the Bizarre Festival in 1998, the band played a much rockier, chunkier version with a straight 4/4 beat.

Then there are the remixes. Or, to be accurate, remakes. For the *Mixed Up* album, 'A Forest' had to be re-recorded for the 'Tree Mix', later released as a single in December 1990 (with the 'Shiver Mix' of '**In Between Days**' on the B-side), because the original master tapes had been lost. And there's the acoustic version, recorded for the extra disc of *Greatest Hits*, the track they chose to supply to *Q* magazine for its *Essential Glastonbury* covermount CD in 2004.

'A Forest' didn't receive universal critical acclaim on its release. Reviewing the single for *NME*, Julie Burchill described Robert Smith as 'trying to stretch a sketchy living out of moaning more meaningfully than man has ever moaned before'.

However, it has top-tier status in The Cure's body of work. It's arguably their most popular song, among their fans and also their musical peers. U2 chose The Cure's original on a covermounted CD for *Mojo* magazine called *U2 Jukebox* in 2005. 'A Forest' came first in a *Slicing Up Eyeballs* poll to rank 225 Cure songs, with 2,984 votes (one place ahead of '**Just Like Heaven**'), and second in a similar poll by *Rolling Stone*.

'A Forest' is The Cure's fifth most-**covered** song. It's been recorded dozens of times, by everyone from London crusty-goth band Creaming Jesus on their *Bark* EP (1990) to a drum & bass version by Italian artist Madaski (1998) to German techno duo Blank & Jones (2003, with a new vocal by Robert Smith himself, who also appeared in the video) to Gigi D'Agostino's electronic instrumental cover (2010) to prog rocker Steven Wilson (2010) to Paul Hartnoll from Orbital's side project 8:58, with folk group The Unthanks on vocals (2015).

The band clearly remain proud of its quality. They've performed it live over a thousand times, making it the most-played song in their repertoire. But no amount of repetition can drain the song of its richness, nor the cultural associations it conjures. When Robert Smith sings 'Running towards nothing/ Again and again and again', one hears distant echoes of *Macbeth*'s famous soliloquy which begins 'Tomorrow and tomorrow and tomorrow, creeps in this petty pace . . .' as the king contemplates the futility of existence after learning of the death of his wife, and awaits his defeat by a forest which moves (Malcolm's forces, disguising themselves as trees from Birnam Wood).

The Cure are a band whose oeuvre invites overthinking, and 'A Forest' invites it more than most. Robert Smith once told *Sounds* that the song was about an actual childhood experience, and later told *Cure News* that it was 'a childhood dream (nightmare) that came true with adolescence', prompting all manner of speculation from fans. He later asserted in *Stand and Deliver* fanzine that the childhood experience story was made up.

'It's just about a forest . . .'

A Letter To Elise

When The Cure premiered 'A Letter To Elise' at their *MTV Unplugged* performance on 24 January 1991, it was the first song from the *Wish* album to be made public. When it was released as a single on 5 October 1992, it was the third and last to be lifted from the album. As such, it can be said to have topped and tailed the *Wish* era.

You might expect, then, that it held a special place in Robert Smith's heart. Not so. He believes it was a terrible choice of third single, one made by the record company. He's also expressed regret that the video, a bog-standard performance clip made by Aubrey Powell (of album cover designers Hipgnosis, an influence on **Parched Art**) during a soundcheck at an American show, was not directed by their trusty **Tim Pope**. The song has been played live only sparingly, and did not make it on to *Greatest Hits* (though it did feature on *Galore*).

It's far from a terrible song: it's quietly lovely, a medium-paced sentimental beauty. Robert has said that the lyric is a 'stream of consciousness' full of 'diverse references', but it seems a fairly straightforward lament for a dying love affair.

> Oh, Elise it doesn't matter what you do
> I know I'll never really get inside of you
> To make your eyes catch fire the way they should . . .

(He has also said that 'the mood is generally resignation in the face of inevitable change', which seems closer to the truth.)

It has been hypothesised that Franz Kafka's *Letters to Felice* was an influence. One also inevitably thinks of Beethoven's *Für Elise* (itself something of a mystery, as it lay undiscovered until after Beethoven's death and the identity of his Elise remains uncertain). However, Robert Smith has said that the title of The Cure song is a nod to **David Bowie**'s 1969 song 'A Letter to Hermione' – his regretful, after-the-fact adaptation of a love letter he never sent to his ex-girlfriend Hermione Farthingale – and that Robert picked the name Elise from French polymath Jean Cocteau's 1929 novel *Les Enfants Terribles*, whose plot strongly features an intercepted letter. (Jean Cocteau had considerable currency in English alternative circles during the post-punk era: dream-pop trio Cocteau Twins named themselves after him, and the sleeve of The Smiths' 'This Charming Man' was a still from Cocteau's 1950 film *Orphée*.)

The single's various formats contained various mixes, but Robert preferred the original MTV version to any of them. Its B-sides were the languorous and atmospheric 'The Big Hand' and, on the twelve-inch, the lively and cryptic 'A Foolish Arrangement', something of a cult fan favourite and the name of a prominent Cure website.

'A Letter To Elise' only reached No.28 in the UK, The Cure's lowest placing for five years, and completely failed to chart in the US, somewhat vindicating Robert's opinion of its unsuitability for single release.

It would be an exaggeration to say 'A Letter To Elise' is the runt of the litter of Cure singles, but it's something of a neglected child.

A Night Like This

When is a Cure single not a Cure single? When is an album track not an album track? 'A Night Like This' occupies an interzone between the two.

The centrepiece of Side 2 of *The Head On The Door*, the song seemed to have a special status bestowed upon it, elevated above the other mere album tracks. In 1985, to The Cure fan world, it certainly felt like a single in all but name; a single *manque*.

For one thing, it had a video. Nothing special, just a standard performance clip with a few spooky tree branches silhouetted behind Boris Williams' head, but a video nevertheless. For another, in the States, Elektra circulated it to radio stations as a promo single (copies of which currently sell for about £25), and it was sufficiently well known in the US for Smashing Pumpkins to record a cover of it for the B-side of their 1996 single 'Bullet with Butterfly Wings' (see **Cover Versions Of The Cure**). And it was the closing track on 1986's *Staring at the Sea* (the CD version of *Standing On A Beach*) despite not being a single, as well as appearing on the video compilation thereof.

One can easily understand why the band might have wished to give it prominence, as it represented a deeper, richer side to *The Head On The Door* than its two frivolous official singles '**In Between Days**' and '**Close To Me**'. It moves with a lugubrious elegance, unhurried, undictated-to by the needs of pop radio. Its pace is almost identical (1bpm apart) to that of '**Charlotte Sometimes**', and its gloomy mood is not dissimilar. Unusually, for a Cure song, it features a saxophone solo (courtesy of **Ron Howe** of **Fools Dance**), adding to its sense of drama. The lyric, sung by a bereft-sounding Robert, describes a break-up happening in real time (and regretted even as it happens):

It goes dark
It goes darker still
Please stay
But I watch you like I'm made of stone
As you walk away

The song's complex heritage may offer further clues to its privileged position. It was, after all, in the set of the first proper concert by **pre-Cure band** Malice at St Wilfrid's School Hall in **Crawley** on 20 December 1976 – the only song in the set that wasn't a cover – making it their oldest-documented original song. However, it would be almost a decade until they actually recorded it. Instead, they took what Robert once described as its 'Roxymusicish' chord sequence and sped it up to create 'Plastic Passion' (the B-side of '**Boys Don't Cry**'), before eventually coming full circle and slowing it down into 'A Night Like This' as we know it. (One fan has created a mash-up of the two songs on YouTube to illustrate the point.)

Not only was 'A Night Like This' played at their first show, but it was, at the time of writing, played at their most recent at Wembley Arena on 13 December 2022, making it the longest-surviving original song in The Cure's live repertoire. It will probably be there at the very end, whenever that comes. Nobody would be surprised if to say goodbye with 'A Night Like This' is the last thing they ever do.

Adventures And Plans

Adventures And Plans was the immediate successor to *The Further Adventures Of TeamCure*, and the immediate predecessor of *Cure News*. Like *Further Adventures*, it consisted of a photocopied sheet of A4 paper with a typed diary in episodic and ellipsis-ridden form from Robert Smith.

Issue 1 (the third newsletter in all) arrived on fans' doormats in early 1986, covering the release of *The Head On The Door* and The Cure's 1985 UK tour, along with the first TeamCure five-a-side football match (see *Queens Park Rangers*) which ended in 'a humiliating 6-3 defeat'. Typical extract: '. . . then we made a french documentary about us in london and

paris (where we were poisoned!)'.

Issue 2 (the fourth newsletter in all), mailed out in late 1986, mentioned the releases of *Standing On The Beach* and the re-recorded '**Boys Don't Cry**', a festival in Holland, a boozy journey to Venice on the Orient Express, and the fact that they considered calling their as-yet-unreleased seventh album *One Million Virgins*.

By now, the content was so sparse and scant that Robert's readiness to hand over to the *Cure News* team was palpable.

Advertising

This ought to be a very short entry. After all, as Robert Smith stated categorically to Suzi Feay of the *Independent* in 1997, the band had never allowed any of The Cure's music to be used in advertising. 'I think the commercialisation of everything is really insidious and really horrible', he told her. And that, it seemed, was the truth, pure and simple.

The truth, however, is rarely pure and never simple. To begin with, one can absolutely understand Smith's distaste for the collision of commerce and music. The eighties were a period when megastars such as Michael Jackson, The Rolling Stones, Tina Turner and Sting could earn millions of dollars from appearing in adverts and/or having their tours sponsored by major corporations like Coca-Cola and Levi's. The Cure had solid reasons for eschewing such tie-ins that went far beyond a basic English disdain for the vulgarity of it all. It's near-impossible for a successful band to completely avoid such link-ups, especially when playing festivals which typically have a sponsor. And The Cure willingly played a small secret gig as part of a competition run by Miller Lite in 1998, at a time when it suited them to loosen up and get match-fit for the album (*Bloodflowers*) they were making.

A major problem with these commercial connections was that once you allowed advertisers to cross your threshold, you surrendered control over how your art would be presented, and what it would become associated with. On 16 November 1984 The Cure's show in Ontario was recorded for the King Biscuit Flower Hour, a syndicated radio show in the US. When the concert was broadcast, it was interrupted by commercial breaks featuring adverts for Reese's Peanut Butter Cups, Budweiser beer and, most appallingly, the US Army. (A double disc LP of the show, intended for circulation to radio stations, can be found for sale online, complete with those ads.) The idea that The Cure's music could be used for recruiting young listeners to be sent off to war sat uncomfortably with the band's principles.

In that pre-internet era, even the most stringent 'No' was no guarantee that your music wouldn't surreptitiously be used for commercial purposes, especially far from the watchful eye of your management. For example, at one point in the 1980s, 'The Lovecats' was used on a deodorant advert in Greece without authorisation. And Brazilian television station Globo ran unauthorised adverts connecting The Cure to Wrangler jeans, twenty times a night. 'I find it really offensive,' Robert told Johnny Black of Q magazine in 1987. 'We've never been sponsored that way. Oh, on odd one-offs we've been sponsored by beer companies. Seven thousand cans of Heineken backstage suits me fine. It's dreadful. In the minds of millions of these people, The Cure and Wrangler are now inextricably intertwined.'

For some unscrupulous advertisers there would be legal consequences. When 'Close To Me' was used in a toothbrush commercial without permission, Robert revealed in Cure News 14, the manufacturers were successfully sued. It wasn't a complete zero-tolerance policy, however . . . as long as the advertisers asked first. In 1990 Robert agreed to allow 'In Between Days' to be used in an advert for Lee Cooper jeans because he wore them. (The same song was licensed for use in a Fiat Punto ad in 2003.)

Such cases were few and far between. The one which caused Robert the most anguish was when one of his most personal – and popular – songs, 'Pictures Of You', was used in a 2007 advert for HP digital cameras. The offer came at a time when the band desperately needed a large sum of money in order to maintain control of their catalogue, as their deal with Fiction/Polydor was coming to an end. 'I'm so against music in adverts,' Robert told NME. 'It fucking killed me even agreeing to that, but it was the only way. The money generated from those adverts went into buying me control of our back catalogue, otherwise it would have been like mortgaging the band.' The advert was slightly tacky, and it jarred to hear The Cure's music used in that tawdry context, but nobody remembers it now. In the long run, for The Cure to preserve their autonomy, it was worth it.

So, The Cure never allowed their music to be used in advertising. Apart from all the times that they did.

Robert's distaste for the whole grubby business, however, didn't dissipate. 'I have the impression everything is tolerated these days,' he told Humo magazine in the 2000s. 'They've all become prostitutes. It's apparently generally accepted that artists lend their music for commercials. Sting does it, Celine Dion, Moby, even Bob Dylan . . . Fuck! That's still not done, in my eyes. I don't want Cure fans to think of toothpaste when they hear "The Walk".'

Alcohol

The Cure are not outwardly a boozy band. Alcohol isn't integral to their music. There are a few references to it in their work – the lyrics to 'The Blood' (see Head On The Door, The), 'Cut Here' and 'Fascination Street', and the title 'Cloudberry' (see Lost Wishes) – but their music isn't intrinsically calibrated for carousing. They aren't The Pogues.

However, it's never been a secret that behind the scenes there's a history of heavy drinking in The Cure camp. Obviously, there are problematic dimensions to this. Lol Tolhurst's alcoholism was undeniably a factor in his diminishing contribution to, and eventual expulsion from, the band. And Robert Smith's own lowest point, circa 1997, saw him too drunk to perform on stage. With that caveat, this section presents a selection of anecdotes – some darker, some more comedic – involving The Cure and alcohol.

'From the very beginning', wrote Tolhurst in Cured, 'I was a blackout drinker.' The recorded facts would seem to bear this out. In November 1978, after a show in the Midlands, The Cure stayed in a hotel for the first time because Polydor's top brass had come along, and bought the band drinks. Unable to pace himself, Lol ended up with his head down the toilet bowl. Later that night, sharing a room with Smith, Tolhurst vomited all over the floor and walls. In Ten Imaginary Years, Robert recalled that he thought this was 'really humiliating'.

Smith himself, however, used alcohol to smooth over social awkwardness of meeting new people, as Siouxsie Sioux confirmed to biographer Mark Paytress in 2003. 'Robert was fond of his booze, as we were,' she said, recalling Smith's first stint as a Banshee in 1979, 'and bringing him on board just accelerated the rate of our consumption . . . Alcohol was a great short cut to the immediate deep friendships that we felt we had to make with Budgie and Robert.'

Meanwhile, Lol's drinking on tour continued to escalate. On 8 October 1979, after a gig in Hull on the Banshees/Cure tour, Lol went missing. Smith and **Steve Severin** became deeply concerned, and went searching the banks of the River Humber using cigarette lighters to illuminate the way. After following a trail of empty bottles, they found him asleep in the bulrushes, refusing to move. They left him there to sleep it off.

In December that year, on a Cure trip abroad, Lol became so uncontrollable after a session of red wine binge-drinking in Eindhoven that, to cut a long story short (see **Pissing**), Robert ended up urinating in Lol's suitcase. 'It was very scary,' said Lol later, 'but I didn't see the connection between my alcohol intake and that dark depressed feeling I carried around with me afterwards, which made me want to drink even more.'

The studio, as well, became a notable venue for band drinking. Witnesses to the making of *Pornography* in 1981 and 1982 speak of a floor-to-ceiling mountain of empty cans and bottles, setting in place a tradition of alcohol-assisted recording that continued through most Cure sessions thereafter. Smith once blamed alcohol for the entire '**Lovecats**' project: 'Composed drunk, video filmed drunk, promotion made drunk! It was a joke.'

And his alcoholic antics often spilled over into more public settings. As he told *NME*, Robert once when inebriated bet a friend that he could go around the outside of a hotel by jumping from balcony to balcony. 'It took about an hour,' he recalls. 'And once I got to a certain point it seemed farther to go back to where I could hear **Mary** screaming. It was lamentable, like one of those *Beavis and Butt-Head* "I bet you can't do that" things.'

Smith was not, however, much of a pub man. As he told *Flexipop!* in 1982, he preferred drinking at home with Mary. 'A great joy is making up cocktails. I mix all sorts of drinks together. Milk cocktails are always best – they sit very well on your stomach. One of the worst I ever invented was called "Dennis the Menace" – it gave me the most chronic hangover I've ever had in my life. It had about seventeen different drinks in it, all mixed up in a pint mug.' (Self-invented cocktails were something of a hobby for Smith: another was the Oracle, inspired by Teletext.)

A culture of excess was becoming normalised by the mid-eighties. In 1986, according to Tolhurst

during his later **lawsuit** against the band, the band and their wives and girlfriends took a ride on the Orient Express and ran up a bar tab of between £1,500 and £2,000. (Although, for ten people, at Orient Express prices, this may not have amounted to a huge volume of alcohol . . .)

The recording sessions for *Kiss Me, Kiss Me, Kiss Me* (1986–87) and *Disintegration* (1988–89) were famously boozy, and – for Tolhurst's Cure career – catastrophically so. But Tolhurst wasn't the only heavy drinker within the band: when asked by *Cure News* in 1988 how many hours a day **Simon Gallup** drank, Robert quipped '25'. In the same publication in 1989, Smith listed his favourite drinks as including red wine, Kirin lager, Bud, Guinness, Bloody Mary and milk. By the end of 1990 he admitted often being drunk before going onstage.

The *Wish* campaign of 1992 was no less liquor-drenched. The topic came up in the thirteenth issue of *Cure News*. **Perry Bamonte** confirmed that Robert was drinking red wine with orange juice (a very basic form of sangria) onstage, and that Perry also did this, whereas **Porl Thompson** preferred his red wine straight. Simon had given up spirits and was only drinking lager (preferring Becks or Fosters), while only **Boris Williams** eschewed booze altogether. 'My worst habit is drinking', Robert admitted, but he had no plans to give up. There's a moment in *Play Out*, filmed that year, when Simon gives Robert a bottle of pear schnapps called Poire Williams, an eau de vie (colourless fruit brandy, often with a whole pear in the bottle) as a gift. Gallup himself, when asked by Johnny Black in 1994 which subject he would choose if he were a contestant on *Mastermind*, answered 'drinking, or the works of Patrick White', and acknowledged that 'one of my hobbies is drinking'.

In 1997, speaking to Suzi Feay in the *Independent*, Robert attempted to rewrite history. 'The group has a reputation for excess, and it has been justified. We were drunkards for quite long periods of time and the group has always been sociable, which doesn't really fit in with what we're supposed to be like. But there have been members of the group who've drunk to excess too often, and it's reduced them to jelly, which is what happened with Lol. I had one last fling in 1989, the year I turned 30.' In reality, 1989 was far from a 'last fling'. Indeed, The Cure's lowest point of 1997 and 1998 was largely alcohol-induced. (And the following year, they had no problem in associating themselves with Miller beer for a promotional gig at London's Forum.)

By 2013, though, those days of drink-fuelled insanity were long behind him, and Robert was able to view his drinking past with a certain perspective. 'I had some kind of road to Damascus experience drink-wise when I was 14,' he told the *Guardian*, 'and it was at the bottom of a glass. In the past, I didn't really give a shit about what I was saying, so I would just be drunk all the time. The only way I could get through a day of interviews was to have two drinks with every interview.'

Smith does, on the whole, seem to have a sensible, balanced and circumspect view of alcohol and its benefits and drawbacks. He doesn't consider drinking to be an evil, nor does he consider blackout drunkenness big or clever. When asked a question in *Cure News* about whether The Cure's frequent discussion of booze may have an effect on their fans, Robert replied: 'I am a bit concerned about the question's correlation/association between alcohol and alcoholism. The two do not inevitably go hand in hand. But hey! Be careful out there . . .'

All Cats Are Grey

The idea that **drug** culture has played an important role in The Cure is not a controversial one. What's perhaps less well known, however, is that The Cure had an important role in drug culture.

On the face of it, the song seems an unlikely contender to soundtrack the dropping of an E. The funereal final track on Side 1 of *Faith*, The Cure's 1981 **gothic** masterpiece, it seems to come from a place of deep depression. It is said to have been partly inspired by the *Gormenghast* novels of Mervyn Peake, and in *Cure News*, Robert Smith explained it as being 'Just a nightmare of being lost/trapped in caves – echoes of the grave and of prison cells and again of growing old.'

Although the lyrics – seemingly about drifting slowly towards death with no particular drama or ceremony – are officially credited to Robert, **Lol Tolhurst** has claimed some input, telling Tim's Listening Party that 'All Cats Are Grey' was somewhat about his mother's death. It's a track to which Tolhurst is clearly attached (his post-Cure band **Levinhurst** covered it), and that is fitting: his gently dolorous keyboards make it what it is.

For the song's connection to ecstasy, we turn to Marc Almond, with whom The Cure shared many things, including a string section (see **Venomettes**) and the writing credits for Marc and the Mambas' song 'Torment' (see **Collaborations**). Famously, Marc Almond and his Soft Cell partner Dave Ball are thought to be the first British people ever to have taken ecstasy, on a trip to New York. And, almost as famously, they did so not to some piece of thumping NYC techno music, but to the sound of one of The Cure's most beautifully morose moments, coming up at the exact moment when 'All Cats Are Grey' was playing, as Marc told me during an interview for the *Quietus* in 2015.

'It [ecstasy] was a very new thing. There was me, the journalist Adrian Thrills, Cindy Ecstasy [Soft Cell's dealer who they once snuck onto *Top of the Pops* by getting her to duet on 'Torch'], Dave Ball and a few other people. And Cindy Ecstasy was the ecstasy girl of New York. I'd never heard of it before in my life, and it was my third or fourth night in New York, and she said "Come round my house, I want to give you something special". So I did, and it was an amazing experience. I remember the record that was playing was *Faith* by The Cure. And I know it sounds weird, but 'All Cats Are Grey' is the most perfect ecstasy record. Whenever I hear that now, instantly it's like I'm on ecstasy. It was very pure then, not cut with anything, and hadn't become the love-thug drug it later became. I love all that, how it turned thugs into love-thugs . . .'

If you take it out of its *Faith* context, and turn a deaf ear to the bleak lyrical content, Marc has a point. 'All Cats Are Grey' is strangely conducive to a cuddle puddle. The chords don't go where you initially expect them to, easing into a major when you're anticipating a minor. It's oddly comforting, like slipping into a warm bath (and without razor blades to hand).

E is for . . . All Cats Are Grey.

Allen, David M.

David M. Allen is the English record **producer** responsible for producing or co-producing every Cure album from 1984 through to 1992, the entire imperial phase of what is generally considered the band's 'classic' **line-up**. He was to The Cure's pop years what **Mike Hedges** was to their **goth** years.

Allen, not to be confused with Gang of Four/ Shriekback bassist Dave Allen, was born in Twickenham in 1959 and began his career while still a teenager, his first released work being a novelty single called 'Monster Ball' by Screaming Lord Sutch. He also helped engineer Devo's 1977 cover of The Rolling Stones' 'Satisfaction' aged just eighteen. Allen's first permanent job came in 1980 when he was hired as an understudy to Martin Rushent at his Genetic Studios in Berkshire, where one of his earliest tasks was to assist Rushent in making the various drum machines and synthesisers 'talk' to each other (a difficult task in those pre-standardisation, pre-MIDI days) to create the Human League's classic 1981 album *Dare*. He also worked on records by Altered Images, Tenpole Tudor and Dead or Alive before beginning his long relationship with The Cure.

As The Cure's most-trusted producer in their eighties glory years, he produced an unbroken sequence of classic albums, from *The Top* through *The Head On The Door, Kiss Me, Kiss Me, Kiss Me* and *Disintegration* to *Wish*, as well as working on the live album *Concert* and live movie *The Cure In Orange*.

Pictures of Allen – nicknamed Dirk by the band – behind a mixing desk in the eighties show him with a shock of black hair, but he is now grey, bearded and wizardly, not unlike his predecessor Hedges. And, like Hedges, he has an impressive CV. In addition to his work with The Cure, he was a prolific collaborator with many other alternative pop and rock acts, including **Associates**, The Sisters of Mercy, The Damned, **Depeche Mode**, The Mission, The Psychedelic Furs and Wire.

In 2010, in an interview with BBC 6 Music's Andrew Collins, he spoke of the long, slow end of his tenure as The Cure's producer. 'The creative working agreement or working relationship between me and Robert was broken by *Disintegration*', he said. (He also claimed it was he, not Robert, who saved the satchel of lyrics from the studio fire.) Though he produced the next album, *Wish*, he was frustrated with the pace of progress, and recommended they should get someone else in to mix it. He did not work on the next album, 1996's *Wild Mood Swings*, at all. However, he remained close to Cure world, physically at least, running his company Blank Multimedia from the same building as **Fiction** and **Xfm** between 1995 and 1997. Interestingly, in the 6 Music interview, he would not rule out working with The Cure again.

In 2014 and 2015 Allen released two albums with The Magic Sponge, a band he formed with Tim Whelan (Furniture/Transglobal Underground), on which he is credited as 'Sweet Faggy Allen'. In 2016,

Allen launched his own boutique studio, Studio 7, in Tottenham with Laurence Loveless, and shipped over Krautrock legend Conny Plank's handmade mixing desk 'The Plank' from Cologne. The desk, which was used to record Kraftwerk's *Autobahn* and Ultravox's *Vienna* among others, has proven popular with British acts including Hot Chip, Clean Bandit, Franz Ferdinand and Years and Years. In 2022, he released his first solo album, *The DNA of DMA*, on Record Store Day, consisting of songs written and produced in 1980 which landed him the job at Genetic in the first place, using many of the same methods and machinery later heard on *Dare*.

Even if the first thing people ask Allen about will always be his past with The Cure, Allen himself has never stopped looking towards the next thing.

alt.end

'alt.end' (all lowercase) is a keyboard shortcut most often used to move to the last cell of a column in a Microsoft Word table. It's also the name of the ninth track on 2004's *The Cure*, released as a **US**-only single.

An indie-dance track sonically similar to Happy Mondays' 'Kinky Afro', it's a break-up song where the break-up is blessed relief rather than traumatic: 'It's a big bright beautiful world out there/Just the other side of this door . . .'

Directed by the Saline Project (as was its sister single '**Taking Off**'), the video for 'alt.end' shows Robert writing up one of his **dreams**, as he is known to do in real life (see **Flexipop!**), then disappearing into a forest to find a spooky girl (even the most casual of Cure fans will get the reference the Salines were making here). The colour palette is the same as on 'Taking Off', but the imagery is far richer: an upside-down Empire State Building, a couple ballroom dancing in a burning house, an Icarus-like angel trapped in a spider's web, and so on.

The single's artwork (drawn by Robert's niece Evie; the cover for *The Cure* was drawn by all his nieces and nephews) depicted a terrifying face with one red eye and one white eye. Like 'Taking Off' (which wasn't released in the US), the B-sides to 'alt.end' are '**Why Can't I Be Me?**' and 'Your God Is Fear'. Released on 18 October 2004, the same date as its rest-of-the-world counterpart, it did not chart.

This, however, came as no surprise: The Cure's career as an American chart act had alt.ended some eight years earlier.

And Also The Trees

The career of Worcestershire post-punk band And Also The Trees is so tightly interwoven with that of The Cure that the latter will always be the elephant in the room whenever the former are mentioned.

Formed in 1979 by two sets of brothers, Justin and Simon Huw Jones and Graham and Nick Havas, the ethereal, gothic-inflected quartet began performing live in 1980, and in the same year sent a homemade demo tape to The Cure. The two bands struck up a friendship, and in November and December 1981 And Also The Trees supported The Cure on a six-date UK tour, by which time original bassist Graham Havas had been replaced by Steven Burrows.

The first musical collaboration between The Cure and AATT camps came immediately after that tour. And Also The Trees' debut album *From Under The Hill*, a cassette-only release that was initially limited to 200 copies, was produced by Robert Smith and **Mike Hedges** in December 1981 at Hedges' Playground Studios, just two months after The Cure themselves had recorded '**Charlotte Sometimes**' there. Their full debut album *And Also The Trees*, featuring several of the songs from that Smith/Hedges-produced cassette, was produced by **Lol Tolhurst** at Crass' studios with engineer David Motion and Lol himself on keyboards, and released on Reflex Records in 1984.

The perception that And Also The Trees were The Cure's pet band (a status they maintained until they were replaced, in the nineties, by **Cranes**) gave their popularity a modest boost, their biggest success coming with the EP *A Room Lives in Lucy*, which reached No.30 in the UK Independent Chart in 1985 (ironically, with no input from any Cure members).

When Robert Smith was asked in 1987 what had happened to them since their collaboration with Lol, he joked, 'They escaped him.' However, only a few years later, Smith himself was helping them out again, when he and *Mixed Up* producer **Mark Saunders** devoted twelve hours (as reported in *Cure News*) to mixing the 7-inch and 12-inch versions of AATT's single 'The Pear Tree'. Thereafter, The Cure's involvement in their recordings ceased.

In the twenty-first century, Simon Huw Jones moved to Geneva where he formed an act called November with Bernard Trontin of The Young Gods and pursued a parallel career as a professional photographer. Justin Jones, meanwhile, formed an ambient dub act called Gods of Luxury, and in 2014 played guitar on a Marc Almond track called 'Impermanence'.

And Also The Trees, with only the Jones brothers remaining from the original line-up, have released albums sporadically and continue to tour. On a few occasions, specifically a trio of special Christmas shows at Hammersmith Apollo in 2014, they have even supported their old friends The Cure.

When interviewed by post-punk.com a month after those shows, Simon Huw Jones reflected on the wildly differing fortunes of the two bands since they first became acquainted. 'Well, I admit it was difficult not to ponder on that once or twice and I suppose the freaky thing is realizing the gulf between their popularity and ours. They have six and a half million Likes on Facebook, for example, and without advertising anywhere can sell out three nights at the Apollo in less than an hour by just announcing it. Impressive. They have written some fine albums and some excellent singles and that once-mighty force that was the music industry swept them up and out of sight, almost . . . but I don't reckon that was ever meant to happen to us . . . It couldn't have for the simple reason that we're not much cop at writing singles and Robert is a bit of a genius at it.'

(For those people to whom this level of information about And Also The Trees is simply not enough, a book called *The Live Chronicles Volume I, 1980–2005* by Achim Jöhnk was published in 2022, with a foreword by Steven Burrows.)

Anderson, Andy

When asked by *Cure News* to describe his former drummer Andy Anderson in one word, the word Robert Smith chose was 'unpredictable'. His life story bears that out.

Clifford Leon 'Andy' Anderson was born on 30 January 1951 to an Afro-Caribbean family in London. His father was a boxer and a part-time jazz drummer at Ronnie Scott's, his mother a singer in a vocal group, and he and his siblings would jam in the hallway in this highly musical household, his eldest brother Colin playing an improvised bass made of a tea chest, broom handle and twine, his middle brother Winston playing piano. A very versatile drummer – he was also skilled on orchestral timpani and kettle drums – he cited Kenney Jones of Small Faces, Mitch Mitchell of Jimi Hendrix Experience and Keith Moon of The Who as his primary influences. He was already a veteran when he was drawn into The Cure's orbit, having made a living as a session musician on jingles and television commercials as well as playing in several bands in the space rock and prog genres. His first release was the album *Xitintoday* by Hawkwind spin-off Nik Turner's Sphynx (on which he is credited as Android Anderson), which was followed by two albums with Gong member Steve Hillage and another with Gong offshoot Mother Gong.

However, he was also active in the new wave scene, playing with M, Techno Twins, Sham 69's Jimmy Pursey and, perhaps most importantly, Brilliant, the alternative funk band formed by Youth from Killing Joke whose 'Coming Up for the Downstroke', co-written by Anderson, appeared on the Batcave compilation *Young Limbs and Numb Hymns*, bringing him into the world of **Goth**. An Anderson-penned song, 'Death Drive', was also recorded by Batcave stalwarts Specimen on a live album.

While his forays into the Batcave would have put him on the radar of Messrs Smith and **Severin**, it was the space rock side of his CV which made Anderson a perfect fit for the two Cure-related projects for which he is best-known: the psychedelic *Blue Sunshine* by **The Glove**, and The Cure's equally lysergic *The Top*.

When The Cure needed a new drummer (**Lol Tolhurst** having decided to move sideways to keyboards) Robert Smith and **Chris Parry** tracked Anderson down at Trident Studios where he was recording with Brilliant. Anderson was already an admirer, having fallen in love with 'A Forest', and the feeling was evidently mutual, as they told him they liked his drumming with Hillage, Pursey and Brilliant. They handed him a cassette to listen to, and invited him to audition. He got the job that day.

Anderson's first public appearances with The Cure were to promote records with which he had no involvement. The first was on 18 March 1983 when the band, now depleted to a duo, needed a drummer and a bassist to perform live on BBC **television**'s *Oxford Road Show*. Anderson was brought in, as was SPK bassist **Derek Thompson**, for the two-song set of '**One Hundred Years**' and 'The Figurehead', both

from the previous year's *Pornography*. Next came a pair of appearances on *Top of the Pops* in July 1983 to mime to '**The Walk**' alongside bass-mimers **Porl Thompson** (first appearance) and **Phil Thornalley** (second appearance), both of whom, like Anderson, hadn't played on that record either. Later that year, however, he returned to *Top of the Pops* with a song on which he actually played: '**The Lovecats**'.

When asked by Radio 1's David 'Kid' Jensen to summarise the virtues of their new member, Smith described Anderson as 'more a free-range drummer than a freelance drummer – a very inventive drummer'. He showed that inventiveness on '**The Caterpillar**', on which the sound of butterfly wingbeats is simulated by Anderson slapping his leather trousers. Using more conventional drumming, his performance on tracks like 'Give Me It' is spectacular.

His contributions to *The Top*, the one Cure studio album on which he appeared, were narcotic as well as musical. As Robert told the *Guardian*'s Dorian Lynskey in 2018, Anderson 'used to make a huge pot of magic mushroom tea (see **Drugs**) at the start of every day and it just went on from there.'

His position with The Cure made him the obvious choice to play drums with The Glove, and it helped that he'd already met Steven Severin and the Banshees already. 'It's a shame we didn't do more,' he told the website A Pink Dream. 'I liked the music on that album [*Blue Sunshine*] a lot. It was a great period musically for us all, and was great fun being a part of it.'

The first fruits of Anderson's work on *The Top* were showcased with a Richard Skinner session (see **Peel Sessions**) in February 1984, another *Oxford Road Show* appearance later that month and Channel 4's *The Tube* in April, before the campaign to promote the album's lead single 'The Caterpillar' began at *Top of the Pops*. The tour to promote *The Top*, however, was ill-fated for Anderson.

The UK leg ran smoothly enough, with the Hammersmith and Oxford dates immortalised on *Concert: The Cure Live*, but when the tour moved abroad, the wheels started to come off. On 18 May 1984, after a show at Théâtre de Verdure in Nice, a sequence of events unfolded in the corridors of a five-star hotel which almost resulted in Anderson becoming a prisoner of the French state. As Lol Tolhurst, talking to *Mojo*, remembered: 'We came back late at night to our very nice hotel. He was walking down the corridor with a boombox on his shoulder, mirror shades on and paramilitary gear. The hotel security challenged him, he told them he was staying there, went to get his key out of his pocket. The security guy thought he was going to do something else, and maced him.' The guard, by all accounts, leapt to assumptions on seeing a black man roaming the plush premises, didn't bother with a verbal challenge, asked no questions, and skipped straight to the macing.

'Andy, understandably, went on the rampage and hammered a door in', Robert told Steve Sutherland in *Ten Imaginary Years*. 'Well, unfortunately, the mayor's daughter just happened to be having an illicit affair with some bloke behind that very door so we had to smuggle Andy out of France in a truck.' A rival version of the story goes that after spending a night in a police cell, Anderson was released without charge on condition that The Cure left town. Either way, the tour continued two days later in Bologna without any cancellations.

The problems escalated again when touring resumed in **Australasia** in September and October. 'The tension on that tour was rife', as Phil Thornalley told Cure biographer Jeff Apter. 'It was very strange and very sad.' These tensions flared after a show at the Hordern Pavilion in Sydney on 12 October. 'He was drinking too much,' Robert told Sutherland. 'I had a big stand-up row with him in a club which turned into a real ruck. It was just one of those arguments that takes place in clubs at two in the morning. Y'know, "You don't give me enough space, man" nonsense. I never really understood it, but I was constantly having to reassure him which I eventually got really fed up with.'

Only three days later, a short three-date tour of **Japan** began. That's when things got even worse for Anderson. The final night, 17 October 1984 in Tokyo, would be his last-ever Cure gig, and the final song of the third encore – 'The Lovecats' – would be the last song he would play with them.

'After the shows,' Robert recalled in *Ten Imaginary Years*, 'I went out to this club with Andy and, again, he went completely berserk. We went back to the hotel and he just went on the rampage. It was about 4.30 in the morning and I was feeling a bit sake'd up so I just said goodnight and went to bed.'

The Cure were staying on a floor sealed off from other guests by security guards. Anderson became embroiled in a fight with one of them. Robert woke to find the police there, with an officer outside every band member's door. 'Apparently,' he told *Mojo* later,

'Andy had attacked Phil, Bill [Chris Parry], Mac [crew member], security guards, anyone . . . He'd just been running through the hotel beating people over the head. He'd just taken the place apart.' Physical force was needed to calm him down, as Lol Tolhurst told Jeff Apter. 'We had a German tour manager, Jade Kniep, who had spent some time in the military, which was fortunate as he was able to restrain Andy so he couldn't hurt himself or others.' Smith found Anderson locked in his room, and was warned by a policeman 'Look out! Wild man in there!' It fell to Robert to tell Andy his tour was over. 'Obviously he wasn't very happy about it but he said, "I respect you, you're the only one who's dared to come and see me".' Arrangements were made to send him home, and The Cure never saw him again. Meanwhile, **Vince Ely** from The Psychedelic Furs was brought in with just five days' notice to fulfil The Cure's imminent American dates.

Looking back on Anderson's stint, Lol Tolhurst told *Mojo*, 'People said to us, 'Oh, you should get Andy, he's a really good drummer', but nobody told us that if we went on the road with him for too long, he went crazy. People who had worked with him before asked us afterwards, "Oh yeah, did he go mental?" Oh, thanks . . .'

Much of the discussion around Andy Anderson – that he was 'unstable', that he was 'mental', and so on – plays into a certain narrative, the 'angry black man' trope. But on many occasions Anderson had cause to be angry.

As a black musician in the overwhelmingly white world of alternative rock, there is no question that Anderson encountered obstacles that few of his peers could comprehend. (It's notable that one of Anderson's first post-Cure projects was Dr Love with Zeke Manyika of Orange Juice, one of the very few contemporaries who could relate to Andy's experience.) Nor is there much doubt that whatever personality traits and mental health issues Anderson already had, these were exacerbated by the behaviour of others towards him. The mace-first, ask-questions-later security guard in Nice was almost certainly motivated by racism, and Robert has acknowledged that similar factors may have played into Anderson's meltdown in Japan. 'There was definitely some issues with racism,' Smith told Alexis Petridis of *Mojo*. 'We were sort of oblivious to it, but when we went to places like Japan, you'd notice things, people's attitudes, how difficult it was for him to get served in clubs. I think it really got to him, it made him frustrated and angry and his behaviour changed as a result.'

The Cure did challenge racist attitudes towards Andy when they encountered them. When asked by A Pink Dream to name his fondest memory of The Cure, Anderson answered, 'Robert and the band being asked, backstage in an interview before a gig in Germany, whether the reason for having a black guy in the band was to do with the fact that at the time we all wore mainly black clothes with silver and white shirts. The whole band said nothing, looked at each other in disbelief, and ended the interview there and then.'

A tremendously talented drummer, Andy Anderson's services were always in demand, even if he was never in one job for very long. After his dismissal from The Cure he worked with a hugely impressive and eclectic list of artists including Iggy Pop, Jimmy Somerville, Peter Gabriel, Midge Ure, the Gun Club, Edwyn Collins, Isaac Hayes, The Last Poets and Mike Oldfield.

In later years he worked on solo projects under the names Prime Data and Front and Centre, making what he described as 'a mixture of house, dubstep, drum & bass and trance', as well as 'trying to create the ultimate pop single and album.'

The nearest he came to a rapprochement with The Cure was a stint with **tribute band** The Cureheads, with whom he parted company after only four months in 2012 when he failed to turn up to the airport for a South American tour. He never went to see the real Cure after leaving them. 'I'm aware of their albums and singles, tours etc.,' he told A Pink Dream, 'but have not been to any as yet. It's good to see the lads are still going strong and doing well.' He clearly held no grudge, and remained friends with Cure crew member **Gary Biddles** and with Lol Tolhurst, even playing in Lol's band **Levinhurst**.

On 17 February 2019 Anderson announced on Facebook that he had Stage 4 terminal cancer. 'No boo-hooing here, just be positive,' he wrote. 'For me it's just another life experience and hurdle that one has to make. . .' Clifford 'Andy' Anderson died on 26 February, just nine days after the announcement. He is the only Cure member to have passed away.

Robert Smith's one-word summary was spot-on. The life and career of Andy Anderson was many things, but it was never predictable.

Animation (band)

We can argue all day about what **Goth** means, and whether The Cure were ever really it, but there can be no question marks over the gothness of Animation. Not to be confused with 'Obsession' hitmakers Animotion, Animation was a project formed by the young Leon Muraglia. Their sole EP, *Frame One* (tracks: 'Secret Life', 'Genevieve', 'Foreign Lands') came out in 1982 as the second and final release on Robert Smith and **Ric Gallup**'s label **Dance Fools Dance** (following the split **Obtainers** and **Mag/Spys** single in 1979). Its ominous bassline, flanged guitar and booming melodramatic vocals tick many Goth boxes, and bear the hallmarks of someone who had definitely heard *Seventeen Seconds* and *Faith* (not to mention several Bauhaus and Banshees records).

This archived quote from Muraglia, now vanished but preserved by the blog *Indepthmusic*, tells a little of the Animation story. 'I played a bit with The Obtainers at school, I knew Robert Smith through The Cure's **Porl Thompson**, who worked at L&H Cloake in town (the record shop). He lived round the corner from me, so I'd often pop round on a Sunday and sit and talk – sounds a bit weird, I know! And sometimes he'd invite me in and give me a guitar to play. He ended up producing and putting out the *Frame One* 7-inch on his label, Dance Fools Dance in 1982. We pressed 500 singles, which Smith left in the back of his **car** (a white Vauxhall VX1800 estate) for a few sunny days when he went on a drinking binge with **Steve Severin** of **Siouxsie And The Banshees** so half of them were badly warped.'

In *Ten Imaginary Years*, Robert told his side of the story. 'It was a bit of a disaster. They'd been playing for two years in Crawley and they couldn't get any other gigs. I thought, if they had a record out, people might take them more seriously but it was terrible and they broke up, so I decided my forte wasn't in that side of the record business after all!'

Many years later, a Leon Muraglia surfaced in Oslo as a kosmische musician, and made an album in 2015 called *Ubi Bene* with Hans-Joachim Roedelius of Cluster and Harmonia. Whether it's the same Leon Muraglia is unclear, but it needs to be noted that one of the tracks is called 'There Is A Huge Duck Standing Right Behind You'.

AOL Sessions

In the days when globally livestreamed concerts still felt like an exciting novelty, The Cure played an AOL Sessions gig on 7 June 2004 at Olympic Studios in London. The AOL Sessions, officially titled Sessions@ AOL, were comparable, in terms of being a promotional tool via a worldwide broadcaster which could reach an international audience in one quick and easy hit, to the *MTV Unplugged* session a decade earlier. (Other bands to perform AOL Sessions included Blondie, My Chemical Romance and Scissor Sisters.)

The **line-up** of Robert Smith, **Simon Gallup**, **Porl Thompson**, **Perry Bamonte** and **Jason Cooper** played a thirty-three minute, seven-song set on a soundstage with no live audience except the viewers at home, the setlist ranging from then-current tracks like '**The End Of The World**' to classic hits like '**Lovesong**' and '**Just Like Heaven**', via fan-fave deep cuts like '**One Hundred Years**'. Surviving footage includes arty overhead shots of the tops of the band's heads, as they stood on patterned red rugs, and the session also involved a brief interview.

The tracks were available individually and as a downloadable bundle on iTunes and, though never officially available as a physical product, the session has been released as an illegal **bootleg** dozens of times.

Argentina

On Tuesday 17 March 1987, The Cure began their first ever South American tour with two nights at Estadio Ferro Carril Oeste, a sports stadium in the Caballito district of Buenos Aires. These shows have gone down in Cure and Argentinian folklore due to the ugly scenes of **violence** that took place at both shows.

The Cure were the first international band to have played at the Ferro Carril Oeste. But they weren't just any international band. They were a *British* band. It was only five years since Britain and Argentina were locked in conflict in the Falklands War, after authoritarian dictator General Leopoldo Galtieri and his murderous military junta ordered the invasion of the islands that Argentinians call Las Malvinas. In the interim, Argentina had made a shaky return to democracy, but there was nevertheless an unmistakable edge to an English rock group playing a concert in Buenos Aires.

Smith, however, was sceptical about media coverage which focused on the geopolitical angle. 'It got distorted because it was Argentina and we're English or British. People thought there was some sort of political overtone to it.' Robert played down the importance of their nationality. 'I think the riots in Argentina would have happened whoever the band was. They'd printed too many tickets. It was nothing to do with us.'

This overselling, certainly, was the catalyst for the trouble. The promoters, one version of the story goes, had sold 30,000 tickets for a 15,000-capacity venue each night. One report even had the numbers at 110,000 and 60,000, but Robert, in a tour diary written for *Melody Maker*, said it was more like 19,000 and 17,000. Associated Press estimated that 23,000 managed to get in.

From the moment they arrived in Argentina, The Cure were greeted like gods. 'For the Argentine public it was a unique event', wrote journalist Oscar Jalil in a superbly thorough 2013 article for *Rolling Stone* and *La Nacion*, 'an Anglo group that arrived at a local stadium at its artistic and popular peak.' As Robert wrote of their journey from the airport, 'there are people everywhere, and we are followed all the way into the city by a bizarre motorcade of horn-blowing-screaming-waving cars'.

If they'd spoken to their old friends **Siouxsie And The Banshees**, they might have had some inkling of what was about to unfold: the Banshees had played in Argentina four months earlier and been drenched in spit for the full ninety minutes of the show, because audiences thought that's how you're meant to behave at a punk concert.

When the day of the concert arrived – a 'hot and dreadfully sunny' day, Smith wrote – there was a febrile atmosphere around the stadium. Local tour manager Fabian Couto, speaking to Jalil, recalled seeing fights outside the venue, and hearing 'an infernal yelling'. One rumour even had it that a rival promoter had paid *barras bravas* (football hooligan firms) to go along and instigate trouble.

The set by support act La Sobrecarga passed off without incident, but it was in the ninety-minute interval that what a police report in *Pelo* magazine described as an 'unstoppable escalation of violence' began. Fans, many of them with tickets but refused entry due to the show being oversold, began breaking in through roofs, fences and walls (one of which was demolished completely). The overcrowding in the stalls forced other audience members to breach a barbed-wire fence and run onto the field. Police reacted by trying to violently repel the crowd, and the crowd fought back with stones, sticks, belts and pieces of metal. A pitched battle erupted, and three police dogs were beaten to death. Thirty people were badly trampled, and a local newspaper the next day, under the headline 'Crónica de la Violencia', printed photos which showed injured people being carried away on makeshift stretchers. Meanwhile, outside the stadium, a hot-dog vendor died of cardiac arrest when his van was attacked by a mob.

Promoter Daniel Grinbank took the stage to appeal for calm, 'because otherwise no more outside groups will come' and play here. His plea had little effect. Eventually, it became clear that the only way to calm things down was for The Cure to actually start the show. Grinbank ordered the band to be ushered onstage. 'I never saw musicians so afraid before going out to play,' Couto told Jalil. But Smith told his band they had to step up and perform.

Just over a week later in Rio de Janeiro, Robert spoke to Johnny Black from Q magazine, and reflected on the Buenos Aires experience. 'We could hear screams and glass smashing from down in the dressing rooms, two hours before the concert began. When we went on stage, it looked like the whole stadium was on fire. Two security men were taken to hospital suffering from burns because fans threw blazing plastic chairs into the security pit.'

If all of that wasn't bad enough, they had to play the same venue again the following night. This time, the police attended in far greater numbers in an attempt to prevent another riot. Organisers had come up with what they thought was a clever idea: to build an enormously tall wooden barrier in front of the stage in order to protect TV cameramen from missiles and to encourage the audience to stand further back. The plan backfired, provoking those who could not see the stage into throwing flaming newspapers over the top, then tearing down the barrier entirely, causing most of the security to flee, leaving the band unprotected.

In his tour diary, Robert wrote:

'The crowd surges forward as we go onstage, and despite the higher barricades and extra police (or more exactly because of the higher barriers and extra police), battle begins.'

As he told Johnny Black, the plan was destined to fail. 'It was madness. They told us that people would back off from the barrier to see the group, but how could

they? There were 17,000 crammed on the pitch alone . . . and when they started ripping the barrier down, security men were hitting the ones at the front with lengths of pipe.'

His diary again:

'By halfway through the set there are several uniformed men on fire, with most of their comrades taking shelter under the stage from the ceaseless and merciless rain of coins, seats, stones and glass.'

Porl Thompson was the first to be hit, a wood and metal crucifix gashing his forehead and causing him to temporarily leave the stage. Eventually, it was Robert's turn. 'When a Coke bottle cracks me full in the face during "10.15" I stop the song and go a touch beserk,' he wrote. Speaking to Johnny Black, he elaborated: 'I spent a minute just screaming at the crowd and the security men. We cut the set short after an hour and a quarter because everybody in the band had been hit by flying objects.'

Smith described the surrounding neighbourhood, as they sped away, as 'not unlike downtown Beirut', and to complete the apocalyptic vision, according to newspaper La Razón the windows of houses adjacent to the stadium were shattered by the volume of the music.

'It wasn't much fun,' the master of understatement later recalled. 'The second night was scary. We were in the middle of it and there was nothing we could do. They brought in the army and there was tear gas. It was very odd. It was a good concert, though. The riots didn't take place inside, so much.'

He admitted that they feared for their lives when the rioting was underway. 'It was the one time I've been really frightened with The Cure, because we were locked in this basement room and we could smell burning, sirens were going off and I thought, We're not going to get out of this.'

For Smith, the root of the problem was structural and endemic. 'The whole place runs on vice and corruption,' he explained to Johnny Black. 'The local police chiefs make regulations that you must have police at concerts, but also that you must pay for them. So, in effect, you bribe them to provide security. The riots in Argentina were really against the police, not against us.'

Smith vowed never to set foot on a stage in Argentina again, a promise he kept for twenty-six years despite frequent visits to neighbouring **Brazil**. When they finally did return, Smith did his English-understatement thing and downplayed the disaster.

'There was a riot, it's true . . .', he told Oscar Jalil, 'but it wasn't Altamont either.'

Arrests

The website Loudwire once gathered together sixty of the most famous police mugshots of rock stars. All the usual suspects – literally – were there: Sid Vicious, Axl Rose, Ozzy Osbourne, Marilyn Manson, pretty much every member of Mötley Crüe, and of course Johnny Cash.

Conspicuous in their absence from this litany of rock 'n' roll bad boys were The Cure. Because they're such politely behaved, well brought-up middle-class Englishmen? Or because most of their misdemeanours occurred in continental Europe where leaked mugshots aren't such a thing? You be the jury.

The band's involvement in **violence**, in their earliest days, tended to be as victims, not perpetrators. However, once they touched down on European soil, they were off the leash. On 25 May 1980 in Rotterdam, The Cure were lucky to avoid arrest when they were thrown out of afterhours drinking bar the Heavy Club when **Lol Tolhurst** urinated in a phone booth thinking it was a toilet (see **Pissing**). Rather than sensibly counting their blessings and calling it a night, they instead went to the beach where Robert Smith and **crew** member Mac ran into the sea, grabbing a 'No Swimming' sign and hurling it into the water. An old woman who lived nearby saw this happen and phoned the police. Before long, the band were arrested at gunpoint, thrown into a van and, according to *Ten Imaginary Years*, had to bribe their way out.

On the same European tour, in Lyon, **Matthieu Hartley** uprooted a small tree and tried to batter down the door to Lol and **Simon Gallup**'s hotel room because he wanted a light for his cigarette. The police were called, and impounded The Cure's van along with all their equipment, obliging them to catch a train to the next date and borrow instruments for the rest of the tour.

Drummer **Andy Anderson** also had run-ins with the police in both France and Japan after hotel flare-ups. Lol Tolhurst, post-Cure, spent a night in a London police cell drunk. And, Robert revealed in *Cure News* in 1994, his own rap sheet included getting arrested in Holland for public indecency, in Luxembourg for criminal damage and in Japan for threatening

behaviour. Each time, he was let off with a warning. He has also been apprehended for vagrancy in **Paris**, and arrested in Germany for pissing against the side of a Mexican bar.

And he seems like such a nice boy.

Artwork

The majority of The Cure's record sleeves have been designed by **Pearl (Porl) Thompson** and **Andy 'Undy' Vella**, mostly under the name of their company, **Parched Art.** Thompson and Vella have typically given The Cure's artwork a distinctive childlike, hand-drawn style which, though ever-changing, is almost always recognisably Cure.

Before Vella and Thompson, **Bill Smith** designed 'Killing An Arab' (originating The Cure logo with the dropped 'C') and the albums *Boys Don't Cry, Three Imaginary Boys* and *Seventeen Seconds*.

Also credited on *Three Imaginary Boys* are Dave Dragon, who had been working on reggae, folk, funk and prog throughout the seventies but had recently turned his hand to a new wave sleeve in the form of Wire's *154*, and Connie Jude, a relative newcomer who had worked for Polydor already on The Jam's *This Is the Modern World*.

The Vella/Thompson era was interrupted almost as soon as it had begun when Ben Kelly, whose solid track record of post-punk sleeves included **Joy Division**, Section 25 and OMD, was brought in for *Pornography*.

Sometimes there have been different configurations, such as 'Lovesong' and *Mixed Up*, which were designed by Vella with paintings by the mononymous Maya (whose only credits are those two records).

It is worth noting that the division of labour between artwork and design is a fuzzy and inexact science, but one can usually surmise that the main image was created by those credited with 'artwork', whereas the superimposition of logos and information, and general layout, is done by the 'design' team.

The twenty-first century saw a new direction, with sleeve design overseen by venerable design house Stylorouge (*Bloodflowers*, *The Cure*), sometimes in tandem with smART (*Bloodflowers*, *The Cure*, *Five Swing Live*), a shady collective whose name has only ever appeared on Cure releases, and is heavily rumoured to be Robert himself.

The Cure's youngest sleeve creators of all were hired for one job in 2004. The artwork, as opposed to design, of *The Cure* was provided by Robert Smith's nephews and nieces: Alice, Benedict, Bethani, Bodhi, Christopher, Ciaran, Darcie, Dames, Nicholas, Noosha, Richard, Samuel, Sarahnearly, Sian, Theodore and Tod. Most Cure record sleeves only *look* as though they were drawn by children. *The Cure* actually was.

Assemblage

Assemblage is the name of a CD box set released in 1991 for the **French** market, featuring the first twelve Cure albums (including the *Japanese Whispers* and *Standing On A Beach* compilations and *Concert* live album) in cardboard sleeves. These sleeves were somewhat clumsily rendered: *Three Imaginary Boys*, for instance, crops off the bottom of the vacuum cleaner.

The front of the box folded out to reveal a large die-cut Cure logo with a multicoloured cardboard wheel underneath which you could rotate to change the logo's colours. There was also a drawer to access the discs made of fake violet silk. It included a sixty-four-page booklet written in collaboration with a French fanzine also called *Three Imaginary Boys*.

The title may be considered a pun of sorts: 'assemblage' means 'assembly' in French but also refers to a blend of grapes in wine-making. It is also, coincidentally, the title of a compilation on the dreaded **Hansa** of early material by Japan, another British band screwed over by that label . . .

Associates

Associates were a Scottish group of the early eighties centred around Billy Mackenzie, a charismatic singer with an operatic vocal range in the style of Russell Mael from Sparks, and guitarist and co-writer Alan Rankine. Critic Simon Reynolds once described them as 'the great should-have-beens of British pop'. Their sparkling, soaring 1982 single 'Party Fears Two' is widely considered the high point of the New Pop movement, and the album from which it came was named Album of the Year in *Melody Maker*.

Their connections with The Cure are many: they shared, at various points, a manager, a label, a studio,

a producer, a bassist and an art designer, as well as going on tour together. Their early careers ran in parallel: both bands were highly regarded on the arty fringes but made inroads into the pop mainstream (The Cure were the first to reach the Top 40, but Associates were the first to reach the Top 10).

Chris Parry became interested in signing them to **Fiction** after *NME* journalist Adrian Thrills made him listen to an Associates tape in the car journey back to London after seeing The Cure in Redhill in late 1978.

In November and December 1979 The Cure and Associates embarked on the Future Pastimes tour together, with labelmates **The Passions**, whose debut single 'Hunted' was the first release on Fiction. By that point, **Michael Dempsey** had been edged out of The Cure and was a member of the Associates. However, the tour was, according to author Tom Doyle in his Mackenzie biography *The Glamour Chase*, 'a disaster' (at least from an Associates point of view, as their sixteen-year-old drummer couldn't play well enough). Incidentally, the Associates subsequently followed in The Cure's footsteps by supporting **Siouxsie And The Banshees** in 1980.

Robert Smith guested on 'Even Dogs in the Wild' (later the title of a novel by Ian Rankin) and the title track of the debut Associates album *The Affectionate Punch*. It was recorded in **Morgan Studios** (*Three Imaginary Boys*), produced by Chris Parry and **Mike Hedges**, with artwork from **Bill Smith**, and released on Fiction on 1 August 1980, making it Robert Smith's first **collaboration** with another artist. Michael Dempsey featured in promotional shots but was not actually on the record. However, having left The Cure he later became a fully-fledged Associate, and co-wrote the 1981 B-side 'The Associate', and the *Sulk* album track 'Skipping'.

Associates split from Fiction in December 1980, their neck-and-neck rivalry with The Cure having apparently become an issue: a case of 'this label ain't big enough for both of them'. Associates publicist Chris Carr, quoted in *The Glamour Chase*, says 'Robert Smith *is* Fiction and as soon as the Associates in any shape or form started to compete, a certain line was toed by Parry. It was definitely Robert Smith that went in and said, 'We're not having it'. I think Chris knew which side his bread was buttered on at that time, and had to kow-tow to that.'

At the height of their pop success, there was always an element of mischief and subversion to Associates. Performing their hit '18 Carat Love Affair' on *Top of the Pops* in 1982, Alan Rankine 'played' a chocolate guitar which he then broke into pieces and fed to the audience. Despite the Fiction fall-out, they maintained a friendship with The Cure at this time, visiting the band during the *Pornography* sessions.

Sulk was followed by a three-year hiatus, fatal for Associates' momentum, during which Rankine and Dempsey both left. 1985's *Perhaps* also had Cure connections: future **Simon Gallup** stand-in **Roberto Soave** played bass, '**Let's Go To Bed**' session man **Steve Goulding** played drums, and **David M. Allen** produced.

After a fourth album *Wild And Lonely* flopped in 1990, Mackenzie made attempts at launching a solo career and at reuniting Associates, but to no avail. When his record label took him for dinner to inform him that he was being dropped, he famously played one last prank. He agreed to everything, as long as they would pay for his taxi home. What they didn't realise was that 'home' didn't mean London. It meant Dundee.

As their careers diverged wildly, Smith and Mackenzie remained on good terms. In a 1990 issue of *Cure News*, Robert cited Billy Mackenzie as someone The Cure had toured with, and with whom he was still friends. In June 1996, Billy made a cameo in a party scene in the video for '**Mint Car**'. This may be his final appearance on screen; on 22 January 1997, suffering depression and devastated by the death of his mother, Billy Mackenzie took his own life.

After his death, Michael Dempsey collaborated with the Mackenzie estate to oversee a reissue programme and protect Billy's legacy. The Cure song '**Cut Here**', released as a single to promote the *Greatest Hits* compilation in 2001, was written in tribute to Billy Mackenzie, expressing Robert's regret at not paying him enough attention on the last occasion they met.

Great should-have-beens perhaps, but the impression left by Associates' fleeting existence is enormous.

Australasia

For a man who doesn't like flying, Robert Smith has made the longest possible plane journey from his local Gatwick Airport on a remarkable number of occasions. The Cure have visited the Land Down Under nine times and counting, and have played in excess of ninety shows in Australia and New Zealand. (Robert played a further seven there as a **Banshee**.)

On their first visit to the Antipodes, which began in July 1980, their New Zealand-born manager **Chris Parry** took his young English charges back to his homeland (and its bigger neighbour) and worked them like dogs. The **tour** was originally intended to involve eight gigs, but that more than tripled, with the band frequently playing two shows per night because promoters had initially underestimated demand. At the first destination on the itinerary, Mainstream Cabaret in Auckland, they played five shows in three nights. Robert didn't mind the insane schedule, and later revealed that after the official shows they sometimes ended up playing in people's garages and basements, still buzzing.

Over in Australia, venues were typically tiny cramped clubs with names like the Bondi Lifesaver, Wollongong Leagues Club and Comb & Cutter Hotel, with equally tiny stages, bringing the band close enough for the audience to vomit on their feet. The tour ended with a final energy-sapping burst of three shows in two nights in Perth, but the band were obliged to stay a further week there, in a hotel overlooking the Indian Ocean, because there were no daily flights back to the UK. For **Lol Tolhurst**, this enforced leisure time was one of his favourite memories of the band, offering the opportunity 'just to have fun and run up and down this beach with white sand like sugar, and you couldn't see anyone in either direction.'

The following year, promoting *Faith* on The Picture Tour in the summer of 1981, their schedule was somewhat more humane: just sixteen shows, with only one double-up. As they told *NME*'s Paul Morley, they were 'experimenting with hedonism' (see **Drugs**) on that jaunt, but the locals were more interested in experimenting with the aerodynamics of lager. Aussie crowds had no patience for the slower, more atmospheric *Faith* material and, according to *Ten Imaginary Years* (see **Books**), 'expected faster, poppier "Fire in Cairo" type stuff'. They showed their displeasure in the easiest way available. 'If a Fosters can hits you,' Smith told Morley, 'then you know that you're in Australia.'

Smith's next visit to the opposite side of the planet came in 1983 as a member of Siouxsie And The Banshees, on a tour during which relations between him and the rest of his side-hustle band became strained. When he returned there in 1984 with The Cure, further tensions erupted into violence as he and drummer **Andy Anderson** had a screaming fight in a nightclub. On this tour, the band were at least playing decent-sized theatres and enjoying a reasonable level of comfort. The schedule, though, was brutal, as Robert recorded in his tour diary. 'Days became blurred. We played 2 concerts in one night in Brisbane, made a **TV** appearance 1200 miles away in Melbourne the next day, and then had to get back up to Brisbane the same night for another show. This particular adventure took 5 separate flights, 2 helicopters, several police escorts(!), and years off our lives . . .'

Perhaps understandably, The Cure took a break from visiting Australia and New Zealand in the second half of the eighties. However, the region was never far from their minds. A newspaper story about the suicide of two fans who had been listening to The Cure while they killed themselves, with the headline 'Gothic Cult Suicide', appeared to point the finger of blame at the band. 'We had this stuck on the wall [during the making of *Disintegration*]', Robert told *Spin* in 1989. 'I know it's tragic, but at the same time it's grimly funny because it obviously had nothing to do with us. We were just singled out.'

Australia's lengthening Cure drought caused 35,000 fans to sign a petition in 1991 imploring them to return. In 1992 they did, for a nine-date tour of large arenas. This time, Robert found an effective way to deal with the long-haul flight, as he told *Cure News*: '[We] flew there but stayed up 72 hours beforehand then took sleeping pills with brandy.'

In 2000 they were back in Aus for six arena shows and a festival, but skipped New Zealand entirely. By 2007, Kiwi fans who felt frustrated by the lack of a Cure gig in fifteen long years drew up another petition (they love a petition in Oceania), and the band duly scheduled an Auckland gig into their tour that year. One of the petitioners, Alastair Ross from Taranaki, was then sent to Melbourne by a television network to interview the band for their only Australasian TV interview.

In 2011, The Cure went back to where it all began – the furthest point away. Sydney Opera House was the scene of a historic reunion when **Lol Tolhurst** rejoined the band for two nights at the beginning of the **Reflections** tour, on which they celebrated the thirtieth anniversary of *Faith* by performing their first three albums in full.

After another arena tour in 2016, which (smartly) began in Auckland to avert any further petitions, they were back in Sydney Opera House in 2019 for another anniversary show, this time performing *Disintegration* in full (plus associated B-sides and outtakes) five times.

All in all, The Cure have given so much time to Australasia over the years that even if it never happens again, it's not The End Of The World.

Awards

It's one of the greatest moments in music television history.

On 29 March 2019 The Cure, having previously been nominated in 2011, were finally inducted into the Rock and Roll Hall of Fame (seeing off the challenge of fellow nominees Def Leppard, Devo, Janet Jackson, John Prine, Kraftwerk, LL Cool J, MC5, Radiohead, Rage Against the Machine, Roxy Music, Rufus featuring Chaka Khan, Stevie Nicks, The Zombies and Todd Rundgren).

During a ceremony hosted at the Barclays Center in New York by Nine Inch Nails' Trent Reznor, who acknowledged The Cure's **influence** on his own band, Robert Smith, **Simon Gallup**, **Jason Cooper**, **Roger O'Donnell** and **Reeves Gabrels** played a five-song set of 'Shake Dog Shake', '**A Forest**', '**Lovesong**', '**Just Like Heaven**' and '**Boys Don't Cry**' as former members **Pearl Thompson**, **Lol Tolhurst**, **Michael Dempsey** and **Boris Williams** looked on.

Just before the performance, TV interviewer Carrie Keagan bounded up to the band on the red carpet, almost hyperventilating with excitement. 'Hi, I'm Carrie!' she beamed. 'It's so nice to meet you! Hi! Congratulations The Cure, Rock and Roll Hall of Fame Inductees 2019! Are you as excited as I am?' Robert turned to look at her, and gave the immortal reply, 'Um, by the sounds of it, no . . .'

The car-crash interview continued for a few more questions, as Smith's bandmates smirked uncomfortably behind him, then Keagan let them go. But it was the 'By the sounds of it, no' moment which went viral. The clip was seen as emblematic of the cultural chasm between American energy and British reserve (see **USA**). It became a news item on ITV's *Good Morning Britain*, introduced by host Susanna Reid as 'When American enthusiasm meets British deadpan'. (Her co-host Piers Morgan claimed to be a massive Cure fan. Reid visibly did not believe him. Nor did anyone else.) In fairness, Carrie Keagan, speaking from Los Angeles, was a very good sport about the whole thing.

In many ways, it may seem surprising that The Cure were there at all. For any serious artist, the idea that something as subjective as aesthetic merit can be measured and quantified, and rewarded with awards, goes against the grain. Music is an art, not a sport. (And the very idea of a Rock and Roll Hall of Fame, always a weird one from a British perspective, derives from American sport.) Awards are nice to receive, and Robert has always been a gracious recipient at ceremonies – his award-receiving face is one with which he's had plenty of practice over the years – but he never gives the impression that he lives and breathes for the sweet validation of a gong. (Especially when that gong is chosen by a committee of mere music industry figures or **critics**, as opposed to the public.)

The first time The Cure truly engaged with the annual awards circus was in 1989 when they played 'Just Like Heaven' at MTV's VMAs (Video Music Awards) but didn't win anything. The following year, at 1990's BRIT Awards, they won Best Music Video for '**Lullaby**'. (Robert didn't have his head turned by the victory: in the April 1990 edition of *Cure News* he called it 'a foolish award'.)

Arguably the most prestigious accolade of The Cure's career came in February 1991 when they won Best British Group at the BRIT Awards. The likelihood of their win had been flagged up by the fact that they had headlined the Great British Music Weekend the previous month at Wembley Arena (as seen in *Play Out*), an event staged by BRITs organisers the British Phonographic Industry and featuring BRITs branding. At the ceremony, where '**Close To Me** (remix)' was also nominated for Best Video and Robert Smith for Best Male Singer, they performed '**Never Enough**' and had their award handed to them by The Who's Roger Daltrey, who expressed relief that he was giving it to a 'real' guitar band: 'I thought I would be presenting this award to a sampler and drum machine.' (Daltrey was not known for his progressive attitudes. In 1980, as a guest host of *Top of the Pops*, he introduced Village People with the words 'watch your backs'.)

At the 1992 VMAs, The Cure won the International Viewer's Choice Award from MTV Europe viewers for '**Friday I'm In Love**' *in absentia*. They were scheduled to play Camden Palace in London as part of the broadcast but withdrew, citing exhaustion.

There then followed a gap of almost a decade in which The Cure quietly and imperceptibly morphed from a band who received prizes for their current work into a heritage act who won Lifetime Achievement-type awards. The first of these was at the Ivor Novello Awards in 2001, where Robert Smith was given the International Achievement Award. In 2003 The Cure were given the *Q* Inspiration Award (another gong awarded to living legends).

In April 2004 The Cure were inducted into the Rock Walk at the Guitar Center in Hollywood, placing an imprint of their hands into the cement. Later that year they were back at the VMAs, winning the MTV Icon award. They received it at a special show on 17 September, recorded at Old Billingsgate Market in London (a building in which your author helped install the flooring during a summer job). The host was Marilyn Manson, who stated that 'The Cure showed me there was more to life than metal.' Guests Blink 182 performed a cover of '**A Letter To Elise**', and were then joined by Robert Smith on their own 'All of This' (the studio version of which featured Robert). AFI played 'Just Like Heaven', Razorlight played 'Boys Don't Cry' and Deftones played 'If Only Tonight We Could Sleep' (which they would later repeat at the **Meltdown Festival**), after which The Cure played an eighteen-song set of their own. It was broadcast, almost inevitably, on Halloween.

In 2007, at Los Premios MTV Latinoamérica (the Latin American version of the VMAs), they won the Influencia Award. It was held in Mexico, which in Cure terms is almost home turf. In 2009 they received the Godlike Genius Award at the *NME* Awards, which had been revived under the aegis of their old pal Steve Sutherland. They played a ten-song set at the awards themselves at London's Brixton Academy, and headlined the accompanying Shockwaves NME Awards Big Gig at the O2 Arena the following night.

In 2020 Robert was back at the NME Awards, winning Best **Festival** Headliner (following a year in which, among other things, they had headlined **Glastonbury**), and performing two songs with Chvrches: their recent **collaboration** 'How Not to Drown' (which had won the award for Best Song in the UK) and The Cure's 'Just Like Heaven'. The same year, Smith and Gallup were back at the Ivor Novellos, picking up the Music Icon Award.

And this incomplete list doesn't even mention the countless nominations, Readers' Polls wins and more obscure accolades that have come their way. The Cure have more awards than most bands could possibly dream of.

But they don't care if you don't.

B

B is for …

Babacar

Babacar, not to be confused with the Ragga MC of the same name, was a supergroup involving the extended Cure family. (Babacar is a common given name in Senegal, the most famous example in the West being yoga teacher Babacar Khane.) Fronted by Caroline Crawley of **Shelleyan Orphan**, they also featured contributions from **Roberto Soave** (**Presence**/The Cure), Jemaur Tayle (Shelleyan Orphan) and **Porl Thompson** (The Cure), with Crawley's partner **Boris Williams** (The Cure/Thompson Twins) on drums.

Their self-titled album and the single 'Midsummer', released in 1998 on their own Mesmer label, showcased their spacious, tranquil alternative folk-pop sound. In 1996 Babacar provided the opportunity for a Cure Reunited moment backstage when both they and Porl's new band **Quietly Torn** were on the bill of that year's WOMAD festival. Caroline Crawley passed away on 1 October 2016.

Ballet

For those who believe in the strict separation of 'high art' and 'low art', the very idea of combining the ultimate 'high' art form, ballet, with the ultimate 'low' artform, rock 'n' roll, is one which invites ridicule. But ridicule, as someone once put it, is nothing to be scared of.

The young Robert Smith's closest brush with ballet was watching a 1976 torture-porn horror flick called *Blood Sucking Freaks* in which a deranged dentist drilled holes into ballet dancers' skulls and sucked their brains out.

However, everything changed in 1982 when the phone rang and it was Nicolas Dixon, choreographer of the Royal Ballet, asking Smith to write some music for them. 'I like ballet,' Smith told *Flexipop!*, 'and I'm going to make a film of **Mary** ballet dancing – but only of her feet. We're going to make it in the garden, but we'll have to be careful that nobody's around because the outfits we wear are pretty provocative. I can't describe exactly what they're like because

Mary's mum buys *Flexipop!*.'

In February 1983, after **Siouxsie And The Banshees** got back from their tour of **Australia**, Dixon rang again. This time, he wanted The Cure to score the music for their forthcoming production of Jean Cocteau's *Les Enfants Terribles*. Even amid the anything-goes chaos of **1983, Robert's craziest year**, Smith suspected that this was too big a task to take on, and instead suggested Dixon should choreograph a performance of 'Siamese Twins' from *Pornography* to be shown on the BBC's arts programme *Riverside*, allowing them to dip their toes into the world of dance.

And so, on 7 March 1983, *Riverside* opened with a unique line-up of The Cure (with **Steve Severin** on bass and **The Venomettes** providing string accompaniment), though anyone who missed the announcement might have struggled to recognise the band, as Robert and **Lol Tolhurst** are barely seen on camera.

To the sound of 'Siamese Twins', the Royal Ballet's Sharon McGorian and Stephen Beagley give a highly literal Dixon-directed routine, in costumes by Michael Pavelka, their arms attached for the first half of it by a fake sleeve of rubber 'flesh' as if conjoined. On the line 'I scream', he screams. On the line 'we all die', she mouths 'we all die'. Meanwhile, an old woman, played by Dorothy Williams, sits in a chair, impassively judging them. It's kind of brilliant, the very definition of 'interpretive dance' and the most 1983 thing ever.

Smith wasn't the only eighties alternative rock star to meddle with the terpsichorean muse. In 1981 David Byrne of Talking Heads collaborated with choreographer Twyla Tharp on an original dance project called *The Catherine Wheel*. In 1988 The Fall collaborated with Michael Clark for the avant-garde ballet *I Am Curious, Orange* starring Leigh Bowery. And The Cure's wasn't even the only episode of *Riverside* to feature rock musicians dabbling in dance. In January 1982, Jimmy Pursey of Sham 69 had given a bizarre two-person ballet to the sound of The Stranglers. In September 1983, Robert's fellow **goth** icon Peter Murphy of Bauhaus would perform an interpretive dance with his partner and future wife, choreographer Beyhan Fowkes, to Bauhaus' 'Hollow Hills', wearing enormous trousers on a sand dune. They were *all* at it.

Although The Cure's effort was well received by viewers and fans, the full ballet project was put on hold indefinitely. However, in a *Smash Hits* feature in October 1983, Dave Rimmer reported that the Jean Cocteau adaptation was still on, and that some of the music had been written already, though Robert was finding it hard going. 'I'll have to finish it in my sleep with all the things I've got coming up,' he told Rimmer.

As late as 1987, the project was still alive, at least in Smith's mind. 'I finished the music,' he told *Cure News*. 'It merely remains for Nicolas Dixon the choreographer to finish the movement. Unfortunately he went missing in Tokyo two years ago – but I haven't lost hope . . .'

There was even an intriguing suggestion in the *Smash Hits* piece that Smith himself might put on a leotard and ballet slippers and do some prancing. However, he found that idea somewhat daunting. 'I can't see it happening somehow. I just don't want to let myself in for that much ridicule.'

Nothing to be scared of, Robert. Nothing to be scared of.

Bamonte, Daryl

Of course, you already know the surname. But you only know who **Perry Bamonte** is because of Daryl Bamonte.

Born on 27 October 1963 in Barking and raised in Basildon, Essex, Daryl Bamonte has held a number of overlapping managerial and technical roles with both The Cure and **Depeche Mode**. He first started working with fellow Basildon natives Depeche Mode as a roadie (Modey?), keyboard tech and tape op in 1980, while he was still at school and before they'd released any records, becoming their assistant tour manager by the mid-eighties.

In 1984, after writing a letter to **Fiction Records**, Daryl was hired by The Cure as a guitar and keyboard tech for the UK and European legs of *The Top* tour. Depeche Mode then offered him a retainer to stay with them, so he managed to set his big brother Perry up with the job of replacing him in The Cure's **crew**, with life-changing consequences for the elder Bamonte.

Daryl also took four months off from Depeche Mode and returned to The Cure camp temporarily in 1985 when he was asked to work on *The Head*

On The Door tour as a keyboard tech, with Perry as guitar tech.

Following two spells of moonlighting with The Cure, Daryl resumed working with Depeche Mode full time, in roles including personal assistant, tour manager and project manager, and is credited on the sleeves of *Violator*, *Songs of Faith and Devotion* and *Songs of Faith and Devotion Live*.

He became a familiar face to DM fans, appearing in the documentaries made to accompany the remastered versions of all their albums from *Speak & Spell* through to *Songs of Faith and Devotion*. He is also seen frequently in the live film *101*, at one point singing The Beatles' 'I Saw Her Standing There' with Martin Gore on guitar and Dave Gahan playing harmonica. In the commentary, he is referred to as 'the fifth member of Depeche Mode'.

In 1994, Bamonte briefly became an *actual* member of Depeche Mode when keyboardist Andy Fletcher fell ill midway through the Devotional Tour and had to go home. Daryl spent a week in a hotel room in Honolulu learning all the keyboard parts from Alan Wilder, then stood in for Fletcher through the band's South American and North American dates.

In 1995 Daryl Bamonte left Depeche Mode to spend ten years working full time with The Cure, in roles including tour manager, project manager and executive producer. He worked on the *Trilogy* DVD, *Bloodflowers*, the self-titled *The Cure* album, the *Join The Dots* box set and several album reissues. On 18 April 2005 he parted company with The Cure's team, just under two weeks after his brother Perry was relieved of his duties.

As a musician, he made two albums in 2011 and 2012 with Depeche Mode drummer Christian Eigner under the name Compact Space, and now plays keyboards with the electronic/post-punk band Permafrost, whose self-description is '4 Norwegians, 1 Baswegian' (a nod to Bamonte's Basildon roots).

Daryl now has his own management company, Bamonte Music Management. He is the label manager of Atlantic Curve, and owner of Angelo Recordings. He has also worked in publishing with Schubert Music Publishing UK for eight years and runs his own company, Archangelo Music. One of Archangelo's signings is **Roger O'Donnell**.

At time of writing he is working with Debdepan, an indie duo comprising Grace Bontoft and Chelsea Tolhurst. (Of course, you already know the surname. But, unlike the Bamontes, they're no relation.)

Bamonte, Perry

'Every private in the French army,' said Napoleon Bonaparte, 'carries a Field Marshal's baton in his knapsack.' The same is true in rock 'n' roll. Many are the members of road **crew** who carry a plectrum in their back pocket, just waiting for a faltering star to flake out so they can step into the limelight. Multi-instrumentalist Perry Bamonte is one of the precious few to have actually made that step.

Born in London on 3 September 1960, Perry Bamonte grew up in Basildon, Essex where he was at St Nicholas Comprehensive School at the same time as Yazoo's Alison Moyet and **Depeche Mode**'s Martin Gore and Andy Fletcher. (This fact was the subject of a May 2022 article in the *Daily Mail* with the headline 'Was This the Most Talented Class in 1970s Britain?') Furthermore, as revealed in *Cure News* in 1999, Perry was once briefly in a band with Mode and Yazoo founder Vince Clarke.

Perry's involvement with The Cure began in 1984. He began as a guitar tech on the album *The Top*, having met them via his younger brother **Daryl**, who was assistant tour manager for Depeche Mode but was also tour managing The Cure. Robert nicknamed him 'Mr Blokey' (until another nickname took hold).

After five years as a Cure crew member, teching and working as Robert's personal assistant, a vacancy in the band suddenly arose in 1990 when keyboardist **Roger O'Donnell** abruptly quit the band for the first time after the Prayer Tour. Perry was elevated from the shadows to become a full member of the band, and locked himself in his room for two months to learn the songs. 'That's dedication', as **Simon Gallup** put it. By December 1990 he had become 'permanent' enough to be featured in The Cure's official 1991 calendar.

Now nicknamed 'Teddy' (apparently because he hangs his head like one), Bamonte mainly played guitar live in what was then a three-guitar line-up, but also keyboards on older material; he played both on *Wish*, on which he was also credited as a songwriting collaborator. When **Porl Thompson** left for the first time in 1993, Bamonte concentrated on guitar (and occasionally six-string bass), with Roger O'Donnell reintroduced on keyboards. Bamonte subsequently contributed to the albums *Wild Mood Swings*, *Bloodflowers* and *The Cure*. And it was Bamonte, along with the similarly tech-savvy Roger O'Donnell, who set up The Cure's official information service online in 1995 (see **Websites**).

Numerous questionnaires and profiles in *Cure News* yield a wealth of personal trivia. For example, Bamonte used to check into hotels under the name Edward Van Menthe. The first gig he attended was AC/DC at Southend Kursaal in 1977, and his first album was the debut by Roxy Music. He collects obscure vintage films. His idea of a good day out is the Tate Gallery. He enjoys reading the poetry of Dante Gabriel Rossetti. He habitually listened to cassettes of Italian baroque music while on tour. He used to have a white rabbit called Bill which accompanied him on the road. His hobbies include remote control cars, fly-fishing and stargazing. He once took a planisphere (star map) and binoculars on tour, and showed **Jason Cooper** Jupiter and its moons through them. Even within a band like The Cure, he cut a cultured, arty figure, with more rounded interests than the average rock star.

Bamonte's initial fifteen-year stint came to an abrupt end in May 2005 when he, along with Roger O'Donnell, was suddenly dismissed from The Cure. According to O'Donnell, the sackings were made via email, then announced on the band's website. At the time, the explanation given was that Robert Smith wished to reduce the band to a three-piece. (However, less than a month later, Porl Thompson was brought back in, making them a four-piece.) Bamonte's brother Daryl, who had been working with The Cure in various capacities, ceased his involvement with them at the same time.

While still a Cure member, Bamonte bought Dulford House in Devon in 1998 after seeing it in *Country Life* magazine, enticed by the sight of peacocks in the garden. The locals, he said, believed he was a member of a Satanic cult. The house was the subject of a *Daily Telegraph* article in 2018 when he put it up for sale. He still lives in Devon with his wife Donna, who runs a livery for retired racehorses.

In the *Telegraph* piece, Perry told the interviewer that he remained good friends with the band. Indeed, the following year, in 2019, he was present at The Cure's induction into the Rock and Roll Hall of Fame (see **Awards**), though he did not perform with them. Then, something extraordinary happened. At the first show of the **Lost World Tour** on 6 October 2022, in Riga, a familiar figure lurked stage-right. Just as suddenly as he had left, 'Teddy' was back in. There had been no big announcement – he wasn't even in the promotional photos for the tour – but he was now a member of the new six-piece Cure.

Perry Bamonte, it turned out, had never entirely put the field marshal's baton away.

Bestival

By 2011, Bestival – DJ Rob Da Bank's carnivalesque weekender held in Robin Hill Country Park, a natural bowl just outside Newport on the Isle of Wight – had established itself as the unofficial end of the **festival** season, in its slot of the second weekend in September.

Expecting the British weather to behave itself at the height of summer is risky enough, but in early autumn it's positively foolhardy. 2011 was a particularly stormy Bestival, with the site lashed by the dying throes of Hurricane Katia, the ground churned to a mudslide under the feet of a crowd of fifty thousand who had largely adhered to the fancy dress theme of 'Rock Stars, Pop Stars and Divas', creating the spectacle of dozens of Michael Jacksons, Slashes and ABBA members slipping around in the swamp. The wind was so strong that Grandmaster Flash's 'The Message' skidded to a grinding halt when the needle blew off his turntable.

The Cure, in their four-piece Smith, **Gallup**, **O'Donnell**, **Cooper** formation, headlined a Saturday bill which also featured PJ Harvey, Paloma Faith, Kelis, Zola Jesus, James Blake, Robyn and Crystal Castles, who disappointed many by failing to drag Robert Smith onstage for a hotly rumoured duet on their 2010 **collaboration** 'Not in Love' (a cover of a 1983 single by Platinum Blonde).

The Cure themselves did not disappoint, and Bestival 2011 has become part of Cure legend. In a two-and-a-half-hour show, denuded of the dry ice which was instantly snatched away by angry gusts the moment it appeared, a hoodie-wearing Robert Smith and his band covered all bases, from the cuddly pop Cure of **'Friday I'm In Love'** to the impossibly pessimistic Cure of **'One Hundred Years'**. They lifted the spirits of the demoralised, mud-spattered audience with a shamelessly hit-packed set of thirty-two songs, even dusting off **'The Caterpillar'**, which hadn't been played live since *MTV Unplugged* in 1991. (Björk, who headlined the following night by playing her latest album with barely any hits to sweeten the medicine, could have learned a lot from The Cure's approach.)

The Cure were still in full flight when the final shuttle bus left the site for Newport. (I can vividly remember **'Boys Don't Cry'**, which opened the second encore, echoing through the trees as it pulled away.) By the time they'd finished completely with **'Killing An Arab'** – retitled 'Killing Another', on this occasion – I was miles away.

Bestival Live 2011 was The Cure's first live album since *Paris* in 1993, and their first to include the entirety of a full-length set. Cramming it all onto two CDs was the job of **Keith Uddin**, who transferred the audio, with mixing by, among others, the elusive **Bunny Lake**. Its **artwork** was designed by **Andy Vella**, and involved white decaying stencil lettering with the holes in the R, A, B and O replaced by hearts, superimposed over a long-range shot of the crowd and the stage.

The album was released on 5 December 2011 by PIAS in the **US**, and in the UK by Sunday Best Recordings, the label run by Rob Da Bank himself, who spoke of his excitement at finally bagging The Cure for his festival. 'Since I was fifteen and backcombing my hair, donning my sister's eyeliner and singing the lyrics to **"A Forest"** into my hairbrush, I've had an unhealthy fascination with The Cure. To say it reached its peak at Bestival 2011 is an understatement, as after seven years of pestering I not only landed The Cure to headline Bestival, but now appear to be putting out one of their live records on my own record label. How strange!' All profits went to local mental health **charity**, the Isle of Wight Youth Trust.

Reviews were largely positive. 'The Cure had pulled off the epitome of the festival set akin to Bowie at Glastonbury 2000 or Macca at Glasto '04, and every bit as legendary,' raved the *Guardian*. *NME* called it the 'set of the weekend', and the *Telegraph* called it 'joyous – truly the stuff of rock-and-roll icons.' For *Uncut*, *Bestival Live 2011* captured 'The Cure at their crowd-pleasing best, an ageless band revelling in their past', and *Under the Radar* suggested that 'the album should serve as both a challenge to younger bands to up their live game and a particularly dynamic treat for fans.' Ian Cohen of *Pitchfork*, however, hated it. 'But while the collection speaks highly of The Cure's professionalism, it never catches spark . . . and while they can't *not* play "Boys Don't Cry", it's performed at a flat-footed "we're gettin' too old for this shit" pace.'

There was no grand concept behind *Bestival Live 2011*. It functions as a live best-of album and a simple souvenir of a legendary set. Robert's rationale, he said, was that 'We had such a great time in the Isle of Wight at Bestival that we wanted to release this show as a way of thanking fans and islanders alike. Bestival IS the best!'

Biddles, Gary

Some members of The Cure **crew** loom larger in the band's history than others, and few have had a more significant role at key moments in their career than Gary Biddles. He was there when they broke up. And he was there when they got back together.

Horley-raised Biddles was a friend of **Simon Gallup**'s who accompanied the band on the Picture Tour in 1981 and ended up looking after their backline. During the *Pornography* sessions he was invariably present, keeping **Lol Tolhurst** company. And to the Smith-Tolhurst-Gallup trio's messy break-up in 1982 he was more than a mere witness; he played an active part.

On the final night of the fraught **Fourteen Explicit Moments** tour on 11 June 1982 at the Ancienne Belgique in Brussels, the band improvised a chaotic one-off song called 'The Cure Are Dead', on which they were joined by various members of **Zerra One** and Biddles. He famously grabbed the microphone and yelled 'Smith's a wanker, Tolhurst's a wanker, only Simon's worth anything in this band . . .' Lol threw his sticks at the back of Gary's head, and it all imploded.

Soon afterwards, Biddles and Gallup formed a band, **Fools Dance** (a successor to The Cry) together, with Biddles on vocals. But he was selfless enough to sacrifice that band's career, essentially killing it off in the autumn of 1984 when he acted as a mediator, arranging for Robert and Simon to meet up for a drink. Smith and Gallup patched up their personal differences, and the former asked the latter to rejoin him. Within a year, Gallup had ended his Fools Dance duties and eased his way back into The Cure. The longest-running partnership in The Cure – that of Smith and Gallup – may never have happened without Biddles' intervention.

In 1987, Biddles briefly re-formed Fools Dance with Jean-Jacques Burnel of The Stranglers on bass and Paul (not to be confused with Porl) Thompson of Roxy Music on drums for a one-off single 'They'll Never Know', after which they split again.

In 1990, Gary Biddles became co-founder and lead vocalist with **Presence**, Lol Tolhurst's first post-Cure band. Essentially, whenever an estranged Cure member wanted to form their own band, Biddles was on hand to help.

In issue 11 of *Cure News* in October 1991 it was reported that Biddles had said vicious things about The Cure, but this rancour was water under the bridge by the time of his death in 2013, and all grievances had been forgotten.

On 17 April of that year, introducing 'A Forest' in Lima, Peru, Robert announced 'This is for Biddles'. The same day, **Andy Anderson** on Facebook remembered him as 'a great friend', and Lol Tolhurst via his Levinhurst account wrote 'RIP Gary Biddles. My friend. We will always love you . . .'

Black Sessions, The

The Black Sessions were a series of live performances broadcast in France on the radio station France Inter in the 1990s and 2000s. The title is a pun on the surname of its host, the now-retired French radio legend Bernard Lenoir.

Significant guests included Arctic Monkeys, Radiohead, The Cardigans, Cocteau Twins, The Divine Comedy, Franz Ferdinand, Nick Cave, Placebo and Pulp, but The Cure are almost certainly the biggest act to grace the Black Sessions stage. The Cure played an eighteen-song set at Studio 105, also known as Studio Charles Trenet (after the singer of 'La Mer'), inside Maison de Radio, the famous circular building on the banks of the Seine, on Friday 15 October 2004.

Unlike their approximate British counterpart, the BBC's **Peel Sessions**, the Black Sessions are recorded in front of an audience of about two hundred people, in one take. That, at least, is the idea. When The Cure played, it didn't quite work out that way.

Although recorded during the promotional cycle for their self-titled twelfth album *The Cure*, the show only included three songs from that album ('Before Three', 'Taking Off', and the single '**The End Of The World**'). It was a career-spanning set, but one which leant towards deeper cuts ('Jupiter Crash', 'Us or Them'), and although six of the songs were singles, only one ('**Lovesong**') counted as a major hit. Clearly revelling in the opportunity to showcase less obvious material, Robert played with audible enthusiasm, and had broken several guitar strings by the final encore of 'The Kiss'.

Where The Cure failed to honour the Black Sessions' one-take philosophy was fourth song 'The End Of The World', which took no fewer than three attempts to get right, due to **Simon Gallup** apparently playing in the wrong key. The two abortive efforts are titled, on some **bootlegs**, as 'The End Of The World (No Good)'. After the lucky third time, Robert sounded relieved. 'We got there . . .'

Blackpool

'When I came down South,' Robert Smith told *Q* in 2000, 'I actually had quite a broad Northern accent and the piss was taken out of me mercilessly at school. That probably didn't help me integrate . . .' The Lancashire town of Blackpool has a special place in the British imagination. What that exact place is depends very much on one's cultural tastes. For some, it is the epitome of all that is brash, trashy, tacky and vulgar. For others, it stands for escapism, freedom and fun. A tourist resort on the shores of the Irish Sea, it is known for its expansive sands, its pier, its Winter Gardens, its Pleasure Beach funfair and its red-painted replica Eiffel Tower. It is Britain's Las Vegas and Coney Island rolled into one. And it is where Robert Smith spent the first years of his life. His favourite childhood memory, he told *Cure News* in October 1991, was sitting on Blackpool beach and **staring at the sea**.

'I have such strong memories of it that I don't know if I would want to go back,' he told Susan Compo of *Spin* in 1993. 'The promenade, the beach, and the smell, it's a magical memory, that evocative time of innocence and wonder.'

Blackpool's heritage as a place of escape and recuperation goes back three hundred years. In the eighteenth century, the wealthier classes of the north of England would travel there by stagecoach for the supposed medicinal qualities of sea bathing. This practice was known, wonderfully, as 'taking the cure'.

The arrival of the railways in 1846 changed everything. Blackpool's growth as a destination for the working classes went hand in hand with the Industrial Revolution. During the second half of the nineteenth century, Lancashire cotton mill owners would close their mills for 'wake weeks' in order to service their machinery. During these weeks, thousands of workers would visit Blackpool. The mills would choose different weeks to shut, thus giving Blackpool a steady flow of tourists during the summer. To this day, it is a popular destination for holidaymakers, daytrippers, and stag and hen parties, as well as having a thriving gay scene.

In musical terms, its main claim to fame – other than as the birthplace of Robert Smith – is as a centre of Northern Soul in the 1970s, the Highland Room of the Mecca Ballroom being an important venue on that underground scene. The town was also extraordinarily good at producing deadpan keyboardists in synth duos: Chris Lowe of Pet Shop Boys and Dave Ball of Soft Cell both grew up there, and were pupils at the Arnold School just one year apart.

Robert has never returned. 'I know that if I went back,' he told *Spin*, 'it would be horrible. I know what Blackpool's like – it's nothing like I imagined it was as a child. I think I would like to go there when I'm older because then I shall probably have similar impressions, because I'd be more decrepit and my eyesight would be so poor.'

Despite the happiest moments of their singer's **youth** being spent there, The Cure didn't once take the opportunity to play a homecoming gig. The closest they got was Preston Polytechnic in November 1979 and the Lancaster University in November 1980. Ironically, Blackpool – the home of 'taking the cure' – is not a place Robert Smith ever took The Cure.

Bloodflowers

'I wanted to make something that would last. If it was the last thing The Cure ever did, I wanted it to be something good . . .'
Asclepias curassavica, or the bloodflower, is a shrub native to the American tropics with a poisonous milky sap which can cause eye injury. No, nothing to see here. Move along. *Bloodflowers* is also an anthology of short stories by Canadian writer W. D. Valgardson, published in 1973. Nope, nothing there either, another red herring.

The title of The Cure's 2000 album *Bloodflowers* employs the metaphor of patches of blood from a fatal wound, which came from a First World War **poem** Robert Smith had read. One possible candidate is the closing lines of Herbert Cadett's 'The Song of the Modern Mars':

Crimson flecks on a sand-coloured mound
Like rays of the rosy morn

And splashes of red on a khaki ground
Like poppies in fields of corn

However, that poem was written about the Boer War, and in any case, the blood/flowers image is not an uncommon one. John Jarmain's Second World War poem 'El Alamein', which speaks of 'flowers in the minefields', is another contender, though again it's the wrong war.

One poem from the First World War which connects flowers to blood is Ivor Gurney's 'To His Love' from 1916, whose final verse runs:

Cover him, cover him soon!
And with thick-set
Masses of memoried flowers
Hide that red wet
Thing I must somehow forget.

Perhaps the most obvious example, however, is John McCrae's 1915 poem 'In Flanders Fields', which helped popularise the association between poppies and remembrance. As poetry analyst G. M. Griffiths wrote of that poem, 'Poppies have been associated with the battlefield since at least the Napoleonic wars, when poppies would thrive and grow on the fields freshly manured by blood. Poppies were also associated with sleep (opium being a poppy derivate) and McCrae, being a doctor, would have been conscious of this: the idea of sleeping under the poppies is revived in the last lines.' The opium poppy is symbolically entangled with sleep and dreams and death – all familiar Cure themes.

Whether the poem which inspired Robert to choose the title *Bloodflowers* is one of the above or none of the above, the poem wasn't the only source. It also, he told *Cure News* in 1999, came from an Edvard Munch exposition on the nature of art.

The prospect of an eleventh Cure studio album is one which Robert Smith originally raised hot on the heels of their tenth; speaking to Suzi Feay of the *Independent* in 1997, he stated that he was contractually obliged to deliver one more (for further discussion of The Cure's contractual obligations, see *Greatest Hits*). He also revealed that the influences for this planned album would include the dance music he had been listening to lately, and the cut-up technique of lyric writing used by David Bowie on *Low*. As time went on, he began talking of the album as 'heavy and dark, somewhere between *Pornography* and *Disintegration*.

The idea that *Bloodflowers* formed part of an 'invented trilogy' with *Pornography* and *Disintegration* is one that he voiced as early as 1997, speaking to Jim Sullivan of the *Boston Globe*. 'The writing is heavier than what I've been writing over the past five years,' Smith said. 'Not gloomier. Just a bit more powerful. Just taking fewer prisoners.' (He would later make that 'invented trilogy' a reality in 2002 by performing *Pornography*, *Disintegration* and *Bloodflowers* back to back at a series of concerts captured on the **Trilogy** DVD.) In another interview, he admitted, 'I felt that **Wild Mood Swings** had very little emotional depth, so I wanted *Bloodflowers* to compete on that kind of level with *Disintegration* and *Pornography* and **Faith**. I wanted it to make people feel something.'

In order to prepare for the project, he listened back to *Pornography* and *Faith* – albums he considered 'my two high points . . . or low points, however you wanna see them' – and played them to the other members of the band, to reinforce the point that he wanted *Bloodflowers* to be as good as those two.

The connection to *Disintegration* was partly a lyrical one, as he told *Xpress* in 2000. 'For me, lyrically, it was like ten years on from *Disintegration*. I wanted to pick up from where I left off and see how much further I'd got . . . which wasn't that much further really (laughs). I found myself obsessed pretty much by the same things. I wanted to pull elements out of what The Cure have done in the past musically and out them into *Bloodflowers*. I wanted to make the archetypical Cure album, really. I wanted it to be the sound of The Cure that I really like, with that melancholy sound rather than the more upbeat pop stuff.' He also acknowledged that approaching the age of forty (as reflected in '39' and 'The Last Day of Summer') was almost as much of a factor as approaching thirty had been when making *Disintegration*.

As the landmark age drew near, Smith began reappraising his old fallback influences, particularly the **literary** ones, by re-reading many of the books which had inspired his younger self and deciding whether they still had any merit. 'I didn't bother . . . throwing books out the window, but I discarded mentally some of the crutches I still had and I thought I didn't really need any more. Some passed the test and others didn't.' And he confessed that he had been in a nostalgic mood, taking stock of his life and career so far (something which he only allowed himself to do once every ten years). 'I don't mark my life by Cure albums, except when I'm making Cure albums. So I sort of thought "since *Disintegration* what have I done artistically and creatively with this band?", and that kind of led into *Bloodflowers*, because I felt I knew what I wanted to do with this marking me hitting forty and this possibly being the last thing that we do, it being the end of a particular part of my life and all that. It all conspired to become the sort of nostalgic, melancholy album that *Bloodflowers* turned into.'

The first proposed release date for *Bloodflowers*, announced in an October 1997 edition of *Cure News*, was spring 1998. That season came and went without the band even entering the studio. (Other dates mooted were February 1999 and April 1999, but it would actually come out almost a year after that.)

Preliminary attempts to work on new material had happened around the time of *Galore* in 1997, but were scrapped. 'We did about six songs in a few weeks and I suddenly had a blinding realisation that what we were doing was rubbish. We were about halfway through the project and I just abandoned it because I thought it was just stale, it didn't sound right . . . It was just instinct. I thought we were heading in the wrong direction.'

In early 1998 Smith came back to the project, and conducted 'endless demos and rewrites' in order 'to get everything just so' before going into the studio. These demos were recorded at his own recently installed home studio, which he had learned to use via 'a very heavy manual-reading session'. Rather than just pick out the ten best songs he'd written, he picked out the songs that felt like *Bloodflowers* songs. He wrote all the lyrics in a three-week burst.

Recording began on 14 September 1998 at St Catherine's Court in Bath, the Tudor mansion owned by Jane Seymour which they'd previously used for *Wild Mood Swings*. At first they made slow progress as they were testing out new technology: 'weird hard-disc recorders, computer editors, etc.' Additional guitars and vocals were recorded at RAK in London in early 1999, with final touches completed at Fisher Lane Farm in Surrey, a studio owned by Genesis. Snooping around, they found the stage sets from Genesis' early tours stored in a barn, complete with costumes on mannequins. It looked, said Robert in an interview with *Humo*, 'like a cross between Madame Tussauds and the Cabinet of Doctor Caligari.' He vowed, there and then, never to use stage sets.

In a revealing interview with Sylvie Simmons of *Rolling Stone* in 1997, he contemplated whether he even needed a band, now that he had a home studio. 'The only reason the group exists is to interpret the songs live,' he answered. 'I've reached a point now where the group is not as important to me.' In the past, he said, he had enjoyed the camaraderie of making albums as a band. 'But, looking long and hard at it, I realised that since *Disintegration* I've been very democratic in my dealings with the group, and sometimes that means musically I've given way, diluted ideas that may have been better . . . So I decided to return to being . . . selfish, I suppose.' To his surprise, the band's other members welcomed this approach. 'I thought there would be a rebellion, but they are actually relieved that I know exactly what I want again.'

And so, *Bloodflowers* came together almost as a Robert Smith **solo album**. Smith would stay in the studio with co-producer Paul Corkett (who had worked on '**Mint Car**', their **cover** of **Depeche Mode**'s 'World In My Eyes' and the **COGASM** track), while **Simon Gallup**, **Perry Bamonte**, **Jason Cooper** and **Roger O'Donnell** would visit, record their parts then leave, allowing Robert to record his vocals on his own. The process favoured the obsessive side of his nature: 'I found myself living and breathing the album.'

On opening track 'Out of This World', Robert – in a voice which doesn't quite sound like Robert – sings, ironically enough, of the joys of being in a band. A somewhat meandering track, but one which features incredible duelling guitar work, it became a regular gig-starter, as Cure album-openers so often do.

Second track 'Watching Me Fall', which describes a **sexual** scenario unfolding on 'a blood-red Tokyo bed', invites the listener to speculate, imagining a one-night stand with a groupie or a sex worker. It was partly inspired, he said, by an article he'd read about Rohypnol, a sedative he took on long-haul flights, and its use as a date-rape drug, and partly by an incident that happened in his own life many years earlier. 'I used some of that [article] and wove it in with this particular experience, then tried to marry it to the idea of what I sometimes perceive as my own decline over the years since *Disintegration*.'

As long ago as 1998, Robert had sung lyrics from the first verse of the still-unrecorded 'Watching Me Fall' over 'Untitled' at the Bizarre Festival, thus directly tying *Disintegration* and *Bloodflowers* together in a live mash-up. The home demo of 'Watching Me Fall', a song which he described as 'very much "Open" Part II' (referring to the first track on *Wish*), was twenty minutes long, and covered his entire career as a kind of 'Seven Ages of Man', but ended up sounding, he said, like Meat Loaf. 'I thought that the scope was a bit too grand – it was supposed to encompass my entire career. In the end I just focused it down to one night; I thought that was long enough.' Even the edited version is eleven minutes long, spooling out inexorably towards its incendiary ending.

With lines like 'The world is neither fair nor unfair . . .' and 'So one survives, the others die . . .', *Bloodflowers*' third track 'Where the Birds Always Sing' echoed '**One Hundred Years**' from *Pornography* (with a title which recalled Public Image Ltd's 'No Birds Do Sing'), Roger O'Donnell's chaotic, scattershot pianos adding textures reminiscent of Mike Garson on Bowie's *Aladdin Sane*.

'Maybe Someday', a song about rekindling an old flame ('I'll see you smile as you call my name/Start to feel, and it feels the same') was anomalously upbeat in this company. It was the one track Robert wasn't sure about as a sufficiently *Bloodflowers*-esque song, but left it in as he wanted 'something naïve-sounding, almost banal' on the album along the lines of '**Lullaby**' on *Disintegration*.

'Coming Up', initially only included on the **vinyl** and the Japanese, Australian and Colombian CD versions of the album, starts like the thrumming of a generator deep in the bowels of a building and continues in a sleazy industrial dance vein akin to Nine Inch Nails for six and a half minutes. With lines like 'It's a snow white original mix and it's fixing me', 'You ask me why I use it/It could be just a way to pass the time' and 'I'm coming up in the dark', it's not too much of a stretch to deduce that it's about **drugs**, though a sexual interpretation just about fits too if you squint.

Perhaps the album's most downcast and desolate number is 'The Last Day of Summer', a meditation on disillusionment and ageing. 'All that I feel for or trust in or love/All that is gone,' Smith sings, repeating that he's 'never felt so old'.

'There Is No If' is the one song not composed specifically for *Bloodflowers*. Smith wrote it when he was nineteen and demoed it several times over the years with an acoustic guitar, but thought he sounded 'like a hippy'. However, when Jason and Roger heard it, they encouraged him to record it properly. (The final version is still mostly acoustic, albeit with some lovely electric soloing near the end.) There is something un-Cure-like in its direct depiction of the heightened romance of young love: 'Remember the first time I told you I love you/It was raining hard and

you never heard/You sneezed! And I had to say it over . . .' but there's a twist. The second half of the song is about the prosaic ordinariness of old love. This time, when he says 'I love you', she doesn't sneeze, she yawns. The unromantic realisation dawns: 'There is no always forever, just this . . .'

'The Loudest Sound', a song whose shuffling drum loops sound like they're informed by trip hop, is another depiction of love turned sour. An elderly couple sit next to each other on a bench, staring at the sky or their feet. 'Side by side in silence/They wish for different worlds/She dreams him as a boy/And he loves her as a girl'. It's a lyric which cleverly manages to be touchingly sweet and tragically grim at the same time.

When *Cure News* asked Robert which song on *Bloodflowers* best described him, he named '39'. A devastatingly self-critical response, as this mechanical metallic funk track begins 'So the fire is almost out and there's nothing left to burn'. A riposte, perhaps, to the Dylan Thomas poem 'Do Not Go Gentle Into That Good Night' – Smith feels as if he couldn't rage against the dying of the light if he tried.

Bloodflowers ends with its own title track. Rolling peals of phased drumming and soporific keyboards provide the backdrop for a dialogue between an optimist and a pessimist. You don't need to be a genius to guess which one Smith plays. Giving one of his most impassioned vocal performances, he insists that dreams always end, waves always break, the sun always sets, the night always falls and flowers always die. (Unlike actual bloodflowers: *Asclepias curassavica* is an evergreen perennial.)

One song which didn't make the cut was the internet-only track 'Spilt Milk', a deceptively upbeat number on which Smith daydreams of a parallel world in which he prioritised 'a house a car a family and friends', wondering aloud if 'I'm wasting all my time' or 'I'm killing all my time' or 'I'm putting off my real life'. As Ned Raggett wrote in the *Quietus*, it 'found Smith's narrative voice grappling with choices and roads not taken', adding 'It's all the more strong for never fully resolving'. Although it wasn't even included on the *Join The Dots* compilation, 'Spilt Milk' would eventually appear on the deluxe 3CD version of *Bloodflowers*.

One notable feature of *Bloodflowers*, even by Cure standards, was the length of the songs. At eleven minutes long, 'Watching Me Fall' may be an outlier, but they average at six minutes. This was never the intention. 'Before we did *Bloodflowers*,' Smith later told *Rolling Stone*, 'I actually wanted it to be a short album, because I find that 70 minutes of one artist is, almost without exception, too much. So I set a target of 45 minutes, but, even cutting it down to nine songs, we were still over an hour. I realise, in hindsight, that it's the songs themselves that probably need trimming back, but I think that they benefit from their length. I've done an edit of 'Watching Me Fall' at home, and I got it down to under six minutes, but it's just not the same song.'

Although artists almost always think their latest album is the greatest thing they've ever done, Smith seemed to actually mean it. 'I was surprised at how good it turned out. I didn't think this line-up was capable of making a record this good,' he said. 'It's quite unusual for a band to be making their best material twenty years after they started. Usually, bands don't do this.'

Although the album was finished in May 1999 its release was delayed because, according to Smith, the record company wanted to release it 'post Millennial fever'. However, bootleg mp3s had begun circulating online long before release, and a buzz grew among the fanbase, which Robert quite liked. Available on CD or quadruple vinyl, it was eventually given a staggered release: 2 February 2000 in Japan, 14 February in the UK and Europe, and 15 February in the USA.

Its artwork, featuring photography by Perry Bamonte, was designed by Stylorouge. Robert's face appeared on the front, his eyes bloody and his mouth murderous. The booklet or inner sleeve had a different arty photo to represent each song, similar to the symbols on *Three Imaginary Boys*.

No singles were released from *Bloodflowers*, much to the record company's dismay, and nor were there any videos. 'In the old days,' explained Robert, 'you used to listen to albums in the dark. That's what I wanted *Bloodflowers* to be. I didn't want to impose pictures onto the record. Because it's kind of an old-fashioned record, in that way.' However, 'Out Of This World' and 'Maybe Someday' were put out as promotional singles, both given radio-friendly remixes by their old producer Mike Hedges, 'a nice way of touching on old Cure history'. The latter became, by some metrics, their biggest radio hit ever, even though in Robert's opinion it was 'the weakest song on the record'. Further remixes of 'There Is No If' (by Jason) and 'The Loudest Sound' (by Robert) were made available on The Cure's website for free.

Reviewers generally didn't have the same high opinion of *Bloodflowers* as Robert did. *Trouser Press* said that it 'feels like a forced recreation of the earlier gloomy classics' and that 'the album sounds completely uninspired, as Smith and company go through the motions of Cure-ness: glacial tempos, despondent lyrics, yadda yadda yadda', adding that 'had Smith paid attention to movie history, he would've known that the third chapter in trilogies always suck, and *Bloodflowers* is definitely the *Godfather III* of this batch', concluding by calling it 'ponderous, laboured and unnecessary'.

Les Inrockuptibles noted that the album featured 'endless songs' with 'dated sounds'. *Melody Maker*'s Mark Beaumont rated the album 1.5 out of 5 in a review titled 'Goth-Awful!' A review in *Rolling Stone* argued that Smith 'can write four bad songs in a row, and Cure albums tend to leak filler like an attic spilling insulation' and concluded that '*Bloodflowers* is half dismissible droning, an unforgivable ratio considering it's only nine tracks long.' On the plus side, *Entertainment Weekly* called it 'one of the band's most affecting works'. And it did receive a nomination at the Grammy Awards for Best Alternative Music Album.

'When we made *Pornography*,' said Smith before its release, 'we didn't have commercial success. I've lived without commercial success and I can live without it again. I don't expect *Bloodflowers* to be a No.1 album around the world. But there will be a great deal of satisfaction from people who are genuine Cure fans.' Robert's expectations were correct. *Bloodflowers* was not a No.1 album around the world. However, it did reach No.2 in Denmark, No.3 in France and Switzerland and No.5 in Sweden and Germany, also making the Top 10 in Belgium, Czech Republic, Greece and Italy. In the UK it reached No.14, and No.16 in the US. In some countries these positions were an improvement on *Wild Mood Swings*, and in the circumstances, with The Cure's profile at a career low, it will have felt like a win.

'It's a pretty goth set', Smith said of the tour which followed *Bloodflowers*. 'There aren't many songs you can dance to . . . It'll please the gothic part of our audience.' (But it did include 'In Between Days' and 'Just Like Heaven' to lighten things up.) One tour wasn't enough for *Bloodflowers*, however. So proud was he of this album that he arranged the *Trilogy* concerts in 2002 to reassert its importance.

And those threats that it might be The Cure's final album? 'It was dramatic for me to say that,' he admitted in *Rolling Stone*, 'but when we were making it, everyone in the group believed that it was the last Cure album. Because I wanted to have that sense of finality. There's no point in making an album like *Bloodflowers* if you really think you're going to do something else. I wanted it to be so that *Bloodflowers* was so perfectly "The Cure" that there was no point making another Cure album. At this moment, I find it impossible to think of making another Cure album. Because I have no need to.'

Despite Smith's belief that 'it would be very courageous to stop the group at such a high note', The Cure did make another album. And then another. 'I was so happy with how it turned out,' he explained to Swiss TV, 'that I wanted to be in The Cure again. So it backfired really . . .'

Robert also told *Rolling Stone* that the experience of making it was the most positive since *Kiss Me, Kiss Me, Kiss Me*. 'I achieved my goals, which were to make an album, enjoy making it, and end up with something that has real intense, emotional content. And I didn't kill myself in the process . . .'

Blue Sunshine

The first and only album by The Glove, the supergroup of Robert Smith from The Cure and **Steve Severin** from **Siouxsie And The Banshees**, assisted by a smattering of auxiliary personnel from both bands' orbits and with **Zoo** dancer Jeanette Landray on vocals (due to contractual restrictions on Robert), was created on a hearty diet of hallucinogens and horror flicks.

Blue Sunshine takes its name from one such video nasty. In the 1978 cult horror movie of that title, Blue Sunshine is the name of a rogue strain of LSD which inspires a spree of killings. Anyone who took those specific tabs of acid in the sixties would suddenly, on the tenth anniversary of dropping it, first go bald and then start stabbing people. For Smith and Severin, the interval between the effect of the **drugs** and acting on it was merely a few hours.

While recording the album at Britannia Row, chosen 'out of irony' because it was **Pink Floyd**'s studio and the album was psychedelic, Smith was theoretically staying at a hotel, but received funny looks from the staff for coming in at 10 a.m. so he tended to stay at Severin's instead, where they would top up their levels of narcotics and cheap shocker

movies. 'I thought it was a real attack on the senses when we were doing it,' Smith told *Melody Maker*. 'We were virtually coming out of the studio at six in the morning, coming back here and watching all these really mental films and then going to sleep and having really demented dreams and then, as soon as we woke up at four in the afternoon, we'd go virtually straight back into the studio, so, it was a bit like a mental assault course towards the end.'

Estimates as to how long the album took to record vary according to who's telling the story, from 'ten days in June' to 'twelve weeks'. In any case, it was created with the help of a shifting cast of extras including **Andy Anderson** (who had already recorded at Britannia Row with Steve Hillage) and **Venomettes** Gini Hewes, Anne Stephenson and future Banshee Martin McCarrick. 'At one point,' Hewes recalled later, 'as Robert was trying to explain himself, he literally fell into the piano and said of the resulting noise, "It goes something like that."'

As Severin told Banshees biographer Mark Paytress, staying focused was a challenge. 'We were a bad influence on each other. It was difficult getting anything done with all the impromptu parties that took place in the studio. I know that Robert's wife regretted him doing the album because she hardly got to see him for months.'

Sometimes the other half of the Banshees would show up. 'Siouxsie and Budgie would often look in on these sessions,' Landray told post-punk.com, 'and they had the sensibilities to know that we were doing something magical, something fantastic.'

In *The Hit* magazine, Smith spoke of the experience in the manner of a Vietnam vet with PTSD. 'Steve and I decided to make a record when I first joined the Banshees as some kind of "art experiment". Although we had a great time making it, it was completely debilitating and aged me about ten years. I think it was due to us bringing out the worst in each other – the most excessive ideas. We spent twelve weeks in the studio but actually recorded for about five days. The rest of the time was spent having an endless party to which we invited a succession of people. It was like a station – once they got really out of it, they'd be moved on and the next batch brought in. In between all this we'd record a piece of piano or drum. After that period with Steve, I was physically incapable of cleaning my teeth. The whole thing was unreal – a dream – and not something I'm likely to repeat in a hurry.' Speaking to Richard Skinner on the *Old Grey Whistle Test*, he echoed those sentiments.

'It was mentally very distressing doing it. It was really good fun but I came out of three weeks in the studio feeling like I'd spent 180 years with him.'

Production is credited to 'Merlin Griffiths' and the album's lo-fi between-song musical interludes to 'The Man From Nowhere'. As neither Merlin Griffiths nor the Man from Nowhere have any credits other than **The Glove**, it is reasonable to assume that they are fictitious, and that what you hear is the work of Smith, Severin and the helpers named above.

Opening track and lead single '**Like An Animal**' has its own section and is, like second single '**Punish Me With Kisses**', atypical of the album as a whole. It's followed by 'Looking Glass Girl' which, with its woozy glissando and clip-clop percussion, could be the incidental music from an unsettling children's drama.

The slinky and slow-motion 'Sex-Eye-Make-Up', which sounds like something off Marianne Faithfull's *Broken English*, is equal parts sexual and surreal, with couplets like 'Or leave me on the stairs with my feet in the air/I think that I'm jazzy like Christ' and 'Inches of glass all shiny and new/Screaming laughing fucks me to death'. Severin later revealed that it was half derived from *Bad Timing*, one of the many films they watched together, and half from a letter in Robert's possession, written by a madman to the Queen (possibly a souvenir from the '**Charlotte Sometimes**' video shoot).

On 'Mr Alphabet Says', Robert breaks the no-singing rule – there's no mistaking that **voice** – delivering impenetrable lyrics like 'You could win your golden teeth/Be a spinning top/Or use a riding crop'. The identity of Mr Alphabet is opaque, as is the meaning of those words. There's a general sense of the circus, perhaps, but it might just as easily have come from another surrealist horror film the duo had watched, or been a product of their acid-rewired minds, which they themselves might struggle to explain in the cold light of day.

'A Blues In Drag', as performed on *Play At Home*, is an atmospheric instrumental for upright bass and piano, reminiscent of Brian Eno's 'Another Green World', and one of Robert's personal favourites (along with 'The Perfect Murder').

The breezy '**Punish Me With Kisses**', as atypical of the album as the other single 'Like An Animal', has its own section. It is followed by the robotic yet languid 'This Green City', which prefigures the Teutonic grace of Propaganda. 'Orgy', with its Arabian strings, sounds the most like something that

might have ended up on a Banshees album and, with relatively straightforward lyrics like 'A tongue explodes in my mouth/A taste of coma and tears' and 'Your face is familiar/From another kill', describes what the title suggests, more or less. It was one of the songs The Glove performed live on the BBC's *Riverside*.

On 'A Perfect Murder', whose harmonic glockenspiel melody is a slowed-down sibling to '**Let's Go To Bed**', Robert is singing again: 'The meeker sleeker circle girls dressed in docile white/ Spinning on a hill they follow the Dracula kite . . .', a couplet which combines the imagery of childhood innocence and Gothic literature (both well-established Cure tropes).

The album ends with 'Relax', a six-minute instrumental combining the delicate sound of the koto (a Japanese stringed instrument) with an ominous Severin bassline and foreign-language film loops.

The **artwork**, by Banshees/Creatures regulars Da Gama, was full of trippy blue and purple spirals and solarised photos, echoing the aesthetic of sixties psychedelia. Released on 9 September, dropping into the New Pop world of **1983**, everything about it felt anomalous and anachronistic. The personnel involved nevertheless guaranteed a certain amount of press coverage. On the week of release, Smith and Severin appeared on the front of *Melody Maker*, both wearing Ray-Bans, like vampires hiding from daylight. Promotion, however, was difficult: when the album was ready, the Banshees were back together and touring in Europe and Israel.

The record was not a hit, rising no higher than No.35. 'Despite the fact that they'd spent too much time and money and effort on it,' said Sioux to Mark Paytress with ill-concealed glee, 'and released it at the most opportune time, The Glove album and single did nothing. It didn't really happen.'

The album has gained a certain cult audience with the passage of time, and with each re-release. The first, on CD, was in 1991 with added tracks 'Mouth To Mouth' ('Like An Animal' B-side) and 'Tight Rope' ('Punish Me With Kisses' B-side), as well as the 12-inch mix of 'Like An Animal'. The second, a deluxe edition from Rhino Records in 2006, contained an extra disc of Robert singing demos of all the songs from the album and the previously unreleased 'Opened The Box (A Waltz)', as well as 'And All Around Us The Mermaids Sang' (aka 'Torment', which Smith and Severin gave to Marc And The Mambas), and an instrumental called 'Holiday 80' (not to be confused with the Human League EP of the same name). And on Record Store Day 2013 the album was released by Polydor in a limited edition of 3,500 numbered copies, on marbled blue **vinyl**.

With the space of a few years, in a 1989 issue of *Cure News*, Robert said 'The Glove project was good deranged fun – an artistic indulgence – but I wish I had sung on all of it. Musically it was fab, lyrically a bit patchy (Severin bits – oops!) but overall I'm proud of it.' Severin, in hindsight, was able to praise Robert's guitar-playing.

Did it achieve its aims? Robert's view flip-flops on that. 'We didn't want it to sound like a self-indulgent album made by two ageing hippies', he said in one interview. In another, he confessed 'Yes, of course it was indulgent, which is why so few people have bought it.'

Blood, The

To most of the world, 'The Blood' is the third track on Side 1 of *The Head On The Door*, and that's where the story ends. In Spain, however, it was released by PolyGram Ibérica in 1986 as a limited-edition single, in a black sleeve with a red blood-spattered Spanish guitar on it, backed with 'Six Different Ways'. (*Very* limited edition: only three or four hundred copies were pressed up, and these **rarities** now sell in the region of £850.)

The song is a maudlin meditation upon lost love, and upon seeking solace in alcohol. 'Tell me who doesn't love/What can never come back?' Robert asks rhetorically at the start. 'I am paralysed by the blood of Christ', runs the chorus, 'Though it clouds my eyes, I can never stop . . .' The inspiration for this, Smith later stated, was a night spent drinking an entire bottle of vintage Oporto wine called 'Lágrimas de Cristo' (the tears, not the blood, of Christ), sometimes also called 'Lacrima Christi'.

Although the drink was Portuguese, the music is Spanish-flavoured. It's one of The Cure's occasional excursions into exoticism (see also 'Kyoto Song' on the same album and, much later, '**The 13th**'). In an interview with *Guitar Player* magazine in 1992, Robert linked it to his interest in Eastern music, and it does indeed have a repeated Moorish motif reminiscent of the flourish at the start of '**Killing An Arab**'. However, the flamenco guitars and castanets make it overwhelmingly Hispanic in mood. (Robert's genuine interest in flamenco extended to going to watch a flamenco group during a day off while touring Spain in 1988.)

A semi-official **video** for 'The Blood' was made in Spain by Gerard de Thame (who went on to be a director of some note, making the videos for Erasure's 'Sometimes', Tanita Tikaram's 'Twist In My Sobriety' and Black's 'Wonderful Life' among others). It is not considered canon by The Cure camp – although it is hosted on their Vevo – and is stylistically very different from the **Tim Pope** clips of that era. When French television programme *Les Enfants du Rock* ambushed Robert with it in 1986, he ventured, tongue in cheek, that the director had 'obviously got some sort of personality crisis'.

It is superb, in fact. Filmed mostly in black and white, it follows a male and female flamenco-dancing duo through an Iberian townscape and the colonnades of a deserted temple, their stamps and swirls leaving blood-red trails in the air. Some of the religious imagery is somewhat heavy-handed – a painting of Christ with blood pouring from a hole in his chest, a cup of communion wine spilling over a Bible – but it goes beautifully with the song, especially after a bottle of wine. *In vino veritas*.

Bognor

Bognor Regis is the sleepy seaside resort in West Sussex that Robert Smith and **Mary** Poole now call home. It is perhaps best known as the place of which the dying King George V, when asked to accord it royal status with the suffix 'Regis' because he had once spent some time convalescing there, is reputed to have said 'Bugger Bognor'.

Robert and Mary moved to Aldwick, a suburb on the edge of Bognor in 1989, and actually attended a meeting in the village hall. 'It was pretty chaotic,' Robert told the *Guardian*'s Dorian Lynskey in 2018. 'I was asked to leave, for no reason other than I wasn't welcome. I thought, "I've made a terrible mistake."'

He soon learned to love the place. In the April 1990 edition of *Cure News*, he said that when he needs to be alone 'I go to the sea and just stare' – one of the benefits of not living in **Crawley**. It is no surprise that someone whose happiest formative memories are of sitting by the sea in **Blackpool** should feel so at peace in Bognor. In the 1992 song 'This Twilight

Garden', from the B-side of '**High**', he paints an idyllic picture of the couple's life there:

I lift my hands from touching you
To touch the wind that whispers through
This twilight garden turns into a world where dreams are real

Talking about Bognor to David **Bowie** on **Xfm** in 1995, he articulated some of the pros and cons of living there. 'I am not accepted at all, but I don't mind that. See, that is the plus side for me. In London it would be easier for me to go out and socialise whereas where I am I retain a sort of anonymity and a distance – not that anyone is really that bothered. I might get Italians on the beach with binoculars, but the locals really haven't taken me to their heart. I would be horrified if they had.'

In the twenty-first century, however, Bognor *has* taken Robert Smith to its heart. Local taxi drivers will proudly tell you that they've had 'that bloke from The Cure' in the back of their cab, taking him to his house in Aldwick. In the Famous Residents display in Bognor's museum, along with one of the King, there is now a photo of Robert Smith.

Books (about The Cure)

The book you hold in your hand is not the first to be written about The Cure. In fact, the number of tomes dedicated to the band runs comfortably into double figures.

The first known example was a slim volume simply called *The Cure*, written by Jo-Ann Green in 1985, which Robert Smith later described as 'utter rubbish'. It was in order to counteract books like Green's, and to take control of their own narrative, that The Cure commissioned an official version.

The book, written by *Melody Maker* journalist and friend of the band Steve Sutherland with the mysterious 'Barbarian' (actually a nom de plume of French writer Lydie Goubard of *Libération*) and designed by **Andy Vella**, was called *Ten Imaginary Years*. It was announced with a Smith-penned insert stashed inside vinyl copies of *Kiss Me, Kiss Me, Kiss Me*, which read as follows: 'P.S. Out and about in late summer 1987 is the very awaited and at last here *Ten Imaginary Years: The Cure Story*. It is the only real Cure book in the world. It is written by Steve Sutherland and Barbarian, and edited by me, so that

you know that every word is true . . .? If you ever wondered what *really* goes on . . . accept no other. Love, Robert, x'

Of course, the ellipsis and question mark are a wry acknowledgement that those two things do not necessarily follow, and that seasoned readers of rock biographies would realise the word 'so' is doing a lot of work. However, what can incontrovertibly be said is that *Ten Imaginary Years* represented the narrative of The Cure that Robert Smith was happy to present to the world in the summer of 1987.

Published by **Fiction** in collaboration with **Zomba**, *Ten Imaginary Years* was largely an oral history from the points of view of the main protagonists (a format which has become standard after publishing sensation *The Dirt* by Mötley Crüe). One of the strengths of this approach is that it graciously allowed former members of The Cure, including those who had perhaps left in acrimonious circumstances, to have their say.

The next official book was *The Cure: Songwords 1978–1989*, a straightforward collection of lyrics published by Fiction with Omnibus. The nineties saw further SingalongaCure product in the form of sheet music books for *Standing On A Beach*, *Disintegration*, *Wish* and *Wild Mood Swings*.

An unofficial biography called *The Cure: Success, Corruption and Lies* (strangely opting for a New Order-related title) by Ross Clarke came out in 1992. The next Cure book, though, had an ambiguous quasi-official status.

The Cure on Record, written by Cure superfan Daren Butler and published in 1994, was not a biography but a guide to The Cure's recorded output, right down to the last catalogue number and record sleeve. Though not published by Fiction, it was assembled with the help of Robert Smith and **Tim Pope**. Butler, the ultimate authority on Cure **rarities**, owns many himself, his most prized being a test pressing of 'Lament' (one of only six in existence), which had previously belonged to BBC radio DJ Janice Long. *Cure News* reported in 1998 that Butler was planning a follow-up book specifically about rarities, but this never saw the light of day. However, he did collaborate with Robert on the biography of The Cure on the band's **website** in 1999.

On the subject of phantom books . . . In 1993, *Cure News* announced that there would be an updated version of *Ten Imaginary Years* in 1995. In 1994, the author was announced as journalist Johnny Black. In 1995, the publication date was put back to 1996. In

1996, the publication date was put back to 1997. The Johnny Black update of *Ten Imaginary Years* never did materialise.

One Cure book did come out in 1997, though: *Catch: Robert Smith and The Cure* by Daniel Patton. And the first years of the twenty-first century saw another flurry of book activity.

Jeff Apter's *Never Enough: The Story of The Cure* was published in 2005, as was Richard Carman's *Robert Smith: The Cure & Wishful Thinking*.

Andy Vella's own photo book *Obscure: Observing The Cure* was published in 2014, with words from *Mozipedia* author Simon Goddard and a foreword from Robert Smith. **Lol Tolhurst**'s *Cured: The Tale of Two Imaginary Boys*, published in 2016, remains the only memoir from an actual member of The Cure. **Tom Sheehan**'s *In Between Days: The Cure In Photographs 1982–2005* was published in 2016. And Ian Gittins' *The Cure: A Perfect Dream*, printed (like the Vella and Sheehan books) in a luxurious large-format hardback, was published in 2018.

Most of the books above have been very useful in the making of *Curepedia* in one way or another. I'm standing on the shoulders of giants.

The most recent Cure books at the time of writing this one were Christian Gerard's *The Cure FAQ: All That's Left to Know About the Most Heartbreakingly Excellent Rock Band the World Has Ever Known*, in 2021, and a further book of Cure photography, *Stills*, by Paul Cox in 2022.

The Cure publishing industry shows no sign of slowing down. Whether you think *Curepedia* is the best, the worst or merely the latest is subjective. What seems objectively certain is that it won't be the last.

Bootlegs

If you take Led Zeppelin, The Beatles and Bob Dylan out of the equation, The Cure are strong contenders to be the most-bootlegged band in the world.

Open up any website listing them for sale and prepare to be astounded, and perhaps slightly depressed, by the unfathomable mass of unofficial and illegal Cure product. To pick a mere handful of examples, almost at random . . .

Lost Wishes & Mixes does exactly what it says on the tin: it's a CD which combines *Lost Wishes* (the instrumental tracks from the *Wish* sessions, originally released on a fanclub-only cassette) with a selection of remixes.

The Cure's show for *The Black Sessions* in 2004 were released on bootleg CD by Sangatte Records, named for the controversial refugee camp on the coast of northern France where riots occurred in the early 2000s. The discs are marked as 'promotional' and claim to be in a limited edition of 2,500 – neither of these things is true.

The label-less *Obscureties* – you see what they did there – is a gathering of various Cure tracks from film soundtracks, tribute albums and so on. Then there's the many-volumed *Razor Rare* series on the California-based, Czech-manufactured Flood label, scooping up everything from Easy Cure demos to **Peel Sessions** to live tracks re-bootlegged, in an audacious crim-on-crim raid, from other bootleg labels.

Athens 2005 Terravibe is a two-song lathe-cut 7-inch single featuring live versions of '**Three Imaginary Boys**' and 'Shiver And Shake', recorded in Greece and allegedly limited to fifty copies. (If you believe that, I have a sack of nails from Christ's cross to sell you.) Also on vinyl – well, very thin vinyl – '**Killing An Arab**' has been released on a clear square flexidisc in Russia. (Which does, to be fair, sound very cool.)

Filmed Cure bootlegs, such as *Until Summer Ends*, a Taiwanese DVD collecting footage from French and German festival appearances in 2004 and 2005, were also popular, at least until the bottom fell out of the DVD market.

With the vast majority of these bootlegs, it's a mystery that anyone would bother parting with money for them. The Cure are not a band who hide their rarities away. In the nineties, perhaps, there was a need for such illicit releases, but not since the bootlegger-busting *Join The Dots* box set in 2004 (and any remaining rarities usually get mopped up by the deluxe reissues of the classic albums).

Nor are The Cure an under-recorded, under-filmed band. They are not inadequately served for official live albums, with *Concert, Entreat, Show, Paris, Bestival Live 2011* and *40 Live (Curætion-25 + Anniversary)* all readily available.

There are plenty of official live videos and DVDs, including *The Cure In Orange, Play Out, Show* (again), *Trilogy, Festival 2005* and *40 Live* (again), not to mention the wide range of Cure concerts, professionally filmed by broadcasters, available for free on YouTube. Unless you were actually there, or the gig has some historical significance, the worth of owning a badly recorded copy of any particular Cure show seems minimal.

That said, every once in a while the bootleggers will dredge up a small piece of gold. One bootleg, called *Play For Today*, is a double vinyl pressing of the gig The Cure played on 31 May 1980 at the Scala in Herford, Germany, home to the 1st Armoured Division of the British Army during the Cold War. This was the show where the band improvised a song called 'Happy Birthday' (bearing no resemblance to the traditional sing-song) for **Simon Gallup**. (It's also on a bootleg called *Strange Days*, and one of those *Razor Rare* discs, among others.) Far from a jolly felicitation, it is filled with terror and dread, as if channelling Public Image Ltd's *Metal Box*, Smith essentially telling Gallup that his youth is over. 'Simon's twenty in half an hour, so this is for him . . .' he announces, then sings a lyric that has been transcribed as follows:

You saw the people
Around you
Getting old
You wake up
The teenage yearn is
Gone for you

And so say all of us.

Bowie

David Bowie was the first pop artist to understand that the shards of a shattered self can form a kaleidoscope. He was the first to understand that masks can tell greater truths than a face. And the first to understand that the key to enduring fascination is constant change. There is a strong case to be made that he is not only the most influential musician of all time, but the most important cultural figure of the twentieth century.

Born David Jones in Brixton in 1947 and raised in Bromley, he recorded under various names in the mid-sixties, such as Davie Jones And The King Bees, Davy Jones And The Lower Third, and The Manish Boys. His first appearance on British television, aged seventeen, was as a spokesperson for the Society for the Prevention of Cruelty to Long-Haired Men (who were actually the Manish Boys, protesting about having been told to cut their hair if they wanted to appear on the BBC). After changing his name to David Bowie to avoid confusion with Davy Jones from The

Monkees, he continued recording with bands such as The Buzz and The Riot Squad. In 1967 he began studying mime under Lindsay Kemp and released a string of solo singles in a twee sub-Anthony Newley, Cockney music-hall style such as 'The Laughing Gnome' and 'Love You Till Tuesday', but struck gold in July 1969 with psychedelic pop curio 'Space Oddity', a Top 5 hit about an astronaut stranded in space, timed perfectly to cash in on the moon landings.

After moving in a hard rock direction with the Tony Visconti-produced *The Man Who Sold The World*, Bowie faded from the public radar for a couple of years, but broke into the Top 3 in 1971 with the superb *Hunky Dory*, featuring such enduring classics as 'Changes', 'Oh! You Pretty Things', 'Queen Bitch' and 'Life On Mars?' It was the next album, 1972's *The Rise And Fall Of Ziggy Stardust And The Spiders From Mars*, which truly elevated Bowie to the stratosphere and defined the glam-rock era. *Ziggy* was a concept album about an alien rock-star messiah who comes to Earth to save the planet from destruction, only to be destroyed by his own ego. In order to inhabit the titular role, Bowie shaved his eyebrows, wore extravagant facepaint, grew his hair into a bright red mullet (though the word 'mullet' didn't exist yet), dressed in theatrical catsuits and capes, and adopted a provocatively pansexual persona on songs like 'Moonage Daydream' and the stand-alone single 'John, I'm Only Dancing' (having already shocked readers of the music press by coming out as bisexual). Ziggymania continued through the next album *Aladdin Sane*, but Bowie stunned fans in July 1973 by killing off Ziggy and breaking up the Spiders from Mars live on stage at Hammersmith Odeon.

After one further album in the glam genre, *Diamond Dogs* in 1974, Bowie again wrongfooted his followers in 1975 with the 'plastic soul' album *Young Americans*, and again with the funk-meets-Krautrock direction of 1976's *Station To Station* and a new persona, the Thin White Duke. He then decamped to Berlin with friend Iggy Pop, producer Tony Visconti and collaborator Brian Eno to work on a trilogy of forward-looking, avant-pop albums: 1977's masterpiece *Low* (originally intended as the soundtrack to his first film vehicle, Nic Roeg's *The Man Who Fell To Earth*), 1978's *'Heroes'* and 1979's *Lodger*. In 1980 he revived the character of Major Tom on No.1 single 'Ashes To Ashes', from the album *Scary Monsters (And Super Creeps)*, generally considered the last of his imperial phase, before ditching art rock altogether, hooking up with Chic's Nile Rodgers and becoming a global pop star on 1983's super-commercial *Let's Dance*.

If you think The Cure weren't paying attention to all this, then you haven't been paying attention to The Cure. Every band of their generation were Bowie's children, and studied his playbook carefully. His shifting personae, his literary influences and lyrical preoccupations with themes of insanity are obvious formative influences on The Cure.

It's become a hackneyed cliché for musicians to talk about having their lives changed by 'the Starman moment', but some things are clichés because they're true. On Thursday 6 July 1972 Bowie performed 'Starman', the lead single from the *Ziggy Stardust* album, on the BBC's flagship pop programme, *Top of the Pops*. The performance caused a sensation, instantly becoming what Americans would call 'a water cooler moment' and what, in the colder British climate, ought to be called 'a kettle moment'. In a time when there were only three TV channels and no video recorders, so that Britons could only watch what was being broadcast at any one time, the performance was seen by fifteen million viewers, and left a huge impression on the young.

There were three things Bowie and his band did to make 'Starman' such a transformative moment. Firstly, his androgynous and alien appearance, with his multicoloured catsuit, cherry-red boots, **make-up** and feathered hair was already enough to have angry dads kicking holes in their television screens. Secondly, on the line 'I had to phone someone so I picked on you', Bowie broke the fourth wall, waggling a pointing finger directly down the camera towards the viewer – an extremely powerful tactic. Thirdly, he casually slung his arm around the shoulder of guitarist Mick Ronson. Incredible as it seems today, a man with his arm around another man was considered shocking in early seventies Britain, when homosexuality had only been decriminalised five years earlier and male-on-male affection was strictly circumscribed by convention. (In their live shows, Bowie and Ronson took it much further, with Bowie pretending to fellate Ronson's guitar.)

At home in **Crawley**, a thirteen-year-old Robert Smith watched in awe. 'I felt that his records had been made with me in mind,' he once told Will Hodgkinson in the *Guardian*. 'He was blatantly different, and everyone of my age remembers the time he played "Starman" on *Top of the Pops*. The school was divided between those who thought he was a "queer" and those who thought he was a

genius. Immediately, I thought: this is it. This is the man I've been waiting for.' *The Rise And Fall Of Ziggy Stardust And The Spiders From Mars* was the first album Robert Smith ever bought. 'I loved the idea that Bowie represented The Other,' he told *Cure News*. 'I was 13 when this came out and it represented everything I wanted the world to be: alien, glamorous and cool.' In an *Entertainment Weekly* interview by Pete Wentz of Fall Out Boy, Smith recalled, 'I suppose what appealed to me even at that young age was how individual he was, that "I don't give a fuck" look.' The following year Robert, by now fourteen, saw his first Bowie concert at Earls Court in London.

Lol Tolhurst, just across town, was also watching and equally impressed. (He and **Porl Thompson** and **Michael Dempsey**, on a break from their job in the chemical factory, once saw Spiders From Mars drummer Woody Woodmansey's U-Boat in a local pub, much to their excitement.) However, it was *Low*, for Lol, which was 'the album that changed everything'. On *Curious Creatures* he praised Dennis Davis' pitch-shifted drumming on that record, and the general mood of alienation, describing it as a 'pivotal' record in his life.

The influence of that despondent Berlin Trilogy mood unmistakably seeped into The Cure's early works, and Bowie's influence is detectable in countless ways, from their appearance to the title of **'A Letter To Elise'** (inspired by Bowie's 'Letter To Hermione'). And there can be no doubt that The Cure paid it forward, providing eighties *Top of the Pops* viewers with plenty of 'Starman moments' of their own.

In 1995, the **Fiction**-affiliated radio station **Xfm** asked Robert to interview Bowie on air. It did not go well. 'I got incredibly drunk before it,' he told Pete Wentz, 'and started arguing with him. It was one of the most awful days I've ever had in my life.' He talked across Bowie for two hours, and, as he later told the *Guardian*'s Dorian Lynskey, 'I think my opening gambit was, "We can both agree you've never done anything good since 1982."' (The same year, The Cure recorded a cover of Bowie's 'Young Americans' for the album *104.9* to support Xfm's application for a Londonwide licence.)

Having made what he assumed was a terrible first impression, Smith was surprised two years later to be invited to perform at David Bowie's fiftieth birthday concert at Madison Square Garden in New York, the only British artist asked to duet with him. Together they performed a thrashy 'The Last Thing You Should Do' from Bowie's forthcoming album *Earthling* (the world premiere of that song), and an acoustic 'Quicksand' from *Hunky Dory*.

'Quicksand' was one of the songs the teenage Robert saw Bowie perform at that 1973 Earls Court show. Duetting with Bowie should, therefore, have been easier than it was. 'I'd learned it phonetically when I was about 14 in my bedroom,' he told the *Independent*'s Suzi Feay, 'and they're completely the wrong words. And when we were walking up to the stage I said, "I know I'm going to sing the 14-year-old's version." He thought it was really funny. He said "If you want, I'll sing your version." I said "No no no no, it doesn't make any sense!" He said "Mine doesn't either . . . "'

The whole experience was a major thrill for Smith. 'That was one of my best moments,' he told Pete Wentz, 'one of my lifelong ambitions.' Speaking to Jim Sullivan of the *Boston Globe*, he said that meeting Bowie offstage completely changed his impression of him. 'I still had an idea of what I wanted him to be like, but I found him to be different and probably not how I imagined him to be. I thought he'd be very cold, aloof, distant, and clever. But he's very genuine. One of the most gratifying things is when another artist that you admire turns around and says they like what you do. When Bowie told me that he liked what I did, that was it for me. I could have stopped.'

Bowie's guitarist that day, and the organiser of the concert, was **Reeves Gabrels**, who would later, after a couple of **collaborations**, be lured into joining The Cure. Smith also met **producer** Mark Plati that day, who had remixed *Earthling* tracks for Bowie and would later produce the new tracks on The Cure's *Greatest Hits*. Continuing the crossover between The Cure and Bowie camps, in 1999 **Jason Cooper** drummed on the demo version of Bowie's 'Seven' (from the album *Hours*), released on a CD single the following year.

And it was the experience of watching Bowie play *Low* in its entirety followed by his latest album *Heathen* at Bowie's **Meltdown Festival** in 2002 which inspired Smith's decision to attempt the *Trilogy* shows, and informed his thinking about his own Meltdown in 2018.

Low is one of the albums, along with *David Live*, that Smith has cited among his favourites of all time, and he has named 'Life On Mars?' as his favourite single (as it reminds him of the first time he danced with **Mary**). He has named Bowie, along with Jimi

Hendrix and Alex Harvey, as one of the 'rogue characters' who were his role models growing up.

'He showed that you could do things on your own terms,' Smith told the *Guardian*, 'that you could define your own genre and not worry about what anyone else is doing, which is I think the definition of a true artist.'

Boys Don't Cry (album)

It's a tried and tested ploy by small record **labels** who have acquired the rights to a chunk of the catalogue of a band with one big song to their name, to whack it all out on an album with that same big song as its title, for maximum marketability. And so, with minimum imagination, the first Cure album to be released in the **USA**, on the PVC label, was called *Boys Don't Cry*.

It's debatable, however, whether *Boys Don't Cry* counts as an album at all, in the traditional sense. It's essentially a cut-and-shut compilation of extended highlights from *Three Imaginary Boys* (which had not been released in America first time around) with non-album singles and B-sides.

The songs which survived from *Three Imaginary Boys* were '**10.15 Saturday Night**', 'Accuracy', 'Grinding Halt', 'Another Day', 'Object', 'Subway Song', 'Fire In Cairo' and 'Three Imaginary Boys'. (Those omitted were 'Foxy Lady', 'The Weedy Burton', 'So What' and 'It's Not You'.) And parachuted in from elsewhere were 'Plastic Passion', '**Killing An Arab**', 'World War' and of course '**Boys Don't Cry**', sitting in classic budget compilation style at the very top of Side 1.

In later years, when Elektra reissued *Boys Don't Cry* on CD, some tinkering was done with the track listing. 'Object', of which Robert Smith is not a fan, was removed and replaced by 'So What'. And *Three Imaginary Boys* outtake 'World War', which Robert deemed 'a nonsense', was also removed from most CD releases, 'probably (possibly) because I hate it,' he told *Cure News*.

The album was released in the States on 5 February 1980. Its **artwork**, itself a blown-up detail from the *Three Imaginary Boys* sleeve, is a vaguely Pop Art approximation by **Bill Smith** of an Egyptian desert scene, with a pink pyramid rising above three green palms against a bright blue sky, as a reference to the song 'Fire In Cairo'.

It eventually slipped out in the UK in the August of **1983, Robert's craziest year**, allowing newcomer fans of '**The Walk**' and '**The Lovecats**' to catch up on some of what they'd missed, but was drowned out somewhat by all the other Smith/Cure/Banshees activity at that time, though it did eventually go platinum (and also went gold in France).

Robert Christgau, originator of the 'capsule review', wrote about *Boys Don't Cry* in his Consumer Guide column in *Village Voice*. Despite awarding it a B+, he sounded underwhelmed.

> The sound is dry post-punk, never pretty but treated with a properly mnemonic pop overlay – I can look over the titles and recall a phrase from all but a few of these 13 songs. Intelligent phrases they are, too, yet somehow I find it hard to get really excited about them. What are we to think of a band whose best song is based on a novel by Albert Camus? Granted, I prefer 'Killing An Arab' to *The Stranger* – the idea works better as a miniature – but that book defined middlebrow for me before I knew what middlebrow was, back when it was holy writ for collegiate existentialists. And the last thing we need is collegiate existentialist nostalgia.

In *Rolling Stone*, Debra Rae Cohen also highlighted The Cure's adolescent **literary** pretensions, writing that the record 'proves they can transcend their Comp. Lit. 201 (Elementary Angst) scenarios.'

Hindsight has been surprisingly kind to *Boys Don't Cry*. Despite not really being an album, it has twice made it into *Rolling Stone*'s list of the four hundred greatest albums of all time. And, in his book *Fear of Music: The 261 Greatest Albums Since Punk and Disco*, Garry Mulholland drily called it 'the ultimate in morose sixth-formers, intellectualising their inability to get laid' and 'the most fun you can have without ever having a hope of taking your clothes off'.

It emerged in 1985 that the title track was Andrew Ridgeley from Wham!'s favourite song of all time. And if you think that piece of trivia was crudely bolted together with the rest of this entry, with no consideration for sequencing, now you know how *Boys Don't Cry* was made.

Boys Don't Cry (song)

'Toxic masculinity'. A widely understood phrase now, first coined by author Shepherd Bliss and developed via the mythopoetic men's movement of the 1980s and 1990s, but non-existent when The Cure wrote 'Boys Don't Cry'. The concept is that societally enforced masculine norms of behaviour are damaging not just for people of other genders but for men themselves. A strand of toxic masculinity runs through a certain type of **Englishness**: stoicism in the face of emotional trauma, the 'stiff upper lip'.

Lol Tolhurst, on the BBC Radio 4 series *Soul Music*, posited a direct connection between 'Boys Don't Cry' and the growth of a healthier attitude towards such matters. 'The Cure are totally responsible in my mind for boys being able to get close to their emotions and feelings . . . As anyone who grew up in 1960s/1970s Britain knows, emotion was not really on the table. It was "stiff upper lip" stuff . . . Most teenage boys in the seventies were repressed in lots of ways.'

Robert Smith, speaking to *Rolling Stone* in 2019, confirmed that this emotional repression was behind the song. 'When I was growing up, there was peer pressure on you to conform to be a certain way. And as an English boy at the time, you're encouraged not to show your emotion to any degree. And I couldn't help but show my emotions when I was younger. I never found it awkward showing my emotions. I couldn't really continue without showing my emotions; you'd have to be a pretty boring singer to do that. So I kind of made a big thing about it. I thought, "Well, it's part of my nature to rail against being told not to do something."'

The idea of social pressure to suppress tears was not new in pop. The Four Seasons, in 1962, gave it a feminine twist with 'Big Girls Don't Cry'. In 1975, the breathy female voice of Kathy Redfern on 10cc's 'I'm Not In Love' urged singer Eric Stewart to 'Be quiet, big boys don't cry . . .' The Cure took that idea and, as Smith told *Rolling Stone*, railed against it. At the Reading Festival 1979, before a super-fast, double-speed rendition of 'Boys Don't Cry' (as if Lol was dying for a piss and wanted to get it over with), Robert pointedly dedicated the song to 'all the macho men in the audience'. (He pronounced it 'makko'.)

'Boys Don't Cry' had been a weapon in The Cure's armoury for a long time. It was one of the four songs on the demo tape recorded at Chestnut Studios, paid for by **Ric Gallup**, that got them signed to **Fiction** by

Chris Parry in 1978. They recorded it as part of their first **Peel Session** in December that year. And it is documented as the opener of their live set as early as 9 February 1979 at the Nashville Room in London, four months ahead of its single release. At that gig, a gang of skinheads turned up intent on **violence**, but their leader was pacified by 'Boys Don't Cry' and calmed everyone down, proof that The Cure's music hath charms to soothe the savage breast.

An irresistible and instantly memorable piece of pop-punk, it was The Cure at their most Buzzcocksian (as Mat Snow of *NME* noted at the time), but the inspiration went back much further than that: Robert, in *Cure News*, called it 'an attempt at a Sixties pop song'.

The song's basic narrative – losing a girl by being a dick, living to regret it, desperately wanting her back – is not exactly uncommon in The Cure's oeuvre, nor in popular music as a whole. But it's the chorus – pitching Robert's emotional vulnerability versus received ideas of masculinity – that really resonates.

The B-side, 'Plastic Passion', was based on the same chords as '**A Night Like This**' but sped up, and included the word 'hyoscine' (also known as scopolamine or Devil's Breath, a **drug** used for treating motion sickness), most likely a leftover from Lol's chemistry studies. It started out, Robert told *Cure News* in 1991, 'as a pastiche of early Roxy Music ("Pyjamarama"-style)'.

The single's **artwork** featured young soldiers, fear in their eyes, marching off to war. The reverse, to depict 'Plastic Passion', featured an advertisement for a blow-up sex doll ('HELGA Never Says No!'). The run-out grooves bore the inscriptions 'But Bill does' on the A-side (a reference to Parry) and 'From the land of a thousand microphones' on the B-side (referring to the number of mics needed to record Lol's drums).

One press ad featured a Vietnam War soldier with the following text printed sideways:

Nowadays, terrorism is a plague happening all over the world. An elite troop, made of commandos, coming from the American army, is training to fight terrorists. The general commandant says 'We will be there to kill'.

Another ad for the single, with accompanying tour dates, was published in *NME* and featured an action shot from a boxing match, with informative ticker-tape up the side:

Red Cross Boxing at the Empress Stadium, Earls Court . . . 2nd round Kilrain retired with split eye . . .

Warfare and macho (makko) sporting pursuits: it all connected, somehow to the battered and bruised emotions of the song's protagonist.

The single was warmly received by critics on its release in June 1979. Giovanni Dadomo of *Record Mirror* and Ian Birch of *Melody Maker* both compared it to The Beatles. Phil Sutcliffe in *Sounds* called it 'their untypical Undertones manque single'. Even *NME*'s noted Curesceptic Paul Morley (see **Desperate Journalist**) wrote 'This is magnificent', and his colleague Jon Savage called it 'a genuine find' when it appeared on **Polydor**'s *20 of Another Kind, Vol 2* compilation ('**Killing An Arab**' had appeared on *Vol 1*). Decades later Bob Stanley, in his book *Yeah Yeah Yeah*, called it 'Palitoy Power Pop' (Palitoy being the manufacturer of tough-guy boys' toy Action Man).

Despite all that critical goodwill, it failed to chart first time around. However, it was to receive a second chance. In 1986 The Cure needed a single to promote the *Standing On A Beach* compilation, and 'Boys Don't Cry' was given a 'New Voice – New Mix' reboot.

There are various notable differences between the 1986 version and the original. On the newer version, the four-chord intro is strummed rhythmically rather than struck, filling the gaps. On the second and third choruses, there is no gap between the words 'boys don't cry' (as compared to the lagged 'boys . . . don't cry' on the original). At the end of the bridge, on the line 'thought that you needed me more', the word 'more' is sung once and allowed to hang, given a bit of echo (as compared to the repeated 'more-more-more' on the original). The drums are also slightly more prominent.

The 1986 12-inch is more complex than either of the 7-inch versions. It starts with just bass and drums for a few bars, before the guitar intro plays for a few further bars with added guitar embellishments, so that it's almost ninety seconds before the vocals come in. The second verse is Robert's voice and Lol's drums only, then Lol's drums on their own for a while, then an echoey chorus, then just the guitar on its own, then the drum comes back in, then the 'I would break down' verse, then a penultimate chorus, half of which is just Robert's voice and guitar, then the bridge, then an instrumental section . . . until the song has become twice as long, but somehow manages to be half as satisfying.

Strangest of all, after going to all that effort, neither the 7-inch nor 12-inch edit of the 1986 version made it onto *Standing On A Beach*, the album it was intended to promote. For that album, the 1979 original was used intact. (In the US, 'Let's Go To Bed' was re-released to promote the album instead.)

For the 1986 single's B-sides, no new songs were written. Instead, they delved back into the archives for two songs as old as 'Boys Don't Cry' itself. One, on the 12-inch, was the daft disco folly 'Do The Hansa' (see Hansa). The other, on the 7-inch, was 'Pillbox Tales' (originally called 'Listen'), which was recorded in 1979 for Hansa but thus far unreleased. The latter is not, as one might suspect, a drug song but a reference to the time Lol Tolhurst and his girlfriend Sarah snuck out for a midnight tryst in one of the hexagonal Second World War machine gun emplacements, known as 'pillboxes', built across Britain in anticipation of German invasion, of which there remained dozens in the fields and woods north of Horley. (Pillbox Tales eventually became the title of a Belgian bootleg compilation of early rarities.) Robert, in a 1991 edition of Cure News, dismissed both B-sides as 'a nonsense'.

A video, directed by Tim Pope, was made for the 1986 version. The Cure – the original trio, bassist Michael Dempsey having been brought back in for the day – appear in shadow form only, with glowing red eyes, behind a backdrop onto which 'The Cure?' is briefly projected, with day-glo gloves popping up at random (in a possible callback to the socks in 'In Between Days'). In front of the backdrop, three young boys perform the song. 'We saw these three boys playing football in the school playing field,' Robert told Les Enfants du Rock, 'and thought they looked remarkably like us at that age.' Another version of the story is that various kids were invited to a dance studio to audition, and asked to play drums. Lol picked someone to look like the younger him ('but he flattered himself'), and they each did the same. In any case, the three children make it a brilliantly effective video. Following their moment of fame, the boys often went to Cure shows and met the band. Only one of them subsequently pursued a career in showbusiness. Mark Heatley (the young Robert Smith) went on to star in the 1988 TV movie Infantile Disorders before leaving the acting industry for a successful career in IT, though he made a return to acting in 2020, voicing the character Mavic Chen in a CGI recreation of a lost episode of Doctor Who.

As well as the video, the single was promoted with a round of television appearances, including one in France with the band all wearing dresses (this, apparently, was Lol's idea). And it became a hit at last, albeit a minor one. Chris Parry was convinced the original would reach the Top 10, but 'It didn't get there because Polydor stitched us up', Robert Smith, promoting the new version, told The Hit magazine. 'In a perfect world, that would have been No.1.' It reached No.22. (It made the Top 10 in Ireland, and also New Zealand, where it had already reached No.22 first time around.) Nevertheless, it proved to newcomers that The Cure always did have pop songs up their sleeve, before the hits came. It's just that the world wasn't listening yet.

'Boys Don't Cry' has had a significant cultural afterlife. It's one of The Cure's most-covered songs, with versions by Scarlett Johansson, Miley Cyrus, Hell Is for Heroes, Reel Big Fish and Razorlight among others, plus a truly horrible breathy rendition by Grant Lee Phillips. In 2016 it was sung in a blind audition on the French version of The Voice by Antoine Galey. (He came third.)

The Cure themselves rarely leave it out of their setlist (it is their second most-played song, behind 'A Forest'), and as well as the two single versions, recorded an acoustic take for MTV Unplugged. 'Right,' said Robert with a wry twinkle in his eye, 'this is the, um, definitive version of "Boys Don't Cry" . . .'

The title has been repurposed many times, including a 2021 novel by Fiona Scarlett, a 2010 novel by Malorie Blackman, a 1999 film by Kimberly Peirce, and a magazine published by Frank Ocean in 2016 to accompany his album Blonde, which was released on his own label, also called Boys Don't Cry. The song has been used in countless films, including The Wedding Singer, 50 First Dates, Nick and Norah's Infinite Playlist, and Friends With Benefits. It has also been used, played backwards, as catwalk music at the end-of-year show at the Antwerp fashion academy. And in 2022 English singer Louis Dunford recorded a song supportive of male mental health issues called 'Boys Do Cry'.

The song lived on as a touchstone of male sensitivity for the emo generation, and Robert Smith believes it has something to say in the context of LGBTQIA+ culture. 'I was singing ['Boys Don't Cry'] at Glastonbury', he told Rolling Stone, 'and I realised that it has a very contemporary resonance with all the rainbow stripes and stuff flying in the crowd . . .'

As long as toxic masculinity exists, 'Boys Don't Cry' will be there to help with the detox.

Brazil

The Cure's eight-date tour of Brazil in the summer of 1987 could not have been more different to the mayhem and carnage that characterised their visit to **Argentina** just a few days earlier.

The previous year had been The Cure's Brazilian breakthrough, *in absentia*. The massive Rock in Rio festival in 1985, whose headliners included Queen, Rod Stewart and Yes, made Anglophone rock hugely popular, and by 1986 newer bands like The Cure and U2 were swept up in the trend. *Standing On A Beach* became a bestseller, '**Close To Me**', '**Let's Go To Bed**' and '**The Walk**' all entered the charts and received heavy rotation on Brazilian radio; the French TV special *Les Enfants du Rock* was screened on a national station; '**In Between Days**' was played on a TV soap; previous albums *Concert* and *The Head On The Door* sold in large quantities; music magazine *Bizz* was deluged with letters about The Cure; national newspapers began writing full-page appreciations of them, and by the end of 1986 they'd sold almost 400,000 albums in South America, the majority of them in Brazil.

By the time The Cure arrived there in March 1987, they were already so popular that they found it impossible to wander around and meet ordinary people because they were always surrounded by security. At a show in Belo Horizonte, armed police had to form a human chain to create a narrow corridor through the crowd for The Cure to walk to the stage. By the end of the gig, the steel barrier at the front was snapping (but the chaos of Buenos Aires was thankfully averted). The final three shows in São Paulo, where their popularity was at its highest, were attended by approximately 20,000 people per night.

Robert and the band were highly appreciative of this rapturous welcome, and reciprocated by giving Brazil the world's first taste of upcoming album *Kiss Me, Kiss Me, Kiss Me*. Lead single '**Why Can't I Be You**' premiered on the second night in Porto Alegre and later featured in São Paulo, where '**Torture**' was also unveiled.

Their first visit to Brazil was considered sufficiently significant for one of the concerts to be broadcast on Brazilian TV, further boosting their profile. Following the tour, sales of *Standing On A Beach* passed a quarter of a million (which was, at the time, more than had been sold back home in the UK).

The Cure's next visit to Brazil was in January 1996, when they began the Swing tour with two dates there, and again Brazilians were treated to an exclusive. Songs from *Wild Mood Swings* were premiered at the opening night in São Paulo, and two days later the band performed six of them for the press in a Rio hotel. Again, the Rio gig was shown on TV. During the encore, Robert wore a Brazil football shirt. On a night off in Rio de Janeiro, as reported by *Cure News*, they decided to enter a local nightclub talent show. Robert drew the short straw and sang Barry Manilow's '**Copacabana**' (a night which inspired the video to 'The 13th').

Roger O'Donnell was as much a fan of Brazil as Robert was. On one occasion he was honoured to meet Ayrton Senna's sister, as an admirer of the late racing driver. In 1999, he uploaded music to his Prizmatic website which wasn't right for The Cure but which had a distinct Brazilian influence (an influence which did, nevertheless, seep through onto The Cure's 1996 single '**Gone!**').

Robert, however, could not always enjoy Brazil in the way he would have wished. He was simply too famous, and too recognisable. 'The group divides itself in two parts,' he told *Oor* in 1999:

Simon (Gallup), Porl (Thompson) and I couldn't enjoy it, the others could. We couldn't escape it, because our haircuts and pale faces showed we were no tourists. We played in gigantic stadiums and stayed in luxurious hotels. But despite all that, you felt like a prisoner inside your hotel room, because there were constantly hordes of fans waiting for you downstairs. Sometimes I felt like running downstairs and screaming: 'Here I am, just rip me to pieces!' To see all those faces of people who lost hope but still stayed around the hotel, from the window of your limousine. It was perverted. I could by no means find it a terrific experience. The shows however are amongst the best we gave. Rich with emotion. You could see how long people had been waiting for it, and how they wanted to suck every last breath out of us. At the same time, that was very frightening. At a certain point, a barrier broke right when we got out of the bus. Suddenly, I found myself lying on the ground with a bunch of people on top of me. I thought: 'What a fucked-up way to die, overwhelmed by sixty million Brazilians . . .'

Bullying

Was there a culture of bullying in The Cure? It's the elephant in the room when discussing the dynamic during the band's imperial phase of the late eighties, and it's a tough subject to deal with.

'It was bullying at its worst,' **Roger O'Donnell** once told Craig Parker from the **website** Chain of Flowers, 'and I am afraid to say I was a part of it. I am very sorry for the part I took in it all, but it was such an entrenched part of the culture of the band it was very hard not to get involved. *Lord Of The Flies* springs to mind. . .'

The 'Piggy' in this analogy is **Lol Tolhurst**. As long ago as **Matthieu Hartley**'s time, Tolhurst was the lightning rod for the band's frustrations. 'Dear old Lol,' said Hartley in *Ten Imaginary Years*. 'He's the master. We beat him up, wind him up, frame him up, but he understands. He knows we have to release our tensions in some way and he's the target.' (Hartley also admitted that he often picked on Lol because he couldn't pick on Robert Smith.)

What started as a family secret began to seep out. As early as 1986, journalists noted that Lol was invariably the butt of **Simon Gallup** and Robert Smith's jokes. In 1987, Robert told ITV's *Night Network* that 'Lol gets persecuted in every one of our **videos**. That's the theme that runs through them all.' It was becoming clear, however, that fiction reflected fact. When asked in *Cure News* who argues with whom in March 1987, almost everyone named Lol, and a year later the same publication included the statement 'everyone hates Lol because he chain-smokes'.

The Lol-baiting went into overdrive, unsurprisingly, circa 1989 and *Disintegration*. In January of that year, Robert answered fan questions in *Cure News*.

Q: What's the funniest thing Lol has ever done?
A: Pretend to be part of the group.
Q: Why do you all victimise Lol?
A: Because he is useless.

Asked to define his relationship with each band member, when it came to Lol, Robert said 'non'. And Robert wasn't the only Tolhurst-taunter: in the band's official tour programme, Roger named Lol as his favourite wooden object.

In the immediate aftermath of Tolhurst's inevitable dismissal, there was a certain amount of measured remorse from his former bandmates. Robert admitted to *Cure News* that the worst thing he did to Lol was to have 'left him unconscious drunk naked in a hotel lift'. Speaking to Belgian magazine *Humo*, he said 'Lol played a certain role in the past – the role of the victim. We constantly criticised him. Bullying Lol was our favourite thing to do in our spare time. Sadly enough, he couldn't even fulfil that part any more in the last two years.' In the same interview, Smith revealed that the reason he was considering a **solo album** was 'because I was fed up with all of those games and all of that bullying. It used to be fun, a real floorshow; top-shelf barbed wire humour. But after a while, it had more to do with a constant attack, and the worst thing was that Lol didn't even react to it anymore.'

A couple of years later, however, Robert had hardened. When asked why he left Lol out of his list of thanks at the BRIT **Awards**, he told *Cure News*, 'Because he did nothing worthy of thanks and I despise him!'

Lol's post-Cure band **Presence** were a particular object of scorn. In 1992, Robert gleefully recited extracts from appalling reviews by *Melody Maker*'s Andrew Mueller. (In the same piece, Mueller noted that The Cure had a Lol Tolhurst dart board on the tour bus, given by a friend.) 'Presence would be better without Tolhurst,' Robert told *Cure News* in October 1991. 'He does nothing except pose ridiculously and look ugly – but even without him they would be at best mediocre.' In the same interview he revealed that he and Simon Gallup had been to see Presence at the Marquee in London that June. 'Simon and I decided we should inform Tolhurst of his uselessness at first hand – so we did.' (He also mocked Lol for putting 'ex-Cure' on Presence adverts.)

In hindsight, Roger O'Donnell, writing on his own website, expressed sadness at the way things had played out:

I think it's pretty much common knowledge how Lol was treated in those days: very very badly. I'm not innocent either, but then again he didn't really do himself any favours, he was drunk most of the time and when he was trying to stay sober we would do all we could to get him drunk again. He barely played anything on the record [*Disintegration*] and I think some of the things he did play I had to play again while he wasn't there. It was pretty sad, looking back, the way he was victimised but it was sort of funny at the time, or was it? He would usually be so drunk after dinner that he would go straight to bed only to get up at about 2 a.m. and come wandering into the studio and say everything sounded like shit. He would then decide he was hungry and would go and cook himself something, which we would all do our best to ruin. He would still eat it, though. . .

In the same piece, Roger went into specifics. 'One of the other amusing things to do was to use Lol's brand new computer, that we made him buy, to draw obscene pictures of him on and then pin them on the wall . . . How old were we?'

In his 1994 **lawsuit** against The Cure, Tolhurst's statement accused other members of waging a campaign of malicious practical jokes, including putting a scorpion skin in his face flannel and (corroborating Roger's account) decorating the studio with cruel cartoons of him, leading to him becoming ill and losing a stone in weight.

He admitted that when under the influence of **alcohol** he sometimes became aggressive, largely stemming from frustrations he felt. 'It was a vicious circle, I drank for confidence, but later, I lost my confidence because of the drink or the constant abuse and I became unable to perform. The other members of the band would constantly play practical jokes on me. As the days wore on, these jokes became more and more malicious.'

Interestingly, in his 2016 memoir *Cured*, Tolhurst doesn't place the blame for what went on anywhere but upon himself. He admits being a drunk who contributed little to the final Cure record to carry his name, and who behaved regrettably himself. (This is classic Twelve-Step rehab speak: former addicts taking 'ownership' of what happened during their addiction, and making amends.) It is clearly a subject on which he still has strong feelings, however. In 2014, Tolhurst made the music for a documentary about bullying by Swedish director Sandra Nelhans called *So It Won't Happen Again*.

Simon Gallup, speaking to journalist Johnny Black in 1994, also ventured the view that Lol brought the bullying upon himself. 'He voluntarily became a scapegoat', Gallup claimed, arguing that Tolhurst perversely enjoyed his role as band punchbag. 'His contribution to the group was minimal to say the least – this is the way he could get attention.' Tolhurst would deliberately try to provoke Gallup, the bassist recalled, with **Perry Bamonte** trying to calm things down, but 'I would punch his [Tolhurst's] lights out.' (It's important to mention at this point that Simon has separately stated that he wishes he had been 'kinder' to Lol.)

When Tolhurst was removed from the equation, he left a victim vacuum. 'I think it was a huge relief after he was gone,' wrote Roger. 'However, I do remember there being a certain uneasiness as to who was going to take his place as the band scapegoat or escape valve. He wasn't missed in any sense, he had become ridiculous and sad. Nobody did take up the role of official scapegoat, and that probably led to the tensions within the band becoming so unbearable during the Prayer Tour.'

Eventually, with the passing of time, the ill feeling became water under the bridge, and Lol was even invited to rejoin The Cure for nine shows in 2011. 'Happily,' wrote Roger on his blog, 'Lol is now healthy and happy and not drinking and hopefully he forgives us for what went on then . . .'

What went on then wasn't good for Lol Tolhurst, and it wasn't good for any of The Cure. Nobody comes out of the bullying saga covered in glory. Both victim and perpetrators have accepted their faults, and to varying extents patched up their differences.

A redemption, of sorts.

Burrows, Sean

Credited as an assistant to the producers on *Kiss Me, Kiss Me, Kiss Me*, sound engineer Sean Burrows had an eclectic track record beforehand, working with Lee 'Scratch' Perry, Eurythmics, Mick Jagger, Iron Maiden and Judas Priest. His role on The Cure album was to record the saxophone parts at Compass Point Studios in the Bahamas, along with Jacques Hermet. After working with The Cure he vanished off the face of the recording industry.

Butcher Billy

It's unsurprising that a man who is essentially a walking comic book character should find himself the subject of comic art. The pages of Pinterest are overflowing with caricatures of Robert Smith by fans with varying levels of talent, and that's before we begin to discuss The Cure's frontman's animated avatar in *South Park* (see **TV**).

There's even been a full-length Cure comic, published by Revolutionary Comics in 1992. The work of editor Todd Loren, writer Jay Allen Sanford, and artists Greg Fox (cover) and Scott Jackson (panels), it's an unauthorised biography (based on 1989's official Cure **book** *Ten Imaginary Years*) which takes as its premise the fact that Robert is terrified of flying. On a plane, he meets Death and his life flashes before his eyes in graphic novel form. (Robert later told *Cure News* he had read the comic and considered it 'excellent' and 'frighteningly true'.)

One comic artist, however, stands tall above all others when it comes to depicting Robert Smith, and that artist is Butcher Billy. Born Billy Mariano da Luz in Curitiba, **Brazil** in 1978, he worked as a graphic designer in an ad agency for many years before adopting the Butcher Billy alias for his illustrations of late seventies and early eighties musical icons in the style of classic Marvel/DC comic book covers.

'As a child of the Eighties', he told the blog MusicOnWalls, 'I was heavily influenced by everything from Saturday morning cartoons on TV to the music coming from the radio. Ian Curtis or Johnny Rotten are as iconic to me as Superman or Batman. Real people or imaginary characters, the incorruptible ideals of perfect superheroes or the human flaws and desires sometimes so desperately depicted in song lyrics – all of those influences affect us to the point of defining our character and personality, career paths and life choices.'

His first series, *The Post-Punk/New Wave Super Friends*, went viral in 2013 with its depictions of heroes including Joy Division, Morrissey, Devo, **Siouxsie** and, above all, Robert Smith, whom he depicted in the styles of *The Joker*, *The Deep* and *Jaws*.

As Billy's fame spread, he continued to paint pop icons (Freddie Mercury, Kurt Cobain, Amy Winehouse, and almost as many images of **David Bowie** as David Bowie had images). He intermittently returned to Robert Smith as an inspirational icon, with images which referenced *Beetlejuice* and *The Lost Boys*.

Meanwhile, his work was picked up by publications including the *Guardian*, *Rolling Stone* and *Vanity Fair*. His pieces were showcased in galleries across the globe, in cities including London, Dubai, Lisbon, New York, Paris, San Francisco, Birmingham, Chicago and Miami, and two books of his art have been published in France. He attracted commercial collaborations with companies including ESPN, Michael Jordan, Foot Locker, British Gas, E Leclerc, Billboard and, fittingly, art supplies manufacturer Winsor & Newton. He has also worked with television shows such as *Stranger Things*, *The Mandalorian* and *Black Mirror*, drawing

images to create excitement around each episode.

However, he just couldn't leave The Cure alone. In 2016, via the online platform Adobe Create, Butcher Billy published *Tales from the Smith*, a series of images which recontextualised Cure songs as retro horror posters: 'Close To Me', 'Boys Don't Cry', 'Pictures Of You', 'A Forest', 'The Caterpillar', 'Friday I'm In Love', 'Lullaby' and 'Disintegration', rendered in classic gore flick style with nods to films like *Friday 13th* and *The Evil Dead*. (Cannily, he made them available to buy as prints and T-shirts.)

They are utterly superb. Despite being completely unofficial and having no input from The Cure themselves, Butcher Billy's images succeed in bringing the songs to life every bit as vividly as any **Tim Pope** video or **Parched Art** packaging.

'This frightening series of strange tales,' the artist explained, 'is an homage to the **goth** legend who truly taught us love and darkness'.

C

C is for …

Camus, Albert

Albert Camus, born in 1913 in Mondovi (now known as Dréan) in Algeria, was a French–Algerian writer and philosopher associated with the ideas of Existentialism, the Absurd and Rebellion, and the second-youngest ever recipient of the Nobel Prize for **Literature**. His novel *L'Étranger* was the inspiration for The Cure's debut single '**Killing An Arab**'.

That novel's title is usually translated in English as *The Outsider* or *The Stranger*. However, in French it carries an added meaning: the phrase 'à l'étranger' means 'abroad' or 'another country'. Published in 1942, at a time when Algeria, where it is set, was still a colony of France, this undercurrent of 'otherness' was not insignificant.

The novel is a first-person narrative from the point of view of Meursault, a man who appears devoid of agency and incapable of empathy; a man who merely exists and is buffeted by events, indifferent to his fate. In the book's crucial scene, as recounted in The Cure's lyric, Meursault and a friend become involved in an altercation with a pair of Arab men. Shortly afterwards, Meursault encounters the men again and, affected by heatstroke and seeing a flash of a knife, shoots one of them dead with a gun he has confiscated from his friend for safekeeping. In the book's second half, Meursault is convicted by a jury, it seems, for failing to show the emotions deemed acceptable by society – for example, grief at the death of his mother – more than for the crime itself. (As Camus summarised it later, 'In our society any man who does not weep at his mother's funeral runs the risk of being sentenced to death.') Meursault is offered a lifeline by a chaplain who tries to convince him that converting to the Christian **religion** will help his appeal, but Meursault, an atheist, refuses. He is executed.

Le Monde rated *L'Étranger* No.1 in their Top 100 books of the twentieth century. It is the ultimate cult classic, one of the core texts for any student Existentialist, along with Franz Kafka's *The Trial*, Jean-Paul Sartre's *Dirty Hands* and Peter Handke's *The Goalie's Anxiety at the Penalty Kick* (even though Camus distanced himself from the term 'Existentialism').

Existentialism was a body of thought developed in the twentieth century and building on the previous ideas of philosophers including Heidegger, Nietzsche and Kierkegaard, which held that existence precedes essence, emphasising the authentic subjective experience of a human in the world as the only real truth, and stressed the importance of action ('to be is to do' being a Sartrean tenet). It is closely linked to the notion of the Absurd, which argues that there is no meaning in the world other than the meaning we give it.

In November 1981, Paul Morley (see **Desperate Journalist**) wrote a Cure feature for *NME*, written in the voice of Robert Smith as paraphrased/imagined by the writer. In the piece, 'Robert' says the following: 'There are no bounds that ANYONE can conclusively fix that can realistically harness us, so therefore you work in the context of the absurd. Life is ABSURD, then death is absurd, a heightened absurdity perhaps less absurd than birth.'

It's fairly certain that Robert, or 'Robert', is alluding to Camus here, especially as the opening paragraphs of the piece mentioned French literature. And Morley, if it was his interpretation of Smith's ideas rather than Smith's actual words, was not inaccurate. 'Killing An Arab' was not, and would not be, The Cure's only early expression of the Absurd. The song '**One Hundred Years**' had not been written yet, but the lyric 'It doesn't matter if we all die' is nothing if not a statement of the Absurd.

Camus developed his ideas further in 1947's *La Peste* (*The Plague*) in which a bubonic plague-like virus strikes the Algerian city of Oran, causing its people to band together in common cause to defeat the threat. It has been read as an allegory for the French Resistance fighting Nazi occupation. It's arguably a superior work to *L'Étranger,* and if the young Robert Smith had read that one instead, and sung 'I am the stranger, killing a virus', it might have saved him a lot of trouble.

Other significant Camus works include *Le Mythe de Sisyphe* (*The Myth of Sisyphus*), 1942, *L'Homme Revolte* (*The Rebel*), 1951, *La Chute* (*The Fall*), 1956, which gave fellow post-punk band The Fall their name, the short story collection *L'Exil et le Royaume* (*Exile and the Kingdom*), 1957, and the unfinished

Le Premier Homme (*The First Man*), still being written at the time of his death and published in 1994.

Robert is known to have read Camus and Sartre as a teenager in French, and once told *Cure News* that philosophically his biggest influences are Camus, Sartre, Kafka and his dad. Camus' connection to The Cure evidently goes further than just one song. Indeed, the immediate precursor to *L'Etranger*, *La Mort Heureuse* (*A Happy Death*), written 1936–38 but unpublished until 1971, is referenced in the song 'M' on *Seventeen Seconds*.

Another point of connection is Camus' love of football. Like Smith (see **Queens Park Rangers**), Albert Camus saw no conflict between being a deep thinker and having a love of the game. Famously, he played in goal for the Racing Universitaire d'Alger junior team from 1928 to 1930, and contrasted the simple rules and clear morals of the sport with the contradictory imperatives of the Church and State. One of his oft-repeated quotations is 'What I know most surely in the long run about morality and obligations, I owe to football.'

Albert Camus died aged forty-six in a car crash on 4 January 1960, driving the luxurious Facel Vega FVS of his publisher Michel Gallimard (who also died) into a plane tree on a long straight stretch of the Route Nationale 5. A death as senseless and absurd as anything in his works.

Carnage Visors

Carnage Visors is the ultimate elusive Cure item: it literally cannot be seen.

When The Cure played Aylesbury Friars on Saturday 18 April 1981, the first night of the Picture Tour – the tour to promote the album *Faith*, which had come out the day before – the advertising promised 'A complete evening including special Cure recorded music, a Cure film and The Cure live on stage for approx 90 minutes.'

That film was *Carnage Visors*, a twenty-seven-minute and fifty-one-second animated short directed by **Ric Gallup**, older brother of bassist **Simon** (and something of a mentor and facilitator to the early Cure). The Cure had commissioned Gallup to create the film with the intention of taking it on tour with them in lieu of a support band. Ric's first attempt at making *Carnage Visors* (the title was meant to be 'the opposite of rose-tinted spectacles'), which had taken

over two months to put together in his garage, had to be scrapped when it came back from the developers because it was too dark to use. He then had just three days to film a replacement version.

Meanwhile, the band – who had not seen the finished film – were obliged to record the instrumental soundtrack 'blind' in one day on 16 March at Point Studios near London's Victoria Station. According to *Ten Imaginary Years*, 'Robert played bass along with a Dr Rhythm drum machine, **Lol** counted out beats on a stopwatch, Simon poured wine into Robert's mouth at two-minute intervals then added bass overdubs. Robert did some keyboards too.'

Fortunately, by all accounts, the soundtrack – a long, portentous, atmospheric piece built around one recurring motif – complemented the film well. Some fans, however, found the whole concept too challenging, and reacted restlessly. It therefore had the added bonus of allowing the band to gauge how volatile a crowd was likely to be on any given night. 'If there was a lot of catcalls and throwing of things at the stage,' Robert recalled later, 'it would wind us up and we'd go out and be really aggressive.'

The film was never officially released. Plans to put it out as a cut-price VHS circa 1987 were abandoned. The only surviving footage online is a thirty-five-second extract, showing a long-limbed robot with a television for a face gazing at itself in a mirror with horror while another mechanical beast looks on. The provenance of this clip is a French TV show from 1985 which ran it during a Cure interview, much to the band's amazement: they had no idea where the producers had sourced the film.

One person from outside The Cure camp, however, managed to get their hands on it. On the *Curious Creatures* podcast, Budgie revealed that he had seen *Carnage Visors* at The Cure's show at the London Lyceum, got hold of a copy, and played it on **Siouxsie And The Banshees**' tour bus.

The soundtrack was a little easier to acquire. It was first released on Side 2 of the cassette version of *Faith*, billed on the artwork of some versions as 'Two Albums on One Cassette'. It was later released on CD when *Faith* was given a deluxe reissue in 2005. However, it has never been officially released on vinyl. A limited-edition test pressing is rumoured to have been made (*Record Collector* even placed it at No.9 in a list of Cure **rarities**), but the rumour is false: Daren Butler's painstakingly accurate *The Cure on Record* (see **Books**) states that '**Fiction** never pressed any vinyl or test pressings', and Robert Smith himself has stated that it doesn't exist.

The Cure returned to the idea of a support film in 1987 on the Kissing Tour with the intro film *Eyemou*, footage of which is far easier to find (and which is therefore far less discussed). In the decades since, the invisibility of *Carnage Visors* means it has taken on a mythology of its own.

Beware of fakes. A full twenty-eight-minute clip ostensibly purporting to be *Carnage Visors* was uploaded to YouTube by a user called encOm511 in April 2020: a mix of vintage stop-motion puppetry, German expressionist cinema and the 1903 Hepworth & Stow silent adaptation of *Alice in Wonderland* stitched together with Ric Gallup's long-armed robot at the end. It's all given a unified feel by overlaying a murky 'vintage' filter, but it seems like a clever hoax. The telltale words 'Comments are turned off' appear directly under the clip. Perhaps conclusively, encOm511's 'About' section says, quite openly, 'All music videos I post are created & subtitled by me.'

Perhaps the real deal is out there somewhere, gathering dust in Ric Gallup's garage, or decaying in Budgie's basement, or lurking pristine in a French television station's archive. Perhaps we'll see it one day. But perhaps it's better for some mysteries to remain mysteries.

Cars

The Cure are not a car-obsessed band. Their many MTV appearances did not include *Pimp My Ride*. Robert Smith is not Bruce Springsteen, despite sharing a penchant for long gigs. And he has never written a lyric about driving his Chevy to the levee, nor a hymn to his little deuce coupe. What follows, however, is an incomplete and inexact history of Robert Smith's cars (and those of certain other Cure members).

Smith's first car, in his late teens, was a Mini which he painted grey. He drove it before the paint had dried, and it ended up covered in leaves. He upgraded to a blue Vauxhall Chevette, but crashed it into a wall on the way home from an early Cure gig and 'nearly decapitated ourselves', forcing the band to borrow their mate Phil from **Horley**'s van, which in turn broke down on the way to their London gig the following night, which they failed to make (much to **Chris Parry**'s displeasure). We also know, thanks to **John Taw**'s photos, that at least one member of The Cure's first line-up owned a British Leyland hatchback, and that it probably wasn't **Michael Dempsey** (as he was in the passenger seat). Dempsey, during his time in **Associates** and possibly The Cure, also drove a Vauxhall Chevette.

By the time of their tour supporting **Siouxsie And The Banshees** in 1979, Robert was driving a green Austin Maxi – literally a **mint car** – but chose to travel in the Banshees' bus while the rest of The Cure crammed themselves into Smith's car.

In 1982, according to Leon Muraglia of **Animation**, Smith drove a larger white Vauxhall VX1800 Estate. By 1985, according to his own diary in *Libération*, he was driving a Jeep. It was this white Jeep which he arranged to be sent to **France** in 1986 circa *The Cure In Orange*, in order to drive around during the *Kiss Me, Kiss Me, Kiss Me* sessions. However, that white Jeep too was written off during a late-night driving escapade through the village of Correns involving the whole band which left it dangling precariously over the precipice of a vineyard.

By the time of *Disintegration* he was driving a black Lada Niva, which he described in *Cure News* as 'a big customised "off-road" thing'. According to **Roger O'Donnell**'s blog about *Disintegration*, 'pretty much the whole band were into 4x4 vehicles at the time, I had a Jeep Wrangler, **Boris Williams** and **Porl Thompson** both had Land Rovers and Robert had a Lada 4x4. Boris, Porl and I all met up at Boris' house and drove up to Reading in convoy together, we even had walkie talkies so we could talk to each other on the way. Very big toys for big boys.' (Roger and Boris are also known to have owned retro MG sports cars circa *Disintegration*.)

The Lada Niva was still Robert's vehicle in 1991 and 1992. That's when the trail goes cold and the car-related revelations dry up. Smith's current motor of choice is not a matter of public record. If you do see him on the roads, however, you're advised to heed the incidents above, and allow him plenty of space.

Catch

'You write good songs', the executives of **Hansa** told Robert Smith before dumping The Cure, 'but there's never a catch.'

Well, there was now.

This anecdote, put about by Smith in 1987, is only

part of the explanation behind the sweetly swaying single they released as their second from *Kiss Me, Kiss Me, Kiss Me*. The lyric, like many Cure songs before it, appears to be about an ever-elusive girl. There's a plausible theory that it has **sexual** overtones ('And even though it felt soft at the time, I always used to wake up sore . . .') But the full story, Smith told *Cure News* in 1998, was rather more elaborate. 'In 1970, aged ten, I fell off my bike and suffered quite severe concussion; sporadically, over the following two years, I suffered fleeting but intense daytime hallucinations of a girl called "Bunny" (see **Bunny Lake**). In 1972 I flew for the first time; a few minutes after take-off the plane hit really bad turbulence and I suffered a very violent attack of nausea and vomiting, along with incredibly severe headache; after this my Bunny visits stopped. In 1984 in NYC JFK airport whilst waiting to pass through immigration I met a girl who was the spitting image of Bunny. Her real name was Anna, we talked very briefly. "Catch" is about this chance encounter.'

Whether you choose to believe this tall tale is a matter of personal taste, but the song itself, with its idyllic, sleepy, shambling charm, has the power to make even the most hardened *Pornography* fan sigh 'Aaahhh'. Small and perfectly formed, at just two minutes forty-three seconds, 'Catch', packaged in a **Parched Art** sleeve depicting watercolour swirls of tadpole-like (or sperm-like) shapes, with 'Breathe' on the B-side and additionally 'Chain of Flowers' on the 12-inch, came out on 27 June 1987. It wasn't a huge hit (No.27 in the UK, No.16 in Ireland, something of a flop elsewhere), but in the context of its parent album it melted the hearts of all those who had a heart to melt.

It didn't receive a huge amount of promotion, apart from a performance on *The Roxy* (ITV's short-lived rival to *Top of the Pops*), but there was, of course, a video. According to both Robert Smith and director **Tim Pope**, the three-day shoot took place on location in the home of a 'Lady Kildare' in Cap Camarat, Provence, France. (Extensive research fails to uncover the existence of any Lady Kildare during that era. She, like 'Bunny', remains elusive . . .) Another account describes the owner as a '94-year-old harpist'. In any case, the video depicts the band strolling through an overgrown hillside garden. As Pope vividly recalled on his website, 'The whole location . . . stank of dog shit. Tortoises were everywhere, cooking in the sun like boil-in-a-bag crustaceans, and we found another room that was just like something Miss

Havisham would have lived in. It was filled with rotting ballerinas' dresses and rag dolls with maggots in. The elderly lady who owned the joint came down the spiral staircase, like Gloria Swanson in *Sunset Boulevard*.'

Smith was pleased with the video, apart from one scene. '**Lol [Tolhurst]** ruined it,' he later complained. 'We made this beautiful video, and this old bastard in coal miner's jeans wanders down the spiral staircase not even bothering to pretend he's playing the violin.'

If he could change one thing about 'Catch', he told *Cure News*, 'I'd leave the coalman violinist out.'

Caterpillar, The

In the 2010s, the British media, from the BBC to the *Daily Star*, regularly ran a scare story to the effect that **drug** dealers were selling Rowntree's Fruit Pastilles injected with LSD. A better metaphor for 'The Caterpillar' by The Cure you could not hope to find: a perfect lysergic pop confection.

As well as being the lead single from *The Top*, 'The Caterpillar' was the first the public heard of their work with long-term producer **Dave Allen**. In both respects, it represented something of a curveball. Coming off the back of Robert Smith's crazy year of **1983**, in which he gorged himself on both psychedelia ('**Dear Prudence**', *Blue Sunshine*) and psychedelics, 'The Caterpillar' was both a logical conclusion and also something of a cul-de-sac.

There are some for whose tastes 'The Caterpillar' may be a little *too* twee and whimsical, but it has grown in stature to become one of the band's most fondly regarded singles. Like '**Let's Go To Bed**', it's a song whose main melody is made of doo-doo-doos. Why are some doo-doo-doos better than others? Somehow, on 'The Caterpillar' it works far more effectively than on 'Let's Go To Bed'. One is charming, the other has a capacity to be irritating. It's almost as if on 'Let's Go To Bed' the doo-doo-doos were sarcastic, with inverted commas placed around them to distance The Cure from such a pop ploy, whereas on 'The Caterpillar' they are sincerely embraced.

The chaotic, atonal violins at the start, played by Robert, sound like the speech of children's television aliens *The Clangers*. Before the song gets going Smith, *sotto voce*, mumbles 'Sunday, Monday, Tuesday' etc., but with some days missing. (He would get all the days of the week in the right order a decade later on a lesser, but more successful, single.) The butterfly wingbeats are, famously, the slapped thighs of **Andy Anderson**'s leather trousers.

In terms of instrumentation, it's acoustic (strummed guitar, piano, congas), adding to the sense of a song teleported forwards from the late sixties heydays of Donovan and Marc Bolan in his magickal faerie phase. Lyrically, it's a fairly simple love song in which Robert is enraptured by a flittingly transient 'caterpillar girl', to whom he will say anything mendacious that might keep her near him: 'I'll dust my lemon lies with powder, pink and sweet . . .'

The **video**, directed by **Tim Pope**, was filmed in the London Butterfly House in the Great Conservatory of Syon Park, in Brentford by the side of the Thames. At that time, Syon Park was the London residence of Hugh Algernon Percy, the 10th Duke of Northumberland. (There is something pleasing about the thought of this Tory peer and honorary colonel of three different army battalions harrumphing from a high window as these disreputable drug-taking socialists and pacifists rampaged around right under his nose.)

Andy Anderson, talking to A Pink Dream, remembered it as 'a great fun day out.' Robert Smith, in **Cure News**, remembered it as the day he discovered blusher for the first time (a landmark moment in the development of his **make-up**). Tim Pope's main memory is that he perpetrated a wind-up on a crew member involving 'a massive pile of Vim' (a British brand of cleaning powder).

The video features **Porl Thompson** and **Phil Thornalley** even though they did not contribute to the song, something which has inevitably happened a few times in Cure history (see also '**Wrong Number**'), given their ever-churning line-up. What it doesn't feature, however, is any live butterflies. The band wanted to walk around in an atrium filled with lepidoptera, but it was the wrong time of year and they hadn't yet hatched from their chrysalises, meaning that The Cure had to settle for cocoons and dried caterpillars on **Lol Tolhurst**'s piano keys, and rapid cutaways to footage of butterflies from elsewhere.

It wasn't the worst butterfly-based miscalculation in rock history, at least: in 1969, The Rolling Stones attempted to release two and a half thousand Cabbage White butterflies into the air at their Hyde Park concert, but poor storage conditions and hot weather meant that most of them fell out of the boxes already dead.

Released on 30 March 1984 with the similarly acoustic-based 'Happy The Man' on the B-side, 'The Caterpillar' came in a **Parched Art** sleeve featuring a Surrealist doodle of eyes, tails and mouths, reminiscent of the 1940s work of Spanish artist Joan Miró. It reached No.14, becoming their third Top 20 hit in a row and earning them a *Top of the Pops* **television appearance** in which all five members sat cross-legged on the floor in matching black trousers and white shirts, in a very T. Rex style.

It received generally warm reviews. *Sounds* praised its 'superpretentious lyric bursting with the kind of colour references which only spring from the use of illegals, all on a voyage into the human zoo'. The most memorable review, however, came some ten years later from the world's greatest music critics, MTV's cartoon dumbass teenagers Beavis and Butt-Head. As well as parodying the song's staccato lyrics ('Peter Piper picked a peck of pickled pepper'), critiquing Robert's make-up ('His lipstick's on crooked') and his **voice** ('How come this guy always has to sing like . . . [*pained howl*] . . . If he didn't do that, he'd be better'), the duo latched onto Smith's refusal to stare down the lens.

> Butt-Head: 'How come this guy won't look at the camera? That pisses me off.'
> Beavis: 'Yeah. Yeah. It's like when you try to get a cat to look at itself in the mirror and it's like, it won't look at itself, and it looks up and down, and you're like, LOOK AT YOURSELF! LOOK AT YOURSELF! NOW! NOW! And it just won't do it . . .'

Charity

There's a certain left-wing position which contends that charity is inherently conservative, in that it places a fig leaf of respectability over a fundamentally corrupt system, allowing a warm glow of munificence to the donor without ever challenging the status quo which has resulted in the need for charity to exist in the first place, and absolving governments of their responsibility to protect the well-being of the public.

This isn't a sentiment you hear often in pop. In 1986, in the immediate afterglow of Band Aid and Live Aid, The Housemartins dared to step out of line with the single 'Flag Day', which began with Paul Heaton lamenting 'Too many Florence Nightingales/ Not enough Robin Hoods' and then taunting 'So you thought you'd like to change the world/Decided to stage a jumble sale for the poor . . .' For the majority of pop stars, the orthodoxy was still that the best way to improve the world was to rattle a collection tin under the noses of their fans. And so, by and large, it has remained.

So where do The Cure fit in? Robert Smith is fully aware of the need for radical change (see **Politics** for details of his views, and of the charities and causes he has chosen to support). However, he is also pragmatic enough to know that he is in the privileged position of being able to help people immediately via the proceeds of his recordings and performances.

For one thing, a proportion of all Cure album royalties goes to good causes ('It's my Catholic upbringing', he told the *Independent*'s Suzi Feay in 1997). And The Cure have given their time to charities since the very beginning: on 16 October 1977, still under their **pre-Cure** name Easy Cure, they played a show at Felbridge Village Hall near East Grinstead with all proceeds going to the Arthritis and Rheumatism Council.

At the height of their eighties fame, they played a show for Mencap at the Camden Palace on 19 November 1985. Mencap were also beneficiaries of the *Entreat* live album in 1991 along with the MS Society, Amnesty International, Cot Death Research, Leukaemia Research Fund, Spastics Society, Dr Hadwen Trust, NSPCC, Imperial Cancer and RNIB.

In 1994, all proceeds from the fanclub-only *Lost Wishes* cassette went to the Portsmouth Down's Syndrome Trust. In 1997 Robert hand-decorated a 'terrifying' mask for a celebrity mask auction for the Prince's Trust.

In 2007, The Cure recorded a cover of John Lennon's 'Love' for the charity album *Instant Karma: The Amnesty International Campaign To Save Darfur*. In 2008 the **Hypnagogic States** EP benefitted the International Red Cross. In 2011 all profits from the *Bestival Live 2011* album went to the Isle of Wight Youth Trust.

In 2013, The Cure invited an Amnesty International 'My Body My Rights' stall along on their South American tour. In 2014 they played two shows for the Teenage Cancer Trust at the Royal Albert Hall.

In 2019 Robert Smith and **Jason Cooper** (along with the mysterious **Bunny Lake**) submitted original pieces of artwork to be auctioned by Heart Research UK. In 2020 Robert auctioned one of his guitars for #ILoveLive to support live event workers affected by the Covid-19 pandemic. In 2021 Robert once again auctioned artwork for Heart Research UK. The same year he auctioned a guitar amp for Milk Crate Theatre, a Sydney charity which supports homeless people using workshops, theatre productions and community outreach. In 2022 The Cure released a series of Bunny Lake Designs greeting cards in aid of World Cancer Fund International.

In addition to all of that, Robert is listed as a celebrity supporter of CAFOD (the Catholic Agency For Overseas Development). That Catholic upbringing, again. And that's without even mentioning the more overtly political causes The Cure have supported, whether tacitly or actively, which include Greenpeace, the Campaign for Nuclear Disarmament and Extinction Rebellion.

In short, barely a month (and never a year) goes by without Robert Smith doing something charitable. And it's always done in the knowledge that, even if such acts cannot by themselves change the world, they can change *someone's* world.

Charlotte Sometimes

'One of the best songs we've ever done,' said Robert Smith when introducing 'Charlotte Sometimes' on French TV show *Les Enfants du Rock* in 1986, 'but one of the worst **videos** we've ever made.'

Penelope Farmer's novel *Charlotte Sometimes*, published in 1969 when Robert Smith was nine or ten, tells the story of a girl who, at night, time-travels half a century back in time to take the place of a girl called Clare, who in turn leaps forward in time to take Charlotte's place. The pair never meet, but communicate by notes left in an exercise book. Charlotte becomes trapped in Clare's era, and struggles to keep hold of her own identity. *Charlotte Sometimes* combines three recurrent Robert Smith themes: **madness**, **dreams** and **literature**.

The BBC's storytelling programme *Jackanory* serialised *Charlotte Sometimes* for children in January 1974. Robert Smith would have been fourteen, so probably not a *Jackanory* viewer (although there wasn't a lot else to do in the seventies, so you never can tell), but The Cure's teenage fans from 1981 – my generation, in fact – would already have been exposed to the story at an impressionable age, increasing the song's potency.

The opening paragraphs of the novel include the words 'By bedtime all the faces, the voices had blurred for Charlotte to one face, one voice . . .' and 'The light seemed too bright for them, glaring on white walls.' Near the end of the book there are people dancing to celebrate Armistice, and a school walk in which Charlotte learns of Clare's fate and begins crying. You don't need much more than a passing familiarity with the lyrics of 'Charlotte Sometimes' to realise how closely Robert based the song on the novel.

The stand-alone single was recorded on 16 and 17 July 1981 in the gap between a run of European festival dates and a North American tour at **Mike Hedges**' newly opened Playground Studio (which Smith named), and co-produced by Hedges and the band. Describing it on Australian radio in August 1981, ahead of its release, Smith said 'The whole thing's aggressive but in a very dreamy way. It's like a distant nightmare. It's threatening, but never comes close enough to threaten. Classic Cure song, I suppose.' His description was accurate. 'Charlotte Sometimes' is a gorgeous slow-to-mid-tempo swirl, with heavily treated guitars that pervade it like a thick mist. So heavily treated, in fact, that some mistook them for synths. (Curiously, the synth-based 1981 Various Artists compilation album *Modern Dance* features 'Charlotte Sometimes', even though it has no synthesisers on it.) **Chris Parry** didn't particularly like it, and thought it sluggish. Robert Smith, however, was so proud of it that he called **Steve Severin** from Auckland to play it to him down the phone, but fell asleep and ran up a phone bill of four hundred and eighty New Zealand dollars. He was right to be proud, though maybe not $480 proud. 'Charlotte Sometimes' is a small-g **gothic** classic, and as close to immaculate as Cure singles get.

So far, so good. That video, though, is another matter entirely. The director, at Chris Parry's suggestion, was Mike Mansfield, silver-haired supremo of ITV children's pop show *Supersonic*. As a television producer he had worked on shows like *Russell Harty Plus* and *Shang-a-Lang*, but his side hustle as a pop video director was starting to take off. He had directed Elton John & Kiki Dee's 'Don't Go Breaking My Heart', Bonnie Tyler's 'It's A Heartache' and Grace Jones' 'Private Life', as well as several videos for Rod Stewart, Sex Pistols and ELO. Most recently, he had helmed Adam & The Ants' costume mini-dramas for 'Stand And Deliver' and 'Prince Charming', which won him The Cure commission. They gave him the book *Charlotte Sometimes* to read, and he came up with

a highly literal storyboard. 'What a mistake,' said **Lol Tolhurst** in hindsight. 'Embarrassing . . .'

The location, at least, had promise. There is a belt of Victorian asylums on the leafy outskirts of London – **Michael Dempsey**, no longer a member of The Cure by the time of 'Charlotte Sometimes', once had a job as a porter at one of them, Netherne Asylum. Holloway Sanatorium, a redbrick gothic pile in Virginia Water, Surrey, was one of the more imposing examples. It was a good choice to stand in for the boarding school in the narrative. It had only closed in December 1980, and quickly became a popular filming location (perhaps most famously used in Bonnie Tyler's 'Total Eclipse Of The Heart' video). Founder Thomas Holloway's original plan was 'an asylum for the middle-class insane', and it's hard to get any more Cure than that.

The casting, however, was appalling. Charlotte, a schoolgirl in uniform, is played by grown woman in lipstick and eye make-up, her anachronistically crimped hair making her look more like a member of Pan's People (or **Zoo**) than a child, and giving the video a queasily exploitative feel from the very start. The identity of the actress, who also plays Charlotte's Victorian alter-ego Clare, has sadly been lost to history. (A myth has sprung up that it was Robert's sister Janet, another that it was **Simon Gallup**'s girlfriend, but neither is true.) The Cure had no say in picking her, and Robert, on *Les Enfants du Rock*, described her as 'uselessly horrible'.

The quality of the recording looked cheap. Apart from exterior scenes, which were rendered in almost psychedelically colourised high contrast, it had a brightly lit, made-for-TV, shot-on-videotape feel (which everyone could have seen coming, if they'd watched those Ants videos).

And the action is unintentionally hilarious. Charlotte – grown woman in a schoolgirl's frock Charlotte, remember – tentatively explores the school while band members lurk ominously around her. She is seen running off with her alternate self, Clare. She then pulls back a sheet on a gurney to discover the body of Clare, who comes to life, causing Charlotte to scream hammily, and run out of the building pursued slowly by a zombie-like Clare brandishing a candelabra.

'When we saw it, we didn't know whether to laugh or cry', said Robert in *Ten Imaginary Years*. 'We wanted a film noir,' he said later, 'and it turned into *that*. It was enough to kill any aspirations to make a decent video. It was one of the worst moments of my life when we saw the 'Charlotte Sometimes' video back.' After this, if Cure videos were funny, at least they were meant to be.

The 'Charlotte Sometimes' debacle had no measurable ill effect on Mike Mansfield's career. He continued to make pop videos, and even re-used the same location for Adam Ant's 'Goody Two Shoes'. His television credits included 1995 TV movie *Tiger Bastable: The Case of the Nazi Mindbender*, whose IMDB description reads 'Maverick private-eye Tiger Bastable is called in by Scotland Yard to investigate the mysterious disappearances of young men and women from English public schools.' (Probably time-travelling to swap places with their alternate selves.)

From The Cure's point of view, the best that can be said is that the experience of visiting the disused asylum had some unexpected benefits. Robert, who had been reading books on mental illness on tour, was fascinated by what he discovered in the asylum's art department, including a 'grotesque skull sculpture' which he took home, and which inspired the song 'The Figurehead' (see *Flexipop!*, see *Pornography*, see *Madness*). Lol, meanwhile, pocketed a green sculpture of a dog drinking from a bowl.

The single's **artwork** was a blurred photo of **Mary**, taken in 1980 by Robert in a Scottish castle. (The cover of '**Pictures Of You**', years later, was the same photo, unblurred.) The B-side 'Splintered In Her Head' was also inspired by the Penelope Farmer novel (as, incidentally, was *The Top* track 'The Empty World'). The 12-inch also included a live version of 'Faith'. It was released on Monday 5 October 1981, with a minimalist press ad that looked like a hand-torn yin and yang. **Polydor** were convinced that it would go Top 10, but they were wrong. (That said, its actual highest position – 44 – wasn't bad for a band like The Cure in 1981.)

It has become one of The Cure's most-venerated singles, but that view wasn't universal at the time. One fan was so disgusted by it that they sent Simon Gallup hate mail. 'When we released the single "Charlotte Sometimes",' he told *Oor* magazine, 'someone sent it back to me, shattered in pieces, with the message: I don't understand how you can do such a thing.'

Maybe they'd seen the video.

Clinic, The

Before *Further Adventures Of TeamCure*, before *Adventures And Plans*, and long before *Cure News*, there was *The Clinic*. This Cure fanzine, made by the band themselves, ran for five issues between 1979 and 1981. A team effort, it was overseen by 'Marg' (Robert Smith's elder sister Margaret), with design by **Lol Tolhurst**, photos by **John Taw**, and input from **Ric Gallup** among others.

Issue 1 relays The Cure story so far (they're very careful to always type 'THE URE' in capitals, but add the dropped 'C' in pen). In the discography, they proudly boast that '**Killing An Arab**' has sold 'over 12,000 copies'. In the trio's individual profiles, Lol calls **Horley** the 'land of 1000 tennis clubs'. And there's a column called *A Personal View Of Paul Morley* by **Simon Gallup** (not yet a member of The Cure) in response to that **critic**'s negative comments about *Three Imaginary Boys* in *NME*, presaging the band's **Peel Session** track '**Desperate Journalist** In Ongoing Meaningful Review Situation'.

Issue 2 involves a tour diary, including their van getting taken apart in a search at a ferry terminal and a jovial account of **Siouxsie And The Banshees**' Aberdeen meltdown. There's also a handwritten plug for '**Jumping Someone Else's Train**' by Marg.

Issue 3 arrives in the aftermath of **Michael Dempsey**'s departure and the arrival of Simon Gallup and **Matthieu Hartley**. Robert writes a very self-critical reflection upon The Cure's place in the scheme of things, beginning 'Up until now The Cure has been, in the eyes of many people, nothing more than a name, an indistinct concept, a group that maybe has depth, but maybe has nothing . . .', and pitilessly taking stock of their 'whimsical' album and 'mechanical' gigs. The lyrics to '**Seventeen Seconds**' and 'Play For Today' are included to pad it out.

Issue 4 has a summary of their foreign **touring**, shines a light on the four members' musical tastes, and includes a promotional piece by Ric about the **Obtainers** and **Mag/Spys** split single on the **Dance Fools Dance** label. There's also Part One of The **Cult Hero** Story, but there never was a Part Two.

Issue 5 breaks the news that Matthieu has left, and otherwise consists mainly of the lyrics from the *Faith* album, suggesting their heart wasn't in it anymore.

It's disarmingly teenage (some of them were still nineteen) and leaves the reader with the sense that these towering gods of alternative rock were, in reality, just kids trying to figure it all out.

Scans of The Clinic's five issues, donated by Ric Gallup, are hosted by the **website** Pictures Of You.

Close To Me

That wonky Tamla beat. That creaking hinge. That ragtime brass. That watery wardrobe. 'Close To Me' had everything, and sealed the deal for me as a Cure fan. For me, and for many others of my generation who had previously enjoyed The Cure's music, this was the song where we fully fell in love.

The second single from *The Head On The Door* bore, for the second Cure single in a row, the detectable influence of Motown. 'It reminds me of "Jimmy Mack",' Robert Smith told *Record Mirror*, referring to Martha Reeves And The Vandellas' hit of 1967. 'That's the sound I thought it should have.' But, unlike the exuberant Detroit clatter of '**In Between Days**', 'Close To Me' contained only the barest rhythmic skeleton of Motown, its minimalist punch-and-snap delivered with exquisite discipline by **Boris Williams** and **Simon Gallup**. From the instrumentation to Robert's up-close-and-personal vocal, it sounds like what it is: a song about claustrophobia. Airless, desiccated, freeze-dried, oppressively intimate.

Incredibly, there was internal disagreement about whether it ought to be a single. The rest of the band were convinced it would be a hit, but Robert wasn't sure. He agreed to put it out, with the addition of a brass section. This was a masterstroke: in its pop single form, the brass section *makes* it. (Which creates a problem for *The Head On The Door*, because the brass isn't on the album version, making for a slightly disappointing interlude in the album's running order when you're expecting the hit.) That brass, coming in like an answer to the musical question posed by each phrase, was provided by a Southend-based, zoot suit-wearing jump jive revival band called Rent Party, whose main trumpeter Laurence Parry later did session work with James Taylor Quartet and Yazz before joining UB40 in the late nineties.

Robert later told *Cure News* it was a song about 'claustrophobic pursuits of the night', and told ITV's *Night Network* 'It's about days when you wake up, and at the end of the day you wish you hadn't because it's been a trial.' He expanded on the theme in *Ten Imaginary Years*, explaining that it was about

feeling 'frustrated, humming with your head under the pillow, like the end of a day where you feel nothing has been achieved and you're in a hurry to get the day over with so you can start the next one. You tell yourself tomorrow you're going to do lots of positive things. But the next day is just like the one before. Sometimes it goes on for weeks.' It was also another of The Cure's many songs based on **dreams**, containing a direct reference to his 'head on the door' nightmare which gave its parent album its title.

The **Tim Pope**-directed **video**, though not without strong competition, is The Cure's best. The action begins on the clifftop at notorious suicide spot Beachy Head, in a wardrobe filled with clothes and The Cure. The doors close with a creak – the same creak used on the single. The first face we see is a trussed-up Simon Gallup, his mouth lit from within by a lightbulb. The camera moves to Boris Williams, clapping out the rhythm. Then **Lol Tolhurst**, playing a tiny Casio keyboard, and then, on the top shelf, **Porl Thompson** picking out notes on an orange plastic comb. Finally, rising up through the jackets and shirts and hangers, Robert Smith. As he sings, we start to see finger-puppets representing each member of the band (made by Pope's company Glo), manhandled roughly by Robert. Intermittently, we're shown external views of the wardrobe, teetering on the edge. Two minutes in, during the trumpet solo, it topples. Down past the chalky cliff, overlooked by a red and white striped lighthouse, to the rocks below.

Instead of shattering on impact, killing everyone inside, the wardrobe miraculously hits the sea and begins to fill up with water, implicitly **drowning** everyone within. It's a masterclass from Tim Pope, with an especially superb acting performance from Robert (as well as the others who, in contrast to him, maintained neutral, understated facial expressions instead of mugging or portraying panic).

It was, however, Robert's least favourite Cure video to make. Partly, this was down to the sheer discomfort of being in water for such a long time. 'It was the most uncomfortable 12 hours that I've ever spent,' he told *The Hit*. 'He [Tim Pope] ended up dropping the wardrobe – with us still in it – into a huge tank filled with 1,000 gallons of water. Watching it you'd think it was fun, but all I could think about was dying a slow, painful death.' The state of the water itself didn't help. 'The water tank was filled from a fire engine,' he told *Night Network*, 'and the water had been sitting there for two and a half weeks. It was revolting. In fact, everyone was ill after that.'

And the digestive system of one member of The Cure made matters even worse. Lol Tolhurst had been for a curry the night before, and the results were toxic. 'Lol's bowels were a problem in a very confined space', Pope later said. In *Ten Imaginary Years* he gave a vivid description of what ensued: 'Suddenly I saw the whole crew retract and the band all shot over the other side of the studio but Lol was just standing there with this bestial look on his face, grinning and I had to go outside and throw up . . .'

After all that discomfort, the video was rarely shown in the UK. 'They're never expressly banned. They're just not shown. If they were banned it would be better. You'd have twice the publicity.' In *Ten Imaginary Years*, Robert recalled 'It worked out really well but he [Pope] was unhappy because it hardly got shown at all, least of all on children's television presumably because they thought it would incite kids to climb into wardrobes and fling themselves off cliffs.' On MTV, however, it went into heavy rotation, much like its predecessor 'In Between Days'.

The single was released on 13 September 1985. The sleeve **artwork** wasn't a classic: a photo of the band trapped underneath (or, in Robert's case, peeping out from) the wardrobe from the video, surrounded by coloured fish shapes, with the band's name and song title upside-down in the bottom corner. The main B-side, 'A Man Inside My Mouth' was, Robert told *Cure News*, about 'the other me' in 'a dream I had. I hope it was a dream!' (One of many, many Cure songs inspired by dreams.) The 12-inch also featured 'Stop Dead' (about 'meeting my match'), and there was also a 10-inch EP which featured all those songs plus 'New Day' ('a drug-induced improvisation').

Now, cover up the next few lines with your hand. Then try to guess what chart position 'Close To Me' – immortal, iconic, universally loved 'Close To Me' – reached in the UK. You'll already have guessed by my phrasing of the question that it didn't make the Top 10. But it's worse than that: it didn't even make the Top 20. Impossibly, for such a famous and popular single, it only got to 24. It was, however, a major hit in **Australia** (reaching No.7).

The song had a second bite at the cherry in 1990 when it was remixed for the *Mixed Up* project, and released as a single with '**Just Like Heaven**' (Dizzy Mix) and '**Primary**' (Red Mix), in a **Parched Art** sleeve covered in salmon-pink fish shapes superimposed on a russet-coloured rendering of the *Quadpus* octopus.

'Close To Me (Closest Mix)' was a reworking by Paul Oakenfold and Steve Osborne with the subtlest of dance elements: the emphasis of the rhythm was subtly shifted from the off-beat to the on-beat, creating a more placid, chill-out feel.

A second video was also made, picking up where the previous one left off. Beginning with the wardrobe's tumble from the cliff, it depicts the band emerging at the bottom of the sea: literally coming out of the closet. Robert plays plastic sax and trumpet, and is attacked by a giant octopus. Simon is harassed by cardboard fish. Porl's musical comb magically changes colour between shots. They all have a fight with the starfish, played by **Chris Parry**, during which Simon's knee made impactful contact with Parry's testicles. (Whether this was accidental or accidentally-on-purpose is open for debate.) Despite the hull of a boat being visible above them, no member swims up to safety.

The remix charted far higher than the original, reaching No.13 in the UK (and 4 in Ireland), although this can in part be explained by the facts that The Cure were a far more established band, 'Close To Me' had had five years to embed itself as a well-loved song, and even though it was the second single from *Mixed Up* (following '**Never Enough**'), its release still came a month ahead of the album itself.

It's The Cure's second most-**sampled** song, with Lady Sovereign, Afroman and Yungblud among the twenty-one artists who have used it to date. It has also been covered by many artists, Mark Lanegan the most prominent. And Robert Smith himself sensed its influence upon a major hit single of the late eighties. In a 1988 issue of *Cure News*, a fan compared George Michael's 'Faith' to it, and Robert seemed to agree, replying 'There is very little worse than an uninspiring thief, particularly who carefully shapes his stubble!'

None of which matters. Because regardless of what it may or may not have inspired, 'Close To Me' stands proud as overwhelming proof of The Cure's sheer pop genius.

COGASM

COGASM – CO for **Cooper, Jason**; GA for **Gabrels, Reeves**; SM for Smith, Robert – was the acronymic alias adopted in 1998 by two current and one future member of The Cure to record a track for the film *Orgazmo* (see **Films, The Cure's music in**), directed by Trey Parker and produced by Matt Stone, the duo with whom Smith also worked on *South Park* (see **TV, The Cure referenced on**). Smith had met Gabrels, **David Bowie**'s guitarist, the previous year while making a guest appearance at Bowie's fiftieth birthday party.

Orgasmo is a daft sex comedy about a Mormon doorknocker who, through an outlandish series of events, becomes first a porn star and then a superhero, armed with the Orgazmorator, a ray gun which induces orgasm in whoever it is aimed at. In satirising The Church of Jesus Christ of Latter-Day Saints, it prefigured Parker and Stone's hugely successful 2011 stage musical *The Book Of Mormon*.

COGASM's contribution to the soundtrack was recorded in the summer of 1998 at RAK Studios, where The Cure had previously recorded *Pornography* in 1982. It was co-produced by Paul Corkett (see **Producers**), who had engineered *Wild Mood Swings* and would later co-produce *Bloodflowers*, and mixed by the Dust Brothers (the LA-based Beastie Boys collaborators, not the UK version who became the Chemical Brothers). 'A Sign from God', written by Smith and Gabrels, is an uptempo scuzzy rock number which tangentially traces the lead character's transformation story, Smith's heavily distorted, Cockney-inflected vocal delivering lines like 'No, not **religion**, I'm talking serious OOBE' (Out of Body Experience) and referencing the then-current Kate Winslet film *Hideous Kinky*.

The soundtrack album, released on Nickelbag Records in 1998, was divided between hip hop (Wu-Tang Clan, Dilated Peoples, KRS One) and alternative rock (Atari Teenage Riot, Smash Mouth, COGASM). Secondhand copies of the album are extremely cheap to buy, making it an easy score for Cure completists.

Although Cooper, Gabrels and Smith were not all Cure members at the time, COGASM arguably marks only the second time a configuration of The Cure had recorded under a false name (the first being **Cult Hero**).

Collaborations

For a band that is so particular about creating their own discrete, ring-fenced musical universe, The Cure – and, in particular, Robert Smith – have been involved in far more collaborations than one would

expect. They started happening almost as soon as The Cure had a record company to pay the bills and a studio to play around with.

The first, in November 1979, was 'I'm A Cult Hero' by **Cult Hero**, the comedy-funk single recorded during downtime at **Morgan Studios** by assorted members of The Cure past, present and future and their families, with local postman Frank Bell on lead vocals. The same year, Robert released a split single by the **Mag/Spys** and **The Obtainers** on his own **Dance Fools Dance** label, and produced the Obtainers tracks himself. That autumn, he played live – a collaboration of sorts – with **Siouxsie And The Banshees** on the *Join Hands* tour. Since then, Robert Smith has been involved in literally dozens of hook-ups and side-projects, whether as a songwriter, a producer, a musician, a vocalist or a live performer.

A Cult Hero gig followed at the Marquee in March 1980. On 3 and 4 April, at the Rainbow Theatre, Robert played guitar with The Stranglers, minus singer Hugh Cornwell but plus an all-star cast (including **Matthieu Hartley** on keyboards), in solidarity with the imprisoned Cornwell. On 1 August, **Fiction** labelmates **Associates**' debut album *The Affectionate Punch* was released, with backing vocals from Robert on the title track and 'Even Dogs In The Wild'.

In 1982 Dance Fools Dance released a second and final record, the Smith-produced EP *Frame One* by **Animation**. That year he also produced *From Under The Hill*, a cassette album by **And Also The Trees**.

In **1983** he began his stint as a full member of Siouxsie And The Banshees, starting with the single '**Dear Prudence**' and ending with the album *Hyæna*. He also collaborated with Banshees bassist **Steve Severin** on the supergroup side-project **The Glove**, recording one album, *Blue Sunshine*. He also collaborated with Severin, **The Venomettes** and choreographer Nicolas Dixon on a **ballet** performance of 'Siamese Twins' for the BBC's *Riverside*, and co-wrote the song 'Torment' with Severin for Marc And The Mambas.

In 1984 he collaborated with director **Tim Pope** on Pope's solitary single, 'I Want To Be A Tree'.

A five-year gap ensued during which Smith was too busy conquering the world to devote any time to side-hustles, but in 1989 he returned to arboreal activity with *The Pear Tree* EP by And Also The Trees, for which he provided remixes.

In 1990 The Cure album *Mixed Up* featured remixes from Paul Oakenfold, François Kevorkian,

Mark Saunders, William Orbit and Bryan 'Chuck' New.

After another gap spent being famous, Smith played on and produced the single 'Jewel' by **Cranes**, a regular Cure **support band**, in 1993.

The Stranglers and Friends: Live in Concert, from that 1980 benefit gig, was released belatedly in 1995, with Robert on 'Get A Grip' and 'Hanging Around'.

In 1997, Robert performed live with **David Bowie** at Bowie's fiftieth birthday concert, featuring future Cure member **Reeves Gabrels**. Later that year, Gabrels returned the favour by appearing live with The Cure in the US, as did Wayne Hussey of The Mission. Gabrels also played guitar on The Cure's single '**Wrong Number**'.

In 1998, with **Jason Cooper** and Reeves Gabrels, Smith formed the supergroup **COGASM** to record a track for the **film** *Orgazmo*.

In 2000, Gabrels album *Ulysses (Della Notte)* came out, with Smith appearing on 'Yesterday's Gone', co-written by the two of them.

The twenty-first century saw a sustained period of busy collaborative activity from Smith, who had begun to look upon the younger generation of artists who had grown up on The Cure with warm, almost paternal affection.

In 2001, Saffron from Republica collaborated with The Cure for the single '**Just Say Yes**' on their *Greatest Hits*.

In 2003, Robert contributed vocals to the Junkie XL track 'Perfect Blue Sky' on the album *Radio JXL: A Broadcast from the Computer Hell Cabin*. He also sang on Blink-182's 'All Of This' on their self-titled album, contributed the song 'Believe' to former Bowie sideman Earl Slick's album *Zig Zag*, sang on Blank & Jones' techno **cover** of '**A Forest**', and provided vocals for Junior Jack's superb Italo-house single 'Da Hype'.

In 2004 he played on former Nine Inch Nails member Chris Vrenna's band Tweaker's song 'Truth Is' on the album *2 a.m. Wakeup Call*. That was also the year he appeared live onstage with Placebo at Wembley Arena, duetting with Brian Molko on '**Boys Don't Cry**'.

In 2005 Smith guested on a cover of the Bee Gees' 'To Love Somebody' on *TheFutureEmbrace*, the debut solo album by Billy Corgan of Smashing Pumpkins. Seven years later, Corgan made a bizarre allegation on Chicago radio station 93XRT that Smith had made a move on him backstage at a Cure show. 'Robert tried to make out with me that night. And that's not a joke,' Corgan said. 'It was the first time I ever met

Robert Smith and he tried to make out with me. I said I only like girls and he said, "That's OK, I'm a girl", and then he threw up practically all over my shoes. That's a true story.' (Whether you choose to believe the Trump-supporting Voldemort lookalike is up to you.)

In 2006, on the Faithless track 'Spiders, Crocodiles & Kryptonite' from their album *To All New Arrivals*, Smith reprised his vocal from '**Lullaby**', which the track samples extensively. The same year, Smith and **Simon Gallup** guested with Korn on *MTV Unplugged*, performing a medley of Korn's 'Make Me Bad' with The Cure's '**In Between Days**'. (The album of the show was released in 2007.)

In 2007 Robert sang on the single 'Please' by Orbital's Paul Hartnoll, from the album *The Ideal Condition*. (Hartnoll would later cover 'A Forest' with his 8.58 side-project.)

In 2008 the *Hypnagogic States* EP handed over remixing duties to the emo generation, in the form of AFI, Fall Out Boy, My Chemical Romance, 30 Seconds To Mars and 65daysofstatic. (Not that the last of those is emo.)

In 2010 Robert returned the favour by singing on 65daysofstatic's 'Come To Me' on their album *We Were Exploding Anyway*. One of the finest Robert Smith collaborations of all time also happened that year: the **Fiction**-signed electroclash act Crystal Castles' 'Not In Love' with Smith on vocals.

In 2011 Robert sang on 'Take Forever' by Japanese Popstars on their album *Controlling Your Allegiance*, then took a three-year break from collaborations.

On the 2014 tribute album *The Art Of McCartney*, The Cure covered The Beatles' 'Hello Goodbye' with the help of Paul's son James on keyboards (and, on the same album, Robert contributed a cover of Wings' 'C Moon').

In 2014 Robert made a surprise appearance at the science show *Brian and Robin's Christmas Compendium*, duetting with Eric Idle on Monty Python's 'Always Look On The Bright Side Of Life'.

In 2015 he made two remixes of 'Vapour Trail' by shoegaze legends Ride (Vapour Mix and Trail Mix), who had supported The Cure in 1991, for the reissue of their debut album *Nowhere*.

There was then a five-year break until 2020 when Smith remixed Deftones' 'Teenager' for their remix album *Black Stallion*. Smith's voice can be heard on the remix. 'It's amazing to hear Robert rework one of our songs and sneak his voice in there,' the band's Chino Moreno told *NME*. 'If you'd have told me that when I was 15 years old, I would have lost my fucking mind and not believed a word you were saying. It was a dream.'

The same year, during Covid-19 lockdown, Robert co-wrote, sang, and played guitar, bass, keyboards and even a music box on 'Strange Timez' by Damon Albarn's project Gorillaz, on the album *Song Machine, Season One: Strange Timez*, which reached No.2 in the UK (the highest-charting album involving Robert Smith for over thirty years). He also appeared with them on a livestreamed virtual gig that Christmas, and joined them in front of a live audience at the O2 in London on 11 August 2021 after lockdown had ended, a show that was free to NHS workers.

2021 saw extensive collaborations between Robert and the Scottish electro-pop group Chvrches. The link-up between the two parties began when Chvrches' manager approached Robert about supporting The Cure on tour. Lockdown prevented that happening, but Robert sent them a demo of a song he'd written on Halloween 2020. That song was 'How Not To Drown', released as a single from their fourth album *Screen Violence*. In an online video interview conducted by Zane Lowe, Chvrches' Martin Doherty said he wouldn't be in a band in the first place if it wasn't for *Disintegration* and *Pornography*. The collaboration continued in 2022 when Robert and Chvrches played two songs together ('How Not to Drown' and '**Just Like Heaven**') at the NME **Awards** (where The Cure had won Best Festival Headliner) at Brixton Academy. Two weeks later, at Chvrches' own Brixton gig, Robert guested on no fewer than four songs in the encore, including those two.

In 2023, Robert conducted one of the most monobrow-raising collaborations of his career when he remixed 'Pretty Boy' by Noel Gallagher from Oasis for the deluxe edition of the album *Council Skies* by Gallagher's band High Flying Birds.

Robert Smith isn't the only one who's dabbled in collabs while an active member of The Cure. During his Cure stint, **Phil Thornalley** spent the autumn of 1983 jet-setting all over the world making albums with the Thompson Twins and Duran Duran. **Lol Tolhurst** produced And Also The Trees' self-titled full debut album in 1984, and played keyboards. **Porl Thompson** contributed to **Shelleyan Orphan**'s *Humroot* in 1992, and worked on his own side-project Swanson's Daughter in 2009 (but the one track uploaded to SoundCloud was later removed). Jason

Cooper drummed on a David Bowie remix in 1999. Reeves Gabrels' side-projects would require a whole separate entry. And in 2023, Simon Gallup performed on the track 'Sabbath' by Evi Vine.

Then there are the collaborations that got away. In a 1991 edition of *Cure News*, Robert revealed he'd nearly worked with **goth**-folk band All About Eve, but it never happened. And ever since working on *Hypnagogic States*, rumours were rife that Jared Leto might record with The Cure – in 2013 Leto tweeted that he'd love to sing with Robert Smith. It has yet to occur.

But plenty of collaborations did, hence the length of this entry. With all that collaborative activity, it's a wonder Robert finds time to make so many Cure albums.

Oh, wait.

Compilations

The Cure are not a band who are under-served when it comes to compilation albums.

The iconic, game-changing best-of album was, of course, 1986's *Standing On A Beach*. But that wasn't the first. *Boys Don't Cry* (1980) was a compilation of sorts, gathering together highlights from *Three Imaginary Boys* with other material from 1978–79 for the US market. So, arguably, was *Happily Ever After* (1981), which bolted *Seventeen Seconds* and *Faith* together into a double disc release for the American market. And *Japanese Whispers* (1983) was a compilation of the singles 'Let's Go To Bed', 'The Walk' and 'The Lovecats' with their associated B-sides.

Nor was *Standing On A Beach* the last. *Galore*, in 1997, picked up where the former left off. *Greatest Hits* (with its *Acoustic Hits* bonus disc), in 2001, cherry-picked tracks from both. The odds-and-ends box *Join The Dots* followed in 2004. And remix album *Mixed Up* (1990) is arguably a compilation, in which case *Torn Down* (2018) also counts.

Then there were fansploitation multiple-CD boxes like *Integration* (US-only, 1990), *Assemblage* (France-only, 1991) and *Classic Album Selection* (Germany-only, 2011). **Australia** also went in for some *Happily Ever After*-style album twinning, with the non-consecutive pairing of *The Head On The Door & Wish* (1996) and *3 For One* (*Faith, Pornography* and *The Top*, 2000). France also did the non-consecutive thing with *Three Imaginary Boys & Faith* (2008) and *Pornography & Seventeen Seconds* (2008). *The Head On The Door & Kiss Me, Kiss Me, Kiss Me* (also France, also 2008) at least made chronological sense.

One true oddity out there is *Pure Cure*, a promotional disc pressed up by Elektra in Canada in 1992 with the catalogue number CURE 1 (which, amazingly, had never been used before). A best-of with emphasis on the more recent works, it featured four tracks from the then-current *Wish*, two each from *Disintegration*, *Mixed Up* and *Kiss Me, Kiss Me, Kiss Me*, two earlier singles in the form of 'The Lovecats' and 'Boys Don't Cry' and, bizarrely, their Doors cover 'Hello, I Love You' from Elektra's Various Artists album *Rubaiyat*. What it didn't include, even more surprisingly, was 'Friday I'm In Love'. If this was an attempt to steer radio stations away from playing that divisive yet ubiquitous song, it failed: they played it anyway.

In truth, the casual, car-journey Cure listener only really needed *Standing On A Beach* and *Galore*. The more involved fan would want those two, *Join The Dots* and all the studio albums plus *Mixed Up* and perhaps a live album or two. And the obsessed completist collector would need all of the above and more, even though the track listings would overlap massively.

It's an expensive business, following The Cure.

Concert

'It looks like a bootleg,' Robert Smith said to Richard Skinner on the BBC's *Old Grey Whistle Test* when asked about *Concert: The Cure Live*, 'and it's supposed to be our version of a bootleg. It's all black and white and very cheap, and was done very very quickly in about four days of mixing. And it's very rough. But I think that's how live albums should be . . .'

The live album is a curious beast. What is it there for? If you want a perfect rendition of your favourite band's best songs, nine times out of ten the studio album is better. If you want a personal memento of a gig you actually attended, then it's very unlikely that the live album will do that for you. And they almost always cheat, avoiding that 'very rough' sound by using sneaky overdubs. Nevertheless, particularly in the 1970s, the making of a live album was considered

by musicians and 'serious' music fans alike an essential rite of passage, to prove that the band 'had the chops' and 'could cut it onstage'.

For a decade or so, they proved bafflingly popular. Highly successful examples included The Who's *Live at Leeds* (1970, UK No.3, two million sold in the US), George Harrison & Friends' *The Concert for Bangladesh* (1971, UK No.1 and US No.2), Bob Marley and the Wailers' *Live!* (1975, certified gold in six countries including the US), Dr Feelgood's *Stupidity* (1976, UK No.1), Peter Frampton's *Frampton Comes Alive* (1976, US No.1, eleven million sold worldwide) and Motörhead's *No Sleep 'til Hammersmith* (1981, UK No.1).

Compared to those, *Concert* was only a modest success, but did well for a band from the alternative sector, a band with a few crossover hits to their name but sustained mainly by a cult following. Released on 26 October 1984, some time after the golden age of live albums, it reached a respectable No.26 in the UK charts.

The album was recorded at the Oxford Apollo and Hammersmith Odeon shows of *The Top* tour in May 1984. As well as being a time capsule to document the Smith, Tolhurst, Thompson, Thornalley, Anderson line-up in full flight, *Concert* captured The Cure at arguably their most gothic and intense. Although it contained six singles, it omitted the two most populist and melodic options, 'Boys Don't Cry' (not played on the UK tour at all) and 'The Lovecats' (only played on the final night at Hammersmith). Highlight: a pummelling, chaotic 'Give Me It', with skronking No Wave sax from Porl Thompson. Lowlight: a slightly flat and listless '10.15 Saturday Night'. What it tells us: Robert didn't talk much (there's precious little chat beyond 'This one's called "The Walk" . . .'). The sound engineer loved the reverb button (in 'The Hanging Garden', lines like 'Catching halos on the moon' are still echoing when Robert has started singing the next one). And it shows us that 'A Forest' was a relatively compact and bijou 6:46 in those days.

Its artwork, designed by a certain 'Toberr' (anagram of Robert), with its Courier-style typewriter font and badly reproduced black and white photos, did indeed imitate the style of a bootleg sleeve, just as *Live at Leeds* had done previously.

The cassette version featured a whole separate album on Side 2, called *Curiosity (Killing The Cat): Cure Anomalies 1977–1984*, comprising, as Robert told MTV, 'all bits of junk that people were asking about'. This, in practice, meant that it gathered together alternate versions of assorted songs, long before *Join The Dots* did a more comprehensive job, notably the previously unreleased 'Heroin Face' (a song Robert described in *Cure News* as 'a nonsense'), all of which later turned up on remastered versions of the relevant albums.

Which is exactly the sort of thing a bootlegger would do.

Cooper, Jason

You don't get to be the third-longest serving member of The Cure without doing something right.

Jason Toop Cooper was born on 31 January 1967 in London and grew up in Bath. From an early age, he was interested in the more avant-garde corners of rock: his first gig, aged just thirteen, was Captain Beefheart & His Magic Band at Bristol Colston Hall in October 1980. He was also a fan of Jimi Hendrix (something he shares with Robert Smith), his favourite song being 'Foxy Lady', covered by The Cure on *Three Imaginary Boys*.

Jason was raised in a musical household. His father, who worked for Virgin Records, gave him a copy of The Cure's *Seventeen Seconds* and he became a fan. 'My favourite memories,' he told Cure biographer Jeff Apter regarding his youth, 'are listening to *Faith* and drinking cider.' He eventually saw them live at the nearby **Glastonbury Festival** in 1990.

Where some drummers might bash away in their bedrooms on a kit their parents wish they'd never bought them, then blag their way into a band, Cooper actually took the trouble to study his craft at Drumtech, now part of BIMM (where he is a patron and visiting artist).

After leaving Drumtech, his first work of any significance was with My Life Story, the orchestral Britpop band of anything up to twelve members, led by Jake Shillingford, whose string section was frequently borrowed by other acts on *Top of the Pops*. Cooper featured on their singles 'Girl A, Girl B, Boy C' and 'You Don't Sparkle', and the debut album *Mornington Crescent*. 'Jason's time-keeping is incredible,' says Shillingford. 'He can sound like a drum machine . . .'

In addition to My Life Story, Cooper took various session gigs, working with Jean-Jacques Burnel of The Stranglers and German house diva Billie Ray Martin of Electribe 101 fame. His final My Life Story commitments were wrapped up in late 1994 (they'd already replaced him by their New Year's Eve gig), because Jason had followed up an interesting-looking small ad in *Melody Maker*. 'Drummer wanted for international band', it read. 'Very famous band needs drummer, no metalheads'. (The address given was that of **Fiction** Records on Charlotte Street, so it wasn't hard to figure out who this 'very famous band' were.)

After the departure of **Boris Williams**, The Cure auditioned several drummers during the *Wild Mood Swings* sessions, four of whom ended up on the record. But it was Cooper, who auditioned to a demo of '**Jupiter Crash**' and was brought back in to try 'From The Edge Of The Deep Green Sea' and 'Disintegration', who impressed Robert Smith enough to win the job permanently.

'When we were auditioning,' Smith told Susan Masters of *Pulse* in 1996, 'the thing that clinched it with Jason was that he wasn't just a drummer. He'd done lots of other things. He'd lived in the Far East for a while and could bring a whole new dimension to the band. We've also had some really great discussions.'

Cooper's first gig with the band came before the album was actually released, on 6 June 1995 in Athens, by which time he'd already inevitably been nicknamed Cooperman. 'It's really great fun to be on tour with Jason,' **Roger O'Donnell** told Masters, 'because he's seeing everything for the first time. We tend to get a bit jaded – "Oh, here we are in LA again" – whereas with Jason, when he's with us, he's never been to the States before so he's really excited.'

Cooper approached the task of joining such an illustrious band with humility and an absence of ego. 'It's a daunting prospect,' he later told *Rhythm* magazine, 'and it's just something that I just try and do as well as I can, and play as well as I can, and if the fans like it then that's fantastic and if they don't then there's not much really I can do.' It was also a job he approached with diligence, studiously listening to old multitracks of previous drummers' recordings to approximate them as best he could.

One thing Jason brought to the band was a familiarity with technology, as Robert, speaking to Jim Sullivan of *Boston Globe* about the single '**Wrong Number**', explained: 'It's something to do with the makeup of the group as it is at the moment, particularly with Jason on drums. He's still in his twenties and doesn't have the hangups [of some older drummers]. A different generation feels kind of threatened by machinery.'

For some Cure fans, none of this would ever be good enough. As *LA Weekly* once noted, there are whole internet forums dedicated to comparing Cooper unfavourably to Williams. One hater has uploaded a 'How to play like Jason Cooper' video of the band performing 'Push' at a festival on YouTube, with on-screen captions like 'Same drum fill again . . .' One recurring complaint seems to be that Cooper's powerful style is too 'rock' for The Cure. He is criticised for riding the crash cymbals too much for some fans' tastes. (In his defence, The Cure are a stadium band now, and a stadium band needs a big beat.) He is also criticised for relying on pre-programmed loops when playing older songs. (In this regard, people often don't know what they want. If a live show sounds nothing like the record, they'll complain about *that*.)

Cooper responds to such criticisms with a calm dignity. 'With anyone who joins a band that's well-established,' he told *Rhythm*, 'there's always going to be people that want the previous drummer, or the drummer before that, but you can't get too hung up on that – or I can't, anyway. I definitely don't dwell on it. All I try to do is play the music with as much conviction as I can and pay respect to the good drum part that's been there before and make it come alive when we play it live.'

Jason Cooper has played on four studio albums, *Wild Mood Swings*, *Bloodflowers*, *The Cure* and *4:13 Dream*, and will doubtless play on a fifth, if it ever comes. In the meantime, he continued to work on outside projects.

In 1998 he formed **COGASM** with Robert Smith and **Reeves Gabrels** for a one-off song on the *Orgazmo* soundtrack. In 1999 he drummed on the demo version of **David Bowie**'s 'Seven' (from the album *Hours*), which ended up as track 3 of the 'Seven' CD single the following year. He also drummed on Bat for Lashes' single 'Strangelove' in 2012, on *Froot*, a Top 10 album by Welsh artist Marina and the Diamonds, in 2015, and on one track on prog artist Steven Wilson's album *The Future Bites* in 2021.

Cooper regularly composes music for film, with former My Life Story cellist Oliver Kraus, operating from a studio in a shed at the bottom of his garden. They won the Best Original Score award at the Solstice Film Festival in 2008 for their score for the horror thriller *From Within*. Their other credits include *Spiderhole* (2009) and *Without Gorky* (2011).

Relatively little is known about Jason Cooper's life outside music. His hobbies, according to *Cure News*, include birdwatching, cricket and swimming. In 1995 his entire record collection was stolen. On 15 May 2004, he married his long-time girlfriend Allison. In the summer of 2019 he took part in a fifty-four-mile charity bike ride for the British Heart Foundation in honour of his drum technician Paul 'Ricky' Welton, who had passed away of a heart attack.

The Cure are not a band who carry passengers. (Well, not since the late eighties.) Almost three decades on, Jason Cooper is still on The Cure's drum stool. That, like his drumming, speaks volumes.

Cover Versions (by The Cure)

'Tonight there's going to be a jailbreak / Somewhere in this town.' Yeah Phil, maybe try the jail . . .

According to **Lol Tolhurst** in *Cured*, that Thin Lizzy classic was the first song The Cure played together. Serial performers and recorders of cover versions in their early years, they dialled it down somewhat for most of the eighties, then got back into the habit with a vengeance in the nineties.

In their earliest **pre-Cure** incarnations, the band's repertoire consisted largely of other people's songs. The second Malice gig, at St Wilfrid's School Hall in **Crawley** on 12 September 1976, consisted almost entirely of covers (and '**A Night Like This**'). They played the aforementioned 'Jailbreak', **David Bowie**'s 'Suffragette City', **Jimi Hendrix**'s 'Foxy Lady' and, as an unplanned encore, The Troggs' 'Wild Thing' with Lol on vocals.

The one and only full gig by spin-off band **Cult Hero**, at the Marquee in London on 23 March 1980, consisted almost entirely of covers from 1973, based on an episode of *Jimmy Savile's Old Record Show* which Robert had taped from BBC Radio 1. (This was long before most people knew what we all now know about Savile.) The set comprised songs originally recorded by Detroit Spinners, David Cassidy, The Ronettes, Thin Lizzy, The Faces, Focus, Sweet, The Strawbs, Slade and Gary Glitter. (This was long before most people knew what we all now know about Glitter.)

That Glitter song, 'Do You Wanna Touch Me? (Oh Yeah)', would become The Cure's most frequent cover song of all time: they played it on at least forty-six occasions between 1980 and 1985, usually as an encore, making up the words to the verses. The second most frequently covered song is 'Foxy Lady', performed at least thirty-six times between 1976 and 2011.

After those two, there's a steep drop-off before you get to the rest. They dug back into Thin Lizzy's oeuvre in 2022 to play 'Don't Believe A Word' six times. In 2019 they ended five of the *Disintegration* anniversary gigs at Sydney Opera House with a cover of 'Pirate Ships' by Wendy Waldman, which they had demoed back in '89. In 2002 they played 'The Faith Healer' by The Sensational Alex Harvey Band, one of Robert's biggest **influences**. They had a brief fling with 'You Really Got Me' by The Kinks, playing it three times in the late eighties. They've played 'Wild Thing' twice: that St Wilfrid's gig in 1976 and again in 1987. They gave 'Paranoid' another outing on 1 December 1978 after being heckle-bullied by bikers at Aston University, but could only half-remember how to play it. Their one-off version of the Lord's Prayer in Aberdeen in 1979, with **Siouxsie** and **Steve Severin** guesting, technically counts as a cover, as the Banshees had done it first at the 100 Club in 1976. They ended a show at Wembley Arena in December 1987 with a seasonal singalong of Slade's 'Merry Xmas Everybody'. They played The Doors' 'Hello, I Love You' live on the *Jonathan Ross Show* in 1991. And – perhaps most bizarrely – an eyewitness claims to have seen them play 'MacArthur Park' by Jimmy Webb, with Robert using his Jazzmaster **guitar** for the first time, in Newport (the Shropshire one, not the Welsh one) in 1979. No audio proof survives, so we'll just have to imagine an inconsolable Robert Smith telling us that someone's left the cake out in the rain.

In terms of actually recording cover versions, it all begins with the **Hansa** sessions in 1977 when Easy Cure were obliged to try out with The Beatles' 'I Saw Her Standing There' and Bowie's 'Rebel Rebel' among others. The first cover by The Cure to make it out into the wild, however, was their absurdist rendition of 'Foxy Lady' on *Three Imaginary Boys*.

The Thatcher years came and went before their next recorded cover, 'Hello, I Love You' for the album *Rubaiyat* in 1990 to celebrate the Elektra **label**'s fortieth anniversary. A year later, Robert admitted to *Cure News* 'We don't really like the Doors.'

The Cure were back on the Hendrix train in 1993, recording 'Purple Haze' twice. The first time was for the launch of the radio station Virgin 1215, on which their version, recorded only twenty-four hours beforehand, was the second track ever played (though the presenter Richard Skinner announced it as 'Hey Joe'). The second time was for a Hendrix tribute album called *Stone Free*.

In 1995 they covered Bowie's 'Young Americans' for an **Xfm** album called *104.9* in support of that station's application for a Londonwide licence. In 1998 they covered **Depeche Mode**'s 'World In My Eyes' for tribute album *For The Masses*. In 2005 they covered John Lennon's 'Love' on Amnesty International **charity** album *Make Some Noise*. In 2005 Robert **collaborated** with Billy Corgan on a cover of the Bee Gees' 'To Love Somebody' on Corgan's album *The Future Embrace*. In 2007 The Cure joined Korn on the nu-metal band's *MTV Unplugged* show for a medley of Korn's 'Make Me Bad' and The Cure's 'In Between Days', released on the album of that session. In 2010 and 2012 they recorded two covers for Tim Burton **films**: 'Very Good Advice' for *Alice in Wonderland* and Frank Sinatra's 'Witchcraft' for *Frankenweenie*. In 2011 Robert Smith recorded a cover of John Martyn's 'Small Hours' on the tribute album *Johnny Boy Would Love This*. In 2014 The Cure contributed two tracks to tribute album *The Art Of McCartney*: a cover of Wings' 'C-Moon' (with Paul's son James) and a cover of The Beatles' 'Hello Goodbye'. And in 2015 Robert covered 'There's A Girl In The Corner' by perennial **support band** the Twilight Sad for the 7-inch vinyl version of that band's single 'It Never Was The Same'.

Soundchecks are a category to themselves: songs The Cure covered for their own amusement, intended neither to be heard by the public nor recorded in a studio. For example, the run-through of the *Mission Impossible* theme with which they soundchecked in Vienna in 1996.

Then there are the ones that got away. In 1997 Smith said, perhaps jokingly, that he'd considered covering Tom Jones' 'What's New, Pussycat?' with Bananarama.

Such is The Cure's fondness for covers that you shouldn't bet against them whipping one out again. But it's very unlikely to be anything by Gary Glitter.

Cover Versions (of The Cure)

The Cure aren't a band whose work invites reinterpretation easily. Robert Smith's lyrical universe is typically so idiosyncratic that nobody other than Smith himself could credibly deliver the words, and he never writes with a view to his songs becoming standards. A small handful of The Cure's more accessible moments, however, have proven transferable to other singers. Their top five most-covered songs, according to the SecondHandSongs website, are '**Lovesong**' (75 times), '**Boys Don't Cry**' (62), '**Friday I'm In Love**' (58), '**Just Like Heaven**' (58) and '**A Forest**' (57).

London-born singer Adele recorded a stripped-down acoustic cover of 'Lovesong' on her planet-steamrollering 2011 album *21*. That album broke records across the globe. It reached No.1 in over thirty countries. It was the world's bestselling album in 2011 and again in 2012. In the UK it is the fourth-biggest seller of all time, and the bestseller by a solo artist ever. In the **US**, it was certified diamond (over ten million copies) and is the best-performing album on the Billboard 200 of all time. It has sold over thirty-one million copies worldwide. And it's the biggest-selling album of the twenty-first century. There's only one problem: Adele's cover of 'Lovesong' is *horrible*. But it's entirely conceivable that The Cure make more money from that Adele album than from their own these days, so nobody's complaining.

While Adele's might be the most lucrative cover of a Cure song, it isn't Robert's favourite. That is Dinosaur Jr's wayward version of 'Just Like Heaven'. Despite its comedic death-metal growls ('YOU!!!') and DJ-confounding abrupt ending, it's a version which genuinely does the song justice. Robert even appeared on the front of the 6 May 1989 issue of *Melody Maker* with singer J. Mascis to promote Dinosaur Jr's version and, on the *Show* album, you can hear Robert 'covering' Mascis' guitar solo – the ultimate compliment. Dinosaur Jr later **supported** The Cure in Pasadena in 1992. In 2014, a double-sided 7-inch **vinyl** single of The Cure's original of, and Dinosaur Jr's cover of, 'Just Like Heaven' was released for Record Store Day on the Rhino label.

Another Cure cover to gain the approval of its originator was Bristolian berserker Tricky's version of '**The Lovecats**'. A stealthy trip-hop take with jazzy pianos and telephone noises for texture, it's a radical reinvention, and it works. As Robert told *Humo*, 'I'm glad to hear a cover that isn't a copy.'

Smith isn't always so generous with his reactions. In 1994, Terry Edwards, trumpeter by appointment to the Britpop movement, released an EP of instrumental Cure covers called *Cure-Ation*. Robert told *Cure News* he 'didn't understand it'. Edwards got away lightly. In 1990, American heartland rock singer John Eddie contributed a sub-Springsteen rendition of 'In Between Days' to *Rubaiyat* (the Elektra compilation which also featured a **cover by The Cure** of The Doors' 'Hello, I Love You'). Robert called it 'absolutely hideous'. Correctly.

Some covers mean more to the coverer than others. In 2018 the Nashville indie singer Morgxn recorded 'Boys Don't Cry', and wrote an essay in *Billboard* explaining that the song helped him to process his grief at the death of his father. 'Everyone knows the iconic guitar riff. But as I pulled up the lyrics . . . I was struck with something so new. So vital. "Boys Don't Cry" is an admission. That boys don't cry . . . boys actually weep. It is OK to show how much it hurts. It is OK to feel unmeasurable [sic] pain . . . and for my father, that I'm sorry for not understanding him before he was gone.'

In 2022, bedroom-pop singer Phoebe Bridgers recorded a piano-based version of 'Friday I'm In Love' and, like Morgxn, felt moved to show her workings. On Spotify's *Under Cover* podcast she explained that she had written the lyrics to the song in her first school notebook. 'I think I even made a little calendar for myself that incorporated the lyrics', she said, acknowledging the song as 'very seminal to me and my music taste' and describing it as 'the best possible summer song'.

Artists who have covered The Cure range from the very famous to the not-remotely-famous. In 1996, on the reissue of their 'Bullet with Butterfly Wings', Smashing Pumpkins included a cover of '**A Night Like This**'. (Robert Smith would later **collaborate** with their singer Billy Corgan on a cover of the Bee Gees' 'To Love Somebody'.) At the other end of the spectrum, one of the more obscure Cure covers is the oddly entrancing piano version of 'A Forest' by Italian jazz trio Diego Morga, Camillo Pace & Lello Patruno on their 2011 album *Chi Ha Fottuto Donald Duck*. However, it doesn't achieve much that French easy listening covers band Nouvelle Vague hadn't already when they covered it on their debut album in 2004.

There have been whole tribute albums to The Cure.

In 1997, **goth** label Cleopatra released one called *100 Tears*, which opened with a version of '**One Hundred Years**' by Nosferatu, whose former lead singer Gary Clarke had by then already left to form **tribute band** The Cureheads. In 2009 *NME*, to celebrate The Cure winning that magazine's Godlike Genius **Award**, gave away a CD of Cure cover versions consisting of a mixture of pre-existing recordings like the Dinosaur Jr one and brand-new recordings, the pick of the bunch being a gloriously unhinged yet respectful run through 'A Forest' by Cumbrian-raised eccentrics British Sea Power (nowadays trading as Sea Power).

Some Cure covers are live-only affairs. For example, Led Zeppelin alumni Page and Plant covering '**Lullaby**' in 1995 with **Porl Thompson** in their band. Or Deftones' version of 'If Only Tonight We Could Sleep', performed in 2004 on The Cure's *MTV Icon* show. Smith later booked Deftones to play his **Meltdown Festival**, and introduced The Cure's own performance of the tune as 'a Deftones song'.

This isn't the only time Robert Smith has got involved with someone else's cover of a Cure song. At Wembley Arena in 2004, he joined Placebo onstage for their version of 'Boys Don't Cry'. (Oddly, singer Brian Molko hogged the vocals, making Smith's cameo somewhat pointless.) And, in 2003, he collaborated with German techno duo Blank & Jones on their electronic version of 'A Forest', contributing a new vocal and even appearing in the **video**.

Robert Smith's reaction to hearing cover versions of The Cure, he told *Cure News* in 1999, is generally to feel flattered. 'Only twice have we stopped a Cure cover . . . and no, I'm not going to say who!'

Cranes

'Cranes look like a Russian peasant band, don't they?' said Robert Smith when asked to compare bands to national football teams. 'They look like they've just travelled across the Steppes barefoot. They get to the semi-finals and everybody says, "Oh, I really like the Russians" then forgets all about them, which is a bit like Cranes. Oh, and I've seen Jim from Cranes drink a whole bottle of vodka, which I thought only Russians could do . . .'

Formed in Portsmouth in 1985, Cranes – centred around the sister-brother duo of singer Alison and drummer Jim Shaw, soon joined by guitarists Mark Francombe and Matt Cope – emerged at the cusp of the nineties. They took their name from a David Leavitt story-within-a-story about an abandoned child who emulates the construction cranes he can see from his bedroom window (and also the fact that the dock at Portsmouth is dominated by cranes).

Their recordings, which combined Alison's helium-high vocals (once compared to the lady in the radiator from *Eraserhead*) with an unsettlingly austere industrial-**gothic** backing, were championed by many writers (myself included) at *Melody Maker* magazine, which put them on the front cover long before they'd developed a significant fanbase. They were once described as 'a dark reproach to the frivolity of the Madchester and Britpop years, their music a quiet but insistent clarion call to solitude and seriousness.'

The acclaim which greeted early releases such as mini-LP *Self Non Self*, the *Inescapable* EP and debut album *Wings Of Joy*, which exhibited the influence of **Siouxsie And The Banshees**' orchestral phase circa *Hyæna* and the etherealism of early Cocteau Twins, brought them to the attention of Robert Smith, who adopted them as, essentially, Support Band by Royal Appointment to The Cure – indeed, both he and **Simon Gallup** named them in *Cure News* as their ideal support band, and Robert described them as 'savagely underrated, a band with a vision'.

Cranes did indeed support The Cure globally on the *Wish* tour of 1992. They missed the show on 15 May at Nassau Coliseum near New York due to problems entering the **USA**. At one extraordinary show on 15 November in Liévin, France, Alison was too ill to sing, so Robert Smith and **Porl Thompson** played her vocal lines on guitar. (Sadly, when Simon Gallup was ill on that tour, Alison Shaw didn't reciprocate the favour by singing his basslines – they brought **Roberto Soave** in instead.)

The Cure's patronage of Cranes continued in 1993 when Smith remixed their single 'Jewel', helping them towards their highest-ever chart position of No.29. Coincidentally, in 1996 Cranes released an album called *La Tragédie d'Oreste et Électre*, based on Jean-Paul Sartre's *Les Mouches* (itself based on a Greek myth), meaning that both bands (see '**Killing An Arab**', see **Camus**) had made records inspired by Existentialist **literature**.

In later years a lightness and liquidity entered Cranes' music, displacing the tumult and terrors of their early work, inviting a wholly new interpretation of the band's name: Cranes are uplifting.

Crawley

The Cure couldn't only have come from Crawley. But they could only have come from somewhere *like* Crawley.

There is a tendency for bands from the featureless hinterland towns in the orbit of London to be London's most devoted mythologisers: Blur (Colchester), Saint Etienne (Horsham/Reigate), Suede (Haywards Heath). Close enough for the capital's light pollution to drown the stars from the night sky, but far enough away for the glow to seem exotic.

Crawley is twenty-eight miles south of Central London and eighteen north of Brighton, forty-three minutes from Victoria by Southern Rail, closer to the coast than the city but within its orbit, neither one thing nor the other. But The Cure, interestingly, don't fit into the glamour-dazzled, Londonophilic pattern of Home Counties bands. Instead, they exemplify another archetype. Theirs is the sound, to quote The Members, of the *suburbs*. It is (see **Englishness** for more about this) rooted in the Commuter Belt, and at the same time universal. As Richard Strange put it in the *Out of the Woods* **documentary**, 'Their music was very English, very Home Counties English, very much about Southern England.' **Lol Tolhurst**, speaking to *Uncut*, verified this sense of suburbia seeping into The Cure's music. 'It was no surprise that we made the kind of music [that we did], because we lived in a very muted, very grey place. We just reflected back what we saw around us.'

Located at the northern edge of West Sussex, Crawley – its etymology is 'crow field' – was an ironworking centre in the Roman period, then spent sleepy centuries as a market town, gaining a rail link to London in 1841 and Gatwick Airport (see **Horley**) in 1945. After the Second World War it was designated as the site of one of the government's New Towns under the New Towns Act of 1946 (which sought to bring jobs and infrastructure to satellite towns in the South East), with the aim of attracting fifty thousand people there. (The population of the borough is now just over 118,000.) The new Crawley swallowed up several nearby villages, hence its strange patchwork of vintage architecture and utilitarian housing blocks.

The influx of new residents included the Smith family, who had first moved to Horley in 1962 then made the short move to Crawley four years later. There, the young Robert attended St Francis Junior School, Notre Dame Middle School and St Wilfrid's Comprehensive School. Lol Tolhurst, though from Horley, also attended St Francis, and Crawley was where most of the future Cure members crossed paths (**Porl Thompson**, for example, was working in a record shop there).

Prior to The Cure's breakthrough, very few figures from Crawley had made a dent on the public consciousness. Ten years before Smith, Tolhurst & co were born, serial killer John Haigh, the Acid-Bath Murderer, was active in the town, putting Crawley on the map for grisly reasons. 1980 was a big sporting year for Crawley, with boxer Alan Minter becoming the undisputed middleweight champion of the world in Las Vegas and decathlete Daley Thompson winning gold at the Olympics in Moscow, but in musical terms the only local band of note were Brett Marvin And The Thunderbolts, better known under the pseudonym Terry Dactyl and the Dinosaurs for their 1972 novelty hit 'Seaside Shuffle'. It was not a town replete with positive role models, musically or otherwise.

'Crawley is grey and uninspiring,' Robert Smith once said, 'with an undercurrent of **violence**.' The main hazard, apart from roaming gangs of psychopathic skinheads, was boredom. 'Crawley is just twenty miles south of London,' wrote Lol in *Cured*, 'but it might as well be another planet. It is a town with no centre and no end, just endless rows of suburban bleakness that blurs into the dark, dank countryside.' Lol speaks of a tedium that was palpable, and Smith concurred: 'It's a dreadful place. There's nothing there.' (In fairness, that may have changed somewhat since. The town now has a League Two football club, and an 855-capacity theatre, the Hawth.)

That pall of nothingness informed The Cure's music. Tolhurst describes Crawley as 'a place where it's always raining and a slate grey sky hangs over everything'. For him, The Cure's music is inseparable from the town it came from. 'It sounds like where we lived', he told BBC Radio 4's *Soul Music*.

Michael Dempsey agreed. 'It was enveloped in this great miasma of apathy,' he said on *Curious Creatures*. 'Nobody was interested or paying attention. They weren't even angry that you were doing anything. It was just disinterest.' Robert Smith felt the same way. 'Growing up in Crawley? That's easy,' he told *Télérama* in 2012. 'It was shit. It's just like any other small town: most people were awful, and some people were really good. And the really good people were my friends.'

Those friends would congregate in a handful of

pubs, chiefly The Rocket, where Robert and Lol would be ridiculed as 'poofs' by the more retrogressive (and plain aggressive) locals. Smith, Tolhurst, Dempsey and Thompson went there for Robert's seventeenth birthday, where they were confronted by National Front skinheads. Fighting between youth tribes was a normal occurrence.

Nevertheless, the **pre-Cure** versions of the band played The Rocket (later renamed The Railway and, later still, The Firecracker) thirteen times in 1977 and 1978. On 19 February 1978 Easy Cure were supported by local punk band **Lockjaw**, featuring **Simon Gallup**, whose audience trashed the place.

Other Crawley venues which hosted the nascent Cure include Worth Abbey and St Wilfrid's School Hall (their first two gigs, while still called Malice), the bandstand on Queen's Square (as seen in the earliest surviving live footage), Crawley College, Montefiore Institute. Finally, on 18 March 1980, The Cure played the Lakeside Inn, where Porl Thompson (re)joined them for a '**Cult Hero**' encore.

Smith lived at his parents' house in Crawley well into the eighties, and his and **Mary**'s families lived in the town well into the twenty-first century, Robert's only reason to revisit a place in which, he has said, he never felt rooted.

'It's really strange in Crawley,' Smith later said. 'They're rewriting history, about what I did, saying I judged battles of the bands and things like that. I didn't do any of that. I fucking hated Crawley.' He quickly caught himself, and added 'I forget this goes on the internet. I fucking love Crawley. Thank you, Crawley.'

Crawley, nevertheless, is proud of The Cure. In 2018, Crawley Museum held a Cure exhibition, and *Cured* is on sale in its gift shop, making it surely the only local museum that sells a book which essentially tells you that the best thing about the town is the road out of it.

Crew

The concept of TeamCure – the idea that the band's extended family unit is bigger than merely the three, four, five or six musicians and extends to include crew and management – is strong within Cure folklore. Some of these figures, like **Chris Parry** and **Gary Biddles**, are significant enough to have earned their

own entries in this book. One crew member, **Perry Bamonte**, even ended up joining the band. Other soldiers in The Cure crew who have served with distinction over the years include (but are not limited to) the following.

The longest-serving member is lighting designer Angus MacPhail, sometimes known as 'Mac', sometimes known as 'Snail'. He joined The Cure crew on the Three Imaginary Boys tour, having been headhunted from the **Generation X** crew, and has been with them ever since. If you've ever enjoyed the use of lighting, silhouettes or projections at a Cure concert, MacPhail is the man to thank.

Another lighting man who served with honour is Roy Bennett, who worked on lighting and set design for the Prayer and Wish tours, as reported in a 1993 issue of *Cure News*.

Security boss Brian 'Headset' Adsett, Robert's personal minder on tour, is a veteran. One of the old **Crawley** Cure mafia, Adsett's connection with Smith goes so far back that he claims he used to stand at the bar and heckle the very young Robert's **pre-Cure band** The Crawley Goat Band. He is also, according to photographer **John Taw**, the vomiting person pictured on a badge he made for The Cure in their early days.

Speaking of photographers, lensman Paul Cox was almost always on hand between 1980 and 1999 to document their tours, and can therefore be considered a de facto crew member. His photos were published in a **book** called *Stills* in the autumn of 2022.

For the last few tours, The Cure's production manager has been Phil Broad. In the eighties, however, the job belonged to Aberdeen-born, Scottish–Polish Marek 'Mick' Kluczynski, a larger-than-life character who began his musical career in the late sixties promoting monthly blues concerts in the Shetland Islands, which obliged him to intervene in fights between oil workers and fishermen drunk on whisky. He allegedly got his big break by winning a card game with Marc Bolan, which somehow led to a job with **Pink Floyd** and their company Brit Row, which in turn brought them into The Cure's orbit. (He was once challenged to drink a pint of whisky by Roger Waters, who bet him he couldn't do it. Waters lost.) For many years, post-Cure, he worked as production director of the BRIT Awards, until his death in 2009. Prior to his career in rock, Kluczynski had worked for the NHS, bringing what **Lol Tolhurst** in *Cured* described as 'insane crofters' into hospital after living alone in the Highlands had driven them mad. 'Apparently the police would escort Mick up to these lonely shepherds' farms,' Lol wrote, 'and open the door of the farmhouse while Mick, armed with a syringe full of some heavy-duty sedative, would run full tilt at the mad crofter, plunge the needle in, and then help drag the sedated shepherd out to an ambulance.' The perfect preparation for working with The Cure.

Tour managers came and went. In 1980, the role was taken by a 'Welsh wizard character' called Lawrie Mazzeo who once tricked The Cure into doing a runner from hotels without paying (only to be apprehended by the police as soon as they checked into the next hotel). Mazzeo had a habit of prioritising restaurant bookings over making sure there was a PA at the venue. In 1985 the incumbent was 'Hoss', real name Mick McGinty, described by Robert in *Libération* as 'a reformed sumo tour manager'. In 1987 it was Malcolm Ross, described by journalist Johnny Black in *Q* as 'delightfully Irish'.

The Cure's entourage circa *Faith* also included a Ted roadie called Elvis who deemed The Cure 'a right bunch of scruffy cunts'. In a 2000 interview, Robert recalled Elvis' stint. 'He had a quiff, and wore drapes and brothel creepers, and he was always playing Elvis when he was driving us. He was really big and tough. We'd say "Turn Elvis off!" and he'd say "If I turn Elvis off, I stop driving."'

Cure crew members have won **awards** for their work. In 2022, the WILMAs (Women in Live Music Awards) honoured Anna Mac and Marie Gallop for their roles as lighting technician and production coordinator respectively.

Perhaps the most prominent tour tech, aside from Bamonte, is Bruno Brunning, also known as 'Billy Bongo'. Brunning joined in 1985, when he was described by Robert as 'a drummer's friend', but by 1989 he was credited as 'keyboard technician', and has functioned as an all-round personal assistant. During the preliminary sessions for *Disintegration*, for example, it was Bruno who set up a simple recording studio in the dining room. His reward was a cameo role in the '**Pictures Of You**' video, in which he wore a bear suit.

That wasn't the only time The Cure crew ended up on **video**. As reported in *Cure News*, the '**Friday I'm In Love**' clip was full of them: 'the extras are all crew including Chris Parry as Indian waiter, **Dave Allen** as props man, Steve Whitfield (assistant engineer on **Wish**) is Mr Mop, Bruno (their PA) and Binky (guitar

roadie) are Laurel and Hardy, and dancing girl is Michi (make-up artist) . . .'

Now that's teamwork.

Critics

'You'd be stupid not to take notice of it,' Robert Smith said to David 'Kid' Jensen in 1983. 'Whether it has any effect is another matter. It's never had any effect on what The Cure do. We usually keep track. People manage to worm their way into the black book.'

Five years later, with The Cure well on the way to becoming one of the world's biggest bands, Smith could afford to take a more relaxed view of critics. 'I never really bother about "reviews" of our records,' he told *Cure News* in 1988 (scare-quotes around 'reviews' his own). 'They are generally based on unimportant criteria and incorrect assumptions of intent. In fact, criticism by fools can actually strengthen your resolve and determination . . .' (He wasn't fooling anyone about the 'never really bother' thing: in 1992, at the very height of *Wish*, he admitted that he and **Simon Gallup** still read *Melody Maker*.)

The first time they encountered a living, breathing critic from the national music press came on 17 September 1978, when *NME*'s Adrian Thrills caught one of their many early appearances at Lakers in Redhill on 17 September 1978. Thrills was unimpressed. However, when the same journalist wrote up an interview with them on 16 December 1978, under the headline 'Ain't No Blues For The Summertime Cure', he praised them as 'an abrasive light metal trio' and 'a breath of fresh suburban air'.

On 27 January 1979, *Sounds* gave The Cure their first music press front cover, with a photo of the band in front of a foetus sucking its thumb and the headline 'Stars In Embryo'. However, when that magazine sent Andy Gill to Sheffield to review them live, he called them 'Three Infuriating Berks'.

Over at *NME*, Paul Morley wrote an infamous review of *Three Imaginary Boys* which took them to task for their 'insignificant symbolism' and 'rude, soulless obliqueness', prompting the **Peel Session** smackdown '**Desperate Journalist** In Ongoing Meaningful Review Situation', but within a year he had jumped on The Cure train, interviewing the band and praising *Seventeen Seconds*.

Sometimes, even their own friends could be barbed in their criticism: *Melody Maker*'s usually extremely favourable Steve Sutherland wrote, of a Hammersmith Odeon gig on the **Fourteen Explicit Moments** tour, that 'the place is too vast, the sound too thin and spineless, the light show too spartan and the songs themselves too intimately miserable to communicate anything other than boredom'. Sutherland went on to write their official biography *Ten Imaginary Years*.

This fairly even pattern of the positive and the negative, more swings-and-roundabouts than slings-and-arrows, continued throughout their career. Truth be told, The Cure have received acres of positive coverage in the press for decades, with only a small percentage of negative reviews. Look at any album entry in this book for evidence.

And Smith is certainly correct that it 'never has any effect' on The Cure (at least in terms of their success or failure). In 1989, *Melody Maker* critic Chris Roberts wrote a spectacular review of *Disintegration* which called it 'about as much fun as losing a limb' and 'the sound of a man finding it all too much, giving in rather gutlessly to the sheer size of the chaos. It's decent of him to share this with us. I mean he could have written some songs or something.' Roberts wrote that 'you'll be lucky to find a tune on here', and that 'They have nothing to say except: please help me I don't understand a thing about the world oh actually it's not important don't trouble yourself go back to sleep.' The thing is, I believe Chris actually *liked* the album. When he talked about 'the whole lazy turmoil', he immediately clarified that 'lazy turmoil is not in itself a criticism'. Regardless of that review, the album went on to sell four million copies. Not that this proves that the critic's reaction was 'wrong' – it is impossible to be 'wrong' about a subjective artistic judgement. But it does put the power of critics, even in that pre-internet age when they (we) were 'gatekeepers' not cheerleaders, into perspective.

Of course, true criticism – in the sense of intelligent appraisal – isn't a banal binary of thumbs-up or thumbs-down anyway. If you want an example of true criticism of The Cure, seek out blogger K-punk (aka Mark Fisher) on the 'ostentatious absenteeism' of Robert Smith, under the title *It Doesn't Matter If We All Die: The Cure's Unholy Trinity*.

There was a flurry of controversy involving the thumbs-down kind of criticism in 2014. On 28 and 29 March that year The Cure played two **charity** shows at the Royal Albert Hall for the Teenage Cancer Trust (having previously done so in 2011). The shows were played in front of 5,272 fans each night who had

paid £100 (standing), £75 (seated) or £50 (obstructed view) to be there. At the time, these were unusually high ticket prices, justified by the charitable status of the gig. It is reasonable to assume, then, that most people in the venue were diehard fans rather than casual gig-goers come to check out The Cure. Doors opened at 6.30 p.m. and there was no support act. Everyone would have understood that it was going to be long. They had even announced on their website that it would be a full three-hour show. And besides, this was The Cure.

One person who didn't appreciate the duration of the journey between 'Plainsong' and '**Killing An Arab**' was Caroline Sullivan of the *Guardian*. In a review which ran on 30 March, she wrote: 'They may be able to play for more than three hours without exhausting their hits, but they've yet to work out how to build up a show: song follows song – an incredible 45 in all – but there are few peaks or teasers, let alone much of the fraught darkness that got them here in the first place.' Her review ended: 'Condensed into 90 minutes, though, this would have been one of the gigs of the year.'

There were, inevitably, angry comments underneath the online version of the article from Cure fans. In response to one of them Sullivan made the fateful error of claiming, 'I have it on good authority that the band have read the review and liked it.' Robert Smith took to Facebook and Twitter to deny this, and whipped out those scare-quotes around 'review' again:

> '*I have it on good authority that the band have read the review and liked it.' Caroline Sullivan . . . WHAAAT?!! SHE WAS COMMENTING ON HER OWN GUARDIAN 'REVIEW' OF OUR EPIC 45 SONG 213 MINUTE FRIDAY RAH TEENAGE CANCER TRUST SHOW*
>
> *TO BE CLEAR – AND ON THE BEST AUTHORITY – THE BAND HAVE INDEED READ THE REVIEW – BUT DID NOT LIKE IT!*
>
> *THE REVIEW WAS – TO PUT IT POLITELY – LAZY NONSENSE . . . swampy . . . numbing . . . yet to work out how to build up a show . . . GULP!!!*
>
> *BUT WE NOW KNOW WHERE WE HAVE BEEN GOING WRONG ALL THIS TIME: Condensed into 90 minutes, this would have been one of the gigs of the year*
>
> *WE PLAY TOO MANY SONGS! DOH! BUT . . . IS IT NOT VERY OBVIOUS THAT WE PLAY OUR OWN SHOWS (AS OPPOSED TO FESTIVAL HEADLINES) FOR FANS OF THE BAND? THAT IS WHY WE PLAY A MIX OF*

SONGS, AND WHY WE PLAY FOR AS LONG AS WE DO . . .

   WHEN WE GO TO SEE AN ARTIST WE ARE FANS OF, WE DON'T WANT THE PERFORMANCE TO END . . . THAT'S WHAT BEING A FAN MEANS . . . ISN'T IT?

   WE HAD TWO FANTASTIC NIGHTS, PLAYING TO GREAT CROWDS FOR A WONDERFUL CHARITY . . . THE GUARDIAN 'REVIEW' WAS SAD BITTER JUNK

   PS. AS FOR THE TORYGRAPH HACK . . . sigh . . . ONWARDS.

The 'Torygraph hack' was the *Telegraph*'s chief rock critic Neil McCormick, who had made similar gripes about being kept up beyond his bedtime, but the *Telegraph* is behind a paywall so McCormick got away comparatively lightly.

Rather than quietly letting the fuss die away, Sullivan doubled down with a self-justificatory *Guardian* column on 1 April. She acknowledged that The Cure had forewarned everyone about the length of the show, and conceded that it wasn't even their longest (that being a fifty-song, three and a half hour epic in **Mexico** the previous year). But 'imagine the intensity', she argued, 'if the show's dark, dreamlike energy had been condensed into a couple of hours.' She also argued that 'the sheer slog of being onstage for more than three hours means that artistry is ill-served by marathon shows', that 'a very long gig . . . has a kind of "let's see how committed you are" aggression', and that 'it's hard to feel excited by the all-you-can-eat ethos', ending with the offer 'OK, Robert. Buy you a drink?'

Things then escalated when *Pitchfork* reported on the back-and-forth between Sullivan and Smith. I even weighed in myself, tweeting about the covenant between artist and audience regarding show length: 'It's what The Cure DO. Their fans understand the deal. No one at the gig left disappointed (except a handful of journalists).'

By now, even the most unaware critic has got the memo that Cure gigs are long. But if one of them complains again, that sound you can hear is Robert Smith's little black book being opened one more time.

Cult Hero

Most bands wait a few years before messing around with spin-offs, side-projects and secret alter-egos. The Cure were already at it within eighteen months of their own first single.

Cult Hero was a short-lived band featuring several members of The Cure past, present and future, fronted by Frank Bell, a friend of the band's older brothers and member of The Cure's 'wrecking crew', who often wore a T-shirt that read 'I'm A Cult Hero'. By day, Frankie Bell was the local postman in **Horley**, but he had always wanted to make a record. The Cure wrote a couple of songs for him, and moonlighted as his backing group.

'We've known him for years,' Robert explained in an Australian radio interview. 'He used to be in the pub and he's really hu . . . *vast*, you see. And he used to think he'd make a really good No.1 matinee idol. So, we just arranged to go into the studio one Friday night, instead of going to the pub . . . Everyone from the pub ended up coming along, and settled down and got completely mortal.'

The studio for the session – drinking and recording – was **Morgan**, where The Cure were recording *Seventeen Seconds*, and the two Cult Hero tracks were produced by **Mike Hedges** (and **Chris Parry**, who is credited as co-producer).

The A-side, 'I'm A Cult Hero', littered with egotistical boasts like 'I walk on water and I don't get wet', 'I'm ahead of my time' and 'My time is coming and it won't be long', was a satire of the delusions and vanities of the new wave scene, in a similar spirit to 'Part-Time Punks' by the Television Personalities (1978) and The Cure's own '**Jumping Someone Else's Train**' (1979).

It slotted comfortably into the 'comedy-punk' or, to use the phrase coined by Garry Bushell in *Sounds*, 'punk pathétique' genre of the late seventies and early eighties, as exemplified by acts such as Splodgenessabounds, Jilted John, John Otway & Wild Willy Barrett, Notsensibles, Die Toten Hosen and The Toy Dolls. The downbeat bathos of Bell's delivery, combined with the use of synths and a disco backbeat, also gave it a similar flavour to Jona Lewie's later hit '(You'll Always Find Me In The) Kitchen At Parties'. One reviewer, according to *Ten Imaginary Years*, called it 'a bit of discofied studio nonsense concocted by the group and a drinking buddy that should never have seen the light of day'.

The B-side, 'I Dig You', had a Dr Feelgood-esque riff and a pub disco backbeat, and a lyric, spoken rather than sung, which ran (in its entirety):

I dig you
You dig me
We dig each other
That's groovy
Oh yeah.

An initial two thousand copies were pressed up and released by **Fiction** in November 1979. In North America, however, it was licensed to the Modulation label and the sides were flipped, with 'I Dig You' promoted to the A-side, and it sold thirty-five thousand copies, becoming an improbable Top 10 hit. A snatch of 'I Dig You' was included on a new wave 12-inch megamix called 'Punk Force Medley' by Waves, released in Canada in 1981, as were 'Grinding Halt' and '**10.15 Saturday Night**' by The Cure. In Canada at least, Frank Bell actually was a cult hero. (The single was also released in New Zealand in 1981, again with 'I Dig You' as the lead track, while 'I'm A Cult Hero' was included on an Australian compilation called *Britannia Waives the Rules*, also in 1981.)

Original copies of 'I'm A Cult Hero' sell for an average of £55 on Discogs, the price depressed slightly by the fact that both Cult Hero tracks now appear on the deluxe reissue of *Seventeen Seconds*.

Taken on its musical merits, the Cult Hero record would be a negligible Cure curio. However, it marks an important moment in the history of The Cure's **line-ups**. Robert Smith was in the process of edging bassist **Michael Dempsey** out of the band, and waited until Dempsey was away on holiday before beginning work on it. In Dempsey's absence, Smith brought in friend Simon Gallup to play bass, as a way of testing whether they would be musically compatible. An *Uncut* article from 2000 suggests this was always the plan, arguing that the record was 'designed as an exercise to break Gallup into the band'. In *Ten Imaginary Years*, Robert all but confirms that this was the pretext: 'I wanted to record with Simon. I never really knew Michael, we never had that much in common.' By the time Dempsey returned from holiday, Gallup had already learned the bassline. (Dempsey did contribute to the record a little: he played some synth with a wine bottle.) Cult Hero also saw the return of Smith's former Malice bandmate **Porl Thompson** to the fold (see **pre-Cure bands**), making it the first time Smith, Thompson and Gallup had all played together.

As a recording act, Cult Hero were done. As Robert told that Australian radio interviewer, they did record one further song, a version of a leftover Easy Cure track called 'See the Children Feel the Children' (see **Hansa**) which was, Robert admitted, 'a bit of a dangerous song', and was never released.

They did, however, play live. There was a dry run at the Lakeside Inn in **Crawley** on 18 March, when Bell joined The Cure for an encore of 'I'm A Cult Hero', as did Porl Thompson, making his live Cure debut. Five days later, Cult Hero played their only real gig, on Sunday 23 March 1980 at the Marquee on Wardour Street in Soho, where The Cure themselves had played a three-night residency just a fortnight earlier. Cult Hero were supporting The Cure's Fiction labelmates **The Passions** on the third of a month of four Sundays they were playing at the venue.

Topped and tailed by 'I Dig You' and 'I'm A Cult Hero', the setlist otherwise consisted of seventies glam, rock and pop **covers** (including 'Whiskey in the Jar', 'Do You Wanna Touch Me?', 'Cindy Incidentally', 'Hocus Pocus', 'Blockbuster' and 'Cum On Feel The Noize'), with 'I Dig You' played a second time as the encore. The line-up included Janet Smith and Simon's then-girlfriend Carol dressed as schoolgirls, as well as two actual schoolboys, **The Obtainers**. Photos taken by **John Taw** show Bell as a heavyset lad in a leather jacket, with Simon, Lol Tolhurst and a stripy-trousered Robert also visible, a circular Cult Hero logo hanging in front of the Marquee's backdrop. On a live recording, the crowd can be heard chanting 'Frankie! Frankie!' in the manner of 'Angus! Angus!' at an AC/DC show.

A coda to the Cult Hero story: Bell joined The Cure onstage five years later on 14 September 1985 at the Brighton Centre – by that point The Cure's nearest thing to a 'local' gig – for an encore of 'I Dig You'.

As an attempt to make Frank Bell into a pop star and to induct Simon Gallup into The Cure, 'I'm A Cult Hero' can be said to have been partially successful. Frankie Bell is still a postman. Simon Gallup is still in The Cure.

Cure News

Cure News was a printed newsletter circulated to Cure fans between 1987 and 1999 as a means for the band to communicate directly with its audience, bypassing the music press. It wasn't the first such enterprise – its predecessors were the shorter-lived *The Clinic*, which ran from 1979–1981, and *Further Adventures Of TeamCure*, launched in 1985 and later renamed *Adventures And Plans* before being wound up – but, with twenty-one issues published over twelve years, was the most enduring.

The newsletter was run by Janie Webber and Chris White, who soon became a regular part of The Cure's travelling retinue, and even featured as extras in the videos for 'The 13th' and 'Mint Car'. It was distributed via the band's International Information Service (a fan club in all but name) from 28 Ivor Place, London NW1, an address it shared with Desire Records, a **Fiction** offshoot which released alternative acts like Raymonde and SPK (whose former member **Derek Thompson** was very briefly bassist in The Cure), and later moved into dance and hip-hop acts like Double Trouble & the Rebel MC. In October 1989 it moved into the Fiction offices on Charlotte Street, but by October 1991 it had relocated to Northolt in the West London borough of Ealing, where it remained until its closure.

Notable features included a penfriend section, regular fan Q&As with the band, the Inspirations section in which Robert Smith explains every song on every Cure album (from Issue 5 onwards, starting with *Three Imaginary Boys*), and photos of fans themselves which, once received, were manipulated and captioned by **Parched Art**.

The band in general seem to have engaged with the *Cure News* process to varying degrees (Robert perhaps most of all), enjoying the freedom to say things they'd never say in the mainstream press, sometimes indiscreet, sometimes mischievous, sometimes questionable in their honesty.

In the beginning, *Cure News* consisted of typed sheets on photocopier paper, crudely stapled together, but over the course of its existence it became more and more slick and well-designed. Issue 11 was the first to feature a photo of the band on the front, the first page previously having consisted of a welcome letter from Janie. (This was also the first issue printed on recycled paper.) Janie retired after Issue 18, leaving Chris in control from Issue 19, and the final two issues, 20 and 21, were printed on glossy paper, like a professional magazine.

The twenty-one issues of *Cure News* are now archived at https://curenews.net/archives.

Cure, The (2004 album)

There is a certain freedom which comes with already having delivered your masterpiece. In the view of Robert Smith, 2000's *Bloodflowers* was exactly that: a statement album, deliberately conceived to be the third part of an imaginary **trilogy** involving *Pornography* and *Disintegration*. With that magnum opus completed, released, toured and filmed live, Smith and his band were now liberated from the weight of expectation (albeit a largely self-imposed weight), and able to work on making 'just' a good Cure album. And what better name for a good Cure album than *The Cure*?

The background to the making of *The Cure* is the three-album deal they had signed with **Geffen** – specifically I Am, the subsidiary **label** run by **Ross Robinson** – following the end of their relationship with **Fiction**. It was almost the end of The Cure, too: Robert had been making a few more of his sporadic cry-wolf noises about splitting up the band and doing something more 'adult' with his life. He didn't. He also said, on the *Trilogy* DVD, that 'I want the next album to be the heaviest album that's ever been made in the history of music.' He didn't do that either. However, the prospect of working with Ross Robinson, the architect of nu metal, did affect the kind of material Smith was writing. 'I started writing really heavy songs,' he told Bill Crandall of *Rolling Stone*, 'because, when you're working with Ross, he's bound to want dark and moody. What became very apparent is that he liked *all* kinds of things we did. He's really into the melodic side of the band and the pop side of the band.'

The Cure **line-up** which made *The Cure* was Robert Smith, **Simon Gallup**, **Roger O'Donnell**, **Perry Bamonte** and **Jason Cooper**. But it didn't end there. One notable feature of *The Cure* is its preposterous executive producer credits. The list of exec prods is like that of a Hollywood blockbuster or a bloated, overcooked hip-hop album, including Jordan Schur (former Geffen CEO and founder of Suretone), **Daryl**

Bamonte, the ever-mysterious Bunny Lake, and Robinson himself.

After recording early demos at Stanbridge Farm Studios in the Sussex countryside, The Cure assembled at Olympic Studios, the former cinema and theatre in Barnes, South West London, which in 1966 was converted into a legendary studio used by rock heavyweights including The Beatles, The Rolling Stones, David Bowie, Led Zeppelin, Prince and Jimi Hendrix (whose 'Purple Haze', later covered by The Cure, was originally recorded at Olympic).

The process of whittling down the track listing was, fittingly enough, a little like the judging of the Winter Olympics figure skating. 'We ended up with thirty-seven demos,' Smith told Rolling Stone, 'and we all sat down and gave everything marks up to 20. We didn't really leave the studio for the last couple of months. We had no visitors. No one was allowed in. It was quite a surreal experience.'

Ross Robinson's career, and the circumstances under which he became The Cure's producer, are detailed under his own entry. His methods in making The Cure, however, are of interest here. In order to help them reconnect as a band, he made them sit in a circle and play. Smith told Rolling Stone: 'He put us in a very confined space, right on top of each other, with eye-to-eye contact. At night, we'd face the other way, light the candles and suddenly it became very real. I would stand up and away we would go . . .'

One story which has circulated about The Cure is that Robinson made the band record every track live as an ensemble, but that cannot be entirely true, as Jason Cooper recalls recording some of his drum tracks separately. 'He had me playing from midnight till 4 a.m. one night on just one song. He won't stop until he gets what he wants.'

Remarkably, Robinson attempted to get the best out of The Cure – grown men several years his senior – by devising a chart on which each band member's performance on each track was rated and logged. 'He holds it up in front of you,' Simon Gallup revealed to Mojo's Johnny Black while the recording was still in progress, 'and you have to say if you think you can do better.' This did not go down well with the bassist. 'I really wanted to punch his teeth in at first. He's been pushing us to the limits. He told me he wanted to see my fingers bleed and, after one take where I thought I'd played really well, he said, "You're not crying!" It's hard to know exactly what he wants out of us, but he gets results.'

Robert Smith, at the time, believed it was worth it.

'Everything we'd done before was going to culminate on this record – that was the mindset that we had when we were in the studio. And I would say that more passion went into the making of this record than all the others combined.' Speaking to Rolling Stone, he said 'This is how I always imagined making records could be. Nothing comes close to what I felt while we were making this album.' In an interview for the AOL Sessions, Smith said that Ross was the first real producer they had worked with since the first Cure album, implying that he considered all the other producers they had worked with in the intervening years to be mere technicians.

(What's Mike Hedges – chopped liver?)

Roger O'Donnell, however, differed in his appraisal of Robinson's methods. In a blog article he wrote, 'It was never a serious atmosphere in the studio and when you think about the album [Disintegration] and how dark it is, I'm sure people think we were sitting around slitting our wrists with candles and chains hanging from the walls. In fact, years later, working with Ross Robinson, he actually thought that's how we should work and he had this presumed idea of what The Cure should act like. It was completely wrong and false and just felt fake, like we were trying to be The Cure. We were The Cure. . . He never really understood that, but that's another story.'

Listening to The Cure now in the light of the above is fascinating. As soon as the laser hits the plastic on 'Lost', The Cure are there, sounding more American than ever before. However, they haven't suddenly turned into Limp Bizkit or Papa Roach. If anything, they've turned into Pavement. 'I can't find myself,' sings Robert in a fatigued, failing voice over lazily strummed, sloppily tuned guitars with (like Pavement themselves) more bum notes than a proctologist's filing cabinet. Smith witnesses a couple of young lovers apparently going through a break-up and imagines their inner lives, trying and failing to project himself into their shoes. 'I can't find myself/In the soul of this stranger in love . . .'

'Labyrinth' is a song of two halves, both musically and lyrically. There's something very 1969 about its distorted vocal and Eastern-sounding guitars and percussion, then midway through it erupts and becomes very Ross Robinson, but also genuinely heavy psych. This mirrors a lyric which depicts the deceptive normality both before and after a catastrophic event, perhaps a house fire:

The house is dark – the room is scarred

The boy is stiff – the bed is hard
The blood is thick – the head is burst
The taste is dry – the kiss is thirst

'Before Three' begins with a yelp of joy but, this being The Cure, the joy is not all that it seems. Over shoegaze-inspired chords, Robert reminisces about 'the happiest day I knew in a sea of gold down next to you' and 'the happiest night I ever had, up next to you on silver sand'. It's laced, however, with the quiet tragedy of knowing when and where you were happiest, the unspoken acknowledgement being that you will never be that happy again: 'we have to keep this night alive' and 'it's hard to hold this night inside . . .'

Next up, at least on certain CD pressings and the double **vinyl** version, is 'Truth, Goodness And Beauty' on which Robert sings the self-excoriating words of an unspecified girl:

Nothing I do is good
And yeah all I am is ugly

'**The End Of The World**', the album's lead single, has its own entry. On the album it's followed by 'Anniversary', a dense and complex track with reverberating pianos rising and falling in the mix, another song about reminiscence, but in which one of its two interlocutors carries a dark secret.

A year ago tonight we lay
Below this same remembering sky
I kissed you
You never wanted me to know

The strangely parenthesised '(I Don't Know What's Going) On . . .', in which Robert's voice is very high in the mix, is another exhilarating but ambiguous love song: on the one hand, 'I am so in love with you', but on the other, 'I am so disturbed by you . . .'

The anti-terrorist statement 'Us Or Them' is one of The Cure's most-discussed late-period songs (and it is considered here more fully under **Politics**). It's noticeable, and perhaps significant, that the lyrics ('Get your fucking world out of my head') echo those of 'The Kiss' on *Kiss Me, Kiss Me, Kiss Me* ('get your fucking voice out of my head').

The synth-led, self-lacerating 'Fake', next on the vinyl but excluded from all CDs except Japanese ones, throws back to 'End' from *Wish*, with Robert's brilliantly brutal, Cnut-like assessment of his own unworthiness for worship: 'I can't fly, I never really could/I just throw my arms out as I fall . . .'

The next two tracks, '**alt.end**' and '**Taking Off**', both have their own entries, as singles. They are followed by the messy 'Never', on which too many elements (including somewhat metallic guitars) trip over each other at once while Robert's voice strains at its very limits: 'She will never be the one . . .'

At ten minutes twenty-one seconds, 'The Promise' is the obligatory very long song on a Cure album, with elongated outbreaks of apocalyptic wah-wah soloing. By contrast, 'Going Nowhere' (excluded from North American pressings) is a tranquil coda, made of beautiful fountain-droplets of piano and elegiac guitars. 'Tell me that you love me again,' Smith sigh-sings, sounding as broken as he did at the start of Side 1. The last sound you hear is Robert's breath, exhaling and inhaling, shivering and shaking with cold or emotion.

Except that if you bought it on double vinyl, it didn't end there. (There is no definitive iteration of the album. It's a complete shambles. There are almost as many versions of *The Cure* as there are of The Cure.) 'This Morning', thematically, throws back to 'The Funeral Party' from *Faith* and forward to 'I Can Never Say Goodbye' from the **Lost World Tour** (and, just maybe, the **fourteenth album**) in its devastating account of death in the family. It features a rare spoken-word interlude from Robert:

I had to think to breathe, my heart bursting in my head. . . We moved in silence through a slowly waking world of pale grey rain. . . And as we drove, a strange sun split the sky. . . In that moment I knew nothing would ever be the same again. . .

If *The Cure* has a cousin in The Cure's catalogue, it's *Kiss Me, Kiss Me, Kiss Me* for the range of darkness and light as much as its elongated running time (71.13). 'This album was recorded live in a candlelit room & mixed very loud in the dark,' read the sleeve. 'We know you should turn down the lights & turn up the sounds for your optimum listening pleasure . . .'

The childish stick-figure **artwork** was drawn by Smith's young nephews and nieces Alice, Benedict, Bethani, Bodhi, Christopher, Ciaran, Darcie, James, Nicholas, Noosha, Richard, Samuel, Sarahnearly, Sian, Theodore and Tod, who were unaware that their drawings, which were supposed to represent 'a good dream' and 'a bad dream', were intended for the album. (The results were coordinated by Stylorouge and smART.)

The album contained a DVD element in the form of a short 'making of' film with three additional tracks: 'Back On' (an instrumental of 'Lost') and 'The Broken Promise' (an instrumental of 'The Promise'), and 'Someone's Coming (Scratch "Truth Goodness And Beauty" Vocal)'. Most of the visual content is mundane – Cooper's kit being set up, Smith scribbling something down with a green pen – but it does offer some insight into the producer's methods, with the band surrounded by tall white candles and huddled around a red Persian rug to offset the clinical varnished pine of Olympic's sound room, Robert's wrists a blur as he shreds, Robinson dancing out his instructions like a conductor-ballerina.

Ultimate Classic Rock deemed *The Cure* 'overlong' and 'a heavier album than fans probably expected (or even wanted) from The Cure'. *Trouser Press* wrote that 'Smith continues to flail a bit artistically on *The Cure*, but sometimes seems on the verge of regaining his equilibrium and inspiration.' They also called it 'the loudest Cure album in some time, at the expense of nuance' and considered Smith's anger on 'Us or Them' to be 'giggle-inducing'.

The Cure was released on 25 June 2004, first in Japan, then Europe, then the **US** – the same pattern as *Bloodflowers* and, due to advances in streaming and file-sharing technology, the last time in Cure history that such staggered release dates would be viable. It was promoted with a lengthy run of appearances at **festivals** across Europe and the Americas, and reached the Top 10s of Belgium, Denmark, **France**, Germany, Italy, Norway, Poland, Spain, Sweden, Switzerland, the UK and the US, and was certified silver in the UK. It would be The Cure's final Top 10-busting, framed disc-earning album (although it remains to be seen what the proposed fourteenth album might achieve).

Hindsight has not, as yet, rehabilitated *The Cure*, and it is generally ranked low on lists. But, for all the Ross Robinson hype, it does exactly what it says on the plastic jewel case. It's *The Cure*.

Curiosa

From the very beginning of their career, The Cure have always played at other people's **festivals**. In 2004, they decided to make their own.

Following the model of Lollapalooza, the nineties touring festival of alternative rock bands launched by Perry Farrell of Jane's Addiction, The Cure parlayed their usual North American tour into something much bigger, creating a double-staged festival called Curiosa which visited twenty-two American cities in the summer of 2004. (It was originally meant to be twenty-three, but Seattle was cancelled.) The main stage also featured Interpol, The Rapture and **Mogwai**, with headliners The Cure playing a short set by their standards, one performance comprising just seventeen songs and one encore of two songs. The second stage had a revolving bill, headlined on alternate dates by Muse and Thursday, with other acts including Scarling, Head Automatica, The Cooper Temple Clause, Auf der Maur and Cursive, offering an interesting snapshot of Smith's **tastes** at the time. It was also a foreshadowing of his **Meltdown Festival** in 2018, which Mogwai also played, and the subsequent Anniversary show (see *40 Live*), where Interpol supported.

Though ticket sales were somewhat disappointing, Curiosa was nevertheless one of the most successful alternative tours in the US that year. As the tour neared its conclusion, Smith took over San Diego radio station 91X for a special show on which he played tracks by the bands on the bill, and explained his rationale for creating it. 'I was wondering what The Cure would be doing next summer in America,' he said, thinking back to his last **US** visit in 2003. 'I knew we were going to be making a new record, and I knew we'd be playing some shows and I really wanted the experience to be something different. I thought that adding in some of the bands that I love, you know, it's a really selfish idea, would just make it a great summer for me. And I also assumed that other people would get into it as well. And that has proven to be the case. It's exceeded all my expectations. It's an absolutely fabulous way for us to spend the summer.' (Amusingly, one of the sponsors of the tour was MAC **make-up**, their voiceovers during the 91X radio show billing themselves as 'makers of fine white face powder and really good black nail polish'.)

Speaking to *Female First* in hindsight, Smith theorised that the timing for a Cure-led alternative package tour was perfect, because the era in which The Cure were uncool had passed, and bands influenced by The Cure were breaking through. 'We were unfashionable pretty much everywhere post-*Bloodflowers*, but suddenly there were lots of young bands who'd grown up listening to *Disintegration*, *Kiss Me, Kiss Me, Kiss Me* or *Wish* and didn't know that you weren't supposed to like us. So we kind of knew it was happening, at some point there's going to be a generation of people who are going to go and form bands who are going to have seen The Cure. I feel slightly paternal towards some of them, the Curiosa thing was almost like me saying, "Come here, my loves."'

The quality of the support acts, said Smith, forced The Cure to raise their own game. 'I felt fucking competitive on that tour, but in a really good way, like, "Now I'll show you what I can do" . . .'

Curious Creatures

Curious Creatures, named for the Emily Dickinson poem 'The Past Is Such A Curious Creature' (as well, of course, as the double Cure/Creatures pun), is a podcast hosted by **Lol Tolhurst** and Budgie in which the former Cure and Banshees drummers reminisce about their respective careers as well as discussing post-punk music in general. Since its launch in May 2021, guests have included Will Sergeant of Echo & The Bunnymen, Tim Burgess of The Charlatans, James Murphy of LCD Soundsystem, and Lol's fellow Cure founder Michael Dempsey. 'You may think you know the territory . . .,' says Lol at the start of every episode, before the pair add in unison '. . . but we drew the map.' Persistent rumours that Lol and Budgie were planning to turn Curious Creatures into a band, featuring guest appearances from several of their famous friends, were proven correct in July 2023 when a supergroup called Lol Tolhurst x Budgie x Jacknife Lee (the latter being the renowned Irish producer whose lengthy CV includes Robert Smith's collaboration with Crystal Castles) unveiled their debut single 'Los Angeles' (featuring James Murphy) on PIAS Recordings and announced an album, also called *Los Angeles*, featuring appearances from, among others, The Edge and Bobby Gillespie. The Curious Creatures podcast is at http://www. curiouscreaturespodcast.com and the spin-off supergroup are at @LolBudgieJCKNF on Twitter and @lolxbudgiexjacknifelee on Instagram.

Cut Here

There are Cure songs that are cryptic, gnomic, enigmatic, Sphinx-like, challenging the listener to read between the lines and come up with a possible interpretation. And then there's 'Cut Here'.

Billy Mackenzie of The Cure's former **Fiction** labelmates **Associates** had committed suicide in 1997. The last time Robert Smith saw him, backstage after a show, he was a little dismissive of his old friend, failing to give Billy the time and attention he deserved. 'Cut Here' expresses Smith's deep regret at that. 'So dizzy Mr Busy, too much rush to talk to Billy,' its sort-of-chorus runs, 'All the silly frilly things have to first get done/In a minute sometime soon, maybe next time, make it June/Until later doesn't always come . . .'

Co-produced by Mark Plati and built on a restless drumming pattern from **Jason Cooper** and a nagging keyboard motif from **Roger O'Donnell**, it was released as a single in October 2001, one month ahead of the *Greatest Hits* album it was intended to promote. It did not make the UK Top 40, though it reached the Top 10 in Spain.

Richard Anthony directed its very conventional video, just a performance clip with a few mirrors occasionally fracturing the image. The band all wear black or charcoal grey suits, as though attending a funeral. As well they might, because – though not a Cure classic for the ages – 'Cut Here' stands as a touching *memento mori* to always make time for your friends while you still can. 'I wish "If only",' sings Robert at the end, 'but "If only" is a wish too late.'

Cuteness

In Japanese culture the concept of *kawaii* translates loosely as 'lovely', 'loveable', 'cute' or 'adorable'. It can refer to people, objects, clothing, animals or fictional characters that have charming, childlike, shy or vulnerable qualities.

A whole *kawaii* subculture has developed, which encompasses such cultural phenomena as anime cartoons and Pokémon, and is particularly popular with teenage girls, both in Japan and the West. It has been successfully exploited by American toy manufacturers like Hasbro (My Little Pony) and Japanese ones like Sanrio (Hello Kitty).

Kawaii is closely related to the aesthetics of neoteny (the idea that attractiveness or beauty depends on the retention of childlike features or attributes), which biologist Stephen Jay Gould believed to be a key element of human evolution. We are genetically hard-wired, the theory goes, to respond emotionally to large eyes set far apart, small noses, full lips and flat, round faces. And it crosses the species divide: it's why everyone loves puppies and kittens.

Robert Smith – specifically the Robert Smith of The Cure's peak of popularity, the Robert Smith of 1983 through to 1992, '**The Lovecats**' through to '**A Letter To Elise**' – is *kawaii*.

This may seem a strange claim to make, as he was not a hairless, harmless dreamboat boy-band member but a grown man pushing (and pushing past) thirty, with body hair and stubble, in a band who wrote dark songs about death, **drugs**, **sex**, **violence** and hatred. Nevertheless, there is something about Robert Smith that sets off the *kawaii* receptors in the brain of many a fan. The band's 'melancholy musings', Cure biographer Steve Sutherland once wrote, 'beg mothering instincts from doe-eyed girl fans'. Writer Simon Reynolds made a similar point when he argued that 'Smith's little-boy-lost aura is a large part of his appeal, especially to the female half of The Cure's fans. Even at 33 he finds it hard to think of himself as a man rather than a boy and says that "Wendy Time", on the *Wish* album, is the first time he's used the word "man" to describe himself in a song.' And in *Vox*, Betty Page wrote that Smith's image 'practically yells "please mother me"'.

A review of a Cure gig in Madrid in *Melody Maker* from November 1992 compared him both to a koala and the Queen Mother (the elderly royal matriarch considered lovable by much of the British public). And *Melody Maker* isn't the only publication to have mentioned koalas: *East Village Eye* called him 'a prophet of gloom [who] is the cuddliest thing this side of the Qantas koala bear; he is cute in a Pillsbury Doughboy sort of way'. On a similar cuddly animal tip, Simon Witter, in *Sky* magazine, described Smith as being 'like Paddington Bear, crossbred with **Siouxsie Sioux**, the morning after a very long night'.

Part of it is to do with his onstage body language: the arms that are never quite fully outstretched, the fingers in his mouth, the pigeon-toed stance, as captured in *The Cure In Orange* (and as discussed in the *Curepedia* entry for that). Part of it is arguably his singing **voice**: Richard Cromelin, in the *LA Times*, wrote about Smith 'delivering erotic reveries and contemplations on mortality in a piping, little-boy voice.' Part of it is his dress sense, wearing oversized shoes, baggy trousers and voluminous jumpers and shirts, like a small boy playing dress-up with dad's wardrobe. (Smith once said he wore crumpled, unironed clothes because 'I think people look more homely and cuddly when they're crumpled, anyway.') And part of it is his **make-up**: those smudged rings of kohl around the eyes that make him look like a bush baby or some other inhabitant of London Zoo's Moonlight World section, and that inexpertly applied lipstick that looks like he's just messily eaten a jam sandwich.

Some of those things Smith cannot help, or does not intend. But he has, historically undeniably played up to his cuteness, with winsome lyrics like 'When I see you kitten as cats' (from '**High**'), with accessories like his white teddy bear, called S-teddy (as revealed in a January 1989 edition of *Cure News*), with which he was pictured on the tour bus in 1992. Or his off-duty clothing, like the Betty Boop T-shirt in which he was once pictured (a human cartoon character wearing an actual cartoon character). Or his television viewing habits, revealed in *Cure News* to be 'live football (QPR), and Tickle on the Tum' (an ITV children's programme).

Robert Smith – the 1983 to 1992 Robert Smith – could almost have been designed by some dastardly doll manufacturer, perfectly calibrated to be adorable. And there is a whole cottage industry of independently made, *kawaii*-friendly Robert Smith dolls. A scan through the first few pages of an Etsy search for 'robert smith cure' on a random day brought up the following: a Robert Smith paper doll, featuring toes turned inwards and outfits including the furry suit from the '**Why Can't I Be You?**' video. A crocheted Robert Smith *amigurumi* doll. A painted Robert Smith peg-man in a Christmas jumper. A Robert Smith cake topper. A Robert Smith glove puppet. A Robert Smith rag doll. A Robert Smith customised Barbie doll. A felt figurine of Robert Smith (admittedly as well as figurines of the other members of The Cure, though one imagines there isn't overwhelming demand for Reeves Gabrels). A plush doll of Robert Smith in his CCCP ice hockey shirt. And a furry doll of Robert in his 'Why Can't I Be You?' bear suit. ('I love my little BOB!!! So cute and perfect!' wrote one happy customer.) And, away from Etsy, there's a Robert Smith Funko Pop! doll (the ones with the massive heads), in two different designs. Robert, put simply, *is* a doll.

But can you be cute and sexy at the same time? Millions of Cure fans, and thousands reading this very chapter, will be screaming in the affirmative. But cuteness and sexiness would appear to be opposite poles, almost impossible to reconcile. In May 1998, an interesting review of a Cure show in Los Angeles appeared in *Cure News*, written by a fan called M. 'Robert was the most scrumptious', wrote M. 'With his nicely teased hair, black blouse, black jeans and big shoes, he danced and moved child-like to each and every song.' The telling phrase is 'child-like'. M then went on to express disgust that some girls in the crowd clearly wanted to have Robert's babies.

M, one imagines, was outnumbered. And it must not be overlooked that Robert Smith was voted fourth Most Sexy Male by *Melody Maker* readers at the end of 1990. Clearly, there are plenty who find Robert Smith legitimately and uncomplicatedly sexy, and plenty who have no difficulty in squaring 'sexy' with 'cute'. Evidently, one can be both things at once. But let's put it this way. Nobody wants to mother **Simon Gallup**.

D

D is for . . .

Dance Fools Dance

Dance, Fools, Dance is, first and foremost, a 1931 MGM crime drama starring Clark Gable and Joan Crawford. The fact that the **Crawley**-based independent record label of the same name never eclipsed the movie is all you need to know.

The indie was set up in 1979 by Robert Smith with **Ric Gallup** to release a split single by the **Mag/Spys**, featuring Ric's younger brother **Simon Gallup**, and local schoolboy band **The Obtainers**. Robert revived the label in 1982 to release a single by another young local act, **Animation**. The failure of this second release to create much of a stir convinced Robert that he wasn't cut out to be a record industry mogul, so he wrapped up the label's activities for good.

Surprisingly, the one Crawley combo who never released anything on Dance Fools Dance were Simon Gallup's other band, **Fools Dance**.

Dazzle

The magnificent 'Dazzle' was **Siouxsie And The Banshees**' fifteenth single, the second to be lifted from their *Hyæna* album, and the third and final single from Robert Smith's stint as a Banshee.

Smith is generally a bit down on his two years in the Banshees. When asked about that era in interviews, he invariably states that the live stuff was great, the recordings not so great. But 'Dazzle', co-written by Robert, proves that he's not *entirely* right about that.

The song had its origins when Siouxsie sent a tape of herself playing a piano part, with the working title 'Baby Piano' (two words which actually appear in the final song), to strings players Martin McCarrick (later to become a fully-fledged Banshee), Anne Stephenson and Gini Ball of **The Venomettes**, and pianist Anni Hogan. This piano motif, scored for strings by McCarrick, became the gradually fading-in overture to 'Dazzle', with additional strings by members of the London Symphony Orchestra.

It was the strings that Robert Smith liked least about it. As he told Brian Johns in the Banshee-ography

Entranced, the song began its life 'like the Glitter Band or Sweet or something, really raw. And then they got in the orchestra.'

But it was also that orchestral element which snagged the attention of fans and critics alike, thanks to the production genius of **Mike Hedges**. In *Smash Hits* Ian Cranna, noting the nautical grandeur of the strings, called it 'an absolutely titanic meeting of *The Onedin Line* and sixties wall of sound'. Those elements can be heard to full effect in the phenomenal '7 Mins Plus Glamour Mix' on the 12-inch single.

Its lyrics were rich with imagery, in typical Siouxsie style ('Skating bullets on angel dust in a dead sea of fluid mercury . . .') They were in part inspired by the film *Marathon Man*, the words 'swallowing diamonds, a cutting throat' referring to a scene in which Laurence Olivier puts diamonds into his mouth. The only mis-step was the repetition of the phrase 'glittering prize', which had been the title of a Simple Minds single less than two years earlier.

Robert Smith officially had a hand in both the B-sides, although on the atmospheric 'I Promise' with its oblique lyrics about crying samurais and flying ravens, his guitars are barely heard, glockenspiels and a child's music box instead taking precedence. The pick of the extra tracks was 'Throw Them to the Lions'. An almost atonal anti-**religion** diatribe ('Come and meet deliverance/Blind faith will set you free' are its first words, 'Your prophet mumbles nonsense/Carved in blocks of stone' its last), it had Smith's serrated scouring guitars at the fore, making it one of the harshest-sounding Banshees tracks from that period.

Released on 25 May 1984 on the Banshees' own Wonderland **label** (via **Polydor**), it was only a modest hit, reaching No.33 in the UK and charting nowhere else. (Most Banshees fans would already have bought the album.)

The seldom-shown **video** for 'Dazzle' – a **Tim Pope** tumult of tumbling raindrops, snowflakes, diamantes and pearls – features Siouxsie heavily, **Severin** a little, Budgie less . . . but Robert Smith, tellingly, is nowhere to be seen. We never see where the guitar is coming from.

He had, essentially, already checked out.

Dear Prudence

Robert Smith's first recording as a member of **Siouxsie And The Banshees**, having stepped in to replace a departed guitarist for the second time, was a turbo-charged cover of one of The Beatles' less famous and less feted songs – Steve Sutherland, in *Ten Imaginary Years*, called it 'a Mansonised version of the old Beatles song'.

The song was written by John Lennon in Rishikesh, India, during The Beatles' 1968 sojourn with Maharishi Mahesh Yogi, and inspired by Prudence Farrow (sister of actress Mia, who was also present). Farrow became so obsessed with Transcendental Meditation that she would rush back to her chalet straight after lectures from the Maharishi to practise, despite being implored by the others to join them partying (hence the lyric 'won't you come out to play?').

'Prudence Farrow got an attack of the horrors, paranoia, an identity crisis and wouldn't come out of her Butlins chalet', Paul McCartney later recalled. 'We all got a little bit worried about her, so we went up there and knocked, "Hi, Prudence. We all love you. You're wonderful!" But nobody could persuade her out.' Farrow 'seemed to go slightly barmy', Lennon said in a 1980 interview. 'They selected me and George to try and bring her out because she would trust us. If she'd been in the West, they would have put her away. . . She'd been locked in for three weeks and was trying to reach God quicker than anybody else.'

According to Farrow: 'I would always rush straight back to my room after lectures and meals so I could meditate. John, George and Paul would all want to sit around jamming and having a good time and I'd be flying into my room. They were all serious about what they were doing, but they just weren't as fanatical as me.' (So fanatical, in fact, that she became a Transcendental Meditation teacher and author herself.)

Agoraphobia, identity crises and **religious** fanaticism, of course, are all very Cure subjects. But the song was not Robert's choice. According to the Banshees' authorised biography by Mark Paytress, 'Dear Prudence' had been recorded at Smith's insistence to document his time with the group. However, drummer Budgie later claimed that the Banshees were all big fans of *The Beatles* (aka the White Album, on which 'Dear Prudence' appeared) except for Smith, but that they settled on that song

because it was the one he knew. **Steve Severin** believed that the track particularly appealed to Smith because 'John Lennon's version sounds a bit unfinished'.

The reason for recording a cover at all, Severin admitted in Brian Johns' biography *Entranced*, was that there weren't any new Banshees songs written and they needed a single out. Siouxsie was familiar with the White Album because her older brother always played it. The Banshees had already recorded 'Helter Skelter' from the same album in 1978, and Siouxsie suggested the idea of recording another Beatles cover after the band listened to The Beatles' music while touring Scandinavia. This time Budgie lobbied for 'Glass Onion', also from the White Album, but was overruled – 'Dear Prudence' it was.

Recording began in Stockholm in July **1983** but was interrupted when Robert, spinning plates like crazy that year, was called away to promote '**The Walk**'. The track was completed at Angel Studios in Islington (where The Cure later recorded *The Head On The Door*), with Robert's sister Janet playing harpsichord.

The power of the track is all in Smith's guitar. Heralded by four hefty whacks of Budgie's snare, the whole thing just *unfurls* in opulent, bejewelled psychedelic splendour as Siouxsie intones Lennon's lyrics with a measured menace. As **cover versions** go, it's a majestically assured example.

Tim Pope made the **video**, having already worked with The Cure and (Siouxsie and Budgie's side project) The Creatures. Filmed in Venice, it mainly features the band cavorting around the canals and bridges, with lots of superimposed watery effects and visual noise.

The shoot was eventful, to say the least. In *Ten Imaginary Years*, Pope remembers them all getting drunk at a local disco where Siouxsie and Budgie had a row while Robert danced to ABBA songs. He then remembers Smith and Severin rampaging around the streets, setting fire to flags and throwing a bottle through a plate-glass window before running off.

At one point in the shoot, Severin was arrested by police for filming without permission. A shot of the bassist being escorted down some steps by carabinieri made it into the final cut. At another point, Budgie drunkenly decided to scale a wall in a pair of canvas two-toed sloth boots that were ill-suited for climbing, and fell, breaking a bone in his foot. After downing half a bottle of brandy to dull the pain, he was whisked away by river ambulance. 'I woke up in a hospital surrounded by surgical amputees with dark hairy skin and big grins all talking a different language,' he told Mark Paytress. 'I knew I wasn't in heaven because I was confused and scared and hurt like hell.' After being patched up, he was delivered back to the video shoot dressed head to toe in crumpled gold Tibetan silk (his costume for the video) with smudged make-up and matted blond hair, looking, in Siouxsie's words, 'like Coco the Clown'.

Rewatching the video armed with these anecdotes is a very different experience to seeing it innocently first time.

Released on 23 September 1983, 'Dear Prudence' was the Banshees' first single on **Geffen** Records in the United States, a **label** with whom Robert would have further dealings down the line. In the UK, with **artwork** by Da Gama, who also worked with **The Glove** and The Creatures, it was released on the Banshees' own Wonderland imprint (via **Polydor**). One of the B-sides was the guitarless, percussion-heavy 'Tattoo', which was Sioux's preferred choice for the A-side, but she was persuaded otherwise. The other, on the 12-inch, was '(There's A) Planet In My Kitchen', a daft experiment full of radio theatre sound effects which might have been better left on the studio floor.

Smash Hits' review was sniffy and patronising: 'Siouxsie always had a bit of the old *Alice in Wonderland* about her,' wrote David Hepworth, 'and it's not surprising that she should choose to revive a Beatles song from their most whimsical period. She's even kept the phasing. But does she know that it was originally written for actress Mia Farrow's sister? Thought not.'

The public, however, were more firmly convinced of its merits. Beatles nostalgia was big in the early eighties in the aftermath of John Lennon's shooting (Roxy Music's cover of Lennon's 'Jealous Guy' had reached No.1), and 'Dear Prudence' picked up plenty of daytime airplay, steadily climbing the singles charts, peaking at No.3 and earning them a prestigious spot later that year on the Christmas *Top of the Pops*. 'It was a surprise,' said Siouxsie later, 'but it didn't really sink in until we'd finished the touring and we were back home for the winter. Then we thought, "Blimey! We got to No.3!"'

For all the chaos of the recording sessions and the video shoot, and for all the wrangling behind the scenes about whether it should even be made, 'Dear Prudence' was Siouxsie And The Banshees' biggest hit. And, at that point, Robert Smith's too.

Dempsey, Michael

One Imaginary Boy.

Michael Dempsey was one of three founder members of The Cure, and the first one out. Born on 29 November 1958 in what was then Salisbury, Rhodesia and is now Harare, Zimbabwe, Dempsey grew up in Salfords, Surrey, two miles north of **Horley**. He attended Notre Dame Middle School, where he first met the young **Laurence Tolhurst** and Robert Smith. Dempsey, like Smith, stayed on for sixth form till the age of eighteen, then rejoined Lol at **Crawley** College, where any creative ambitions were drummed out of him. He wanted to be a journalist, but was advised to do Business Studies instead. Upon leaving, Dempsey ended up working at Netherne psychiatric hospital, working as 'a porter in a lunatic asylum', as he put it on the *Curious Creatures* podcast.

He was known around town for riding a 50cc Fantic Caballero motorbike (or, later, a Honda) and wearing a black leather jacket. He was also, importantly, the owner of a brown Guild bass, which qualified him to join Smith, Tolhurst and fellow schoolmate Marc Ceccagno in their fledgling **pre-Cure** bands. Dempsey was there right through Obelisk, Malice and Easy Cure to the final name-change.

As soon as The Cure began to become public property rather than local heroes, Dempsey was made to feel that he didn't quite belong. At a gig on 25 October 1978 at the Windsor Castle on Harrow Road, London, **Chris Parry** told Dempsey that his **image** needed work. 'Dempsey looked a dork so I told him so', Parry recalled in *Ten Imaginary Years*. 'Dempsey wore corduroys, Hush Puppies and a grandpa jumper.' (To be fair, Parry was almost as scathing about the appearances of Smith and Tolhurst.)

Dempsey, who was named as Mick when their first **Peel Session** was played and also in The Cure's first cover story (*Sounds*, Jan 1979), holds a couple of unique or almost-unique claims in Cure history. He sang backing vocals on '**Killing An Arab**' (it's very rare for Cure songs to feature BVs.) He is the only person other than Smith to sing lead on an officially released Cure track, namely their **cover** version of Jimi Hendrix's 'Foxy Lady' on *Three Imaginary Boys*, an album on whose **artwork** he is generally thought to be the Hoover.

His playing posture was very different from that

of the man who would eventually hold down The Cure's bassist position long-term. 'He was very much the new wave bass player who could play his bass at pelvic level,' said Dempsey of **Simon Gallup**. 'I could never do that. I had to have it under my chin like some sort of funkster . . .' (Indeed, if you look at Dempsey on the **'10.15 Saturday Night'** video, he plays his instrument at a very upright, almost forty-five-degree angle.)

As for his bass style, it might actually have been too good for The Cure in their first phase (just as **Porl Thompson**'s guitar playing was too good for them). *Sounds*' Mick McCullough, watching a Cure gig at the Moonlight Club, believed Dempsey's bass 'steals the evening's honours', which won't have gone down well with his bandmates. When asked by *Cure News* to give one-word descriptions of every member of The Cure, past and present, Robert Smith summarised Dempsey as 'fussy'. Whether that applied to his fretwork or his personality is debatable.

In this band of misfits, Dempsey was a misfit. A relatively introspective and guarded character, he didn't share Smith and Tolhurst's tastes or lifestyles. 'Simon and Robert both had a liking for Indian food,' he said in *Ten Imaginary Years*, 'and it was my undoing. I hated it.' And, as Lol Tolhurst recalled, 'Michael always used to take as many vitamin pills as possible and yet he was always ill.'

There was low-key friction between Dempsey and Smith when they toured with **Siouxsie And The Banshees**. 'One morning he came down to breakfast,' Smith later said, 'and The Cure and the Banshees are all sat at a table and there wasn't room for him. I thought "Oh no, this is going to be the last straw" . . .'

In the end it was Robert's back, not Michael's, which broke. And the difference was musical rather than personal. 'I think the final straw came when I played Michael the demos for the next album,' Smith told *Uncut*, 'and he hated them. He wanted us to be XTC part 2, and – if anything – I wanted us to be the Banshees part 2. So he left.'

Left, or was sacked? One fact that isn't questioned by anyone is that Dempsey was unimpressed by the *Seventeen Seconds* demos. Lol Tolhurst remembers Dempsey being 'non-committal' about them, and believes that Dempsey's playing style wouldn't have suited the minimalism of the new material anyway. 'I remember [Robert] saying he wanted to make the next album really boring,' said Dempsey in *Ten Imaginary Years*, 'and I couldn't quite grasp that concept.'

Smith decided the Hoover sucked, and went round to Gallup's house to tap him up. On the *Curious Creatures* podcast, Dempsey claimed that Smith had a long phone conversation with him (though Robert does not remember this). The most common version says that it fell to Lol to break the news to Michael that he was out. In any case, the bassist became the first of the original trio to part company with The Cure, and no attempt was made afterwards to contact Dempsey and make peace.

Michael Dempsey's departure was announced in *NME* on 10 November 1979. The *Crawley Advertiser* printed a rumour that he was about to form a band with fellow fancy muso Porl Thompson, but he ended up joining a band from the other end of Britain.

Dempsey had begun moonlighting with **Associates** while still a member of The Cure. 'I remember foolishly saying to Robert: they're really really good!', he said on *Curious Creatures*. The transfer from Cure to Associates was smooth: they were also signed to **Fiction**, they were produced by **Mike Hedges** who was The Cure's regular producer too, and Dempsey even ended up supporting The Cure with his new band on the Future Pastimes tour.

In Chris Parry's opinion, Dempsey was 'a very eloquent bass player', and he was better able to express that eloquence in the context of Associates. His work on their classic 1982 album *Sulk*, including the singles 'Club Country' and 'Party Fears Two', was sublime.

Initially, according to *The Glamour Chase*, Tom Doyle's biography of Billy Mackenzie, Dempsey's clipped southern vowels and suave demeanour proved a curiosity to the Scottish duo. However, it wasn't long before he found himself on the wrong side of another clash of personalities. It didn't help that Dempsey crashed Mackenzie's Mercedes; nor, according to *The Glamour Chase*, did the fact that he was not a cocaine enthusiast. He and Associates co-founder Alan Rankine both left, leaving them as essentially a Mackenzie solo vehicle.

Dempsey flitted from band to band after that. In 1982 he performed with Roxy Music on a European tour, and appears in their 'Avalon' video. Then he joined Liverpudlian band The Lotus Eaters in time for their one big hit, 'The First Picture Of You'. In 1988 he appeared on the album *Laughter, Tears and Rage* by Act, a synth duo signed to Paul **'Desperate Journalist'** Morley's label ZTT and fronted by Morley's wife, ex-Propaganda singer Claudia Brücken.

He had a brief reunion with The Cure in video form, and also only in shadow form: his is the silhouette playing bass behind the backcloth in the 1986 'Boys Don't Cry' video. He also reunited with a post-Cure Lol Tolhurst twice: first in the early nineties with **Presence**, on whose demos he performed as well as co-writing some of the songs, and then in 2007 with **Levinhurst**, on whose third album *Blue Star* he appeared.

Dempsey has his own music publishing company, MDM, and has worked on many soundtrack projects for film and television. In 1992, for example, he wrote and recorded a soundtrack for *Swan Song*, a sixteen-minute animated short film (of which a clip can be seen at the BFI's ScreenOnline site), which was the graduation video of Carolina Lopez Caballero from the West Surrey College of Art and Design in Farnham, performed by Jesus Gonzalo and the baroque trio Parnaso Español. The soundtrack was circulated as a handmade yellow cassette tape to friends, which makes it one of the most niche Cure-related rarities possible.

And, speaking of rarities, a small but fascinating archive of memorabilia from Dempsey's days in The Cure and Associates can be found at his long-dormant personal website, mdmmedia.com.

Depeche Mode

Depeche Mode are the one band to whom The Cure can look sideways as equals: fellow eighties survivors turned arena-filling giants of alternative music, with a truly international reach. Formed in Basildon, Essex in 1980, Depeche Mode – original line-up Dave Gahan, Martin Gore, Andy Fletcher and Vince Clarke – were one of the most successful synthpop bands of the era, scoring major hits with their second and third singles 'New Life' and 'Just Can't Get Enough'. When musical genius Clarke left in November 1981 to form Yazoo, replaced by Alan Wilder, many assumed the band were doomed. However, Martin Gore immediately became the band's main songwriter and delivered a constant stream of hits.

In 1985, The Cure and Depeche Mode found themselves thrown together by fate, fleeing for their lives. Melina Mercouri, a former actress turned politician, was the Greek Minister of Culture and, with her French counterpart Jack Lang, had devised the idea of an annual European City of Culture. The first

recipient of this honour was the Greek capital, and Rock In Athens music **festival** on 26 and 27 July was a major part of the celebrations. The two-day festival, held in the Panathenaic Stadium (scene of the first modern Olympics in 1896), was The Cure's biggest to that point, with an expected crowd of fifty thousand. Depeche Mode played the first day, and The Cure, due to play the second day, came along to check out the site. In scenes similar to those which would unfold when The Cure visited **Argentina** two years later, thousands of counterfeit tickets had been sold, leading to pitched battles between locked-out fans and police and security, and fans throwing chunks of concrete over the backstage fence. Matters escalated when headliners Culture Club faced a barrage of homophobic abuse directed at singer Boy George, and rioting broke out. The Cure were forced to escape the **violence** with Depeche Mode in the back of a truck, forcing their way through the angry mob. (The Cure nevertheless played the festival the following day, on a bill headlined by surprise guests The Clash playing their last-ever gig.)

As the eighties wore on, Depeche Mode's once-sunny synthpop sound became noticeably *noir* on singles like 'Master And Servant', 'Blasphemous Rumours', 'A Question Of Time' and 'Never Let Me Down Again', as well as the albums *Black Celebration* and *Music For The Masses*. Their lyrical themes followed down a similar path: manipulation, deceit, corruption, sadomasochism, **religious** hypocrisy, **drug** addiction, suicide.

It's notable that Depeche Mode's period of greatest success, with the singles 'Personal Jesus' and 'Enjoy The Silence' and the album *Violator* in 1989–90, maps onto The Cure's own commercial high point. In some ways, the two bands had made reverse journeys in order to get there: The Cure started dark then went pop, and Depeche Mode started pop then went dark. But they both, by embracing all sides of their respective back catalogues, ended up in roughly the same place.

There are also connections in terms of personnel. **Daryl Bamonte** was a member of Depeche Mode's technical and managerial team before moonlighting with The Cure, and later made the switch to The Cure's **crew** full time. His older brother **Perry**, whom Daryl introduced to The Cure, had been in the same class as Martin Gore and Andy Fletcher at school, and was once briefly in a band with Vince Clarke. And **Steve Lyon**, producer of *Wild Mood Swings*, had previously worked on two Depeche Mode albums.

As is the case with The Cure's other parallel travellers, **New Order**, Robert isn't above slinging the occasional barbed comment at Depeche Mode. In a 1991 issue of *Cure News*, Smith dismissed them as 'formularised'. If that sideswipe ever reached the Basildon band, they held no hard feelings. In 1992, Depeche Mode flew in specially to see The Cure's Pasadena Rosebowl concert on the *Wish* tour. And, two years after that, Gahan, Gore, Wilder, Daryl Bamonte and Robert Smith all attended the Italy vs Ireland match in the USA '94 World Cup (a game won 1–0 by Ireland in one of the biggest shocks in World Cup history, the solitary goal scored by Ray Houghton).

Robert managed to find at least one Depeche Mode song which wasn't too formularised for his liking; The Cure **covered** 'World in My Eyes' for the tribute album *For the Masses* in 1988. Depeche Mode have yet to repay the compliment, but if 'Reach out, touch *Faith*' isn't a Cure reissue slogan waiting to happen, then someone's missing a trick.

Desperate Journalist

Quis custodiet ipsos custodes? (Who watches the watchmen?)
– Juvenal

Paul Morley is the greatest music writer of his generation. Born in 1957 in Farnham in Surrey, he grew up in Stockport, Greater Manchester, making almost the exact reverse journey to that of the infant Robert Smith. The first record he owned as a child was 'Ride A White Swan' by T. Rex. As a teenager he began writing for fanzines in Manchester, and then became a contributor to *NME*. Factory Records boss Anthony H. Wilson famously took Morley to a funeral home to show him the dead body of **Joy Division**'s Ian Curtis, an incident depicted in the film *24 Hour Party People*.

In 1983 he formed the avant-garde pop group Art Of Noise with Gary Langan, J. J. Jeczalik, Anne Dudley and Trevor Horn. The same year, with Horn and Jill Sinclair, Morley launched the record label ZTT (Zang Tumb Tuum), best known for giving the world Frankie Goes to Hollywood. Morley was their media manipulator, responsible for the big concepts and the small print, and vice versa.

His anthology *Ask: The Chatter of Pop* is a masterclass in the art of the interview. He has since written many books, one of the finest being 2004's *Words and Music*, an oblique history of pop which uses as its central conceit an imagined car journey with Kylie Minogue towards a virtual city made of sound. And he has become one of Britain's foremost cultural **critics**, appearing in endless music **documentaries**, including *Out of the Woods* (about The Cure).

Back in 1979, while working for *NME*, Morley reviewed The Cure's *Three Imaginary Boys*. Morley wrote that the album 'does a lot less than please, and a lot more than irritate', that 'they make things much worse than they could be by packaging this insubstantial froth as if it had some social validity', that 'the lads go rampant on insignificant symbolism and compound this with rude, soulless obliqueness' and that 'The Cure are absolute conformists to vaguely defined non-convention'.

The Cure considered Morley's review to be 'word salad', and retaliated in a hilarious and ingenious manner, just a week after publication. During their second **Peel Session**, recorded on 9 May 1979 and broadcast on 16 May, they recorded a reworked version of their song 'Grinding Halt', retitled 'Desperate Journalist in Ongoing Meaningful Review Situation', with lyrics that parodied Morley's written style, quoting directly from his review, and also mocked his *NME* colleague Ian Penman.

A mystery review
Of word salad
Is written by my friend
Ian Penman
He uses long words
Like semiotics and semolina
But I countered
With enigma
And metropolis.

(According to a retrospective Cure piece in *Uncut*, although Morley's review had angered Smith, he also partly agreed with it.)

A year later, in June 1980, with the hatchet buried and the water under the bridge, Morley had become quite favourably disposed towards The Cure, and interviewed them circa *Seventeen Seconds* under the headline 'Days of Wine and Poses'. Still, the legend of *that* Peel Session lived on (to the extent that Desperate Journalist, a London indie band influenced by post-punk, took their name from it).

The Cure had, in one playful, satirical stroke,

adapted Juvenal's idea and posed a modified version of his question. *Quis recognitores ipsos recenset?* (Who reviews the reviewers?)

Disintegration

The first words are 'I think it's dark and it looks like rain'. The last are 'I'll never lose this pain.'

Even by Cure standards, *Disintegration* – their eighth studio album, considered by many to be their ultimate masterpiece – was doom-laden. Much of this was rooted in personal factors. Robert's state of mind was overshadowed by a dark cloud in the shape of his impending thirtieth birthday (in April 1989), a looming chronological milestone which seems to have troubled him far more that it would the average person.

The prospect of ageing troubled him deeply. Reaching thirty seemed to him to encapsulate wider feelings of inadequacy and futility. 'I'm still talking about getting older,' he told Dutch magazine *Oor*, 'and about how it always seems that what you do doesn't really seem to make any sense, because these kind of feelings never seem to reach a climax, but rather a lowest point.'

As *Uncut* later put it, 'the date [his birthday] had started to assume a mythical significance for him. Smith was convinced that he was fast approaching a cut-off point of old age – and his reaction was once again to withdraw into himself.' Looking back on that era in 2002, Robert told Swiss television that he hated turning thirty so much that he had a full 'breakdown'. This wasn't the first time that the arbitrary arrival of an age with a zero at the end troubled him. 'I was 20 when I made it [*Seventeen Seconds*],' he said in *Ten Imaginary Years*, 'and we were all realising that we were no longer young . . .'

He was also deeply affected by the fact that two teenagers from New Zealand (see **Australasia**) had recently committed suicide while listening to The Cure. According to *NME*, 'the band kept a cutting of the news story pinned to the studio wall while recording.'

Lastly, it didn't help that Robert had plunged himself into one of his intermittent LSD phases. As Stephen Dalton later wrote in *LouderSound*, 'Smith conceived this milestone album in a fog of depression and hallucinogenic **drugs**.'

Interestingly, when the fourteenth edition of

Cure News from 1993 reached *Disintegration* in its ongoing series of album recaps, Robert was for once unable to fulfil the usual 'Inspirations' section, on the grounds that 'all these songs are too personal for me to talk about.' It was, evidently, closer to the bone than most.

These personal factors, however, were only part of the story. Smith had made a conscious aesthetic decision to steer The Cure away from the bright pop flavours of much of *Kiss Me, Kiss Me, Kiss Me* and back towards the sombre intensity of their early eighties work. As he told *Oor*, 'When *Kiss Me* was finished, it was time for reflection. I wanted to sing songs with more depth again. Our new album is in a certain way a reference to The Cure of a few years ago.' He added '*Disintegration* means a return to our minimalist recording style. First, I wanted to go back to the terrain we explored with *Faith* and *Pornography*.'

This was all part of The Cure's ongoing cycle of reaction and counter-reaction. 'We tend to go in big circles and big spirals,' he told MTV in 1990, 'and it was inevitable that we'd slip out of being a pop group again . . . I was missing doing songs with the group that had a bit more depth and emotion to them . . . and the concerts having a certain intensity. I wanted to drag the band back into doing something that hurt a bit more.'

The length of the album was another conscious decision. By the end of the 1980s, the Compact Disc was on the way to becoming the dominant format for music, particularly in the United States where CD sales passed vinyl sales for the first time in 1988 (and would pass cassette tapes by 1992).

A CD holds eighty minutes of music, and *Disintegration* lasted seventy-two minutes and twenty-seven seconds. 'I wanted to be able to stretch songs again for 8 or 9 minutes,' he later explained, 'and no easy short pop songs. I wish I'd had some more time with *Faith* to experiment a bit more with certain songs, but we were stuck with the fact that an LP side cannot be longer than 20 minutes.'

Rather than make it The Cure's second double vinyl LP in a row, Smith kept it as a single disc but chopped two songs ('Last Dance' and 'Homesick') from the CD and cassette versions. They were only reinstated many years later when deluxe editions of *Disintegration* came out on double 180gm vinyl in 2010, 2018 and 2021.

The album's running time wasn't the result of uncontrollable creative diarrhoea, nor an inability to edit. It was an aesthetic decision. As he told Ted Mico of *Spin* at the time, 'It's our old idea of producing a thematic album, so you sit down and listen to it end to end on your own. This gave us the time to draw out sections and underplay sections. Rather than having to make the point in three or four minutes, we've allowed ourselves seven minutes. In that sense, the minimal way of recording, it goes back to our earliest stuff rather than *The Top* or *The Head On The Door*, where we tried to cram everything in. Those albums were good and they worked, but this is supposed to be a bigger-sounding record.'

The extra space facilitated by the album's length allowed it to become what it is. It's an album to luxuriate in, to slowly synchronise with, to allow its pace to dictate your own heartbeat. For Robert, it was intended as a solitary listening experience. 'The *Kiss Me* album was an album you could listen to with other people,' he told *Rapido* in 1989. '*Disintegration* is an album you listen to on your own.'

And it was an album which, at least to begin with, he created on his own. In the new house in London to which he and **Mary** had recently moved, he began writing songs while, by all accounts, taking significant amounts of acid. Seven existing demo tracks that didn't make the cut for *Kiss Me, Kiss Me, Kiss Me* were considered, but only two or three were actually worked on, due to Robert's belief that 'our next stuff has to be very different'.

He wasn't the only member of the band who had been writing demos, however. Keyboardist **Roger O'Donnell**, on his website, once wrote an in-depth blog gathering his memories of the making of *Disintegration*. When the band met up, O'Donnell himself remembers bringing an hour's worth of music for what would end up being a very keyboard-heavy album, and all other members (even **Lol Tolhurst**, to a limited extent) came armed with ideas of their own.

The gatherings happened in two main chunks, one in early 1988 and one in late summer, both at Brushford Barton, **Boris Williams**' elegantly sprawling country house in Devon (a property so large that it is now a venue which hosts open-air theatre), twelve miles from the nearest town and theoretically safe from distractions.

In practice, however, they found plenty of ways to distract themselves. Robert bought a pool table from a small ad in a local paper, and had it set up in Boris' hallway ('mainly', Roger wrote, 'because we were unable to win our way on to the table at the local pub'). There was also clay pigeon shooting,

boules, cricket and table tennis. There were frequent barbecues, and much drinking, as the house had a beer cellar (which wasn't an ideal situation for a band with Lol Tolhurst in it). If they didn't feel like cooking, they'd order pizza from a local place called Poppins. 'The restaurant was owned by two gay guys,' Roger wrote, 'who thought it would be hilarious to cover one delivery of pizzas with magic mushrooms and not tell us. It was quite funny but we had no idea what was going on. I thought I was losing my mind . . .'

Somehow, amid this gently bucolic chaos, an unusually large crop of songs was harvested by the end of the two stays. 'It was weird with *Disintegration*,' Robert later told the *Chicago Tribune*. 'We actually had more stuff than we did for the *Kiss Me* double-album. We could quite easily have done a triple-album. But it could have become almost unlistenable, really. Some of the stuff we didn't put on the album was very "noisy", just like slabs of noise.' At the end of the Brushford Barton sessions, having whittled an initial thirty songs down to twelve, the core of what became *Disintegration* was nailed down.

Recording began in mid-October 1988 in £2,000-a-day Hook End Manor, a sixteenth-century Elizabethan country house in Checkendon, a few miles north of Reading. This half-timbered rural pile is said to have been built for the Bishop of Reading in 1580, but this cannot be true, as that post was not created until 1889. However, it may have belonged to Thomas Whyte, the Archdeacon of Berkshire (the equivalent role) in that era. A more recent wealthy owner was financier Sir Charles Clore, whose millions funded the collection of Turner paintings at Tate Britain.

The first musician to take over the property was Alvin Lee of sixties and seventies blues-rockers Ten Years After, who built a studio inside called Space. It has changed hands several times since. Lee sold it to David Gilmour of The Cure's boyhood heroes **Pink Floyd**, whose album *The Final Cut* was recorded there, and whose famous inflatable pig from the cover of *Animals* was stored in one of the outbuildings. The house is believed by some to be haunted, and in 1987 the Gilmour era allegedly came to an end because his wife could no longer stand the ghosts. Clive Langer and Alan Winstanley, producers of Madness and Morrissey among many others, took it over and renamed it Outside. Later still, it was taken over by Trevor Horn who rebranded it Sarm Hookend and hailed it as 'the best residential studio in the world'.

The Cure arrived during its Langer-Winstanley

phase, and it was Morrissey who had been there directly before them to make the single 'Ouija Board, Ouija Board' whose video, starring Kathy Burke and *Carry On* stalwart Joan Sims, offers extensive views of the Tudor interiors of Hookend, with its dark wood-panelled rooms, black-beamed ceilings and oak staircases, as well as its twenty-five-acre grounds, including Britain's oldest monkey puzzle tree. (For the insatiably Cure-ious, a twenty-two-minute film from 2017 of the building's now semi-derelict interiors by UrbEx filmmakers Exploring with Fighters shows a gravestone eerily propped against a wall in the basement, bearing the name of a seven-year-old called Little Jack, along with the date 17 April 1909.)

Not long after The Cure's arrival, disaster struck. An unattended heater in Robert's room caught fire. The studio's own fire extinguishers proved insufficient to quell the flames, and the fire brigade were called. According to Roger's blog, 'Robert had opened the window in his room as he is always hot and likes fresh air, one of the cleaning ladies went in the room and shut the window and thought it was cold so put the heater on! We were at dinner and somebody smelt smoke, it's lucky the entire house didn't burn down as it was very old and all made of wood.'

Lol's room, next door, was undamaged and he was able to stay put. Robert's room, though, was a charred, blackened mess, forcing him to relocate to living quarters elsewhere on the estate. Everything in his room had been destroyed.

Well, almost everything. It could have been a lot worse. Robert's entire lyrics for the album were in the room in a leather satchel. According to Roger's first draft, **Perry Bamonte** (Robert's personal assistant at the time), made a brave effort to save them from the flames but all was lost, leaving Robert with only his memories of the lyrics. However, O'Donnell later learned that the lyrics *had* been rescued.

But by whom? That is the question. In 1990, Robert gave a radio interview in which he claimed the whole band had formed a chain with towels to enter the burning bedchamber, and the lyrics were indeed saved but the whole wing of the house was burnt down.

However, producer **David M. Allen** gave his own account when speaking to BBC 6 Music's Andrew Collins in 2010. Allen claims that between using up all the fire extinguishers and waiting for the fire brigade to arrive, it was he who ran into the house to save the satchel. 'Anyone who knows me knows I'm mad enough to do that . . . When I dropped the satchel on

the floor, it burst into flames.' His valour, he stated, was fuelled by a desire to avoid repeating a situation on *Kiss Me, Kiss Me, Kiss Me* when he had to wait around for six weeks for Robert to finish the lyrics. As O'Donnell summarised it, 'Believe what you want, I was there and I still don't know the truth . . . or rather, the truth was lost over the years . . .'

A typical working day, when not firefighting, involved an initial session between 4 p.m. and 8 p.m., then a long dinner which, according to Roger, 'was a huge ritual with lots of drinking and storytelling and laughing', then a much longer, open-ended session until as late as 8 a.m. before sleep. A typically nocturnal Cure *modus operandi*, which meant that band members saw little sunlight. Roger would go cycling in the woods after breakfast just to escape for a while.

The atmosphere in the sessions, by most accounts, was oppressive. Robert had ceased speaking to the rest of the band, later admitting that 'I actually wanted an environment that was slightly unpleasant . . . I became very isolated and went into one of my non-talking modes. The others thought I'd lost the plot. They were still caught up with the idea that we were becoming a really famous band, and they weren't grasping that the music I wanted to make was incredibly morose and downbeat.'

Then there was the Lol situation. By Tolhurst's own admission, only 'an idea or two' of his made it onto *Disintegration*, but his 'mental fog' prevented him from contributing more. And, while Robert worked largely in solitude, there was plenty of time for the rest of the band to engage in The Cure's favourite sport of Lol-baiting. While some of this amounted to **bullying**, it was also a response to his habit of consuming so much **alcohol** at dinner that he fell asleep, then turning up to the studio drunk at 2 a.m. telling them that everything sounded rubbish. The band presented Robert with an ultimatum: Lol had to go.

Eventually, there was no choice. As the band gathered to hear the final mixes at RAK Studios, Lol stood up, after several beers, and announced 'half of it is good but half of it is shit', arguing that some songs sounded like The Cure but others did not. (He now considers it 'quite a wonderful album'). Lol was out, and contacted his lawyers. The Cure, crediting him only with 'other instrument' on the sleeve, released the most successful album of their career.

Disintegration, a name which they eventually settled on in January 1989 after toying with the working titles *A Dream Of Deception* and ***Wild Mood Swings***, began in majestic fashion.

The unhurried, stately intro of 'Plainsong' is a classic Cure album opener. For two and a half minutes there are no vocals, and you almost want it to stay that way: the audacity of beginning an album with an instrumental overture would be quite a statement.

When Robert does start singing, his second word is drowned in echo, as is much of the song, symbolic of one of the album's themes of communication breakdown. The lyric, he told *Oor*, 'enlightens different aspects of an obsession'. That obsession, framed in the format of a dialogue, appears to be with ageing and death:

I think I'm old and I'm feeling pain, you said
And it's all running out like it's The End Of The World, you said
And it's so cold, it's like the cold if you were dead . . .

The bridge is deeply ambiguous: 'Sometimes you make me feel like I'm living at the edge of the world', Robert sings, before ending with 'It's just the way I smile, you said . . .'

Plainsong in the religious sense (it's a term for a style of Gregorian chant and other Catholic liturgy) is typically monophonic. 'Plainsong' in The Cure sense is all about the chords. On the day of recording, when Robert was so hungover that he could only communicate via handwritten notes, Roger recalled that 'He played the big chords. They were very Robert, just sort of playing every note you could at the same time. The song is in C, so it's all the white notes and just about every one of them was played in that song.' It's a song in which Roger himself is to the fore, with its backward piano sounds played on the studio's Bösendorfer grand, and a booming bass that is actually O'Donnell's synth.

This grandiose intro is followed by a version of '**Pictures Of You**' that lasts an extraordinary seven and a half minutes. (Even the single, which has its own entry, is nearly five.) This in turn is followed by 'Closedown', which continues with the same tempo and chords and key as 'Pictures Of You', giving the album a feeling of unity that continues throughout. Only eight lines long, it begins 'I'm running out of time', and ends 'If only I could fill my heart with love'.

Robert told *Oor* that it was written a long time ago, 'which explains why it sounds so gloomy', but it isn't as if the more recently written material was full of good cheer.

'**Lovesong**', the world-conquering single (which,

like all the singles, has its own entry), is next. Short and sweet, at three and a half minutes long, it's the only track on the album with a classic pop song run-time.

'Last Dance', Robert told *Oor*, is about the disappointment he felt after a meeting with someone from old times who's not like he or she used to be anymore. A song about trying and failing to rekindle a relationship, dotted with interesting words like 'punctual' and 'abasement', it ends on a sorrowful note:

But Christmas falls late now, flatter and colder
And never as bright as when we used to fall
And even if we drink, I don't think we will kiss
In the way that we did when the woman was only a girl

In context, '**Lullaby**' strikes an ever so slightly jarring note, its pantomime creepshow narrative too trivial somehow for the context which surrounds it, although musically it's not too anomalous, and along with 'Closedown' and 'Untitled', it's almost exactly the average bpm of 94.5.

The big bad monster bassline of '**Fascination Street**' is next, then it's 'Prayers For Rain', statistically the average *Disintegration* song, both mean and median, in terms of length, but the second-fastest (117 bpm).

Robert had bought a CD of sound effects which he used on the record, to Roger's dismay. 'I hated them and fought against them, I hate anything that's too literal and why do you need thunder and rain on a song called "Prayers For Rain"? Isn't it obvious?'

It's actually 'The Same Deep Water As You' that has the storm sound effects, which top and tail what is, at nine minutes nineteen seconds, the longest song on an album that isn't exactly lacking in long songs. Although it was never a single, it was voted seventh best Cure song by *Rolling Stone* readers. Speaking to *Spin*, Robert connected it to early, dark Cure classics like 'Siamese Twins', 'Faith', 'Figurehead' and 'Seventeen Seconds'. Barbara Ellen, in *NME*, called it 'devoutly reminiscent of "**All Cats Are Grey**"', and the *Guardian*'s Ben Hewitt hailed it as 'one of The Cure's most breathtaking compositions'. It was, Robert said, 'about the expectations people have from you, and how you never can live up to those expectations.' He admitted having cried during the recording of it, but '[that] doesn't mean anything. It's even a bit embarrassing that I could care so much about those lyrics at that time.'

The title track 'Disintegration', the fastest (122 bpm) and second-longest (8.18) was uncharacteristically major-key and upbeat, but not lyrically. 'It's my scream against everything falling apart, and my right to quit with it when I want to,' Robert explained. *Rolling Stone* theorised that it was a forewarning that his drug habit might kill him, highlighting the lyrics:

> I leave you with photographs, pictures of trickery
> Stains on the carpet and stains on the memory
> Songs about happiness murmured in dreams
> When we both of us knew how the end always is

Highly regarded by fans, it was the highest-ranking album track (at No.8) in a poll of favourite Cure songs conducted by *Slicing Up Eyeballs*.

'Homesick', a song 'about the attraction of forbidden fruits', is generally acknowledged as the only song with a significant input from Lol Tolhurst, having begun life as one of his demos (though it was then reworked by Roger and **Simon Gallup**). 'I think we only chose it to make Lol feel like he wasn't being left out,' O'Donnell wrote in his blog. Its working title was 'The Tale of the Lonely Badger' or 'The Unknown Badger' because, according to David M. Allen, The Cure's technician Bruno Brunning (see **Crew**) was upset to find a dead badger by the side of the road in Devon, leading to a ribald band in-joke about how the badger ended up that way. 'Homesick', like 'Last Dance', was not included on the vinyl edition of the album, appearing only on the CD and cassette. However, on the deluxe 2010 reissue of *Disintegration* one can hear an alternate version on which the band reprise a band argument from legendary bootleg *The Troggs Tapes*.

The final track, 'Untitled', coming as it does (on CD and cassette) after 'Homesick', feels like coming home, its chords approaching like warm hugs.

The most striking thing about the album, once you'd heard it all the way through, was that feeling of unity. Click tracks were used, and all of Boris' kick drums were replaced by Allen with a sample of one hit he'd played, adding to the sense of sameness. Most tracks didn't stray far from the average of 94.5 bpm, and the most common key is A minor, in which four of its twelve tracks – 'Lovesong', 'Last Dance', 'The Same Deep Water As You' – are played. The average length is just under six minutes, but half the songs are considerably over that length (with the compact and bijou 'Lovesong' bringing the average down).

The **artwork** from **Parched Art** featured, unusually, a picture only of Robert. (His mouth had been on the front of *Kiss Me, Kiss Me, Kiss Me*, but that was an extreme close-up.) For a band album, the artwork made it look a lot like a solo one, causing a certain amount of unrest within the band. The picture was a Polaroid by **Andy Vella**, who had used the camera on a photo shoot in Ireland and decided he liked the softness of the colours.

Unbelievably, with hindsight, *Disintegration* was initially considered by their **US** label Elektra to be commercial suicide. As Robert told *NME*, 'They thought I was being "wilfully obscure", which was an actual quote from the letter.' He later told *Uncut*, 'This was one of my blackest moments. I thought it was my masterpiece, and they thought it was shit. They'd turned up expecting *Kiss Me* Part 2, and they got *Pornography* Part 2.'

Reviews were not unanimously positive either. Jim Bohen of the *Daily Record* called it 'ponderous', Chris Roberts of *Melody Maker* called it 'about as much fun as losing a limb' and complained of its greyness and listlessness, and Barbara Ellen of *NME*, in a broadly favourable review, worried that 'one is left fearing for Smith's present state of mind. Surely a psyche shattered this profoundly could only resume play as a mosaic.'

It struck a chord with the public, however, especially in the US, where it propelled them to stadium-filling size. As *Rolling Stone* later put it, 'This was no longer the cool cult group beloved by your older brother, but the band you heard all over the radio and blaring out of kids' cars in the parking lot of the mall. Robert Smith posters went up on teenagers' walls all over Middle America.'

It entered the charts at No.2 in the UK and 14 in the US, and became the band's most commercially successful album, selling more than three million copies. Interestingly, in the UK the singles releases from it followed the classic pattern – high placing for the lead single, then steadily lower for those that followed ones – but in the US they went the other way: 46, 31, 2. (Note: 'Fascination Street', not 'Lullaby', came out first in the States.)

On the *Disintegration* tour, actually named the Prayer Tour ('That word calls up the idea of believing and by that means points out in a sublime way to the Faith-era', explained Robert), all the album's songs were played at every show, but not necessarily in album order, and were interspersed with other songs. However, it's an album The Cure have revisited on more than one occasion in its entirety. In Brussels and Berlin in 2002 they presented *Disintegration* with *Pornography* and *Bloodflowers* as part of a *Trilogy* (under which name the concerts were released as a DVD the following year). They also marked the album's thirtieth anniversary in 2019 by playing it for five nights at the Sydney Opera House, along with associated B-sides and outtakes like 'Esten' and 'Delirious Night'.

A deluxe reissue in 2010 came with an additional disc of rarities, demos and instrumentals, a live disc titled *Entreat Plus*, and a further selection available online only. The vinyl reissue, now a double, reinstated 'Last Dance' and 'Homesick'.

Posterity has been just as kind to *Disintegration* as the cash registers were at the time. Four of the Top 10 favourite Cure songs of *Rolling Stone*'s (predominantly American) readers are from *Disintegration*, and it was ranked by *Ultimate Classic Rock* and *Far Out* magazine as the band's best.

Whatever trauma Robert Smith may have felt at turning thirty, the resulting album turning The Cure into the biggest alternative band on the planet can only have softened the blow.

Documentaries

Needless to say, many filmmakers have jumped at the chance to make a documentary – a 'rockumentary', if you will – about The Cure.

Most television channels with a reasonable arts budget will, at some point, throw some money at summarising the career of one of the world's most venerable and respected bands. One of the earliest examples was the BBC's thirty-minute *That Was Then . . . This Is Now* episode in 1988 in which a short-haired Robert Smith talked us through The Cure's decade-long rise. A much later attempt by another reputable broadcaster was *The Story of The Cure*, made in 2004 by Canadian channel MuchMoreMusic with reasonably professional production values and original interviews by presenter Bill Welychka interspersed with archival clips.

The most satisfying Cure documentary – inevitably, given its unprecedented access to, and cooperation from, the band – is the 1991 film *Play Out*, which has its own entry in this book. However, the existence of a definitive, official documentary hasn't deterred

others from opportunistically chopping together a few interviews with fans, journalists and musicians then slapping Robert's face on the front of a DVD case.

One of these is 2004's completely unauthorised *Out of the Woods*. Although cheaply made, with no permission to use any actual Cure music but instead featuring incidental music done in a 'Cure' style, it is actually quite interesting, with contributions from Paul '**Desperate Journalist**' Morley, Richard Strange, **Steve Severin**, Janice Long and producer **Steve Lyon**. A similar project, 2007's *The Cure: Rock Case Studies*, did at least have an archival interview with Robert Smith and footage of the band circa *The Top* performing on Channel 4's *The Tube* to lend value to the film.

Then there are completely homemade efforts. *Untitled Documentary Film Series*, for example, is an exhaustive five-part YouTube compilation of Cure clips sourced from YouTube itself. Perhaps the most interesting amateur Cure film, however, is one which has yet to be completed. *Push: A Cure Fan Documentary* is a project involving hand-held footage of **fans** following the *Bloodflowers* tour (the premise being that this was allegedly a farewell tour). The film is still looking for funding, but the website contains a teaser clip.

However, the ultimate Cure documentary may soon be upon us. In December 2017, **Tim Pope** tweeted, 'So, 2018 will see me collaborating with Robert on a feature-length, chronological documentary of The Cure's history from the 1970s via present day to the future. Robert himself will tell the story and this will work alongside other events for the band's 40-year celebration.' He continued, 'The film to which I will bring my own style of jiggery-pokery will use as well as "old favourites" a cornucopia of material from Robert's collection which has never been seen before: Super-8; interviews; bootlegs; rare performances; behind-the-scenes, blah. Updates "as and when".'

The following March, at a film event called r7al (Rencontres 7e Art Lausanne) in Switzerland, *Variety* reported that Pope again spoke about the project. 'I want to make a film like *Goodfellas* where Robert is narrating the film in a first-person way,' he said, 'and it is like crazy and we are on this journey.'

He added that The Cure documentary is unlikely to be finished this year (meaning 2018). Five years later, Pope's rockumentary, if you will, has yet to materialise. But watch this space. (Even a blank space is more watchable than some of the documentaries out there.)

Dreams

There are few things more tedious than other people telling you about their dreams. Unless they're Robert Smith's, and he's turned them into a song.

In 1797, the Romantic **poet** Samuel Taylor Coleridge experienced an opium-induced dream during which he composed the entire poem *Kubla Khan*. Upon waking, he was interrupted by a knock at the door, and subsequently could not recall the poem's intended ending. As he wrote upon the eventual publication of the unfinished work in 1816, referring to himself in the third person:

> On awakening he appeared to himself to have a distinct recollection of the whole, and taking his pen, ink, and paper, instantly and eagerly wrote down the lines that are here preserved. At this moment he was unfortunately called out by a person on business from Porlock, and detained by him above an hour, and on his return to his room, found, to his no small surprise and mortification, that though he still retained some vague and dim recollection of the general purport of the vision, yet, with the exception of some eight or ten scattered lines and images, all the rest had passed away like the images on the surface of a stream into which a stone has been cast, but, alas! without the after restoration of the latter!

Robert Smith is very much not at home to persons from Porlock. As he revealed in his 'Welcome to the Working Week' diary in *Flexipop!*, 'I lay in bed for an hour or so thinking about the dreams I'd had during the night. I've taught myself to remember my dreams and write them all down, because they help me to write songs. I sometimes read one of my dreams before going to sleep at night too, so that I can carry on having the same dream from one night to the next.'

The title track of *Three Imaginary Boys* in 1979 was the first of countless songs inspired by Robert's dreams. The number of Cure songs explained in *Cure News* by Robert simply as 'a dream' almost became a running joke. They include 'A Man Inside My Mouth' from the B-side of '**Close To Me**' (1985), 'Like Cockatoos' from *Kiss Me, Kiss Me, Kiss Me* (1987), 'A Foolish Arrangement' from *Wish* (1992), and 'Return' and 'Strange Attraction', both from *Wild Mood Swings* (1996), as well as 'Adonais' (also inspired by the poetry of Shelley and the actor Brandon Lee, see **Films**) from the B-side of that

album's lead single '**The 13th**'.

Sometimes the title makes it plain: 'The Dream' from the B-side of '**The Walk**', for example, or 'A Japanese Dream' from the B-side of '**Why Can't I Be You**'. Other examples of Smith drawing upon the oneiric realm for lyrical inspiration include 'Close To Me' itself ('If only I was sure that my head on the door was a dream . . .') and, also from *The Head On The Door*, 'Kyoto Song' which begins 'A nightmare of you / Of death in the pool / Wakes me up at quarter to three . . .' (a lyric which arguably also belongs under **D is for Drowning**).

Then there's the whole tangled conundrum of *Music For Dreams*. Brian Johns' biography of **Siouxsie And The Banshees** reveals that this title was in play as early as 1982: 'Soon after **Blue Sunshine**, Smith said there had been drunken discussions of **The Glove** making a purely instrumental *Music For Dreams* album but this never materialised.' This title was also touted as the name for the instrumental companion album to *Wish* in 1992, and was mooted in 1994 as the potential title of a Robert Smith **solo album**.

One album that doesn't contain any dream content is *Disintegration*. 'There aren't, as was the case in the past, any songs based upon my dreams,' Smith told *Oor*. 'More like nightmares in broad daylight!' However, he did tell *Cure News* that '2 Late', one of the songs from the *Disintegration* sessions which didn't make the cut (but did turn up on the extra disc of the 2010 reissue) was, you guessed, about 'a dream'.

Without doubt, one thing he has historically shared with Coleridge is a prodigious intake of mind-altering **drugs**, which will undoubtedly have facilitated some spectacularly vivid dreams. In one, he told *Libération*, he dreamed that he was pregnant.

Sometimes he would find other ways to feed his dormant imagination. 'I watched a video of a film called *The Shout*,' he told *Flexipop!*, 'which gave me wonderful "mental" dreams that made me wake up a few times. I don't ever have nightmares as such, because even dreams that scare me I enjoy . . .'

Sometimes, dreams can be a theatre of revenge. In his *Libération* diary, he reports feeling distressed at being woken up by builders in the flat upstairs blasting out Nik Kershaw's new single 'When A Heart Beats' on Radio 1, then goes into a dream in which he's a serial killer and Nik Kershaw and the builders are his victims. A few days later it happens again and the song is 'Torture' by King.

And, speaking of torture, he once told *Cure News*

that the worst form of psychological torture he could imagine would be 'Constantly waking up then waking up and then waking up . . . always in a dream, or would this be any different?' (This anticipated, by two decades, a famous sketch by Scottish comedian Limmy.)

Above all, Smith's sleeping self provides a rich seam of song material. As often as he draws upon **literature**, **zoology** or drowning for lyrical inspiration – even more, perhaps – he draws upon the nocturnal emissions of his unconscious. It all adds up to a Freudian nightmare. Or a dream.

Drowning

Thalassophobia is defined by the United States National Library of Medicine as 'a constant and intense fear of deep water such as the ocean or sea'. Aquaphobia, a related condition, is defined by *Medical News Today* as 'a fear of water itself [which] can include a fear of being in any body of water, including small ones'.

By any reckoning, Robert Smith must be rock's most prominent thalassophobe and aquaphobe. From the very beginning of his career to the present day, references to drowning and metaphors involving a watery death abound in The Cure's works.

As early as 1980, on 'In Your House' from their second album *Seventeen Seconds*, Robert was singing 'I drown at night in your house, pretending to swim'. The following album *Faith*, in 1981, had 'The Drowning Man' as its penultimate track, drawing its entire narrative from the gothic **literature** of Mervyn Peake:

> Starting at the violent sound
> She tries to turn
> But final
> Noiseless
> Slips and strikes her soft dark head
> The water bows
> Receives her
> And drowns her at its ease

'Lament', a 1982 song premiered on a flexidisc given away with *Flexipop!* and re-recorded for the B-side of '**The Hanging Garden**', would appear to be another drowning song: 'Today there was a tragedy under the bridge . . . A man slipped away, waving a last vanilla smile . . .' The same year, 'A Strange Day' on the album *Pornography* included the words 'I close my eyes / Move slowly through drowning waves . . .'

In 1985, *The Head On The Door* concluded with 'Sinking', a titular metaphor which speaks for itself. For all its giddy romance, what's often overlooked about 1987's '**Just Like Heaven**' is that it ends with a drowning:

> Alone above a raging sea
> That stole the only girl I loved
> And drowned her deep inside of me

In 1989, the single '**Pictures Of You**' from *Disintegration* featured the intriguingly chosen words: 'Remembering you how you used to be / Slow drowned, you were angels'. The same album featured 'The Same Deep Water As You', whose second verse begins 'The shallow drowned lose less than we . . .'

In 2008, two B-sides featured drowning lyrics. On '**The Only One**' flipside 'NY Trip', in a verse about skating, Robert sings, 'Yeah I'm in love with you cold / Any warmer and I drown . . .' On 'Down Under', B-side of '**Sleep When I'm Dead**', he sings of being lured to the depths by sirens' song: 'Around the sea-green pool we spin / Mermaids sing songs to pull us in . . .' And as recently as 2021, 'How Not To Drown', his **collaboration** with Chvrches, begins 'I'm writing a book on how to stay conscious when you drown.'

There are, doubtless, others. It's easy to see why drowning is such an oft-used metaphor. As well as being a particularly horrific way to die, it implies helplessness and surrender to forces far greater than oneself. Interestingly, Robert is known (via his *Libération* diary in 1985) to be a fan of Kate Bush's *Hounds Of Love*, an album whose entire second side is a concept piece called *The Ninth Wave* about a woman stranded at sea, desperately trying not to drown.

If Robert's drowning thing is rooted in a genuine fear – thalassophobia or aquaphobia – rather than fascination, he must be a sucker for punishment. The Cure have 'drowned' in **videos** not once but twice: the first (in '**Close To Me**') shows them falling off a cliff in a wardrobe which fills with water, and the second shows them under the sea trying to fight their way upwards to the surface.

And that fear can only have been exacerbated when photographer Richard Bellia (whose silhouette of Robert adorns the cover of *Curepedia*) made him get into a swimming pool in Switzerland, fully clothed.

Drugs

If The Cure are not outwardly a boozy band (as per The *Curepedia* entry for **Alcohol**, and I'm doubting the veracity of that statement even as I type this), then they *are* outwardly a druggy band, and drugs *are* integral to their music.

It was on their first visit to **Australasia** that the band first explored the limits of altered states. 'Experimenting with hedonism as a path to enlightenment,' Robert recalled. 'I think The Cure came to that decision when we were in New Zealand. Hedonism is the only way, we decided, a total sensory input or overload, exploring and pleasing every sense!'

Speaking to *NME*'s Paul Morley (of **Desperate Journalist** fame) in November 1981, Robert said, 'It's an old idea, that derangement of the senses. There were the Romantics and the nineteenth-century French Surrealist **poets** reaching these decisions . . .'

He needed to be careful, though, with his choice of drug. 'I was taking a lot of coke during the making of that album [*Faith*],' Robert told *Uncut* in 2000, 'and it was a very difficult and cranky atmosphere. Everything we did was wrong. I was permanently red-eyed and bitter and *Faith* didn't turn out how I wanted it to at all. I remember finishing the vocals off at Abbey Road and just feeling incredibly empty.'

Trips to the **US** were chemically enhanced affairs in The Cure's early days. Their first visit in 1980 ended with the band getting so high that they rode around on the bonnet of a local videographer's VW Beetle in Boston. Their second in 1981 nearly took a catastrophic turn when Robert and **Simon Gallup** took four times the recommended dose of Quaaludes in a club and, they believe, 'nearly died'.

What they hadn't yet tried, according to contemporary interviews, were psychedelics. 'Anything that has been recorded by us and released has been done without us ever having hallucinogenic drugs,' said Robert in a radio interview in Melbourne in August 1981. 'But at the same time, if you listen to a song like even "**Three Imaginary Boys**", people come up and say "Hey, you must have had a really good trip when you were doing that." The only thing I don't understand is how that can be levelled as a criticism . . .'

In late 1981, Smith began staying at **Steve Severin**'s house in London and got heavily into LSD. As Severin remembers in Mark Paytress' official **Siouxsie And The Banshees** biography, 'Robert was doing a lot of chemicals at the time, particularly acid . . . I think he found it creatively very useful.' Many of the lyrics for **Pornography** were written while walking around London, hallucinating. He later told *Cure News* that during the making of the album itself, 'I discovered the notion of massive quantities of very serious drugs . . . Me and Simon egged each other on to lower and lower depths.' A typical day of recording would start with a tab of acid and degenerate from there. 'I must confess that I don't remember making a lot of *Pornography*,' Robert told *Guitar Player* magazine in 1990. 'We probably drank and took more drugs than we should have – an interesting process, but one that would kill me now. In the period between 1982 and 1984 I was looking for something. I went a bit weird for a while, but in quite a positive way.' With remarkable irresponsibility, one magazine, quoted in *Ten Imaginary Years*, encouraged Smith to take even more drugs. 'Robert Smith seems to be paying the price for his heavy boozing these days – he's getting quite chubby. Better stick to your favourite Peruvian snuff, Rob – at least there's no calories in it . . .'

The period in 1982 between the end of the Fourteen Explicit Moments tour and the making of '**Let's Go To Bed**', when The Cure barely existed, was an equally mind-altered time. In *Cure News* Robert remembered being awake for four days, and hallucinating even without the aid of chemicals. He was sleeping on Severin's floor (when he slept at all). He felt 'dislocated', and missed having a group around him. 'All of which conspired to make me paranoid, jumpy, upsetting and obnoxious . . .'

Mary tried to step in to help. Robert's drug intake was unquestionably one of the exacerbating factors which made 1983 into his craziest year. However, when he began working with Severin on the project that would become **The Glove**, his drug use, which had widened to include opium, became a more enjoyable experience. 'Acid made me feel very connected to Severin. We had a fantastic time making The Glove album. We were living in a *Yellow Submarine* cartoon world. We'd walk round London, and when you're taking acid with someone you really like, it's really funny. It was a very upbeat time and it got rid of all the bad stuff that happened while I was making *Pornography*. It was liberating not having to conform to the same thought patterns. You think, "Fuck me, I can think and act in different ways."'

The influence of hallucinogens ran through into the making of **The Top**. During The Cure's set at

Meltdown, comprising a chronological setlist with a song from each year, Robert followed a performance of 'Bananafishbones' by remarking 'You can tell when the serious drugs started to kick in.'

The Cure's drug use appeared to have tailed off somewhat in 1984, 1985 and 1986 while they became internationally famous, and in 1987 Robert was claiming to have given up. 'I just realised one night,' he told *Q*'s Johnny Black, 'I can remember it clearly, that I couldn't go on like that, or I'd end up a complete halfwit. The funny thing is, when I stopped, so did the band. It was like, since I didn't ask for it to be around, nobody else bothered. As a result, the whole character of the band has changed.'

This, however, was exactly the same period when they appeared on *Les Enfants du Rock* in drag, a decision Smith later blamed on drugs. 'We've done things that were so odd,' he later told *Télérama*. 'Particularly in **France**, where we used to do some of the Saturday night **TV** shows and wear dresses. We were so stupid, and we genuinely didn't really care, because we were so drunk and we were taking so many drugs . . .' Soon afterwards, he also wrote the majority of *Disintegration* while taking large amounts of LSD.

In a moment of clarity, speaking to *Oor* magazine in 1989, he expressed regret at his decade of excess. 'I hate myself for the quantities of drugs I've taken in the past, and the amount of alcohol I've drunk. Most of it was escapism: trying to get rid of the idea that everything is futile and pointless.'

Like a lot of people at the turn of the nineties, Robert got into ecstasy, circa *Mixed Up*. However, the demonised 'dance drug' of tabloid headlines did nothing for his footwork. 'I can't dance without E and I can't dance with it,' he later told *Blah Blah Blah*. 'I'm not a gregarious person who responds to that atmosphere. If I take E, I'd rather listen to Mahler on my own.' His use of MDMA was, however, social when the occasion demanded. He told *Cure News* that 'we took lots of ecstasy' in Dublin at the end of the *Wish* tour in December 1992.

In the middle of that decade, the band's drug use eased off again. '99% of the time we're normal,' Simon Gallup told Johnny Black in 1994. 'We don't have orgies. We don't do drugs – well, we *have* done . . .' Later, as Robert entered his forties in the new millennium, the idea of that kind of chemical abandon became less appealing because, he told Swiss television, 'the recovery times got longer.'

Robert's beliefs on the ethics of drugs are strongly libertarian. 'I think all drugs should be decriminalised,' he told *Cure News* in September 1994, 'and heroin regulated – all the others are fine! Certainly no worse than alcohol . . .' (This attitude is consistent with The Cure's involvement with the Hugh Cornwell benefit concert in 1979 – see **Collaborations**.) In the same issue, Simon Gallup advised 'Do what you do, as long as you can take it. Don't do it to show off.' Meanwhile, **Porl Thompson** was in favour of legalisation, but considered drugs 'a waste of time'.

A fascinating insight into The Cure's views on drugs came when Robert and Simon hosted a phone-in on Californian radio station KROQ in 1992 (see also **Sex**). A caller asked whether magic mushrooms are dangerous. Smith and Gallup argued passionately that lead emissions are a worse problem, highlighted the hypocrisy regarding people's comfort with drinking alcohol and discomfort with tolerating drugs, argued that a natural organism such as psilocybin and a chemical product such as LSD are not the same, claimed that cocaine, heroin and barbiturates are the worst and most addictive whereas taking hallucinogens and smoking a joint are relatively harmless social recreation, and entered into a verbal duel with the show's co-host Dr Drew in which, again, they argued against prohibition.

Many Cure songs are, Robert has confirmed, inspired by drugs. 'A Short Term Effect', the druggiest song from *Pornography*, their druggiest album, is, he told Cure News, about 'a drug and its effect – short-term, I thought.' Others with a confirmed narcotic origin are 'Icing Sugar', '**Hot Hot Hot!!!**', 'Babble', 'Out of Mind', 'From The Edge Of The Deep Green Sea' and 'The Big Hand'. The majority of these are positive or, at least, equivocal. One unambiguously negative song about drugs is 'Numb' from *Wild Mood Swings*, which begins

> He doesn't want to know what's going wrong
> Because he's in love with a drug
> One that makes him numb
> One that stops him feeling at all

Perhaps it's wisest to end in a similar vein to the balanced 'be careful out there' message which concluded the **Alcohol** entry. 'It's great,' Smith said of drug-taking to Banshees biographer Mark Paytress, 'but when it takes over, you can find yourself encountering mental problems. There are people from that era, one or two that were close to The

Cure, who went seriously mental. They never really recovered . . .'

Dutton, Michael

Michael Dutton is a sound engineer who began his career at **Morgan Studios** in the late 1970s. *Three Imaginary Boys* by The Cure was only his fourth job, having cut his teeth providing 'tapes and tea' for The Enid on *Aerie Faerie Nonsense* in 1977. He also engineered **'Boys Don't Cry'**, *Seventeen Seconds* and *Faith*, as well as **Associates'** *The Affectionate Punch* and The Passions' *Michael & Miranda* – basically, anything that came through Morgan on **Fiction** Records and involved **Chris Parry** or **Mike Hedges**. Not long after his final sessions with The Cure, Dutton switched his attention to an entirely different genre and became an acclaimed sound engineer in the world of classical music, working with the likes of Michael Nyman and the Balanescu Quartet and overseeing new recordings of the works of Elgar, Delius, Vaughan Williams, Prokofiev and Stravinsky. He also reissues vintage classical and jazz recordings on his labels Dutton Epoch, Vocalion and Dutton.

E

E is for …

Early Gigs (attended by The Cure)

As **Crawley** was within striking distance of both London and Brighton, Robert Smith, **Lol Tolhurst** and the other teenaged future members of The Cure were fortunate enough to see most of their rock heroes live, and some of those heroes saved them the trouble of travel by actually playing in Crawley.

Almost incredibly, Robert Smith – aged just eleven and taken there by his older brother – saw as his first gig his hero **Jimi Hendrix** play the Isle of Wight Festival on 30 August 1970. Within three weeks, Hendrix would be dead.

By the time he was thirteen, Robert was already going to gigs on his own. On 5 April 1972 he saw Status Quo at the Brighton Dome. He is unsure, he later told *Cure News*, whether Quo or jazz-fusion troupe the Mahavishnu Orchestra was his first gig flying solo. Asked that question by the same publication on a different occasion, he was uncertain whether it was The Sensational Alex Harvey Band – another of the young Robert's heroes – or Thin Lizzy or the Mahavishnu Orchestra or blues-rock guitar virtuoso Rory Gallagher.

Alex Harvey played several London shows in 1973, including two at the Marquee, and one at the Greyhound in Croydon (later a Cure haunt), but does not appear to have headlined Brighton Dome that year. However, on 6 June SAHB did play there as support to Slade. Thin Lizzy didn't play Brighton at all that year, so if Robert saw them it was probably at the Top Rank, not the Dome, on 29 November 1972. The Mahavishnu Orchestra played the UK twice in 1972, at Crystal Palace Bowl on 25 August and Paris Theatre, London on 2 September, then toured the UK the following year but didn't play Brighton, the nearest show being the Rainbow Theatre in London on 30 June 1973. And Rory Gallagher played the Brighton Dome on 12 February 1973. In any case, it looks like Quo are the winners.

Other members of The Cure also answered the 'first gig' question in 1999. For **Simon Gallup** it was King Crimson or The Incredible String Band ('both shit!'). For **Perry Bamonte** it was AC/DC at Southend Kursaal on 19 March 1977. For **Jason Cooper** it was Captain Beefheart at Colston Hall, Bristol on 26 October 1980.

One thing we know for certain is that on 12 May 1973, Robert – just turned fourteen – saw **David Bowie**, backed by The Spiders From Mars, on the *Ziggy Stardust* tour at Earls Court in London, playing almost the entirety of his new album *Aladdin Sane*. Smith had now completed the triumvirate of his formative heroes: Hendrix, Harvey, Bowie. (Also in the audience that night was a fifteen-year-old John Beverley, later to become better known as Sid Vicious.)

In 1977, Lol Tolhurst, **Michael Dempsey** and **Porl Thompson** would by chance overhear former Spiders drummer Woody Woodmansey and his new band U-Boat soundchecking in a Crawley pub.

The punk era was a particularly fruitful time for gig-going for the Crawley contingent, and 1977 was a big year in Crawley itself. On 5 February 1977 The Jam played Crawley College, supporting Little Bob Story, and Robert and Lol both went. On 18 February, The Stranglers – with whom The Cure would later perform onstage in aid of their imprisoned singer Hugh Cornwell – also played the college, and played the Leisure Centre on 30 September that year. The **pre-Cure** gang, by now playing their own **early gigs** as Easy Cure, also went to see The Stranglers at the Red Deer in Croydon on 5 January. (The Cure have also claimed The Clash played Crawley in 1977, but there is no record of this show.)

Croydon was a regular stomping ground, where they saw bands from Thin Lizzy to Can at the Greyhound. (There is no record of Can playing the Greyhound, but if The Cure say they saw Can at the Greyhound, who are we to argue?). Future tour mates **Siouxsie And The Banshees** played there several times (6 November 1977, 12 February 1978, 7 May 1978, 12 November 1978), and The Cure attended more than one. On 26 November 1978, The Cure would play the Greyhound themselves, supporting **Generation X**.

Buzzcocks at the London Lyceum on 10 March 1978 is perhaps the last time Easy Cure would go on a group outing – within a fortnight they'd slimmed down to a trio and rebranded as The Cure.

Such frequent gig-going wasn't cheap, especially if you liked a drink. The Cure liked a drink. To get more bang for his buck, Lol got into the habit of sneaking 200% proof **alcohol**, stolen from the laboratory at his workplace Hellermann's, into gigs to pour into his pint.

Pretty soon, Easy Cure – or The Cure – were earning enough money from playing live to buy all the booze they liked.

Early Gigs (played by The Cure)

With their shorter, sharper, punkier name, and with the elaborate guitar stylings of **Porl Thompson** out of the picture (for now), The Cure entered the spring of 1978 needing to establish their new identity and their new, minimalist sound.

Robert Smith had prepared for the dawning of the new era with a shopping spree. On 17 April he bought a Bontempi organ, the (in)famous Woolworth's Top 20 **guitar**, and a WEM amp. 'The sounds on Elvis Costello's *My Aim Is True* album were really cheap,' he said in *Ten Imaginary Years*, 'and they were the sounds I wanted.' They had those **John Taw** promotional photos, ready to use on posters. (One of them, showing the trio standing solemnly by a graveside, is now comically reminiscent of the 'too much perspective' scene from Graceland in *This Is Spinal Tap*. But that didn't exist yet.) They had the **artwork** (with the help of **Ric Gallup**), they had the merch (those 'vomiting' badges). They were good to go. They just needed to break out of their local area.

The Easy Cure show at **Crawley**'s Montefiore Institute Hall on 22 April had brought an end to the **pre-Cure** era, and Robert Smith, **Michael Dempsey** and **Lol Tolhurst**'s first gig as The Cure, minus Thompson, took place at their familiar stomping ground, The Rocket, on 18 May. Three weeks later they played Lakers Hotel in Redhill (another established Easy Cure haunt), then on 9 July they were back at The Rocket for the strangest of shows: a pseudo-**religious** ceremony called Mourning the Departed later described by Robert as 'a séance in the pub', with priest costumes, 'crucifix' guitars, creepy organ backing tapes, and a cameo from 'the departed' himself, Porl Thompson (who had barely

been gone five minutes) pouring a pint over Lol's head.

With that cathartic rite out of their system, The Cure knuckled down to 'normal' gigging, as well as gigs in Merstham Village Hall, The Buccaneer in **Horley** (with **Simon Gallup**'s band **Lockjaw**), and Redhill Lakers another seven times (sometimes as support to bands like The Vapors, or local jazz-funk-reggae fusion act The Hotpoints).

This was part of the problem: their patch was parochial, their reach restricted. The furthest away they'd gigged, in any of their incarnations, was Orpington in Kent (as Easy Cure). And Orpington, with all respect to Orpingtonians, was hardly a hotbed of rock 'n' roll and, though officially part of the London Borough of Bromley since 1965, didn't *really* count as London. They needed to get themselves to the Smoke.

This all changed at one of those Lakers gigs on 27 August 1978 when **Chris Parry**, having already listened to *that* demo tape (and presumably eaten *that* digestive biscuit and drunk *that* cup of tea), and having already met them face to face in Mayfair, came down to check them out live. Parry liked what he saw, and signed them to **Fiction**. More importantly, in the immediate term, he got them out of Sussex and Surrey.

In order to 'toughen them up', Parry first sent them to the University of Kent in Canterbury on 5 October 1978, where they shared a bill with Wire (who had a profound **influence** on The Cure's thinking). Then came The Cure's first London gig.

The Windsor Castle – trading as the New Windsor Castle at the time – on Harrow Road was already a venue with musical heritage when The Cure played a run of four consecutive nights there from October 25 to 15 December 1978. An early Victorian pub with stuccoed windows and a castellated parapet, it had seen its heyday in the 1960s when The Rolling Stones and The Who played. In the seventies, it received a shot in the arm from the punk and new-wave movement, with The Jam, The Ruts, The Stranglers and Dr Feelgood all playing there prior to The Cure. The year after The Cure's residency, U2 would play an early London gig there, The Psychedelic Furs would play several times, and Dexys Midnight Runners would make their London debut. Joe Strummer drank there, and The Clash song 'Protex Blue' is named after the brand of condoms in the gents' toilets. And Iron Maiden once refused to play as the pub was empty, leading to them being banned for life. It wasn't purely a music venue, however: on Fridays, The

Windsor was especially busy, as it turned into a strip pub. Whether this bumped up The Cure's attendances or took half the audience away is unrecorded. But, as the band were supporting pub-rock also-rans The Young Bucks, and the ticket price was 50p, the strippers probably made more money. (Don't bother looking for The Windsor Castle if you're doing some Cure tourism: it's since been converted into a block of apartments and a restaurant.)

By the time they played legendary punk pub venue The Hope and Anchor in Islington on 19 December, however, the place was packed due to coverage The Cure had received in the *NME*. But The Cure didn't give the best account of themselves in front of an audience of music press readers wondering what all the fuss was about. Robert had flu, and was dosed up on Disprin and Night Nurse. He collapsed halfway through the gig, with a temperature of 102.

The next London gig on 22 December barely went any better. On the day that '**Killing An Arab**' was released by **Small Wonder**, The Cure were booked to support The Pirates at The Music Machine in Camden (later known as the Camden Palace and, later still, KOKO). The Pirates were the recently reformed rock 'n' rollers who were previously the backing band for Johnny Kidd of 'Shakin' All Over' and 'Please Don't Touch' fame, who had died in 1966. Their audience of Teds and greasers didn't know or care who The Cure were, and that was reflected in the advertising, which didn't even name them specifically, listing only The Pirates '+ support'. To make matters worse for The Cure, they couldn't even get in, despite having dashed up directly from an afternoon gig at the Upjohn Pharmaceuticals Christmas Party in Crawley in order to be there. 'My dad worked there and pulled strings to get us booked as the cabaret,' Robert later remembered. 'It was really funny – we got no reaction at all! We played for 25 minutes, got very drunk, then drove like madmen to The Music Machine where we sat outside for two hours because the bouncers wouldn't believe we were the support group to The Pirates.' (The next time The Cure played The Music Machine, on Fiction's Future Pastimes tour a year later, there were no such problems – they were headliners.) The Cure's final London show of 1978, at the Marquee supporting Ultravox, was closer to their comfort zone, crowd-wise. And they didn't get locked out.

The vital thing was that Chris Parry had got them used to playing London. But this early phase of The Cure's career, when they were scrappy amateurs playing local pub gigs with isolated forays into the Smoke, *really* ended straight after that Windsor Castle residency when they ventured outside the capital on their first **tour** of the UK in November 1978, supporting **Generation X**.

And *that* went well . . .

Ely, Vince

In a peculiar foreshadowing of his stint with The Cure, Vince Ely got his first big job in rock through the unreliability of another drummer. When The Psychedelic Furs were offered a **Peel Session** in June 1979 on the strength of a demo tape they'd sent to the BBC, their drummer was late. John Peel helped them advertise for another, and Ely was the successful applicant.

Ely had already been in other bands, notably the notorious Moors Murderers, whose membership also included Chrissie Hynde, Steve Strange, Topper Headon and punk icon Soo Catwoman, and who played at The Roxy and supported The Slits. Their controversial song 'Free Hindley' was never released, but gained them a significant amount of outraged media coverage. (Ely also played alongside Strange in another band, The Photons.)

It was with The Psychedelic Furs, though, that he made his name, playing on their first three albums, including the classic *Talk Talk Talk* (engineer: **Phil Thornalley**), and singles including 'Sister Europe', 'Love My Way' and the original 'Pretty In Pink'. Unusually for a drummer, his timing was a little off: he left before their two big albums *Mirror Moves* (1984) and *Midnight to Midnight* (1987), and their global hit in 1986 with the re-recorded film version of 'Pretty In Pink'. In the meantime, he drummed with artists including Ministry and Robyn Hitchcock (a collaboration which continued after his Cure days). He rejoined The Furs in 1988 for another couple of years, just after interest in them had peaked.

The call to help out The Cure in their hour of need came when **Andy Anderson** had departed, amid much mayhem, leaving the band drummerless with a North American tour looming. The job was first offered to Mike Nocito, who had co-engineered *Pornography* with Thornalley, but he passed. When Thornalley then suggested Ely, he was pushing at an open door: Robert Smith was an admirer of The Psychedelic Furs and had been obsessed with their drum sound.

After hastily learning The Cure's set, Ely stayed for just eleven dates. His first Cure gig was on 22 October 1984 in Vancouver, his last on 4 November in Houston. He was unable to complete the tour, and his departure left The Cure in yet another predicament, forcing them to hire and rehearse another drummer in forty-eight hours. **Boris Williams**, another friend of Thornalley's, stepped in.

Since leaving The Psychedelic Furs for a second time, Vince Ely has remained a mostly private individual, dividing his time between Spain and Sussex, and devoting his energies to rehoming and adopting Podenco dogs.

The End Of The World

The best Cure single since the eighties?

'The End Of The World' was the lead single from twelfth album *The Cure*, and their first not to be released on **Fiction** (it was on new **label Geffen**). It was also the first the world had heard from their work with **Ross Robinson**, and took everyone by surprise by being as far from nu metal (Robinson's usual genre) as humanly possible. Instead, it captured The Cure at their lightest and flightiest. It's uncomplicatedly lovely.

A song about miscommunication between two devoted lovers – 'Me, I don't show much', it admits, and 'Me, I don't say much' – it nevertheless emphasises the love between them with the repeated phrase 'I couldn't love you more' (a phrase previously used on 'Home' from the B-side of '**Mint Car**'). Its unusual time signature, with verses played in a repeated pattern of three bars of 4/4 followed by one bar of 2/4, creates a jumpy, jittery, hesitant feeling which assists the already-fiendish catchiness of its melody.

The **video** was directed by Floria Sigismondi, the prolific Italian–Canadian director whose CV already included the remarkable videos for Christina Aguilera's 'Fighter' and Marilyn Manson's 'The Beautiful People', as well as numerous **David Bowie** songs, and who would later direct the rock biopic *The Runaways*. Beautifully lit, and shot in Sigismondi's trademark glitchy stop-motion style, it features Robert walking around a house in which everything falls apart, spills and shatters, until he and the rest of The Cure are left scrambling through a pile of wood, bricks, tiles and debris. It begins with an

animatronic sparrow landing on a window ledge with a worm in its mouth, a nod to the closing scene of David Lynch's *Blue Velvet* with the beetle-munching bird. It ends with the house reconstructing itself as Robert goes back inside, and a rag doll resembling **Mary** appearing on the radiator (the lady in the radiator being another Lynchian trope, this time from *Eraserhead*), the implication being that even if domestic bliss disintegrates, everything is fixable and happy endings are possible. It's probably The Cure's best video that isn't by **Tim Pope**.

The first of the single's two extra tracks was the harrowing 'This Morning', seven minutes long, slow and sombre as a funeral march. It recounts a last visit to a dying elderly relative in a brightly lit hospital ward. Again, it's a song about miscommunication, or lack of communication:

> Years go by
> Didn't really say that much at all
> And moments just fly
> Didn't ever really touch at all
> Weeks always run down
> Didn't really get that close at all

It manages to be brutally raw by being so plainly descriptive, a balance very few songwriters could strike. It also features a rare spoken moment from Robert when the news of the death comes through:

> The dawn call was broken, short, disconnected, far away. . . I couldn't understand too much of what was being said. . . A matter of minutes, peacefully, so sorry. . . I had to think to breathe, my heart bursting in my head. . .

After that, the other extra track, 'Fake', a self-lacerating song about admitting to your lover that you are not what you pretend to be, felt relatively cheerful.

The **artwork**, a line drawing by one of Robert's young nieces or nephews, as per the entire *The Cure* project, depicted a pair of disjointed figures, fittingly enough for the contents of all three songs.

'The End Of The World' reached a respectable No.25 in the UK (their first Top 40 hit since 'Mint Car' in 1996), and made the Top 20 in Italy. More than that, however, it reminded the world that nobody could write a pop song quite like The Cure when they were on form.

Englishness

As English as rain. And as universal, too.

There's a moment in the first episode of the rebooted *Doctor Who* from 2005 which, in an elliptical way, goes some distance towards explaining the paradoxical specificity and universality of The Cure. 'If you're an alien,' a sceptical Rose Tyler, played by Billie Piper, asks the Ninth Doctor, 'how come you sound like you're from the North?' The Doctor, played by Salford-born Christopher Eccleston, replies 'Lots of planets have a North . . .'

Lots of countries have a **Crawley**. You don't need to actually live on the Sussex-Surrey border in order to identify with The Cure. Suburban angst is a global phenomenon, and as long as you're from somewhere *like* Crawley, The Cure are speaking your language . . . even if they are not speaking your language. Nevertheless, the question of the extent to which The Cure exude Englishness – and the effect that has had on their music's reach – is a fascinating one.

There is a particular pall of melancholy which hangs over the English soul. It's especially prevalent in the Home Counties, the dreary soulless towns of the Commuter Belt from which The Cure arose. It's made up of boredom and alienation, of ennui and thwarted ambition, the quiet miseries of lower middle-class life. It's a mood of resignation and defeat, a sense of 'Don't get your hopes up, because this is as good as it's going to get.' It's a feeling which casts its shadow over the comedy of Tony Hancock, the poetry of Philip Larkin, and the writing of George Orwell. And it's there in the music of The Cure.

But, crucially, The Cure are *non-specific* in their Englishness. 'We don't sing about issues that are socially relevant, particularly,' Robert once said. 'So that they're not placed in England. If you get caught up in singing about social and political issues in England it tends to alienate a lot of people.' Unlike their eighties rivals The Smiths, whose songs are so full of the hyper-local minutiae of English life that there's barely room for anything else, The Cure's lyrics are never set in England *per se*. (With a handful of exceptions, like 'Kyoto Song' or 'Club America', Cure songs aren't explicitly rooted in a particular location at all.) They are the polar opposite of Little Englanders. Indeed, their rejection of a certain type of Englishness – the stoicism and 'stiff upper lip' which is supposed to be part of the national character –

inspired one of their signature songs, '**Boys Don't Cry**'.

In some ways, The Cure give off a whiff of Englishness in a way they cannot realistically control. There is an indelible Englishness to Robert Smith's **voice**, of course. Unlike many English rock stars, he doesn't Americanise his voice to sing in a stereotypical mid-Atlantic drawl. Nor does he go too far the other way and force an exaggerated Mockney accent. (The Cure are not Madness, or Blur, or Sham 69, or Small Faces.) His vowels are simply those that are naturally his, as a product of the suburban South East of England.

Furthermore, the sum total of the way The Cure present themselves – the hairstyles, the clothes, the **make-up**, the **artwork**, the **videos** – adds up to the archetypal English post-punk band in the eyes of, for example, American fans (see **USA**), whether the band actually wish to be that or not.

There's a theory that it is precisely The Cure's pervasive, drizzly gloom that is appealing to people in hotter, sunnier lands. In **Mexico**, for example, that English greyness is perhaps as exotic to a certain kind of person as the vivid colours of Mexican culture are to the English.

Crucially, though, The Cure's Englishness is low-key, vaporous, a background mood rather than a defining feature. Vitally, there are no lyrical obstacles to 'getting' The Cure. Anyone who has ever felt sadness or loneliness or regret, or felt their precious grip on reality slipping away, can find something in The Cure's music that resonates.

And that's why almost anyone, from the north or south of this planet or any other, can understand The Cure.

Entreat

When freebies go wrong . . .

In July 1989, at the end of the European leg of the Prayer Tour, The Cure played three nights at Wembley Arena. (One of them was my first-ever Cure gig.) All three shows were recorded, and eight tracks – all of them songs from *Disintegration* – were compiled into a live album called *Entreat* (their second live album after 1984's *Concert*).

Its title was a pun, the word itself meaning to implore or beg, but also echoing the near-homonym 'a treat', something given as a surprise gift. Because

Entreat was first given away for free on CD or cassette in branches of FNAC, **France**'s equivalent to WH Smith, in the autumn of 1989 whenever someone bought a copy of one of The Cure's back-catalogue reissues. In May 1990, the same happened in branches of HMV in the UK.

The fan reaction to this freebie was not as grateful as you might expect. As Robert Smith explained in *Cure News*, 'This caused ill feeling with fans who wanted to be able to buy it separately. In the end, this was done, with money going to **charity**.' This compromise, to pacify angry Cure completists who didn't want to have to re-buy an old Cure album just to get the free live one, seemed to satisfy everyone, and the commercially released version of *Entreat* made it to the Top 10 in the UK and New Zealand, and Top 20 in Austria and Germany. (A longer edit, titled *Entreat Plus* and including a live version of every song from *Disintegration*, came with the *Disintegration* deluxe reissue in 2010.)

The Cure were on prime form at those Wembley shows, match-fit after a forty-eight-date run but not exhausted (they still had North America to come). Robert is especially impressive when delivering the rolling, ranting lines towards the end of 'The End' without pausing for breath. In 'Prayers For Rain' he holds a note on the word 'rain' for twenty-two seconds, like a **goth** Bill Withers dreaming of a not-so-'Lovely Day'. (In fact, Withers' note only lasts eighteen seconds, so Smith wins.)

The album itself is of a high quality, if somewhat clinical, taken straight from the sound desk by engineer Smudger and mixed by Bryan 'Chuck' New, with many songs almost indistinguishable from their studio versions apart from brief washes of applause between tracks. There's minimal banter (''Kyou. This is "Closedown" . . .'), meaning that the recordings are unlikely to come from the final night, when Robert went into almost Jarvis Cocker-esque banter overdrive.

Figuring out which copy you own is easy. The sleeve featured a photo of Robert in a voluminous shirt with his hands in the air, as if being held at gunpoint. In France the shirt was tinted pink, in the UK yellow, and on the eventual commercial release, blue.

Ironically, the most expensive copies now are the originally free ones. The pink French version goes for around £33 on Discogs, the yellow British ones for £11, but the retail blue ones for less than £4. You almost can't *give* them away.

Eyemou

Carnage Visors wasn't the only time The Cure used an intro film to set the atmosphere before a concert. On the Kissing Tour of 1987, each show was directly preceded by a short five-minute film called *Eyemou*, projected onto the front-of-stage curtain. Directed by **Porl Thompson** and **Andy Vella**, it consisted sonically of abstract sounds and interference, and visually extreme close-ups of Robert's lipstick-smeared mouth, and occasionally his flickering tongue or bared fangs, with intermittent flashes of his pupils, as he mouthed semi-audible words. This, he told *Cure News* the following year, was 'a recital of an ancient Japanese tea ceremony (**Parched Art** being obsessed with tea and contemplation)'. It has never officially been released in any format, but survives in fan footage of the tour.

F

F is for . . .

4:13 Dream

4:13 Dream is half the album it could have been. Literally.

In July 2007, Robert Smith spoke to *Billboard* at a time when The Cure's thirteenth album was still slated for October that year. 'What will probably happen,' he told them, 'is that a double album will come out like a limited edition, mixed by me. A single-disc version, which I assume will be primarily chosen by the label, might get mixed by someone else in order to have a different thing. There's a concern Cure fans will feel like they have to get both, but the fact is, I've agreed to sell the double version at a single album price, because I feel that strongly about it. It is almost impossible to get a double album nowadays. I naively thought my standing as an artist would push aside all objections, but the world gets ever more commercial as it turns.'

In the background to all this multi-format mayhem was a power struggle between Smith and **Geffen**. He had written thirty-three songs and wanted to release a double, but after relatively poor sales of *The Cure* in 2004 he was not in a strong negotiating position. As a result, the version of *4:13 Dream* that we have heard is but a fraction of the record he intended.

Amid the turmoil of this tussle between artist and corporation, everything got delayed, including a **US** tour for the autumn of 2007 which was postponed till the spring of 2008. In the *Billboard* interview, Smith put the delays down to his lyrical perfectionism. 'I've gone through so many revisions, probably more than all of the other records put together. I just wanted to get the tone right to reflect how I am at the age I'm at.' The themes, he promised, would be contemporary and topical. 'There are songs about relationships, the material world, **politics** and **religion**. They're very upfront and dynamic. People will be surprised how stripped-down and in-your-face the record is . . .' Some of the music, however, dated back to demos he'd recorded in the mid-1980s.

4:13 Dream was recorded at Parkgate Studios, a residential set-up in the village of Catfield, East Sussex, a mile from the site of the Battle of Hastings. Parkgate had previously been used by Paul McCartney, Def Leppard, Blur, and The Cure themselves for '**Wrong Number**' (**Reeves Gabrels**' first session on a Cure track) and demos for *Bloodflowers*. The Cure were the final band to use Parkgate: the complex, which was made up of converted Victorian cottages, was in the process of being converted back into private luxury homes while The Cure were there.

The album was produced by **Keith Uddin**, who had previously worked as an engineer on the 'Acoustic Hits' disc of *Greatest Hits* and also assisted with various deluxe reissues. The Cure **line-up** was the keyboardist-free quartet of Robert Smith, **Porl Thompson** (making one of his sporadic returns to the fold), **Simon Gallup** and **Jason Cooper**. Listening to the album, one can hear the familiar players do their familiar things. There's Thompson doing his scintillating guitar, there's Gallup doing his looming, probing bass, Cooper doing his Jason Coopering, and of course, there's the unmistakeable wounded wail of Smith. But it was not a happy camp. Smith described the sessions as 'the most intense and difficult three months that I have spent with other people who I thought I knew', and the record as 'the most fraught album I've ever been involved in.' (As Nitsuh Abebe pointed out in a *Pitchfork* review, these are 'both claims that, considering the rest of this band's biography, are really saying something'.)

The title carries echoes of *4.48 Psychosis*, the experimental play about clinical depression by Sarah Kane, who took her own life over a year before it was ever performed. (A review in the *Guardian* described it as 'a 75-minute suicide note'.) This, however, is likely to be coincidental. Smith's explanation was simply that The Cure were a four-piece and this was their thirteenth album, with thirteen songs on it. The numerical element also related to the promotional gimmick of releasing one single a month, on the thirteenth of the month, for four months in the run-up to its release. 'Because it's the thirteenth studio album,' Smith told MTV, 'I thought "Let's introduce the number and see what we can do with it." I thought "Let's have four singles and release them on the thirteenth of every month then release the album."' MTV themselves assisted with the singles campaign, filming the live **videos** for each of them, namely '**The**

Only One', 'Freakshow', 'Sleep When I'm Dead' and 'The Perfect Boy' (each of which has its own *Curepedia* entry).

In the process of whittling the thirty-three songs down to thirteen, Smith excised the gloomier numbers in favour of the more polished and upbeat ones, with a view to releasing the gloomier ones as a separate album (which, it transpired, would never materialise).

It opens with the paradoxically under-produced yet over-produced 'Underneath The Stars', keyboard glissandos clashing with demo-quality drums as Smith, his voice excessively disguised with backmasked echo effects, imagines himself and his lover lying back on a boat or raft, contemplating the infinite.

After the far perkier 'The Only One', the first of the album's four singles (both in album sequence and release order), 'The Reason Why' is equally upbeat, but the musical mood is contraindicated by the first line, 'I won't try to bring you down about my suicide' (which might be the most comically Cure-ish opening gambit since 'It doesn't matter if we all die' from **'One Hundred Years'**), but the rest of the lyrics are somewhat Cure-by-numbers (it must be the twentieth Cure song with lines about 'falling through the stars'), even if the unnamed person who, in reported speech, tells Robert 'you're holding on to nothing left of something gone' has a delicious turn of phrase.

After the punchy 'Freakshow', single two (both in album sequence and release order), 'Sirensong' is a divine 2.22 interlude in waltz time as Robert sings, enraptured, of a girl with 'golden hair', 'silver skin' and 'crystal eyes'. The spell is only partially broken by the realisation that the middle of those three attributes makes her sound like a pickled onion.

The almost-unhinged 'The Real Snow White', a song fuelled by wayward romanticism and barely suppressed lust, could fit onto any of the band's best albums. 'It was a tricky gun to load, and I didn't get to fire' doesn't take much decoding (see **Sex**), and nor does the repeated refrain of 'You've got what I want'. The ending, 'It's only for the night/And I will give it back tomorrow/I swear', the last two words delivered in a bizarre drawl, is among the oddest on any Cure song.

Despite being made by an **English** band with an English producer in the English countryside, 'The Hungry Ghost' sounds like some Bostonian indie rock act with Steve Albini at the faders. Its lyrics are a word-collage at times, prioritising pleasing assonance over meaning ('Kimono coral floral print/Exclusive tint and cut reclusive . . .'), but it appears to be about avaricious consumerism, the 'ghost' of its title the human compulsion to acquire material goods.

'Switch' is the second track on *4:13 Dream* to summon thoughts of 'One Hundred Years', but does so via the drum pattern rather than the lyrics. A full-pelt track on which Thompson gets to fully let rip with the effects pedals, it expresses Smith's fear of losing his sense of self.

After 'The Perfect Boy', the third single in album sequence and the fourth in release order, 'This. Here And Now. With You.' conjures the head-spinning bewilderment of a moment of passion, but allows moments of exquisite lyrical focus: 'I bite your mouth so fearfully and slow/The taste of summers yet to shine . . .'

Following the single 'Sleep When I'm Dead' (fourth in sequence, third in release), 'The Scream' begins, counterintuitively, at a whisper (vocally and instrumentally) before building to a literal scream of horror as Smith finds himself in a nightmare made all the more vivid by the conviction that 'this is not a dream'.

Finale 'It's Over', like 'Open' and 'End' on *Wish*, is one of those Cure songs whose title is a winking acknowledgement of its position on the album. Hectic, hurtling and headlong, it's another Cure song about entropy, about things going wrong:

> A nagging sense of shame I can't explain
> An acrid taste of smoke and blood and tears and drugs
> And every inch of me is raw

It would be Porl Thompson's final bow as a recording member of The Cure and he rose to the occasion with fingertip-scorching fretwork.

The **artwork**, by **Parched Art**, featured two abstract faces, one of them with a downturned mouth and blood dripping from the eyes (in a possible callback to the **Fourteen Explicit Moments** tour). The typography, designed by **Andy Vella**, involved a variation on the classic dropped 'C' logo. The sleeve listed jokey pseudonymous credits such as handclaps by 'The Catsfield Sub Rhythm Trio', and percussion by 'Smud' (Smith himself, perhaps; see also 'Smudger' on the *Entreat* credits).

In a mostly positive review in the *Independent on Sunday*, Simon Price called it 'a set of songs that develop slowly, like Polaroid pictures.' *Trouser Press* detected complacency, saying of this 'archetypal Cure album' that 'its only major drawback is the sense that Smith has thrown in the towel on challenging himself or his following, now content to simply give the people what they want.' For Andy Greenwald of *Entertainment Weekly*, this was business as usual: 'Smith once again indulges in his patented bipolar cocktail of feedback-drenched swoons . . . spiked with bursts of giddy pop'.

In the *Guardian*, Dorian Lynskey wrote of this 'admirably taut and vibrant' album that 'though nothing here scales classic heights, everything is either spry and charming . . . lush and stately . . . or fierce and churning'. In *NME*, Martin Robinson wrote that 'This album suggests a re-engagement with the popular music scene, if not an act of war.'

Nitsuh Abebe, reviewing *4:13 Dream* for *Pitchfork*, argued that 'for a "pop" record, a lot of tracks here seem poorly framed, even half-baked, as if Smith's "spontaneous" approach – his attempts to capture the raw energy of his demos – have kept him from putting as much attention into the organisation of his songs, the flow of the parts, the clarity of the melodies, the lucidity of the lyrics, or even the firmness of the ideas behind them.'

And John Doran of the *Quietus* took the album to task for its production, which, he wrote, 'stinks worse than a fourteen-year-old's wank sock after a rainy Bank Holiday weekend in Southport', adding that 'they could have dragged the guy who sleeps on the roundabout near my house down to the studio, given him loads of ketamine and strapped boxing gloves on him and he would have done a better job.'

The release date was meant to be 13 September 2008, but was pushed back, with the **Hypnagogic States** remix EP taking the September slot instead. *4:13 Dream* eventually came out on 27 October, making an absolute hash of the whole triskaidekaphile concept. It made the Top 10 in Belgium, **France**, Italy and Poland (where it went gold). In the US it reached a creditable 16, but in the UK a disappointing 33. Across all territories it was The Cure's least successful album since *Pornography*, and in the UK their least successful since *Three Imaginary Boys*.

In fan and critic polls, it tends to average out as the worst Cure album. For Robert, this is unfair, and a reflection merely of its place in the timeline rather than its quality. 'I honestly feel that [*4:13 Dream*] had better songs on it than most of the early stuff,' he said with hindsight, 'but the earlier songs have a certain something. They exist in another continuum. When we

play "**In Between Days**", "**Just Like Heaven**", "**The Lovecats**", they mean something culturally. Whereas "The Hungry Ghost" from the last album doesn't mean something culturally. But to me it is much, much better.'

The album was performed in its entirety only once, at Piazza San Giovanni in Rome on 11 October 2008 as part of a broadcast by the ever-helpful MTV. (They encored with a hits set.) The *4:13 Dream* material then melted away into the rest of the live set, and by the time of their North American tour the following April only four songs from it made the cut.

The labyrinthine saga of the non-release of the other tracks in some form or other, be it on a single album putatively titled *4:14 Scream* or a double called *4:26 Dream*, is detailed in the entry **fourteenth album**. Whether any of the **unreleased songs** will ever emerge is uncertain.

All we can say for certain is that *4:13 Dream* is the final Cure album . . . to date.

40 Live

The Cure played only two concerts in 2018. Each of them was filmed, and gathered together in a 2DVD, 4CD box set entitled *40 Live (Curætion-25 + Anniversary)*. One was the closing night of Robert Smith's **Meltdown Festival** in the relatively intimate 2,700-capacity Royal Festival Hall on 24 June, the other their enormous fortieth anniversary show in Hyde Park, London on 7 July. 'Meltdown's going to be doom and gloom,' Robert told the *Guardian*'s Dorian Lynskey beforehand, 'and Hyde Park's going to be hands in the air.'

Another thing Smith promised for the Curaetion-25 show at Meltdown was a line-up of previous bandmates, setting fans' imaginations racing. **Lol**? **Pearl**? **Boris**? **Matthieu**? In the event, the only old friends Robert unveiled were songs rather than humans. Split into two halves, titled *From Here to There* (which ran chronologically from the band's earliest days to the present) and *From There to Here* (which reversed the journey), the setlists consisted of Robert's personal favourites, with one song per set from each Cure album. These tended towards the deeper cuts, with only seven of the twenty-eight songs being singles. The format allowed Robert to have a little fun with Cure history, remarking after

'Bananafishbones' from *The Top* that 'You can tell when the serious drugs started to kick in.' A new-ish, unreleased song 'It Can Never Be The Same' (first performed live in 2016), its title emblazoned across the body of one of his guitars, closed Part 1, and Part 2 began with another, 'Step Into The Light' (left over from the *4:13 Dream* sessions, and also premiered in 2016). For everything he said about doom and gloom, and for all the wilful obscurity of some of his choices, the closing run of 'Primary', 'A Forest' and 'Boys Don't Cry' wasn't exactly hands-in-your-pockets.

At the sold-out anniversary show in Hyde Park, the crowd of 65,000 was the second-largest audience The Cure have ever played to at one of their own gigs, as opposed to a festival crowd (the first- and third-largest both being in Mexico). The show was part of the British Summer Time series of gigs, which had attracted controversy after charging higher prices for admission to the Golden Circle near the stage, with a large semicircular barrier keeping the general admission ticketholders well away from the action. The Cure, uniquely and heroically, stipulated that this policy would not apply to their show, with the same £72.95 ticket price for everyone (still an eyewatering amount, especially when you added the £9.80 booking fee) and that whoever got there first could get the Golden Circle wristbands.

They were supported on the main stage by Interpol (survivors of Curiosa), Goldfrapp, Editors, Slowdive and Pale Waves. The second stage was headlined by Ride, with Lisa Hannigan, The Twilight Sad (who had played Meltdown the previous month) and This Will Destroy You. The third stage was an entirely Meltdown line-up of Kathryn Joseph, Kælan Mikla and pg.lost.

When The Cure took the stage under the fake foliage of the BST canopy for a two-hour-plus retrospective of their entire career, beginning with the perfectly chosen opener 'Plainsong', the sun was still in the sky and the temperature a very un-British 28 degrees. Between 'High' and 'A Night Like This', Robert apologised for not saying anything yet. 'I honestly can't talk until the sun goes down. It's taking all my energy not to dissolve into a pile of dust . . .'

He wasn't lying about the 'hands in the air' thing – eighteen of the show's twenty-nine songs were singles. On the fortieth anniversary (or near enough) of their first-ever gig as The Cure, they played a crowdpleasing show, hailed on the subsequent film trailer as a 'legacy-defining gig', whose encore ended with five songs which took it all back to the very

start: 'Boys Don't Cry', 'Jumping Someone Else's Train', 'Grinding Halt', '10:15 Saturday Night' and 'Killing An Arab' (the latter a decision with which Smith struggled, this being the anniversary of the 7/7 bombings).

The film *Anniversary*, directed with a dusty, pollen-haze aesthetic by Tim Pope with co-director Nick Wickham, an experienced maker of live concert movies who had also worked on *Trilogy* in 2003, was shown in cinemas. (Various fans have cheekily added themselves as 'Audience Member' to the castlist on IMDB.)

Anniversary was packaged together with *Curætion-25* in both film and audio forms, in an Andy Vella-designed box with a big neon pink '40' on the front as *40 Live (Curætion-25 + Anniversary)*, thereby constituting The Cure's sixth and seventh live albums and eighth and ninth live films (depending on what you count). To clock up that many, you need to have been around a very long time.

Towards the end of the anniversary show, when the sun had dipped below the Kensington horizon and the temperature had cooled enough for him to speak, Smith mused on his band's longevity. 'If you'd asked me then what I thought I'd be doing in forty years' time, I couldn't have told you it was this.'

Faith

Fittingly, for a record that is largely about belief (or the absence thereof), *Faith* is an album surrounded by an almost religious aura. It is, whether or not its creators welcome this description, one of the sacred founding texts of gothic rock, as are at least two other Cure albums. (*Fact* magazine rated it the third-best gothic record ever made.)

The album was, to a large extent, a meditation on ideas about faith itself, about religious indoctrination, and about the elusive and ultimately futile human search for eternity. Robert had literally written lyrics in church. 'I asked myself questions about the people around me,' he recalled in *Ten Imaginary Years*. 'Why some of them devoted their whole lives to something they would only get after death.' Speaking to *NME*'s Paul 'Desperate Journalist' Morley on the same topic, he said '. . . there will always be the nagging truth that you're sacrificing your senses to the ideal of purity when in fact you might be wrong in the end.'

Grief was another major element. Robert Smith and

Lol Tolhurst both suffered close family bereavements during this period. Robert's grandmother had died suddenly in the run-up to the recording, and Lol's mother was diagnosed with terminal cancer and would die while Lol was touring the album. 'Around the time of *Faith*,' Lol told *Record Collector* later, 'there were a couple of things that happened to me and Robert that were quite upsetting. My mother was ill, and Robert's grandmother – who he was pretty close to – died. Both myself and Robert went to a Catholic school, and were very heavily immersed in religion up until our teens. Organised religion tells you one thing, then as life unfolds you realise that there's an individual interpretation you can put on events. So there were a lot of personal things that went into that album.' The Cure began using their music for emotional catharsis, opening a floodgate that would never close again. In a UK radio interview in 1981, Lol said 'It sounds like a contradiction in terms, but we do have a certain joy from getting rid of our melancholy feelings by singing them.'

Smith has cited **Pink Floyd** circa *Ummagumma* and Nick Drake as **influences** on *Faith*, but also religious music. 'I like a lot of music that is built around repetitions,' he told *Record Mirror*, 'Benedictine chants particularly, and Indian mantras. These musics are built around slow changes, they allow you to draw things out. When the first album came out, critics started referring to the early songs as "pop" classics. I don't really want to be tagged as a band that writes "pop" classics. Beethoven didn't write three-minute "pop" songs and he wrote some good music . . .'

The band were, at this point, reduced to a trio of Robert Smith, Lol Tolhurst and **Simon Gallup** after the departure of **Matthieu Hartley**. The line-up lent itself to minimalism, forcing the issue of what the successor to *Seventeen Seconds* would sound like. For the second album in a row (or the third, if you count his engineering on *Three Imaginary Boys*), the producer was **Mike Hedges**, hitting a rich vein of form for goth-adjacent albums: the same year, he produced Bauhaus' *Mask*, and the following year *A Kiss In The Dreamhouse* by **Siouxsie And The Banshees**.

For an album which is, like *Disintegration* and *Pornography*, often hailed for its unity and cohesion (a hater might say 'sameyness'), *Faith* had a fractured genesis. After a couple of weeks of rehearsal, the first abortive demo sessions took place at **Morgan Studios** between 27 and 29 September 1980, where

the band and Hedges recorded early versions of **'Primary'** and **'All Cats Are Grey'** which, Smith later said, sounded 'slow, plodding . . . very dead' when what they wanted was 'funereal'. In a UK radio interview, Smith said it was a mistake to begin recording in the same studio as *Seventeen Seconds*, because a lot of the emotions held over. They resumed at Morgan between 2 and 11 February, but were unhappy with the sound, and tried a number of other studios – Red Bus, Trident, the Roundhouse and Abbey Road – making it a five-studio album.

Much of the album was being written in the studio, which inevitably had financial implications. **Chris Parry**, who had promised not to get involved, witnessed the spiralling chaos and stepped in, overseeing the booking of studios. 'The **drugs** were coming, the demands were coming, lyrics were being written on the studio floor . . . I could see that they couldn't carry on like that.' Parry then began turning up to the actual sessions, because they were taking far too long, and he wanted it wrapped before it went even further over budget.

The sombre, subdued sound they arrived at was never the plan. 'When we first started, it was supposed to be louder and more aggressive than anything we'd done before,' Smith told a radio interviewer. 'Because that was how we felt at the time. It's not as aggressive as it should be, really. It's just that while we were making it, things . . . changed. Simple as that . . . We'd go in to record a song and it turned out radically different to how we imagined it would.'

Smith's drug habits at the time played into the mood. 'I was taking a lot of coke during the making of that album,' he told *Uncut* in 2000, 'and it was a very difficult and cranky atmosphere. Everything we did was wrong. I was permanently red-eyed and bitter and *Faith* didn't turn out how I wanted it to at all. I remember finishing the vocals off at Abbey Road and just feeling incredibly empty.'

As Smith conceded in *Ten Imaginary Years*, 'We laid down the tracks in a completely disinterested way, as if someone else was doing it and not us. But whenever I started to sing, the whole atmosphere went black.' Fun was a scarce commodity. 'There's only ever been one period of The Cure when there was no humour involved and that was fifteen years ago now,' Robert told *Blah Blah Blah* in 1996, 'around the time of *Faith* and *Pornography*. Why? It was just the way we were. Simon and I did have fun but it was all incredibly drug and alcohol-fuelled. There was a feeling of desperation and anger and frustration. I went haywire.'

Mike Hedges, too, was not immune to the pervading gloom. 'It was a dark, dark, dark record,' he told *Sound on Sound*, 'and when you work on something like that you're not laughing and smiling the whole time. You get heavily affected by the music, and by the time we finished it I was on the verge of a nervous breakdown. God, was I depressed. I mean, we didn't fight or anything in the studio. It was just bloody miserable. You know, we'd have a drink and relax between sessions, but we took the recordings themselves very seriously. Robert had a cathartic outpouring of emotions on that album, and because of that it affected all of us.'

Side 1 begins with the heavily flanged Simon Gallup bassline of 'The Holy Hour', a song written by Robert Smith while sitting listening to Catholic mass in the brick-built, Grade II-listed Friary Church of St Francis and St Anthony in **Crawley** on a Sunday evening, 'trying to make sense of the communal response and faces' (*Cure News*). In the lyric, Smith finds it impossible to feel what everyone else feels. 'I kneel and wait in silence', he sings, 'I sit and listen dreamlessly'. In the final verse he yells in distress:

I stand and hear my voice cry out
A wordless scream at ancient power
It breaks against stone
I softly leave you crying

From the very start of *Faith*, his faith is what he's lost. The song ends with two desolate tolls of a church bell, recalling the opening title track of Black Sabbath's self-titled debut. (It's conceivable that this is coincidental. But it isn't likely.) Lol Tolhurst, playing that synth-bell during the **Reflections** shows, 'almost fell over with the wave of emotion', he told Tim's Twitter Listening Party.

Lead (and only) single 'Primary', which has its own entry, was the first song written for *Faith*. It was, Robert told *Cure News*, about 'toying with the idea that it may be better to die very young, innocent and dreaming . . . or even to murder as a gift.'

'Other Voices', another track prominently featuring a lugubrious bass rumble from Gallup (praised by Tolhurst as 'awesome . . . so precise but funky too'), was later explained by Robert as 'Blotting out the world through the eating of forbidden fruit? Deafened by lust?' The lyrics do indeed suggest **sex**, with phrases like 'You brush past my skin, as soft as fur', 'Commit the sin, commit yourself', 'Pulsing in

my swinging arms'. Some of the lines, like 'Come around at Christmas/Smile at me slyly, another festive compromise . . .' were actually written by Tolhurst. A foggily filmed, fish-eye-lensed promotional **video** was made for 'Other Voices' by Bob Rickerd (who had also filmed 'Primary'), but it was never released as a single. Lol remembers the shoot as 'A little scary! We were in sort of gauze cage to film it filled with smoke to make the lights soft. Suffocating!' The song has subsequently, Robert told *Cure News*, been used as the background music to BBC programmes 'about cars etc'.

'**All Cats Are Grey**', a track whose cultural importance has earned it a separate entry in this book, rounds off Side 1. One of two songs inspired by the novels of Mervyn Peake, it features Smith on keyboards and piano, with no guitar at all. In *Cure News*, he described it as 'Just a nightmare of being lost/trapped in caves – echoes of the grave and of prison cells and again of growing old'. On Tim's Twitter Listening Party, Lol revealed that its title was a phrase that his mother Daphne had used.

At the beginning of Side 2, those Benedictine influences come through strongly on 'The Funeral Party'. There is something hymn-like about the steady cadences of Smith's vocal, set against a miasma of elegiac synths. It is, said Robert, 'about the death of my grandparents, and ultimately, I suppose of the death of my parents, and then me . . .' In the very first verse, he imagines his grandparents' buried bodies. 'Two pale figures ache in silence/Timeless in the quiet ground/Side by side in age and sadness . . .' Performing it live was challenging. 'At the same moment in "The Funeral Party",' Smith recalled, 'everyone on stage went "gulp!".' Nevertheless, a tape of the band playing it live was played at Lol's mother's funeral.

The two sides of *Faith* have a beautiful symmetry: on each of them, the second of four songs is a fast one. 'Doubt', like 'Primary', is urgent and uptempo, with Smith singing in a strangely petulant, punk-like Cockney yelp. It is, he wrote, about 'expressing the anger and frustration at the pointlessness of everything (at the time?), trying to fight the waves of absurdity.' Almost immediately after its release, it was the one song Robert threw under the bus. 'Seven good tracks and one that's not so good – "Doubt",' he said in a 1981 radio interview. 'I like it for the exact reasons that Robert doesn't,' countered Simon. 'It sounds manic.'

'The **Drowning** Man', although utterly different in

genre, is similar to Kate Bush's 'Wuthering Heights' from three years earlier in the sense that it narrates a piece of Gothic literature in precis form. It recounts a death scene from Mervyn Peake's *Gormenghast*. The character Lady Fuchsia Groan, described by Robert as 'a very unfortunate, sad character', is in melancholy mood brought on by the death of her father and the knowledge that her lover, Steerpike, is a murderer. Perched on a window ledge, she stares out at the floodwaters surrounding the castle in which she lives. A knock at the door startles her, she bangs her head, and falls into the water and drowns. This incident is described in plain and literal terms in Smith's lyric:

    Starting at the violent sound
    She tries to turn, but final, noiseless
    Slips and strikes her soft dark head
    The water bows, receives her
    And drowns her at its ease . . .

The broader meaning of the song, Smith told *Cure News*, was 'mourning the death of innocence, the death of blind love'.

It's an astonishingly atmospheric track, Smith's voice drenched in echo by Hedges, his spindly guitar figures set over a shuffling rhythm from Tolhurst and Gallup. 'This is a style that The Cure made all our own,' said Tolhurst on Tim's Twitter Listening Party, 'a sort of shuffling/motorik beat that pushes and pulls the rhythm so it feels like it's standing still but moving at the same time', going on to compare it to 'A Forest'. In a piece on Cure deep cuts for the *Quietus*, journalist Ned Raggett vividly described the track thus: 'Robert Smith's anguished vocal rises and fades into distances like air bubbles in murky water, his skittering guitar and the spare rhythm section work of Simon Gallup and Lol Tolhurst an audio portrait of utter desolation.' In 2018, 'The Drowning Man' was the track selected by Robert Smith from *Faith* to be remixed for the *Torn Down* compilation.

'Rape me like a child,' Smith sings on *Faith*'s closing title track. 'Christened in blood/Painted like an unknown saint/There's nothing left but hope.' A song about religious abuse? Perhaps not. It is, said Smith in *Cure News*, 'Self-explanatory. As optimistic as I could get, it does, or should, offer a note of HOPE.' (If that's his idea of optimism . . .

'Faith' is another medium-slow track, with very faint hints of Joy Division's 'She's Lost Control' about Gallup's bassline. *Faith* was the first album by The Cure to feature a six-string bass guitar, an instrument also used by Peter Hook of Joy Division. 'The whole

Faith album has six-string bass', Smith told *Guitar Player*. 'I think when people talk about the "Cure sound", they mean songs based on six-string bass, acoustic guitar and my voice, plus the string sound from the Solina. Joy Division/New Order and The Cure both got into the sound at the same time.'

Like many Cure songs (hello 'Plainsong', hello 'Push', hello 'The Kiss'), 'Faith' is in no hurry for Robert's singing to start, developing patiently for two minutes ten seconds before the vocal comes in. He's mostly despondent, barely able to summon the energy to enunciate, although on the line 'please say the right words' he actually becomes animated for a few seconds. It ends with Robert repeating 'There's nothing left but faith' (a line he once considered the best he'd ever written) several times until, the final time, the instruments have dropped out and it's just him, distant and distorted, a ghost of himself.

'The album is all quite grey and downbeat,' said Andy Vella to Natasha Scharf in her book *The Art of Gothic*, 'so we wanted a cover that reflected that.' For the *Faith* artwork, Vella and his Parched Art partner Porl Thompson came up with an image which, with its amorphous grey shadows, could to the untrained eye have been a ruined priory or deserted farmhouse seen from grass-level, but could equally have been abstract shapes, like a Rorschach blot designed to test the viewer's imagination. It was, in fact, an image of the ruins of Bolton Priory in the fog, created via darkroom trickery, applying a solarisation effect to a negative.

Bolton Priory, on the banks of the River Wharfe in North Yorkshire, was an Augustinian monastery built in 1154 but dissolved by Henry VIII in 1539. As well as tying into the general theme of religious faith, Bolton Priory had significance for Robert Smith. 'When I was a kid, I used to play beside it on my holidays. It's hundreds of years old, and the way it is on the cover is the exact image I'd retained of it. It's one of my oldest memories.' (Fiction hated it.)

Faith was released on 14 April 1981. In the US, it was bundled together with *Seventeen Seconds* on 9 September with the grimly ironic title *Happily Ever After* (which Jim Green of *Trouser Press* called 'as misleading a title as the late Ian Curtis' band being called Joy Division'), a contrast exaggerated by that album's artwork, which features a sports field of brightly coloured, flag-waving cheerleaders. *Faith* was remastered in 2005 as part of Universal Music's Deluxe Edition series. The new edition featured 'Carnage Visors', demos and live tracks as well as the non-album single '**Charlotte Sometimes**'. It also included a few never-before-released tracks (in demo form, all instrumentals). On Record Store Day 2021 it was reissued as a limited-edition picture disc.

Reviews of *Faith* ranged from the caustic to the cautiously positive. *Sounds*' John Gill picked up on the Krautrock influences, comparing it to La Düsseldorf and Neu! and, alluding to religious faith itself, concluded '*Faith* requires a personal act of involvement, the reward being a sense of belonging'. *Melody Maker*'s Adam Sweeting called it 'a sophisticated exercise in atmosphere and production', concluding that 'It's gloomy, but frequently majestic, never using brute force where auto-suggestion will do. You may not love it, but you'll become addicted to it.' *NME*'s Ray Lowry, in a review accompanied by a picture that still had Matthieu Hartley in it, tore the album apart, opining that 'it says absolutely nothing meaningful' and likening it to Pink Floyd (a comparison which wouldn't have hurt the band anywhere near as much as it was meant to). *Creem*'s Iman Lababedi made a similar comparison, but more positively, calling it 'arty (in an early Pink Floyd manner)'. And *Record Mirror*'s Mike Nicholls wrote that 'The Cure remain stuck in the hackneyed doom-mongering that should have died with **Joy Division**', criticising its 'spineless meanderings' and calling it 'hollow, shallow, pretentious, meaningless, self-important and bereft of any real heart or soul'.

The album reached No.14 in the UK, No.9 in the Netherlands and, remarkably, No.1 in New Zealand (a feat they would never achieve again). It was their most successful album to date. Chris Parry, however, was disappointed that it didn't spawn any hits ('Primary' stalled outside the UK Top 40).

The Cure promoted *Faith* with the Picture Tour, on which they were supported by **Ric Gallup**'s film, *Carnage Visors*. 'Those songs had a downward spiral effect on us – the more we played them, the more despondent and desolate we became,' said Robert in *Ten Imaginary Years*. 'Most of the time, I left the stage crying.' Critics almost invariably compared the tour to a religious ceremony, and the band decided to own it, posing for a photo in front of a church sign which read 'This church offers FAITH' (actual caps).

In the Netherlands, they toured in an actual circus tent, moving it from town to town. In Sittard on 24 June 1981, just before the encores, Lol was told to phone home. On doing so, he learned that his mother had died. The band went back onstage. Lol was able to play for about one minute, then simply sat immobile. After returning to the UK for his mother's funeral, Tolhurst took the decision that the band needed to recommence the tour or he would go mad.

Faith's legacy is assured. It remains a hugely influential touchstone of alternative rock. However, some critics remain unconvinced. 'The Cure's sound became a dolorous fog on *Faith* and *Pornography*,' wrote Simon Reynolds. 'Smith's forlornly withdrawn vocals, the listless beat and the grey-haze guitars made for some of the most neurasthenic rock music ever committed to vinyl.' (He says that like it's a bad thing.) Bob Stanley, in *Yeah Yeah Yeah: The Story of Modern Pop*, wrote that '*Faith* may as well have been called *Even Closer*. The Cure took Joy Division's angst and channelled it in a more teenage, sulky way.'

The Cure themselves couldn't leave it alone. In 1983, when they'd moved on to new sounds and a new line-up, they performed the album in full at the Elephant Fayre in Cornwall, which they were headlining, as an unannounced warm-up on the second stage. In 2011, they performed it in Sydney, London, Los Angeles and New York as part of the **Reflections** shows.

In 1998, Smith offered his own reflections on *Faith* in *Cure News*. 'I was probably obsessed with the idea of faith because I thought that if I found something to believe in, it would sort out all my other problems. And I didn't.' Nevertheless, he rated the record highly. 'This is one of my favourite three Cure albums. It was written at a time of ever-deepening depression, and was intended to explore the whole notion of "faith", but it ended up as a testament to near complete disbelief, and led me on and down – enter *Pornography*...'

Producer Mike Hedges was brutal in his assessment. '*Faith* is more intense than *Seventeen Seconds*, more atmospheric, darker, grey, misty. Most of the songs are songs to hang yourself to.'

Fans

In The Cure's 1989 song 'Prayers For Rain', Robert Smith sings of an 'infectious sense of hopelessness'. Something about The Cure's sense of hopelessness has, over the years, proven an incredibly infectious and durable virus.

Music **critic** Simon Reynolds has written of 'their abiding mega-cult following – a vast legion of the unaffiliated and disillusioned', describing them as 'suburbia's lost dreamers'. For Robert Smith, The Cure's appeal to their fans comes down to empathy, a sense that your own emotions are reflected by the songs. 'Sometimes,' he told the *Chicago Tribune* in 2019, 'when you're feeling miserable and you listen to miserable music, it comforts you, because you feel there's someone who understands. You're not alone.'

Debora Parr and Marion Little are two long-term Cure fans from the UK who regularly travel great distances to follow the band, often doing several dates on a European tour. For Debora and Marion, the social aspect of Cure fandom – the sense that, as Robert puts it, 'you're not alone' – is of huge value. 'The meet-ups before and after shows between fans is as important as the shows itself,' Marion says. 'We have formed so many amazing friendships as a result of following tours, or meeting in forums online.'

For Marion, what characterises Cure fans is kindness:

> I find Cure fans are incredibly generous. Whether it be sharing gigs with others via recorded copies of gigs, or going live during shows so others can experience it too. We all work together to make sure everyone who wants a ticket to a gig can get one. We club together on sale days and divide and conquer, planning it like a military operation. Ticket sales days are incredibly stressful and tickets fly out the door, so pre-planning with other fans is key to success. If you miss out, everyone tries to help each other to find a ticket. When magazines and suchlike come out, fans will buy extra copies to send to fans in other countries. During **Lol Tolhurst**'s book signings, many books were signed for fans in corners of the globe that were not covered by Lol's book tour.

For Debora, inclusivity is part of the appeal. 'I like the gender and age mix at gigs. Gender-wise it's about 50-50. So many other bands of that era have a predominantly male audience – a lot of the ones I go to, anyway. And there is a real age range too, from old punks who would have been there at the start to baby **goths** having their "first Cure gig" experience.'

Are Cure fans 'goths', then? It's not quite that simple. By 1989, 'Cureheads' had mutated to become distinct from goths as a youth tribe. A famous RTÉ item featured an interview with half a dozen young Cureheads on Dublin's Grafton Street who wore rosary beads 'to annoy grown-ups'. And Cure shows nowadays do attract everyone from emo kids to metallers to very mainstream music fans.

The more hardcore fans, though loyal, aren't slavishly so. 'There's always going to be people who like us because of what we look like,' Robert once said, 'but at the same time, I do think we have a higher percentage of people who do listen to what we do. And are very critical of what we do, as well. We've always had a very critical audience. Which at times can get annoying, but it's generally a good thing to have.'

The Cure are responsive to fan opinion, to an extent. In the late eighties they went through a phase of sending a **crew** member (often it was **Perry Bamonte**) into the crowd with a video camera to ask which songs they would like to hear. The band would then watch the footage in the dressing room, and sometimes alter their set accordingly. As **Chris Parry** explained to *Q*, '[Robert] does have this very highly developed sense of audience. Like all good artists, he lives in other people's perceptions.'

Some fans are loyal to a particular version of The Cure, and will not tolerate any deviation. Circa *Japanese Whispers*, Robert began receiving hate mail from former fans who felt betrayed by the success of The Cure's pop singles. 'I really detest them,' Robert said in *Ten Imaginary Years*. 'It's like we're their pet band, and how dare I tamper with our mysterious image? I never asked for blind devotion. I resent it because they're trying to shrink me into a one-faceted person who's only allowed to produce one style of music.' **Roger O'Donnell**, however, gets the mentality behind it. 'I think a lot of Cure fans struggle with the **success** of the band,' he once said. 'They want it just to be for them, and I understand that.'

Sometimes, devotion can reach unsettling extremes. Circa 1983 The Cure were regularly followed by two Japanese girls nicknamed Doom and Gloom who used to stand and cry in front of the band whenever they got the chance. At a Cure gig in Los Angeles in 1986 a fan, clearly suffering from some form of mental illness, clambered onto the stage and began slashing at their own body with a knife. 'It was pretty serious,' Robert later said, 'but perhaps some of the crowd who'd smoked too much dope might've thought it was some sort of art installation.' In 1993, a group of fans started camping in *Simon Gallup*'s garden.

Some subjects divide fan opinion. Often the arguments involve pitting one current Cure member against another from a different era. '**Boris Williams** was in the band 1984 till 1993,' says Marion Little. '**Jason Cooper** has been with The Cure since 1996, so significantly longer than Boris was ever with them, yet many Cure fans see Boris as the only true Cure drummer and poor Jason is constantly compared to him, many believing that Jason simply cannot match Boris playing on songs that Boris originally played on. Personally I think it's a load of old rubbish, and I absolutely love Jason's style . . .'

Debora Parr has seen a similar division around guitarists. 'There is also a lot of debate about whether **Reeves Gabrels** is a good fit for the band. There is a lot of loyalty to **Pearl Thompson** and a lot of people find Reeves a bit too classic American rock style, too many widdly solos etc. Whereas some people lap this up . . .'

Debates on certain recurring topics rage online. According to a thread on the **website** Curefans, these include: 'Robert's **hair**', '*Disintegration* is great', '*Wild Mood Swings* sucks', 'Robert's **shoes**', 'Simon is cool – and hot', 'We love *Trilogy*!', 'Robert's hair Part 2', 'Porl sucks', 'Porl rules', 'Robert's lipstick', 'Porl sucks Part 2', '*WMS* sucks (again)', '*The Cure* sucks', 'Robert & **Mary** – sweethearts forever', '*Disintegration* is the best album ever made, really', 'Keyboards vs no keyboards', 'Robert's hair Part 3', 'More about keyboards vs no keyboards', 'Robert's . . . socks?', 'Simon is hot', 'Simon is cool', 'Don't you think that 'It Used to Be Me' should have been an album track?', 'Robert's shoes Part 2', 'Porl sucks – or rules? Whatever', and 'Robert's hair Part 4000'. (I mean, this was pretty much the working structure for *Curepedia*.)

Debora Parr confirms this. '"What do you think of *WMS*?" posted in a group will get about 300 comments, still. If you are making a new fan friend, you have to establish where you stand on the *WMS* position first! Personally I can't stand it . . . According to some, this characterises me as a miserable humourless goth that is expecting everything to be *Pornography* Part 2.'

Certain Cure songs are apparently popular with the band (evidenced by their disproportionate number of appearances in the live set) but unpopular with the fanbase. For Marion Little, '**Wrong Number**', 'Hungry Ghost', 'Club America' and '**Friday I'm In Love**' come into this category, 'but they do also provide an opportunity to pop to the bar or loo in an otherwise long show . . .' It also facilitates an in-joke between Marion and her fellow fans: '[We do] "Wrong Number" face . . . Many of us like to take photos of ourselves pulling a face during "Wrong Number"!'

When you've been to as many Cure shows as she

has, you are able to spot patterns, such as certain pairings of songs in the running order. 'We also look out for the bookend sets,' says Marion. 'If the set starts with "Open" then you know it will finish with "End", if the set starts with "Plainsong" you know it will finish with "Disintegration", and so on.'

The Cure are unusually good with fan relations, beyond merely canvassing customer opinion with a video camera. Lol Tolhurst has spoken of Robert's 'wonderful ability to talk to each fan of the band', remembering that 'People lit up as he talked to them, and he had that charismatic way of making each one feel as though they were the only one that mattered.' For Lol, it's a mutual dynamic. 'One reason I feel The Cure's fans have been so loyal is because they understand that we are equally committed on the other side of the equation.'

The attitude of Cure fans has changed over the years. Marion Little believes newer, younger fans are less critical. 'They haven't lived through the different incarnations of the band so they tend to whinge about these things less than seasoned fans.' Debora Parr agrees. 'I think the newer fans have a more open mind about the later stuff. They don't just automatically write off everything after *Disintegration/Wish* as rubbish.'

There is a visible age divide, Debora has noticed. 'You see some real baby goths properly dressed up at gigs, much more than us old bastards. Makes you proud.' Robert Smith, too, has noticed this divide between the elder Cureheads and the kohl minors. 'The best part about playing live is seeing how weird the audience has become,' he told *Chicago Tribune*. 'The less mobile people with grey hair in the back, and down in front the people with glitter on their faces . . .'

Their devotion didn't ease off, even at The Cure's **lowest point**. On the Swing Tour, Simon Gallup noticed, a car followed them for miles and miles, with the fans sleeping inside it each night. And, he said on the *Trilogy* DVD, some fans are so tenacious in their touring that they become familiar faces. 'It's got to the point where we know about 50% of them by name . . .'

Robert Smith is one of a tiny handful of musical icons – Ian Curtis, Kurt Cobain, Richey Edwards – who have transcended their era and will always *mean* something. Generation after generation of alienated adolescents, 'those picked last for basketball' as *Details* magazine put it, will continue to discover him.

'He's a very attractive personality, as peculiar and odd as he is,' said Paul Morley (see **Desperate Journalist**) in the *Out of the Woods* **documentary**. 'And at stages in teenage life, someone like Robert Smith, in the great pop sense, is the kind of guy you'd want to be your hero. He seems to live out your fears and live out your vulnerabilities. He's created an alternative lifestyle. He rejects authority, he *looks* like he rejects authority, he sings about mysterious things . . .'

This sense of identification, Robert Smith believes, is what attracts fans to The Cure. 'I think the kind of fame the group enjoys is fame through understanding,' he told *Cure News*. 'Most people feel they know us because they know about us – it is a kind of affinity, not worship. At least I hope . . .'

The positive effect that The Cure's music has on fans is, he said, the whole reason for doing it. 'Thinking, sometimes knowing, that some of our songs have affected people as they have affected me, is the most fulfilling part of The Cure. It makes the world turn a tiny bit slower.'

Fascination Street

It's all about that bass. 'Fascination Street' might be **Simon Gallup**'s finest five minutes. The muscular, machine-like rumble of the bassline is what made it a stadium-ready monster.

If you listen carefully, it's a little like the **'Close To Me'** bassline, but in a minor key and a bad mood. (It's also similar in rhythm and feel to the bass riff from 'Right Place, Wrong Time' by New Orleans voodoo-blues maestro Dr John. Though this is almost certainly a coincidence, it's a very neat one. But we'll come to that.)

That bassline is offset by a descending four-note arpeggio on Robert Smith's guitar that's strikingly similar to one played by John McGeoch on 'Israel' by **Siouxsie And The Banshees** – a song Robert would have played live in the double digits of times in 1983 and 1984 (it's the opening song on live album *Nocturne*).

'"Fascination Street" is booze and **drugs**, let's just say', Robert explained to *Oor* in 1989. But it's a song which makes narcotic excess and **alcoholic** abandon sound strangely bleak and hollow. It's about the feeling of chasing a kick that's illusory, and the knowledge before even heading out for the night that you're never going to find it. 'Pull on your face, just

pull on your feet', he begs his companion, 'pull on your hair, pull on your pout', even though they both know the fun they crave will evade them. 'Because I feel it all fading and paling and I'm begging/To drag you down with me, to kick the last nail in . . .' he sings, and 'let's move to the beat like we know that it's over . . .'

The origin of the song was a visit to New Orleans, where The Cure played a show at the Lakefront Arena at Lake Pontchartrain, north of the city, on Monday 27 July 1987. As Robert told *Cure News*, there had been a 'band adventure' on Bourbon Street. 'I was getting ready to go there,' Robert remembered later, 'and I thought, "What the fuck do I think I'm going to find?" It's about the incredulity that I could still be fooled into looking for a perfect moment.'

New Orleans is the world's greatest drinking city. (And a contender for the world's greatest city, full stop.) It's the birthplace of jazz, music seeps from its pores, and it's almost impossible to have a bad time there. The Cure's mistake, though, was going to Bourbon Street, the US equivalent of Marbella or Faliraki on a Friday night. Bourbon is indeed a dystopian hellscape, full of frat boys from out of state drinking day-glo Hand Grenade cocktails and trying to get girls to take their tops off in exchange for some cheap beads. It's not just that it's for tourists: it's for the *worst kind* of tourist. For the true NOLA experience they should have headed for a boozy night on Frenchmen or Decatur, or left the Quarter altogether for the backstreets of Marigny or Bywater. But then we would never have heard 'Fascination Street', in all its disillusioned majesty.

There is nothing of New Orleans in the **video**. It was filmed in a disused power station in South London, made up to look like an abandoned theatre with scant props (a red British telephone box, a lamppost, a street sign). The band all look freezing cold – a state it is almost impossible to achieve in actual New Orleans. **Roger O'Donnell** is particularly beautiful, with a perfectly pale face, jet-black coiffure, neckerchief and Nehru collar, but he looked too good for Robert's liking, and a re-edit was made with less of Roger in it. It ends, for no obvious reason, on a long, lingering close-up of **Porl Thompson**'s face. It's **Tim Pope** at his least inspired and most cursory, and Robert hates it. But there was a reason for that 'Will this do?' feel, according to **O'Donnell**. 'In those days,' he later wrote, 'videos were incredibly expensive lavish affairs which took hours and hours to film and edit. Robert and Tim Pope had a very big idea for the video for "Lullaby" which was very expensive, but they had a plan to offset the expense by shooting the video for "Fascination Street" very cheaply and doing them side by side. I think they were shot one after the other, and the budget combined.'

'Fascination Street' was released on 18 April 1989 in North America only, where it – not 'Lullaby' – was chosen as the lead single from *Disintegration*, as it had been used on the **film** soundtrack *Lost Angels*. Its B-sides were 'Babble', a fast song about claustrophobia and boredom punctuated by backwards noises recorded from the television and, on the 12-inch and CD versions, 'Out Of Mind', a mid-tempo throwback to the dense, dark sounds of the *Pornography* era, on which Smith compares his mental state to zoochosis (see **Zoology**). The CD also included an extended remix of 'Fascination Street', later included on *Mixed Up*, which takes four minutes before the vocals even come in, but subdues the song's best feature: its bassline.

The **artwork** is as throwaway as the video: just the band's name and the song title stencilled over some flowers left over from *Disintegration*. It reached No.46 in the Billboard chart, and became The Cure's first track to reach the top of the newly created Modern Rock Tracks chart (based on radio airplay), where it stayed for seven weeks.

However, 'Fascination Street' looms larger in popular culture than its chart status would suggest. (It's given its name to a film production company in Los Angeles, run by documentary maker Nasar Abich Jr, and a recording studio in Örebro, Sweden run by heavy-metal producer Jens Bogren.) It's also a bigger feature of The Cure's live repertoire: their eleventh most-played song, with over six hundred outings.

Because it isn't about underwhelming chart positions, forgettable videos and uninspiring sleeves, nor even bad nights out in New Orleans. It's all about that bass.

Favourite Songs

What are The Cure's favourite songs by The Cure? What are The Cure's least-favourite songs by The Cure?

Recency bias is a factor. Musicians will invariably tell you that their latest album is the greatest thing they've ever done. The converse of this is that when the dust has settled, often at a distance of decades,

they're more able to clearly see when something wasn't up to scratch. With that temporal caveat in place, here follows an incomplete timeline of Robert Smith's statements on which Cure songs he loves – and hates.

In 1987, Robert named his favourites as 'Faith', 'Sinking', 'Accuracy', '**Charlotte Sometimes**', 'The Figurehead', '**A Forest**', 'Shake Dog Shake', '**In Between Days**' and 'If Only Tonight We Could Sleep'. A year later, in *Cure News*, he repeated his love for 'Faith and 'The Figurehead', but chose 'Object' from *Three Imaginary Boys* as his least favourite Cure track.

With another five years to think about it (and a whole load of new material to consider), he told *Cure News* in 1993 that the best songs he had ever written were 'From The Edge Of The Deep Green Sea', 'Faith', 'Open', 'End', 'Same Deep Water As You' and '**Just Like Heaven**'.

In 1994, asked by the same publication to list The Cure's best B-sides, he named 'Happy The Man', '2 Late', 'Harold And Joe' and 'This Twilight Garden', while **Simon Gallup** went with 'Babble' and 'Fear of Ghosts', and **Perry Bamonte** chose 'Twilight Garden', 'Big Hand' and 'New Day'. In the same issue, Robert revealed that the reason that the CD version of *Boys Don't Cry* had lost the song 'World War' was 'probably (possibly) because I hate it.'

Readers learned, in 1995, that Smith's favourite Cure lyric used to be 'There's nothing left but faith' (from 'Faith') but was now 'Please stop loving me, I am none of these things' ('End').

In 1998, the old 'favourite Cure songs?' question came up again, and this time, 'off the top of my head', he listed 'Bare', 'Disintegration', 'Treasure', 'Faith', 'From the Edge Of The Deep Green Sea', 'Trust' and 'Scared As You'.

And, in 1999, the whole band were asked to nominate their favourite song to perform live. Robert picked 'Disintegration', Simon 'From The Edge Of The Deep Green Sea', Perry 'Faith', **Jason Cooper** 'Homesick' and **Roger O'Donnell** 'Prayers For Rain'.

On the subject of live performance, should we read anything into statistics? There's an element of crowd-pleasing to Cure setlists, of course: there are certain songs they surely feel obliged to play, whether or not they're in the mood. With that caveat, here are The Cure's ten most-played songs.

1. 'A Forest'
2. 'Boys Don't Cry'
3. 'In Between Days'
4. 'Play for Today'
5. 'Just Like Heaven'
6. '10.15 Saturday Night'
7. 'The Walk'
8. 'Killing An Arab'
9. 'Three Imaginary Boys'
10. 'Primary'

But if you don't trust statistics, you can't necessarily trust words from the horse's mouth, either. Robert Smith once said that 'Let's Go To Bed' is one of his favourite songs to perform live. And if you believe that, you'll believe anything.

Festival 2005

Released by **Geffen** on 27 November 2006, *Festival 2005* is a live DVD which does exactly what it says on the tin, capturing The Cure at summer **festivals** in Spain, Belgium, **France**, Switzerland, Sicily, Hungary, Germany, Greece and Turkey.

In many ways, it ticks all the expected boxes: **artwork** by **Parched Art** (big multicoloured letters made of live photos), mixing by **Keith Uddin**, and so on. What makes it unique, however, is that it was to a large extent fan-created. Not only was it edited together by superfan and author Daren Butler, but **fans** actually held the camera.

As the DVD box explains: 'In 2005 a nascent Cure trio of Robert Smith, **Simon Gallup** and **Jason Cooper** celebrated the return of former guitarist **Porl Thompson** with a series of nine eclectic headline festival shows across Europe. The quartet's unique blend of passion and power proved to be a thrilling combination, and the summer set a new benchmark for Cure live highs. *Festival 2005* presents a selection of these performances captured by a mix of fans, crew and on-the-night big-screen cameras.'

Though by no means the most definitive nor the most satisfying video record of The Cure live, it is arguably the most authentic in terms of accurately representing a fan's-eye experience of seeing The Cure at a festival.

An EP featuring three of the songs – '**alt.end**', 'Push' and '**In Between Days**' – was also made available.

Festivals

How did The Cure become the ultimate festival band?

It didn't happen overnight. Their training started early. In fact, The Cure's very first gig outside the UK was a festival, Sterrebos near Groningen in the Netherlands on 29 July 1979 in the middle of the afternoon (quickly followed by their second, an indoor gig at the Groningen venue Simplon that same evening). They were back in the Low Countries for the Bilzen Jazz Festival in Belgium on 17 August 1979.

By the time they made their UK festival debut at Reading on 24 August 1979, they were almost festival veterans. They were halfway up the bill of the main stage that day, beneath The Police, The Tourists, Motörhead (with whom they shared a trailer) and Wilko Johnson. A rough **bootleg** recording survives, and they broadly went down well, apart from the odd shout of 'wanker' from the rockers. Robert, in a tight red top, dedicated a super-fast '**Boys Don't Cry**' to 'all the macho men in the audience' (he pronounced it 'makko'), and 'Do the **Hansa**' to 'everyone who hates disco'.

They were back in continental Europe a fortnight later for the Rotterdam New Pop '79 festival, which they headlined in front of a crowd of ten thousand, and of which footage survives – perhaps the earliest with the original trio of Smith, **Tolhurst** and **Dempsey**.

Into the eighties, The Cure's festival appearances became . . . *eventful*. In June 1980 a festival in Rettel descended into **violence**, with the crowd tear-gassed by police, and headliners Roxy Music refusing to play. At Werchter in 1981 they used '**A Forest**' as a weapon to protest against headliner Robert Palmer's petty timekeeping. And in 1985 Rock in Athens descended into another riot, which The Cure had to flee in the back of **Depeche Mode**'s truck.

Nevertheless, The Cure and festivals became synonymous. Almost every year's **touring** schedule involved several summer festivals, and four or five tours were literally called the Summer Festivals. Their biggest repeat customer is **Glastonbury**, which they have headlined a record four times.

In 2004 The Cure even created their own touring festival **Curiosa** (which might as well have been called Robertapalooza), and in 2018 they not only played Robert Smith's indoor **Meltdown Festival** but also BST in Hyde Park (see **40 Live**), which too can be considered Cure-ated. A year later, Pasadena

Daydream – a one-day festival with many Cure favourites on the supporting bill – also had Smith's fingerprints all over it.

The Cure's festival-headlining game is strong, and has been officially immortalised twice: on film by *Festival 2005* and on CD by *Bestival Live 2011*. They know they're good at it, and so do bookers. This once-awkward, antagonistic alternative act have become the perfect unifying everyman band. Everyone loves a bit of Cure, and if they do descend into the darker depths of their back catalogue (or their latest album) during the set, everyone knows they'll unleash a hit-packed final stretch sooner or later.

Robert Smith enjoys it as much as the crowds. 'If we're playing outdoors in the summer,' he said on the *Trilogy* DVD with dry self-awareness, 'I find it pretty difficult to feel miserable. Not that I want to . . .'

Fiction

'Over the four years The Cure have worked with Fiction and **Polydor**,' Robert Smith told *International Musician* in 1983, 'they've realised that the more they pressure us to do something, the less likely it is that it'll get done. They've learned to tolerate me like an awkward but inexpensive halfwit in the corner. The fact that we've never been in debt to a record company has allowed us a great deal more freedom than most bands . . .'

Five years before this qualified endorsement of the **label** which was The Cure's home for most of their career, Robert Smith was busy writing letters. They came with a biscuit, a teabag, and a tape. The letter read: 'We are The Cure. We have no commitments. We would like a recording contract. Listen to the tape.' The tape contained the demo recordings **Ric Gallup** had paid for. The tea and biscuit was, he was hoped, a friendly gesture which would make A&R persons at record companies look more kindly upon The Cure and, at the very least, press Play.

In almost every case, it didn't work. The **Crawley** postman – quite possibly Frank Bell from **Cult Hero** – delivered rejection letters from Phonogram, EMI, Virgin, Island and the BBC.

Almost every case. One man liked what he heard. **Chris Parry**, a New Zealander who had become frustrated with his successful but restrictive A&R job at Polydor, was about to quit the company and go solo with his own label, taking Ita Martin with him. He summoned The Cure to London on 10 August 1978 (see Parry's *Curepedia* entry for full details of that day's drink-fuelled meeting), and – after seeing them play at Laker's in Redhill on 27 August – he signed them to his new label on a six-month deal.

When they first met, the label had no settled name. Parry's original preference was either Night Nurse (which The Cure vetoed) or 18 Age (to which The Cure asked, quite reasonably, 'What happens when we turn 20?'), before all parties agreed on Fiction Records, with the company slogan 'Beats Tired Reality' (as seen on the sleeve of '**Killing An Arab**').

Though Fiction was under the autonomous control of Parry, it had the financial, manufacturing and distribution might of Polydor behind it. In this regard, it is a classic case of a faux-indie label. This species also includes the following seemingly indie imprints: Blanco Y Negro (Warner), Caroline (EMI/Universal), Creation (Sony), Dedicated (BMG/Arista), Deltasonic (Sony), Fauve (Sony), Indolent (BMG/RCA), Matador (Atlantic), Seed (Atlantic), Two Tone (Chrysalis), V2 (Virgin). All of these have, for some or all of their existence, been owned and/or distributed by a major label while presenting as an indie in terms of its aesthetic and roster, exercising varying degrees of autonomy but maintaining a general vibe and aura of 'indie-ness'. But Fiction came first.

Once it had a name, it needed a logo. The first, a spiky, triangle-based, very new-wave design, was created by **Bill Smith** but later replaced by the iconic blobby, painted-looking version from **Porl Thompson** and **Andy Vella** (yet to call themselves **Parched Art**).

With a name, a logo, a band and financial backing, all it needed was a premises. Fiction's earliest homes were both in Willesden: Parry and Martin ran it from a room within **Morgan Studios** for a time, and from 14–16 Chaplin Road, just around the corner (nowadays occupied by a business called Unity Music Offices & Bedroom Studios), but its most famous and longest-running home was at 97 Charlotte Street in the heart of Fitzrovia. It also, at the height of its success, ran an office in New York at 850 7th Avenue, a twelve-storey block now occupied by everything from a Thai spa to a farm insurance office.

Though The Cure were synonymous with Fiction and were the label's flagship band, they were not the only act on its roster. The first act to release a record on Fiction were actually Mod band Purple Hearts (see '**Jumping Someone Else's Train**'), and they were soon joined by **The Passions** and **Associates**, both of whom ventured out with The Cure on the label's

Future Pastimes package tour of November 1979. Fiction also released one-off curious like **Tim Pope**'s 'I Want To Be A Tree' and Cult Hero's 'I'm A Cult Hero'. In the late eighties and early nineties, a second wave of Fiction artists were signed: Eat, The God Machine, and Die Warzau.

Though technically a Polydor subsidiary, Fiction itself had a subsidiary in the form of Desire Records, which released alternative acts like Raymonde and SPK (whose former member **Derek Thompson** was very briefly bassist in The Cure) and, later, dance and hip-hop acts like Double Trouble & The Rebel MC.

For a couple of years between 1989 and 1991, Fiction HQ was home to *Cure News*. Fiction also became a publisher of Cure **books** such as *Ten Imaginary Years* and *Songwords 1978–1989* as well as assorted Cure sheet music, and its song-publishing wing represented acts such as Stereo MCs and Cameron McVey. Its most lasting legacy outside of The Cure, however, was in helping to set up the London indie radio station **Xfm** (now Radio X).

In the late nineties, Robert Smith became frustrated with restrictions placed upon him regarding the release of Cure music. 'It's like being back at school,' he complained. 'I'm 40, and I have to get permission to put my own music on the web.' On 14 February 2000, having wriggled free via the contractual obligation album *Greatest Hits*, The Cure allowed their contract with Fiction to lapse. A year later, Chris Parry sold the dormant label to Universal.

In 2004, Universal revived the Fiction brand under the control of Paul Smernicki, Joe Munns and Beastman 'to give Universal a bit more of a guitar stronghold', and released records by artists including Snow Patrol, Cure **collaborators** Crystal Castles, Tame Impala, Death From Above 1979, The Maccabees, Kaiser Chiefs, Elbow, White Lies, Guillemots and Yeah Yeah Yeahs.

An impressive roster. But did any of them send a teabag and a biscuit?

File

Rarities from Robert Smith's stint in **Siouxsie And The Banshees** are themselves rare, given the brevity of his tenure, but *File* is one of them. A 7-inch single circulated free to members of the Banshees fan club, which was called The File, it contained 'Head Cut' (from *Juju*) and a new song, co-written by Robert,

called 'Running Town', recorded live at the band's second night at the Royal Albert Hall on 1 October 1983 (and therefore effectively a *Nocturne* outtake). A feral, wayward uptempo track built around a serrated descending riff from Smith, and featuring lyrical references to The Beatles' 'Helter Skelter' (itself covered by the Banshees at the Royal Albert Hall), the song was also performed live on Channel 4's *The Tube*. Membership of The File in 1983 cost £3.50. Copies of *File* now sell for an average of £105.

Films (The Cure referenced in)

When you're an icon, it's tempting for others to borrow your iconography. And you can't always control the way in which they borrow it.

Robert Smith has been referenced, in all but name, in the look of several characters from cinema. The earliest, and perhaps most obvious, is *Edward Scissorhands*. In Tim Burton's classic **gothic** romance from 1990, Vincent Price plays a mad professor – part Frankenstein, part Gepetto – who creates a son from body parts, leather and metal but dies before he can finish the job, leaving the boy, Edward (played by Johnny Depp), without proper hands, and with sharp blades for fingers instead. A local couple take him in, and he becomes a neighbourhood celebrity, excelling at hairdressing and topiary. He falls in love with their daughter, Kim (played by Winona Ryder), with tragic consequences. With his black clothing, deathly white face and shock of wild black hair, Edward strongly resembled Robert Smith. It's an established fact that Tim Burton is a massive Cure fan (he once said, 'Their music has always been inspirational to me somewhere, in anything I've done'), and that the look of Edward was directly inspired by Robert. Burton even invited The Cure to record the soundtrack. As **Roger O'Donnell** recalled on his website blog about *Disintegration*, 'Another thing I remember, but I don't know how widely known this is, was that Tim Burton had asked Robert for The Cure to do the soundtrack to *Edward Scissorhands* and the script was lying around the studio. I don't know why we didn't, or what happened . . .'

One film with a Robert Smith-informed central character did end up having The Cure's music on the soundtrack: *The Crow*. It has not gone unnoticed that the character of rock-star-turned-superhero Eric Draven from this 1994 superhero movie bore similarities to Smith, which became more pronounced when The Cure's own favoured filmmaker **Tim Pope** directed the sequel, *The Crow: City of Angels*, in which the mantle of the Crow is taken up by mechanic Ashe Corven. The first Crow film featured the specially written song 'Burn' (see **Films, The Cure's music in**). Furthermore, their B-side 'Adonais' was written with actor Brandon Lee, who died while playing Eric Draven in the first film, in mind.

Then there's the film in which the lead character basically *is* Robert Smith: *This Must Be the Place*. Named after a Talking Heads song, this 2011 drama stars Sean Penn as Cheyenne (a name inspired by **Siouxsie Sioux**), a former rock star with wild black hair and bright red lipstick who retired following the death by suicide of two of his fans. He has been living in Dublin for twenty years but, following a failed attempt to reconcile with his father in New York, finds himself becoming a Nazi hunter, travelling across America on the trail of elderly war criminals. Director Paolo Sorrentino, another huge Cure fan who had seen them live several times, confirmed that the character of Cheyenne was inspired by the fact that Robert Smith continued to dress as Robert Smith even when off-duty, deep into middle age. 'Here was a fifty-year-old who still completely identified with a look which, by definition, is that of an adolescent. But there was nothing pathetic about it. There was just this one thing that, in the movies and in life, creates an incredible feeling of wonder: the extraordinary, a unique and thrilling exception.'

A number of film titles have referenced The Cure. *Boys Don't Cry*, directed by Kimberly Peirce, is a 1999 biopic about Brandon Teena, a trans man from Nebraska (played by Hilary Swank) who is murdered in a transphobic attack. (A **cover** of 'Boys Don't Cry', performed by Nathan Larson, appears in the film.) In his book *Spaceships Over Glasgow*, Mogwai's Stuart Braithwaite reveals that Robert Smith once told actress Chloë Sevigny, who co-starred in the film, that *Boys Don't Cry* had made him cry. *Just Like Heaven* is a 2005 supernatural romcom starring Reese Witherspoon. (Katie Melua's cover of 'Just Like Heaven' appears over the opening credits, and The Cure's original over the closing credits.) And *In Between Days* was the title of a Korean coming-of-age drama by So Yong Kim in 2006.

The Cure and their songs have even been used as a plot point. 'In Between Days' is in the charming 2013 coming-of-age film *Sing Street*, in which the teenage protagonists go through a very obvious 'Cure phase'.

Mike Leigh's *Career Girls* (1997) tells the story of two women, one of them very Smith-like in her look and demeanour, who reunite six years after leaving university and attempt to bond over their shared love of The Cure. (One of them even uses The Cure's music as therapy.) With Smith's permission, Leigh used six Cure songs in the film.

Speaking to Jim Sullivan of the *Boston Globe*, Smith gave his reaction to the way he is treated by Leigh's film. '[I'm] this iconic figure who doesn't change. There's a part of the film when they see a poster for "**The 13th**" and one of them says, "Is he still doing that?" Like I'm an unchanging man in a changing world. It was very weird, because it was wrapped up in what I represented at the time, which was a kind of disaffected youth, and I was perceived as being the same now. It's weird, because I know I'm not. I realise it's there, but to see it up there on the screen, to have it driven home like that. I've never really felt like that, even when I was 17 or 27 . . .'

That's the trouble with being an icon. Anyone can hang your image anywhere. And it means whatever they want it to mean.

Films (The Cure's music in)

The music of The Cure has proven irresistible to film directors as an aural shortcut to a certain mood. (Usually, though there are exceptions, one of elegiac melancholia.)

There are two categories of film in which The Cure's music appears: 1) those where The Cure's pre-existing music was borrowed, and 2) those where the music was written and/or recorded bespoke for the purpose of the film.

Literally hundreds of the former category exist, but the earliest example is almost certainly the use of 'Grinding Halt' on the superb proto-Riot Grrrl movie *Times Square* (1980) from the same Robert Stigwood stable that brought the world *Grease* and *Saturday Night Fever*, trying to do the same for punk/new wave that *Saturday Night Fever* did for disco and *Grease* did for rock 'n' roll. (It failed, culturally and commercially, but it's very watchable.)

Teen dramas seemed the most obvious home for Cure songs in the eighties, 1989's *Lost Angels* (starring Beastie Boy Adam Horowitz), which used '**Fascination Street**', being one example.

Mike Leigh used no fewer than six Cure songs – '**The Lovecats**', 'The Upstairs Room', '**The Walk**', '**Let's Go To Bed**', '**The Caterpillar**' and 'Just One Kiss' – in *Career Girls* (1997), a film which also uses The Cure as a plot device (see **Films, The Cure referenced in**).

In 1998, Adam Sandler sang '**Boys Don't Cry**' in the eighties-set romcom *The Wedding Singer*, signalling that The Cure had, at least in part, become a signifier of nostalgia as well as all the other baggage they entail.

Their music could still evoke menace, such as the use of 'Watching Me Fall (Underdog Remix)' in *American Psycho* (2000). Or magnificence, as when 'Plainsong' appeared in Marvel's *Ant-Man* (2015). Increasingly, however, their music became a staple of twenty-first-century romantic comedies. For example, '**Friday I'm In Love**' appeared in both *He's Just Not That Into You* (2009) and again in *About Time* (2013).

'**Close To Me**' appeared in a school disco scene in *Son of Rambow* (2007) and, in a not-dissimilar vein, '**In Between Days**' features in both the charming Dublin-based coming-of-age film *Sing Street* (2013), in which the teenage protagonists go through a very obvious 'Cure phase', and François Ozon's romantic drama *Summer of '85* (2020). The film was originally meant to be called *Summer of '84* until Robert Smith intervened. 'I absolutely wanted to use their song 'In Between Days',' Ozon told the *Guardian*'s Jonathan Romney, 'and he said, "Sorry, but that came out in 1985." So I changed the title, and he let us have the song.'

The most-used Cure song in film, however, as with television, is '**Pictures Of You**', which has appeared in *One Perfect Day* (2004), *Starter for 10* (2009), *Café de Flore* (2011), *The Vow* (2012), *White Bird in a Blizzard* (2014) and *Me You Madness* (2021) to name but six, although it's being chased down by '**Just Like Heaven**', with five appearances under its belt.

Then there's the second category of music written and/or performed specifically for the film in question. This nearly began in spectacular style in 1990 when The Cure came close to recording the entire soundtrack for Tim Burton's **gothic** tragicomedy-romance *Edward Scissorhands* (see **Films, The Cure referenced in**), as Prince had done for Burton's previous film *Batman* a year earlier, but the idea came to nought. Smith did, however, eventually work with Burton for his 2010

remake of *Alice in Wonderland*, contributing a wonky **cover** of the Sammy Fain and Bob Hilliard song 'Very Good Advice' (first voiced by Kathryn Beaumont on the 1951 Disney version) to the spin-off album *Almost Alice* (with a vocal credit given to the elusive **Bunny Lake**), and again for the 2012 stop-motion horror-comedy *Frankenweenie* on the spin-off album *Frankenweenie Unleashed! Music Inspired by the Motion Picture*, slurring through an enjoyably demented cover of Frank Sinatra's 1957 hit 'Witchcraft'.

The first film for which The Cure provided a brand-new song was dark superhero flick *The Crow* (1994), whose source material – a cult comic by James O'Barr – featured a titular lead character whose look was partly inspired by that of Robert Smith. The song, 'Burn', was **Boris Williams**' last recording as a full member of The Cure. 'It sounded (purposefully) like an "old" Cure song (*i.e.* from ***Pornography***, '**The Hanging Garden**' in particular!)', Robert told *Cure News*, and he wasn't kidding. Ned Raggett, choosing it as one of The Cure's finest deep cuts in the *Quietus*, described it as 'a dark jewel of a song' and 'majestic and nervously uneasy at the same time'.

They were back in the superhero soundtrack game the following year when 'Dredd Song' appeared over the closing credits of *Judge Dredd* (1995), wittily beginning with the words 'Never say it's over, never say the end . . .' (When Robert saw the finished film, he thought it was terrible.)

In 1997, side project **COGASM** (**Jason Cooper**, **Reeves Gabrels**, Robert Smith) recorded 'A Sign From God' for the twisted comedy *Orgazmo*, a film by Trey Parker and Matt Stone (who would later recruit Robert to the voice cast of their enormously successful cartoon series *South Park* – see **TV, The Cure referenced in**). And 'More Than This' (not a cover of the Roxy Music hit) was a new Cure song written for 1998's film version of *The X-Files*.

With all this film-related activity, it's a wonder that Robert has never crossed the line into taking charge of an entirely self-created cinematic project. In 1997, Robert revealed to *Rolling Stone* that he had ambitions in that direction: 'I want to dedicate myself to sculpture and film music.' By 2000, things had escalated. He'd written a treatment for a film of his own, and was making instrumental music for it. He'd written the characters, wanted the music to reflect them, and was considering putting it out with a booklet explaining it all. 'If it doesn't work,' he said, 'I'll do another Cure album.'

He did another Cure album.

Five Swing Live

Five Swing Live was a limited edition EP of songs **recorded** live on the last three dates of the Swing Tour of December 1996 at Sheffield Arena, Manchester NYNEX and Birmingham NEC. They were recorded by Steve Whitfield, who first worked with The Cure on their **cover version** of The Doors' 'Hello, I Love You' in 1990 and went on to engineer *Wish*. The five songs, 'Want', 'Club America', '**Mint Car**', 'Trap', and 'Treasure' were all, as the title implied, from the *Wild Mood Swings* album. It was The Cure's fourth live release of the 1990s, coming after *Entreat* (1991), and *Show* and *Paris* (1993), but would be their last for fourteen years.

Released in June 1997, the five thousand copies of *Five Swing Live* were only available via The Cure's **website**, at a time when 'surfing the web' was still a somewhat niche pursuit. The individually numbered card-sleeved CDs bore the unusual **Fiction** catalogue number of FIXCD.COM 1. The **artwork**, a high-contrast black, yellow and red live photo, was credited to the enigmatic and Cure-specific smART. Copies are now worth an average of £67.

The album was dedicated to the memory of **Associates** singer Billy Mackenzie, who had passed away in January 1997. A Wordsworth inscription on the sleeve demonstrated Robert's love of **poetry**: 'The music in my heart I bore, long after it was heard no more.'

Flexipop!

Flexipop! was a British monthly music magazine which launched in May 1980 and positioned itself as an edgier, more piratical, renegade rival to the leading pop publication *Smash Hits*. Founded by ex-*Record Mirror* writers Barry Cain and Tim Lott, aged twenty-four at the time, it was printed on a cash-in-hand, brown envelope basis using spare capacity on porn baron David Sullivan's presses. (Sullivan, as well as making his fortune from adult movies and magazines, also set up the *Sunday Sport* newspaper, and is now a co-owner of West Ham United.)

Flexipop!, in the words of Lott, was 'trashy, puerile, brash, vulgar', and a deliberate reaction against the seriousness of writers like Paul Morley (see **Desperate Journalist**) and Ian Penman at *NME*. It

often photographed stars in suggestively sexual or sadomasochistic poses. Even more so than the mildly mischievous *Smash Hits*, it mocked the stars, as seen in cruelly hilarious comic strips about Adam Ant and Toyah, as well as a strip about the adventures of a toilet. These were the work of cartoonist Mark Manning (who would later find fame as heavy rock singer Zodiac Mindwarp).

One controversial aspect of *Flexipop!* was its comedic use of 'pinheads', in other words sufferers from the neurodevelopmental disorder microcephaly (as seen in Tod Browning's *Freaks* and, more recently, *American Horror Story* season 4) as visual mascots and cartoon characters. 'Our mascot', Cain said later, 'became an obscure cartoon figure called Zippy the Pinhead. Our motto was "Pure Pulp for Pinheads".'

Flexipop! gave far more coverage than its poppier rival to alternative bands such as The Cramps, The Birthday Party and The Cure. The Cure's first appearance in *Flexipop!* came in Issue 13, December 1981. Robert reminisced about his first ever gig – fronting the **pre-Cure band** Malice at his school's Christmas concert – that turned into a disaster, and waxed lyrical about Christmas in general.

One regular section in *Flexipop!* was Welcome to the Working Week, a seven-day diary written by musicians themselves. Robert supplied an especially memorable example in Issue 21, August 1982. The article's own standfirst read 'Robert Smith of The Cure has the weirdest week in the entire history of this page. God is it weird . . .' (It left such an impression on me that I tore it out, folded it up and carried it around in my school blazer pocket so that I could re-read it whenever I needed to.)

The text was superimposed on Edvard Munch's *The Scream*, opposite a photo of Robert perched halfway up a tree, with **Mary** hugging the trunk. The fact that Robert's week had two Thursdays and no Tuesday was presumably a mere typo (and, if not, he'd got the hang of the days of the week by the time of '**Friday I'm In Love**'. The really bizarre stuff unfolded when you read the content.

The diary takes place in the first week in nearly two years that he's been able to stay at home in Crawley at his mum and dad's house. (His parents were away visiting his brother in Wales.) He begins his Wednesday by waking up at 10.30 a.m. and writing down his **dreams** to assist with songwriting. He drinks coffee all day to stop himself eating. He goes to the hairdressers, 'which was probably the worst move of my life. I had it put into zig-zag crimpy bits and it's ended up looking like a hat. Before, it was all straight and sticking out. It made me look really mental, which was really great because no-one came near me.' At three o'clock in the morning he goes for his nightly walk in an ornamental park. 'It's quite a refreshing feeling – you never know if someone's going to jump out and hit you. It's nice having fear for a while.'

The following day he deliberately goes out for another walk during a torrential thunderstorm in just a T-shirt, then comes home soaking wet to watch some shows he's recorded off the television: 'a few short cartoons, a programme about learning to play the guitar and some early morning shows for Arab-speaking people.' (He had been trying to get the local video shop to rent him snuff movies, to no avail.) He sits in the garden with Mary till four o'clock in the morning, talking.

Friday he spends clearing out his rubbish tip of a bedroom, then replying to fan letters. 'I always make my replies obtuse, obscure and brief. I think that people always treasure them more when they can't understand what they mean.' He reveals he's been reading David Cooper's *The Language of Madness* and *Sanity, Madness and the Family* by R. D. Laing and Aaron Esterson, inspired by the experience of filming the '**Charlotte Sometimes**' video in a disused asylum. These books, in turn, fed into the lyrics on **Pornography**, notably 'A Short Term Effect'.

'In the afternoon,' he says on Saturday, 'there was a football match on telly, so I sat in the garden and watched it through the window.' (This doesn't seem weird at all now. It did then.) He speaks of his plans to make a film of Mary **ballet** dancing 'but only of her feet'. Then Smith Sr. turns up. 'Mary and I were playing football in the garden this evening when suddenly my dad appeared in the doorway – we hadn't seen him for days – and he started to take pictures with a camera. That was a bit embarrassing, because Mary only had a see-through blanket on . . .'

He reveals that he and Mary dress up a lot when they're alone. 'Today I dressed up as my mum and cooked a curry. There's always an undercurrent of insanity which goes on in private.' The make-believe continues on Sunday, when 'We spent part of the day pretending to be an old couple'. Monday is spent recording some *musique concrete* of 'trains, planes birds and trees' for use in a song, and drinking cocktails made of milk and **alcohol**.

On the final day he drives to London to see *Star Wars* and *The Empire Strikes Back* at the Odeon, Marble Arch (later the venue for the premiere of *The*

Cure In Orange). 'There were only four other people in the whole cinema – a mum and dad and their two children. The children started running up and down and I couldn't think why they were doing it. Then I realised that the soundtrack was in quadrophonic and they were starting at the front and running to the back to follow the spaceships shooting overhead. So I decided to join in and spent the rest of the time running up and down this huge, empty cinema.' Then he goes to get drunk with **Steve Severin** at **Siouxsie And The Banshees**' studio, cabs it back to **Fiction** and collapses into bed.

In the eyes of this teenage reader, the idea that adults were allowed to live in this quietly deranged manner was something to cherish. (Robert contributed another week-in-the-life diary to French newspaper *Libération* in 1985 that was far more sensible and mundane: for example, Mary and Robert going to see Santa Claus in Selfridges, going to a firework display in the rain, and going to see the Vienna Boys Choir. It's very unlikely that French schoolchildren ripped that page out and folded it into their pockets.)

Flexipop!'s USP was the free, brightly coloured flexidisc affixed to the front – a precursor of the cover-mounted CDs later attached to rock mags – typically featuring one song by a contemporary band. On Issue 22, in September 1982, it was The Cure's turn.

Flexipop!'s approach about the disc came at a pivotal moment in The Cure's history. One thing Robert didn't mention, in his Welcome to the Working Week, is that it took place at a time when there quite possibly wasn't a Cure at all. In the aftermath of the chaotic and ill-fated **Fourteen Explicit Moments** tour, **Lol Tolhurst** was taking an extended sabbatical and **Simon Gallup** had quit altogether (for the time being). At this point, more than at any other, The Cure was Robert Smith and Robert Smith was The Cure.

The song he chose to record was a doom-laden track called 'Lament' which he had composed while away with Mary on a camping trip in Wales. In the absence of any actual Cure musicians, Smith asked Severin to help him record it at London's Garden Studios, making it essentially a precursor to **The Glove**. 'I was surprised I was writing again,' Smith said later, 'but pleased . . .'

The track, four minutes and thirty-one seconds long, is more of an experiment than a song, built around a drum machine, a schoolchild's recorder and Smith's meandering guitar lines, and the quality is that of a demo. Robert's wailed vocals are mostly indecipherable, though when he and Tolhurst re-recorded it for one of the B-sides of '**The Walk**' (later available on *Join The Dots*), it had a lyric about a drowning ('Today there was a tragedy/Underneath the bridge . . .'). It does have its fans: a 2019 article by Wren Graves on the website Consequence named the *Flexipop!* version of 'Lament' as one of The Cure's 10 Best Deep Cuts.

The cover-mounted flexi, sellotaped over the face of ABC's Martin Fry, came in flimsy green see-through plastic. The disc played at 33 rpm, with a label that had a small circle to show where the listener ought to place a 1p coin to weigh it down, and a promise that 'This flexidisc is made of high-quality vinyl and will not damage your stereo system'. What it omitted to mention was that your stereo system might damage the flexidisc, as would pretty much any solid object with which it came into contact. Longevity and playability are not strongpoints of any flexi, which is probably why copies of 'Lament' are not especially prized **rarities**, except as colourful pieces of memorabilia, selling at about £15. That said, some copies were made on red plastic rather than green, and in 2022 someone on Discogs was trying to sell one of those for £587.

Flexipop!'s uniqueness was undermined when *Smash Hits* also started giving away flexidiscs, but ultimately *Flexipop!* was the architect of its own downfall when it began pushing too hard against the limits of what was socially acceptable. One notable transgression was a Letters page edited by a woman known only as the Baroness, who often appeared dressed as a dominatrix in stockings and suspenders, and told readers they were mentally ill or that she wished they'd die in a car crash.

The mock photo-love stories, featuring guest stars (e.g. Altered Images, Bad Manners, Bow Wow Wow) were also a source of controversy. One month, in an uncanny echo of the *Oz* magazine obscenity trial, Mark Manning was left in charge when the editors were away, and ran a photo story called 'Bad Bax 2', starring psychobilly band The Meteors, using real blood and meat from the butchers. Cover-ups were hastily added when the editors returned, but the magazine was still withdrawn from sale by retailer WH Smith for two issues, and circulation halved. Eventually, in 1983, the magazine was shut down for obscenity. The last page of the last-ever issue: an advert for '**Like An Animal**' by *The Glove*.

Former editor Barry Cain keeps the *Flexipop!* spirit

alive on social media, and there is an archive of the magazine's output at www.flexipop.com. A *Flexipop!* book, with Robert Smith on the cover (and containing his Welcome to the Working Week), was published in 2017.

Whatever else *Flexipop!* achieved during its brief life, there's a case to be made that it accidentally kept The Cure alive.

Fools Dance

After the end of **Matthieu Hartley**'s short spell in The Cure, he and Stuart Curran, a former bandmate in **Mag/Spys** along with **Simon Gallup**, formed The Cry (sometimes just known as Cry). When Gallup's own first spell in The Cure ended, he too jumped on The Cry life-raft.

In early 1983 a five-piece version of The Cry, comprising Gallup, Hartley, Curran, singer Ian Fuller and drummer 'Tot' (Paul Thompson, not *that* one, formerly of Roxy Music) began gigging, playing a show in Lingfield, Surrey and another at London's pay-to-play dive The Rock Garden in April. There was a Cry cassette tape, but they never released anything commercially.

An upheaval in The Cry line-up, with Fuller and Tot going on to form Walking Floors then Hartley leaving in August 1983, gave the remainaing duo of Gallup and Curran the opportunity to rebrand themselves Fools Can Dance, bringing in former Cure roadie **Gary Biddles** on vocals. This new trio was augmented by saxophonist **Ron Howe**, then drummer Pete Gardner (ex-Let's Eat Cake), having managed with a drum machine for a while. Their first date with this new line-up was in August 1983 in Reigate, not far from **Crawley**. At a show in Bath in October, one reviewer called their sound 'a flatly paced plod'. Before long, doubtless concerned about the similarity of their name to that of neo-classical 4AD group Dead Can Dance, Fools Can Dance lost the 'Can' and became simply Fools Dance.

An early publicity photo shows the core trio of Gallup, Curran and Biddles all sporting magnificent **gothic** manes of **hair**. One review of a Fools Dance gig noted that Biddles 'could be mistaken for you-know-who from 20 yards' (while accepting that he didn't try to sound 'like HIM'). As Ron Howe acknowledged in a 2003 interview, 'Gary Biddles was seen as the ultimate Robert Smith clone at that time'.

Howe also admitted that 'we played up Simon's role in The Cure to the fullest extent', and indeed no Fools Dance gig listing was complete without the C-word.

The extended Crawley/**Horley** mafia of Cure associates were heavily involved in Fools Dance. Brian Adsett, friend of The Cure and later their head of security (see **Crew**), was road manager, with **Ric Gallup** doing the lighting. Carol Thompson, Simon's girlfriend, sister of **Porl** and Mag/Spys and **Cult Hero** backing vocalist, was also involved, helping to create a Fools Dance tour programme which featured a personal profile of Simon which ended with the words 'Be Pure, Be Vigilant, Behave' (the catchphrase of *2000AD* comics character Torquemada, later repurposed by Manic Street Preachers as a lyric on their single 'PCP').

Gallup was, Biddles acknowledged in an interview with *Libération*, the main songwriter, though they all chipped in. At gigs, Gallup emerged as a secondary singer, taking lead vocals on 'The Ring', of which *Sounds* wrote: 'Simon's vocal power . . . sends sparks down your spine and leaves one with the satisfaction of knowing that there are two possible frontmen in the band.'

Fools Dance toured extensively in Europe in 1984, and were especially popular in the Netherlands. An indication of their growing status is that at one show they were supported by The Cult. At one show in Belgium, Howe recalled, they bought a load of petrol station flowers and threw them at the audience to dispel their moody goth image.

It all ended when Gallup was tapped up by Big Cure. Gary Biddles had selflessly engineered a pub session with Gallup and Robert Smith, which resulted in Gallup being gradually eased back into the fold for *The Head On The Door*.

No Fools Dance records were released while Simon Gallup was a member. However, recordings made during that period did come out subsequently. The self-titled *Fools Dance* EP was released by Dutch label Universe Productions in 1985, and shows them to be a decent, competent mid-eighties goth band in the vein of Clan of Xymox, UK Decay, Danse Society or The Bolshoi, with heavily flanged guitar atmospherics and reverbed vocals. The somewhat *Faith*-like 'Happy Families Waiting (at the Skylab Landing Bay)', sung by Gallup, is probably their best track. The artwork was even more shameless in pushing The Cure connection than Fools Dance ever were in their lifetime: a circular sign on the front said 'SIMON CURE GALLUP'.

A further EP *The Priest Hole*, released in 1986 on the Lambs to the Slaughter label, consisted of the songs from the first EP rejigged in a different order. Biddles then made an attempt to reform Fools Dance with Jean-Jacques Burnel of The Stranglers and Paul 'Tot' Thompson, releasing the far more professional-sounding *They'll Never Know* EP in 1987, which had a touch of The Psychedelic Furs and Julian Cope to it. He then gave up.

Biddles' post-Fools Dance life is detailed in his own entry. The same applies to Ron Howe and Matthieu Hartley. Peter Gardner joined Lefaye, who supported The Cure (see **support bands**) and remained, according to *Cure News*, Simon's 'drinking buddy'. Stuart Curran still gigs in the Surrey area in a band called The Flashing Blades.

And Simon Gallup is Simon Gallup.

Fourteen Explicit Moments

'I wanted it to be the ultimate "fuck off" record', Robert Smith once said of **Pornography**. If that's the case, then Fourteen Explicit Moments was the ultimate 'fuck off' tour.

In hindsight, they should have taken a break. The Cure had played 119 shows in 1981, across thirteen countries and three continents, and the first quarter of 1982 was spent making their fourth album in a relentless storm of **drugs** and discord. But taking a break wasn't how The Cure operated. To quote the 1425 translation of *Isaiah 48:22*, 'peace is not to wicked men'. Or, in the more familiar 1574 John Calvin version, 'there is no rest for the wicked'.

On 18 April 1982, The Cure set out on the most catastrophic **tour** of their career. The initial fourteen dates – the Fourteen Explicit Moments of the tour's title – were in Plymouth, Reading, Bristol, Brighton, Southampton, Sheffield, Newcastle, Glasgow, Edinburgh, Manchester, Birmingham, Norwich and Leicester, winding up in London on May Day. They were supported by cockatoo-haired corporate rockers **Zerra One** and a film called *Airlock* (see **Carnage Visors** for their previous cinematic support act), described by a reviewer in *Sounds* as 'an ill-illuminated and badly focused amateur movie'.

The tour's *mise en scène* was both innovative and aggressive. Lighting engineer Mac (see crew) projected colour washes onto the screens, while risers and amps had mirrored fronts so audiences could see themselves (and be dazzled). As **Lol Tolhurst** wrote in *Cured*, '[The stage] was confrontational compared to what had come before . . . [It] comprised screens that were remotely operated to come down over the drum kit which was placed to the side of the stage. They also covered other areas of the stage to create different effects. It was stark to say the least . . . The effect was similar to sitting in a pub or club with a mirror bar . . . A little disconcerting for the audience, which was part of our intention.'

The band's appearance was of a piece with this disconcerting intent. The big **hair** – crimped, gelled and sprayed – began on this tour, and their **make-up** was deliberately grotesque. They streaked lipstick not just across their mouths but under their eyes, so that when they began sweating under the house lights, it appeared that they were crying blood.

The reviewer from *Sounds*, after witnessing the Bristol gig, wrote: 'Whoever did the lights are worth every penny of their doubtlessly large fee, magnificent yet simple with immaculate use of spots, three screens and a bit of back projection, all made to look like there's nothing to it but with an almost *Close Encounters*-type exhilaration inbuilt.' They also likened it to **Pink Floyd**, which was closer to the truth than they probably realised: The Cure had hired Pink Floyd's actual lighting rig and PA via production manager Mick Kluczynski, who also worked for Floyd's production company Britannia Row.

The live set was remorselessly harsh, usually incorporating seven of *Pornography*'s eight tracks, unleavened by any pop tunes. ('**Boys Don't Cry**' wasn't played once in 1982.) Some shows ended with 'Forever', an improvised jam with the repeated, echo-laden refrain 'all I have to do is kill her'. ('Forever' remained a classic example of an **unreleased song**, until live recordings were added to the deluxe reissues of *Faith* and *The Top*.) Others ended with the even longer freeform finale 'All Mine' (also unreleased until the deluxe *Pornography*). It also saw The Cure bring a little technology into their armoury. As Lol said on Tim's Twitter Listening Party, 'For the *Pornography* tour, we took a reel-to-reel tape machine for the drum track on "**One Hundred Years**" and for background sounds on the track "Pornography". The first time we hadn't played everything you heard from the stage live. Now it's commonplace . . .'

Reviewing the show in Brighton on Robert's

twenty-third birthday for *NME*, critic Richard Cook wrote of 'an assault powered by an almost ecstatic vitriol', detecting that the tour was 'set to pitilessly lambast their audience.' Cook continued: 'It's all very skilfully deployed: a bruisingly clear sound of scathing force, a clockwork, Pavlovian lightshow, a variegation of light and shade in the song order that builds to the unmitigating force of "Pornography" itself as the climax.' He found the singer, however, to be 'stubbornly static and spellbound by his microphone', and perceptively noted that 'Smith, on his birthday, looked dejected and tired.'

On 5 May, just four days after the final UK show at Hammersmith Odeon, they began the European leg – retitled the Pornography Tour – which called at Rotterdam, Amsterdam, Nijmegen, Zwolle, Groningen, Utrecht, Grivegnée, Turnhout, Berchem, Deinze, Genk, Berlin, Düsseldorf, Neu-Isenburg, Aachen, Hamburg, Köln, Mulhouse, Strasbourg, Montreux, Pau, Toulouse, Montpellier, Aix-en-Provence, Lyon, **Paris** (two nights), and Schifflange, finishing in Brussels on 11 June. Twenty-nine days on, eight days off.

The reason for this punishing schedule was partly financial. The cost of Pink Floyd's gear, coupled with relatively low gig fees, meant, as *Ten Imaginary Years* put it, that 'profit margins were low and they had to play almost every night to make it viable.'

Low attendance, too, chipped away at morale. At Düsseldorf Philipshalle, for example, they played to a two-thirds empty room. 'It must be said that not many people turned up,' Lol later told *Record Collector*. 'I recall large halls with about 50 to 100 people in them, and that didn't help matters.' And the emotionally draining nature of the *Pornography* material left the singer exhausted: according to Lol, Robert would sometimes collapse on the floor and lie there for thirty minutes after a show, because he'd put so much effort into it.

All of this led to an atmosphere of simmering tension between Smith, Tolhurst and **Gallup**. It boiled over in Strasbourg on 27 May. By this point, Simon and Robert were barely on speaking terms, and an almighty row erupted in a nightclub afterwards. Unsurprisingly, **alcohol** was involved. Depending on which version you believe, either Simon thought Robert was getting free drinks and therefore refused to pay for his own, or a barman mistook Simon for Robert and asked Gallup to settle Smith's tab. In any case, Robert came over to see what was going on. 'Simon was so wound up that no one could talk to him,' Robert later recalled. 'He was screaming at the barman, this young kid who was nearly in tears. By himself, Simon would never have behaved like that but he was surrounded by the road crew so he was behaving the way he thought a rock 'n' roller ought to behave . . . He didn't want to pay for his drinks because he thought I wasn't paying for mine. I told him to shut up, and he punched me.' A fistfight, described by Robert as 'an enormous ruck', broke out. 'It was the first time he really laid into me . . .'

After this explosion of **violence**, Robert said 'that's it', went back to the hotel, packed his suitcase, grabbed his passport, and flew from **France** back to London on the 6.30 a.m. flight the next day. He was home in **Crawley** by 10 a.m. Simon Gallup also flew home later, leaving Lol Tolhurst the only member of The Cure still on the tour with Swiss, French and Belgian gigs still to be completed. A plan was even hatched, at one point, of persuading Zerra One to pretend to be The Cure for the remaining gigs.

Fortunately, the Strasbourg fight happened at a time when the band had a three-day break. In the meantime, Robert's father Alex convinced him that he had to return to the tour. 'For me it was over and out. But when I unexpectedly showed up home, my dad wouldn't let me in. 'You have a responsibility as an entertainer,' he said. "People have bought tickets, get yourself back on tour."'

Smith flew back to join Tolhurst, as did Gallup. Inevitably, the remaining dates were even more fraught with tension than the previous run. It all came to a head, again, at the final show on 11 June at the Ancienne Belgique in Brussels. The band ended the encore with a messy, improvised ten-minute jam called 'The Cure Are Dead'. Zerra One joined in, and roadie **Gary Biddles** was on vocals, inventing words on the spot and making strange howling noises. According to some versions, Smith decided to play drums, so Gallup grabbed Smith's guitar, leaving Tolhurst having to play bass. And, depending on who you believe, either Robert Smith threw drumsticks at the back of Simon Gallup's head, or Lol Tolhurst threw drumsticks at the back of Gary Biddles' head. Biddles announced: 'Smith's a wanker, Tolhurst's a wanker, only Simon's worth anything in this band!' (Other versions have Biddles using the C-word about Smith. Sadly, the only surviving recording cuts off before it happens.) The gig was over, the tour was over, and The Cure seemingly were over, too. 'That night . . . felt like death,' Tolhurst later wrote. 'It was the death of that version of The Cure.' Smith slept

through the journey home, and nobody spoke. He and Gallup would not see each other for another eighteen months. Tolhurst and Smith eventually regrouped as a duo, but for a while it appeared that The Cure were genuinely finished.

In a tour programme for his post-Cure band **Fools Dance** (which also featured Gary Biddles), Simon reflected on his reasons for leaving. 'It's just basically that Robert and I are both really arrogant bastards, and it got to such an extreme. I suppose you just can't have two egocentrics in a band and Robert was sort of "the main man". At one time I did bear a lot of malice on them. But now it controls me about as much as getting up in the morning. It was just three years' experience.' Many years later, on the *Trilogy* DVD, Simon spoke about it again. 'When we did the *Pornography* tour, it did change my personality. It changed me into someone I didn't like. I changed into a really nasty piece of work. But you can't just blame it on songs. It was a time of experimenting with things which, by their very nature, change a person's personality.'

In the immediate aftermath Smith, according to an interview he gave to *Uncut* in 2000, suffered a nervous breakdown. He returned to his parents' home in Crawley, and refused to speak for two weeks. He also dried out, and reflected on what had happened. 'I'd seen the ugly side of my own nature,' he admits. 'I'd seen how vile I could become, but at the same time I realised "It doesn't have to be like this."'

After a quick visit to Playground Studios in Camden to visit **Siouxsie And The Banshees**, who were putting the final touches to their masterpiece *A Kiss In The Dreamhouse* with The Cure's old producer **Mike Hedges**, Robert and Mary ran off to Wales for a camping holiday without telling anyone where they'd gone. 'I just wanted to disappear,' he later explained.

In other words, he fucked off.

Fourteenth Album

Will it ever happen?

Hopes of a fourteenth album by The Cure have been raised, dashed, delayed, teased, trailed and trashed throughout the ever-lengthening interval since 2008's *4:13 Dream*. Here follows an incomplete timeline of those hints and promises, announcements and de-announcements, revelations and backtracks.

The first time Robert Smith openly spoke about the prospect was at a French press conference in July 2012. He revealed that he'd been composing songs and sending them to **Simon Gallup** for his feedback, and that something was about to happen. 'We've got a month's gap between festivals, and this **line-up** of The Cure will be recording, for the first time.' Pressed on when these recordings might be released, he became tetchy. 'Eventually, of course we'll do something new. But so what? I've grown out of that. I don't care *when* we do it. As long as it's good, it doesn't really matter.'

The same month, in the same country, he reaffirmed that issue of quality control. 'We've done so much,' he told *Télérama*, 'that I have to be convinced that what we do is as good. It has to be better. Because otherwise, what's the point? I don't want to just keep making music because that's what I do. That isn't what I do. I still want to grow old feeling that I'm an *artist*, not someone who's in a band. There's a subtle difference. My younger self is crying at that, but there's a grain of truth in it. I wouldn't want to sully the earlier works by feeling that I could do better.'

In 2014, some specifics began to emerge. In February, *Pitchfork* ran a news story, based on a press release, to the effect that The Cure would be releasing a new record that year, tentatively titled *4:14 Scream*, supposedly recorded at the same time as *4:13 Dream* and originally planned as the second half of a double album (an idea with which **Geffen** refused to comply). However, in March the same website, under the headline 'Robert Smith Doesn't Sound Too Enthusiastic About The Cure's Next Album', was forced to backtrack somewhat in response to an interview Smith had given to **Xfm**.

'We're in a weird predicament,' he said, 'in that I've finished singing and mixing an album that was made by a band that no longer exists.' (**Porl Thompson** had left, **Roger O'Donnell** had returned, and **Reeves Gabrels** had joined.) 'I'm not sure it happens that often. This band is trying to make an album with this line-up, and it's an album that I'm tempted to make, that's really different to anything else we've done. So, trying to be convinced that I should release the second half of what is an effectively an album that came out in 2008, it's a bit of a sore point, really, to be honest, amongst this current line-up.' However, he stuck to the story that the album would probably appear that summer, although he did not intend to perform songs from it live. 'I just never sang it,' he added, 'because I couldn't be bothered. I just didn't think the words were good enough.' He told the station that over the past eighteen months he had rewritten the lyrics and started recording them.

On 1 April 2014, a day on which one is advised to take anything with a pinch of salt, *Pitchfork* once again ran a Cure story, based on a blog post in which Robert clarified his earlier comments, explaining that he thought *4:13 Dream* was an excellent album but that cramming it all onto a single CD meant that roughly half the tracks had to be left on the shelf. 'And my plan this sunny spring Monday at the end of March is to get to the point in the next month or three where we can release: 1. A Limited Edition *4:26 Dream* double CD album of 26 songs (all remixed) – i.e. the original *4:13 Dream* sessions concept album (including the 'instrumentals with words') – of which 10 tracks or more will be previously unreleased . . . 2. a Ltd Edition *4:14 Scream* single CD album of 14 previously unreleased songs, albeit some of them may also be on *4:26 Dream* . . . but these *4:14 Scream* versions will all have words and vocals . . .'

Meanwhile, Robert had been telling the *NME* that he thought *4:14 Scream* was a dreadful title, but that he would probably be keeping it. '**Andy (Vella)** who does our covers has done a really great album cover for it, a kind of pastiche of me doing a scream, so maybe we'll keep it. It's one of those reverse psychology things, where it's so bad it's good.' He also blamed their now-former label Geffen for the delay. 'It was just pure bloody-mindedness [sic] why the tracks weren't included on the last album. I was so fucking angry that [the label] wouldn't release a double album. I wouldn't give them the other songs.' Those 'one to three months' passed, however, with no sign of either the double-disc *4:26 Dream* or the single-disc *4:14 Scream*. In fact, it was another two years before there was any sign of activity in terms of new material.

On the first date of their 2016 American tour, at New Orleans' Lakefront Arena on 10 May, The Cure premiered two unreleased songs. 'It Can Never Be The Same' is a lengthy, keyboards-dominated, mid-paced song of regret about a break-up which would fit nicely onto *Disintegration*. 'Step Into The Light' is a superb diatribe in 6/8 time against **religious** belief which deserves to be more widely heard. Both are said to have been intended for *4:14 Scream*. Live recordings of both songs ended up on the *40 Live (Curætion-25 + Anniversary)* box set. After that, however, there have been no further sightings of *4:14*

Scream activity, and the trail on that project goes mysteriously cold.

In June 2018, ahead of the Smith-curated **Meltdown Festival**, Robert spoke to the *Guardian*'s Dorian Lynskey. 'I've hardly written any words since [*4:13 Dream*],' he told him. 'I think there's only so many times you can sing certain emotions. I have tried to write songs about something other than how I felt but they're dry, they're intellectual, and that's not me.' When asked whether he'd be disappointed if there was never another Cure album, he replied, 'I would now, yeah. Because I've committed myself to going into the studio and creating songs for the band, which I haven't done for 10 years. Meltdown has inspired me to do something new because I'm listening to new bands. I'm enthused by their enthusiasm. So if it doesn't work, I'll be pretty upset, because it will mean that the songs aren't good enough.' Smith also told Lynskey he had been revisiting unused old lyrics with a view to repurposing them, but 'some of them don't make any sense to me anymore. It would be weird if I felt the same as I did when I was in my 20s. I'd be mental!'

In August 2019, in an American interview syndicated to the *Chicago Tribune* and *Los Angeles Times*, he announced that an album was in progress, and that he would be working on it during a break in touring. 'We're going back in [to the studio] three days after we get back from Pasadena for me to try and finish the vocals, which is, as ever, what's holding up the album. I keep going back over and redoing them, which is silly. At some point, I have to say "That's it".'

He once again credited the experience of working with younger bands at Meltdown with inspiring him. 'Something clicked inside my head: I want to do this again. It came as a bit of a shock to me, to be honest. No one really believed me until we started recording.' He also told the interviewer that the loss of close family members had affected the mood of the music. 'It's very much on the darker side of the spectrum. I lost my mother and my father and my brother recently, and obviously it had an effect on me. It's not relentlessly doom and gloom. It has soundscapes on it, like *Disintegration*, I suppose. I was trying to create a big palette, a big wash of sound.' Lastly, he revealed that the album's working title was *Live from the Moon*, 'because I was enthralled by the 50th anniversary of the Apollo landing in the summer. We had a big moon hanging in the studio and lunar-related stuff lying around. I've always been a stargazer . . .'

Later that month, he spoke to *NME*. 'I feel intent on it being a 2019 release,' he said, 'and would be extremely bitter if it isn't. At some point I will have to say 'This is it', otherwise we'll just keep recording like we have done in the past. It never gets any better. We're due one more session, then we're done.'

There were, he said, eight songs already written which formed the core of the album. The lyrics, he said, were 'more true', 'more honest' and therefore 'a little bit more doom and gloom.' He spoke of a wish to express the darker side of his recent experiences, 'but in a way that will engage people. Some of the albums like *Pornography* and *Disintegration* are kind of relentless. I leavened *Disintegration* with some songs like "**Lullaby**" and "**Lovesong**", but I think this one is more like *Pornography* because it hasn't got any of those songs that lighten the mood at all.'

He then mused about the probable reaction such an album would receive. 'If it does turn out like that, I think it's going to alienate any kind of pop audience we still have. I think fans for a certain type of music that The Cure make will love it. That's the dichotomy of the paradox: they will love the fact that it's merciless.'

He even found himself thinking beyond this album to the one after. 'Roger thinks that this is the last album but I think that every album we do is the last Cure album. It may well be, but if there's another bunch of good songs then there's no reason not to follow it up. What do we do if we've got seven good songs leftover? Wherever it ends up, it will be an honest decision. There's no record company involvement. It's just us doing it. No one is pulling the strings . . .'

Two months later, in a *Rolling Stone* interview in October 2019, he expanded on his thoughts about the moon landing that inspired the new album's working title. 'I was 10 at the time, and I can remember standing out in the back garden with my younger sister and my dad, looking at the moon, and he was explaining to me what was going on, that there were men up there. And I thought, 'Yeah, yeah' – an early skeptic. Then I was thinking, what is the world going to be like in 50 years, and it just dawned on me as we turned into 2019, good grief, is this it?'

He then spoke about the 'downward slide' the world has been on since the optimism of the sixties and seventies. 'What it [the moon landing] represented to my generation – I was on the cusp of turning into a real person – was the possibilities that were out there. It seemed like suddenly a switch was clicked and the world changed. It's very disturbing.'

So, when would *Live From The Moon* see the light of day? The intention, he said, was to bring the album out on the anniversary of the 1969 landing, therefore 20 July 2019, 'complete with NASA crackling vocals and stuff', but that date had already passed. They'd already done a four-week session at Rockfield Studios in South Wales (famous as the place where Queen made 'Bohemian Rhapsody') surrounded by moon memorabilia and with a glowing lunar sphere hanging from the ceiling – 'I even bought a 1969 guitar to play on it just to get the vibe going' – but the main cause of the delay was, once again, the words. 'In a funny way, I was trying to achieve nostalgia for a world that never happened. And I think that's still what I want the world to be. That's why I'm struggling a little bit with the lyrics.'

Over the course of the year, Smith became dissatisfied with the new songs as they stood, and convinced that they could be improved. 'I don't think the tone of it is going to change, but I think I'll probably structurally change some of the bits. Rather than editing the stuff inside a computer, I'd rather we just play it again.' He told the interviewer that they were planning a ten-day session in Paris or Los Angeles to complete the work. 'It'll be a rush mix. It's really just down to me to finish the words. We seem to keep rewriting songs. I don't think I've quite nailed some of them. I've sung most of it, but I think it has to be the best thing. I can't do the whole, "That'll do." I've never felt that with a Cure album, but with this one in particular, I think we've waited more than 10 years, and I can't just think, "Oh, that'll do."' He offered a revised release date. 'Realistically, it's going to be November because there's no way it can get mixed in under three weeks.' It did not come out in November.

The moon album having seemingly burned up on re-entry, work appeared to have begun on another album. In 2020, Roger O'Donnell spoke to *Music Week*. 'I'm sure what's going on now [Covid-19] is going to delay it, but it's pretty much finished. But who knows what's going to happen tomorrow? We wouldn't be able to promote it with shows or anything at the moment. It's an amazing record though, I can tell you that . . .'

In June 2021, in a joint interview with **collaborators** Chvrches, Robert told Zane Lowe that something could be coming out 'next year' (i.e. 2022). 'I've always wanted to do an hour's worth of noise,' he told Lowe. 'And I didn't want it to be like, The Cure, you wait ten years and we bring out an album that's just like, noise. That's like, NO!' (Comments

he made a year later to *Rolling Stone* about his solo album having begun life as 'literally just feedback' may suggest that the noise idea was never intended for The Cure.) He then revealed that the band had *two* albums in the pipeline: the 'relentless doom and gloom' one and a more upbeat one, which were 'both very close to being done.'

Almost a year later, one of the albums – publications seemed confused about which – at least had a name. The title *Songs Of A Lost World* was revealed during the NME **Awards** in March 2022. Each album would have a ten-track running order (although this had expanded to twelve by the time he spoke to *Rolling Stone* in May), and the **artwork** was already designed. Mixing of the doom-and-gloom record would, he said, begin on 1 April, and a September release date was possible, with vinyl production backlogs cited as the only potential reason for a delay.

Speaking at the Ivor Novello Awards on 19 May 2022 (at which he and Simon Gallup walked onstage to some new Cure music), Robert admitted he was getting cold feet about the cheerful album. 'While there are a handful of really good songs, I've kind of fallen out of love with others so we're going to have to record another four or five, perhaps. If it gets finished, it's very upbeat. It's the flip-side to the first one.' (Note the 'if' . . .) The first one, he promised, was imminent. 'We *will* be releasing a new album. I get fed up of saying this now! We will be playing from October, and the new album will be out before then . . .' (The new album was not out before then.)

There is no law which states that Robert Smith is obliged to give the world a fourteenth album. It's fine for The Cure to carry on being one of the world's greatest live acts. It's not as if he has a questionable work ethic. He's been a prolific collaborator, and he's worked on anything up to five albums, to varying states of completion. Only a tendency to be overly self-critical, or a tendency to lose interest and want to move on to the next thing, has hindered their release.

However, it clearly bothers him that it's yet to happen. On 4 February 2022 he tweeted to his 161,000 followers, 'WE WILL BE PERFORMING SONGS FROM A NEW ALBUM WHEN WE NEXT PLAY . . . OR WE WON'T BE PLAYING AT ALL! AND I REALLY WANT TO PLAY . . . SO THAT MEANS . . . X', adding '. . . IT MEANS MY DESIRE TO RELEASE A NEW ALBUM IS OVERWHELMING! X' In *NME* he doubled down, echoing the thoughts of many a Cure fan. 'I'd rather it just came out. I can't stand the anticipation . . .'

He was, in this case, true to his word: when they next played, there were new songs. The opening night of The Cure's European tour in Riga on 6 October 2022 contained two new songs, 'Alone' and 'Endsong', and the third night in Stockholm introduced another called 'And Nothing Is Forever'. Later shows introduced two further songs, 'I Can Never Say Goodbye' and 'A Fragile Thing'. The tour itself was hurriedly rebranded **The Lost World Tour** on social media.

He wouldn't make all that fuss, and not deliver an album. Would he?

France

'Sometimes it's Spain, sometimes Italy, but usually, France is our best European country . . . From a very early age, from our second album, French people just got it.'

When Robert Smith told *Cure News* in May 1988 that he had once climbed around the outside of the Paris Hilton Hotel from balcony to balcony on the seventh floor at 4 a.m. in the rain, it was merely the latest in a long line of Cure escapades that seem to happen with disproportionate frequency in France.

On 5 June 1980, at least according to official biography *Ten Imaginary Years*, they ended up missing a gig at Lyon university because they got lost in the mountains. Once at the hotel, **Matthieu Hartley** proceeded to uproot a small tree and tried to batter down the door to **Lol Tolhurst** and **Simon Gallup**'s room because he wanted a light for his cigarette. The police were called (see **Arrests**), and impounded The Cure's van along with all their equipment, forcing them to catch the train to Belgium and borrow instruments for the rest of the tour.

This anecdote does not tally exactly with known facts: The Cure actually played Le Bataclan in Paris on 5 June 1980, and did not play in Belgium next. But *something* clearly happened. And they clearly didn't have a lot of luck in France that year. On 14 June they played a **festival** in Rettel where there was a riot, police tear-gassed the crowd and headliners Roxy Music refused to play.

On 30 September 1981 in Caen, they leapt into the crowd to confront restless audience members (see **Violence**), a regular feature of Cure shows at that time, then got back onstage and carried on playing.

On 18 May 1984 in Nice, **Andy Anderson** was wrongfully attacked by a hotel security guard and went on a rampage which nearly saw him imprisoned and the tour cancelled.

Then there was the ever-spiralling mayhem in France in late 1985, recounted by Robert in Issue 1 of *Adventures & Plans* in typical lower-case style:

france was groovy (except in grenoble where laurence sang (?) 'wild thing' to commemorate 9 years of The Cure on stage and then we went to monte carlo and lost and simon spent the whole time dressed as santa claus singing 'hello old lady' and **boris** set hotels on fire and montpelier and toulouse were fun and then everyone in the world came over to dance on the last night at the bercy in paris and it was glorious and we went out and got emotional and then gatecrashed and played at the staff party in our hotel and then we came home . . .

And it was in France that The Cure played what is considered their worst-ever concert, on 25 July 1998 at Théâtre Romain de Fourvière, Lyon (see **Lowest Point**), which counts as an escapade of sorts.

Despite, or because of, these chaotic *événements*, a love affair developed between that country and The Cure. They were fully-fledged celebrities in France, with limousines and police outriders, by 1986 – long before they attained anything like that status in the UK or the **US**. (I can verify this. Walking around Paris in 1988 in full gothic hair and make-up, I was heckled by someone singing '*Show me show me show me* . . .', the opening words of '**Just Like Heaven**', such was The Cure's fame there. That never happened in London.) On one occasion, The Cure's bus was held up for an hour on the Franco-Belgian border because customs guards wanted autographs – something which also happened in **Mexico**. 'We're adopted sons,' Smith told *Record Mirror* in 1986. 'We're not an English group who are coming to play in France . . .'

Robert speaks a little French, and does sometimes introduce songs in that language when playing a Francophone country. As a teenager, he read **Camus** and Sartre in the original language. He has named Notre-Dame Cathedral as his favourite building in the world, and Paris Bercy his equal favourite venue for acoustics and atmosphere (along with the LA Forum).

Lol Tolhurst, too, is a Francophile. On the ill-fated **Fourteen Explicit Moments** tour, he met a French girl called Anne and went to live there for several months, firstly on Rue Cadet in the 9ème arrondissement in Paris before travelling around France to Montpellier, then over into Spain to Figueres, Cadaqués and Port Lligat (on something of a Dalí pilgrimage).

France was the location for a number of important Cure recordings. In 1983, the Studio des Dames was chosen to record 'The Lovecats'. In 1986, *Kiss Me, Kiss Me, Kiss Me* was recorded at Château Miraval in Correns, soon after the filming of *The Cure In Orange* in a Roman amphitheatre in the South of France. In 1993, The Cure released a live album, *Paris*, recorded at **Le Zénith** in the French capital the previous October. In 2004, they gave a radio concert in Paris as part of **The Black Sessions** series for France Inter.

The Cure were on French television long before they were on British television. Their first-ever **TV appearance** was a concert broadcast on the French show *Chorus* in December 1979, including an early version of '**A Forest**' called 'At Night'. On 11 April 1982 they played a thirty-minute set without an audience for a show called *L'Echo des Bananes* (similar to Britain's *The Old Grey Whistle Test*) at Studio Davout, where classic albums including Nico's *Desertshore* and Serge Gainsbourg's *Cannabis* had been recorded (and where parts of Echo & The Bunnymen's *Ocean Rain* would later be made). And, as a member of **Siouxsie And The Banshees**, Robert took part in a performance of the Christmas carol 'Il Est Né Le Divin Enfant' on French television in 1982 (even though he did not play on the Banshees' recording of it, on the B-side of the single 'Melt!').

Robert has also been a regular presence in the French print media. In December 1985, left-wing national newspaper *Libération* ran a week-in-the-life diary, written by Smith (see also: *Flexipop!*), under a standfirst which described him as 'le Rimbaud de Crawley'.

'There's a sensibility about us that the French understand,' le Rimbaud de Crawley once theorised. 'We're not that English.'

The Cure and France, clearly, have a friendly understanding. If only the French had a phrase for that.

Freakshow

The shortest Cure single ever? No, not *quite*. But it is the second-shortest.

At two minutes thirty-two seconds, 'Freakshow' was the first sub-three minute Cure single for twenty-one years (the previous one being '**Catch**' in 1987, at

2:43). It is beaten in brevity only by the band's debut single '**Killing An Arab**' (2:21) a full three decades earlier. For comparison, it is shorter than '**Boys Don't Cry**' (2:35), '**Jumping Someone Else's Train**' (2:55) and '**In Between Days**' (2:57).

The second of four singles released on the thirteenth of every month in the summer of 2008 in the run-up to *4:13 Dream* (see also 'The Only One', 'Sleep When I'm Dead' and 'The Perfect Boy'), 'Freakshow' is characterised, more than anything else, by its curtness. There's no intro and no outro. The first words, 'I can't believe it', are the first thing you hear. The last thing you hear is 'stop'. With no chorus as such, just relentless verses laid over one pleasingly crunchy repeated alt-rock riff pattern, it's a song which gets in, does what it needs to do, and gets out again.

The song made its live debut in **Mexico** City on 22 October 2007, originally under the title 'Don't Say Anything'. Like the other pre-*4:13 Dream* singles, it didn't have a video other than its monochrome MTV performance, but they did perform it on *Jimmy Kimmel Live*, where the last couple of bars were drowned out by a 'Powered by the Pontiac Vibe' sting, infringing The Cure's anti-**advertising** policy.

Released on 13 June 2008 with **Parched Art** watercolour **artwork** of a green eye, and the superior 'All Kinds Of Stuff' on the B-side, it didn't trouble many chart compilers, but did reach No.30 in **France** and, for the second single in a row, No.1 in Spain.

The shortest description of a single in *Curepedia*? No, not *quite*. But it is the third-shortest.

Friday I'm In Love

For people who don't particularly know or like The Cure, 'Friday I'm In Love' is *the* Cure song. In 1992, the year of its release, Robert Smith described it as 'a throw your hands in the air, let's get happy kind of record' and 'a very naïve, happy type of pop song.'

Its origin story varies depending upon whom Smith is telling. In *Cure News*, he said it was 'written in 15 minutes on a sunny Friday afternoon outside the Boat Inn in Oxford.' He told *Guitar World* a different version. 'I remember driving home one Friday afternoon to have the weekend off. And I started to think of this really great chord sequence. I was about 20 minutes away from the studio. So I turned around, went back to the studio and everyone was still there.'

They recorded it that night. Robert played a

twelve-string, **Porl Thompson** played the spindly lead part, and **David M. Allen** eventually pitched it up from D major to D sharp via Varispeed, to give it an imperceptible added pop sparkle. Its cadences and rhythms made it a sibling to '**Just Like Heaven**' and a cousin to '**In Between Days**' (albeit not as likeable as either).

It clocked in at three minutes and thirty-eight seconds, as though the result of an exercise in writing a radio-friendly pop song to sell its parent album *Wish* to the world. 'I've always been aware enough to know you've got to sugar the pill a little bit,' Smith told *Guitar World*, 'but not in a banal way.' He himself admitted there was a slightly cynical methodology at play. 'I mean, 'Friday I'm In Love' is not a work of genius, it was almost a calculated song. It's a really good chord progression, I couldn't believe no one else had used it and I asked so many people at the time – I was getting drug paranoia anyway – "I must have stolen this from somewhere, I can't possibly have come up with this." I asked everyone I knew, everyone. I'd phone people up and sing it and go, "Have you heard this before? What's it called?" They'd go, "No, no, I've never heard it . . . "'

Perhaps surprisingly, the lyrics were not yet written when the first version was recorded. They'd nicknamed it 'Friday' because of the day of the session, and Robert took that title and ran with it. 'I thought, why don't I do a song about that Friday feeling? It's a thing you have at school, and lots of people work at jobs they don't really enjoy. So that Friday afternoon feeling is something you look forward to.' Again, the writing process was a calculated exercise, and one which Smith found unusually hard. 'Genuinely dumb pop lyrics are much more difficult to write than my usual outpourings through the heart,' he told *Spin*. What he came up with was a simple days-of-the-week song, placing it in the same tradition as the Easybeats' 'Friday on My Mind', Alexander O'Neal & Cherelle's 'Saturday Love', Craig David's 'Seven Days', Neil Sedaka's 'Calendar Girl' and the ancient English nursery rhyme 'Solomon Grundy'.

He was, initially at least, proud of the finished article. '"Friday I'm In Love" is a dumb pop song,' he admitted in *Spin*, 'but it's quite excellent actually because it's so absurd. It's so out of character – very optimistic and really out there in happy land. It's nice to get that counterbalance.'

The **video**, filmed in Shepperton by **Tim Pope**, won a MTV Europe viewers' poll for best video of the year, and reportedly took only three hours to make. This can't include the clean-up operation, because 'Friday I'm In Love' surely rivals '**Close To Me**' for the title of The Cure's messiest video ever.

It begins with Pope sat astride a rocking horse and dressed as a clown, shouting directions through a plastic megaphone in a high-pitched voice after inhaling helium. The band then come galumphing down a fire escape and onto the set, shrug off black suits to reveal their stage gear and, with a bass drum skin that reads 'The Cures' perform the song in front of an ever-changing series of theatrical backdrops (a tropical island, an industrial townscape, an English country garden, a dockyard). Band members dress as characters from **French** silent filmmaker Georges Méliès' *The Eclipse, Or the Courtship of the Sun and Moon*, with Porl in a turban-like headdress and a gold crown and **Simon Gallup** in a wedding veil. Meanwhile **crew** members Bruno Brunning and Binky masquerade as Laurel and Hardy while larking about with a big brass bed, David M. Allen wrangles the props, **Chris Parry** appears as an Indian waiter pushing a snack trolley, pints of lager are spilled everywhere, and everyone is pelted with a beach ball, fake snow and whatever else comes to hand. For one blink-and-you'll miss it moment there's a small flying pig, perhaps a reference to **Pink Floyd**, or perhaps the idea that pigs might fly before The Cure wrote a song as cheerful as this.

The **artwork** by **Parched Art** was a twist on the *Wish* sleeve, with that album's blue disc on a red background transformed into a heart. A coloured vinyl version with a PVC cover was also available. The B-side 'Halo' featured backing vocals from Caroline Crawley of **Shelleyan Orphan**. The 12-inch additionally featured 'Scared As You', with 'Friday I'm In Love (Strangelove Mix)' rounding off the CD.

It was released on 15 May 1992 as the second single from *Wish*. Two of the formats were released on a Friday instead of the customary Monday, meaning that it entered the British charts at a lowly 31. However, it eventually rose to No.6 in the UK, as well as reaching No.18 in the **US**, their second-highest position ever in both countries (behind No.5 hit '**Lullaby**' in the UK, and behind No.2 hit '**Lovesong**' in the US). It would be their final Top 10 hit in the UK, where it was certified platinum, and their final Top 40 hit in the US. It was also a major hit in Ireland and New Zealand.

The first time it was performed live was in Bradford on 21 April 1992, but the first time they actually played it on a Friday was three days later on 24 April at Glasgow Barrowlands. Within a couple of months, the song's success was giving Robert mixed feelings. Introducing the song in Pasadena on 27 June he said 'Some people think we make mistakes with certain songs. We're not sure if this one is or isn't . . .' By November, when they played London Olympia, Robert was audibly bored and tired while singing it.

This is understandable. Of course, nobody held a gun to his head and forced him to write it, so he had nobody else to blame. But once it was out there in the world, its ubiquity became an unstoppable juggernaut. For people who don't particularly know or like The Cure, 'Friday I'm In Love' is *The Cure* song. 'The people who like "Friday I'm In Love" aren't actually fans of The Cure,' Robert told *Musikexpress* in 2000. 'They're not the ones who buy my records.'

To this day, if you hear a Cure song on daytime radio, it's 99% certain that 'Friday I'm In Love' will be what you hear. 'It's always been paradoxical that it's pushed down people's throats that we're a **goth** band,' Smith told *Mojo*'s Keith Cameron. 'Because, to the general public, we're not. To taxi drivers, I'm the bloke that sings "Friday I'm In Love". I'm not the bloke who sings "Shake Dog Shake" or "One Hundred Years".'

It's a song which broadcasters expect them to play. When 'Friday I'm In Love' was absent from their planned setlist for VH1's Hard Rock Live in 1999, *Cure News* reported, it caused an argument with the producers.

Speaking to Fall Out Boy's Pete Wentz in *Entertainment Weekly* in 2006, Robert admitted that he had begun to despise some of The Cure's biggest hits, this one included. 'For a long time, I didn't like certain songs because I thought, "You're to blame, you bastard. You made me popular." "Friday I'm In Love" is a perfect example of that.' (That said, it was a regular encore on the **Lost World Tour** in 2022.)

Its cultural impact continues to resonate. In 2009 it featured on the soundtrack to *He's Just Not That Into You* (see **Films**), and *About Time* in 2013. In 2015 it was **covered** by Yo La Tengo. And on Friday 28 May 2021, The Sofa Singers – a hundreds-strong international choir set up during Covid lockdown to collaborate on a different classic song each week via a Zoom call – turned their attention to The Cure. The song: 'Friday I'm In Love'. The choice made perfect sense, as it ticks two boxes: everybody knows it, and it's easy to sing along to.

Love it or hate it, 'Friday I'm In Love' is still massive. Any day of the week.

Further Adventures Of TeamCure

The Further Adventures Of TeamCure was an official newsletter sent out by the fan club circa 1985, a successor to *The Clinic* and a precursor to *Cure News* (TeamCure being a catch-all term for The Cure and their **crew**). It existed for two instalments under that name, and a further two under a different name, before *Cure News* took over.

Typically printed on two sides of a sheet of A4, the contents consisted of rambling recollections from Robert Smith in lowercase letters with scant punctuation. Issue 1 comprised a tour diary about The Cure's recent visits to **Australasia** and Japan, alluding with classy gentleness to the **Andy Anderson**'s meltdown and departure. The hunt for a new drummer was detailed (resulting in the temporary hiring of **Vince Ely** of The Psychedelic Furs, who was given just one day to rehearse for the upcoming American dates), then *another* hunt for a drummer when Ely left (this time resulting in the longer-term employment of **Boris Williams**, who also had just one day to rehearse). The back page announced the departure of **Phil Thornalley** and the return of **Simon Gallup**, thus neatly tying up the loose ends of the line-up chaos that had afflicted the band over the last year, and reassuring fans who had been following it all in the weekly music press that there was still a Cure to be a fan of.

Sample extract: 'the last 2 weeks of the tour slipped into a very hazy and muddled city . . . we fell down the stairs in buffalo . . . we arrived in washington half an hour after we were due onstage . . . the pa system blew up in boston . . . we went over niagara falls in a barrel . . .'

Issue 2 covered a European tour, detailing further Cure chaos in a similarly amiable style: 'It is in this famous ancient resort [Viareggio] that boris gets very tired and attempts to drown the rest of the group by stealing a boat and driving it into them as they are having a relaxing 3am sea swim. happily he fails and he is keelhauled.'

Robert's ongoing newsletter narrative resumed, at least for two instalments, under the name *Adventures And Plans*.

G

G is for ...

Gabrels, Reeves

Reeves Gabrels did not get his job in The Cure because he's part of the **Crawley-Horley** mafia. Reeves Gabrels did not get his job in The Cure because he looks the part. Reeves Gabrels did not get his job in The Cure because he's a friend of a friend. Reeves Gabrels did not get his job in The Cure because he's a **crew** member's brother. Reeves Gabrels did not get his job in The Cure because he happened to be in the studio at the right time. Reeves Gabrels did not get his job in The Cure because he saw an ad in the press and smashed the audition.

Reeves Gabrels got his job in The Cure because Robert Smith knows excellence when he sees it. He was just what The Cure needed: not so much a musical Swiss Army Knife as Doctor Who's sonic screwdriver.

Both the oldest (born 1956) and newest (joined 2012) member of The Cure, Gabrels grew up in Staten Island, New York in a working-class family. His mother was a typist, his father a deckhand on tugboats. At the age of thirteen he began learning guitar, taught by a friend of his father, Turk Van Lake (who had played with jazz legends Benny Goodman, Buddy Rich and Sarah Vaughan). He studied at the Parsons School of Design and the School of Visual Arts, during which time he took further tuition from John Scofield, a jazz guitarist who had played with Miles Davis, Herbie Hancock and **Bowie** collaborator Pat Metheny. His focus of attention turning away from his art and design studies and towards guitar, Gabrels moved to Boston to study at the Berklee School of Music. In Boston he joined a number of bands, such as The Dark, Life on Earth, The Atom Said, The Bentmen, Modern Farmer (whose bassist David Hull later joined Aerosmith), and Rubber Rodeo (whose producer Ken Scott had previously worked on David Bowie albums like *The Rise And Fall Of Ziggy Stardust And The Spiders From Mars*). Unwittingly, Gabrels was spiralling ever nearer to Bowie's orbit.

Gabrels' first professionally released recording was the single 'Someone Won't Believe It' by the obscure Massachusetts indie act Christopher Jones Band in 1983. His second, third and fourth, with Scouse art-rockers Deaf School, sixties icon Sandie Shaw and little-known rock band Too Happy, followed in 1988. His fifth would have a far higher profile.

Reeves Gabrels first met David Bowie in 1987 when Gabrels' then-wife, Sara Terry, was working as a publicist on Bowie's disastrous Glass Spider Tour. At the end of the tour, Terry gave Bowie a tape of Gabrels playing guitar. Having listened to it, Bowie called Gabrels with an invitation to work together. Bowie admitted that he had 'lost his vision', and was searching for ways to get it back.

They first collaborated in 1988 when Bowie enlisted Gabrels to help with a seven-and-a-half-minute rearrangement of the *Lodger* track 'Look Back in Anger' for a performance incorporating film projections and dance from the avant-garde troupe La La La Human Steps, as part of a benefit for the Institute of Contemporary Arts in London. Bowie praised Gabrels' rearrangement as 'a hard-edged wall of guitar sound'.

In 1998 Gabrels was a founder member of the band Tin Machine, the suit-wearing hard rock band in which Bowie pretended that he wasn't, to quote Ziggy, 'the special man' and was just one of the guys, along with the brothers Tony and Hunt Sales (sons of American comedian Soupy Sales) who had previously worked with Bowie on Iggy Pop's *Lust For Life*. During Tin Machine television appearances, Gabrels played his guitar with a vibrator. The BBC's *Top of the Pops* banned the use of the vibrator, so Gabrels instead mimed with a chocolate eclair.

When Tin Machine disbanded in 1992 after two studio albums and a live album, Gabrels stayed on as a Bowie sideman. With his jazz training, Gabrels brought a highbrow/avant-garde/experimental pedigree with him, and pushed Bowie to re-explore his experimental side. Bowie credited Gabrels with using the powerful phrase 'stop doing it', meaning that Bowie should stop feeling obliged to play the old hits, and to once again function as an artist. Gabrels participated in a creative renaissance from Bowie which included the albums *Black Tie White Noise* (on one song only), *1. Outside*, *Earthling* (on which he played synth as well as guitar) and *'hours . . .'* (on which he added drum programming to his roles). He co-produced the latter two.

During the Bowie years, Gabrels continued to work with other artists. He toured with Free and Bad Company singer Paul Rogers, recorded with The Mission, Alisha's Attic, Public Enemy, Jeffrey Gaines, The Rolling Stones and Natalie Imbruglia (on the **Phil Thornalley**-produced album *Left of the Middle*), and made an album with his old band Modern Farmer.

In 1995 he released his first solo album *The Sacred Squall of Now*, featuring contributions from Nirvana's Dave Grohl, actor Gary Oldman, and Frank Black of Pixies (whose 'Cactus' was covered by Bowie on his first post-Gabrels album *Heathen*), and has released, in total, eight albums in his own right, either under his own name, or with his band Reeves Gabrels and His Imaginary Friends, or in collaboration with David Tronzo or Bill Nelson.

Gabrels quit Bowie's band four days before the *'hours . . .'* tour, leaving the singer frantically scrambling to find a replacement – a predicament to which The Cure, and indeed **Siouxsie And The Banshees**, can relate. (Page Hamilton from the alt-metal band Helmet stepped in.)

Reeves Gabrels first met Robert Smith when Gabrels was the musical director and organiser of Bowie's fiftieth birthday concert in January 1997, at which Smith duetted with Bowie on 'Quicksand' and 'The Last Thing You Should Do'. They kept in touch, and Smith and Gabrels **collaborated** on a song, 'Yesterday's Gone', for Gabrels' solo album *Ulysses (Della Notte)* with Smith on vocals, which wasn't released until 2000. Gabrels' first appearance on a Cure record came later that year when he and Bowie remixer/**producer** Mark Plati were brought over to the UK to work on the single '**Wrong Number**' (a collaboration which later resulted in **Jason Cooper** travelling in the other direction to work with Bowie). Gabrels then appeared as a guest guitarist on several dates on The Cure's US tour that autumn, his first being at the American Legion Hall in Los Angeles on 28 October 1997, playing on '**Close To Me**' and 'Wrong Number'. In Philadelphia on 29 November he joined them for '**Never Enough**', and the following night in Fairfax for several songs, and again in San Jose on 8 December, his last Cure appearance for fifteen years.

In 1998 Smith, Cooper and Gabrels worked together again in the one-off side project **COGASM**, recording the song 'A Sign from God' for the soundtrack to the **film** *Orgazmo*. The time wasn't yet

right, however, for Gabrels to become a member of The Cure. **Perry Bamonte** was well-established as their guitarist, and when Bamonte's first stint came to an end, Cure legend (and Smith's brother-in-law) **Porl Thompson** slotted straight back in.

In his post-Bowie, pre-Cure era, the much-travelled multi-instrumentalist Gabrels continued doing session work (for artists from David Coverdale to Godhead), made an album with heavy metal supergroup X-World/5, worked on the music for the video game *Deus Ex*, and played live with the New York punk band Jeebus. In 2001 he worked with Ozzy Osbourne on a track called 'Black Skies', intended for a video game called *Ozzy's Black Skies* which was shelved due to the 9/11 attacks and later released, minus the Gabrels/Ozzy track, as *Savage Skies*.

In 2012, Gabrels received a phone call from Robert Smith. Porl Thompson had left (again), and The Cure needed a guitarist. Gabrels agreed. With all respect to **Vince Ely** and **Boris Williams**, it was the first time a 'name' musician had joined The Cure with an established reputation and a major body of work behind them. Not since Gerard Houllier headhunted Gary McAllister for Liverpool in 2000 had a major team made such an inspired signing of an old pro.

Gabrels diligently learned The Cure's material, and gave much consideration to which guitars he should use for each song (a decision process he explained in detail on his Facebook page). His first show as a full member of The Cure was at the Netherlands' Pinkpop **festival** on 26 May 2012.

Gabrels' extra-curricular activites have continued during his Cure tenure, including frequently working with improvisational Boston instrumental group Club d'Elf, and contributing to the album *Fistful Of Devils* by fellow Bowie alumnus Earl Slick. (Incidentally, in 2004, Robert Smith had contributed to Slick's album *Zig Zag*.) In 2018 Gabrels married Susan Van Wie Kastan, who is now his business manager.

Though he has yet to appear on a Cure studio recording since 'Wrong Number', he features on the live films and albums *Anniversary* and *Curaetion-25* (packaged together in the *40 Live* box) and only a fool would claim he hasn't made a difference.

With his sensible black shirts and cropped, balding white hair, Reeves Gabrels is an unshowy, unobtrusive figure (the days of vibrators and eclairs are long gone) who doesn't *look* very 'Cure'. But, since his introduction to the band, there has been an unquestionable increase in the expansive enormity of their live sound. You might not notice Gabrels when he's there, but you'd notice him if he wasn't.

And that is why Reeves Gabrels has a job in The Cure.

Gallup, Eden

The first time Eden Gallup was seen on film, he was still a baby, being carried by his father **Simon** in the 1991 documentary *The Cure – Play Out*. Thirty years later, Eden would, metaphorically speaking, carry his father (or, at least, his gear).

Born on 16 March 1990 with Robert Smith as his godfather, Eden almost didn't make it that far: as *Cure News* revealed in 1995, he terrifyingly 'had tubes coming out of him in hospital'. Details of his childhood and wellbeing were relayed to fans on a semi-regular basis in that publication: for example, Simon enjoying taking him to Chessington World of Adventures in 1992, the rather sweet revelation in 1993 that Simon was now doing his drinking in a pub called Charlie Chalk (actually the name of a children's play area attached to Brewers Fayre pubs), and the news that Eden had suffered a serious salmonella scare in 1994. It became common, for a while, for fans to throw teddy bears for Eden onstage at Cure shows. Nobody guessed that Eden Gallup would one day be onstage at Cure shows himself.

His earliest forays into the family trade happened when he was aged just fifteen, forming his first band, Violet Vendetta (a name shared, coincidentally, with a goth wrestler from Staffordshire). This alternative rock/metal four-piece, still extant, opened for The Cure in **Mexico** in 2019, a show which was released as an album, *Live At Foro Sol*. Their debut studio album is expected in 2023. Eden also has an experimental noise side project called Serpent Ride, which released the album *Invaders* in 2018.

By the 2010s he was technically proficient enough to be drafted into The Cure's **crew** as his father's bass tech. And, on two occasions in 2019, he stepped up to actually play bass for them. His first show as substitute bassist was in Japan on 28 July, making him the second Cure crew member (after **Perry Bamonte**) to make the transition to playing with the band.

The substitution was not announced beforehand, but a tweet from The Cure's official account that night explained: 'A serious personal situation affecting our bassist Simon arose after the Paleo Festival show

on Thursday, and as a consequence Simon was unable to travel with us to Japan. Very reluctant to disappoint our wonderful Japanese fans, and after much discussion, we decided to go ahead with our Fuji Festival headline on Sunday with a very brave and very excellent Eden Gallup filling on bass. We are all very grateful to Ed for reaching out across the generational divide to help us out, and join him in welcoming his dad back for our seven remaining summer festival shows.'

Footage from Fuji shows him playing '**A Forest**' in his dad's customary low-slung style, in front of his 'BADWOLF' amp, with utmost confidence. In a post-gig interview for Japanese television, Robert was full of praise for him. Later that year, on 12 October at the Austin City Limits festival in Texas, Eden gave another assured auxiliary performance, the band once again citing a 'serious personal situation' as the cause of Simon's absence.

Since then, in addition to his own musical endeavours, Eden has continued teching for his father, working in The Cure's backline crew throughout the **Lost World Tour**. And if they ever need a ready-made substitute as a moment's notice, they now know they can simply reach out across the generational divide, and he'll be there.

Gallup, Ric

The Cool Older Brother is such an established trope in popular culture that it's almost a cliché: the wise senior sibling who's been there, done that, and can mentor and educate the young upstarts with a few steers in the right direction and a few loaned LPs. Robert Smith had 'The Guru', and **Simon Gallup** had Ric.

Born on 11 October 1953, seven years before his bass-playing brother, Richard 'Ric' Gallup played an almost incalculable role in the formation and development of The Cure.

On Saturdays circa 1976 Ric worked in a record shop – where else does a Cool Older Brother work? – within the **Horley** branch of Radio Rentals, where Robert Smith and assorted other members of the various **pre-Cure** formations would hang around. It was via Ric and that record department that Smith properly met Simon Gallup, who he sort-of knew from the pub. Ric would bring hip, obscure, culty records down from London to gently indoctrinate the younger generation into the ways of prog, Krautrock and jazz (his eclectic tastes including Nick Drake, Faust, Captain Beefheart, Scott Walker, Chet Baker and Hawkwind – music for 'heads', essentially).

One afternoon, Ric saw The Cure (in their Smith, **Dempsey**, **Tolhurst** incarnation) skulking around looking disconsolate after their failed dalliance with **Hansa**, and – according to Lol in *Cured* – said 'I'll give you £50 if you go and make a demo'. The trio gladly took the bribe to get out from under his feet, and on 27 May 1978 went to Chestnut Studios in Haslemere to record an eight-track demo (which cost just under £50, allowing a little spare for beer money), featuring '**Boys Don't Cry**', 'It's Not You', '**10.15 Saturday Night**' and 'Fire in Cairo'.

At this point Lol Tolhurst was a trainee chemist and Michael Dempsey was working as 'a porter in a lunatic asylum' (as he put it on *Curious Creatures*), and there was a sense that these demos were a final roll of the dice. Robert sent the tapes, with a tea bag and a digestive biscuit, to all the major labels he could think of. They all came back accompanied by rejection letters, except the one, **Chris Parry** from Polydor, who was about to launch his own **Fiction** label and wanted to meet them. With the help of those Ric Gallup-funded demos, The Cure's career was about to properly begin. It isn't too much of an exaggeration to say 'No Ric Gallup, no Cure'.

Ric's involvement with The Cure didn't end there. When **Porl Thompson** left the Easy Cure, Ric took over the design of The Cure's gig posters. He was also closely involved with many other Cure-related bands in the **Crawley** area. He designed **artwork** for Simon's bands **Lockjaw** and **Mag/Spys**, and co-founded (with Robert) the **Dance Fools Dance** label, which released a Mag/Spys single (split with **The Obtainers**) on which Ric produced the Mag/Spys' tracks. Ric also later designed promotional materials for **Fools Dance**, Simon's band during his spell away from The Cure, and took charge of the lighting at their gigs. His tentacles are everywhere in Cure-world.

He is also directly responsible for the ultimate elusive Cure item, *Carnage Visors* (the animated film, with an instrumental soundtrack by The Cure, that the band took on tour in 1981 rather than having a support act).

From the mid-1980s onwards, Ric became the regular lighting designer for Cure affiliates **And Also The Trees**. He was also something of a technical wizard: he once built a homemade synthesiser for his friends' band, The Escalators. Nowadays a

photographer and filmmaker, he has a uniquely florid way of expressing his frustration with the idiocy of humanity on social media, one typical Facebook pronouncement being 'Grunt forth in ignorance, I'll not swallow your corporate semen'.

Gallup, Simon

Simon Jonathon Gallup, The Cure's low-slung bass hero, resident **sex** god, second-longest serving member and for many years the owner of the greatest **hair** in **goth**, was born on 1 June 1960 in Duxhurst, Surrey. He grew up in **Horley**, where he studied at Horley Infants and Junior schools and Balcombe Road Comprehensive, leaving with no qualifications and taking a job as a plastics mould dipper in nearby Smallfield, 'near Hell'. In a tour programme for **Fools Dance**, the band with whom he played in between his first and second stints in The Cure, he had this to say about his early life:

> Most people born in this year [1960] suffer from the same faults, having to grow up in some of the most poignant times in youth culture. Too young to be a hippy, too old to be affiliated with Punk Rock led to a generation of children playing AC/DC records with a mixture of Van Der Graaf Generator, Kiss and Alex Harvey.

The first record Simon Gallup ever owned was a cover of the *Batman* theme. (Gothic mood, killer bassline – it figures.) Genesis in 1973, however, was the best show he's ever seen.

At Balcombe Road, his favourite subject was Environmental Science. He didn't know the members of **pre-Cure** bands Malice or Easy Cure from school – they went to a different one – but he did know them from around town. He first met Robert Smith in 1976 in the Crawley branch of Radio Rental, where Simon's older brother **Ric Gallup** ran the record department, he knew **Lol Tolhurst** because Lol's girlfriend Sarah was at Balcombe Road, he knew **Porl Thompson** because he was dating Porl's sister Carol, and they all just generally knew each other 'from the pub'. In *Ten Imaginary Years* Gallup summarised his life in his late teens as working in a factory from 7.30–5.30, playing bass for a couple of hours, spending the rest of the evening with Carol, and ending each week 'down the pub with my 18 quid'.

That bass-playing was, at first, with punk band

Lockjaw, who were managed by Simon's other brother David, with Ric designing the artwork. Lockjaw gigged with Easy Cure on more than one occasion, and Robert and Simon became friends. The pair would ask DJs to play 'Night Fever' by the Bee Gees so they could disco dance together while Lockjaw's punk followers pogoed about.

When that band fizzled out after two singles, Simon went on to form the **Mag/Spys** (aka Magspies or Magazine Spies), managed by Ric, who also gigged with Easy Cure/The Cure. The Mag/Spys recorded at **Morgan Studios** in downtime during The Cure's preliminary sessions for *Seventeen Seconds*, for a split single with **The Obtainers** on Robert and Ric's label **Dance Fools Dance**. At the same time in the same studio, the **Cult Hero** single 'I'm A Cult Hero' was being made, with Simon Gallup moonlighting on bass. By the time either the Mag/Spys single or the Cult Hero single were released, however, Simon Gallup was already a member of The Cure, headhunted from the Mag/Spys along with keyboardist **Matthieu Hartley**.

In the background to this was the fact that relations between Smith and Cure bassist **Michael Dempsey** had become frosty, with Dempsey unimpressed by Smith's demos for *Seventeen Seconds*. Smith suspected that Gallup would be more fun to work with and, unbeknownst to Simon, the Cult Hero session was a tryout. His first gig as Cure bassist was on 16 November 1979 at Eric's in Liverpool, the opening night of **Fiction Records**' Future Pastimes tour. When the final sessions for *Seventeen Seconds* were held in January 1980, Gallup was fully integrated.

His musical impact was immediate: his bassline on '**A Forest**', the solitary single from *Seventeen Seconds*, is one of The Cure's immediately recognisable moments. '**Primary**', the lead single from third album *Faith*, was entirely built on the duelling basses of Smith and Gallup and Tolhurst's drumming (Matthieu Hartley having been edged out), and Gallup's contributions to 'The Holy Hour', 'Other Voices', 'The Drowning Man' and the title track were exceptional. The dark, brooding sound of their fourth album, *Pornography*, relied hugely on Gallup's contributions.

However, **touring** life with The Cure was difficult. Long periods of the Picture Tour (for the *Faith* album) were spent in uncomfortable silence, and by the time of the **Fourteen Explicit Moments** tour of 1982 (for *Pornography*), tensions were becoming unbearable.

The emotional intensity of the material, combined with an unusually hot early summer, shredded the nerves of Smith, Gallup and Tolhurst. 'Unfortunately,' Simon later recalled, 'Robert and I took it out on each other.' Rather than back away and allow each other space, they resorted to deliberate provocation. 'What had really been a jovial experience,' Simon remembered, 'became an aggressive one and there was a real viciousness, real vindictiveness in some of the practical jokes that were being played.' The effect of this on the live show is disputed, even by Robert himself: 'We couldn't bear each other any more but it made us good on stage,' he once said, but he has also asserted that 'People hated those concerts . . . even most Cure fans.'

What's certain is that it all exploded into **violence** on 27 May 1982 in Strasbourg with a fistfight between Gallup and Smith in a bar, causing both men to fly home. The tour did resume a few days later, but Gallup travelled separately with the road **crew**. The final show in Brussels on 11 June 1982 ended with an onstage meltdown, and Gallup didn't see The Cure for another eighteen months. 'The pressures of having to keep up the intensity and aggressive sentiments of *Pornography* turned Simon into someone different,' Lol Tolhurst stated in *Ten Imaginary Years*, 'though, at the time, I don't think he noticed. Or didn't want to . . .'

Back in the UK, after a short break, Robert and Lol carried on recording without Simon. Simon, meanwhile, was living at Fiction because he'd temporarily split up with Carol. He only found out he wasn't in The Cure when a **fan** rang up asking which studio Robert and Lol were in. There had been no communication from Robert to discuss the matter. It was assumed, from Smith's side, that the split was obvious. 'It would have been a pointless call,' Robert later recalled, 'because I had no intention of playing again at all. I was just fed up and, effectively, at that point, The Cure had stopped.'

When the new-look Cure began having hits, Simon felt 'bitter and sour' and thought 'That should be me' when he saw them on *Top of the Pops*. 'On the outside,' as Robert remembered it, 'people were saying "That horrible Robert Smith has chucked out Matthieu after Michael, and now the bastard has thrown out his best friend."'

Meanwhile, Gallup considered his options. At one point he was offered a job as a roof tiler, but he declined. 'I'm scared of heights,' he later said, 'and I don't like getting up.' Instead, he formed another band with Matthieu Hartley and former Cure crew member **Gary Biddles**, originally called Cry and then Fools Dance. In a Fools Dance tour programme, Gallup reflected on the catastrophic tour which led to his leaving The Cure. Gallup had one further prank to play on the main man. He posted a copy of 'I'm A Moody Guy' by Shane Fenton (later known as Alvin Stardust) through Robert's door, snapped in half so he couldn't play it. (Robert, perhaps making an in-joke, later named it as his favourite record of all time.)

However, at the end of **Phil Thornalley**'s stint, The Cure were again short of a bassist. Gary Biddles generously brokered a pub meet-up between Smith and Gallup (even though it effectively meant the end for Fools Dance). As Smith told *The Face* shortly afterwards, 'After about 18 months of not seeing him, I thought "This is silly, I can't not like him any more", so one night I went to this pub where we all used to drink and I knew he'd be there. It was quite funny, cos when I walked in, it all went quiet, just like a Wild West film, but I just walked up to him and started talking to him.'

Robert invited Simon to play on demos of some new songs The Cure were recording at F2 Studios in London, and he was back in the fold, playing his first gig back in the band on 20 June 1985 at Barcelona's Studio 54. Those new songs became *The Head On The Door*, and Simon's bassline on that album's second single '**Close To Me**' was, if anything, even more iconic than that of 'A Forest'.

Simon Gallup's contribution to The Cure was visual as well as musical. Simon had the most immaculate gothic hairstyle, and he had it before Robert (as proven by photos of The Cry playing The Rock Garden in 1983). Gallup was very particular about his **image**, and unwilling to compromise his look in the face of hot weather: in an **Andy Vella** photoshoot on Copacabana beach from March 1987 (average temperature: 30 degrees), Robert is in a sensible and climate-appropriate T-shirt but Simon is defiantly wearing a long black coat. He looked impossibly cool onstage: as Michael Dempsey once put it, 'He was very much the new wave bass player who could play his bass at pelvic level. I could never do that . . .' And if Gallup didn't say much in public – he once sat alongside Robert for an entire *Rápido* interview in 1989 without uttering a word – it was because he didn't need to: he silently radiated sexiness, becoming the ultimate goth pin-up, eclipsing even his own lead singer. As Robert once told *Record Mirror*, 'My idea of hunkiness is Simon.'

But his musical contribution *is* immense. As much as **New Order**'s Peter Hook or PiL's Jah Wobble, Simon Gallup must be credited as someone who pioneered the use of the bass as a lead instrument within alternative rock in the post-punk era, and is arguably the most successful exponent of that style. On some Cure songs, like '**Fascination Street**' as well as the aforementioned 'A Forest' and 'Close To Me', Gallup's bass is the star. He is also a significant contributor to The Cure's **songwriting**: as Robert confirmed on Swiss TV in 2002, '75% of the music is me, 25% Simon or sometimes someone else.'

One night, during the recording of *Kiss Me, Kiss Me, Kiss Me*, Robert's fiancée **Mary** ripped up some paper and threw it over Simon and Carol like confetti, and predicted 'You are going to get married, aren't you?' They were. Simon and Robert talked about having a double wedding, but **religious** complications – Robert and Mary being Catholic, Simon and Carol not – precluded it. 'But it just meant two parties instead . . .' Robert was Simon's best man, Simon was Robert's best man. Guests at Simon's wedding included Bananarama, whom he had met when they both appeared on the same **TV** show in the Netherlands, and with whom he had sometimes partied at the Wag Club.

Simon and Carol had two children together, Eden (born 1990) and Lily (born 1992). **Eden Gallup** is now a member of The Cure's crew as well as a musician in his own right, and Lily Gallup is a photographer living in Los Angeles. Simon and Carol later divorced, and in 1997 Simon married his second wife Sarah, with whom he has two further children, Evangeline 'Evie' Gallup (born 2000) and Ismay Gallup (born 2007).

In the 1990s and 2000s, Gallup lived just outside Crowborough, a low-key celebrity hotspot in East Sussex on the edge of the Ashdown Forest of *Winnie the Pooh* fame, a town also home to the likes of David Jason, Cate Blanchett and Tom Baker. (He once named his favourite pubs as the Coopers Arms in Crowborough and the Anchor Inn in Hartfield.) He has since relocated to Andover in Hampshire.

Thanks to questionnaires in *Cure News*, we are privy to a wealth of disparate information about the sometimes-taciturn bassist. He is 5ft 11ins tall, and has brown eyes. He has 'a short fuse', and at one point took up meditation. (These two facts may not be unconnected.) He supports Reading FC (who, coincidentally, play in the same colours as Robert Smith's beloved **Queens Park Rangers**), was once a season ticket holder, and has often draped a Reading flag over his bass amp. He got his first tattoo – a heart with a dagger through it – in New Zealand and has never looked back. His **alcoholic** drinks of choice are Guinness, Jameson's, vodka & grapefruit, and lager. His favourite food includes cheese and tomato rolls and goulash. His favourite films include *Peter Pan*, *Irma la Douce*, *Star Wars*, *Willy Wonka*, *A Streetcar Named Desire* and *Excalibur*, and his favourite actors include Vivien Leigh and Jacqueline Bucknell. His taste in **literature** includes *Something Wicked This Way Comes* by Ray Bradbury and *Wuthering Heights* by Emily Brontë, his favourite author, after whom he once named one of his dogs. He is also a fan of Alan Moore's comics *V for Vendetta* and *Swamp Thing*. His favourite bands and musicians include New Order, John Martyn, The Clash, The Chieftains and Kate Bush, whose 'Cloudbusting' he once named as his favourite music video. He has a taste for metal and hard rock acts like Iron Maiden, Thin Lizzy and Rush, and has also spoken highly at various times of The Sisters Of Mercy, Chumbawamba, Ride, My Bloody Valentine and Slowdive. He rarely **collaborates** outside of The Cure, but has worked with LA alt-rockers Beauty in Chaos and singer-songwriter Evi Vine. He takes an interest in military aviation, even though he hates flying, and has a RAF roundel tattoo. He has been horse riding and learned mandolin. His favourite scent is patchouli. He currently has a black pug called Bear.

His main obsession outside of The Cure is cycling. He likes to ride on the South Downs and the Ridgeway (an ancient track considered Britain's oldest road, which in its current form runs from Overton Hill in Wiltshire to Ivinghoe Beacon in Buckinghamshire). He has cycled Sommet Mont Ventoux (one of the most gruelling stages of the Tour de France). He rode the London–Brighton bike race in 1993, and has taken part in **charity** fundraising rides. He once cracked a rib falling off his bike in March 1997 and was absent for a few Cure engagements. Bikes he has owned include the Kona Explosif and the Brooks B17, and he currently rides an Orange. (*The Cure on Orange* joke writes itself.)

A paragraph for the gear geeks . . .

For most of his career, Simon Gallup's bass of choice has been a Gibson Thunderbird IV. However, he has also had basses specially made by Dick Knight, and has used a six-string Fender Bass VI for The Cure's more melodic requirements. He has also played a Fender Precision, a Fender Jazz,

a Rickenbacker 4001, a Music Man StingRay, a Washburn AB10 acoustic, a Kramer acoustic, an Epiphone Jack Casady and an Eccleshall 335. His collection of Boss pedals comprises the BF-2 Flanger, the CE-5 Chorus Ensemble, the MT-2 Distortion, the DD-3 Digital Delay and the NS-2 Noise Suppressor. In 2004 Gibson designed a special red Thunderbird bass to celebrate twenty-five years since Simon (first) joined The Cure. And in 2011 Schecter released a Simon Gallup signature model, based on their Ultra Spitfire bass, personalised in black and red with the number '1979', an image of Simon's heart-and-dagger tattoo, a red rose, and a picture of a Spitfire fighter plane.

Since rejoining The Cure for the first time in 1985, Gallup has taken a number of breaks, some of them enforced, some of them not. In November 1992, on the *Wish* tour, he fell ill after several months of suffering from pleurisy, and was hospitalised. He missed twelve dates while **Roberto Soave** stood in.

What's less well publicised is the fact that he also left the band for two months in May and June 1995, when the band were working on *Wild Mood Swings*. 'I'd been drinking too much,' he later explained, and was weighing up the competing responsibilities of the group and his young family, concluding that 'I can't do both anymore.' After two months, Robert phoned him up as a friend, to see how he was, not just to ask him back in the group. But he *was* back in the group.

Then, in July 2019, Gallup missed the Fuji Rock Festival in Japan due, it was announced on Twitter, to 'a serious personal situation'. This time, Eden Gallup stood in. Later that year, at Austin City Limits in October, The Cure tweeted that 'another serious personal situation affecting our bassist Simon arose yesterday, and as a consequence, he had to return to the UK.' Again, Eden stepped in.

The most worrying case, for Cure fans, came on 15 August 2021 when Gallup publicly announced on Facebook that 'With a slightly heavy heart I am no longer a member of The Cure! Good luck to them all . . .' Underneath, he explained, somewhat cryptically, that he was 'fed up of all the betrayal'. This out-of-the-blue resignation stunned fans, causing outbreaks of mourning for what looked like the end of the band. However, two months later, the matter seemed to have been quietly resolved. On 15 October, responding to a fan's query about whether he was in The Cure, he tweeted 'Yes I am.'

If you look at the bare facts, Simon Gallup has been in and out of The Cure like a sewing machine needle.

But it's long been the case that without Simon, it just wouldn't be the same. Simon is 'the heart of the live band,' Robert told *NME* in 2019. 'He's always been my best friend . . . It's weird that over the years and the decades he's often been overlooked . . . And yet he's absolutely vital to what we do.'

And if Simon Gallup really left, as Robert Smith told the *Guardian* in 2018, then 'it wouldn't be called The Cure.'

Galore

Galore – The Singles 1987–1997 is The Cure compilation nobody – neither the band nor the public – really wanted. Picking up where *Standing On A Beach* left off, it's a fairly strong album on paper, being a straightforward collection of the singles from *Kiss Me, Kiss Me, Kiss Me*, *Disintegration*, *Mixed Up* and *Wild Mood Swings* in chronological order, including such mega-hits as '**Lullaby**', '**Lovesong**' and '**Friday I'm In Love**', mostly in their single remix or radio edit forms. However, it landed at a moment when interest in The Cure was at an all-time low, not least among The Cure themselves.

The rather ugly **artwork** was a Perou photograph of a baby eating an ice cream on a beach. Robert Smith later told *Cure News* the child was 'an "agency" baby – I picked it out of a catalogue – weird!' One might interpret it as a conceptual nod from designer **Andy Vella** to the old man on the sleeve of *Standing On A Beach*, as if he has de-aged to infancy, Benjamin Button-style.

Released on 28 October 1997, it reached No.31 in America (where it eventually sold half a million and was certified gold), No.37 in the UK, and didn't break into the Top 30 anywhere else. Its sales were only a quarter of those of *Standing On A Beach*.

Speaking on Swiss television in 2002, Smith revealed he had considered **splitting** the band up after *Galore* (a statement to be taken with a pinch of salt, as he's been threatening to split up The Cure for almost as long as there's been a Cure). In an interview with *X-Press*, he revealed the full extent of his disillusionment. 'Bringing *Galore* out, though, was a pretty pragmatic decision. My heart wasn't in it when we did *Galore*. I got disenchanted really because the record company wanted a **Greatest Hits** and I wanted *Standing On A Beach* Part 2, a documented CD of 'These are the last ten years of singles by this band'.

I would never claim it to be a Greatest Hits or Best Of or anything. They quickly saw that this wasn't the big TV-advertised Cure album they were hoping for, and they just pushed it out very gently. So I think with that whole year I got into a bit of a strop really, with The Cure and all it stood for. It wasn't going in the right direction for me.'

In historical terms, *Galore* is of interest chiefly for its one new song, '**Wrong Number**', which marked the debut of **Reeves Gabrels** on a Cure recording. Other than that, let's pretend it never happened. Nothing to see here, move along.

Geffen

Geffen is a record **label** founded in 1980 by music industry executive David Geffen, formerly the founder of Asylum Records and later a Warner Bros film executive, initially as a subsidiary of Warner Records before being acquired first by MCA and then Universal. Its first two releases were Donna Summer's *The Wanderer* and John Lennon's *Double Fantasy*. It then went on to become one of the major players in 1980s and 1990s rock and pop, particularly in the **US**. All of **Siouxsie And The Banshees**' releases during the Robert Smith era were on Geffen in the States, as were The Cure albums *The Cure* and *4:13 Dream* (via its subsidiary alternative imprint Suretone). The Cure had a brief falling-out with Geffen over the overpricing of the *Hypnagogic States* EP on iTunes, before the label acceded to Robert's request to lower the price. He also held them responsible for the band's failure to release the proposed *4:14 Scream* as their **fourteenth album**.

Geffen is now more of a puppet label than a stand-alone company. David Geffen, meanwhile, has been named as both the owner of the most valuable art collection in the world and, by not-for-profit website The Conversation, one of the most polluting individuals in the world, second only to Roman Abramovich, due to his fondness for luxury super-yachts (one of which he bought from Abramovich). Super-yachts have been the target of campaigns by Greenpeace, one of The Cure's favourite **charities**. There is something pleasing about the idea that by putting out music by The Cure, Geffen has been inadvertently funding the very people who would like him to quit his yacht habit.

Generation X

Generation X were a second-wave punk band formed in London by Bromley Contingent member Billy Idol (later to become a peroxide Presley for the MTV generation) and Tony James (later of Sigue Sigue Sputnik and The Sisters of Mercy). By late 1978 they'd already scored a Top 30 album and two minor hits with 'Your Generation' and 'Ready Steady Go' and appeared twice on the BBC's *Top of the Pops*, who viewed them as the acceptable face of punk (the punk band who weren't going to smash up the dressing room), and were just about to drop their biggest single 'King Rocker'. They were rising stars, and the lucky support band riding their coat-tails on their November and December **tour** of the UK were The Cure, making their first foray outside London and their Surrey/Sussex home patch.

The tour was run on a tight budget, with The Cure driving back to sleep on the floor of **Chris Parry**'s house near Watford most nights to save cash. On the opening night in High Wycombe, the Generation X road manager tried to charge The Cure for using the PA and lights. They refused, and instead used their own Yamaha A40 speakers which they'd previously used for pub gigs, with Robert operating a H/H mixing console onstage to get the right levels (using a friend in the audience to signal 'up' or 'down') and, in a delicious throw-forward to the *Three Imaginary Boys* artwork, two standard lamps for lighting. Rather than infuriate the Generation X crew, it impressed them. The sound engineer Nigel and lighting guy Mac let them use the real gear for free the following night, and Mac would later defect and join The Cure's **crew** full time.

A particularly eventful show, according to *Ten Imaginary Years*, was at Halesowen Tiffany's on 30 November. (This date is not verified anywhere else, so the anecdote is of debatable accuracy.) Allegedly, the band were attacked by skinheads at the gig. Then, while staying in a hotel for the first time because **Polydor**'s top brass had come along, they overdid the record company's bar tab and **Lol Tolhurst** ended up vomiting all over the floor and walls of the room he was sharing with Robert, which Robert found 'really humiliating'.

The more well-documented incident, however, happened on 3 December in Bristol when, in an incident recounted in full in the entry **'Pissing'**, Tolhurst urinated on Generation X's lead singer. After one further date at Dunstable California Ballroom on 5 December The Cure were kicked off the tour, having played just seven shows, and Generation X completed their nine remaining dates of 1978 without them.

There may have been some in the audience for that initial run of seven shows who thought The Cure pissed all over Generation X. They had no idea how right they were.

Glasgow, Live in

Glasgow Barrowland is said – at least by Glaswegians – to be the greatest venue in the world. This 1930s ballroom in the strongly Catholic East End of Glasgow (rebuilt in 1958 after the original 1934 building was destroyed in a fire) is famed for its curved, cross-hatched blue and cream ceiling, its bouncing sprung dancefloor of Canadian maple, its iconic neon fresco of shooting stars, and above all, the roar of the crowd. (In 2023 *The Barrowland Roar* was the name of a BBC Scotland documentary about the venue.)

It was notorious for gang fights as much as music. It became part of a particularly bleak period of local history when a serial killer known as Bible John, who recited Old Testament scripture to his victims, targeted three women who had all been for nights out at Barrowland. It has featured in countless works of fiction, on screen and page, adding to its mythology. Almost every major touring act passed through its 1,950-capacity hall at some point, including Robert Smith's hero **David Bowie**. It is fabled as the sort of place where if you put in a good performance the audience will give you a raucous response, but if you don't, they'll let you know about it.

The Cure's first trial by fire at Barrowland was on 25 August 1984 (having already performed at the Glasgow Apollo earlier in the year), and they passed the test, with bodies pinging about in the moshpit like molecules in Brownian motion. We know this because the BBC was there to capture it.

Barrowland was often the location for filmed shows (The Smiths, for example, were filmed there for Channel 4's *The Tube*), and The Cure's show was a special BBC promotion, with tickets that read 'BBC TV presents'. Despite being an English band, The Cure were a good fit for Glasgow and Glasgow was a good fit for them. They'd already visited the city earlier that year to play the Apollo, and their popularity in Scotland is disproportionately high. (A Scottish singles chart exists, separate from the UK chart, and The Cure's placings are invariably higher.)

The gig went out live as part of a *Rock Around the Clock* all-dayer of concerts and documentaries on BBC 2, curated by the makers of the *Old Grey Whistle Test*. (Earlier in the day, The Cure's rivals/fellow travellers **New Order** had played live from London.) In that week's *Radio Times*, The Cure's show was listed 'Robert Smith and his exciting band bring their musical menagerie including '**The Lovecats**' and '**The Caterpillar**' to Glasgow's Barrowland Ballroom for a live concert.'

In the event, 'The Lovecats' was not played by Robert Smith's exciting band, but it was an otherwise hit-packed show which included '**Primary**', '**The Walk**', '**The Hanging Garden**', '**One Hundred Years**', '**A Forest**', '**The Caterpillar**' and '**10.15 Saturday Night**'. After only an hour, which in Cure terms is barely a warm-up, it was over. But warmed up they certainly were, with Robert in a smart grey suit and buttoned-up white shirt that made him sweat under the lights. Fourteen songs were played in all, the last of which, 'Forever', was not broadcast, the credits having rolled during '**Killing An Arab**'.

It is of historical interest because, for most British viewers, this was the first taste of a Cure concert on free-to-air **television**. It also had international reach, reshown in other territories including Japan. *The Cure Live in Glasgow* was later put out as an unofficial bootleg DVD, bundled together with the songs from the Paris Théâtre De L'Empire show from 1979, but as it's easily available on YouTube, there's no reason for buying it.

Glastonbury

The Glastonbury Festival is accorded a special place in the British cultural firmament. Founded by Somerset farmer Michael Eavis, and co-organised latterly by his daughter Emily, the original Pop, Blues & Folk Festival at Worthy Farm, Pilton in 1970 was headlined by Tyrannosaurus Rex and attended by just 1,500 people. It has since swollen from its origins in the hippie underground to an annual (except for occasional years when the fields lie fallow) extravaganza which now attracts approximately 200,000 people (roughly the same as the entire population of Portsmouth, Rennes, Pamplona, Rostock, Padua or Salt Lake City). It covers all genres of music (except metal), and also encompasses many other performing arts. It has raised money for charities and political causes such as CND, Greenpeace, Oxfam and Water Aid.

Two developments in the 1990s changed the nature of the festival: the erection of a sturdier perimeter fence in 1992 (followed by a 'superfence' in 2002) to keep out New Age travellers who had become accustomed to getting in for free, and the arrival in 1997 of sponsorship from the *Guardian* and extensive **television** coverage by the BBC. Glastonbury has since become a more middle-class, family-friendly affair, though it does retain some of its countercultural flavour. Although there are dozens of other large music **festivals** every year in the UK, none of them receive as much publicity or commentary as Glastonbury.

If it sometimes feels as if Glastonbury has been officially decreed 'Britain's festival', then it also sometimes feels as if The Cure are 'Glastonbury's band'. The Cure aren't the artists with the most Glastonbury appearances. They're behind Van Morrison (8), Elvis Costello (6) and Primal Scream (5), and are tied in fourth place with Coldplay and Lily Allen. However, as headliners they are unbeaten – only Coldplay, with four headlining appearances, are their equal (and one of Coldplay's four was unplanned, as replacements for The Strokes).

By the time The Cure made their first appearance in 1986, there had already been a changing of the guard: the hippies were stepping aside and a new generation was moving in (headliners in 1984 were The Smiths, and in 1985 Echo & The Bunnymen.) On the day of their show, the band's tour bus arrived during a rainstorm to a swamp-like site, populated by a crowd of 75,000 caked in mud. The Cure's love of football (see **Queens Park Rangers**) meant that they delayed going onstage in order to watch France v Brazil in the World Cup quarter final which went to extra time and penalties. When they finally stepped out onto the Pyramid Stage, walking on to the sound of 'Relax' by **The Glove**, the rain stopped, and their light show – augmented by an electrical storm – cast green rays on the remaining drips of water. The Cure's set, broadcast live on BBC radio, is remembered as one of their iconic shows. Although most of their pop hits to date (apart from '**The Lovecats**') were dotted through the setlist, the third and final encore – the title tracks of *Faith* and *Pornography* – was an uncompromising one.

Their next appearance, in 1990, was memorable

for all the wrong reasons. For a start, they took the stage in broad daylight, there being no overrunning World Cup match to use as a pretext for tardiness (Cameroon's famous 2–1 victory over Colombia was all wrapped up by 8.30 p.m.). 'It's a shame,' Robert later told MTV. '[Daylight] makes the set a lot more laid back . . . We're a lot more aware of how hideous we look. We tend to keep our heads down more.' The show had barely begun when a girl at the front, where there were no crush barriers, collapsed and had to be given the kiss of life. The incident 'shocked us a bit too much to really get into the set', Robert told *Cure News*. A helicopter landed during 'Shake Dog Shake' to take the girl away, and a member of festival staff attempted to warn Robert to stop playing, but he didn't understand the message. 'It was very weird,' he told Swiss television in 2002. 'I thought I was imagining the whole thing.' He described that year's festival as 'badly organised – I thought "what am I doing here?"'

In the aftermath, Robert felt certain that The Cure would never play Glastonbury again. Five years later, however, they did. The Cure were Sunday night headliners, with most of their set broadcast on BBC Radio 1 and highlights shown on Channel 4. Prior to their set, Robert watched and loved Supergrass, and took the time to see **Porl Thompson** (who had left The Cure the previous year) perform with Page and Plant. Porl then joined The Cure for the final song, 'End'.

The 1986, 1990 and 1995 sets were all pressed up on vinyl (the first two) and CD (the third) for internal BBC use (see *In Concert*), and eleven songs from 1995 were also sent to the **US** for radio broadcast on a set of CDs which also included Veruca Salt and Simple Minds, copies of which sell for around £88.

Following a twenty-four-year gap, The Cure returned to Glastonbury in 2019. After closing a relatively sombre main set with 'Disintegration', Robert told the crowd he needed to exit the stage for a couple of minutes 'to get my pop head on', then delivered a mercilessly poptastic, hit-packed encore of **'Lullaby'**, **'The Caterpillar'**, **'The Walk'**, **'Friday I'm In Love'**, **'Close To Me'**, **'Why Can't I Be You?'** and **'Boys Don't Cry'**. They'd come a long way since the bleak *Faith/Pornography* finale of 1986.

When a band absolutely owns the Pyramid Stage like that, it isn't so much a case of The Cure being Glastonbury's band. It's Glastonbury being The Cure's festival.

Glove, The

They'd been talking about it for years.

Robert Smith and his closest friend outside The Cure, **Steve Severin** of Siouxsie And The Banshees, first discussed a **collaboration** during the *Faith* sessions. Long before Smith became a fully-fledged Banshee himself, while both bands were forging their separate paths, some sort of Smith–Severin project looked increasingly likely. There was such a similarity between the way they used melodies and structures, Severin later told *Melody Maker*, that it was 'inevitable' that they would one day work together.

In mid-1982, said Severin in the *Out of the Woods* **documentary**, Smith began turning up at his house laden with various bottles of **alcohol**, and would make cocktails while they watched videos. Their first collaboration came soon afterwards, in the form of an early version of The Cure's 'Lament', given away free as a flexidisc with *Flexipop!* in September 1982. As this was made by Smith, Severin and no one else, it was a Glove track in all but name, though credited to The Cure.

Though The Glove were mainly active during **1983, Robert's craziest year**, they actually made their first recordings in November 1982, on an early version of **'Punish Me With Kisses'**. In a similar manner to the way Duran Duran fractured into two factions, Arcadia and The Power Station, in 1985, the Banshees spent much of 1983 divided into The Creatures and The Glove. (The difference being that, unlike Duran, the Banshees kept going throughout, as did The Cure.) They'd written 'Punish Me With Kisses' while the Banshees were recording their album *A Kiss In The Dreamhouse*. 'We just wrote a song together at that time,' Severin told *No.1* later. 'It's not as if we're some sort of reaction to The Creatures.'

The name The Glove was a nod to The Beatles' acid-infused cartoon film *Yellow Submarine*, a favourite of Smith and Severin, in which prime antagonist the Blue Meanie sends out the Dreadful Flying Glove as his executioner. A fitting name, as that sort of **drugs**-drenched sixties psychedelia, along with what Severin later called 'that kind of Britishness epitomised by the Avengers and Dirk Bogarde in Modesty Blaise', was intrinsic to The Glove aesthetic.

In Mark Paytress' official Banshees biography, Severin recalled that Smith was doing 'a lot of chemicals' at the time, from LSD to opium, and found it enhanced his creativity. Smith also said that acid made him feel 'very connected' to Severin.

'We'd walk round London, and when you're taking acid with someone you really like, it's really funny. It was a very upbeat time and it got rid of all the bad stuff that happened while I was making *Pornography*. It was liberating not having to conform to the same thought patterns. You think, "Fuck me, I can think and act in different ways."'

There were two key elements fuelling The Glove: drugs and horror, mixed together into a heady cocktail of inspiration. As *Record Collector* retrospectively put it, 'Steve and Robert gorged themselves on an unhealthy diet of pulp videos, junk magazines and various chemical stimulants, in an effort to overload their senses.'

They watched an estimated six hundred films in the run-up to, and making of, The Glove's first (and, so far, only) album. These included Dario Argento's *Inferno* and *Tenebrae*, Abel Ferrara's *Driller Killer* and *Ms. 45: Angel of Vengeance*, as well as *Videodrome*, *Bad Timing*, *The Brood*, *Evil Dead* and *Helicopter Spies*. They would also buy hundreds of glossy magazines and cut them up to make day-glo murals.

This period of hibernation, Severin claimed in Mark Paytress' book, was fortuitous for Smith. 'The timing was good because he'd got himself a dodgy perm. It was a complete disaster and made him look like Kevin Keegan, so he needed those three months in hiding so that he could grow his hair back.' (In reality, Smith was never out of the public eye for anything like three months, but the idea of him with Keegan hair is priceless.)

Originally, the plan was for The Glove to be a fictitious band (perhaps along the lines of Gorillaz, with whom Robert collaborated many years later). However, Smith and Severin faced obstacles in launching any sort of band at all. **Chris Parry** initially tried to block the project, because he'd spent five years building up The Cure. 'I didn't want Robert to sing on the album,' Parry recalled in *Ten Imaginary Years*, 'because it would have been too like a Cure record and it would have damaged **Fiction** – someone else would have got the royalties while he was still under contract to me.' **Simon Gallup**, too, was unhappy with the idea of Smith going off with Severin. 'I'd always prided myself on being his confidant, and I wanted it to stay that way.'

Although Severin, speaking to *No.1*, pretended it was a deliberate decision to have a different vocalist – 'Robert's voice sounds too distinctive . . . actually,

he sometimes sounds as if he's crying' – he was putting a positive spin on the situation. Smith was contractually prevented from being the singer.

The frontperson they hired was Jeanette Landray. Born in Liverpool on 4 March 1960, Landray moved to London at the age of sixteen with her then-boyfriend Budgie, drummer with Big in Japan, and later The Slits, and later still, the Banshees. Landray herself had been in Scouse band Jaqui & Jeanette, known for their 1979 new wave reggae track '194 Radio City', since released on various Liverpool-centric compilations.

By the time of The Glove, Landray was a member of *Top of the Pops* dance troupe **Zoo**. (What's great about that is . . . imagine you were writing an A-Z of The Cure, and were really struggling with the letter Z.) She had also appeared as a nurse in **Pink Floyd**'s video for 'The Fletcher Memorial Home', escorting a Soviet general onto a croquet lawn to meet Mrs Thatcher.

Landray was known to Severin through Budgie. 'I was a good friend of Steven's,' she told post-punk.com, 'and I asked him if I could sing for the record, and he said, "You can't sing!" I replied, "So?" And so it was. . .'

For the making of the album *Blue Sunshine*, its contents, its release and its reception, turn to the separate entry that covers it. The same applies to the singles '**Like An Animal**' and '**Punish Me With Kisses**'.

The Glove never properly performed live, apart from a handful of television appearances, including the BBC's *Riverside* (playing 'Orgy' and 'Punish Me With Kisses') and their mimed turn during the Banshees' Channel 4 film *Play At Home*. 'Don't forget,' Severin explained to *No.1*, 'that [*Blue Sunshine*] was recorded during the night and we were sometimes drunk or worse. We'd just sort of stagger over the keyboards and record something. That's one reason why we're not going to play live. There's no way that we can hope to recreate some of those moments on stage. No way.'

'Big In Japan' wasn't just a Scouse supergroup that once had Budgie in it. It was The Glove's claimed *raison d'être*. 'The Glove was always aimed at Japan, actually,' said Robert in *Ten Imaginary Years*. 'We really liked it there when we went with the Banshees so we decided we'd be this mysterious Western group and do this short disco tour of Japan with **Lol** as the support act, but it didn't come to anything. I don't think **Polydor** even released the album in Japan!' (They did. Its Japanese catalogue number is 28MM 0315.)

When The Glove failed to be big anywhere on earth, the project quietly fizzled out. There were drunken discussions of The Glove making a purely instrumental album called *Music for Dreams*, which never materialised (though the title stayed with Smith as a possible name for his oft-promised **solo album**). However, rumours of a second Glove album flared up again in 2010 when Severin gave an interview to Nottingham-based *Left Lion*. 'It's just a matter of time,' he said. 'Making space for it means effectively shutting down The Cure for six to nine months. That's a huge machine with many people depending on it for their livelihoods so timing is key. One day, I hope.'

In the post-Glove era, Landray appeared as a dancer in British horror film *Underworld*, then resurfaced in 1986 fronting the short-lived, Mick Ronson-produced alternative rock band Kiss That, who made one album, *Kiss and Tell*. She also choreographed videos for Tears For Fears, **Depeche Mode**, Flesh For Lulu and Duran Duran, and worked with ITV dance troupe Hot Gossip. She later briefly formed a band with her then-husband, session drummer Chuck Sabo, and is now a painter, last known to be living in Florida on a farm with a rescued horse.

Severin later said that he regretted involving Landray, and the feeling was mutual, Landray telling Banshees biographer Brian Johns that she felt 'very much a third party' during The Glove sessions. (However, in another interview, she said they 'never suffocated me, they let me experiment', and were 'easy to work with'.)

And what of The Glove, now that the dust has settled? 'It was totally self-indulgent,' admitted Severin in *Out of the Woods*. 'That was the whole point of it . . .'

Gone!

There were two world-famous pop stars wearing LA Kings ice hockey shirts in the mid-1990s. One of them was Snoop Doggy Dogg. The other was Robert Smith.

The fact that Smith wore such a seemingly un-Cure garment as a fashion item in the video to 'Gone!' tells you a lot about this off-kilter, anomalous single. In just about every way, they were stepping outside their own established norms.

The fourth and final single from *Wild Mood Swings*, 'Gone!' – the second Cure single to feature an exclamation mark in its title – was released in December 1996 to little fanfare. It was an unusual choice, to say the least. Written in a lurching, wonky waltz time, it had a Swinging Sixties feel, **Roger O'Donnell**'s keyboards reminiscent of Georgie Fame or Brian Auger or Alan Price, with carefree horns adding a slight Latin feel.

The lyric saw Smith berating himself for his own lethargy and apathy, trying to give himself a motivational kick up the backside:

> Sick as a dog and six times as mean
> You don't want to sing you don't want to play
> You don't want to swing you don't want to sway
> All you want to do is nothing

Later, with droll sarcasm, he explained: 'I was trying to reflect the get-up-and-go mentality that I am so well known for.'

Its **video** – semi-live, semi-candid, with much backstage larking around – was shot at the LA Forum by Steven Hanft. We see Roger frying a fish in a pan that's too small for it (summoning memories of the *Spinal Tap* sandwich incident), an outdoor tea party scene reminiscent of the T. Rex movie *Born to Boogie* (or, indeed, the **Banshees** episode of *Play At Home*), and the band's mums in Edwardian frocks and bonnets, doubling as the horn section. At the end Robert, wearing that hip-hop hockey shirt, drives off in a Volkswagen Beetle. (The car is orange, not mint. The *other* flavour of Christmas chocolate stick.) The video didn't get seen much, perhaps because of **Simon Gallup**'s 'Thick As Shit' T-shirt as much as any anti-Cure agenda or their fall from fashion. In Robert's estimation, it 'doesn't really work'.

The **artwork** by **Parched Art**, in keeping with other *Wild Mood Swings* singles, was a photograph of a tin toy, this time a clockwork boy holding a red suitcase. This being the mid-nineties, it was released in a CD1 and CD2, with the extra tracks being remixes of songs already available on *Wild Mood Swings* (**The 13th**', **This Is A Lie**', **Strange Attraction**') or, in the case of CD2, merely remixes of 'Gone!' itself.

With no compelling reason for fans to buy it, and despite a live **TV** performance on *Later . . . With Jools Holland*, the single limped to No.60 in the UK charts and so the *Wild Mood Swings* campaign ended with a whimper.

Goth

Q: How do you know if someone's a goth?
A: Ask them if they're a goth, and they'll say, 'No.'

This, of course, is the logic of the mediaeval ducking stool. If they drown, the witch is dead. If they don't drown, it's witchcraft so burn them at the stake. Nevertheless, it's a peculiar fact that almost every band typically associated with goth – including The Cure, and especially **Siouxsie And The Banshees** – strenuously denies having anything to do with it.

But we're getting ahead of ourselves. Goth, a musical and style movement fixated on morbidity, dark romance, twisted sex, the occult, horror and death, is – ironically – the subculture that refuses to die. Since its origins in the early eighties, goth's continuing influence is arguably bigger than ever in the 2020s, and can be felt not only in music and fashion but in the aesthetic of films, television, literature, art, comics, even gaming. The sign of any successful subculture is the proliferation of spin-off sects, and goth now has dozens, from pastel goth to EGL (elegant gothic Lolita) to cybergoth to trad goth (i.e. those staying true to the eighties look). And there's an ever-growing industry of goth nostalgia, from museum exhibitions to books to box sets.

The term 'gothic rock' was first coined in 1967 by John Stickney of *The Williams Record* in 1967 to describe The Doors, and the term was used in the same year to describe The Velvet Underground. However, it was in the late seventies that it began to be applied to the bands who shaped the sound and style of goth as we know it. In July 1978, *NME*'s Nick Kent used it about Siouxsie And The Banshees, and in September 1979 Joy Division's (see **New Order**) manager Anthony H. Wilson described them as 'gothic'. Before long, no review of Joy Division was complete without the G-word.

When writers spoke of 'gothic rock', the comparison being made was with gothic **literature**, implying that the artists involved were conjuring an atmosphere of menace, mystery and dread similar to that created by the writing of Horace Walpole, Edgar Allan Poe, Mervyn Peake, John William Polidori, the Brontë Sisters, Mary Shelley and Bram Stoker.

The Banshees and Joy Division, however, were precursors. The record considered to be the first true goth release is Bauhaus' 'Bela Lugosi's Dead', a sprawling, adventurous nine-minute post-punk dubscape over which singer Peter Murphy paid melodramatic homage to the 1930s *Dracula* actor, released in August 1979. The Northampton quartet, whose drummer Kevin Haskins has been a guest on *Curious Creatures*, were the band who codified the sound and style of goth in their short career (which ended in 1983, though they have reformed several times since), namely guitars drenched in chorus, flange and reverb effects, deep, rumbling basslines and dramatic, theatrical vocals.

Visually, goths were monochrome peacocks and dark dandies, clad in fetish wear and Victoriana, with big, backcombed and crimped **hair** and startling **make-up** consisting of pallid greasepaint and feline Cleopatra eyes. It's an **image** that was made internationally famous by Siouxsie Sioux (though she may reject the term 'goth' just as much as Robert does) and Robert Smith. The psychology behind the goth look was about externalising your alienation and differentiating yourself from mainstream society. To quote a track from the Banshees' classic *A Kiss In The Dreamhouse*, 'Confound that dowdy flock with a sharp-honed nerve / Because we're painted birds by our own design'.

There are solid socio-historic reasons why the youth of Britain were receptive to doom-laden music at that time. A pervasive, palpable sense of dread was ever-present in the early 1980s. The Soviet Union had invaded Afghanistan, and for the first time since the Cuban Missile Crisis of the 1960s, there seemed to be a clear and present danger that the Cold War was about to turn hot. For anyone growing up in that era, it was not a question of *if* we were all going to die in a nuclear holocaust, but *when* we were all going to die in a nuclear holocaust. Pop had three broad responses to the certainty of our imminent annihilation. One (favoured by New Romantics like Duran Duran) was to party like there's no tomorrow, because there might *not* be a tomorrow. Another (favoured by the likes of The Specials, The Jam, The Beat and UB40) was to protest against the lunacy of our warmongering leaders. A third was to make music which, whether consciously or otherwise, captured that creeping fear. This third category included The Cure's *Seventeen Seconds*, *Faith* and especially *Pornography*, all three of which are formative gothic rock releases.

The biggest names associated with eighties goth, along with The Cure, the Banshees and Bauhaus, are The Sisters Of Mercy, The Cult, Killing Joke, Nick Cave (with The Birthday Party or The Bad Seeds), The Mission and Fields Of The Nephilim. One might also add The Cramps, the American band whose horror-comedic schlock 'n' roll schtick was often described as 'gothabilly'. However, there was a whole second stratum of artists beloved by goth devotees, such as Specimen, Flesh For Lulu, Virgin Prunes, Alien Sex Fiend, Danielle Dax, Xmal Deutschland, Gene Loves Jezebel, Sex Gang Children, Ghost Dance, Clan Of Xymox, Danse Society, The Bolshoi, Christian Death, March Violets, The Chameleons, UK Decay, Skeletal Family and dozens more.

Though the *music* of goth may have been infused with dread, the *scene* was all about decadent celebration. The epicentre of London's goth subculture was the legendary Batcave – a club which, let the record state, Robert Smith sometimes frequented – in Soho. Launched in 1982 by Specimen members Olli Wisdom, Jon Klein and Jonny Slut, with production manager Hugh Jones and DJ Hamish MacDonald at the Gargoyle (later known as Gossip's) at 69 Dean Street, the Batcave ran for three years and attracted regulars including Marc Almond, **Steve Severin** and Nick Cave. The music and style of the Batcave was celebrated in a 2023 box set and book, *Young Limbs Rise Again*.

There was also an important outpost of goth in the North, with Leeds clubs like F Club and festivals like Futurama creating a rich hotbed for bands like The Sisters Of Mercy, Southern Death Cult and New Model Army.

The Batcave era coincided with Smith's stint as a Banshee. 'When I joined Siouxsie And The Banshees,' he told *Female First*, 'I was aware that I was stepping into a Goth band, in that Siouxsie was a Goth icon. I became a *de facto* Goth icon around that time. When I was with the Banshees I made the point of wearing pyjamas – I wore a blue stripy pyjama top. I wanted to make a point I was not part of this world. I used to go drinking with Severin in the Batcave around that time, and there's nothing more Gothic than drinking in the Batcave in 1983 with Steve Severin. But I would be wearing pyjamas . . .'

In the later eighties and early nineties, there was a shift among the goth scene towards tougher industrial and EBM (electronic body music) sounds which had been percolating in Europe (Einstürzende Neubauten, Front 242), North America (Ministry, Nine Inch Nails, Front Line Assembly, Skinny Puppy) as well as the UK (Test Dept, Scraping Foetus Off The Wheel, Nitzer Ebb). Later still, the goth scene mutated and melded with metal, with Marilyn Manson being the most obvious fusion of the two subcultures (which were

once poles apart). To this day, if you see someone who looks a bit goth, they're as likely to be into Slipknot as Siouxsie.

The Cure, for a time, were seen as a soft option, derided by hardcore goths for abandoning the dark stuff and writing pop hits. 'I remember just for a while,' Robert later said, 'Goths were outraged that people would think we're a Goth band. They hated us because we'd kind of jumped ship, they thought. Because we sounded like we do on *Pornography* and the next thing we do is '**Let's Go To Bed**' and '**The Lovecats**' and '**The Walk**' and all these sort of stupid pop singles.' In more recent years, however, that has flipped around again, and newer generations of goths revere The Cure as founding icons.

Whether goths love or hate The Cure is a matter of indifference to Robert Smith. He has repeatedly distanced himself from the movement, over a period of several decades. Speaking to Robert Sandall of *Q*, he described goth music as 'incredibly dull and monotonous, a dirge really.' To the *Guardian*'s Louis Pattison he complained that 'It's so pitiful when "Goth" is still tagged onto the name The Cure. It's only people that aren't Goths that think The Cure are a Goth band . . . We were like a raincoat, shoegazing band when Goth was picking up.' To *Time Out* he recalled, 'We got stuck with it at a certain time when goths first started. I was playing guitar with Siouxsie And The Banshees, so I had to play the part. Goth was like pantomime to me. I never really took the whole culture thing seriously.' And he once insisted to a Belgian magazine that 'The Cure, contrary to what music encyclopaedias will tell you, are not Goths.'

Other members of The Cure have been more relaxed about the description. **Roger O'Donnell**, in a fan Q&A, said 'I think Robert was the only one who ever got upset about the band being called Goth. I never cared, and it's a bit hard to dispute really isn't it? I mean, even if The Cure didn't think they were Goth, their audience did.' **Lol Tolhurst**, on *Curious Creatures*, stated 'What I would maintain is that we were the fertile ground that grew the Goth era'. Indeed, in September 2023, Tolhurst published his own book on the topic, *Goth: A History*.

Robert, however, is not having it. In an interview with *Blah Blah Blah*, he vented his frustration. 'The biggest misconception about The Cure is that we're a Goth band. We were never Goths . . . I hate the way every album is dismissed as more of the same thing. We mix lots of sounds and types of music but it always comes down to the hair and the lipstick and the gloom. We played a concert recently in **France** and Blur were supporting us. The whole front ten rows were diehard Goths. They were giving Damon shit and screaming at him, so he started chucking water over their hair. He said "The more you shout, the more water I'm gonna pour over you, and you'll all look stupid when Robert comes out . . ."'

In a 2019 interview with *Rolling Stone*, he went further. 'I don't think of The Cure as a Goth band. I never have. I grew up in a world where Goth hadn't quite been invented in the way that we know and love it.' He accepted that The Cure's music chimed with goth audiences, but 'was I responsible for Goth? No. And if I was, I'd be very happy. But I wasn't.' He continued: 'I'm aware we played a part in it, and I think that we're part of the history of Goth, without question, but like a footnote. The Cure just aren't a Goth band.'

He could, however, see positives in the scene itself. 'I love subcultural stuff like that, where people have a vision of what the world should be, how they should be. I think it can be really charming. There's a slightly sinister edge to subculture-ism, but generally speaking, it's a good thing. It helps people feel they belong to something at the time that they probably feel they need to belong to something. And I'd rather Goths than skinheads. And I also like the fact that it represented kind of "other". It's a dangerous thing to look like a Goth. In certain parts of England, you run the risk of a beating if you look like a Goth, which I think is fucking outrageous. So in that sense, I feel a community of spirit with Goths and other subcultures who choose to live an alternative lifestyle. But I wouldn't consider myself to be a part of it.'

To *Female First*, he pondered the way in which the association between goth and The Cure first arose in people's minds. 'When we did the *Faith* album in 1981, Goth hadn't been invented then, we were actually a "raincoat band". We were inventing goth with that album and *Pornography*. But we weren't, we were just playing emotional music. I was feeling a bit desperate at the time, the band as a whole was a bit despairing, we thought it was going to end with *Pornography*. The record label had given up on us and the crowds were pretty much non-existent. We went around the world and played to the same 500 people everywhere we went and we couldn't see how we were going to play to more. And we were taking vast amounts of very strong **drugs** and actually didn't really give a shit. And that, somehow, gave rise to Goth . . .'

Try as he might, Robert will never be able to shake the tag. (The *NME Originals* magazine on goth in 2005, for example, had Smith's face on the front.)

Ultimately, though, this disconnect between intention and reception is perfect. There's nothing so gothic as an unrequited love story, and this is one. Because The Cure may not love goth, but goths sure do love The Cure.

Goulding, Steve

When **Lol Tolhurst** switched from drums to keyboards before The Cure's three 'fantasy singles' – '**Let's Go To Bed**', '**The Walk**' and '**The Lovecats**' – he left a drummer-shaped hole. That hole was filled, initially at least, by Steve Goulding.

Born in South London in 1954, renowned session drummer Goulding was a former member of Graham Parker & the Rumour who had co-written Nick Lowe's 'I Love The Sound Of Breaking Glass', played on 'Watching The Detectives' from Elvis Costello & The Attractions' *My Aim Is True* (an album the younger Robert Smith had admired), as well as 'Whole Wide World' by Wreckless Eric and 'I Knew The Bride' by Dave Edmunds. Basically, pick up any pub rock record from the late seventies, and chances are you're hearing the drums of Steve Goulding. He also performed with **David Bowie** on *The Johnny Carson Show* and in the concert scene from the film *Christiane F.*

Goulding was drumming with **Associates**, a band whose career intertwined with The Cure's in various ways, alongside former Cure bassist **Michael Dempsey** when the call came to help out with The Cure's new single. Despite its robotic sound, 'Let's Go To Bed' has a human drummer, and that drummer is Steve Goulding. He also drummed for The Cure on the session (see **Peel Sessions**) they recorded for BBC Radio One's David 'Kid' Jensen in October 1982, playing 'Let's Go To Bed', 'Just One Kiss' and '**One Hundred Years**'.

In the mid-eighties he joined Leeds post-punkers The Mekons, and also toured with Gang Of Four, Thompson Twins (what is it with The Cure and Thompson Twins drummers?) and Roxy Music, reuniting with Dempsey for a European tour and the 'Avalon' video. In 2011 he reunited with Graham Parker & The Rumour, and appeared in the Judd Apatow film *This Is 40*.

Gray, Howard

Alvin The Aardvark And The Fuzzy Ants. That's the band you *won't* know Howard Gray from. Born in Sydney on 15 July 1962 and raised in Liverpool, Howard Gray formed ATA&TFA at the age of fifteen, with a line-up which also included his own brother Trevor and Norman '**Noko**' Fisher-Jones, later bassist, albeit briefly, with The Cure.

Gray got his first job in music in 1980, while still in his final year of school, working at Richard Branson's residential studio The Manor (where, many years later, The Cure would record *Wish*). His early assignments were chiefly with Virgin-associated new wave acts such as Public Image Ltd and Orchestral Manoeuvres In The Dark. He later broke away to become Steve Lillywhite's engineer on records by Simple Minds, XTC and The Pretenders, and also worked on UB40's mega-selling *Labour Of Love*.

It was Gray who engineered *The Top*, assisting **Chris Parry** and **David M. Allen**, and subsequently *The Head On The Door*, on which he co-produced 'Kyoto Song'.

In 1990 he reunited with Noko, and Trevor Gray, to form the electronic dance act Apollo 440 who scored a number of hits including 'Ain't Talkin' Bout Dub', 'Lost In Space' and 'Stop The Rock' during the Big Beat craze.

Although their paths never crossed while working with The Cure, it's interesting from a Cure perspective that Gray ended up tampering with the work of **Mike Hedges** when Apollo 440 were brought in (under the alias Stealth Sonic Orchestra) to remix several tracks by Manic Street Preachers (themselves later hand-picked by Robert Smith for his **Meltdown Festival**). He also had a near miss with **Porl Thompson** when Apollo 440 remixed 'Come With Me' by Puff Daddy featuring Jimmy Page, just after Thompson had ceased to be part of Page's band.

Everything is connected, even if the connections are sometimes tenuous.

Greatest Hits

The contractual obligation album is an established part of rock 'n' roll lore. In order to terminate their legal ties, whether with their record label or some other interested party, an artist submits what is typically a sub-standard album, sometimes under duress, usually intending it to be the final release under their current agreement (or, occasionally, the penultimate, to speed things along), while keeping all their best material back for the golden day when they are finally free.

As long ago as 1980, it was already such a cliché that Monty Python released a comedy record called *Monty Python's Contractual Obligation Album*, which was exactly that. In 1975, Lou Reed delivered *Metal Machine Music*, an entirely instrumental album of challenging abstract noise, largely to annoy RCA (for whom he would make just one more record). *Rolling Stone* described it as sounding like 'the tubular groaning of a galactic refrigerator', and it has repeatedly been listed among the worst albums of all time. In 1977, under the terms of his divorce from Anna Gordy Gaye, Marvin Gaye was obliged to pay half the royalties from his next album to his ex-wife. He responded with a wilfully weird and uncommercial release called *Here, My Dear*. (Both the Lou Reed and Marvin Gaye albums have since been critically rehabilitated, to varying degrees.)

Led Zeppelin's odds-and-ends compilation *Coda* was released in 1982 to fulfil their contract to Atlantic and cover a tax bill, but few fans find much merit in its contents. Mike Oldfield's 1990 album *Amarok* consisted of one hour-long instrumental track with no melodic moments which could be isolated as a single to market it. Oldfield's intention was to persuade Virgin to release him from his contract. It succeeded.

And then there's Prince, the all-time don of trolling the record label. In 1993, angry with Warner Bros' ownership of his masters and their refusal to release his prolific output at a suitable pace, he changed his name to an unpronounceable symbol. In 1994, he appeared at an awards ceremony with the word 'slave' written on his face. In 1996 he delivered the final album he owed them, *Chaos And Disorder*, and refused to promote it. It was the lowest-selling album of his career. Warner let him go.

There can be no doubt that The Cure were conscious of these precedents when they were looking to wriggle out of their deal with **Fiction**, hence the *Greatest Hits* album that nobody wanted. Created under the condition that Robert Smith could choose the songs himself, it was released in November 2001, only four years after *Galore*, their 1987–97 compilation, and featured no fewer than eleven of the same tracks. While it would have been almost impossible to provide a satisfactory overview of The Cure's singles discography without spilling over onto two CDs, the list of major songs omitted from *Greatest Hits* is eyebrow-raising: '**Killing An Arab**', '**Jumping Someone Else's Train**', '**Primary**', '**Charlotte Sometimes**', '**The Hanging Garden**', '**The Walk**', '**The Caterpillar**', '**Catch**', '**Hot Hot Hot!!!**' and '**Fascination Street**' all failed to make the cut. It did, however, find room for '**Wrong Number**', one of the new tracks already used as buyer-bait on *Galore* but nobody's definition of a Greatest Hit, having peaked at 62 in the UK chart. The extra tracks this time, forcing fans to shell out, were the sweetly heartbreaking '**Cut Here**' and the awful '**Just Say Yes**', each of which has its own entry.

There was, however, a bigger piece of buyer-bait than those two new songs, at least for the early birds. Ever since the advent of *MTV Unplugged* in 1989 (on which The Cure had appeared in 1991), the acoustic hits album had become almost as much of a music biz cliché as the contractual obligation one. A limited-edition 2CD version of *Greatest Hits* came with an extra disc entitled *Acoustic Hits*, recorded on 13 August 2001 at Olympic Studios, London by the line-up of Smith, **Gallup**, **Cooper** and **O'Donnell**, with **Boris Williams** brought back in to help out on percussion. Engineer **Keith Uddin** made the first of many appearances in Cure credits, while the mysterious and possibly fictional Jay Cocks is credited with 'musical assistance', as are the non-fictional engineers Philippe Rose and Jonathan Shakhovskoy. The sessions were filmed by Richard Anthony for posterity. A straight A/B comparison of songs like '**Boys Don't Cry**' and '**Just Like Heaven**' on *MTV Unplugged* and *Acoustic Hits* shows relatively little difference, leading fans to wonder why *MTV Unplugged* wasn't released as an album itself. To date, it never has been. Eventually, however, *Acoustic Hits* was released as a stand-alone double LP on Record Store Day 2017.

Even the **Stylorouge**-designed sleeve, featuring a photo of Robert, taken by Rob O'Connor, with Robert's hands in the foreground and white stars dappled around him, doesn't feel very 'Cure'. For all its acoustic reworkings and extra tracks, an air of pointlessness hung over *Greatest Hits*. But The Cure had fulfilled their contractual obligation, and were free from Fiction. That was all the point it needed.

Guitars

Guitar geeks, this one is for you. Everyone else, skip to the next entry.

Robert Smith began learning classical guitar from the age of nine from a student of John Williams, playing an acoustic with nylon strings. 'My sister was a piano prodigy,' he told *Guitar Player*, 'so sibling rivalry made me take up guitar because she couldn't get her fingers around the neck. I learned a lot, but got to the point where I was losing the sense of fun. I wish I'd stuck with it. I still read music, but it takes me too long to work through a piece . . .'

It wasn't long before he felt the pull of the more rock 'n' roll thrill of the electric guitar.

He got his first electric in December 1972, aged thirteen. That guitar was the infamous Woolworth's Top 20, made in Japan by Tiesco in sunset red fading to black at the edges, which would almost invariably go out of tune mid-gig. He would later take the Top 20 to **Morgan Studios** to record *Three Imaginary Boys*, along with a small WEM combo amp. Manager **Chris Parry** was horrified at the cheapness of Smith's equipment, and took him out to buy a 1964 Fender Jazzmaster. To Parry's dismay, Smith immediately installed the pick-up from the Woolworth's guitar on the Fender, and played this mutant hybrid on the album. 'It's a brilliant guitar', he told *Guitar Player*, 'though I actually bought it because of how it looked.' (Appearance, as well as sound, has always mattered to Smith: in 2014 he was playing a 'map-shaped' National Newport Val-Pro 88, purchased partly 'because of how it looked'.) He also refused to get rid of his amp until it fell apart after the guitar solo on the title track. Smith acquired another Jazzmaster around this time, which was customised in 1985 by an art student called Lisa and nicknamed 'Fish', becoming one of his favourite guitars.

Another favourite, he later told *Cure News*, was the Fender six-string bass he was given during the *Faith* sessions by **Mike Hedges**. (This, he said, was the one guitar he would save from a fire.) Other guitars Smith was seen playing in the early eighties include the Fender XII he used with **Siouxsie And The Banshees**, and a prized Vox Teardrop which **Lol Tolhurst** managed to break not once but twice during the making of *The Top*.

A full inventory of Smith's guitar collection in 1984 was published in *Further Adventures Of TeamCure*: Fender Jazzmaster (x2), Fender Stratocaster, Music

Man StingRay bass, Ovation Breadwinner, Fender Precision bass, Rickenbacker fretless bass, a fretless six-string bass, the Woolworth's Top 20, the Vox Teardrop, a Gibson Chet Atkins and an Epiphone semi-acoustic.

The Epiphone was probably the big red EA-250 he wielded a couple of years later on *The Tube* while performing '**Hot Hot Hot!!!**'. His collection of six-string basses grew to include a Fender Bass VI which he played on '**Pictures Of You**'. And the Gibson was probably the Chet Atkins Country Gentleman he played on *Wish*. 'It's brilliant!' he enthused. 'It's the first guitar since my very first Jazzmaster to sound exactly how I want it to.'

His collection continued to expand in the nineties. Circa 1995 his new acquisitions, according to *Cure News*, included a Gretsch Tennessee Rose (from **Perry Bamonte**), an old Gibson ES-335 Stereo, and two Takamine acoustics (a six-string and a twelve-string). By 1997 these were joined by a five-string banjo, a Coral sitar, an Ovation twelve-string acoustic, a PHD Custom bass, a Yairi classical, a Gibson SG custom and two Mosrites (a single neck and a double neck). In 1999 he acquired even more, including a Gretsch Black Falcon, a Mosrite Venture and a Music Vox Acoustic. Many of his purchases were from a London shop called Vintage and Rare (which was also frequented by **Porl Thompson**).

In 2005, Smith linked up with manufacturers Schecter to design a custom guitar called the UltraCure. Based on the pre-existing Schecter Ultra, it features a chambered mahogany body in plain black, a twenty-four-fret neck with moon- and star-shaped mother of pearl inlay blocks, and Seymour Duncan '59 pickups. They tend to sell for around £1,299. Robert himself frequently uses them live, along with a twelve-string version and a six-string bass version.

Robert isn't the only Cure member to get involved with special editions. Porl Thompson also had a custom guitar made by Shecter, the Porl Thompson Corsair, while Perry Bamonte had one made by Aria, the BB (Bamonte Baritone) series, and Collar City Guitars of New York have made a Reverend **Reeves Gabrels** Dirt Bike Royale Jr custom, initially as a one-off prototype.

With all those fancy instruments in his artillery, one might assume Robert to be an exhibitionist muso, desperate to demonstrate his virtuosity to the world. In fact, his unshowy (and underrated) style is quite the opposite. He once signed a guitar for the Hard Rock Café with these words: 'PLEASE DON'T SHOW OFF.'

H

H is for ...

Hair

In the summer of 1985, a paper published by geophysicist Joe Farman and meteorologists Brian Gardiner and Jonathan Shanklin in *Nature* magazine alerted the world to an alarming depletion of the ozone layer above the Antarctic, with the finger of blame pointed at CFCs (chlorofluorocarbons). In the summer of 1985, The Cure released their British breakthrough album *The Head On The Door*.

In the summer of 1987, the Montreal Protocol was ratified by 197 nations with an agreement to cap production of chlorofluorocarbons. In the summer of 1987, The Cure released their worldwide breakthrough album *Kiss Me, Kiss Me, Kiss Me*.

Towards the end of 1989, production of CFCs was banned worldwide. Towards the end of 1989, The Cure's biggest-selling album *Disintegration* was released.

In the mid-1990s, ozone layers in the atmosphere were observed to have stabilised and began to recover. In the mid-1990s and 2000s, The Cure's popularity waned and began to dip.

Of course, you don't need to be a scientist to know the difference between causation and correlation. These parallel trends – of the rise and fall of The Cure's record sales and the rise and fall of global concern about CFCs – *could* just be coincidental. But there's one salient fact that links the two closely matched lines on the graph, and it is this. CFCs were the main aerosol propellant in hairspray. *Boom*. There it is. There's your smoking gun.

While it would be unfair to blame the hole in the ozone layer entirely on Robert Smith, **Simon Gallup** and the other members of The Cure, it's fair to say that if there's one **award** The Cure richly deserved to pick up, it's one for lifetime services to the hairspray industry.

If you were there, you know. Boots Extra Firm Hold Unperfumed for everyday use on a student budget. Shockwaves or Elnett if you could afford it. For the true connoisseurs, Insette Spikey, if you could source a supplier. (There was this one chemist up in Wood Green. It was worth the trek.) And, only if you were absolutely desperate and stuck in the arse-end of nowhere with no shop other than a newsagents, Cossack or Harmony which made you smell like Peter Wyngarde or Farrah Fawcett (delete as appropriate).

Oh, everyone had a fit of conscientiousness and tried the non-aerosol pump-action Vidal Sassoon atomiser, but it wasn't the same. If you wanted to achieve your goal of looking like Smith or Gallup, or **Siouxsie Sioux**, or maybe Kevin Haskins from Bauhaus, or Martin Degville from Sigue Sigue Sputnik, or, if you were really in the know and ultra-ambitious, Jonny Slut from Specimen, then you needed your fix of those sweet, sweet chlorofluorocarbons. Sure, backcombing and crimping were also part of the ritual, but without a guilty ozone-killing can of hairspray, you were doomed. It's a **goth** thing. You wouldn't understand.

Robert Smith is, as Andrew Mueller wrote in *Melody Maker*, 'the only rock star with a famous silhouette'. And, while an important component of that silhouette might be his oversized **shoes** (the other entry where I quoted Mueller), the most important component is his oversized hair.

If we're going to be really nerdy about it (and why stop now?), there are actually *two* iconic Robert Smith hairstyles. Or, at least, two variants on a theme. One of them is the famous exploding crow's nest style, as copied by Edward Scissorhands. (Think: '**Close To Me**' video.) The other is basically that, but with a lovely graduated undercut up the nape of the neck, blending diagonally into the tousled top. (Think: '**Why Can't I Be You?**' video.) For a brief period, circa 1991 and the *Play Out* film, Robert sported a blend of the two, using a butterfly clip to give the impression of a short back and sides while the top was the usual haywire haystack.

In the very early days of The Cure, Robert was achieving results without the use of professional hair products. 'The best way to make your hair stick up in the air', he told Australian cassette magazine *Annual Report* in 1981, 'is using soap and water. And not to wash it. People say not washing your hair is dirty, but really it's clean. Because you don't get fleas if you don't wash your hair, because fleas like to live in clean hair. And then you can do lots of nice things with it. You'll never have to use the phrase "I've washed my hair and I can't do a thing with it" ever again . . .'

From then on, the development of the Robert Smith hairstyle can be traced via photo shoots and music videos. Circa *Pornography*, on the **Fourteen Explicit Moments** tour, the big hair made its first appearance (inspired, he later said, by the skyscraping quiff sported by Jack Nance as Henry Spencer in David Lynch's surrealist horror film *Eraserhead*).

During and after his second stint in the Banshees during **1983, Robert's craziest year**, his hairdo began to find its classic shape, as seen in the video for '**The Lovecats**'. By the time of *The Top* tour the following spring, **Tom Sheehan** caught up with the band in Bologna and photographed them among mediaeval ruins and equestrian fountains, allowing us to give a precise date to the point at which his hair had grown out into the iconic thatch: 20 May 1984. (Meanwhile, during his hiatus from The Cure as a member of **Fools Dance**, Simon Gallup developed a remarkable gothic mane which actually exceeded Smith's. As a matter of fact, photos of pre-Fools Dance configuration The Cry at The Rock Garden in April 1983 show that Gallup actually had the giant hair *first*.)

Other members of The Cure followed different paths. **Lol Tolhurst**'s thick puff of dark curls only seemed to expand or contract, never going full 'Cure'. And **Porl Thompson**'s tousled, tentacular style (and, later, shaven head with tattoos) was a style all of his own. It was Gallup and Smith who rocked the shock of hair that inspired a generation (several generations, in fact) of copycats. Into the nineties, the hair of some members of The Cure seemed to subtly expand the longer they'd been in the band. **Roger O'Donnell**, **Perry Bamonte** and **Jason Cooper** had all definitely been at the crimpers and canisters at various points, as if there was a certain Cure coiffure that was contractually stipulated for all newcomers.

In 1986, Robert became so sick of media commentary around The Cure being reduced to hair-lips-hair-lips that he chopped it all off, as shown in the big reveal at the start of *The Cure In Orange*. The legions of imitators were also a motive. 'The fans were beginning to look more like me than I do,' he told Michael Azerrad of the *St Louis Post Dispatch*.

The great shearing, as shocking to eighties goth kids as Elvis Presley's army buzzcut had been to fifties rock 'n' rollers, was self-inflicted. 'I did it myself, one night,' he told ITV's *Night Network* the following year. 'Then I woke up the next day and I'd

forgotten that I'd done it. Which was a very horrifying experience . . .' (In 1987, he also gave us another insight into his styling methods, recommending KMS gel and backcombing instead of the use of soap.)

Of course, he grew it all back. 'I'd find it difficult to sing some of these songs without this hair,' he told Azerrad. 'I'm always unhappy about my physical appearance, and I feel most comfortable looking like this – it's my way of facing the world.' By the time of '**The Only One**' in 2008, he was comfortable enough with his tonsorial trademark to reference it in his lyrics: 'I love what you do to my head/It's a mess up there . . .'

Nowadays, Robert Smith seems content to let his hair do its own wild thing, without over-reliance on primping products.

The ozone layer says 'Thanks'.

Hanging Garden, The

The fact that The Cure's manager thought 'The Hanging Garden' was the best option for a radio-friendly single from *Pornography* tells you everything you need to know about *Pornography*.

'Under pressure from **Chris Parry**', said **Phil Thornalley** later, 'we worked on "The Hanging Garden" to add something more catchy.' The quest to turn the sow's ear of that song into the silk purse of a hit single ate up a disproportionate amount of energy and effort. 'I think we spent more time on that [than the rest of the album],' said Thornalley, 'trying to make it more palatable to radio programmers.'

'The Hanging Garden' was a cacophony of rumbling drums and quasi-psychedelic guitars, with cryptic couplets such as 'Catching haloes on the moon/Gives my hands the shapes of angels . . .' Impenetrable, indigestible, uncompromising and dense, it sounded more like a tangled rainforest of vines and lianas than a neatly ordered lawn. **Lol Tolhurst**'s thunder-rolls on the floor toms with his mallets were some of his finest work. It's one of the outstanding achievements of the Smith-**Gallup**-Tolhurst incarnation of The Cure.

The lyric was written, said Robert Smith in *Ten Imaginary Years*, when he was at his parents' house, heard some cats having sex outside in the garden, and 'It made me go strange. I wanted to go out in the garden, so I did. Stark naked. Stupid.' Later, he would explain it as being 'about the purity and hate of animals fucking'. With its imagery of slaughter, and Smith's traumatised vocal delivery, it doesn't take long for the mind of the listener to imagine a double meaning to the song's title: not just a display of Babylonian horticulture but a garden where hangings take place.

The **video** was filmed among the fountains, foliage and statuary of York House, a seventeenth-century stately home in Twickenham that had been home to English dukes, Austrian counts and French comtes. Its last private owner – Sir Ratan Tata, who laid the Italian-style garden – was the patriarch of the Tata family of industrialists, best known in the UK for owning the steelworks at Port Talbot in South Wales. In 1965 the house was acquired by the local council, and has been the municipal offices of the London Borough of Richmond upon Thames since, its sunken lawn now occasionally used as an open-air theatre. In pop-cultural terms it is most notable for providing the location for the sanatorium scenes in the Michael Caine film *Alfie* (yet another link between The Cure and asylums). The site is directly adjacent to Pete Townshend's Eel Pie Studios, where Robert would find himself again a year later recording *Hyæna* with **Siouxsie And The Banshees**.

In her influential 1964 essay 'Notes on Camp', Susan Sontag defined camp as 'seriousness that fails'. The video for 'The Hanging Garden' by The Cure was so filled with failed seriousness that it's the very definition of camp. 'For the "Hanging Garden" video,' Robert recalled years later, 'we got two people who did Madness videos but it was a really awful video. They wanted to make us look serious, and we wanted them to make us look like Madness.' The end result achieved the worst of both worlds.

The team was led by Chris Gabrin of Limelight Productions, who had directed the last three Madness videos, as well as 'Wot!' by Captain Sensible, 'Nuclear Device' by The Stranglers, 'Wham! Rap' by Wham!, 'Don't Go' by Yazoo and 'Time (Clock of the Heart)' by Culture Club, and who went on to work with the Thompson Twins, Five Star, Pat Benatar and the Go-Go's. Comedy was his forte: bands sending themselves up. The Cure weren't quite ready to carry that off, yet.

Not that the video is funny (at least, not intentionally so). But it is one of those painfully hyper-literal eighties videos (see Dire Straits' 'Romeo & Juliet' for the ultimate example), as satirised so brilliantly by Erasure's 'A Little Respect'. They're, er, 'hanging' in an ornamental garden. In order to

highlight the line 'wearing furs and masks', they all wear masks, and at one point Lol has to wear a tigerskin rug. When 'the animals cry', we zoom in on the face of a worried-looking lion statue. And so on.

At other moments, statues, sometimes wearing ivy, randomly appear and disappear. There are day scenes, night scenes, scenes shot through red, green, purple or blue filters, and scenes filled with a waft of smoke. There are jump-cuts of statues' faces from weird angles (a very eighties trope) and, for no apparent reason, there's a wandering armadillo.

Strangely, 'The Hanging Garden' wasn't even the only video by a British alternative rock band that year to feature an armadillo scuttling across the screen: 'Rock The Casbah' by The Clash, directed by Don Letts, entered the charts on 26 June 1982 – just three weeks before 'The Hanging Garden' was released – with a video featuring a meaningless cingulate. For a brief moment in the summer of '82, random armadillos looked like becoming another signature trope of eighties videos, along with swinging lightbulbs, cauldrons of burning oil and Venetian blinds.

Released on 12 July 1982 with sleeve displaying a bleached-out, slanted photograph of the trio in white masks on an otherwise-black sleeve, from the same session as the blurred image on the front of *Pornography*, 'The Hanging Garden' came in two formats: a normal single with '**Killing An Arab**' on the B-side, and a gatefold double pack billed as 'A Single', featuring '**One Hundred Years**' on the B-side, with a second disc of '**A Forest**' and 'Killing An Arab', both recorded live in Manchester. It was the first Cure single released in Japan, a nation they would not visit till two years later. In the UK it reached No.34, a respectable position for an alternative band at that time, and their first sniff of the Top 40 since 'A Forest' itself.

It was not universally well received. In *NME*, Adrian Thrills called it 'a dismal exercise', adding that 'The Cure have drifted disappointingly and indulgently from the idyllic pop invention of their younger days', seemingly unable to deal with the fact that they weren't just rewriting '**Boys Don't Cry**' for ever. In 2013, in his pop history *Yeah Yeah Yeah*, Bob Stanley wrote that 'singles like "**Charlotte Sometimes**" and "The Hanging Garden" packed in an album's worth of melancholy and flanged guitars inside three minutes, but it was all somehow powdery and a little slight. The Cure were more about stubbing your toe than taking your life.'

What seemed undeniable was that a record like 'The Hanging Garden' stood little chance of becoming a hit. And yet, somehow, it was.

Hansa

The very first time The Cure had any dealings with a record company, their fingers were burned.

Hansa Records was a German **label** founded by Peter and Trudy Meisel, Peter also being one of the founders of Berlin's legendary Hansa Studios where **David Bowie** recorded most of his Berlin Trilogy (*Low*, *'Heroes'*, *Lodger*), the acoustics of its main room, the Meistersaal, famously proving invaluable in the recording of the title track of *'Heroes'*.

The record label wing of Hansa Musikproduktion, distributed by Ariola, was mostly known for signing German acts, but occasionally released British or American rock acts in the 1960s, including Thirteenth Floor Elevators, The Troggs, The Hollies, The Herd, Shadows Of Knight and Norman Greenbaum. In the late seventies, however, Hansa had hit a slump, with only the world-conquering pop act Boney M shifting significant units. They needed fresh blood.

In April 1977 Hansa placed an advert on the back page of *Melody Maker*, looking to recruit English bands. The exact contents of the ad differ according to who's talking. **Michael Dempsey**, speaking to *Record Collector* and *Curious Creatures*, thinks it said 'Do you want to be a rock 'n' roll star?' with a picture of a woman draped over a motorcycle. Robert Smith, in *Ten Imaginary Years*, thinks it was a picture of a woman in tight hotpants bending over a drumkit with the caption 'Wanna be a recording star? Get your ass up – take your chances!'

Either way, the unbelievably sexist ad caught the eyes of Easy Cure, as the **pre-Cure** configuration was still calling itself, and they sent Hansa a tape and a photo. Dempsey believes the tape and photo were sent separately, and that Hansa only showed an interest when they saw the photo. In the light of what transpired, this seems all too credible. Five days later, on 5 May 1977, Robert received a telegram from Hansa's Kathy Pritchard asking him to call them urgently.

Just over a week later, Easy Cure auditioned at **Morgan Studios**, London (where, only two years on, they would record *Three Imaginary Boys*). Hansa A&R boss Steve Rowland was watching, and

phoned a few days later to sign them. His interest, the band suspected, was visual more than musical. As Michael Dempsey remembered it on *Curious Creatures*, they weren't even filmed playing live, but miming to something. 'In retrospect,' said Robert in *Ten Imaginary Years*, 'their only interest was in the way we looked. They thought they could turn us into a teen group like [Hansa-signed pop act from Pontefract] Child. I don't think they even listened to our tape – they just liked the photo.' In *Record Collector*, **Lol Tolhurst** corroborated this: 'At our audition, they seemed much more interested in the way we looked than how our songs sounded, which should have been a red flag.'

Five days later, Easy Cure were offered a contract. As Dempsey told *Curious Creatures,* 'Robert got his father to get the Upjohn legal department to cast an eye over the Hansa contract, but they weren't versed in media law.' After much debate, they signed.

The deal was the subject of much excitement locally. Under the headline 'ROCKING' TO THE TOP, the *Crawley Observer* reported that of 1,400 bands who had replied to Hansa's ad, sixty auditioned, and eight were offered contracts. Easy Cure's contract was for five years, renewable annually, and their first single would come out on Atlantic. 'There were so many other bands that we didn't pin our hopes on it,' Robert told the paper. 'It all happened so fast, but now we are really looking forward to making our first record . . .' (The *Crawley Observer* listed the **line-up** as Smith, Tolhurst, Dempsey, **Porl Thompson** and **Peter O'Toole**, but O'Toole had left by the time the sessions began, with Smith moving to lead vocals.)

Hansa set Easy Cure up with sessions on 11 October and 15 November 1977 at SAV (Sound and Vision) Studios in London. The Meisels wanted them to record **cover versions**, sending them tapes of songs including 'I Fought The Law' (Sonny Curtis) and 'The Great Airplane Strike' (Paul Revere & The Raiders), but were not interested in hearing Easy Cure's own songs. Although they did record a couple of covers, 'I Saw Her Standing There' (The Beatles) and 'Rebel Rebel' (David Bowie), they mainly refused, and recorded original material instead. 'It got to the point where we would have been [comedy covers act] the Barron Knights of Punk', Robert said to *NME*'s Adrian Thrills in The Cure's first interview.

Five tracks from those Hansa sessions can be heard online: 'See The Children, Feel The Children' written from the point of view of a paedophile and part-time Santa Claus who tries to abduct children (later recorded, but never released, by **Cult Hero**), 'I Just Need Myself', 'I Want To Be Old', 'Listen' (which later became 'Pillbox Tales' on the B-side of the re-recorded '**Boys Don't Cry**') and 'Meathook'. They're scrappy and raw, but packed with vigour and wit.

They also recorded 'I'm Cold' (which ended up as a B-side of '**Jumping Someone Else's Train**'), 'Little Girl', '**10.15 Saturday Night**' and a radically slower early version of '**Killing An Arab**'.

In January 1978 they recorded another session at PSL Studios with Trevor Vallis (an engineer at Mayfair Studios who went on to work with pop acts like Bucks Fizz, Hazell Dean and Sinitta). Songs recorded this time included 'Plastic Passion' and 'Smashed Up', which Robert called 'the worst song we ever recorded'. As an omen of how doomed the Hansa hook-up was, Lol was hit on the head by a London bus on the way, and staggered away bleeding into a pub to drink a brandy to get over the shock. He was given a sticking plaster, he recalled, by a passing Rastafarian.

The Hansa bosses were unimpressed by what they were hearing, and refused to release 'Killing An Arab' as a single. 'They'd had some success with Child,' Lol told *Record Collector*, 'and perhaps they thought we could be like them, but when they heard us they said, "Not even people in prison would like this!"'

'Hansa wanted to sign us on the basis of what we looked like,' reflected Robert in *Uncut* in 2000. 'They were the label with Boney M and Donna Summer [not true – Donna Summer was never on Hansa] and they wanted to get in on the punk thing. They weren't a cutting-edge label, I was aware of that, but I thought that once we got in the studio and recorded our songs they'd just have to release them.'

Neither side was happy with the deal, and on 29 March 1978 Robert managed to negotiate a separation with Hansa under the terms of which the band would keep the rights to all the songs they'd recorded.

In the immediate aftermath of the separation, Porl Thompson left the band to attend art college, and the remaining members renamed themselves The Cure. Robert sent out a tape with the demos from the Hansa sessions, accompanied by a note which read 'We are The Cure. We have no commitments. We would like a recording contract. Listen to the tape.'

In place of The Cure, Hansa signed art-glamsters turned New Romantic intellectuals Japan, who had also auditioned at Morgan. (In new wave terms this is analogous to Decca missing out on The Beatles but still getting The Rolling Stones.)

One lasting relic from the whole debacle was the song 'Do The Hansa', a berserk piece of punk-funk in which The Cure vented their feelings against the label, and which starts 'Ein zwei drei vier!' (exactly the same shout which ended the Hansa demo of 'Listen'/'Pillbox Tales'). In *Cure News* in 1988, Smith explained 'doing the Hansa' as 'get a fake tan, wear ill-fitting "designer" clothes, gold, particularly on your little finger, and dance without feeling – this is doing the Hansa, as far as I can remember.'

At the Reading Festival in 1979, Smith dedicated the song to 'everyone who hates disco'. 'Disco sucks' was a regressive and regrettable tendency within punk and post-punk, but for Smith it was personal. (It's worth remembering that later tracks like 'I'm A Cult Hero', '**Hot Hot Hot!!**' and '**Let's Go To Bed**' had disco elements, not to mention the *Mixed Up* project, so his hatred can't have been that strong. But it's also worth remembering that Robert told BBC Radio 1's David 'Kid' Jensen 'I despise disco'.) Whether he meant it or not, 'Do The Hansa' actually crept into the Billboard Disco Chart when a re-recorded version was included on the B-side of the 'Boys Don't Cry' remake.

Aside from that (excellent) track, the ultimate upshot of the Hansa fiasco was that The Cure walked away with a professional-quality demo tape of most of the best songs in their repertoire (plus one of the worst), at no cost to themselves, and with no obligation to Hansa or to anyone else.

Which raises the question: who really got burned?

Happily Ever After

Happily Ever After was a US-only double package of **Seventeen Seconds** and *Faith*, released on A&M on 8 September 1981 and containing all eighteen tracks from those two albums. A review in the *Virginian Pilot* described it, actually quite accurately, thus: 'Sometimes they sound like Gang Of Four meets **Pink Floyd**, acid rock for the industrial age.'

The **artwork** was a photograph of a team of flag dancers, known in America as a 'color guard' or 'flag corps', on a sports field, in the red and yellow colour scheme of the children on the front of '**Primary**'. It was designed by **Ben Kelly**, who was previously associated with Factory Records and who had designed the sleeves for 'Red Frame/White Light' by

Orchestral Manoeuvres In The Dark and 'Love Will Tear Us Apart' from **Joy Division**. He would later collaborate with The Cure again on *Pornography*.

As a catch-up collection for American newcomers, *Happily Ever After* did the job. The best thing about it, though, is its deliciously ironic title.

Hartley, Matthieu

Matthieu Aiden Hartley – or 'Matty', as he was known during his brief tenure as Cure keyboardist between November 1979 and August 1980 – was born on 4 February 1960 in the Surrey village of Smallfield, three miles east of **Crawley**, and raised in **Horley**, where he was a schoolfriend of **Simon Gallup**'s at Balcombe Road Comprehensive. Before being hired by The Cure, he worked as a hairdresser by day and a member of Gallup's band the Magazine Spies, aka **Mag/Spys**, by night. He was known to **Lol Tolhurst** and Robert Smith for walking around Horley with a different brightly coloured hairstyle every week.

When Gallup was headhunted to replace **Michael Dempsey** on bass, Matthieu came with him, in a double signing similar to Tottenham Hotspur's decision to sign Argentinian stars Osvaldo Ardiles and Ricardo Villa together in 1978 to help each of them settle.

Hartley was brought into the band to 'colour in' the sound, as Lol Tolhurst put it. (Robert Smith later put a harsher spin on it: 'They brought a new dimension to the group – pissheads.') He owned a Korg Duophonic synth which, importantly, could play two notes at once unlike the primitive monophonic ones which still dominated the market. However, he was invariably obliged only to play one key at a time, under instructions from the boss. 'My role was reasonably detached,' he said later. 'I wasn't an integral part of the band but I wasn't on probation either. I just did what Robert told me to do.'

He played on just one Cure album, *Seventeen Seconds*, on which his notable contributions include the ominous background notes on '**A Forest**' and the memorable keyboard riff of '**Play For Today**', which is still sung by fans whenever the band play it in concert. He also took part in extra-Cure-icular activities such as the **Cult Hero** single (which was, in fact, the first Cure-related record on which he appeared) and the gig in April 1980 during which he and Robert **collaborated** with The Stranglers at the Rainbow Theatre in solidarity with singer Hugh

Cornwell, who was incarcerated in Pentonville Prison on a drugs charge.

Hartley's first Cure show was at Eric's in Liverpool on the opening night of the Future Pastimes tour. He subsequently toured the UK, America, Europe and **Australasia**, his final show being at Raffles Hotel in Applecross, Western Australia. His life as a touring member of The Cure was characterised by volatility. At the gig on 31 May 1980 in Herford, Germany (see **Bootlegs**), a rowdy audience of British soldiers spat so much beer at Hartley that he threw his synth at them. In **France**, he uprooted a small tree and tried to batter down the door to Lol and Simon's room because he wanted a light for his cigarette. In Australia, he chased Robert through a hotel, kicked a door down and beat him over the head because Smith had woken him up by playing music. Smith retaliated by kicking Matthieu's door down, and later suggested that Hartley was just grumpy because he couldn't find vegetarian food in Australia. As easily the tallest member of The Cure at that time, he was not someone to be trifled with. He was, evidently, a man with a hair trigger.

Chris Parry found Hartley 'overbearing' and 'boorish'. Robert, in a 1990 issue of *Cure News*, described him as 'unreasonable'. Clearly, his personality did not fit, and a certain distance began to open up between Hartley and the rest of The Cure camp. He didn't join the other members in leisure activities like jogging and swimming, and would often isolate himself with a bottle of vodka for company.

The beginning of the end of Hartley's spell in The Cure boiled down to that classic cliché, 'musical differences'. He wanted to add *too much* colour to *Seventeen Seconds* which, Lol later said, was intended to be 'muted, almost monochromatic'; Hartley had a tendency to 'overcomplicate the music'. Furthermore, he was inclined to move in a pop direction while Robert Smith was intent on a darker path. 'I realised the group was headed towards suicidal, sombre music', Hartley said in *Ten Imaginary Years*, 'the sort of thing that didn't interest me at all.'

There was, too, a more prosaic reason: 'Matthieu snored,' Lol later recalled. 'At the time, we couldn't afford single rooms and that was fatal.' On a yacht trip on a day off, the decision was made that Hartley had to go.

Rather than tell him immediately, they gave him the cold shoulder in a manner that would nowadays be described as constructive dismissal. On one occasion, he was made to sit in the back of the van with the gear, rather than the front with the band. 'I was treated strangely, childishly,' Hartley said later. 'Robert stopped talking to me. So did Lol. I'd had enough.' After the end of the Australian tour, back in the UK, Matthieu phoned Robert to tell him he was leaving, saving Smith the trouble. It was, he said, done 'amicably'. The Cure were a trio once again.

Hartley remained friends with Gallup, and even attended a Cure Christmas party. When Simon left The Cure for the first time, he and Hartley were reunited in The Cry, who mutated into **Fools Dance**. After that group disbanded when Gallup rejoined The Cure, Hartley released his own synthpop EP *Gate Crashing* in 1987 under the name Matthieu. Nowadays based in Hove, he has continued making music intermittently, including contributing to an album by local musician Derek Luckhurst in 2005. He is now a member of a sixties-influenced psych-pop group called The Speak, fronted by Nick Endacott-Gibb, the biological son of Bee Gee Maurice Gibb.

Personality clashes aside, Matthieu Hartley can perhaps be considered in hindsight to be a case of right guy, wrong time. Only three years later, a keyboardist with the urge to add some pop colour to The Cure's sound would have been just what they needed.

Head On The Door, The

The one that *everyone* had.

After maxing out their cult status as makers of 'serious' albums, then flirting with the frivolity of the pop single, *The Head On The Door* was the album on which the record-buying public trusted The Cure to deliver satisfaction on both counts. In Britain, at least, this album was the breakthrough.

It was, not coincidentally, the first album recorded by what many still view as The Cure's ultimate **line-up**: Robert Smith, **Simon Gallup**, **Porl Thompson**, **Lol Tolhurst** and **Boris Williams**. Gallup had been lured back in to play bass after **Gary Biddles** invited him to have a drink with Robert Smith, effectively bringing an end to Gallup and Biddles' band **Fools Dance**. Thompson had been enticed into playing guitar and other instruments on *The Top* tour after contributing some sax to that album, and Williams had been hired on drums midway through that tour, replacing *Vince Ely* (himself a replacement for **Andy Anderson**). The Cure were, after a dangerous spell of just being Smith, Tolhurst and whoever they could beg to help them out, a real band again.

In 1985, this new line-up began demoing new songs at F2 Studios on Tottenham Court Road in London before switching to Angel Studios in Islington (where Robert had previously recorded '**Dear Prudence**' with **Siouxsie And The Banshees**) for the album proper, with producer **David M. Allen** and engineer **Howard Gray**.

Paradoxically, it is the first Cure album where every song is credited to Smith and Smith alone (he sat down at the start of 1985, so the story goes, and wrote the whole thing in two weeks flat), but it also feels more like a *band* album than anything The Cure had done in a long while. The reality may be more complex than the credits would suggest. In a *Guitar Player* interview, Smith admitted that 'Simon thinks up brilliant melodies. A lot of the pop stuff we've done, like *The Head On The Door*, are more him than me.' And though drummers rarely receive songwriting credits, the inventiveness of Boris Williams' contribution is immense. In many ways he is the low-key star of the album. The way they worked, too, was more band-like than previous releases: the songs on *The Head On The Door* were recorded together as live takes, rather than capturing each element separately.

Looking back on the making of the album in *Rolling Stone* in 2004, Smith credited the importance of the other members. 'During the demos of *The Head On The Door*, I knew that this was the band. The album's got a real fantastic freshness to it, and it was a really pleasant environment. All the girlfriends got on well, and the band became much more like a family. That old gang mentality was growing a little bit stale. By this time I was 25 and realised I should grow up a bit.'

It wasn't all smiles. Lol's blackout drinking worsened circa *The Head On The Door*. But they also found other uses for booze. An enormous Scalextric track was set up around the studio, and they set the cars on fire by filling them with **alcohol**. (Recreation was as important as creation: a surviving photo of an overflowing ashtray on the studio console tells its own story.) And Lol had toys of his own: for the making of the album, he had acquired a Yamaha RX15 Drum Machine and an E-mu Emulator II.

One unusual tactic Smith had adopted was to pin guidelines to the studio wall for each song, in the vein of Brian Eno's 'Oblique Strategies' when recording Bowie's *Low*. For example, 'Sinking' had the instructions 'We must cry by 6pm tonight.'

The album begins with the crashing, chiming bittersweet jubilation of its lead single '**In Between Days**', the success of which, along with the album's next single, made *The Head On The Door* the first Cure album to warrant an 'Includes the Hit Singles' sticker. It was, Robert told *Cure News*, 'about trios – days, people, places, ages . . .', and came into existence due to a guitar purchase. 'I bought a good metal six-string acoustic,' he told *Rolling Stone*, 'and as soon as I picked it up I started playing the chords to 'In Between Days'. I'd never really bothered playing one, because I'd never owned a good one.' (For all other information on 'In Between Days', visit its own *Curepedia* entry.)

Next up is 'Kyoto Song', its atmospheric plinking and tinkling loosely Japanese in sound. Robert had once played two shows (in one night) in Kyoto with the Banshees in February 1983, and told *Cure News* it was about 'a night spent on someone's floor – **Steve Severin**'s I think'. In the lyric, he is woken at a quarter to three by a nightmare of 'death in the pool' which may or may not be about cannibalism (see **Dreams**).

'**The Blood**', Portuguese wine-inspired and Spanish flamenco-flavoured, also has its own entry, as it was technically a single (in Spain, at least, in very limited quantities), with its own non-**Tim Pope** video. 'It's a very cheap Portuguese wine,' Smith told *NME*'s David Quantick, defending the song from having ludicrous lyrics. 'It's a very heavy drink that all the workers drink . . . it's about 12p a bottle. I was given a bottle of it and I drank it, and I noticed the label, which is the Virgin Mary with Baby Jesus under one arm and a bottle in the other hand. It was completely brilliant . . . This is drunk by hundreds of thousands of people, and it's a pretty visionary drink, really!'

'Six Different Ways' recycles a piano motif from '**Swimming Horses**' by Siouxsie And The Banshees (as *Record Mirror*'s Andy Strickland noted at the time), but in a more jovial and approachable manner. In a *Rolling Stone* interview, Smith credited the new line-up with making it possible. 'Porl has always been a great guitarist, and Boris is an extraordinary drummer. We could never have attempted "Six Different Ways" before, because we never had a drummer who could play 6/8 time. It was a great feeling to be in a band that played well. I thought, "God, we could jam – should we so desire."' The song was, Smith said in *Cure News*, about multiple personalities, though he gave *Rolling Stone* a more prosaic explanation for its title: 'A lot of the lyrics came out of really weird conversations that we were having in the studio. We had this fatuous argument about how many ways there were to skin a cat. The inanity was staggering. And someone said, "There are definitely six different ways." And it just seemed like a nice title because of the 6/8 time.'

Closing Side 1, 'Push', written about 'a train journey home', is a song of two halves. It begins with exhilarating, ecstatic descending guitar motif, accompanied by big tom rolls (possibly gated) from Boris, and carries on that way for 2.23 of its 4.30 runtime before Robert finally sings 'Go, go, go!' In a rare radio appearance, **Mary** introduced 'Push' as one of her favourite Cure songs.

Starting Side 2, 'The Baby Screams' (it's about 'trying to make a dream real') is a track which could almost fit amid the madness of *The Top*, but it's reined in by the subtle electronic, disco-like pulse underneath. As Alfred Soto wrote retrospectively in the *Quietus*, 'the density of the arrangement overcomes the high romantic luridness of Smith's lyrics. "Strike me, strike me, dead" and "Heaven, give me a sign" sound more desperate when a guitar's going apeshit on one speaker.'

Next up is the 'breathy electro Motown bop' (as *Record Mirror*'s Andy Strickland described it) of '**Close To Me**', a song about 'the disappointment of dreams made real'. As well as giving the album its title ('If only I was sure that my head on the door was a dream'), it was the album's second single, and has its own entry in *Curepedia*. In its un-remixed album form it lacks the wardrobe squeak at the start and the intermittent horns near the end, making the song somehow even more intimate and claustrophobic (if not as much fun). Your mind inevitably fills them in.

'**A Night Like This**', by contrast, is huge. 'The words were written in the rain,' explained Smith. 'I was upset . . .' It features a sax solo from **Ron Howe** of **Fools Dance** which, wrote Steve Sutherland, sounds like it belongs on a Hall & Oates record. As the single-that-never-was (complete with a video), it too has its own *Curepedia* entry.

The penultimate track is the underrated and under-discussed 'Screw' (written about '**drugs**', Smith helpfully explained). It was built on an extremely filthy funk-rock bassline from Gallup which had just a suggestion of Grandmaster & Melle Mel's 'White Lines (Don't Don't Do It)' and therefore Liquid Liquid's 'Cavern', and is probably a better example of Cure-go-funk than '**Hot Hot Hot!!!**' on the next album along.

The closing 'Sinking' (about 'despair at getting older and less true') is, at almost five minutes, the album's longest track, and the nearest to something that might have appeared on *Faith*, taking its own sweet time to build an atmosphere and arrive at a fittingly subaquatic sound.

At a pleasingly compact thirty-seven minutes and

forty-six seconds, *The Head On The Door* was The Cure's shortest album since *Faith*, and they would never release another sub-forty-minute studio album again.

The **artwork** by **Parched Art** consisted of a blurred Polaroid photo of Robert's sister Janet, almost indistinguishable as a human form, taken by Porl Thompson. The writing on it, **Andy Vella** later explained, was achieved by experimenting with bleach. The inscription on the run-out groove of the vinyl, '50 Times A Night' and 'They Do It', referred to tigers.

A 2006 reissue of *The Head On The Door* contained Robert's home demos and the F2 demos of all the album's songs, B-sides and hitherto-unreleased tracks from those sessions, the most interesting unearthed rarities being 'Mansolidgone', its title referring back to '**The Lovecats**' and its jazzy stylings too, and the breezy and sweet 'Lime Time', its descending synths too similar to 'In Between Days' for inclusion.

The Head On The Door received generally positive reviews. Andy Strickland of *Record Mirror* called it 'the first real Cure LP for some time', while Steve Sutherland of *Melody Maker* focused on its variety, calling it 'a neat ragbag of the arbitrary – each song a separate piece from a different jigsaw' and 'a compilation of possibilities'. It was *Melody Maker*'s Album of the Year.

Released on 30 August 1985, *The Head On The Door* was a **success**. As well as delivering two immortal and much-loved hit singles, it reached No.7 in the UK and went gold. In the Netherlands it went to No.3. It also made the Top 10 in **Australia** and **France** (where it also went gold), and narrowly missed out in New Zealand. In the **US**, it reached a modest 59, which was nevertheless by far their highest position to date, and also went gold there.

As a commercially acceptable alternative pop record, its timing was perfect for the arrival of Modern Rock radio in the States, and the magnificent Tim Pope **videos** made The Cure regular faces on MTV and put them on the brink of breaking America. In France, it was the album which propelled them to stadium level. It was ranked third in The Cure canon by *Ultimate Classic Rock* and fourth by *Far Out* magazine. And that seems fair – it's probably everyone's third or fourth favourite Cure album.

'I think The Cure really started again at this point,' Robert Smith told *Uncut* in 2000. 'There was a real sense of being in a band for the first time since *Seventeen Seconds*. It felt like being in The Beatles – and I wanted to make substantial "Strawberry Fields"-style pop music. I wanted everything to be really catchy.'

Its success, he told *Cure News*, made him feel vindicated 'after watching all these other people who were really shit sell bucketloads of records', adding that 'everything we'd done up to that point was re-evaluated. Suddenly, we were an important group.'

Hedges, Mike

'Mike Hedges, who started off engineering for us and is now co-producer, is totally deranged,' said Robert Smith on Australian radio in August 1981. 'If we left it up to him to produce, it would be really demented. They [Hedges and **Chris Parry**] have huge arguments, and we all crowd round and listen. The music is taken to a very . . . not superficial but *immediate* level when Chris is talking. He hears things as if they're being played on the radio. He hears things as singles, or as a first-time listener. Which is why it's much more valuable bringing him in to listen to a song rather than working with him. Because he's got a very good ear. And Mike Hedges is the other extreme. He's always wanting to go really over-the-top . . .'

Tall, bearded and wizard-like, Mike Hedges is the genial genius of post-punk production. Born in Nottingham in 1953 to a Catholic family, Hedges grew up in Zambia where he was educated at a Jesuit school, but returned to the UK in 1969. He was working in Haywards Heath as a squash coach when he was offered a job at **Morgan Studios**, initially as a tea boy, tape op and general assistant. One of his first engineering jobs was the soundtrack to the Andrew Lloyd-Webber/Tim Rice musical *Evita* in 1976. Because the older members of Morgan staff weren't keen on punk and new wave, Hedges had a clear run at that sector, and jumped at the chance to work with The Cure. As an eyeliner-wearer at the time, as well as sharing a **religious** upbringing, he clicked with the band, and worked closely with them for three years, providing a counterpoint to Parry's pop instincts (as explained by Robert above). He engineered '**Killing An Arab**' and *Three Imaginary Boys*, then co-produced *Seventeen Seconds* and *Faith* with the band, all at Morgan, as well as the '**Charlotte Sometimes**' single at his own newly opened Playground Studios in Camden (which Robert Smith named). On the podcast *Curious Creatures*, **Lol Tolhurst** and Budgie both credit Hedges with being very open to experimentation and very interested in new technology and techniques in the post-punk era. He also advocated the power of minimalism: 'Mike helped us understand,' said Lol, 'that less is more.'

Hedges stepped away from The Cure after *Faith* because, as he told *Sound on Sound* magazine, 'It was so introspective and depressing, it did us all in.' His role as The Cure's go-to producer was taken, after a brief **Phil Thornalley** interlude, by the equally wizardly **Dave M. Allen**. Hedges would later work with Robert again, however, on the **Siouxsie And The Banshees** albums *Hyæna* and *Nocturne*, and co-produced the **And Also The Trees** demo tape *From Under The Hill* with Robert in 1982.

Outside of his Cure-related achievements, Hedges became one of the truly great producers of the 1980s and 1990s. 'Party Fears Two' by **Associates** and 'The Story of the Blues' by Wah!, two of the pinnacles of the New Pop of the eighties, were his handiwork, and he worked extensively with artists like Marc Almond and Everything But the Girl. In 1990 he bought the Château de la Rouge Motte in Normandy and turned it into a residential studio, installing the mixing desk from Abbey Road which was used on **Pink Floyd**'s *The Dark Side Of The Moon*. Key Hedges productions from the nineties include McAlmont & Butler's 'Yes' and Manic Street Preachers' *Everything Must Go* album. On the twentieth anniversary of the latter, the Manics' bassist Nicky Wire described him as 'this father-like presence', while singer James Dean Bradfield recalled Hedges' unique and unforgettable way of making a first impression: a flaming handshake. 'He'd dipped his hand in calvados and set it on fire, because that's how he greeted every band . . .'

In the 2000s Hedges moved his operation to Westside Studios, complete with the Abbey Road mixing desk, and worked on the music for *Harry Potter* films among other things. He was reunited with The Cure in 2005 for their **charity cover version** of John Lennon's 'Love'.

He retired in 2017.

Hendrix, Jimi

If you trawl through hundreds of Robert Smith interviews, one thing which soon becomes clear is that his most frequently cited **influence** is Jimi Hendrix.

Hendrix was the pioneering guitar alchemist who took the base metal of blues and turned it not merely into gold but into some hitherto-undiscovered futuristic quicksilver alloy from a distant planet. Born Johnny Allen Hendrix in Seattle on 27 November 1942, James Marshall Hendrix first played guitar at the age of fifteen. After a short spell in the **US** Army, the result of a couple of joyriding convictions following which he was given the choice of military service or jail, the reformed teenage delinquent began a career as a session player and sideman with artists including The Isley Brothers and Little Richard. However, it was only when Chas Chandler of The Animals brought Hendrix to London in 1966 and formed The Jimi Hendrix Experience around him that his fame exploded and he earned his reputation as the greatest guitarist of his (or, indeed, any) generation, blitzing the capital's stages with psychedelic blues riffs from his Fender Stratocaster and King Vox-Wah pedal, and causing the most celebrated guitar heroes of the day, from Eric Clapton to Jeff Beck to Peter Green (though not Jimmy Page), to fall at his feet in awe.

The three studio albums Hendrix released in his lifetime – *Are You Experienced* (1967), *Axis: Bold As Love* (also 1967) and *Electric Ladyland* (1968) – were recorded at Olympic Studios in London, in the same room where The Cure would later record their 2004 album *The Cure*. The first of these albums contained 'Purple Haze', as **covered** by The Cure in 1993.

Hendrix's dynamic live performances were literally incendiary: his onstage gimmicks included playing the guitar with his teeth, playing it behind his back, and on one occasion in March 1967 setting fire to it with lighter fluid at the London Astoria (where The Cure would launch *Bloodflowers* in 2000). Word of his showmanship and musicianship reached far beyond the London scene when he played **festivals** such as Monterey Pop (1967), Woodstock (1969) and Isle of Wight (1970), his final UK show.

At the time of his barbiturate-related death in a London hotel on 18 September 1970 aged only twenty-seven, Hendrix had been telling people that he was working on music that could 'heal people'. Because this was Jimi Hendrix talking, nobody laughed.

One of the audience members at the Isle of Wight festival was a young Robert Smith, attending his first-ever gig aged just eleven. He was taken there by his older brother Richard, nicknamed The Guru, who had already indoctrinated Robert into the ways of Jimi via the family record player. 'Jimi Hendrix has always been my idol,' Robert once told *Guitar Player*, 'though I absolutely hate "Crash Landing", "Midnight Lightning" and all that. I remember first hearing [posthumous album] *The Cry Of Love* on a really good stereo when I was 11. I listened with headphones on maximum, just deafened by this stunning stereo picture. It was one of those moments that's stuck with me through my life.'

Speaking to Will Hodgkinson in the *Guardian* in 2003, Smith outlined the impact that the persona of Hendrix had on his childhood mind. 'Hendrix was the first person I had come across who seemed completely free. When you're 9 or 10, your life is entirely dominated by adults. So he represented this thing that I wanted to be. Hendrix was the first person who made me think it might be good to be a singer and a guitarist – before that I wanted to be a footballer.' In an interview with **France**'s *Télérama* in 2012, he expanded on that theme. Discussing his idols **David Bowie**, Alex Harvey and Jimi Hendrix, he said 'They were rogue characters. People who lived a life that was really wild and colourful. I didn't want to be them, but I wanted to be someone who lived in a world that was of my own making.'

If you drop in on almost any Robert Smith interview which discusses his tastes and influences, from any era of The Cure, Jimi's name will crop up. Circa *The Top*, Smith's listening habits involved Frank Sinatra, Erik Satie, **Joy Division** and Jimi Hendrix. In 1987 he listed 'Purple Haze' among his favourite songs, and did the same again in 1989. In 1992 he told *Cure News* that *Axis: Bold As Love* by Jimi Hendrix was one of his favourite three albums. In the same publication in 1995 he stated that he wanted some Hendrix (among other things) played at his funeral. And in 1998 he again listed a Hendrix album among his five favourites, though this time it was *Are You Experienced*.

But how did all this love of Hendrix feed into The Cure's music? Initially, not very much at all, barring a comedy cover of 'Foxy Lady' on *Three Imaginary Boys*. And their 'Purple Haze' cover fifteen years later, which they can be seen hashing out in the tour van on the '**Pictures Of You**' video shoot, isn't entirely serious either. But Hendrix's fiery fretwork audibly left its mark on Smith's playing style. Maybe not on the hit singles, but delve into almost any Cure album from *The Top* onwards and there'll be at least one showpiece track where Robert Smith, **Porl Thompson**, or Smith and Thompson combined, let rip with some sky-kissin' flamethrower Hendrixisms.

Jimi Hendrix himself may have flared fast and burned out in five years flat. As an ongoing inspiration informing Robert Smith and The Cure, however, he's a constant.

High

When Robert Smith was a child, he believed he could fly. He is not alone. It's a remarkably common delusion among children, particularly the more imaginative ones, to believe that they could fly, or at the very least, to refuse to see why they couldn't, through sheer willpower and concentration. From *Peter Pan* to *The Snowman*, the ability to fly is a popular trope in children's fiction. The Swiss psychologist Jean Piaget, in his *Theory of Cognitive Development*, characterised this belief that thoughts can directly affect the outside world as 'magical thinking'. In children, Piaget found, magical thinking is at its peak between the ages of two and seven. Christina Bethell, director of the Child and Adolescent Health Measurement Initiative at the Johns Hopkins Bloomberg School of Public Health in Baltimore, believes magical thinking can be a common sign of psychological trauma. 'It's a form of dissociation,' she told *US News*, 'a coping skill that enables the mind to disconnect from overpowering experience. It's one of the most common things that happens when children have a trauma. If they're unable to process it, they dissociate and indulge in magical thinking. It can lead to bad decisions and dangerous situations.' Magical thinking usually dissipates in adulthood, although arguably lives on in phenomena such as religious prayer, superstitious behaviour, and the New Age self-help fad of 'manifestation'.

'High', a song about 'a girl that swims in a world of magic show', was inspired by a child called Dorothy, the daughter of one of Robert Smith's friends who, like the younger Robert, believed she could fly and, like the older Robert, had an interesting turn of phrase ('sky as a kite' being one example which Smith borrowed as the song's opening line).

The majority of the lyric, however, functions as a straightforward and somewhat cutesy love song, Smith expressing his adoration with the use of his go-to feline references ('When I see you kitten as a cat, yeah as smitten as that, I can't get that small . . .'). When performed live, it's one of a number of songs ('**A Forest**' being the most famous example) where Robert sometimes sings completely different words.

Simon Reynolds praised 'High' for its 'gilded, glazed guitar mosaics', comparing it to shoegaze (a musical movement which was partly inspired by The Cure's earlier works), but it doesn't have the shoegazers' commitment to noise-in-itself, instead using shoegaze-esque effects merely as a subtle flavour note. (The B-side, 'This Twilight Garden', with its dreamy and delicate textures, is far closer to true shoegaze.) In a 1992 interview with *Guitar Player*, Robert revealed that the song came from a musical idea of **Simon Gallup**'s, and compared its looped, repetitive structure to sampling. 'I work out parts that work all the way through a song. It can be nice to go from a chorus back to a verse, but have the same part come in on top of it. It's The Cure version of sampling, really. "High", one of Simon's songs, has the same basic phrases all the way through – you can put any of them almost anywhere, and they'll still work.'

The **video**, filmed in **Mexico** City on a very hot day and, according to Robert in *Cure News*, 'a total nightmare from bottom to top', was shot by **Tim Pope** in extreme high contrast, with Robert clambering over fantasy-looking ruins while the band play around him. At several points, the lyrics are depicted literally: for 'I can't lick that far', a long lizard tongue spills from his mouth. For 'It makes me bite my fingers through', he bites his fingers and they stretch like rubber. And, near the end, he is actually 'sky as a kite', flying through the clouds on a giant kite, in a Jesus Christ pose. If Jesus wore high-top trainers.

In hindsight, it feels counterintuitive that 'High' was the lead single from *Wish*, an album that has receded into the popular memory as 'the album with "**Friday I'm In Love**" on it'. But lead single it was, released on 16 March 1992 in a **Parched Art** sleeve with **artwork** depicting a strange one-eyed red jellyfish-lobster creature against a blue sky. As well as 'The Twilight Garden', the 12-inch and the CD single included another shoegaze-inspired track, 'Play', while the US CD single used *Wish* album opener 'Open'.

'High' reached No.8 in the UK, and fared even better in **Australia**, Ireland, Italy and New Zealand, where it reached the Top 5, and flew as high as No.2 in Portugal. Statistically, then, it was a considerable success. Critically, too, it has its fans. A 2018 article by David Ellis in the *Evening Standard* praised 'High' for its 'stunning yet simple guitar riffs and lush arrangements', Smith's 'jubilant' delivery and its 'dexterous and playful' lyrics, describing it as an 'utterly lovely, loveable thing', and ranking it the eleventh best Cure song of all time.

Such things are, of course, subjective. But in any sane universe, 'High' is not the eleventh best Cure song of all time. It might not even be the eleventh best song on *Wish*.

Horley

'If you lived here,' said an estate agent's sign by the side of the railway track just north of Horley station in the 2000s, 'you'd be home by now.'

From 1962, Horley was home to the Smith family, who had moved south when Robert was three, and stayed there until 1965 when they moved to nearby **Crawley**. A commuter town of 22,000 people, Horley was an obscure Sussex settlement until the opening of Gatwick Airport in 1958, where five years later **US** President John F. Kennedy would arrive in England to be greeted by Harold Macmillan. Since then, Gatwick has seen a massive expansion of runways and terminals. If you live in Horley, you either get used to the sound of the planes or you leave.

Horley has, since the Second World War, never not been represented by a Conservative MP. This, alone, would have made the various left-leaning members of The Cure who grew up, worked and socialised in Horley feel anomalous and alienated. But they made the best of it. As teenagers, prior to The Rocket in Crawley, they would hang out in the Cambridge pub in Horley, which had a Pong machine and occasional DJs, and where fights would often break out between rival youth tribes.

Even after they'd left the area completely, Robert still remembered certain aspects of Horley with fondness. In the diary he kept for French newspaper *Libération* in 1985, he wrote 'The two purest institutions in the south of England: the Kings Head pub and the Curry Inn Indian Restaurant.'

Horley. 'If you lived here, you'd be home by now.' You can say that about anywhere.

Hot Hot Hot!!!

The first of The Cure's two Exclamation Mark singles ('**Gone!**' being the other), funk-rock romp 'Hot Hot Hot!!!' was, like the rest of **Kiss Me, Kiss Me, Kiss Me**, recorded at night in Château Miraval in the South of **France** with producer **David M. Allen**, with the band in a condition of considerable narcotic disrepair. According to Robert Smith in *Cure News*, the lyric was 'espousing the general delights of "altered states of consciousness".'

The effects of whatever varieties of **drugs** and **alcohol** were in their systems acted as a distorting filter for their musical intentions, which were, Robert told a French interviewer, for it 'to sound like Chic'. There is recognisably a touch of 'Good Times' to **Simon Gallup**'s bassline, but the overall effect is clunky, not funky. (Smith's other comparison, to Louis Armstrong, is harder to hear, except in his occasional vocal growl.) The peak of the Madchester movement, and the associated trend for indie bands to suddenly discover a 'dance element to their music' was still a year away in early 1988, so The Cure can at least be said to have anticipated that curve (although they'd been there already, five years earlier, with '**The Walk**' and '**Let's Go To Bed**'). The general daftness of the session is encapsulated in Robert's shrieking impersonation of French crooner Charles Aznavour's 'She' (a song he later revealed he used to sing in the bath) at the very start before the music kicks in, and the uncredited presence of French locals joining in on its 'Hey, hey, hey' chorus.

The **video**, by contrast, was relatively restrained by Cure and **Tim Pope** standards. Filmed in monochrome, it captures the band in a retro setting, with each musician wearing a smart suit on an individual circular riser, and Robert in Ray-Bans sporting the short-cropped **hairstyle** unveiled in **The Cure In Orange**, and singing into a vintage spring suspension microphone. At certain points the band operate marionettes of themselves, and there are cutaways to the obligatory extras in animal costumes and fancy dress. It ends with the entire band pretending to have dwarfism by kneeling on their Converse trainers, an idea which, like **Lol**'s blackface in '**Why Can't I Be You?**', probably wouldn't fly now.

Released on 8 February 1988 and remixed by François Kevorkian (who also did the 12-inch remix of 'Why Can't I Be You?'), in a black **Parched Art** sleeve with a shoal of flying fish shapes as the **artwork**, its B-sides, depending on the format, contained alternate mixes of the A-side, a remix of 'Hey You!', or both. In the **United States** the CD single was released in a longbox, just in case you really wanted a shelving headache.

It received little airplay on UK radio, and poor reviews from **critics**; *NME*'s Steve Lamacq called it 'spuriously welcoming, but basically a tragedy of trenchfoot' and ended with the backhanded compliment 'Even I know [Smith has] better stuff hidden in that mop of his'.

It rose no higher than No.45 in the UK charts, the first Cure single since 'Let's Go To Bed' six years

earlier to fail to crack the Top 40 (though it did reach 18 in Ireland and 8 in Spain). By this time its parent album had already been out for ten months, and there was little incentive for fans to buy the single.

Although it was a fixture in The Cure's setlist as recently as 2016, it is only an occasional visitor nowadays, played just twice on their most recent tour and twice on the tour before that, suggesting it's a song on which Smith and his bandmates have gone cold-cold-cold.

Howe, Honkin' Ron

A bit-part in The Cure's discography is better than no part at all, and **Horley**-based saxophonist Ron Howe holds the rare distinction of having played saxophone (or, indeed, any woodwind instrument) on a Cure track (**Porl Thompson**'s turn on *The Top*'s 'Give Me It' is another rare instance, along with Andrew Brennen's work on **Kiss Me, Kiss Me, Kiss Me**).

Howe originally trained to be a welder at **Crawley** College before becoming a member of Gallup's mid-eighties band **Fools Dance**, adding prominent and lengthy sax breaks to songs like 'The Ring' (on which his improvised solo takes up more time than Gallup's vocal). Howe was nicknamed Don Diddy Don Don by Simon Gallup – perhaps a reference to Don Howe, a venerable servant to Simon's beloved Arsenal as a player and a coach, and possibly a play on the garage rock classic 'Have Love, Will Travel'. Either way, that first Fools Dance EP actually featured a track called 'The Don Diddy Song'.

His most listened-to work, however, will inevitably be his guest appearance on '**A Night Like This**' from *The Head On The Door*, popping up at the two minute forty-five seconds mark for a thirty-second solo – like the goth equivalent of Steve Norman's showpiece turn on Spandau Ballet's 'True' – with additional sax squawks as the song ends.

Honkin' Ron Howe, as he calls himself on his Musicians' Union profile, went on to play with electro-goth band Box Office Poison in the nineties, who had a sideline in cover versions of cult sixties film and TV themes. In 2019, under his own name, he covered the theme from *The X-Files* for a compilation on the Future Legend label.

Still active in the Horley area, he specialises in rhythm & blues, listing Junior Walker, King Curtis and Manu Dibango among his influences, and hosts a tip-sharing Facebook page called Demystifying the Saxophone.

Though never anywhere close to becoming a fully-fledged Cure member – he doesn't even appear in the 'A Night Like This' video – his place in Cure history is secure. In 2020, during Covid lockdown, he reprised his famous solo for charity on a socially distanced reworking of 'A Night Like This' with Cure **tribute band** The Cureheads.

Hyæna

The sixth album by **Siouxsie And The Banshees**, *Hyæna* is one of their finest. (Fans will argue all day about the actual finest – *A Kiss In The Dreamhouse* is a personal favourite – but *Hyæna* must be somewhere in the reckoning.) It's of interest to *Curepedia* because it is also the only studio album they made with Robert Smith. (Smith himself later deemed *Hyæna* a 'mistake'. But musicians are rarely the best judges of their own music . . .

One of Robert Smith's conditions for rejoining the Banshees at the end of 1982 had been that they documented his second stint with a record. The hit single **'Dear Prudence'** had been the first instalment, but he wanted an album to his name as well.

The circumstances of its creation were inauspicious to say the least. Smith was already running on empty, his health and energy levels tipping dangerously into the red by the second half of **1983, Robert's craziest year**. Starting in the summer, *Hyæna* was recorded 'in spare moments' at Genetic Studios, a barn at the bottom of legendary producer Martin Rushent's garden in Streatley near Reading with **Mike Hedges** at the controls, and took ten or eleven months in total. Large parts of it were recorded concurrently with The Cure's *The Top*, meaning that Smith would typically finish work with The Cure at Eel Pie Studios in Richmond then get a taxi to Reading to join the Banshees, arriving still full of **Andy Anderson**'s magic mushroom soup and God knows what else, metaphorical matchsticks propping open his sleepless eyelids. (In this respect, Smith's status as something of a junior partner within the Banshees was both a blessing and a curse. On the downside, he wasn't expected to make the big decisions. On the upside, he wasn't being invited to make the big decisions.)

The state he was in, and his limited availability, caused friction. 'I could understand their frustration with me not being there all the time,' he said in *Ten Imaginary Years*, 'but I got a bit fed up with their dismissive attitude towards what I was doing in The Cure.'

The other three Banshees found themselves easily distracted by the curry house across the road. 'It was so frustrating,' said Smith. 'I'd turn up and they'd all go out for an Indian and leave me alone in the studio with Hedges saying "Right, you've got three hours. When we come back, we want to hear a guitar part."'

Most of *Hyæna* was composed in the studio. According to Budgie, it was the first time they'd gone into the studio with virtually nothing. For inspiration, they had a variety of 'strange little musical toys', like an autoharp, delivered to the studio.

Robert had his own opinions as to where *Hyæna* ought to go. 'After **The Glove** and playing around with the psychedelic thing, it was time The Banshees got raw again and I thought that was the way it would go. It shouldn't have been *A Kiss In The Dreamhouse* Part 2. Lots of stuff came from me and Sev just staying up all night, playing and recording this and that, really rough and very powerful.' (**Steve Severin** would later play down Smith's input, claiming 'Robert wasn't making much of a creative contribution. He tended to turn up and just play along.')

By November 1983 Robert had finished his guitar parts, but there were still creative choices to be made, and he found himself at odds with the others. 'We had a few disagreements about the production,' he told Richard Skinner on the *Old Grey Whistle Test* in 1984. 'When it got to the final stages, I started thinking in slightly different ways, sound-wise. Everyone did, but I didn't have the stamina to argue with the Banshees en masse. There were too many people, I thought, in the studio at the end, so I thought one less would make it easier . . .'

His old pal Mike Hedges being present as producer ought to have helped. Hedges had already worked on the first three Cure albums (two of them as producer), as well as engineering the Banshees' previous album *A Kiss In The Dreamhouse* and producing the debut by Banshees side project The Creatures, so he was a logical choice and an easy fit. However, Smith wasn't necessarily happy with Hedges' treatment of those 'rough and powerful' ideas he and Severin were coming up with: 'the production smoothed it all out', he complained in Brian Johns' Banshees biography *Entranced*.

The smoothing out of those songs was achieved in part by the auxiliary personnel: Robin Canter, a classically trained oboist more used to playing Handel and Haydn, and the Chandos Strings (now Radio 3 regulars under the name Chandos Baroque Players), whose only previous non-classical work was a couple of records by folk singer A. J. Webber. But their instruments were used judiciously, to sharpen the edges of the melodies more often than to dull them.

After the stunning overture of '**Dazzle**' (the strings-heavy single which has its own entry), second track 'We Hunger' was also notably not very guitar-centric (strangely for an album with which Smith wanted to leave his mark on Banshees history). Instead, strings and exotic percussion dominate, with Sioux spinning an extended metaphor involving the feeding frenzy of creatures from locusts and leeches to hyaenas (unnamed, but implied) to humans carving their dinner, comparing all to the vampiric greed and gluttony of consumerism.

'Take Me Back', which began with Robert messing about on a piano, has Budgie's marimba to the fore. Its lyric reads like a short story, its conclusion unresolved: a woman on a night out in the big city feels unsettled and displaced, and demands to go home, only to find when she gets there that 'where you come from isn't always home'.

'Belladonna', one of two songs with lyrics by Severin, is as deceptively optimistic as its title (Italian for a beautiful woman, but also a deadly nightshade-derived poison, used by Livia in ancient Rome to murder Augustus, by the real-life Macbeth to halt the English army, and by the captors of Solomon Northup, author of *Twelve Years a Slave*). While woodwind trills prettily like birdsong, Sioux sings of sirens or mermaids luring the unwary to being devoured by sharks, with some of her most poetic imagery referencing *The Tempest*: 'Five fathoms deep/The lovers leap/The lanterns of skin/Summon us in . . .' The staccato piano tumult of '**Swimming Horses**', another single with its own entry, bookends Side 1.

It isn't until the start of Side 2 that Robert's guitar is foregrounded. On 'Bring Me the Head of the Preacher Man', a narrative set in frontier times with imagery of desert heat, dry bones, vultures, vipers and tequila worms, Smith's fingerwork twirls in sinister Spaghetti Western figures (in a manner that would be much imitated in the later eighties by goth bands like The Mission and Fields Of The Nephilim), Roxy Music-esque clarinet midway through adding to the maelstrom.

'Running Town', discussed under the *File* EP, is next. It was one of three songs, along with 'Bring Me the Head Of The Preacher Man' and 'Blow The House Down', which had premiered on Channel 4's *The Tube* in February. With its cryptic mentions of Martians and rattlesnakes and drowned refugees, it continues the theme of nature red in tooth and claw, and humanity *in extremis*.

This continues on the frenetic 'Pointing Bone', the second song with lyrics by Severin, with its references to hummingbirds, jaguars and flamingos, as Sioux conjures a scene of ritual sacrifice: 'And slaughter grins on a pleasure spike/When held on high by the riverside/Like a torn-throat child in a jackal hide . . .'

'Blow the House Down', with its Celtic folk flavours, alludes to cult horror classic *The Wicker Man*, with thunderstorm Foley effects, chaotic violins and lines about 'bishops falling from the windows'. And there it ends. ('Dear Prudence' was included on the American edition, and on deluxe reissues, but not on the UK original.)

The **artwork** was designed by Da Gama, the prolific team formed by Alex McDowell and John Warwicker (who had previously designed various Banshees singles sleeves, as well as releases by The Creatures and The Glove), using a superb painting by Maria Penn, one of the more interesting peripheral figures in the Banshees universe. Penn was a Native American artist, much-travelled but originally from Portland, Oregon, who once painted a portrait of Duke Ellington, and studied under (and later married) Cubist Willy Hempel, a graduate of the Bauhaus school. Her first husband was Lionel Stander, an actor in many Pre-Code Hollywood films including *A Star Is Born*, and a civil rights activist (along with Maria) who was blacklisted as an alleged Communist under by the House Un-American Activities Committee but made a return in later life in films such as Sergio Leone's *Once Upon a Time in the West* and TV series *Hart to Hart*. (Incidentally, Ava Stander, daughter of Lionel Stander, was a regular at legendary Goth haunt the Batcave, regularly frequented by the Banshees.) Maria Penn's painting for *Hyæna*, in vivid purples and blues, depicted two clawed, fanged animals entangled in either an embrace or a fight to the death. In Mark Paytress' Banshees biography, Penn is described by Sioux as 'this strange Indian woman who was like a female shaman. She was supposed to be on a higher spiritual plane, though I thought she looked like a bag lady. When I met her for the first time, she looked at me strangely and started waving her fingers in the air. All very odd. She was probably checking out my aura.'

Photography was by Anton Corbijn, the Dutch photographer and filmmaker now famous for his grainy black and white album sleeves and videos for U2, **Depeche Mode** and The Killers, and for feature films like Ian Curtis biopic *Control*, but in 1983 just another jobbing rock snapper.

It was released on 8 June 1984 on their own Wonderland label (via **Polydor**) in the UK, and was the Banshees' first record on **Geffen** in the **US**. It came just three weeks after the Creatures' *Feast*, which may have harmed its sales somewhat, assuming audiences' hunger for new Siouxsie product was finite.

In a strangely fantastical review in *NME*, Biba Kopf praised Sioux for 'queening it rather splendidly, marshalling massive blocks of orchestral noise and sending them to do battle with marvellous queenly irresponsibility'. In *Creem*, Roy Trakin ventured the theory that the production was aimed at overdue acceptance by the American market: 'you won't find the catchy minimalism of Siouxsie And The Banshees on US radio, so *Hyæna* tries to adapt the band's basic gloom *und* doom to the dictates of modern pop and rock, turning its existential angst into heavy metal/ new wave rituals.'

Hyæna had an indirect influence on The Cure, specifically pop singles like '**The Lovecats**' and '**The Caterpillar**', if only by default. 'A lot of what would have gone into The Cure went into the Banshees,' Robert told Richard Skinner on the *Old Grey Whistle Test* in 1984, 'which left pop for The Cure to meddle with. So it did have an effect.'

Hyæna's biggest critics are the people who made it. 'I had to finish *Hyæna* because I wanted to stay friends with Severin,' said Robert in *Ten Imaginary Years*. 'Of the ten songs finally chosen, four are good and six are boring.'

Severin later said 'I think about half of it's up to scratch. We were aiming for something that was almost impossible – to try and get an LP out of a band that didn't really exist. And Robert's desire to be a pop star ground everybody down to one of the lowest points the band's ever had.'

Siouxsie, after Smith had quit the band, was disparaging of his efforts, cackling as she told *Record Mirror* 'Fat Boy Smith has nothing to do with our album except that he plays on it.'

No matter. *Hyæna* has aged better than its creators give credit. The listener is having the last laugh.

Hypnagogic States

Hypnagogic States is a remix EP featuring the four singles which had been released in rapid succession in the summer of 2008 in the lead-up to *4:13 Dream*, namely '**The Only One**' (lead track), '**Freakshow**', '**Sleep When I'm Dead**' and '**The Perfect Boy**', as well as an exclusive fifth track called '**Exploding Head Syndrome**'. It was, therefore, something of a miniature reprise of the *Mixed Up* project.

The choice of remixers leant heavily towards the emo scene (see **Mexico**) which had been partially **inspired by The Cure**, with Jade Puget of AFI, Gerard Way of My Chemical Romance, and Patrick Stump and Pete Wentz of Fall Out Boy all featuring. The other two remixers were Jared Leto's band Thirty Seconds To Mars and Sheffield math-rockers 65daysofstatic.

The latter were responsible for 'Exploding Head Syndrome', a twenty-one-minute techno megamix of the previous four tracks which exists only on this EP. EHS is a real medical condition involving an auditory hallucination in which the sufferer 'hears' loud bangs which do not exist externally and are not audible to anyone else, typically while they are falling asleep. This ties in with the EP's title, a hypnagogic jerk (or hypnic jerk) being a sudden contraction of the muscles experienced when falling asleep, causing the sufferer to wake with a start.

Released on 13 September 2008 in an understated word-based **Parched Art** sleeve, the *Hypnagogic States* EP reached No.1 in Spain. All proceeds were donated to the International Red Cross (see **Charity**).

The iTunes version featured a bonus track, 'The Only One' (Remix 65 by 65daysofstatic). However, it was publicly disowned by the band. As *NME* reported at the time, 'The Cure urged fans in September to boycott iTunes and not buy their *Hypnagogic States* EP from the online store. Writing on his personal blog, singer Robert Smith accused iTunes of ripping off the band's fans by charging £7.99 for the EP, which contains five remixes of the veterans' first four singles from their new album.'

Smith urged fans to wait until the iTunes price had dropped to £4.00 before purchasing. Meanwhile he wrote to **Geffen**, their **label**, protesting that the pricing was 'totally fucking wrong'. A spokesperson explained that the EP had been priced as an album in error, and four days after its release the issue was resolved.

I

I is for . . .

Image

When we speak of The Cure's 'image', what do we mean?

Do we mean the **make-up**? 'It's half vanity and half theatricality,' Robert said in a Japanese interview. 'Because I haven't really got much of a mouth. I'm very featureless. I wish I had that kind of mouth. It's not particularly glamorous or flattering. I don't apply it very well.'

Do we mean the **hair**? 'I prefer myself with hair like this,' said Robert in the same interview, 'because it helps me get away with a lot of things. People approach me in a different way . . . Also, **Mary** doesn't speak to me for the first six months of cutting my hair off.'

If The Cure's image simply means both those things, with each having their own *Curepedia* entries, then Robert accepts a degree of premeditation. 'Obviously we think about what we look like,' he said in a 1988 television interview. 'Everyone does. It's impossible not to have an image. If you have a choice of clothes in the morning, you make a choice for various reasons. Either you wanna look a certain way, or you want other people to perceive you a certain way. Everyone's conscious of image. I think it's just that we relegated it to its proper position. Rather than elevate it to something whereby the image is more important than what you were doing . . .'

In their earliest days, The Cure considered themselves 'anti-image', going as far as to avoid having photos of themselves (other than blurred ones) on the front of their record sleeves for many years in order to cultivate anonymity and mystique. In an interview with *Melody Maker* in 1982, Smith acknowledged in hindsight that this was 'probably a big mistake, not establishing ourselves as personalities earlier on.'

If The Cure didn't care about their image, their manager certainly did. **Chris Parry**'s early impressions were negative, as he recalled in *Ten Imaginary Years*: '**Dempsey** wore corduroys, Hush Puppies and a grandpa jumper. Robert had a coat that he wore a lot which looked very nondescript, and Lol [**Tolhurst**] used to turn up wearing any sort of trousers and shoes, a white shirt, and a bit of a beard. And I thought "These guys are a dog's breakfast. The music is great but they look shit."' (The band didn't appreciate being told what they should wear, but nevertheless accepted money from Parry to buy new clothes.)

It wasn't until the *Pornography* era that the now-famous Cure image of messy scarlet lips and big backcombed hair began to emerge, and by *The Head On The Door* they'd fully nailed it down, global icons of **goth** style. But even then, it never felt completely . . . *designed*. In 1987 Robert admitted that his mum knitted his jumpers, and in 1988 he said, 'Everyone who's been in the group is quite scruffy. Porl [**Thompson**] is quite clothes-conscious. Porl's quite smart.'

Speaking to *Female First*, Smith gave reasons both psychological and pragmatic for looking the way he does. 'I hide behind what I look like with the make-up and the hair,' he admitted. 'I know I do, I'm self-aware enough to know why I'm still doing it. It's uncomfortable on the very few forays into real life that I have, getting petrol and shopping, but I've had it my entire life. I'm with a girl who likes the way I look and when I don't look like I look she doesn't like me as much, it's that simple.'

But do we mean something else when we talk about The Cure having an 'image'? Do we mean their *public* image as deities of doom? Their reputation for misery and depression? If so, The Cure have contravened their own image on dozens of occasions, from leaping around in football kits for a photo shoot (see **Queens Park Rangers**) to releasing daft pop songs with even dafter **videos**. It's analogous to actors who play 'against type', like De Niro switching from drama to comedy in films like *Meet the Parents*, or Jim Carrey going the opposite way in *The Truman Show*. There is a power in that. But in order to weaponise that power, you need to have the image in the first place.

Perhaps we mean a combination of all of the above: the lugubrious look *and* the gloomy disposition. As the *Guardian*'s Dorian Lynskey wrote in 2018, 'Since 1983, the sooty eyeliner, blood-smear lipstick and cobwebbed forest of hair have made him a human logo, transmuted, through the work of people such as Tim Burton and Neil Gaiman, into visual shorthand for the morbidly romantic. He looks like The Cure sound.'

In his blog essay *It Doesn't Matter If We All Die: The Cure's Unholy Trinity*, K-punk (aka Mark Fisher) also read symbolism into The Cure's appearance. 'Robert Smith's *look* – that clown-faced Caligari ragdoll – was a male complement to **Siouxsie**'s. And as with Siouxsie's, Smith's bird's nest backcomb, alabaster-white face powder, kohl-like eyeliner and badly applied lipstick is easily copied; a kit to be readily assembled in any suburban bedroom. It was a mask of morbidity, a sign that its wearer preferred fixation and obsession above "well-rounded personhood".'

In a 1990 interview with *NME*, however, Smith denied that there was too much calculation at play, and that most people are comfortable with the apparent contradictions in The Cure's image (whatever that may mean). 'I don't sit around building a persona,' he insisted. 'I go and shop in Tesco's, pushing my trolley around, and the shop assistants don't go "Eh, what's Robert Smith doing in Tesco's? He's an existential miserable bastard, and didn't I see him on *Top of the Pops*?"'

In Between Days

The drum is everything.

The first that anyone heard of **Boris Williams**' tenure on The Cure's drum stool was the thunderous double-roll with which he introduced 'In Between Days'. It's pure Motown. It could be the fill at the start of 'Ain't Too Proud to Beg', 'This Old Heart Of Mine' or 'Dancing In The Street', played by a Funk Brother like Uriel Jones, Benny Benjamin or Richard 'Pistol' Allen. But it's Boris Williams *in excelsis*, announcing his arrival – and the lead single from *The Head On The Door* – with a joyous clatter and crash.

The song began its life, though, on the guitar. 'I bought a good metal six-string acoustic,' Robert Smith told *Rolling Stone* in 2004, 'and as soon as I picked it up I started playing the chords to "In Between Days". I'd never really bothered playing one, because I'd never owned a good one.'

This is easy to imagine happening. Written in G, there's no bridge, no middle eight, just a simple two-chord verse of G and C and a two-chord chorus of Am and D, before resolving back to G and C again. Robert once called it 'what **"The Caterpillar"** should have

been'. It's a perfect pop song, one of those songs that feels so logical – each chord following the one before – that it's hard to imagine a world in which it didn't already exist. It's almost as if it's written itself.

There were dissenting voices, however, who argued that the song *did* already exist, and that whoever had written it, it wasn't Robert Smith. Danny Kelly of *NME* accused The Cure of nicking it from **New Order**: 'The monstrous scale, nerve and cynicism of Smith's plagiarism, in a world where most claim unique creative genius (Dahling), has, oddly, to be admired.' New Order's Peter Hook has also accused Smith of lifting the linear jangle of 'In Between Days' from both 'Dreams Never End' (1981) and 'Love Vigilantes' (1985). Given that *Low-Life*, the album on which 'Love Vigilantes' appeared, came out in April 1985 and 'In Between Days' in July 1985, this seems likely to be pure coincidence: The Cure's recording would almost certainly have been in the can by the time they could have heard New Order's. However, that 'In Between Days' had absorbed the feel of 'Dreams Never End' from four years earlier, even unconsciously, is more difficult to deny. (It's also, of course, impossible to prove.)

The lyrical narrative of cheater's regret – 'And I know I was wrong when I said it was true that it could have been me, and be her, in between without you' – is a classic Cure trope, and begging a mistreated lover to return was a throwback to **'Boys Don't Cry'**.

The main B-side, 'The Exploding Boy', was all about 'excess', Robert told *Cure News*, and was autobiographical, as he said in *Ten Imaginary Years*: 'I drink too much, eat too much, think too much . . . ha! I'd like to explode. It would be a beautiful death.' With similar high-speed strumming and thunderous tubthumping to the A-side, it felt like a sister song to 'In Between Days'. In the *Slicing Up Eyeballs* fan poll of favourite Cure songs, it was the highest-ranking B-side, coming in at No.56 with 535 votes.

The 12-inch also featured the strings-laden 'A Few Hours After This', which was 'about a party I went to', as Robert told *Cure News*. It 'was supposed to be a party song but went wrong', he said in *Ten Imaginary Years*. 'We could fall outside into the busy night,' he sang, 'we could roll around, and find our upside down . . .' The American version had the oil-dark, openly sexual funk of 'Stop Dead' on the B-side: 'You said I tasted right/And swallowed me alive . . .' In 1988 it was issued on the short-lived CDV format with live versions of 'Six Different Ways' and 'Push' as well as the video, but very few people had the technology to play it.

Apart from *NME*'s accusations of plagiarism, 'In Between Days' was positively received by critics. In *Smash Hits*, it was Single of the Fortnight: 'It bounds away at breakneck speed to the rhythm of strumming guitars and a simple little keyboard melody which goes round and round. Even the morose voice of Robert Smith singing about growing old and losing girlfriends can't stop it sounding bright and lively in a Cure-ishly whimsical way.'

Filmed on 18 June 1985 at Fulham Studios, the studio set up by production designer Ged Clarke and used by eighties luminaries including Duran Duran, A-ha, Spandau Ballet, Simple Minds, Eurythmics and Boy George, the video for 'In Between Days' was an instant classic.

Robert wanted it to be like an old black and white Beatles or Dave Clark Five clip from the sixties, but director Tim Pope had other ideas: 'I see it all swooping, really sick-inducing', he told Smith. The conceit was to make it look as if the band were filming it themselves. One trick was the famous shot from the headstock of Porl Thompson's guitar, staring down the fretboard at his fingertips (later reprised on *The Cure In Orange*). This was done using a fairly hefty camera (this being the eighties), attached to the guitar but dangling on a wire with a studio hand in the rafters taking the weight, operated by Pope who frantically ran around following Thompson's movements. The guitar with the camera attached was a fake one, with a different-coloured strap to the one Porl plays when roaming around camera-free (a continuity error which annoyed Robert).

The other gimmick was the swinging camera. It was this which made 'In Between Days', as Robert told ITV's *Night Network* in 1987, 'the most dangerous video we ever made'. Pope's assistant Jamie Reid hacksawed a hole in the side of a steel shopping basket into which the camera was placed. It was then suspended on a trapeze of Kirby wires, with Robert tasked with manually swinging the camera towards and away from his face. However, the weight was misjudged, and the swinging camera in a cage nearly decapitated the singer. 'It came very close to ending all Cure videos because it missed my head by this much . . .' (Tim Pope actually sustained a black eye from the eyepiece bashing him in the face.)

And this was only the first of three layers. The second involved the band with their faces painted in lurid day-glo colours, filmed under ultraviolet light by assistant director Barry Wasserman (aka 'The Bear', who went on to work on films including *The Witches*, *Hard Candy* and *Harry Brown*). The video flickered between the black and white and fluorescent realms, as if the latter were an alternate reality. Sometimes, as in the closing shot of a prone, grinning Smith, the colourful version was superimposed onto the monochrome, lending his face an eerie, malevolent quality.

The third layer? *Socks*. Tim Pope and his production designer Alex McDowell (soon to leave for Hollywood and work with Steven Spielberg and Tim Burton) had been experimenting with animated colour splashes in post-production for a couple of years, starting with Strawberry Switchblade's 'Since Yesterday', and in The Cure's 'In Between Days' they went into overdrive. The video began with an explosion of brightly coloured sock shapes erupting from Lol Tolhurst's piano. What did it all mean? Robert certainly didn't know. 'The only thing I never understood about all the videos we've made with Pap [Pope] were the socks,' he told *Night Network*. Could they have been an in-joke at the expense of Chris Parry, who – as Lol and Budgie revealed on an episode of *Curious Creatures* – never wore socks? It's as good a theory as any other. Whatever the truth, this wasn't the end of it: two videos later, 'Boys Don't Cry' featured day-glo gloves, as a callback to 'In Between Days'.

The video cost £8,000 to make, but more than repaid its cost, as it went into heavy rotation on MTV, helping the single break into the Billboard Top 100 for the first time in The Cure's history . . . just. It made No.99.

Released on 16 July 1985, with artwork by Parched Art which used a photo of the band in neon facepaint taken at the video shoot by Andy Vella, 'In Between Days' became The Cure's fourth consecutive Top 20 hit (though their last for four years), reaching No.15. It was also a hit in Australia, reaching 16 there.

It's a frequently covered song, with versions by artists including Kim Wilde, Superchunk, The Rifles, Paramore, Ben Folds and Get Cape. Wear Cape. Fly. At Robert Smith's Meltdown Festival, Manic Street Preachers performed it live and dedicated it to him. At Korn's *MTV Unplugged*, they were joined by Robert Smith and Simon Gallup for an acoustic version of the song. It was remixed for *Mixed Up* by William Orbit as the 'Shiver Mix', which also appeared on the B-side of 'A Forest (Tree Mix)' in France.

It was used prominently in François Ozon's *Summer of '85* (see **Films, The Cure's Music In**), which was originally to be called *Summer of '84*. 'I absolutely wanted to use their song "In Between Days",' Ozon told the *Guardian*'s Jonathan Romney, 'and he said, "Sorry, but that came out in 1985." So I changed the title, and he let us have the song.' *In Between Days* was also the title of a Korean coming-of-age drama by So Yong Kim in 2006 (see **Films, The Cure Referenced In**).

'In Between Days' is one of The Cure's half-dozen most famous songs, and their third most-played song live. In concert, especially at any festival that is partially populated by the non-obsessed, it's always been an easy way to bring the entire crowd back on board after a sequence of challenging deep cuts.

When Boris Williams (or any of his successors) hits that intro, it's like hitting a home run.

In Concert (BBC recordings)

If you want to hear 'Six Different Ways' played six different ways, you're in the wrong place. But if you want to hear '**In Between Days**' and '**A Forest**' played four times almost identically, or '**A Night Like This**', '**Let's Go To Bed**', '**The Walk**', '**Close To Me**', '**Charlotte Sometimes**' and '**A Strange Day**' three times, from one indoor venue and one rock **festival**, then the BBC's *In Concert* series is your friend.

Back in the age of physical media, it was customary for the BBC to transfer any notable concerts they had recorded for broadcast onto discs to be circulated around their radio stations and kept in the library for future repeats. The Cure were recorded for the BBC's *In Concert* series on five occasions, all of them whittled down to just under an hour in length (which, being The Cure, means between eight and ten songs) for easy scheduling, with massively overlapping track listings. These discs, stored in sober brown cut-out sleeves with a BBC Transcription Services label bearing the expiry date of the BBC's licence to use them (typically five years), were intended for internal BBC use but have inevitably fallen into the hands of Cure collectors.

The first one is a much-bootlegged show from the NEC in Birmingham in 1985, introduced by Richard Skinner. The **artwork**, if you can call it that, is a black

and white photo of Robert Smith with biographical sleeve notes which mug him off for joining **Siouxsie And The Banshees** when he should have been concentrating on the day job.

The 1986 recording is from the **Glastonbury Festival**, with a black and white photo of the whole band this time, and sleeve notes which refer to 'the eccentric Mr Smith'.

The 1988 disc was actually recorded in December 1987 at, again, the NEC. This time it helpfully includes thirty seconds of applause at the start and end, to provide Partridge-like local DJs with an underlay as they talk up to the news. At the time of writing, there's a copy of this one on sale on Discogs for £465 but the seller is, frankly, having a laugh.

In 1990 The Cure were at Glastonbury again, and the BBC were there too, ready to transfer their performance onto another internal LP. This one revolutionises the Beeb's artwork game by bringing a bit of beige and blue into the mix, and the blurb inside gets the timeline wrong, claiming Smith quit the Banshees to concentrate on The Cure in 1982. You simply cannot trust the mainstream media.

By the time of the 1995 recording, again from Glastonbury, the BBC had switched to using CDs for such purposes, and the disc has almost no artwork beyond the titles and running times in Times New Roman, though it does tell you when it's safe to start fading each song without trampling over Robert's vocal.

As Cure **rarities** go, these utilitarian, functional discs are about as boring as can be. Nobody's framing those to put on their wall. Nobody's showing them off to their guests. And if you think they're worth £465, then I've got a bridge to sell you.

Influenced (by The Cure)

Robert Plant once called The Cure 'the last great English rock band'. **Lol Tolhurst** once called them 'virtual inventors of alternative rock music'. If Plant and Tolhurst are correct, then it's hardly surprising if dozens of younger acts have been influenced by them.

One of the earliest notable groups of Cure devotees to make it big themselves were Duran Duran, who often used to attend Cure gigs. Unfortunately, Robert

Smith didn't reciprocate the love, often using them for easy target practice in the press. 'It was generally Duran Duran,' he later recalled, 'which is sad because they loved us and used to come to our shows. However, they represented everything we hated: the whole glamorous eighties consumer bullshit; this horrorshow we were up against.'

Other bands who have acknowledged a Cure influence include My Chemical Romance, **Mogwai**, Muse, Marilyn Manson and Manic Street Preachers, and that's just the Ms. Oh, another one: My Bloody Valentine. Their 'What You Want' is a homage to The Cure's '**Just Like Heaven**', as leader Kevin Shields told the *Guardian*'s Alexis Petridis. 'I had the pleasure of telling Robert Smith that once and he looked at me like he didn't believe me . . .'

The Charlatans' Tim Burgess, on 'Only Took A Year' from his 2020 solo album *I Love The New Sky*, incorporated his love of The Cure into the lyrics: 'What's your favourite Cure LP? I like *Pornography* . . . but it could be any one of three . . .'

In 2006, Pete Wentz of emo band Fall Out Boy interviewed Robert for *Entertainment Weekly* and told him The Cure had changed his life. In 2019, at their Rock 'n' roll Hall of Fame induction (see **Awards**), Nine Inch Nails' Trent Reznor spoke of The Cure's influence on his own band.

It's not unreasonable to assume that anyone who has ever **covered** The Cure is influenced by them at least to an extent (so, everyone from Dinosaur Jr to Tricky to Smashing Pumpkins to Deftones), and the same goes for anyone who has **sampled** them (so, everyone from Massive Attack to Digitalism to Faithless to Mindless Self Indulgence to Yungblud).

Then there are artists whose songs bear such a strong resemblance to The Cure that it can't be a coincidence: the similarity of Babyshambles' 'There She Goes' to '**The Lovecats**', for example, or 'Dreaming of You' by The Coral to the same song.

After fading from coolness for a while circa Britpop, there was a resurgence in hip young Cure soundalikes at the start of the twenty-first century. The Rapture's Luke Jenner did a Robert Smith wail throughout their debut album *Echoes*. Black Kids completely nailed The Cure's cadences on their single 'I'm Not Gonna Teach Him How To Dance With You'. And as for Canadian band Hot Hot Heat, the clue's in the name.

'The tipping point was a few years ago,' Robert told *Female First* in 2008, 'when suddenly bands were coming up who weren't afraid to namecheck The Cure. We were unfashionable pretty much everywhere post- *Bloodflowers*, but suddenly there were lots of young bands who'd grown up listening to *Disintegration, Kiss Me, Kiss Me, Kiss Me,* or *Wish* and didn't know that you weren't supposed to like us. So we kind of knew it was happening, at some point there's going to be a generation of people who are going to go and form bands who have seen The Cure.'

Speaking to *NME*, he added: 'I feel slightly paternal towards some of them. The **Curiosa** thing, when we played with Interpol, Mogwai, The Rapture and Muse was almost like me saying, "Come here, my loves." I felt fucking competitive on that tour, but in a really good way, like, "Now I'll show you what I can do . . ."'

Frankly, it may be easier just to list the bands who have *not* been influenced by The Cure.

Influences (on The Cure)

Every piece of music an artist ever hears is, arguably, an 'influence'. If something is awful, it drives you to be the opposite. If something is forgettable, it drives you to stand out. And it goes without saying that the majority of the music Robert Smith actually likes (see **Tastes**) is an influence, in some way or another, upon The Cure. This entry, however, will concentrate on those artists which have been specifically cited as inspirations.

Smith's formative Holy Trinity, of course, are David Bowie, Jimi Hendrix and Alex Harvey. Bowie and Hendrix both have separate *Curepedia* entries. But The Sensational Alex Harvey Band merit further examination here.

SAHB, as they were known in brief, were formed in 1972 by Glasgow-born Alex Harvey, a former tombstone-maker and Freemason (one of the few to have actually worked in masonry) who had sung in blues and soul bands in the sixties as well as joining the pit band for the flower-power musical *Hair*. By the time he recruited members of Tear Gas, a prog rock band, to form SAHB he was already thirty-seven. That same year, Harvey's younger brother Les was electrocuted in a freak accident while performing with the band Stone The Crows onstage in Swansea.

The Sensational Alex Harvey Band blended Weimar cabaret and hard-edged prog rock, with Harvey bringing a leering menace and sense of subversion to covers of Tom Jones' 'Delilah' and Jacques Brel's 'Next' (memorably performed on the *Old Grey Whistle Test*) as well as their own material such as 'The Boston Tea Party', 'Faith Healer' and 'Give My Compliments To The Chef' (the last two named by Robert Smith as two of his favourite songs of all time). Speaking to Will Hodgkinson of the *Guardian* in 2003, Smith said, 'Alex Harvey was the physical manifestation of what I thought I could be. I was 14 when I first went to see him, and then I followed him around to all the shows. He never really got anywhere, even though he had something so magical when he performed – he had the persona of a victim, and you just sided with him against all that was going wrong. I would have died to have had Alex Harvey as an uncle.'

Almost as much of a star as Alex Harvey, the hoop-jerseyed frontman, was guitarist Zal Cleminson, who wore theatrical costumes and the white facepaint of a mime artist. Cleminson's justification for the **make-up** was strikingly similar to that of Robert Smith: 'The mime face came about with bigger gigs – more people could see what I was up to.' (Compare to Robert's 'I've got quite ill-defined features and I just wanted to make more of them . . . I need to wear it onstage because if I didn't no one would know where my mouth was.')

When Alex Harvey left in 1976, the rest of SAHB gigged under the brilliant name of SAHBWA – The Sensational Alex Harvey Band Without Alex. He later rejoined, but died of a heart attack in 1982 on the day before his forty-seventh birthday.

Another less-discussed influence on The Cure are Wire, the art-rock quartet formed in London in 1976 whose debut album *Pink Flag* is considered a post-punk classic, and whose drummer Robert Gotobed is in no way an influence on the title of a 1982 Cure single. **Chris Parry** booked The Cure a gig with Wire supporting at the University of Kent on 5 October 1978, and the bands co-headlined Aylesbury Friars on 30 June 1979. Smith was, he recalled in *Ten Imaginary Years*, impressed by Wire's stark white lighting, black clothes and 'rigid, dramatic' music, and was spurred into improving The Cure's own act. As he told *NME*'s Mat Snow in 1984, 'The group that really made me re-evaluate how I did things was Wire. We played with Wire in Canterbury, and I thought they were a really brilliant group – they were so powerful. We were headlining and they supported us, and I was really horrified when they finished. I realised I wanted to do something like that, so that was the first time

when everything was slowed down, and everyone really liked it. That way of constructing things and the way I like to hear things continued.'

The influence of Joy Division (and **New Order**) barely needs explaining, but it is explained anyway in the entry for **New Order**. However, a Cure record which many might assume bore their influence, Robert told Mat Snow, did not. 'For *Pornography* the reference point was not Joy Division at all but the first Psychedelic Furs album which had, like, a *density* of sound, really powerful. And I wanted to see what we would do given that sound.'

The Cure's specific influences differ from album to album. For *Seventeen Seconds*, Robert said, 'I wanted it to be inspired by Nick Drake with the clear, finished sound of **Bowie**'s *Low*'. For *Faith*, he told *Record Mirror*, it was **Pink Floyd**'s *Ummagumma*, Nick Drake (again), Benedictine chants and Indian mantras. For *Wish* it was the unlikely pairing of the Human League's 'Human' and shoegaze band Chapterhouse's 'Mesmerize'.

Much of The Cure's inspiration, of course, is non-musical. Robert is stimulated, he once told *Cure News*, by everything 'from Baudelaire to Tommy Cooper'. The Cure's **literary** inspirations (**Albert Camus**, Mervyn Peake, Patrick White, J. D. Salinger, Penelope Farmer et al) are detailed elsewhere in this book, as are their poetic touchstones (Dylan Thomas, Sylvia Plath, Christina Rossetti, T. S. Eliot), and the importance of horror films on **The Glove** is also documented.

Some apparent influences on The Cure turn out to be purely coincidental. 'The first time I ever heard the Buzzcocks,' Smith told *NME*, 'was when I was singing. It was the first time I'd sung – it was in a pub in Crawley – and afterwards someone came up and said, Are you the singer with the Buzzcocks? And I said, Who are they? And this kid gave me this single, which was 'Orgasm Addict'. And I took it home and played it and I thought, God, this is uncanny, cos it was exactly how I sang.' Robert and **Lol Tolhurst** then began going to Buzzcocks gigs, 'but at that time what we were doing was already formulated to a degree.'

Robert makes a distinction between music which puts him in a creative frame of mind and music which directly feeds into The Cure's work. 'I've always liked Joy Division,' he told *NME*. '*Closer* is probably my favourite record – although from day to day it changes, I mean some days I'll choose a Frank

Sinatra album. Depends what I felt like when I wake up. It's more *inspirational*, I think, things like that on me. Like Captain Beefheart is inspirational, but I don't think there's a direct effect. There's a difference between influence and inspiration.'

Integration

The 1990s were the high point (or low point) of fan exploitation. Record **labels** would routinely rinse every last penny or cent from fans by issuing multiple formats of every single, with CD1 and CD2 and cassette and vinyl and, later, Minidisc ensuring maximum revenue and the highest possible chart position. The Cure, through no fault of their own, were caught up in that trend at the very start of the decade. In 1990 Elektra, their label in the **United States**, elected to gather together the four CD singles from *Disintegration* – 'Fascination Street', 'Lullaby', 'Lovesong', 'Pictures Of You' – in a longbox featuring a detail from the *Disintegration* sleeve with a purple wash, and call it *Integration*. A big red sticker on the front promised '17 rare Cure tracks', but their **rarity** was debatable given that each of the singles was freely available and only a year old. All four singles were in their original jewel cases, and the only unique selling point – other than that ghastly purple box – was a folded poster of a clumsily cropped colour photo of the band. Nothing about *Integration* was very 'Cure'. It is not listed on The Cure's official discography. No wonder.

J

J is for . . .

Japanese Whispers

'Originally,' **Lol Tolhurst** told *Record Collector* in 1993, 'the album was compiled to feed the different markets which didn't have the different singles. But the record company got greedy . . .'

Japanese Whispers was a 1983 compilation album gathering the A-sides and B-sides of '**Let's Go To Bed**', '**The Walk**' and '**The Lovecats**', initially put together for sale in Japan and Germany, its title being a play on the children's game Chinese Whispers (known in the US, and increasingly in the UK, as Telephone, due to its offensive connotations) and the lyrical reference to a Japanese baby in 'The Walk', as well as a nod to one of its intended markets. However, it was also on sale, as Tolhurst noted, in the **USA** and in the UK, where it was advertised in *Smash Hits* as 'a special low-price album', costing £3.99 in Woolworths. (It was re-released as a picture disc in 2021 for about £20, which translates to a not-so-special £6.68 in 1983 money).

The B-sides included were 'The Dream', 'Just One Kiss', 'The Upstairs Room', 'Speak My Language' and 'Lament'. Strangely, 'Mr Pink Eyes' from the 12-inch of 'The Lovecats' was omitted, even though the album's running time was just twenty-eight minutes and twenty-seven seconds and could easily have accommodated another song.

The Rob O'Connor/Stylorouge **artwork**, created using a collage supplied by Robert, featured six cherubs with song titles emanating from their mouths. (On the back, the words spilling from their lips were 'Javanese Hipsters? Janet's Slippers? James Flipper? The Cure?')

Released on 16 December 1983, it reached No.26 in the UK (eventually certified silver), broke into the Top 20 in **Australia** and **France** (for the first time in each) and the Top 10 in New Zealand, and also made the Billboard Top 200.

If bought together with *Boys Don't Cry*, it offered a relatively painless way to acquire The Cure's early singles without digging through crates of second-hand **vinyl**. It was rendered somewhat obsolete by the arrival of *Standing On A Beach* in 1986, unless you really, *really* wanted those B-sides.

Join The Dots

. . . aka the Bootleg Slayer.

One thing that's very clear about Robert Smith – see **Ticketmaster** for further evidence – is that he hates to think of his fans having to spend excessive amounts of money just to enjoy The Cure's music. Although it was compiled and released by **Fiction** after the end of The Cure's association with that label, there is no question that the book-shaped CD box set *Join The Dots: B-Sides And Rarities 1978–2001 (The Fiction Years)* came from the same desire to do the right thing: after all, it was compiled and remastered by Smith himself. As well as telling a secret history of The Cure's music, it ensured that no longer would fans have to buy illegal **bootlegs** from the internet or shady market stalls, or pay inflated prices to dealers in rarities, in order to hear The Cure's less accessible past material.

Essentially, *Join The Dots* did for B-sides what *Mixed Up* did for 12-inch versions: made them available to people who weren't millionaires and didn't have unlimited time to go crate-digging. Of its seventy tracks, ten were previously **unreleased**, and a further twenty-five were appearing on CD for the first time. Previously, the *Unavailable B-Sides* tape on the double cassette of *Standing On A Beach* had gone some way to mopping up stray songs. Subsequently, many odds and ends from the vaults would end up on deluxe editions of reissued albums. But, at the time of its release, *Join The Dots* did an invaluable job of, well, joining the dots.

Its four discs were divided chronologically: Disc 1 (1978–1987), Disc 2 (1987–1992), Disc 3 (1992–1996), and Disc 4 (1996–2001). The opportunity to own digital versions of tracks like 'Do The Hansa', 'I'm Cold', 'Mr Pink Eyes' and 'The Exploding Boy' was timely. Some tracks, however, were a little superfluous. The inclusion of the Bob Clearmountain remix of 'How Beautiful You Are', for example, was barely different enough from the *Kiss Me, Kiss Me, Kiss Me* version to merit inclusion. And there was probably no need for three versions of their **cover** of 'Hello, I Love You', nor two of 'Purple Haze' and 'Signal To Noise'. That said, the two versions of

'Lament' make for an interesting compare/contrast, so these things are subjective. On the whole, it used its disc-space wisely, and did a great job of gathering disparate later tracks from **film** soundtracks such as 'More Than This' and 'Dredd Song'.

The **artwork** featured the famous **Andy Vella** photo of Robert from behind, from the 1986 version of '**Boys Don't Cry**', with the backdrop tinted orange instead of grey. The box contained a seventy-six-page booklet including track-by-track commentary, a complete discography of the Fiction years and rare and previously unseen photographs. (They genuinely are seldom-seen snaps to this day, outside the context of the booklet, where they are adorned with aesthetically pleasing sploshes of **Parched Art** paint.)

The reviews were mostly lukewarm to negative. 'This 4-CD sprawl does The Cure's reputation no real favours', said *Mojo*. 'About halfway through this four-disc set,' wrote *Pitchfork*, 'most people will turn off *Join The Dots*.' *Billboard* spoke of 'joyous discoveries to be had', while *No Ripcord* argued that 'three CDs of good-to-great music is a pretty acceptable ratio'. *Austin Chronicle* wrote that 'Any complaint with this set begins and ends with the list price of $54.98. Beyond that, no Cure freak can do without it.' *Trouser Press* made a valid criticism: 'While this would've been the perfect place for 'Hey You!!!' – the track from the vinyl version of *Kiss Me, Kiss Me, Kiss Me* that was left off the CD – to make its digital debut, what's here is a remix, leaving the original hard to find.' And *Uncut* wrote 'This run would undoubtedly be shown to greater effect on a more succinct collection', missing the point somewhat. *Allmusic* got the balance right: 'It, admittedly, may be a bit too much for someone who isn't quite a big devotee of the band, but it's a veritable godsend for those who've been waiting for this for years.'

Released on 26 January 2004, *Join The Dots* crept into the UK Top 100, narrowly missed out in the **US**, but remarkably, given its price and its niche nature, made the Top 30 in **France**.

The booklet ended with a quote from Robert Smith. 'The first thing I always did when I got a new single was flip it over and play the other side. I always hoped the B-side would give me another version of the artist. Something as good as the A-side but somehow different. I expected great B-sides from the artists I loved . . .'

The Cure, on many occasions, delivered on that expectation. *Join The Dots* is proof.

Jumping Someone Else's Train

The Chords. The Co-Stars. The Gents. The Inmates. The Jam. The Lambrettas. The Look. Makin' Time. Merton Parkas. Nine Below Zero. Purple Hearts. Secret Affair. Squire. The Truth.

Between 1979 and 1983, a full-scale Mod Revival took place in the UK in the immediate vacuum after punk. All the bands above were involved and more, but one towered over all the others in terms of success and cultural impact: The Cure's **Polydor** labelmates The Jam, from neighbouring Surrey. A whole generation of secondary schoolboys started wearing parkas, Sta-Prest trousers, V-neck knitwear and bowling shoes in imitation of the band's frontman Paul Weller. The richer ones, if they were old enough, rode Italian scooters.

Along with the Two-Tone ska revival (with whose audience it overlapped somewhat), the Mod Revival was the defining youth subculture of the turn of the eighties. The Who's film *Quadrophenia*, depicting the Mods vs Rockers violence of the May Bank Holiday 1964, was released in November 1979, permanently encoding the style and ethos of the revived tribe.

Inevitably, as an up-and-coming new wave band in the same era, The Cure had various encounters with the Mod Revivalists (for example, an open-air gig in Carshalton Park with Secret Affair and Merton Parkas). But, even more than The Jam, who were already well-established with a string of hit singles and albums by the time The Cure began to emerge, one band were a clear and present menace to The Cure's prospects: Purple Hearts. **Chris Parry** had signed Purple Hearts to **Fiction**, and they beat The Cure to the punch in terms of getting a record out on the label: their 1979 debut single, 'Frustration', was the Fiction's second release and The Cure's *Three Imaginary Boys* was the third (**The Passions**' debut single 'Hunted' was the first.) They were the second band, after The Cure, to have an album out on Fiction with 1980's *Beat That!*, produced by Parry. Improbable as it may seem now, at the time they were The Cure's direct rivals in terms of record company priorities.

Robert Smith was highly sceptical of the Mod Revival, and chose The Cure's third single as a forum for expressing his thoughts. 'It ['Jumping Someone Else's Train'] was a reaction to the Mod movement that was going on at the time,' he later confirmed. 'That explains the sub-Pete Townshend opening chord . . .'

The 'someone else' refers to the original Mods of the sixties and also to the early adopters of the 1979 revival. The lyric addresses itself to the bandwagon-jumpers and trend-followers, attacking their conformism ('If you walk in the crowd, you won't leave any trace') and disparaging their motives ('If you pick up on it quick, you can say you were there'). The final verse nails the tail-chasing futility of following fashion:

> It's the latest wave that you've been craving for
> The old ideal was getting such a bore

The track was recorded in **Morgan Studios** in mid-September 1979, during the enforced break in **Siouxsie And The Banshees**' *Join Hands* tour, on which The Cure had been the support band, caused by the sudden departure of two Banshees, guitarist John McKay and drummer Kenny Morris. While The Cure were recording, Siouxsie and **Steve Severin** turned up at Morgan to ask Robert Smith to fill in on guitar for the remaining dates, having already replaced Morris with Budgie from The Slits but failed to audition a satisfactory guitarist. He accepted.

During her visit, Siouxsie contributed whoops and yelps to B-side 'I'm Cold', originally a **pre-Cure** song, on which Smith's own vocals – 'My body may be made of fire, but my soul is made of ice' – is covered in so much reverb that the words are barely distinguishable.

'Jumping Someone Else's Train' is also notable as being **Michael Dempsey**'s last stand. His final contribution to The Cure was a strong one: Dempsey's busy bassline, which has a hint of The Jam's similarly rail-themed 'Down in the Tube Station at Midnight' (he later said there was 'a little bit of The Jam in there') propels the song along.

A **video** was made retrospectively in 1986 by **Tim Pope** for inclusion on the *Staring At The Sea* VHS. It consisted purely of a sped-up driver's eye view of the railway line between London Victoria and Brighton, condensing a one-hour train journey to two minutes forty-eight seconds. The choice of route was significant: not only did it pass through **Horley** and **Crawley** (and therefore the stretch of track on which The Cure stood in their early **John Taw** promotional photos), but it was the same journey Phil Daniels' character Jimmy made in the closing stages of *Quadrophenia* to the sound of The Who's

'5:15', feeling increasingly disillusioned with the Mod movement.

Released on 2 November as a stand-alone single in a Pop Art-inspired sleeve featuring dozens of cut-out lipsticked smiling mouths, it received only moderate reviews, failed to chart anywhere, and represented a musical dead end for The Cure. But Robert Smith had made his point. And, within a year, Purple Hearts were dropped.*

*There's a bizarre addendum to this. In 2022, a one-sided feud erupted between The Jam and The Cure. In an interview with *Record Collector*, The Jam's former frontman Paul Weller launched into a strange Modfather vs Gothfather tirade. In response to an interviewer's suggestion that 'Pretty Boy', a single by Weller's friend and former collaborator Noel Gallagher, bore a resemblance to '**A Forest**' by The Cure, Weller said 'I can't fucking stand them. Fucking fat cunt, with his lipstick on still and all that bollocks. He's my age as well isn't he? He's a fucking knob-end, man. I don't like him. I wouldn't work with him. There you go, there's someone I wouldn't work with. I'd fucking slap him or something.' (Gallagher, incidentally, was only too happy to **collaborate** with The Cure: his next single, 'Dead To The World', was remixed by Robert.) Smith had done nothing to provoke this attack – well, at least, not recently. (There was a 1985 interview in which Smith stated 'you'd have to be particularly stupid to believe someone like Paul Weller' on matters of **politics**.) Indeed, the bands shared much in common, as well as both being signed to Polydor by Chris Parry: The Cure borrowed The Jam's gear during the *Three Imaginary Boys* sessions, Tim Pope directed videos for Weller's post-Jam band The Style Council before working with The Cure, and on at least one occasion The Cure soundchecked with a cover of The Jam's 'English Rose'. In response to Weller's attack, **Roger O'Donnell** rushed to Robert's defence, tweeting 'I've always thought, as Spike Milligan said, people who live in glass houses should pull the blinds down before removing their trousers . . . Mr Weller?' Robert himself, however, maintained a dignified silence. It's worth noting that while The Jam enjoyed a great deal of **success** before The Cure started having hits, The Cure went on to be far more successful internationally than Weller. Perhaps his eyes are a shade of pretty green . . .

Just Like Heaven

'The best pop song The Cure has ever done . . . All the sounds meshed, it was one take, and it was perfect.'

This is how Robert Smith described 'Just Like Heaven' to Johnny Black in *Blender* in 2003 and, if anything, he's understating his case. The gloriously giddy, wondrously romantic 'Just Like Heaven' is a musical miracle, one of those songs that you can't imagine fell from the hands, mouths and brains of mere humans but must somehow always have been there, an eternal element of the universe.

The song began life as a demo written in the two-bedroom flat Robert shared with Mary in Maida Vale. It was influenced, albeit accidentally, by another yearning indie-pop classic from the previous decade. 'Although I didn't realise it at the time,' he told Black, 'the structure is actually very similar to a song called 'Another Girl Another Planet' by The Only Ones, which I can still vividly remember hearing on the radio late at night in the mid-seventies. The main difference is that as the song progressed, I introduced some different chord changes which give it that slightly melancholic feeling.'

When the band began working on the song in the South of France during the Kiss Me, Kiss Me, Kiss Me sessions, Smith was impressed by the energy that drummer Boris Williams had brought to it, and decided that the instruments should be introduced one by one. And so, on the finished version, we first hear Williams' drums and Simon Gallup's bass, then Porl Thompson's guitar (strumming chords at first), then Robert's twelve-string, then Lol Tolhurst's keyboards, then Porl's guitar (lead, this time), then everything in unison for four bars, with Porl's extraordinary solo, all the way up and down the scales and back again, leaving the listener reeling before we've even heard Robert's vocal: 'Show me, show me, show me how you do that trick . . .'

While the song was still in its instrumental form, Smith smartly gave it to the French TV show *Les Enfants du Rock*, who had asked The Cure to provide them with a theme tune. Robert was already convinced that the song would become a single, and this was a way of ensuring that millions of viewers would already be familiar with it when it came out.

'Some of it's to do with Mary,' said Robert, when asked to explain the lyric he eventually wrote to match the music. 'Some of *all* the songs are to do with Mary . . .' In *Cure News*, he said it was about 'a life-altering night of magic and trickery' spent at Beachy Head in

1980. And the trick? That, he told Johnny Black, had a double meaning. On one level, it was about the thrill he got as a child from bamboozling his friends with a couple of magic tricks he had learned. 'But on another,' he said, 'it's about a seduction trick, from much later in my life . . . The song's about hyperventilating – kissing and fainting to the floor.'

Speaking to Belgian magazine *Humo*, he expanded on that 'life-altering night', which he spent with a group of friends on that Sussex clifftop. 'We'd been drinking, and someone thought it would be cool to go for a walk. But suddenly the fog came in and I lost sight of my friends and could not see a hand before my eyes. I thought I might fall down the cliff if I moved another foot, so I had to sit down until dawn. Later I heard my friends didn't even look for me . . . The bastards! Their explanation: "Ah, it was nearly 5 a.m. and we thought it'll be light soon . . ." I remember thinking to myself that I had to enjoy the moment. You know, get an involuntary glimpse of the real Beachy Head, try to learn something. I also heard voices . . . I nearly started believing in ghosts.'

Whether it's to do with prestidigitation, seduction skills, abandonment or all three, the overwhelming feeling it conveys is that of one person being utterly, devotedly in love with another.

For the video, director Tim Pope went down a literal route, showing the band performing on what appears to be Beachy Head. It was actually a fake clifftop his team had mocked up at Pinewood Studios, cleverly blended with footage of the real Beachy Head left over from the 'Close To Me' shoot, although Robert had a bit of fun kidding *Humo* that they'd returned to the notorious suicide spot, and that he'd visited a cosy pub and a souvenir shop where 'you can buy T-shirts with the cliffs on it and a little black dot jumping off it.' During the piano break, there's a dream sequence in which Mary herself appears in white robes and headdress. 'I didn't want someone that I'd be uncomfortable with,' he said. 'And I can't really imagine grabbing hold of someone other than Mary.' They dance a devil-may-care, vertiginous whirl on the edge of the cliff. 'It's supposed to look like *Dance of the Vampires*, the Roman Polanski film,' he explained. It ends with Robert, having been 'licked into shape' by daylight, clambering precariously towards the cliff edge and peering over it, as rocks tumble towards the waves below. (The video is also notable for featuring Roger O'Donnell for the first time, though he did not play on the record.)

Packaged in a Parched Art sleeve with abstract swirling shapes encircling a central circular void,

'Just Like Heaven' was backed with the somewhat undercooked 'Snow in Summer' on the 7-inch, with the alternately naïve and passionate 'Sugar Girl' added on the 12. (The American market got 'Breathe' and 'A Chain Of Flowers', both previously used on the UK release of 'Catch', instead.)

Released on 5 October 1987, it got no higher than No.29 in The Cure's home country (where, bafflingly, none of the *Kiss Me, Kiss Me, Kiss Me* singles broke the Top 20), though it did eventually go gold. In the **US**, more importantly, it reached No.40 for the first time, providing a platform from which they would build towards '**Lovesong**' going all the way to No.2.

Reviewers at the time weren't unanimously bowled over. In *Melody Maker*, David Stubbs described it as 'a colourful, fluttery, fussy thing', adding that it 'turns my face green, as if having consumed too many truffles.' However, a critical consensus later grew around its greatness. *Uncut* later called it 'one of the most sublime pop songs Smith had ever written', and in 2004 it made *Rolling Stone*'s list of the five hundred greatest songs of all time. It's consistently highly rated by Cure **fans**: it was No.3 in *Rolling Stone*'s poll of The Cure's greatest songs, and No.2 in a similar poll by *Slicing Up Eyeballs*.

It's been **covered** many times in many languages, by artists as famous as Katie Melua and The Lumineers, but the most memorable surely is the slacker-grunge rendition by Dinosaur Jr. The Massachusetts band recorded it in 1989 for a compilation album, but decided it was too good to give away, and kept it for themselves, releasing it as a single on SST. It's notable for the extremely incongruous heavy metal death-growl with which Mascis delivers the word 'You!' in the chorus, and for its abrupt ending which makes DJs look like fools. Robert has said it is his favourite cover of a Cure song ever. 'J Mascis sent me a cassette, and it was so passionate. It was fantastic. I've never had such a visceral reaction to a cover version before or since.' Smith also stated that the Dinosaur Jr version has 'influenced how we play it live'.

My Bloody Valentine's 'What You Want', from their classic 1991 album *Loveless*, is a homage to 'Just Like Heaven', as MBV's Kevin Shields told the *Guardian*'s Alexis Petridis in 2021. 'I had the pleasure of telling Robert Smith that once and he looked at me like he didn't believe me . . .' There is also a superb and completely unofficial electronic dance remix of 'Just Like Heaven' by London duo The Penelopes, released online for free in 2014.

It has, like several Cure songs, percolated through into popular culture. It gave its name to a 2005 rom-com starring Reese Witherspoon (for which Melua recorded her cover), and it was beamed from Houston to outer space as a wake-up call to the crew of Space Shuttle Discovery in 2016 at the request of astronaut Piers Sellers, who was a fan.

One often wonders, when an artist has recorded a truly immortal song, whether they know it at the time, as they stagger blinking into the daylight outside at the end of the session, stunned by what they've just done. In the case of The Cure and 'Just Like Heaven', they knew. 'When I wrote it,' Robert Smith told *Rolling Stone*, 'I thought, "That's it. I'll never write something as good as this again." I remember saying to the others in the studio, "That's it. We might as well pack up." Thankfully, we didn't.'

Just Say Yes

Coming from a band as **drugs**-fuelled as The Cure, it's tempting to imagine 'Just Say Yes' as a belated subversive riposte to Just Say No, the anti-drugs campaign fronted by First Lady Nancy Reagan (and immortalised in a hit single by the cast of British school drama *Grange Hill*). If only the reality were that interesting, or that much fun.

Musical quality is subjective, of course. Each person's opinion is as valid as every other's. That's the beauty of it. However, the glaringly obvious awfulness of a song like 'Just Say Yes' is so difficult to ignore that it borders on an objective truth.

A **collaboration** between Robert Smith and the Nigerian–British singer Saffron (Samantha Marie Sprackling) from the alternative pop band Republica, 'Just Say Yes' was, along with 'Cut Here', one of the two new tracks on 2001's contractual-fulfilment album *Greatest Hits*. Eagle-eyed Cure devotees would have come across the title, if not the track, already: in *Cure News 21*, published in December 1999, 'Just Say Yes' was mentioned as a song which had been recorded (*sans* Saffron) for *Bloodflowers* but rejected. Leaving it off *Bloodflowers* was absolutely the correct decision: it would have sat very awkwardly amid the atmosphere of that album, and perhaps even destroyed it.

The song is a forgettable piece of techno-pop, lent a slight Indian flavour by its sitar sounds and tabla drums, its lyrics a banal and basic hymn to positivity and spontaneity, like something out of a Nike advert: 'Just say yes! Do it now! Let yourself go! Just leap!'

If you're one of the vanishingly small minority of Cure fans who loves 'Just Say Yes', don't be angry: it isn't just this author who considers it shockingly poor. In the fan poll conducted by website *Slicing Up Eyeballs* it was The Cure's lowest-ranked single (and positioned 183rd of the band's 225 songs). Its only chance of escaping Worst Cure Single status is a technicality: arguably it wasn't a single at all, as it couldn't be bought separately from *Greatest Hits*, but was released to radio stations as a promotional single under the non-standard catalogue number JSY1, with a video to accompany it.

That video is a fairly standard performance clip, with a little goofing around: a mouse costume, some instrument-swapping (during which **Roger O'Donnell** pretends to hurt his finger on **Jason Cooper**'s drum kit), and an *Alice in Wonderland* 'Eat Me' medicine bottle (harking back to Robert's appearance in *Play At Home* with **Siouxsie And The Banshees**) and a Garden of Eden-esque green apple as props. Saffron commits to it with maximum energy, as she does on the single itself.

That energy is what she was hired to provide. For Robert Smith, working with a co-singer was a highly unusual move: it was The Cure's first duet on record, only Robert's second duet ever (having previously sung live with **David Bowie**), and Saffron was only the second guest artist on a Cure record after guitarist **Reeves Gabrels** (himself later a full member of The Cure) on '**Wrong Number**'. As duets go, it's an unorthodox one: rather than trading lines or verses, or even harmonising, both singers sing (or shout) all the lines in the same tune at the same time – they actually shared the same vocal booth – until the very end when Robert yelps a petulant solo 'YES!' The reason for this became clear later. 'When we re-recorded "Just Say Yes", I wasn't able to sing,' Robert admitted to an Italian interviewer. 'That's why I asked Saffron to do it. I wasn't able, I had torn my throat.'

Spare a thought for Saffron in all this. Republica were on hiatus following the collapse of their record label, just four years after the height of their own chart success with the hits 'Ready To Go' and 'Drop Dead Gorgeous'. She'd already collaborated with The Prodigy and, with her band on ice, would later guest with Jeff Beck, Deepsky and Junkie XL, but working with The Cure meant more. She was, as she revealed to MTV's Ray Cokes when she and Robert were interviewed together, a lifelong Cure fan. 'The Cure

have always been with me, they span generations . . . I'm very lucky and honoured to have sung on a Cure record.' She named *The Head On The Door* as one of her favourite albums in *Louder Than War* and, speaking to *Monstagigz*, said of The Cure 'It's some part of my being, my soul, of who I am and my band. The songs mean so much and [Robert's] an inspirational figure and a genius songwriter.'

Saffron had attended many Cure gigs, most recently the *Bloodflowers* show at Wembley Arena, but didn't actually meet Robert until a Smashing Pumpkins gig where, she told MTV, she broke the ice by talking about the piglet on Robert's knapsack, because her own nickname – given to her by Gary Numan and his wife – was 'Piglet'. (Robert immediately denied owning such a knapsack.) When he phoned her to suggest working together, she told *Monstagigz*, she initially believed it was her ex-boyfriend, and greeted him with 'What the fuck do you want?', till he replied 'It's Robert Smith from The Cure!'

Working with one of her heroes was nerve-wracking, she admitted. 'I don't get nervous, I just get butterflies, adrenaline . . . but somebody like Robert Smith?' Saffron performed the song live with The Cure at a show in Paris, during which she asked Robert if her lipstick looked OK. His own **make-up** being famously inexact, the messy-mouthed singer's reply was, 'Are you taking the piss?'

She later described herself as 'so lucky' to have duetted with Robert Smith, and remembered the project as 'a precious moment' in her life. It's unfortunate that this precious moment involved one of The Cure's weakest songs; one which should probably never have seen the light of day.

As *Greatest Hits* was The Cure's final album for **Fiction/Polydor**, and 'Just Say Yes' their final single of any sort for a company with whom the band's relationship had irretrievably deteriorated, the awfulness of 'Just Say Yes' can perhaps be interpreted as a deliberate fuck-you.

If so, it's nevertheless a somewhat self-defeating one. The purpose of any Greatest Hits album is, to a large extent, to provide new listeners with a Beginner's Guide to an artist's oeuvre. The purpose of a promotional single and video is to lure them into purchasing that album. With that in mind, 'Just Say Yes' starts to look like a monumental act of self-sabotage. For anyone who had never heard The Cure before, a first encounter with 'Just Say Yes' might have put them off for life.

If you're tempted to give it a play, heed the words of Nancy Reagan. Just say no.

K

K is for ...

Killing An Arab

Has any debut single ever caused so much trouble?

'Killing An Arab' was always in the running to be The Cure's first single. Indeed, their immediate **pre-Cure** incarnation Easy Cure broke up with **Hansa** precisely because the German label refused to release the track.

On 20 September 1978, **Chris Parry** booked The Cure into Studio 4 at **Morgan** in Willesden, with **Mike Hedges** as engineer and Parry himself as producer. By daybreak on the following day they'd recorded 'Killing An Arab', '**10.15 Saturday Night**', 'Fire In Cairo', 'Plastic Passion' and 'Three Imaginary Boys'. The first two tracks provided the A and AA-side of The Cure's vinyl debut.

The song was a case of nineteen-year-old Robert Smith wearing his reading on his sleeve, as young men do. He had read the classic Existentialist novel *L'Étranger* (*The Stranger* or *The Outsider*) by **Albert Camus** in the original French. Smith made the strange, and in many ways catastrophic decision to foreground the ethnicity of the man shot dead by Meursault, the novel's protagonist, in both the chorus and the title. The band, management and label can't not have known that the title was provocative, nor can they have been unaware that focusing on the race of Meursault's victim placed a particular emphasis that wasn't there in Camus' novel. These decisions had far-reaching consequences. But we'll come to that.

The song itself was a perfectly reasonable piece of post-punk, with an ersatz Maghreb curlicue from Smith's guitar at the start and end giving it a sense of location, **Lol Tolhurst**'s bash-crash drumming very high in the mix, and backing vocals from bassist **Michael Dempsey** (a rare case of a Cure record featuring a voice which isn't Robert's).

The **artwork** from **Bill Smith** depicted a pair of psychotic staring eyes and the first instance of the classic dropped-C Cure logo. The music press advert, designed by Parry (a blurry, reversed image of an old man's face) actually listed '10.15 Saturday Night' above 'Killing An Arab'.

The song was initially released on 22 December 1978 on indie label **Small Wonder** for the first fifteen thousand copies (because **Polydor** didn't want to release any Cure product just before Christmas) then reissued by **Fiction** two months later. Polydor also included it on their Various Artists compilation *20 of Another Kind* in 1979, in between tracks by the more straightforwardly punk acts such as Sham 69 and Stiff Little Fingers, meaning that 'Killing An Arab' became many people's first exposure to The Cure, beyond those who actively went out and bought the single. No **video** was filmed at the time, but **Tim Pope** retrospectively made one in 1986 for inclusion on *Staring At The Sea*, starring veteran fisherman John Button, whose face appeared on the front of *Standing On A Beach*.

The single elicited a decent ripple of appreciative coverage in the UK music press, including an interview by Adrian Thrills in *NME* on 16 December 1978 under the headline 'Ain't No Blues for the Summertime Cure' which described the band as 'an abrasive light metal trio' and 'a breath of fresh suburban air'. Ian Birch in *Melody Maker* compared the Arabic motif ('Moorish-flavoured guitar pattern') of 'Killing An Arab' to the Chinese motif used by **Siouxsie And The Banshees** on 'Hong Kong Garden' the same year, the first time the bands had been mentioned in the same breath. It wouldn't be the last. There was even a front cover story in the 27 January 1979 issue of *Sounds* by Dave McCullough, with the interview, headlined 'Starts in Embryo', conducted in the Natural History Museum with the band, at their own request, photographed in front of a pickled foetus sucking its thumb. The Cure, as a public entity, were up and running. And that's where the trouble began.

It didn't help that Robert had told Adrian Thrills that 'the song's dedicated to all the rich Arabs who go to **Crawley** College discos to pick up the girls', before clarifying what the song was really about. 'It could have been a Scandinavian or an English bloke – the fact that he killed an Arab has nothing to do with it really.' Nor did it help that *NME*'s news pages re-ran only the first half of that quote, without the Camus clarification, in a news story the following week. Nor did it help that *Music Week* erroneously listed the song as 'Kill An Arab', lending it an even more misleading emphasis. (**John Peel**, at least, seemed to know his Camus; playing a session version of 'Killing An Arab' on his BBC Radio 1 show, he said, 'Defensively, of course . . .')

As early as 9 February 1979, before the Fiction re-release was even out, a gang of racist National Front skinheads turned up at The Cure's gig at London punk venue the Nashville Rooms, distributing leaflets and hell-bent on **violence**. Word reached Kingston Polytechnic, where The Cure were due to play the following night, and Robert was told he couldn't play 'Killing An Arab'. He explained the song's **literary** background, and they relented. A whole year of having to issue denials ensued, and by the time of their show in Oxford on 26 September he was wryly introducing the song as 'Family favourite "Killing An Arab"'.

The controversy died down until the song's inclusion on *Standing On A Beach* in 1986. The enthusiasm with which many xenophobic **US** DJs played the song prompted the band to add a sticker to North American releases which read: *The song 'Killing An Arab' has absolutely no racist overtones whatsoever. It is a song which decries the existence of all prejudice and consequent violence. The Cure condemn its use in furthering anti-Arab feeling.* Smith also requested that radio stations should not play the song.

In 1991 the issue flared up again when the first Gulf War between Iraq and the US (and its allies the UK, **France**, Saudi Arabia and Egypt) broke out over the former's invasion of Kuwait. The unwanted radio play went into overdrive, and Robert was forced to hold a press conference to explain that the song was a reference to *L'Étranger* and not an Islamophobic anthem. 'It was totally surreal,' Smith told the *Guardian*'s Dorian Lynskey later, 'explaining Camus to a sea of utterly bemused faces.'

When the second Gulf War began in 2003, The Cure stopped playing the song in America after becoming aware of 'idiot DJs dusting it off'. Robert then had a rethink. 'When it started happening,' he told *Rolling Stone* later, 'I'd be tearing my hair out literally, like, what the fuck? How can I counteract this? So I figured the best way would be to start playing it again. In a funny way, it diminishes it . . . It becomes a song again, rather than a title.'

One way in which Smith has defused the song's negative power, while still being able to perform it, has been by altering the lyrics. Throughout the summer **festivals** of 2005, it became 'Kissing An Arab'. In 2011, as immortalised on their *Bestival Live* LP, it was 'Killing Another'. At other times it has been 'Killing An Arab'.

In fact, Smith was changing the words as long ago as 1980, for not especially political reasons. When The Cure played SO36 in Berlin on 28 May that year, Robert won over the crowd by singing 'Killing Kevin Keegan' instead. (Three weeks earlier, local football team Hertha Berlin had been thrashed 6–0 by Keegan's Hamburger SV, on the way to getting relegated – Keegan scored.)

The most difficult decision they had to face was whether to play it as part of their headlining set at 2019's British Summer Time festival in London's Hyde Park when celebrating forty years of The Cure (see *40 Live*). 'I just wanted to reclaim it,' he told *Rolling Stone*. 'I thought if I can't do it now with the 40th anniversary of it, that's it. What am I going to do, pretend I never wrote it? I've reached an age where I think if people misunderstand it and don't bother to try and understand what the song is about, then tough shit, really. I've given up explaining. Go read Albert Camus. I mean, go read Albert Camus anyway, because he wrote some great books . . . It's been misappropriated, and I thought I should take it back. In modern parlance, I should own that song again.'

The show was on 7 July, the fourteenth anniversary of the 7/7 Islamist terrorist atrocities, and a commemoration had taken place in Hyde Park on the morning of the show. In Robert's view, there was therefore 'a certain poignancy' in playing the song. 'I was showing the others [the setlist],' he told *Rolling Stone*, 'and everyone was looking me like, "Are you fucking mad? Of all days and of all times to play that? Why are we doing it now?" So I sat down and explained, "Let's not fall into that trap. This is not about killing Arabs . . . "' Smith believed that it would have been 'a cop-out' to not end The Cure's fortieth anniversary show with '10.15 Saturday Night' and 'Killing An Arab', the two sides of their first single. That is exactly how they ended the show.

In hindsight, Smith accepted that to some extent he had brought the trouble upon himself. '"Killing An Arab" is a song about many things,' he told *Rolling Stone*, 'but essentially, it's about the value of human life and the value that other people give to their own life and to others. It's a complex subject distilled very badly into a three-minute pop song. I could probably write a better one now, but I don't think it would have the same authenticity. Probably one of my few regrets in life is actually calling it "Killing An Arab". If I'd called it "Staring at the Sea", none of the controversy would have ever happened. No one would have bothered with it . . .'

Kiss Me, Kiss Me, Kiss Me

In the aftermath of punk, the double album had been discredited. It was, along with double-necked guitars and double-length limousines, viewed as a disgusting habit of millionaire prog-rock dinosaurs, associated with enormous artistic self-indulgence (and not, as the artist presumably hoped, evidence of their unbounded creative genius).

The Cure, equal parts **Pink Floyd** and Buzzcocks, were on the fence about such things, and broadly unbothered by incurring the wrath of the post-punk credibility police with the odd bit of hippie excess.

The first punks to break ranks were The Clash, who intended *London Calling* (1979) to be a double album but were refused permission by CBS, then retaliated by making *Sandinista!* (1980) a *triple* album. They were roundly mocked for doing so.

By 1987, however, such concerns were starting to fade. Two significant double albums – both, coincidentally, from Minneapolis – emerged at the start of the year. The first, in January, was Hüsker Dü's *Warehouse: Songs And Stories*, and the second, in March, was Prince's *Sign 'O' The Times*. By the time The Cure delivered theirs, in May, the path had been cleared. (And a year later, now that it was definitely safe to do so, U2 followed suit.)

Around this time, Robert Smith was going through an unusually prolific phase, even by his own standards. He was living in a small two-bedroomed flat in Maida Vale with **Mary**. One room was for sleeping in, the other for music. And he set himself rules about songwriting. 'Just about the only discipline I had in my life was self-imposed,' he told Johnny Black in *Blender*. 'I set myself a regime of writing 15 days a month, otherwise I'd have just got up in the mid-afternoon and watched TV until the pubs opened, then gone out drinking.'

Work on *Kiss Me, Kiss Me, Kiss Me* began almost immediately after the end of the European leg of the Beach Party Tour, as immortalised by *The Cure In Orange*, in August 1986. After Orange, they stayed in the South of **France** and shared a band holiday together at Le Mourillon on the Côte d'Azur – a sign that this was a relatively stable and harmonious **line-up**. Their wives and girlfriends – Mary, **Porl Thompson**'s girlfriend (and Robert's sister), Janet, **Simon Gallup**'s girlfriend (and Porl's sister) Carol, **Boris Williams**' girlfriend Cynde and **Lol Tolhurst**'s

new American girlfriend Lydia (who had been introduced to him by Cynde) – came out to join them. The band and their partners were unable to enjoy any privacy, however – a throng of fifty Cure fans gathered outside the hotel and stalked their every move.

Their next move was to Draguignan, to a studio owned by Jean Costa (an arranger, songwriter and trombonist who had worked extensively with Johnny Hallyday) to refine the songs they had demoed earlier in the year at Boris' house. Costa was at the controls, and would serve glasses of pastis at the end of each session. In his memoir *Cured*, Lol Tolhurst remembers it as a harmonious time, comparable to the 'band camp' days at Robert's house when they were kids. Actual kids, however, had followed them and were sat outside the studio listening. It was time to move on, one more time.

There is a long and rich history of British artists recording landmark albums in French châteaux. In 1971, The Rolling Stones went to Château Amicitia (by then renamed Nellcôte) to make *Exile On Main Street*. In 1976, **David Bowie** went to Château d'Hérouville to begin work on *Low*. And in 1995, Manic Street Preachers went to Château de la Rouge Motte to record *Everything Must Go*.

Château Miraval is a mansion with a vineyard attached, in the village of Var, midway between Aix-en-Provence and Cannes. It had been operating as a part-time recording studio since 1977 when a desk was installed by its owner Jacques Loussier, a renowned jazz pianist who had performed with Charles Aznavour (as interpolated by Robert Smith on **'Hot Hot Hot!!!'**). It would later be owned by Brad Pitt and Angelina Jolie. In 1979, Pink Floyd went there to record *The Wall*. In 1986, Lol Tolhurst went there and fell off one.

Alcohol, inevitably for a band like The Cure living in an actual vineyard, was a major feature of the sessions. 'I'd go outside every day and sit on my rug with a bottle of water,' Smith told Johnny Black, 'and try to finish a lyric by six o'clock, at which point Simon would come out with a pint of chilled Guinness – we'd brought our own supply – which would signify that the bar was now open.' It was estimated that one hundred and fifty bottles of wine were consumed in one week by The Cure and their entourage, much of it by Tolhurst, whose drinking was now so serious that he was often unable to play. On one occasion, he had a row with Lydia and woke up face-down in the vineyard.

On the whole, however, it was an idyllic time. 'The dinners were really pleasant occasions,' Robert recalled in *Rolling Stone* in 2004. 'The girls were there, so the conversation was kind of elevated above what it usually is when it's just a bunch of blokes.'

Everything was fine as long as they stayed inside Miraval. However, Robert had arranged for his white Jeep (see **cars**) to be sent over to France so he could drive around. (Fans, inevitably, had scrawled messages to him on the paintwork.) Before long, that Jeep was written off completely during a late-night driving escapade through the village involving the whole band, which left it dangling precariously over a precipice. 'There we were,' Robert told *Cure News* later, 'hanging upside down in a ditch, and I could smell petrol. I thought we were going to blow up because Simon had a lit cigarette in his hand and I was too shocked and hurt to move.'

Co-producing the album was their now-regular rider of the faders, **David M. Allen**. With Allen at the helm, the band recorded the songs live rather than building them from pieces, which contributed, Smith said in 1988, to the album being the best they'd ever made. There was also an uncharacteristic speed and spontaneity to proceedings. 'After we'd finish recording for the day,' Smith told *Rolling Stone*, 'I would go and sit down in the woods and write another song. And they were done so fast. We didn't fuck about with production; there's a quite touchingly naïve sound on some of the songs.'

For quality control – always an issue when a band is suffering from creative diarrhoea and heading towards a double disc release – they often sought a second opinion. 'We use to have this thing called "the panel",' Smith recalled, 'and all the girls would sit on the sofa in the back of the control room and give the songs marks out of ten – so there was a really big female input. They wouldn't like "Fight", which was really not a girly song. But the more male members of the band were like, "This is rock! This is what we should be doing, not this other wussy stuff." "Shiver And Shake" was my male kind of song. "The Perfect Girl" was a very female song. I think that's probably why the album had such a huge appeal, and why it did so well.'

The first song passed by the panel, or at least the first on the LP's running order, was 'The Kiss'. A bold, ambitious opener, which sounded like the black smoke billowing from some great conflagration, 'The Kiss' was a statement of intent. It's one of many Cure songs that goes on for so long without a vocal that you assume you're hearing an instrumental, with nearly four minutes of squalling guitar (inspired, Smith confirmed, by his hero Jimi Hendrix) before the vocals come in. And when they do, they are profoundly **sexual**.

Your tongue is like poison
So swollen it fills up my mouth

But it is also deeply twisted, with lines like 'Get your fucking face out of my head' (words later paraphrased on 'Us Or Them' on *The Cure* in 2004) and 'I wish you were dead'. In *Cure News*, Smith summarised it as 'the sickness of lust'.

It was followed, in stark contrast, by '**Catch**', the album's second single (which has its own *Curepedia* entry), exemplifying the 'touchingly naïve' aspect of which Robert spoke. The purposeful 'Torture' was a narrative from inside a sex dungeon:

It tortures me to move my hands
To try to move at all
And pulled
My skin so tight it screams

Later the lyric runs 'Hanging like this, like a vampire bat'. It was, as Smith wittily put it, about 'abasement in a basement'.

The fourth track, closing Side 1, was utterly magnificent. 'If Only Tonight We Could Sleep' unfolded like curlicues of burning incense for nearly five minutes over a sparse rhythm track which sounded like a slow-motion rattlesnake. Stripped down, atmospheric and intoxicating, it was a mesmeric track, and one which, at almost five minutes long, vindicated the decision to let these songs breathe for as long as they needed to. Smith explained its lyric as being about 'a slow and happy death' (a possibly unintended reference to **Camus**). It was covered by **Deftones** on the MTV Icon special in 2004, and again at Robert Smith's **Meltdown**.

Side 2 began with the first song anyone heard from the album, the brassy blast of '**Why Can't I Be You?**' (not only the lead single but the first song premiered in concert, on three occasions on the French tour). Robert described it as 'me bemoaning my inelegance? Or being jealous of someone else's poise?' (It has its own *Curepedia* entry.)

The lyric to 'How Beautiful You Are', musically a dry run for '**Lovesong**', was adapted from a short story by Baudelaire, 'The Eyes of the Poor'. In the story, the narrator recounts a glorious romantic day spent in **Paris** with his lover, culminating with an evening in a luxurious new café. A poor man and his ragged children walk past, gazing in awe at the splendour. Instead of showing compassion, the narrator's lover asks him to get the maître d' to send them away. The scales fall from his eyes. In his lyric, against some thematically appropriate French accordion, Smith takes that disillusionment one step further: 'You want to know why I hate you? Well, I'll try to explain . . .'

In 'The Snakepit', the album's longest song at nearly seven minutes, Smith recounts what he described as 'a bitter experience'. In the first verse he's 'kissing you hard like I've got very important business', and in the second he's 'out in a car and it's just full of stupid girls'. Interestingly, 'The Snakepit' begins with the couplet 'Well we're a mile under the ground/and I'm thinking that it's Christmas', while the next track 'Hey You!!!' begins 'Hey you! Yes, you, yes you/The one who looks like Christmas', putting a more positive spin on the same metaphor. Another drum-crashing Fauxtown tune in the 'Why Can't I Be You?' vein, 'Hey You!!!' was described by Robert as 'a party song'. Its very brief lyric (the song is the album's shortest at only 2.22) is essentially a youth club chat-up line, following the Christmas couplet with 'Come over here and kiss me'. It features saxophone from Andrew Brennen, recorded separately by Sean Burrows at Compass Point, Nassau. (Brennen is still active, playing weddings and other occasions in the West Palm Beach, Florida area.) 'Hey You!!!' was left off the CD, but included on the **vinyl** – a rare case, in the history of music retail, where it is CD-purchasers, not vinyl-lovers, who get screwed over. (It was reinstated on the 2006 reissue.)

Side 3 began with '**Just Like Heaven**', the third single to be taken from the album, and simply one of The Cure's greatest ever songs. It broke them into the **US** Top 40 for the first time, greatly assisting sales of the album. (And it has its own entry in *Curepedia*.)

The metallic, abrasive 'All I Want' was, Smith said, about 'sex', and fourth single 'Hot Hot Hot!!!' (the album's funked-up fourth single, which has its own *Curepedia* entry) about '**drugs**!' No wonder, then, that the third track on Side 3, the tranquil and restrained 'One More Time', was dedicated to 'mourning the loss of innocence'.

'Like Cockatoos' began with a similar oscillating sound to **Siouxsie And The Banshees**' 1985 single 'Cities In Dust' (with which Robert had no involvement), before moving into a naggingly memorable bass-and-guitar pattern over which Smith sings one of his many **dream**-based lyrics in which a woman walks through a surreal nightscape where blood falls like rain.

Side 4 begins with 'Icing Sugar', on which Andrew Brennen also plays saxophone, over rolling drums straight out of The Surfaris' surf-rock classic 'Wipe Out'. A love song of sorts, it could equally be interpreted as yet another about drugs. There was no such ambiguity about 'The Perfect Girl', in which a giddy Smith, over chocolate-box violins and guitars which recall '**Dear Prudence**', expresses his devotion

to a 'strange girl' who seems to 'come from another world'. It's not unpleasant, but doesn't do anything that 'Just Like Heaven' or 'Catch' haven't already done better. However, 'A Thousand Hours', summarised by Robert as 'why can't I be me?', is ravishingly gorgeous, a forlorn lament about his own emotional numbness topped and tailed by the desolate cry 'For how much longer can I howl into this wind?'

The penultimate track is the dense diatribe 'Shiver And Shake', which does exactly what it promises. Smith pours out unbridled vitriol at someone who is 'a waste of time', 'just three sick holes that run like sores' and 'a slug on the floor' and makes no secret of his desire to 'smash you to pieces'. It was almost immediately assumed to be about Lol Tolhurst, a suspicion which was confirmed in *Cure News* in 1992 when Smith described it as 'an appreciation of Lol, and others like him'.

The album ends with the mid-paced 'Fight', drenched (ironically enough) in Tolhurst's synths, with a lyric of defiance, summarised by Smith as 'never give up never give in if you're determined'.

Every lyric was written by Smith, but musical composition was shared around the group. 'Icing Sugar' and 'The Perfect Girl' came from Gallup, 'Like Cockatoos', 'Fight' and 'The Snakepit' from Thompson and Williams (who wrote together).

The album's then-gargantuan 74.35 running time allowed it to use every colour of The Cure's stylistic palette. 'In a strange way,' Robert told *Oor* in 1989, '*Kiss Me, Kiss Me, Kiss Me* was a logical follow-up to the singles album. It was a showing off what we were capable of, but with new numbers.' Simon Gallup added 'It was our K-Tel album!' (referring to the British record label famed for its Various Artists pop compilations), to which Robert jokes 'Our disco album'. All of this may, however, have been an attempt to post-rationalise. The real reason it was a double album, he later told *Rolling Stone*, was that they were having so much fun that they didn't want to stop.

The reddish-orange **artwork** by **Parched Art** is a luridly intimate close-up of Robert's lipsticked mouth (and the reverse is an equally zoomed-in photo of his iris). In a 1991 issue of *Cure News*, Robert said he enjoyed how 'disgusting' it is. The image, of course, echoed the album's title. '[The title] was a reaction against so much emphasis being placed on my mouth,' he explained. 'That's why there's so much red. It's become such a focal point that I thought by taking it to the extreme it would deflate the whole thing.' (Given that one title under consideration, according to

Adventures And Plans, was *One Million Virgins*, the artwork could have been a whole lot worse.)

Kiss Me, Kiss Me, Kiss Me was released on 26 May 1987, and was in some territories accompanied by a limited-edition orange vinyl EP featuring the songs 'Sugar Girl', 'Snow In Summer' ('not one of my favourite songs, this didn't really turn out right'), 'Icing Sugar (Weird Remix)', 'A Japanese Dream' ('something that happened while recording **The Glove** album'), 'Breathe' and 'A Chain Of Flowers' ('a story Simon told me once'). A further unused song, 'To The Sky' (which Robert didn't particularly like) was put out on a **Fiction** sampler. The album was reissued in 2006 with all the usual demos and alternate takes, and came out again on lipstick-red vinyl on Record Store Day 2013.

In a highly favourable review at the time, *Rolling Stone* picked up on the obvious Minneapolitan comparisons from early '87.

> This two-record, eighteen-song set is about reaching inward. The Cure is trying to deepen and refine an existing sensibility rather than reach outward to expand it. On previous efforts, guitarist and singer Robert Smith has flirted with everything from conceptually orchestrated studio pop (*The Top*) to sarcastic dance tracks ('**Let's Go To Bed**'); now that The Cure has evolved into an actual band, he's able to consummate those eclectic desires. *Kiss Me* is a breakthrough all right. For the first time, The Cure's music is relatively unfettered by pretension and indulgence, and the results are remarkable.

This uncharacteristic nod of approval from one of the big beasts of the American rock press was significant, and was borne out by the album's chart performance. It reached No.6 in the UK, No.4 in Germany and Austria, No.3 in the Netherlands and Switzerland and No.2 in France. It went gold in the UK, France, and Portugal. In almost every country, it was their highest-placed album so far. Most impressively, it was their first Top 40 album in America, reaching No.35, and continued to sell throughout the year as a slow-burner, ending the year as America's hundredth bestseller (no mean feat in so vast a country) and eventually earning a platinum certification to mark a million sales.

The Kissing Tour introduced one new face to the band: Boris Williams' long-time friend, keyboardist **Roger O'Donnell** (who had not played on the album itself), whose presence allowed Porl Thompson to concentrate on guitars rather than helping Lol on keyboards. Technically, O'Donnell's earliest Cure

recordings are the handful of live tracks from that tour which ended up on the deluxe reissue.

The tour was enormously successful, bringing them to bigger venues than ever before (typically arenas rather than theatres). This upward step wasn't one that Smith enjoyed particularly, and he spoke of his intention to stop the group for a while after the Christmas 1987 shows, stating that 'I want to make things small again for The Cure'. Speaking to *Rolling Stone* in 2004, he recalled 'I remember on the *Kiss Me* tour we were in Los Angeles, and there were girls taking their clothes off and lying down in front of the bus to stop us from driving away. And I remember thinking, "This isn't really what I imagined I would be doing with this band . . ."' The circus surrounding the making of the album and the touring of it left its mark on all of them. 'I don't really think we recovered for about eighteen months,' he later said. 'Everything we did was tainted with a slight bit of insanity.'

Kiss Me, Kiss Me, Kiss Me, though arguably patchy (as double albums almost invariably are), delivered a high hit rate of classics to add to The Cure canon.

Any album which includes 'Just Like Heaven', 'Catch', 'If Only Tonight We Could Sleep' and 'A Thousand Hours' is worthy of its place in the pantheon. Mary considered it their best since *Pornography*. Hindsight has generally been kind to it: *Far Out* magazine ranked it second in The Cure catalogue, and *Ultimate Classic Rock* sixth.

With *Kiss Me, Kiss Me, Kiss Me*, Robert Smith had achieved the once-impossible. He'd tackled the previously *verboten* format of the double album, and come up smelling of roses. But then, perhaps the only difference between a punk and a hippie is the **haircut**. Smith dodged the issue of taking sides by getting rid of his entirely, which may have been his secret. 'The best thing I did,' he told MTV in 1990, 'was I shaved my head before we started recording, and that had a really big impact on the way I thought about things . . .'

Speaking to the *Chicago Tribune* in 2018, Smith had no regrets about the decision to make such an abundant, expansive, stylistically diverse record. 'In the end, what happened was the pop songs absorbed some of the more atmospheric elements of the slow songs, and the slow songs got a bit more tuneful. Looking back, I'm glad it turned out like it did.'

And so were millions of fans.

L

L is for …

Labels

If it isn't true to say that when one thinks of The Cure one thinks of **Fiction**, it's certainly true that when one thinks of Fiction one thinks of The Cure. But that's far from the whole story.

Of course, Fiction wasn't even The Cure's first label. They signed a deal with **Hansa** (via Ariola) with no records issued, then a one-off deal with independent label **Small Wonder** for the first batch of '**Killing An Arab**'. The long Fiction era followed, but Fiction was a subsidiary of **Polydor** rather than a true stand-alone indie, as was Wonderland, through which **Siouxsie And The Banshees**' records were released in Robert Smith's time with that band, as was the sole album by **The Glove**.

Even Fiction/Polydor didn't have the exclusive rights to The Cure during that long partnership. To zoom in on just one case study, the *Boys Don't Cry* album was initially released on PVC Records in the US, but on North American Records in Canada, and later, Elektra, and later still, Passport Records. In Japan it was on Vap. In Australia and New Zealand the same album was initially on Stunn (the label of Terry Condon, a friend of fellow New Zealander **Chris Parry** who acquired the licensing rights for Fiction in **Australasia**) and later reissued on Sire. However, these are all official versions. *Boys Don't Cry* was also widely **bootlegged** in the Communist bloc at a time when Western pop music was banned. In Poland alone, it was released on labels including, but probably not limited to, Takt, MG, Mag Magic, Edico, Reggae, Deck and ALF.

The Cure's EP of **Peel Sessions** from 1978 was released in 1988 on Strange Fruit, the independent label set up by John Peel himself with Clive Selwood, as were many other artists' Peel Sessions by special licence from the BBC. Other anomalies include **charity** releases such as their **cover** of John Lennon's 'Love', only available as an mp3 but technically a 'single', with Amnesty International credited as the label. Or tribute recordings, such as the version of The Beatles' 'Hello Goodbye' with James McCartney, made available as an mp3 via the short-lived Sony imprint Arctic Poppy (which also included the track

on *The Art of McCartney* compilation). Indeed, once you begin to factor in the use of The Cure's music on compilation albums, or on **film** soundtracks, the list of labels expands exponentially.

Much of the complexity of The Cure's label history takes place in the American wing of their discography, where seemingly different labels are often shopfronts for the same major conglomerate, giving the illusion of contract-hopping where none actually takes place. A quick timeline: *Happily Ever After* was on Herb Alpert's A&M label, as was *Faith*. Seymour Stein's Sire put out *Japanese Whispers* and *The Top* (and associated singles). *The Head On The Door* went straight through Elektra, as did *Standing On A Beach* and all American albums right through to *Galore*. (Elektra also reissued older albums such as *Faith*.) In 2000, when Robert allowed The Cure's contract to lapse, he spoke of the relief of no longer having to consult 'three teams of lawyers from Elektra, Universal and Warner Brothers' whenever he wanted to do anything – Warner being the owners of Elektra, Universal the owners of Polydor (and ultimately, therefore, Fiction).

Out of the frying pan and into the fire? Before long, The Cure signed with **Ross Robinson**'s label I Am, a subsidiary of **Geffen**, for a three-album deal, the first of which was 2004's *The Cure*. By the time of 2008's *4:13 Dream* the ground had shifted, and the label was now Suretone via Geffen. The label on which the next Cure studio album will appear is anyone's guess.

Live albums also muddy the waters. Rob Da Bank's Sunday Best put out *Bestival Live 2011*, the *40 Live (Curætion-25 & Anniversary)* box set was released by Eagle Rock, and the not-illegal (if not exactly official) *Red Light District* was on Wicker Man.

And then there's Rhino. A label specialising in reissues, Rhino put out the *Join The Dots* compilation of **rarities** in the US, as well as a single of The Cure's original of, and Dinosaur Jr's cover version of, '**Just Like Heaven**' on double-sided 7-inch vinyl for Record Store Day 2014. Rhino also put out the American version of *Torn Down* in 2018 – an album which, to bring things almost full circle, was put out in Europe under the revived Fiction label.

When it comes to labels, it's probably easiest to

group Cure releases under two headings: Fiction, and Non-Fiction.

Lake, Bunny

Does Bunny Lake actually exist? That is the question posed by Otto Preminger for the majority of his 1965 psychological thriller *Bunny Lake Is Missing*, in which a woman, played by Carol Lynley, claims that her infant daughter has vanished. It is the conclusion of Superintendent Newhouse, played by Laurence Olivier, that she didn't exist: the girl was never there.

Does Bunny Lake actually exist? That is also the question posed by various Cure artefacts bearing the name. Bunny Lake, for example, is credited with having executive-produced *The Cure*, and remixed *Torn Down*, but has not worked on any other artists' records (a comparison being the **artwork** credit smART, which also appears exclusively on late-period Cure releases), prompting a minor frenzy of speculation.

Eagle-eyed fans also noticed that Bunny Lake is credited with recording and/or engineering Robert's contribution whenever he's been obliged to supply his vocal remotely on **collaborations** with American-based artists (or, during Covid lockdown, British ones). These include Crystal Castles' 'Not in Love', Japanese Popstars' 'Take', Blink 182's 'All Of This' and 65daysofstatic's 'Come To Me', Robert's remix of Deftones' 'Teenager', his appearances on Gorillaz' 'Strange Timez' and Chvrches' 'How Not To Drown', and his solo track 'Witchcraft' on the *Frankenweenie Unleashed* soundtrack (see **Films, The Cure's music in**).

Just who is this shadowy lagomorph? The clues have been scattered like Easter eggs throughout the twenty-first century. Whoever it is, their talents evidently extend beyond the studio. In October 2019, The Cure's Instagram account announced that 'Robert and Jason (and the ubiquitous Bunny Lake!) have submitted original pieces of artwork to the @heartresearchuk #anonartproject'. The post used the hashtag #bunnylake, which in turn leads to several other Cure-related posts, demonstrating that the Bunny Lake in-joke has been adopted by some of the more clued-in Cure fans.

Bunny Lake's involvement in The Cure's activities became even more official in July 2022 when the band tweeted, 'The Cure releases a series of Bunny Lake Designs Greeting Cards! Write your love away in these one of a kind greetings cards with bedazzled seashells, blazing pearls, and romantic hidden hearts.' There is now a whole subsection on the 'Shop' part of The Cure's website selling Bunny Lake designs (with profits going to the **charity** World Cancer Fund International).

There are red herrings. Bunny Lake, for example, was also the name of a German electronic pop act led by Christian Fuchs in the 2000s, though this has no apparent connection to The Cure. But Occam's Razor seems to point in one clear direction. In perhaps the biggest clue, Robert himself has been seen with a cut-out from the Preminger film's poster on his guitar.

One intriguing theory is that Bunny is **Mary**. (Lake, Poole, get it?) She has an eye for décor and an interest in voluntary work, which tallies nicely with the greetings card range. Another is that Bunny Lake is the same imaginary girl, also called Bunny, that Robert hallucinated as a child (see '**Catch**').

Or, at the end of the trail of Easter eggs, wearing a bunny mask like Frank from *Donnie Darko*, do we simply find Robert Smith himself?

Largest Audience

The Cure's days of performing to twenty people and a dog in **Crawley** and **Horley** pubs must have seemed a lot longer than ten years ago when, on 8 September 1989, they played Dodger Stadium in Los Angeles. According to *Cure News* issue 11, the crowd was 75,000-strong, The Cure's biggest audience to date, excluding festival sets. While one of these statements was factually correct, the other has to be an exaggeration: Dodger Stadium's capacity for concerts is 50,000.

In any case, the band have since surpassed that number on several occasions, and by some distance. On 21 April 2013 they played to 57,304 at Foro Sol in **Mexico**; a record which was then broken by their show in front of 65,000 at London's Hyde Park on 7 July 2018, only for *that* record to be broken by another show at Foro Sol on 8 October 2019, attended by up to 70,000 people.

While none of these shows gets anywhere near the Top 30 highest attended concerts of all time (the current record holder being 220,000 for a show by Italian singer Vasco Rossi in Modena in 2017), the upward curve demonstrates that The Cure are more popular as a live act than at any point in their career.

Lawsuit

Addiction is a disease, and while addicts don't decide to be addicts, the decisions addicts do make are terrible ones.

In the second half of the eighties, **Lol Tolhurst** fell into a downward spiral of **alcoholism** which radically reduced his musical input into The Cure's recordings, and created poisonous divisions between himself and the rest of the band. In 1986 he had signed a new contract which demoted him from the favoured status of a partner with Robert Smith to that of the band's other members, **Simon Gallup**, **Porl Thompson**, **Boris Williams** and, later, **Roger O'Donnell**. This, Smith and manager **Chris Parry** believed, was more than fair, given Tolhurst's ever-decreasing musical contribution. Eventually, Tolhurst was fired by a letter from Robert Smith in 1989, and did not participate in the Prayer Tour to promote *Disintegration*, an album on which he had barely played a note.

In the immediate aftermath of his ejection from The Cure, Lol had formed his own band, **Presence**. In an item about Presence on the television show *Rapido* in March 1991, Lol was asked how he felt about the falling out with Robert. 'I can't say what he's thinking,' he replied. 'I'm not inside his head. Yeah, it hurt me, for sure. But I'm not going to start a big fight about it. Because it's not worth it. I'd rather be a gentleman about it all.' He added, tellingly, 'I hope that in the next year or so, people will see that I wasn't the complete monster he made me out to be.'

But Lol *was* going to start a big fight about it.

Three years later, in February 1994, Lol Tolhurst attempted to sue The Cure over what he believed were outstanding royalty payments, also claiming joint ownership, with Smith, over the name The Cure.

Despite a phone call three months earlier from Chris Parry in an attempt to persuade him to call it off, Lol was adamant about going ahead. The civil case opened at the Royal Courts of Justice on the Strand, presided over by one judge, Mr Justice Chadwick, with no jury. The hearing lasted for three weeks, with Tolhurst spending three days in the witness stand. Smith and Parry made the case for their defence. Meanwhile, it was reported in *Cure News*, Simon Gallup and **Perry Bamonte** watched from the public gallery.

The essence of Tolhurst's claim was that he was owed royalties from *Kiss Me, Kiss Me, Kiss Me* and *Disintegration*, and also that he had been tricked by Robert Smith and Chris Parry into signing that 1986 contract which, he believed, he had signed to his manifest disadvantage without receiving proper information or advice, relying on Smith who had become the active and dominant member of the band. He requested that the agreement be set aside, and requested an account of the money he believed he was owed. Though no figure was put on this claim, it was estimated that it could run into millions, as the period in question covered two multimillion-selling hit albums.

The Cure gave a sixty-page counterstatement which included the claims that Lol frequently had to be sent home in a taxi before the end of recording sessions because he was too drunk to play, that by the time they recorded *The Head On The Door* his drinking made him unable to contribute, that he needed a row of coloured dots on the keyboard during gigs to help him play despite having promised to learn to play properly, and that the new contractual arrangements had been fully explained to him, the crux of the matter being that because of his behaviour it was inappropriate for him to continue earning more than The Cure's other three members.

During the hearing, Smith called Tolhurst 'a tired, shambling shadow of his former self' and expressed sadness at witnessing 'the rapid decline of someone who I had known and liked since my schooldays.' The final straw, Smith said, came during the demo sessions for *Disintegration* when he saw Tolhurst sitting in a chair reading a book with a drink and a cigarette. 'For the first time it became obvious that there was no conceivable reason for his presence.'

Tolhurst fired back, alleging equal or greater unprofessionalism and heavy drinking from Smith and Gallup, alleging that they often each drank five bottles of wine per night in the studio, and telling a story of the incident in 1986 when The Cure were filmed travelling to Venice on the Orient Express by the *Old Grey Whistle Test*, running up a bar bill of between £1,500 and £2,000 in one night (the insinuation being that they were all as bad as he was).

He also argued that he was being victimised (see **bullying**), which exacerbated his drinking problems. He cited the story of the other members carrying out malicious pranks such as placing a scorpion skin on his face flannel. 'I was drinking very heavily and was the butt of everyone's jokes and aggression,' he stated. 'As a result of the continuous abuse and criticism, I became very ill and lost over a stone in weight. It is correct that when I became drunk, I sometimes became aggressive, largely stemmed by [sic] the frustrations which I felt. It was a vicious circle, I drank for confidence, but later, I lost my confidence because of the drink or the constant abuse and I became unable to perform.'

In a September 1994 issue of *Cure News*, Robert described being in court as 'Listening to perjury', adding in November 1995 that 'The preparation involved was tiring and time-consuming, but I actually enjoyed the hearings themselves – seeing the smug slug squirm made up for a lot.'

The music press had a field day. *NME* thought it was all a bit of a laugh: their news report on the court case was accompanied by a Top 10 of alcohol-based Cure songs with titles like 'Chardonnay Sometimes' and '10-15 Pints on a Saturday Night'.

At 2 p.m. on 16 September 1994, Lol Tolhurst's legal case against Robert Smith, Chris Parry and **Fiction Records** was dismissed. Tolhurst decided not to appeal. Judge Chadwick ordered him to pay 75% of his earnings to cover legal costs. Leaving the court, Robert, Chris and the rest of the band drove past Lol, who sat on the pavement looking utterly dejected.

The case undoubtedly took its toll on The Cure. It's surely no coincidence that there was a four-year gap between 1992's *Wish* and 1996's *Wild Mood Swings*, the longest interval of their career. But it hit Lol hardest of all, costing him an estimated £650,000 which took him a decade to pay off.

Reflecting on the case in 1996, Robert Smith told *Pulse* magazine 'I don't feel bitter about it. I actually feel quite sorry for him, but I don't think he's capable of working with anyone. When he was with us he didn't do any work, so the idea of having him back as a vacuous human being would be completely pointless.'

In his autobiography *Cured*, Tolhurst conceded that he 'wasn't well mentally' at the time of the case and that, encouraged by his lawyers, he set out on a path of 'big, stinking, loud, dark revenge'. He also accepted that during the period in question, he was indeed 'rapidly becoming a liability'.

Speaking to *Vice* in 2016, Lol took a phlegmatic and philosophical view of the whole debacle. 'If I hadn't left the band and hadn't done the big court case and lost millions of dollars, then I'd perhaps have a nicer house to live in or whatever, but I might

not have my son because I wouldn't have been sane enough to be a father.'

An unexpected coda to the story is that while promoting *Cured* at the Latitude Festival in 2016, Tolhurst revealed that he and Smith were on friendly terms again, and that Robert, in a gesture of goodwill, had given Lol all the money he lost in the court case.

Smith, it seems, had taken no pleasure in defeating Tolhurst. As **Tim Pope** told the *Quietus* in 2019:

I remember a funny thing with Robert on the day: even though he won the case, he wasn't happy about it. He knew that his old friend had been advised by people that he should do this. Why? Because lawyers made money. And the judge turned to Lol on the day and said, 'You don't actually know why you're here, Mr Tolhurst, do you?' Lol is a very sweet man, a very lovely man, and I think it was a very hurtful time. I was very pleased to hear that Robert and him became friends again.

Least Favourite Songs

Robert Smith's least favourite Cure songs, like his favourites, undoubtedly change just as often as yours do. However, as a snapshot of his personal hates, he told *Cure News* in September 1994 that the songs from his own catalogue he liked the least were 'World War' (from the *Boys Don't Cry* album), 'Pillbox Tales' (from the 1986 '**Boys Don't Cry**' single but originally written circa *Three Imaginary Boys*), 'Do The **Hansa**' and (early live track) 'Heroin Face', on the grounds that 'none of these four songs have any real meaning'. He has also stated that he hates 'Object' (from *Three Imaginary Boys*). In each of these instances, all relatively obscure cuts from The Cure's formative years, you can understand his discomfort. It's the same discomfort everyone feels when they see photos of themselves as children or adolescents, half-formed and uncool. However, one of Robert's dislikes is far more famous and far less easy to sweep under the carpet. '**Friday I'm In Love**', he told Fall Out Boy's Pete Wentz in *Entertainment Weekly* in 2006, is a song he came to loathe. 'I thought, "You're to blame, you bastard. You made me popular."'

Let's Go To Bed

'If everybody stayed in bed for ten years,' Robert Smith told *NME*'s Paul Morley in 1981, 'then everything would be alright.'

'Let's Go To Bed' was the first of what Smith called The Cure's 'fantasy singles' – attempts to reimagine The Cure as a pop group (the other two being '**The Walk**' and '**The Lovecats**'). In the aftermath of the disastrous **Fourteen Explicit Moments** tour, which resulted in **Simon Gallup**'s first departure from the band and left The Cure slimmed down to a duo of Smith and **Lol Tolhurst**, everything was up for grabs, including the group's future direction.

It was manager **Chris Parry** who challenged Smith to write a pop hit, telling them that he wanted the band to release 'a fun single' in order to destroy the myth of The Cure. This idea appealed to Smith, who at that point wanted to destroy The Cure anyway. (In fact, the singles ended up reviving them.) Parry called them the 'Art Under the Hammer' sessions, and 'a ploy to confuse the fuck out of anyone who'd hitherto known and liked The Cure'. Speaking to Radio New Zealand later, he recalled 'I convinced [Robert] that there was a place for The Cure which was in pop, forget all the **Goth**, forget all that stuff, just have fun, let's just write a few pop songs, you write the pop songs, produce them, and we'll see what happens. And if it doesn't work, you can walk away from the contract.' (This last promise is one on which he reneged . . .)

In the autumn of 1982 Smith locked himself away in Strongroom Studios on London's Goldhawk Road, and demoed 'Let's Go To Bed', recycling a little bit of leftover melody from 'Temptation Two', a vocal version of an instrumental called 'Temptation' which had been demoed for *Pornography*. Smith and Tolhurst then recorded it properly over four days in Island Studios at Royal Chiswick Laundry Works (Island Records being part of the same Polygram umbrella as **Polydor** and therefore **Fiction**).

Tolhurst came armed with a new toy. He had taken a beginners' course in synthesisers with a Musicians' Union-recommended tutor, intending to move from drums to keyboards, and bought himself a brand new New England Digital Synclavier, the sampler used on Michael Jackson's *Thriller* (which cost anything up to $200,000).

Were The Cure now, therefore, a synth duo? Not quite, not yet. For one thing, they brought in **Steve Goulding**, former drummer with Graham Parker, Nick Lowe and Elvis Costello and a lynchpin of the pub rock world, to play live drums on the single. For another, Robert Smith plays plangent guitar chords in the background of the otherwise synth-based track.

The song is a nagging, consciously irritating piece of dislocated dance, built around repetitive doo-doo-doos. Tracks like 'It's Not You' and 'Object' on *Three Imaginary Boys* had already expressed a very cold, very punk view of **sex** as something transactional and dispassionate, and 'Let's Go To Bed' continued that theme:

All of this then back again
Another girl, another name
Stay alive but stay the same
It's a stupid game, stupid game

Smith, however, cautioned against reading too much into it: 'It's a foolish title, and the lyrics don't mean a thing.' The song's awfulness, it seems, was essentially deliberate: 'Musically, I mixed in everything bad I'd heard for years,' he told *Ten Imaginary Years*, 'but even when we'd recorded it, I still didn't think it was horrible enough. So Bill [Chris Parry] remixed it and there it was.'

Parry's initial reaction on hearing the song was horror, even though the pop experiment was his idea. 'When I took "Let's Go To Bed" to Fiction and played it to them,' Robert remembered later in *Rolling Stone*, 'it was like silence. They looked at me, like, "This is it. He's really lost it." They said, "You can't be serious. Your fans are gonna hate it." I understood that, but I wanted to get rid of all that. I didn't want that side of life anymore; I wanted to do something that's really kind of cheerful. I thought, "This isn't going to work. No one's ever gonna buy into this. It's so ludicrous that I'm gonna go from Goth idol to pop star in three easy lessons."'

Nevertheless, Parry was determined to plough ahead with the project. Smith was so unhappy with the track that he lobbied to have the single released under the name Recur, so as not to sully the good name of The Cure. Parry went against Smith's wishes. 'The whole point,' he argued, 'is that we want to come out with an irreligious record, and it has to be put out under The Cure or it's a waste of time.' In interviews set up by Parry to promote the song, Smith trashed it, and even told BBC Radio 1's David 'Kid' Jensen – who had broadcast a session version of the song on 1 November 1982 (see **Peel Sessions**) – that 'I despise it'.

One positive which did emerge from 'Let's Go To Bed' was the **video**: a first-time collaboration with **Tim Pope**, hired because Smith, Tolhurst and Parry had enjoyed the Soft Cell videos on his showreel. Filmed at his own studios in St John's Wood, it was the start of a long and fruitful relationship.

As The Cure had been burned too many times by bad videos, they came up with their own script, but allowed Pope freedom to interpret it. The duo lark about in a lopsided room. Robert sings to a pair of eggs with faces on, then smashes them. The names Marion, Mary and Muriel descend from the ceiling on banners. There's a beach ball, a Christmas tree and a piano, and lots of paint. There's a pratfall at the end when Lol falls through the top mattress of a bunk bed, almost landing on Robert who has rolled out of the way at the last second. It's all very . . . *symbolic*.

Lol draws the short straw and has to do some interpretative dancing, like Roland Orzabal de la Quintana in Tears For Fears' 'Mad World' video, often in silhouette. In order to achieve this, Pope made Tolhurst dance naked behind a screen to throw the right kind of shadow. 'He always makes me do something strange or uncomfortable,' Lol later complained. Not that Robert escaped being forced outside his comfort zone: Pope pushed him to act up, for the first time. 'I saw him as a clown,' Pope said, 'funny but also tragic.'

Robert, in a television interview in 1988, reflected on the clip. 'I think it achieved exactly what we wanted to achieve, which was to make me and Lol look completely stupid. We just wanted to shatter all the illusions everyone had about us. Which was us being very remote, sullen, moody, constantly living in darkness, hanging upside down.' (The **artwork**, however, consisting of a black and white photo of Robert in the dramatic shadows of a Venetian blind, went some way to preserving that image.)

The single was released on 19 November 1982, with 'Just One Kiss' (from the same sessions) on the B-side. Robert Smith bet Chris Parry that 'Let's Go To Bed' would not be a hit. On the terms of the bet, if Smith was right Parry would free him from his contract to allow him to make a **solo album**. Smith won – the single only reached No.44 – but Parry denied ever agreeing to the bet. (It was also re-released, instead of '**Boys Don't Cry**', in the States to promote *Standing On A Beach*.)

It did, however, make inroads in the **US**, rising high on the Billboard Disco Chart. 'Suddenly,' Smith told *Rolling Stone*, '"Let's Go To Bed" was turning into a big hit, on the West Coast particularly, and we had a young, predominantly female, teenage audience. It went from intense, menacing, psychotic Goths to people with perfect white teeth. It was a very weird transition, but I enjoyed it. I thought it was really funny. We followed it up with 'The Walk' and 'The Lovecats', and I just felt totally liberated.'

Has Robert reconciled himself with the song in hindsight, then? He once named it as one of his **favourite songs** to perform live. He may have been joking, but it is The Cure's twelfth most-played song. And nobody's forcing him to play it.

'Let's Go To Bed' is by far the lesser of the three 'fantasy singles'. But The Cure had got their video director, and they'd got over their phobia of writing a pop song – an ailment from which they never suffered again.

Levinhurst

Manila-born Cindy Levinson met **Lol Tolhurst** in 1989, shortly after his dismissal from The Cure, via a mutual friend, while she was working as a hairdresser in Hollywood. They began a relationship, and Lol credits her with helping him survive his struggles with **alcohol** addiction. They married in 2002, and shortly afterwards, formed Levinhurst (a portmanteau of their surnames). 'He heard me singing in the house,' Levinson told a Filipino radio station, 'and he was just like, "let's start a band together".'

With Lol providing drums and keyboards, they recorded their first album, 2004's *Perfect Life*, as a trio with Californian composer Dayton Borders and released it on the independent label Full Contact. On *The Grey EP* (2006, on What Are? Records, founded by former EMI A&R man Rob Gordon) they were down to a duo, but with one very special guest: **Michael Dempsey**, who gave the song 'Never Going To Dream Again' an 'Imaginary Boy Mix'. Furthermore, the EP's lead track was a cover of '**All Cats Are Grey**' from *Faith* (a song which Tolhurst feels is particularly 'his'). Dempsey contributed some further mixing to second album *House By The Sea* (2007, also What Are?), and by the time of third album *Blue Star* (2009, self-released) he was a full writing, touring and performing member. *House By The Sea* also featured guitar from Lol and Cindy's then sixteen-year-old son Gray Tolhurst (now a member of his own band,

Topographies), and guitar and bass from Eric Bradley of The Young Royals (formerly Melt). They toured, with Dempsey on board, in 2010.

On tracks like 'Another Way', 'Sargasso' and 'Mau-Mau', Levinhurst's shadowy, steady-paced alt-pop is unmistakeably Lol. It hasn't always received positive reviews. A review on Allmusic praised *House By The Sea* for its 'continuity and vision', but pointed out that 'there's a fine line between continuity and humdrum homogeneity', and concluded that it 'bumbles into the realm of sleep-inducing monotony by the time the fifth track rolls around.'

Levinhurst, with Michael Dempsey's involvement and that 'All Cats Are Grey' cover among other things, haven't exactly shied away from highlighting The Cure connection. But even without those things, you'd probably figure it out.

Like An Animal

The debut single by **The Glove**, the **1983** project comprising Robert Smith, **Steve Severin** of **Siouxsie And The Banshees** and **Zoo** dancer Jeanette Landray, with its drum machine pulse, **New Order**-ish high-end bassline and skyscraping vocal, sounds a lot more cheerful than its subject matter.

'Like An Animal' was inspired by a true story of the slow mental disintegration of a woman living in a tower block in New York. 'She started dropping small things onto people's heads and progressed to finally throwing a washing machine on top of some unfortunate,' Severin explained in *No.1* magazine.

Sings Landray:

One mile in the air that's where she lives
Her body looks so thin and pink and small
Dropping eggs from nervous shaking hands

'Like An Animal' was released on the Banshees' Wonderland label on 12 August 1983. The **artwork** by Da Gama featured an enormous blue and yellow spiral, which was repeated on the label of the record itself, meaning that when you played it at 45rpm, looking at it had a somewhat hypnotic effect, like being serenaded by Kaa, the python in the Disney version of *The Jungle Book*. The B-side, 'Mouth To Mouth', a love song with a cannibalistic twist reminiscent of 'I Hold Your Hand In Mine' by Tom Lehrer, sounded like Hall & Oates in a torture

dungeon. No music video was made for the song, and it slipped out to little fanfare, reaching 52 in the charts.

Many years later, in an interview with post-punk. com, Jeanette Landray revealed her bandmates' methods for drawing a suitably unhinged vocal performance from her. 'There was a time when my singing of "Like An Animal" was not getting crazy enough, and all of a sudden, I hear this soft voice singing from behind a couch. I walk over towards the voice and it's Robert on all fours singing "Diamonds Are A Girl's Best Friend"!'

Line-Ups

What is the classic line-up of The Cure? It's a debate as old as time. It's inevitably a much-discussed topic whenever fans get together online or in person, given that The Cure have had more members passing through their ranks than The Grateful Dead and, when you add in all the various temporary members, are only one short of Fairport Convention.

With any band, one answer to the question will always be the Original Line-Up. So, if you're a *Three Imaginary Boys* purist, Smith–**Tolhurst**–**Dempsey** will always be definitive, and every one since an interloper.

Another answer is the One Where They Found Their Sound. The line-up of Smith–Tolhurst–**Gallup** lays claim to that accolade (with an honourable mention to **Matthieu Hartley**), for delivering *Seventeen Seconds*, *Faith* and *Pornography* and thereby nailing The Cure's early **gothic** period.

The One Where They Made My Favourite Record is deeply subjective, of course. If your greatest affection is for '**The Lovecats**', then the short-lived, six-month-long configuration of Smith–Tolhurst–**Thornalley**–**Anderson**, which only played ten gigs, is the one for you.

Equally subjective is the First One You Saw. If you didn't catch The Cure live till *Wild Mood Swings*, then to some degree Smith–**Bamonte**–Gallup–**Cooper**–**O'Donnell** is always going to be 'your' Cure.

Of course, it's also possible to play *Fantasy Football* with Cure members, inventing a dream line-up that never actually existed at any one time, by putting together a pretend Cure from a pick 'n' mix of alumni. Smith–Thompson–Dempsey–O'Donnell–Anderson?

Smith–Bamonte–Gallup–Hartley–Tolhurst? The permutations are endless.

One way of measuring the definitive line-up which is objective and incontrovertible is to look for The Longest-Lasting One. The current Cure line-up of Smith–Gabrels–Gallup–O'Donnell–Cooper have been together for over a decade (and counting), making them the most stable line-up of all. This line-up deserves respect and gratitude for keeping The Cure alive. Thanks to these five, we still have a Cure to enjoy. Their power as a live act is unquestionable, and they might, just might, give us a **fourteenth album** one day.

Another approach is the One From The Band's Golden Age. But that only raises the question: what *was* the golden age? If The Cure had an Imperial Phase, to quote Neil Tennant's famous description of the era when the Pet Shop Boys could do no wrong and everything they released raced up the charts, then it covered the *Disintegration* and *Wish* albums and associated singles and, while those records were made by slightly different line-ups, we might be getting somewhere.

We've been dancing around the issue here. Let's cut to the chase. We all know, in our heart of hearts, what the answer is. When *The Head On The Door* was reissued on heavyweight vinyl in 2020, the promotional blurb began: 'Featuring what many consider to be the classic Cure line-up of Robert Smith, Porl Thompson, Lol Tolhurst, Simon Gallup and *Boris Williams* . . .' This, while not an official endorsement as such, is not a statement with which many would take issue. The Smith–Tolhurst–Gallup–Thompson–Williams line-up, which coalesced in April 1985, only lasted for three years. In those three years, however, it delivered *The Head On The Door* and *Kiss Me, Kiss Me, Kiss Me*, as well as being captured on film in *The Cure In Orange*. Furthermore, this version of the band, with the core of Smith, Gallup, Thompson and Williams, arguably endured for almost a decade, with Roger O'Donnell (who could be bothered) substituted in for Lol Tolhurst (who couldn't) during *Disintegration*, and Perry Bamonte coming in when O'Donnell left for the first time, finally concluding when Porl Thompson left at the end of the *Wish* cycle.

If this isn't too much of a cop-out, perhaps it's possible to hedge our bets by talking of *three* distinct 'classic' Cure line-ups.

First: Smith–Tolhurst–Gallup.

Second: Smith–Tolhurst–Gallup–Thompson–Williams.

Third: Smith–Gallup–Gabrels–O'Donnell–Cooper.

If you don't agree, find your nearest Cure fan, and fight it out.

Literature

The Cure are one of the great pedagogic bands. Along with **David Bowie**, Kate Bush, The Smiths and Manic Street Preachers, they are one of a handful of acts whose works are most likely to send fans running off to the library to delve into the literary sources behind the songs. (**Poetry** has been a rich source of inspiration to Robert, and has its own *Curepedia* entry.)

Three works of fiction, in particular, are famously associated with Cure records. The first is **Albert Camus**' Existentialist classic *L'Etranger* (aka *The Outsider* or *The Stranger*), whose narrative inspired the band's debut single '**Killing An Arab**', which in turn caused them no end of trouble.

The second is Mervyn Peake's *Gormenghast* novels, a **gothic** trilogy following the travails of an earl called Titus Groan, which inspired the songs 'The Drowning Man' and '**All Cats Are Grey**' from *Faith*.

The third is Penelope Farmer's supernatural time-travel novel *Charlotte Sometimes* which inspired, obviously, '**Charlotte Sometimes**' as well as its B-side 'Splintered In Her Head', and *The Top* track 'The Empty World'.

But there are plenty of others. 'M' from *Seventeen Seconds*, according to **Lol Tolhurst** on Tim's Twitter Listening Party, 'has an obvious connotation [Mary] . . . and a literary one as well'; that literary connotation appears to be Albert Camus' *A Happy Death* (an originally unpublished precursor to *L'Etranger*). On the same album, 'At Night' was, Smith has stated, inspired by the Franz Kafka short story of the same name. 'Bananafishbones' from *The Top* is a reference to J. D. Salinger's short story *A Perfect Day for Bananafish*. 'How Beautiful You Are', on *Kiss Me, Kiss Me, Kiss Me*, was inspired by a short story by Charles Baudelaire. The 1992 single '**A Letter To Elise**' was partly inspired by Jean Cocteau's *Les Enfants Terribles*. And 'Lost', from 2004's *The Cure*, was inspired by philosopher Thomas Nagel's *View from Nowhere*. 'I was actually tempted to steal the title for this album at some point,' Robert told the *Manila Times*. 'The idea of the book was this concept of stepping outside of yourself. And in order to do that you had to recognize who you were in the first place . . .'

This is only scratching the surface. (One Cure fan, Pete Smith, has devoted an entire **website** cureious.co.uk to the literary influences behind The Cure, with the intention of turning it into a book.)

Other books of which Robert has spoken highly, or at least acknowledged reading, are *A Song of Stone* by Iain Banks, *Something Wicked This Way Comes* by Ray Bradbury, *Arcanum 17* by André Breton, *Naked Lunch* by William Burroughs, *The Castle* by Franz Kafka (whom Robert once described as his biggest influence philosophically, along with Camus, Sartre and his dad), *Les Chants de Maldoror* by Comte de Lautréamont, *The Chronicles of Narnia* by C. S. Lewis (which Robert's father read to him as a child, and which at one point Robert would re-read every Christmas), *Lolita* by Vladimir Nabokov, the complete works of Salman Rushdie, *The Aunt's Story* and *The Solid Mandala* by Patrick White (whose novel *The Vivisector* has been proposed by some fans as an influence on '**The Lovecats**', and whose work Robert once said he would choose as his specialist subject on *Mastermind*), *The Drug User* by various, and the Book of Revelation.

In 1985, Robert told *The Face* that he was considering writing a book of short stories himself. 'I decided last year that if I put together all my attempts at writing a book I'd have a book of short stories with no endings. It'd be like 50 first pages in paperback. I've known the title for ages. Every story is different but they all have the same title. Mary thought of the title actually. It's called *The Glass Sandwich*. I get very serious about it when I feel myself slipping. It's a good mental exercise, but most of the stories aren't very entertaining . . .' (He was still writing it, he told *Cure News*, as of January 1988, but it never materialised.)

Even without *The Glass Sandwich* to bite into, there will be fans out there whose bookshelves are (Titus) groaning with the works which inspired the songs of The Cure, and with other books that they subsequently discovered after investigating the Robert Smith reading list. And that's genuinely one of the most valuable things a band can do.

Lockjaw

In the seventies, British children were conditioned to be afraid of many things. Dark and lonely water. Traffic. Retrieving a frisbee from an electrical substation. Some of these fears took the form of folk demons. The Colorado beetle, devouring our potato crops. Dutch elm disease, decimating our woodlands. Milk thieves called, for some reason, Humphrey (rather than Thatcher). Rabid dogs, usually depicted as coming from France. And the muscle spasm condition tetanus (contractable by, for example, stepping on a rusty nail), commonly known as lockjaw.

Lockjaw was also the name of an antagonist-turned-ally in bulldog form from Marvel's *Fantastic Four* comics, first appearing in 1965.

Lockjaw was, therefore, an absolutely kickass name for a punk-rock band. And the punk-rock band who snapped it up came from **Horley**, their original line-up consisting of vocalist Bo Zo (Gary Bowe), guitarist Micky Morbid (Stuart Hinton), drummer Oddy Ordish (Martin Ordish), and a bassist with the classic punk pseudonym of Andy Septic (**Simon Gallup**). Their first name, however, was the rather more psychedelic The Amazing Doctor Octopuss.

The band, managed by Andy/Simon's older brother David Gallup with promotional **artwork** from his other brother **Ric Gallup**, lasted for just two years, 1976–1978. Inevitably, operating in the same small area as Robert Smith, **Porl Thompson** and **Lol Tolhurst**'s various **pre-Cure** bands, their paths eventually crossed.

On 19 February 1978 Easy Cure played the Rocket pub in Crawley, supported by Lockjaw. Robert Smith remembers Lockjaw as sounding 'more hardcore and Clash-like' whereas Easy Cure were 'more melodic like Buzzcocks', and this reflected itself in their respective followings: Lockjaw's punk crowd trashed the place.

Nevertheless, the two bands formed a certain kinship. In April 1978 they all met for drinks, starting at 5 p.m. and carrying on till two in the morning, and became good friends. They began gigging together (The Cure now having lost the 'Easy'), for example in Brighton on 14 July 1978 and at The Buccaneer in Horley on 12 August 1978. A flyer for the latter can be seen on **Michael Dempsey**'s personal website. According to Martin 'Oddy' Ordish on the Bored Teenagers site, 'we used to do gigs together using the incredible line "I KNOW AN EASY CURE FOR LOCKJAW"'.

One way in which Lockjaw stole a march on The Cure was in actually getting a record out. In 1977 they'd sent a tape to Raw Records, the Cambridge-based independent label founded by record shop owner Lee Wood, notable for releasing 'Johnny Won't Get To Heaven', the debut single by The Killjoys, featuring Kevin Rowland (later the leader of Dexys Midnight Runners). This resulted in Lockjaw's debut single 'Radio Call Sign', in which Bo Zo sounds very cross about radio DJs, with 'The Young Ones' (not the Cliff Richard song) on the B-side (cat no. Raw 8), in November 1977. Its artwork was a door key with the word 'JAW' spelt out in the teeth. 'Putting that record out was a big mistake,' Septic – I mean, Gallup – told journalist Steve Sutherland later. 'We sent a tape to Raw Records and they thought we were this really good suburban punk band, but we were actually shit. If I see any [copies] around today, I break them.'

By the time of their second single, Lockjaw had been joined by Steve Mushroom (Steve Musham) on guitar, while Micky Morbid (Stuart Hinton) had rebranded himself as Stupendous. The single followed a similar anti-media theme to the first. A demo cassette tape, funded by Raw Records, was recorded on 12 November 1977 at Spaceward Studios in Cambridge, featuring two versions of 'A Doonga Doonga', 'I'm a Virgin' and 'Journalist Jive'. (A copy is on display at **Crawley** Museum.) All three songs made it onto vinyl in early 1978 (cat no. Raw 19), with 'Journalist Jive' – a tirade against the printed press – as the A-side. (Perhaps uncoincidentally, Simon Gallup has had a lifelong distrust and disdain for the music press.) The artwork this time was a mock-up of a tabloid newspaper with the subheading *You had better get some pictures of Spiderman in action, Parker, or you're fired!!!!!!*

'Journalist Jive' was reviewed in *NME* by Max Bell, who called it 'a misdirected missile . . . Who wants to hear songs about journalists anyway?' (Robert Smith clearly did – see '**Desperate Journalist**'.)

And there the recorded history of Lockjaw ends. Damaged Goods would later reissue both singles, and in 1993 three Lockjaw tracks resurfaced on a compilation CD called *Raw Records: The Punk Singles Collection*. The current whereabouts of Hinton and Musham are unknown. Martin Ordish still lives in Horley and plays drums in covers band The Tax Players. Bowe and Gallup went on to form **Mag/Spys**. But that's another story.

Lost Wishes

Lost Wishes is a limited-edition cassette EP of instrumental tracks, sold to fan club members in 1994 at a price of £4 each, with all proceeds going to the Portsmouth Down's Syndrome Trust **charity**. Its roots lie in the *Wish* sessions, and in the aborted plan to release an entirely instrumental companion album called *Music for Dreams*. It was given the **Fiction** catalogue number FICCS 50.

The tape's opening track 'Uyea Sound' is named for the village of Uyeasound (all one word) on Unst in the Shetland Islands, the most northerly inhabited island in Scotland, and the strait of Uyeasound, the body of water it overlooks, itself named for the now-uninhabited island of Uyea. Uyeasound is home to a ruined Hanseatic trading house, the ruined Muness Castle, a youth hostel, a church and not a lot else. It is best known for the incident in 1745 when two girls from Uyea rowed to the nearby island of Haaf Gruney to milk their cows, but were caught in a storm on their return and blown all the way to Karmøy in Norway, never to return. They married Karmøy men, and their descendants, with the family name Dyrland, still live there. The track 'Uyea Sound', however, brings to mind a far less stormy sea. This restful piece of music evokes a becalmed bay, the sun glinting gently off the water. Originally called 'Old Scotland', it was based on a demo idea from **Porl Thompson**.

The Scottish and Nordic theme continued with the similarly tranquil 'Cloudberry', named after a liqueur also known as *lakkalikööri* (see **Alcohol**) made from a fruit which proliferates in the Highlands, Scandinavia and other northern climes (the Finnish version of the €2 coin has a cloudberry on it).

The darker, more turbulent 'The Three Sisters', based on a **Perry Bamonte** idea, could be interpreted as a third Scottish reference; the Three Sisters are mountain ridges on Glen Coe, though there are also Three Sisters in the geographies of Canada, Australia and Ireland.

The gorgeously delicate finale, 'Off To Sleep', came from a **Simon Gallup** demo, illustrating the democratic way in which the songwriting was spread around in the *Wish* sessions.

One interesting aspect of *Lost Wishes* is that the music appears somewhat influenced by the then-recent shoegaze movement, which itself was influenced by early Cure, and which in turn would feed into post-rock bands such as **Mogwai**, who are

Cure favourites, creating a virtual spiral of **influence**.

Lost Wishes has been much-bootlegged, and original cassettes nowadays sell for around £70. However, there is no longer any need to buy either, as all four tracks were included on the 2022 deluxe edition of *Wish*.

Lost World Tour

To English football fans, the phrase 'Euro 2022' marks the end of the longest-ever gap between their national team (of any gender) winning a tournament. To Cure fans, it marks the end of the longest-ever gap between their favourite band playing a gig. For this, at least until it was belatedly rebranded the Lost World Tour on social media, was the official name of The Cure's continent-spanning tour in the autumn of 2022.

That absence from **touring** – just six days short of three whole years – was at least partly forced upon The Cure by Covid-19 lockdown, their previous show being at Zilker Park in Austin, Texas on 12 October 2019 and the following one being at the Arena Riga on 6 October 2022, the opening night of the European tour which had been announced the previous December to much excitement.

That opening night in Latvia contained two huge surprises. Firstly, the set was bookended by two brand new songs, raising renewed hopes of a **fourteenth album** (and sending the hashtag #thecurelostworld22 trending). The excellent opener 'Alone', built on just two chords, had a valedictory feel reminiscent of **David Bowie**'s 'Where Are We Now?' and appeared to express Robert Smith's fears that The Cure were running on empty. A guitarless Smith began 'This is the end of every song that we sing/ The fire burned out to ash, and the stars grown dim with tears/Cold and afraid, the ghosts of all that we've been . . .', and lamenting that 'hopes and dreams have gone . . .'

The grandiose ten-minute closer, 'Endsong', took six minutes to even get to the vocals, but then reprised the mood and theme of 'Alone', dwelling on regret at things left undone: audible fragments included 'remembering the hopes and dreams I had, and what I had to do . . .' (At one show in Zagreb, Robert became so emotional when singing 'Endsong' that he shed tears.)

In Stockholm, a third new song was debuted: 'And

Nothing Is Forever'. A bittersweet ballad about being together at the moment of death itself:

> And slide down close beside me
> In the silence of a heartbeat
> You'll wrap your arms around me
> In a murmured lullaby

On 20 October in Krakow, a fourth new song was introduced. 'I Can Never Say Goodbye', dominated by a beautiful piano motif from **Roger O'Donnell**, was about the loss of Robert's brother. 'Something wicked this way comes to steal away my brother's life'.

A fifth new song, 'A Fragile Thing', joined those four in Assago, Italy. With another delightfully delicate O'Donnell piano intro giving way to a slowly churning Gallup bassline, it was a song recounting a dialogue of recrimination and regret between a couple whose love is in danger of disintegration due to absence and distance: 'All this time alone has left me cold and sad and lost . . .', 'Every time you kiss me I could cry . . .'

The other major surprise was that there were six people on stage. Robert Smith, **Simon Gallup**, Roger O'Donnell, **Jason Cooper** and **Reeves Gabrels** were all present as expected, but there was also a new face at stage-right, on additional keyboards and guitar. Or, rather, an old face, as it was none other than **Perry Bamonte**, playing his first Cure gig since 2004. Bamonte's return was a closely guarded secret until showtime in Riga: he had not appeared in any of the promotional photographs for the tour (suggesting, perhaps, that his reintroduction was not a done deal when the session took place).

Other than that, the 145-minute, twenty-five-song set was classic Cure, ending with a crowdpleasing, hit-packed second encore of '**Lullaby**', '**Close To Me**', '**The Walk**', '**Friday I'm In Love**', '**Just Like Heaven**' and '**Boys Don't Cry**'.

After that opening night in Latvia, the Lost World Tour travelled onwards through Finland, Sweden, Norway, Denmark, Germany, Poland, Austria, Czechia, Hungary, Croatia, Italy, Switzerland, Spain, Belgium, Netherlands, Ireland, Northern Ireland, Scotland, England and Wales, snaking back and forth through some of those countries twice or three times, culminating with three nights at Wembley Arena in London, scene of their first-ever UK indoor arena show way back in 1985. Despite snowstorms and rail disruption, and despite Robert having suffered a bout of 'McFlu' in Glasgow, those three London shows were triumphant, and the final night was the longest of the tour, at 177 minutes and thirty-two songs.

Support on all dates came from Scottish band The Twilight Sad, who had previously toured with The Cure in 2016 and been guests at Robert Smith's **Meltdown Festival** in 2018, as well as appearing at the Hyde Park show in 2018.

The North American leg of the tour in the summer of 2023 (followed in the autumn by a South American leg) was the highest-grossing of the band's career. Their thirty-five shows in the **USA** and Canada grossed $35.7 million and sold over 547,000 tickets, easily eclipsing their previous highest-grossing tour, Wish, in 1992, and bringing in over double the earnings of their 2016 visit. This was achieved despite – or, perhaps, because of – Robert Smith's determination to keep ticket prices low, and his much-publicised battles with **Ticketmaster**. This unprecedented success, along with renewed talk of a fourteenth album, signalled that The Cure – as a live act and, just maybe, a recording act – were back with a vengeance.

Lovecats, The

All cats aren't grey.

If one song symbolises The Cure's shift from sombre shades of monochrome into glorious Technicolor, it is 'The Lovecats'.

Released in October 1983, it was the third and final instalment of The Cure's trio of 'fantasy singles' – the stand-alone singles with an atypically pop flavour – and the most successful. 'Rather than continue in the vein that The Cure had been pursuing,' Robert Smith explained to David 'Kid' Jensen on BBC Radio 1, 'we decided to have a complete break and just make some singles, just for the fun of it.' Two decades later, speaking to *Uncut* magazine, he ascribed a deeper motive to the experiment: 'I decided to bring out some music that would destroy the whole myth of The Cure, and alienate the audience that had come to surround us.'

Following a series of **US** dates, The Cure – temporarily whittled down to an official core of Robert Smith and **Lol Tolhurst** but abetted by producer **Phil Thornalley** on bass and new drummer **Andy Anderson** – stopped off in **France** for La Musicomanie festival in Britanny during August, a month when over half of France traditionally takes its holidays and cities become eerily quiet. Rather than head straight home to London, they decided instead to detour to a semi-deserted **Paris** to record a single.

The sessions took place at Studio des Dames, a Polygram-owned studio mostly associated with French pop luminaries such as Sylvie Vartan and Johnny Hallyday, located at 44 Rue ses Dames in the 17*ème* arrondissement, not far from Place de Clichy, at that time a somewhat sketchy district which never went to sleep. The Cure instantly assimilated into this milieu, throwing what became, by all accounts, 'a five-day party' populated by locals they'd only just met. When they did retreat to recharge their batteries, a good night's sleep was not guaranteed: one night during their Parisian sojourn their hotel caught fire, and they came back from the studio to see mattresses being thrown out of the windows.

Something of the chaos and spontaneity of the situation found its way onto the record. 'The studio in Paris was an old record company studio, like Abbey Road,' Lol Tolhurst told *Record Collector* in 1993, 'with instruments lying around. All the instruments on that session were acoustic, the opposite to what we'd done with "**The Walk**".' Those instruments included several that The Cure had never used before. Tolhurst learned to play the vibraphone, Andy Anderson used brushes on his drums, and Phil Thornalley tried double bass for the first time, fumbling his way around messy scales filled with bum notes. Footage from the session shows them figuring it all out. Tolhurst felt, as they toyed with the studio's in-situ jazz gear, that they were 'firing on all cylinders'.

They were, after all, in the perfect place to capture the sound Robert Smith wanted. According to Thornalley, he was aiming for the feel of the Hot Club de France, the jazz collective founded in 1931 whose most prominent members were Django Reinhardt and Stéphane Grappelli. The latter frequently recorded at Studio des Dames. It's not inconceivable that the instruments The Cure picked up had previously been used by Grappelli sidemen and Hot Club alumni. 'I thought it would be slinky to record there,' Smith later explained.

The result was a piece of lopsided ragtime and jittery jazz, whose lively sonic palette included the clinking of glass bottles and onomatopoeic miaows on the fretboard, and earworm-creating 'ba ba da' scatting on the chorus from Smith. It was, *Record Collector* later said, 'an instantly likeable piece of kitsch swing'. At the time, Smith was already slightly disdainful about the whole thing. 'A pretend jazz single' was how he described it to 'Kid' Jensen.

For a seemingly throwaway pop song, however, 'The Lovecats' was rich with allusions to other artforms. First of all, if it sounded cartoonish, that was not an accident: the single knowingly echoes several cartoons. For example, the line 'Not broken in pieces like hated little meeces' is a direct reference to the Hanna-Barbera character Mr Jinks whose catchphrase, whenever tormented by his rodent nemeses Pixie and Dixie, was 'I hate those meeces to pieces'.

Another Hanna-Barbera cartoon cemented the connection between cats and jazz. In *Top Cat*, the action takes place in Hoagy Alley (named for Hoagy Carmichael), the show has a famous jazzy theme tune, and the gang are depicted playing makeshift jazz instruments. *Top Cat* was broadcast (as *Boss Cat*) in the United Kingdom from 1962, and would have been an inescapable part of Robert Smith's childhood, as would Mr Jinks through his appearances on *The Huckleberry Hound Show*.

An honourable mention must also go to *The Pink Panther*, whose appearances in the 1960s Peter Sellers films and the spin-off cartoons were accompanied by Henry Mancini's famous slinky jazz theme.

One cartoon, however, informed 'The Lovecats' above all others. In 1970, when Robert Smith was eleven, Disney released the film *The Aristocats*, a film which – like *Top Cat* and *The Pink Panther* before it – played on the idea that cats are inherently jazzy creatures. The word 'cat' itself, of course, has jazz connotations, 'cat' being standard jazz/beatnik slang for a person, a particularly cool dude being a 'hepcat'. ('The Lovecats', Smith told 'Kid' Jensen, was packed with 'early Sixties beatnik' jargon.) In *The Aristocats*, the jazz cat trope plays out most notably with the song 'Ev'rybody Wants To Be A Cat', which appears in a sequence featuring a motley crew of jazz cats, their leader voiced by real-life jazz musician Scatman Crothers, having a deranged house party, playing double bass, piano and trumpets in a manner not dissimilar to 'The Lovecats' video. (The Cure had learned the whole soundtrack to *The Jungle Book* off by heart during the Future Pastimes tour, so Smith and Tolhurst evidently had a fondness for a Disney-jazz singalong.)

Phil Thornalley has confirmed that *The Aristocats* influenced the feel of 'The Lovecats', and Smith himself has confessed that the Disney film was an inspiration – 'It was supposed to sound like *The Aristocats* or something, late night Paris' – and that he 'knew all the words by heart'. Steve Sutherland, in the book *Ten Imaginary Years*, states that Smith

even bought the film, which – if true – would be an impressive investment, as it wasn't released on VHS until the 1990s, meaning that Smith would have needed to hunt down a projection reel.

Aside from the 'low' culture of cartoons, the lyric also displays more highbrow influences. Some fans have theorised that it is inspired by the novel *The Vivisector* by Australian author Patrick White, in which a man drowns a sackful of cats. Smith was an admirer of White's work, but given the novel's bleak themes and the song's playful mood, a direct connection seems unlikely. The song's literary roots lie instead in poetry.

The first verse opens with the line 'We move like caged tigers', which slip through the streets 'while everyone sleeps, getting bigger and sleeker and wider and brighter'. This carries echoes of William Blake's 1794 poem 'The Tyger': 'Tyger, tyger, burning bright, in the forest of the night . . .' 'The Tyger' was at large, culturally, in the early 1980s: Marianne Faithfull recited the poem in her 1981 song 'Eye Communication', and Duran Duran recorded an instrumental named 'Tiger Tiger' in 1983, the same year as 'The Lovecats'. (Duran Duran, incidentally, were all Cure fans and often attended their gigs.)

Another obvious poetic inspiration is Edward Lear's 1871 nonsense poem 'The Owl and the Pussycat'. In Lear's verse, the titular feline and strigiforme 'went to sea in a beautiful pea-green boat', and serenade one another: 'What a beautiful pussy you are', the owl sings to the cat, and the compliments are returned. The chorus of 'The Lovecats' begins 'into the sea, you and me' and the self-flattering line 'we're so wonderfully wonderfully wonderfully wonderfully pretty' is repeated twice.

The nocturnal dancing cats in T. S. Eliot's 'Song of the Jellicles' are another likely influence, as is the 1939 collection from which the poem came, *Old Possum's Book of Practical Cats* (later adapted for the musical *Cats*, which premiered in 1981).

Cats in general were prowling through popular culture in the early eighties. Stray Cats' similarly retro-jazzy, double bass-heavy 'Stray Cat Strut' was a hit in April 1981.

And cats, of course, are a recurring Cure theme: think of 'Let's Go To Bed' with its 'perfect as cats', of 'High' with its 'kitten as cats', as well as the afore-alluded 'All Cats Are Grey'. Not long after 'The Lovecats', Mat Snow of *NME* asked Smith if being a cat appealed to him. 'It does, yeah, but just because they seem to do very little except make little funny noises, and fuck, and eat, and sleep . . .' (Around the same time, Smith had taken to wearing a white sweat shirt adorned in Keith Haring-style cat prints, sent by an American fan wrapped around some magic mushrooms with a note that read 'from your wife'.)

'The Lovecats' was released as a stand-alone single on 18 October 1983, catalogue number FICS 19, with a running time of 3.33. A superb 12-inch mix clocked in at 4.37. For those too dozy to buy either, it would also eventually end up on mini-LP *Japanese Whispers*. B-side 'Speak My Language', improvised from a bassline Robert Smith hummed to the band during those same Parisian sessions, also had a loosely jazz feel. The 12-inch also included the frenzied, piano-led 'Mr Pink Eyes', a phrase Smith came up with to describe the state of his appearance in the mirror when waking with a hangover. After a harmonica solo, possessed by the spirit of the Hot Club, he exclaims 'It's got to be jazz! That's what she wants . . .' (The words 'It's got to be jazz' could also be found on the sleeve.) All three songs were premiered in a radio session (see **Peel Sessions**) for David 'Kid' Jensen on 21 September 1983.

The video for 'The Lovecats', directed once again by **Tim Pope**, conveyed the giddy whirl of the song perfectly, and unveiled the all-new, smiling, colourful, polka-dotted Cure. 'I think that [fun] side of them was always there, but was never brought out,' Pope told Adam Sweeting of *Spin* in 1987. 'It really hasn't been imposed on them. Robert tends to put out silly singles that don't represent the whole thing of The Cure, so it's easy to make silly films of silly songs.'

Shooting took place at 1 England's Lane, a large but derelict townhouse in the Belsize Park area of North London. In order to secure the keys, Tim Pope convinced the landlord that he was interested in buying it. Once they had the place to themselves, The Cure crew did exactly what they'd done while recording the song in the first place: they threw a party. Over three floors. 'We invited lots of people,' Pope told Steve Sutherland. 'I did all the close-ups first and, by the time we came round to doing the group sequences at about four in the morning, everyone was totally out of their heads.'

The video, which features a slightly different recording of the song with added brass, takes place in a chaotic living room with furniture, mirrors and birdcages arranged at haphazard angles. Smith looms up into the lens as Pope spins around. Tolhurst mugs into the camera from behind a ramshackle piano.

Thornalley plays on despite a large lampshade falling on his head. Anderson somehow remains suave in the corner.

And then there are the cats.

The video was originally meant to feature over thirty real live cats as well as several taxidermied ones. But it was, literally, like herding cats. The real cats were scared of the stuffed ones, and ran off. In the end, only one live cat – a kitten, on Robert Smith's knee – is seen on screen.

One scene involved Lol walking down the street in a full furry costume in the dark, accidentally startling one of the locals. 'I terrified an old Rastafarian at about six in the morning,' he later recalled. 'He was walking along the street and I came out of nowhere in a cat suit. He must have thought he'd had too much herb!'

At 7 a.m. the crew took the keys back to the landlord, job done. One of The Cure's most iconic videos was in the can.

Propelled by that video, as well as substantial radio play, 'The Lovecats' became The Cure's biggest chart hit to date. Beforehand, Robert later admitted, 'there was a lot of debate that it would be commercial suicide'. It proved the very opposite. 'Let's Go To Bed', the first of the 'fantasy singles', had failed to crack the Top 40. 'The Walk' made it to No.12. But 'The Lovecats' crept catlike all the way to No.7. It got The Cure back onto *Top of the Pops* (with **Porl Thompson** standing in for the unavailable Phil Thornalley on double bass). Critically, too, it was a success: Steve Sutherland's review in *Melody Maker*, which namechecked Vincent Price, Herman Munster and Jean Cocteau, hailed it as Single of the Year.

Despite its success (or, perhaps, because of it), Robert Smith seemed curiously un-invested in the song. He cancelled interviews to promote it, and turned down a prime-time TV talk show. Performing it on *Top of the Pops*, he forgot the words. (He would later have a chance to redeem himself on that show's Christmas edition, on which he appeared twice: once with 'The Lovecats', and once as a Banshee with '**Dear Prudence**'.) 'It's a one-off,' he told Richard Skinner on the BBC's *Old Grey Whistle Test*. 'There will be no Lovecats follow-up, no Lovedogs.'

'The Walk' had already made The Cure persons of interest to hugely influential teen music magazine *Smash Hits*, but 'The Lovecats' made Robert and Lol worthy of a colour centrespread (with the song's lyrics down one side). 'Being alive', he told the mag, 'is quite nice at the moment', in a direct reversal of The Cure's doomy image.

All of this meant that 'The Lovecats' was a Trojan Horse for many younger fans who had never heard The Cure before. Older diehard fans, however, were appalled and wrote letters to Robert accusing him of abandoning his principles. His old friend and collaborator **Siouxsie** Sioux jokingly agreed: 'Anyone who writes a song called 'The Lovecats',' she said, 'has got to be a bit soft . . .'

Smith himself seemed quick to distance himself from the song. He described it to *Rock & Folk* magazine as 'an amateurish pop song' and said it was 'far from being my favourite song'. He also blamed **alcohol**: 'Composed drunk, video filmed drunk, promotion made drunk! It was a joke.' By the end of the decade, The Cure had dropped it from their live set, and it remained unplayed throughout the 1990s.

As well as the question of whether it's any good, the song is also at the centre of a perpetually burning controversy among The Cure's more pedantic followers: is it 'The Lovecats' or 'The Love Cats'? The discography sends us mixed signals. On the front cover of the *Japanese Whispers* LP, for example, it's Lovecats, and also on the inner sleeve and the label. On the track listing of the *Japanese Whispers* cassette, however, it's Love Cats. On some versions of the CD box it's Lovecats, on others Love Cats (and the same discrepancy applies to the discs themselves). Currently, The Cure's YouTube channel has it as Lovecats. There is no definitive answer, but for the most legitimate rendering we must surely defer to the original 7-inch sleeve by **Parched Art**, on which the 'e' and the 'c' of 'Love' and 'Cats' are very close together (whereas the 'e' and 'c' of The Cure, directly above, have a gap between them). The label – the printed silver **Fiction** version with the Porl Thompson scrawl, not the generic **Polydor** release – also clearly says 'Lovecats' with a capital 'L' and a lower-case 'c'. For the purposes of *Curepedia*, then, we're going with 'The Lovecats'. (That sleeve, incidentally, was made using wire models photographed under UV light, wearing cat 'masks' made from photos of two of **Andy Vella**'s own cats.)

The song's ability to reach the parts that other Cure songs couldn't was instant. A show on Australia's ABC radio used it as a programme ident, and a deodorant manufacturer in Greece used it – without permission – on a TV **advertisement**.

According to actress Molly Ringwald, director John Hughes worked on a film script based on 'The Lovecats'. After wrapping *The Breakfast Club*, she told Vanity Fair, 'he gave me a mix tape of what the soundtrack was gonna be. Which was pretty much Dave Brubeck, with the last song by Bob Dylan.' (The title 'The Lovecats' did end up being used as the name of an episode of *Degrassi* spin-off *Degrassi Minis*.)

Overplayed and over-familiar it may be to some, but 'The Lovecats' is one of the two or three Cure songs that most non-Cure fans can name. It's one of their most-recorded songs, with artists including Tricky, Supergrass side project The Hotrats, Paul Anka, Tanya Donelly, The Futureheads and Jamie Cullum and Katie Melua all having performed or recorded **cover versions**.

Smith was especially impressed by the Tricky cover. 'It sounds as it was to be expected: weird and wonderful,' he told *Humo*. 'Tricky has slowed down the skipping happy rhythm to a kind of death march, but that doesn't surprise me. Maybe he's listened to the lyrics: in fact, this song is not about cats but about a suicide pact between two lovers. Hence the text 'into the sea, you and me . . .' My idea of a lovesong. That's probably why he made it into a duet. I liked the contrast between the dark lyrics and the summery rhythms, and liked at the time how a dark song like that became a hit. But OK, maybe Tricky is just more consequential than me. I knew he was a fan. And I'm glad to hear a cover that isn't a copy.'

It's also been **sampled** by several hip-hop acts including Spain's Los Chikos del Maíz and UK DJ and rapper Charlie Sloth, and interpolated by Mindless Self Indulgence on 'Tornado' from their 1999 debut album. Furthermore, it has been noted that The Hoosiers' 2008 single 'Cops And Robbers' is very similar to 'The Lovecats', as is Babyshambles' 2007 single 'There She Goes'. The song also has its paw-prints all over The Coral's 2002 hit 'Dreaming Of You', whose Laurence Easeman-directed video featured someone in a bear suit playing a trumpet, and the band emerging from a cramped phone booth onto a beach, both very Cure/Tim Pope tropes.

By the twenty-first century, The Cure had made their peace with this 'amateurish pop song', and reintroduced 'The Lovecats' to their live set. In 2014, Robert Smith even played a unique brass-backed version with the Hackney Colliery Band as part of Brian and Robin's Christmas Compendium of Reason, a show held at Hammersmith Apollo by scientist Brian

Cox and comedian Robin Ince. It now stands as The Cure's sixty-eighth most-played song, respectably halfway down the league table.

To some, 'The Lovecats' will always be claws down a blackboard. To many others, it's the cat's whiskers.

Lovesong

He could have just bought her a necklace.

'Lovesong' was, Robert Smith said soon after its release, a 'wedding present' to his wife, Mary. Unusually for a Cure single, it does exactly what it says on the tin (or in the title). Speaking to *Chicago Tribune* about this uncharacteristically direct, heart-on-sleeve song, he confessed 'It's taken me ten years to reach the point where I feel comfortable singing a very straightforward love song. In the past, I've always felt a last-minute need to disguise the sentiments or put a twist on them. It's actually one of the most difficult songs I've had to sing . . . It's an open show of emotion. It's not trying to be clever. And it's difficult to do, because you run the risk of being laughed at.'

If you play 'Lovesong' on The Cure's official Vevo, a caption appears during the intro which says 'pensive post-punk music'. As a description of this muted, subdued, understated, mid-paced melody, that works as well as any. Said to be based on an idea from Simon Gallup, musically and structurally it is in the vein of 'How Beautiful You Are' from *Kiss Me, Kiss Me, Kiss Me*, which has been described as 'a dry run' for 'Lovesong'. (Incidentally, the title is listed sometimes as 'Love Song' but, as with 'The Lovecats', we're going with the joined-up original rendering here.)

Lyrically, it's one of the simplest in The Cure canon. Each verse has the same structure: 'Whenever I'm alone with you, you make me feel like I am (X) again', where (X) is, in sequence, 'home', 'whole', 'young', 'fun', 'free' and 'clean'. The chorus repeats the phrase 'I will always love you', preceded by the caveats 'However far away/However long I stay/Whatever words I say'. And, apart from an unlisted whisper of Frank Sinatra's 'Fly Me to the Moon', that's it.

This musical wedding gift, following the engagement gift of 'Just Like Heaven' a couple of years earlier, had an important role on *Disintegration*, Robert believed. 'That one song, I think, makes many people think twice. If that song wasn't on the record, it would be very easy to dismiss the album as having a certain mood. But throwing that one in sort of upsets people a bit because they think "That doesn't fit".'

The video was intended to be filmed in Wookey Hole Caves, a subterranean geological feature in Somerset opened as a tourist attraction in 1973 by the Madame Tussauds group and used as a location by *Doctor Who* in 1976. However, the owners trusted Tim Pope and The Cure less than they did Tom Baker and the Cybermen, and permission was denied. (Other sources have the intended location as the nearby caves at Cheddar Gorge.) Instead, Pope built a studio replica of the caves, complete with artificial stalagmites and stalactites made of polystyrene and plaster.

Robert sits slumped against a pretend-limestone column, a lute or balalaika-looking instrument propped up nearby, singing the song while examining the back of his hand. The rest of the band, including Roger O'Donnell who had his own sub-cave with a running waterfall, are barely seen until the final quarter, glimpsed between the columns. At one point, a row of multicoloured socks is briefly visible hanging from the cave roof, a Cure in-joke and a callback to the 'In Between Days' video. It was, in Roger's estimation, 'all in all one of the more painless of Tim's videos to make'. (O'Donnell kept one of the stalagmites, and still has it in his studio.)

Unusually, the sleeve wasn't designed by Parched Art. Instead, Smith chose some artwork by Maya (who also did the *Mixed Up* sleeve), involving a post-Fauvist painting of the faces of two lovers pressed so close together that one of the three eyes is shared between them. (Like 'Siamese twins', one might say, were that phrase still current.)

Coupled with the breezy but half-formed and forgettable '2 Late' on the B-side and, on the 12-inch, the doomy, O'Donnell-penned 'Fear Of Ghosts', 'Lovesong' was released on 21 August 1989 and became, by some measures, The Cure's most successful single of all time, rocketing to No.2 in the US where it was held off the top only by Janet Jackson's 'Miss U Much'. Incidentally, the No.3 spot that week was occupied by another English alternative rock band, Love And Rockets (comprising former members of goth heroes Bauhaus), with their single 'So Alive'. (In the UK 'Lovesong' reached a less impressive No. 18.)

According to O'Donnell, the band weren't especially keen on the song. For the first thirty-six dates of their fifty-two-date European tour in 1989, they didn't even play it, and even on the last stretch it wasn't a constant fixture. They didn't want it released but, following heated discussions, **Chris Parry**'s belief that it should be a single prevailed. Parry's instincts were correct: 'Lovesong' finished what the American success of *Kiss Me, Kiss Me, Kiss Me* had started, sealing the deal for The Cure as stadium-filling icons of alternative rock.

'Lovesong' has been **sampled** a few times, most notably by Wiz Khalifa in 2008 on his track 'Low Riding Freestyle'. However, it's as a modern standard, recorded by others, that it has had a truly significant afterlife. 'Lovesong' is easily The Cure's most-**covered** song, having been reinterpreted by at least eighty-six other artists. Tori Amos opened the floodgates in 1992, and since then it's been covered by, among others, 311, Anberlin, The Big Pink, Death Cab For Cutie, Jack Off Jill, Snake River Conspiracy and, most lucratively of all, Adele. Her 2011 album *21*, on which 'Lovesong' was the penultimate track, was a worldwide No.1, the bestselling album of all time on the Billboard charts, certified platinum ten times over, and sold thirty-one million copies globally.

Which has to be worth a few necklaces.

Lowest Point

When was The Cure's lowest point? These things are intensely subjective, and fans will have a multitude of answers. (The particularly rabid ones will be outraged at the suggestion that The Cure even *have* low points, as opposed to a succession of highs.) Robert Smith himself, however, has an opinion on this.

'We did **festivals** in '97 and '98,' he told Swiss television in 2002, 'and I thought they were the low point of The Cure's life. Because we were just turning up, playing festivals, and I was getting drunk and I had no reason to do it.'

This is a view which is shared by many Cure fans. The period around the Summer Festivals tour of 1998 comes up again and again in discussions around the band's absolute nadir, and the common cause seems to have been **alcohol**.

The trouble began, as Robert suggests, in 1997. One eyewitness at the Boston show, by the Reddit name Squishedgoomba, reported that 'he [Smith] was so intoxicated he forgot the words to '**Pictures Of You**'.' But it was in the summer of 1998 that

things really went off the rails. The band's European jaunt began in Zeebrugge on 18 July, and zig-zagged through Austria, **France** and Italy before reaching Lyon on the 25th for one of the most notorious shows in Cure history.

The Théâtre Romain de Fourvière is one of the most spectacular venues on earth. A genuine Roman amphitheatre, not dissimilar to the one in **Orange**, it is oriented in such a way that the Alps are visible in the distance through the stage, often providing a natural pyrotechnic backdrop in the form of lightning storms. However, on 25 July 1998, The Cure squandered the grandeur of the location by giving one of the most shambolic shows of their career.

On the fan-made footage that survives, the warning signs are visible from the beginning, like Chekhov's gun, with several bottles of what looks like wine or beer (definitely not mineral water) arranged on the front of **Jason Cooper**'s drum riser. The effects of what had clearly been a day of heavy drinking are apparent almost immediately, with Robert appearing bewildered as if under the effects of heavy dissociatives. He is unable or disinclined to sing a large chunk of '**One Hundred Years**', and on '**Just Like Heaven**', perhaps unable to remember the real words, begins to improvise: 'used to show you how I felt, used to show you what it meant, but never more, but never more . . .' Later, he misses his cue to come in on 'In Between Days' due to spending too long fumbling the changeover to his acoustic guitar, and also appears to forget the lyrics to 'From The Edge Of The Deep Green Sea' and '**Wrong Number**'.

The strangeness reaches a peak with '**Disintegration**' at the end of the main set. Robert at first wanders around aimlessly, barely remembering to sing, and then crouches on the floor at the front of the stage, making physical contact with the audience (a very un-Robert thing to do). He pokes his tongue out, and at one point he sticks his finger into his mouth, as though miming an attempt to make himself vomit, then pops it into the hand of a fan. Returning to centre stage, he begins throwing his microphone stand around, and eventually appears to be in tears as he lingers stage-right, needing to be coaxed into the wings by crew.

The traditional finale of '**A Forest**' is even more of a car crash. Robert doesn't even play his guitar for the first three minutes because he has a glass of red wine in his right hand. He eventually drops the drink on the floor, and a roadie has to clean it up. The ending is so chaotic that **Simon Gallup** stops playing altogether for a while, because it's not clear whether Robert's even playing the same song. He improvises lyrics, repeating the phrase 'I need you'. Eventually, after fifteen minutes, Simon signals to Jason to put the song – and the crowd, and the show – out of its misery.

After a gig the following night in Rothenburg, the tour took a two-week break before recommencing on the Iberian Peninsula with a show on 7 August at Zambujeira do Mar in Portugal. The following night, in A Coruña, it became clear that the fortnight's hiatus hadn't changed anything. During a free beach concert on the Praia de Riazor, Robert at one point lay down flat on the stage while singing, staring at the Domus (a brand-new science museum). He later explained that he was just amazed by the beauty of the sunset in the bay of A Coruña.

The shows in Dresden, Hildesheim and Gampel passed without significant incident, but the show at the Bizarre Festival in Koln on 22 August lived up to its name. Fortunately, or unfortunately, it is preserved for posterity in high-quality video, as it was broadcast by German music show *Rockpalast* (which was sponsoring the festival).

As per the Lyon debacle, Robert plays endless bum notes (when he plays notes at all) but on this occasion Smith wasn't the only inebriated member: several others also seem almost as drunk as he is, and the performance is staggeringly sloppy. The band sound under-rehearsed, and not like a band on the twelfth date of a tour, playing material they ought to know inside-out. The intro to '**Lullaby**', for example, sounds like a school band learning it for the first time, and Simon messes up the bass part to '**10.15 Saturday Night**', a song which had been in The Cure's set for two decades.

At one point during 'Disintegration' – evidently a danger song, if only due to its late position in the setlist – Robert falls over on his backside, while keyboardist **Roger O'Donnell**, perhaps the only sober member, smilingly shakes his head in disbelief. Then, in the encores, during 'Untitled', Robert sings lyrics from 'Watching Me Fall' (from the then still unreleased *Bloodflowers*), but it's unclear whether this was a deliberate choice or an absent-minded error. Obviously bands have the right to alter and improvise around their own material, and Robert had a history of doing this. But, given the state of the previous shows in 1998, a question mark was bound to hang in the air.

The ill-fated tour ended in Brno in the Czech Republic on 23 August. The Cure would demonstrate, at two surprise secret shows later in the year, that they could still deliver a decent live show: the first was a short hits set at the wedding of MTV's Ray Cokes in St Tropez on 19 September (with the band in suits), and the second was a gig sponsored by Miller Lite (see **A is for . . . Advertising**) on 11 October at London's Kentish Town Forum in front of a small crowd of competition winners. As far as the majority of European festival-goers were concerned, however, 1998 was The Year It All Went Wrong.

So, what was eating Robert Smith? What was the cause and effect, the chicken and egg? Was he depressed because he was drinking? Was he drinking because he was depressed? Was he depressed because *Wild Mood Swings* – just two years in the rear-view mirror – had been so negatively received, and drinking to forget? It is tempting to resort to armchair psychology. It is, however, telling that only one song from *Wild Mood Swings* ('Treasure') was played on the whole tour, and even that was only heard twice in fifteen dates. Robert himself subsequently said he was 'disillusioned' with the band at this point, and that his reason for doing these shows at all, with no new album to promote, was 'just because I wanted to be on stage.'

If the adulation of European fans was what he craved, to reassure himself that The Cure still mattered, and the stage was his safe place, it doesn't appear to have worked: watch the footage and you will not see a happy man.

The general consensus, however, is that the phase was over within a couple of years and The Cure were back on course. 'By the Dream Tour which was 2000,' said a Boston fan, 'it seemed like he got his shit together.' A renewed sense of purpose – and *Bloodflowers* – was just around the corner.

Lullaby

If The Cure are the band who put the 'creepy' into '**Crawley**', then no Cure song crept and crawled quite like 'Lullaby'.

Arachnophobia – the fear of spiders – is one of the more common phobias. A survey conducted in America by the National Institute of Mental Health found that an average of 30% of adults suffer from it. Other studies have found that it may be as high as 55% in women, and 18% in men.

The fear of spiders is not an entirely illogical one. There is a sound evolutionary basis for being wary of creeping, crawling, potentially venomous creatures. Around thirty of the fifty thousand known species of spiders on earth are poisonous to humans. Of the six hundred and fifty species found in the UK, twelve have a bite strong enough to pierce human skin, with the false widow the most venomous. In 2022, a baby in Ireland was taken to A&E after being bitten by a false widow. Reactions to a spider bite can include inflammation, latrodectism (a combination of pain, muscle rigidity, vomiting and sweating, caused by black widow bites), necrosis and, very rarely, in cases such as the funnel web spider of **Australia**, death.

Fear of spiders is encultured into humans from infancy in most societies (think of the nursery rhyme Little Miss Muffet), and exacerbated by their alien appearance and unpredictable movements. One fascinating folk myth is that of tarantism, a form of hysteric behaviour and involuntary twitching related to chorea, St Vitus' Dance or the dancing mania of mediaeval times, believed to result from the bite of the wolf spider or *lycosa tarantula*. This myth, which arose in Southern Italy in the eleventh century, gave rise to the Italian dance form the tarantella.

Robert Smith, along with **Simon Gallup**, confessed to *Cure News* in 1994 that he suffered a terror of large spiders. One common treatment for phobias such as arachnophobia is exposure therapy (gradually increased contact with the source of fear), but a more controversial technique is flooding (immediate and overwhelming exposure). In 'Lullaby', and particularly its **video**, Smith opts for the latter.

One of the first new songs Robert unveiled to the band during the preliminary *Disintegration* demo sessions at **Boris Williams**' house, 'Lullaby' was to become the most famous expression of arachnophobia in pop. The arachnid which stalks the sleeping Smith is no common or garden variety, but a supersized, human-scale one. The 'spiderman' who will be 'having me for dinner tonight' is not the Stan Lee-created superhero of the Marvel universe, but a bogeyman invented by a Smith family member.

In a 1998 issue of *Cure News*, Smith revealed that when he was young he had a 'very strange' uncle, also called Robert, who delighted in finding ways to scare his nephew witless. These included whispering grim stories in his ear, often involving a boy-eating

creature called the Spiderman. One night the uncle actually climbed through Robert's bedroom window after dark to scare him. (In other versions of this anecdote, including one repeated in *NME*, it was actually Robert's father who told the spider tales, in song form, and would end them with warnings like 'Sleep now, pretty baby – or you won't wake up at all.') In an interview with *Oor*, Smith said the song 'Lullaby' was more broadly about the fear of sleeping, and a Robert Sandall article in *Q* in 1989 claimed that **Tim Pope** believed it to be an allegory about Smith's **druggy** past.

In a *sotto voce*, semi-spoken, semi-whispered tone, Smith sings of this invasive entity with 'candy-stripe legs' who comes 'softly through the shadow of the evening sun, stealing past the windows of the blissfully dead' (a beautifully poetic turn of phrase) into the victim's bedroom. Something in his intimate, gasping delivery, and in lines as vividly sensual as 'His arms are all around me and his tongue in my eyes', almost seems to welcome the imminent devouring, to relish it, to *eroticise* it, even.

Meanwhile, pizzicato strings and chopped guitars follow the stealthiest of drum beats. It's no surprise that this is one of The Cure's most-sampled songs: like The Jesus And Mary Chain's 'Sidewalking' (March 1988), or **Siouxsie And The Banshees**' 'Peek-a-Boo' (July 1988), something about the cadences and rhythm pattern of 'Lullaby' acknowledges hip hop, while not being *of* it.

The video, made by Tim Pope on a London soundstage on 9 August 1989 with feature film production values and, at a cost of £80,000, not far off a feature film budget, was extraordinary, almost eclipsing the song itself.

Both Smith and Pope had independently visualised 'Lullaby' in terms of certain scenes and characters from David Lynch's *Eraserhead*, and the storyboard they came up with equalled that cult masterpiece for eeriness that lingered in the memory.

Robert, a boy in striped pyjamas, languishes in the brass bed of what looks like a Victorian convalescence ward. He is haunted by the rest of The Cure, dressed as (and moving like) mechanical toy soldiers from Napoleonic times, draped in cobwebs and playing marching band instruments, while an actual bird-eating spider stalks across the floor. Then the Spiderman himself, also played by Robert, with grotesque charcoal marks across his mouth and eyes, appears on the ceiling. What unfolds is like something from a horror film, when an increasingly cobwebbed Robert is first ravaged by the arms of his own alter-ego, then disappears into a set of furry black mandibles. (As Roger O'Donnell later recalled, 'Robert being pushed through the mouth of a giant spider . . . was all rather sexual. In fact as they pushed him through it the first time I very humorously shouted out "it's a boy" which made everyone laugh.)

The video was banned in the US, deemed too frightening for the age group it was aimed at. In Britain it received the accolade of Best Video at the BPI Awards in February 1990, an occasion which turned out to be O'Donnell's last public appearance with the band before leaving and then rejoining in 1995.

Released on 10 April 1989 as the lead single from *Disintegration* (in the UK, at least), the single's artwork by Parched Art involved the band name and song title spread in candy-striped curlicues over a blurred photo of a tarantula. The B-side was 'Babble' and, on the 12-inch and CD, 'Out Of Mind'. For details of these, see 'Fascination Street', which in the US had taken pole position from 'Lullaby' in the schedule of singles from *Disintegration*, and had swallowed up its UK B-sides (meaning that when 'Lullaby' finally did come out in the US, it was coupled with live versions of 'Homesick' and 'Untitled' that would later appear on *Entreat*).

It was a hugely successful record, reaching No.5 in the UK, their first Top 10 single since 'The Lovecats' six years earlier, and remains their highest-charting (if not biggest-selling) single in the UK. It was a major hit nearly everywhere else – Germany, Ireland, Netherlands, New Zealand, Spain – except the US.

The band celebrated their chart success with a party at Boris Williams' house, and got so drunk that they had to drive to London the following day to perform the song on *Top of the Pops* with horrific hangovers. As Roger later remembered, 'Robert wanted us all to dress up like the tin soldiers in the video but either we refused or they couldn't find the uniforms.' (They would eventually accede to the uniform code when performing 'The 13th' years later.) Robert himself wore an approximation of the 'Spiderman' make-up, to the horror of the show's producer who told him he would have to take it off or The Cure would not be allowed to perform. Robert refused, and negotiations ensued between Fiction and the BBC. Eventually the performance went ahead, in front of a studio audience who reacted with granny-claps and occasional inane whoops like it was

'Hi Ho Silver Lining' or something. The compromise reached was that there were no close-ups of Smith (who admitted in *Cure News* that he was still drunk during filming), and only of O'Donnell and Porl Thompson.

An extended mix of 'Lullaby' appeared on The Cure's 1990 remix album *Mixed Up*, and an acoustic version on the *Acoustic Hits* disc of *Greatest Hits*. Its strangest appearance on an album, however, was a German various artists compilation called *Gänsehaut & Herzklopfen* (Goosebumps & Heart Palpitations) in 1990, subtitled 'Romantic Hits Of Love'. If 'Lullaby' is Germany's idea of a romantic hit of love, one can only put it down to the language barrier.

'Lullaby' has become embedded in popular culture, used in television shows including *Misfits*, *Fresh Meat*, *Being Human*, *American Horror Story: Hotel*, *Dead Of Summer*, *Entourage*, *90210*, *Cold Case*, *Bates Motel* and *Chilling Adventures of Sabrina*. It's been sampled by Just Jack, Akala, Faithless, Rachel Stevens and Motionless In White (see Samples for details). And it's been covered by Editors, Kate Walsh, and a dozen bands you've never heard of.

But the live cover by Led Zeppelin alumni Page and Plant in 1995, with Porl Thompson himself on guitar, is the one that's having all the others for dinner tonight.

M

M is for ...

Madness (Insanity)

Robert Smith: Janitor of Lunacy.

Surrey is the buckle on the Asylum Belt. In the eighteenth century, dozens of dismal but grand-looking mental hospitals sprang up across London's doughnut-shaped hinterland. Consequently, the countryside around **Crawley** and **Horley** is peppered with Victorian institutions where patients, in less-enlightened times, were incarcerated and left to rot.

Cane Hill, where **David Bowie**'s half-brother Terry was a patient, lay a dozen miles to the north. (The American release of *The Man Who Sold The World* featured a drawing of Cane Hill on the front cover.) Even closer was Netherne Hospital, where **Michael Dempsey** held down a position as a porter before The Cure became a full-time job.

Other picturesquely named institutions in the ring around the capital included Bethlem Royal Hospital (aka the infamous Bedlam), Caterham Imbecile Asylum, Colney Hatch Lunatic Asylum (which once, under a later name, housed Adam Ant), Earlswood Asylum for Idiots, and the Fifth London County Council Pauper Lunatic Asylum.

It is, perhaps, impossible to grow up in the vicinity of these imposing, forbidding edifices without becoming curious about their inhabitants, and about the topic of mental illness in general. It is unsurprising, then, that so many of Robert Smith's lyrics touch upon themes of madness. 'I feel more natural in the company of people who are mentally unbalanced,' he once told *The Face*, 'because you're always more alert, wondering what they're going to do next . . .'

In the early eighties he took an active, academic interest in the subject. 'On the *Faith* tour,' he said in *Ten Imaginary Years*, 'I'd started to read books on clinical insanity, psychiatry, asylums, y'know, mental health in general. I thought about what sort of existence one must have in care, about the way you get treated and I thought, if I'd been alone, that could have happened to me. Instead of singing to an audience, I could've found myself singing to a wall.'

The Cure spent a day in a ruined Surrey asylum in 1982. Holloway Sanatorium, a redbrick **gothic** pile in Virginia Water, was chosen by director Mike Mansfield as the location for the (famously terrible) **video** for '**Charlotte Sometimes**'. In Holloway's heyday, the cruel method of 'dry-packs' was used to suppress troublesome patients. According to a 2008 MA thesis by Kim Jacks of West Virginia University on the nineteenth-century Weston State Hospital, where similar methods were used, 'a dry-pack had the person's body being enveloped in dry blankets for one to three hours . . . allowing no freedom of movement of the ankles or elbows or hands.' ('Wet-packs', on the other hand, 'involved laying a naked person on three blankets wrung out of cold water, and wrapped and bound around the patient from the neck down.') One Holloway patient, Thomas Weir, died while rolled up in a dry-pack.

Such were the ghosts with which The Cure were waltzing that day. The video shoot did have its upsides, however. They wandered into the asylum's derelict art department, and discovered all manner of fascinating artefacts. **Lol Tolhurst** took away a green sculpture of a dog drinking water. Robert Smith took a 'grotesque skull sculpture' which inspired the song 'The Figurehead' on *Pornography*:

> A scream tears my clothes as the figurines tighten
> With spiders inside them
> And dust on the lips of a vision of Hell
> I laughed in the mirror for the first time in a year

In his singularly bizarre 'Welcome to the Working Week' diary for *Flexipop!* in 1982, Robert wrote 'Friday was this week's day of madness for me. There's always one day in the week devoted to the subject.' He revealed that the video shoot had caused him to read two further books on the subject: *Sanity, Madness and the Family* by R. D. Laing and Aaron Esterson (1964) and *The Language of Madness* by David Cooper (1978).

Laing was a controversial Scottish psychiatrist who wished to normalise madness, arguing, for example, that schizophrenia is a 'strategy' employed by an individual who is not 'ontologically secure' in order to avoid 'losing his self', and that mental illness can be understood as a 'transformative episode' which can involve a 'shamanic journey' from which the traveller returns with important insights. Laing's fellow anti-psychiatrist David Cooper viewed madness as a liberating force: 'Madness is permanent revolution in the life of a person . . . a deconstitution of oneself with the implicit promise of return to a more fully realised world'.

These books, Smith told *Flexipop!* readers, fed directly into his lyrics. 'When I came across *The Language of Madness* in a bookshop, I noticed that it had a drawing by a mental patient which looked very like this head [the effigy from Holloway], so I bought it. That book has actually inspired some of the lines on the *Pornography* album, especially in a song called "A Short Term Effect" – "a charcoal face bites my hand" – that was a nightmare that one of the patients had. He would draw people in charcoal, and they would come to life in his dreams.'

In 1983, Robert expressed further thoughts on madness to Mat Snow of *NME*. 'I would like to go into an area of mental health, that sort of area, and psychiatry. Not clinical psychiatry, *alternative* psychiatry – I don't know. It's just something I find very, er, *horrifying*.'

He would like, he told Snow, to do something physical to help, or perhaps for The Cure to draw attention to the subject as a group. 'There's a vast amount of people who've either committed themselves to mental hospitals or been committed for nothing. It just intrigues me – but not in a dilettante sort of fashion. Just something inside makes me feel a bit sick.'

Over the years Smith has, on many occasions, raised money for **charities** related to mental health or mental disability. In 1985 The Cure played a concert for Mencap (who also benefitted from the proceeds from *Entreat* in 1991). In 1994 the *Lost Wishes* cassette raised money for the Portsmouth Down's Syndrome Trust. All profits from *Bestival Live 2011* went to mental health charity the Isle of Wight Youth Trust. And, in 2020, Robert performed 'In Your House' from *Seventeen Seconds* as part of an online version of the variety show *Nine Lessons and Carols for Curious People*, raising money for causes including mental health charity Mind.

In the interview with Snow in 1984, Smith said that he did not believe that he himself was mentally ill. 'No, I'm really stable', he insisted, 'but a lot of it is through mental discipline. I spend a lot of time controlling urges which would in a society supposedly as liberal as ours be thought of as really dubious. We're in a very Kafkaesque situation where you have to control your urges.'

Performing live with The Cure, he believed, was a form of cathartic therapy. 'Some nights I can go off stage and go really mental, completely losing sight of who I am, what I really think. It feels like inducing a sort of self-derangement, which is great. You feel elated and really clean, but I just think that obviously most people haven't got that. They go home and punch somebody out or put their head through a pane of glass . . .'

Mag/Spys

Mag/Spys, sometimes known as the Magazine Spies or MagSpies, were a **Horley** punk band formed in 1979 out of the ashes of **Lockjaw**, and notable for being **Simon Gallup**'s last band before joining The Cure for the first time.

The original line-up, in addition to Gallup on bass, comprised former Lockjaw members Gary Bowe (aka 'Bo Zo') on vocals, Stuart Hinton (aka 'Micky Morbid' or 'Stupendous') on guitar and Martin 'Oddy' Ordish on drums, with the later addition of Matthieu Hartley on keyboards.

They gigged around **Crawley** and Horley with Easy Cure/The Cure, as Lockjaw had done before them and, like Lockjaw, were managed by **Ric Gallup**, Simon's older brother. In *Ten Imaginary Years*, Robert Smith remembers them playing 'fairly icky pop songs'.

In October 1979 Smith invited them up to London, with Simon Gallup's girlfriend Carol Thompson (sister of **Porl**) in tow to provide backing vocals, to record those fairly icky pop songs at **Morgan Studios**. The sessions, produced by Smith, took place in between takes of the **Cult Hero** single, which itself was recorded during downtime in The Cure's *Seventeen Seconds*, meaning that time was at a premium, perhaps explaining the tracks' rushed, lo-fi sound. Two of the tracks were released on the flipside of **The Obtainers**' 'Yeh Yeh Yeh'/'Pussy Wussy' on Robert and Ric's **Dance Fools Dance** label (catalogue number GLITCH 1), in an extremely limited edition of one hundred copies.

The first, 'Lifeblood', features an over-cranked drum machine and frantic punk-pop chords, with busy bass work from Gallup. At one minute and twenty-nine seconds, terseness is its saving grace. The second, 'Bombs', is just as fast, with the chorus 'Ooh ooh wee dropping bombs on everyone I love/

Ooh ooh wee dropping bombs on power and glory'. Both tracks have since appeared on compilations of obscure British punk: 'Lifeblood' on *England Belongs To Me Vol 2* and 'Bombs' on *Bloodstains Across The UK 2*. Two further Mag/Spys songs, 'Dishonour' and 'Gary's Gone To War', are known to have been recorded but were never released.

The tenth edition of Croydon-based fanzine *Chainsaw* broke the news that 'Two members of the Magazine Spies, Simon Gallup and Matthew [sic] Hartley, have left the group and joined The Cure – the Mag Spies are continuing with a new line-up.' Gallup and Hartley, who had jumped ship in November 1979, were replaced by Stuart Curran from local band Crime on guitar and keyboards and Rik Kite on bass. The new-look Mag/Spys supported The Cure at the Marquee in London in March 1980, and in July the split single with The Obtainers was finally released, in paper sleeves with stickers on, hand-made by Ric.

Later that year, they broke up. Curran and Hartley (whose brief tenure in The Cure had come to an end in September) formed The Cry, whom Simon Gallup would later join in 1982 before they changed their name to **Fools Dance**.

Make-Up

Perfection is overrated.

There's a particular Cure photo shoot, circa 1984, which just doesn't look right. It's of the Smith, **Tolhurst**, **Thompson**, **Thornalley**, **Anderson** line-up which toured *The Top*. The landscape-oriented picture of this five-piece Cure can be found everywhere from the centrespread of *Smash Hits* magazine to The Cure's Japanese tour programme to countless unofficial knock-off posters to Anderson's *Rolling Stone* obituary. (From the same shoot, one often sees a photo of Robert alone with his face cradled coquettishly in his hands.)

They're all wearing expensive suits, and their **hair** looks unusually groomed. But what stands out as especially unnatural and un-Cure-like is the make-up. In these pictures, Robert Smith's lips look professionally glossed rather than haphazardly applied. His eyeliner is symmetrical rather than raccoon-smudged. His foundation is as perfect as porcelain. It's a type of make-up (or makeover) which implies the subject's death, making them resemble an embalmed corpse carefully painted by the undertaker for an open-casket funeral rather than a living, breathing human. It's as if a stylist has tried to make Robert into something he isn't, namely an immaculate mannequin like Nick Rhodes, David Sylvian or Boy George, primed to be just another marketable British Invasion pretty-boy pin-up.

The reason this handful of photos from the eighties look so wrong is that most Robert Smith photos *aren't* like that. From his very earliest experiments with make-up, it was never about looking pretty, or perfect. 'I've been putting on make-up since I was at school,' he told *The Hit* magazine, 'to inspire a reaction – which was usually against me.' In a French interview, he added that the reaction was often one of mockery. 'I learnt it myself through trial and error. If people laughed, I knew it was working . . .'

In the *Three Imaginary Boys* and *Seventeen Seconds* eras, Smith's face was largely slap-free, but footage of the Werchter festival in 1981 and also the '**Primary**' video show him already wearing heavy eyeliner. The reason, he explained, was that 'I've got quite ill-defined features and I just wanted to make more of them'. In that same interview with *The Hit*, he added that 'I need to wear it onstage because if I didn't no one would know where my mouth was. It became more gruesome as the band progressed so I decided to tone it down . . .'

That gruesomeness kicked in on the **Fourteen Explicit Moments** tour, when the whole band smeared lipstick not only on their mouths but their eyes, so that it would melt under the lights and slide down, giving the terrifying impression that their eyes were bleeding.

The psychology of dramatic make-up in alternative and **goth** subcultures, particularly among men, is often about throwing down a visual challenge to the world. It sends out a paradoxical dual message: 'Notice me, but keep your distance.' For those who feel themselves at war with the world, it is literally *warpaint*.

And Robert's make-up looks as though he's been in the wars: he once described his lipstick style as 'like someone's punched me in the mouth'. It's comparable to the moment in **David Bowie**'s 'Boys Keep Swinging' video when Bowie, in drag as a beehived catwalk model, rips off her wig and smears her lipstick sideways with the back of her hand. (In Mark Paytress' official biography of **Siouxsie And The Banshees**, **Steve Severin** claims that Smith borrowed Siouxsie's lipstick one night in a London nightclub called Legends and 'smeared it wonkily around his lips, that's how he got his trademark look.')

His skills progressed through trial and error: during 'The Caterpillar' video shoot, for example, he learned how to use blusher. He also developed certain brand loyalties: his favourite lippy, in the late eighties, was Crimson Scorcher by Mary Quant. The reason for wearing it, though, inevitably faded and habit took over: the longer you wear make-up, the more you do it *because* you do it. 'I've long stopped noticing that I put that lipstick on,' he told *Humo* in 2000. 'It's automatic, a ritual. And also a bit of a mask – I feel more at ease on stage in make-up.' And the world had become more accepting and less obsessive about his decision to wear it. 'The days when MTV did an hourly update on my make-up are thankfully long gone. That kind of silliness is no longer necessary.'

Any suggestions that Smith's *maquillage* is about pretty-boy perfection, he insists, are as far from the target as the tip of his lipstick. 'It's not so much vanity,' he once said. 'It's too grotesque to be vanity. It's *theatricality*.'

Martin

In the spring of 1986, on a promotional trip to Paris, The Cure found themselves having to mime on French television (see **France** and **TV**). However, **Boris Williams** and **Porl Thompson** were away on holiday, so **Lol Tolhurst** had to pretend to play drums for the first time in two years. His place on keyboards was taken by the mononymous Martin, Lol's flatmate at the time, who worked in a solicitor's office in the city. This makes him perhaps the shortest-lived 'member' of The Cure: not even a one-gig wonder but a one-song wonder, his moment of glory even shorter than **Derek Thompson**'s two-song reign.

Mary

Relationship goals.

That's a phrase you hear a lot, about Robert and Mary. They are that deeply unusual thing in the world of rock 'n' roll: a couple who have stayed together. As he told William Shaw of *Blitz* in 1985, Robert Smith is a man who has fallen in love only once.

Mary Theresa Poole was born on 3 October 1958

and grew up in **Crawley**. It was at St Wilfrid's Catholic School that she met Robert during a drama class. Pupils were told to choose a partner for an activity, and Smith plucked up the courage to ask her. They've been together ever since.

Having old-fashioned ideas about monogamy and devotion was considered uncool in the post-punk era, and Robert knew it. 'On a personal level,' he told Paul **'Desperate Journalist'** Morley in *NME* in 1981, 'Love and romance are the most important things. Once you're in love you're treated as someone who's an outsider, almost. Because I've been in love, I've been derided by people in a very personal way and what we've done as a group has been put under pressure because of that.'

But Mary was his refuge from *all that*, and his accomplice when he needed to escape. After the **Fourteen Explicit Moments** tour in 1982, for instance, they went camping together in Wales. A year later they did the same but in the Lake District, to clear their minds and get away.

Cool or uncool, Robert didn't shy away from talking about his relationship. In 1985, when they were living in a flat in Maida Vale, he was interviewed by *The Face*, and gave some insight into the peculiar Smith-Poole home life. 'I made a video of us the other week. I left a video camera in the corner of the room and after a couple of hours you forget that it's on, and I was quite horrified at the amount of rubbish we say to each other. It's like listening to mental people. The thing is, we've known each other for so long that I don't have to finish saying things. It's got down to one word, and she knows what I'm going to say.' (He also revealed their shared love of dressing up: 'I don't dress up anymore. Mary does, though. She used to dress as a witch to scare little children and she likes to practise on me.')

In 1985, *Zig Zag* magazine ran a piece poking its nose into Robert and Mary's private affairs. 'My relationship with Mary is what most people would consider to be "liberal", but not in that horrible contrived sense', he said, leaving the question of what sense he *did* mean 'liberal' to the imagination of the reader. 'Obviously from what I do and what she does, we spend time apart. If I'm on tour, she doesn't come with me because she doesn't like that side of it.' He went on to explain that she didn't enjoy people fawning over him because she remembered when nobody cared who he was, and that he didn't enjoy people ignoring her as if she were just another fan. 'We understand each other,' he concluded, 'which is why we've been together so long . . .' The same year, in a diary he wrote for French newspaper *Libération*, Mary goes missing for several days and explains, when she reappears, that she'd been skiing.

When Robert proposed to Mary, in Miraval during the recording of *Kiss Me, Kiss Me, Kiss Me*, she thought he was joking. But on 13 August 1988 they were wed, at Worth Abbey, a 1930s Benedictine monastery in Sussex once used in the BBC2 reality show *The Monastery*. 'I didn't get married to make a statement,' Smith later said. 'Me and Mary wanted all our families to be together that we might not see again. The main reason was to have an emotional day to remember. The actual state of being married doesn't make any difference to either of us.' He didn't have a stag night, he joked in *Cure News*: 'I had a stag decade'. The day itself, he said, was the best of his life. 'It was perfect. Everyone shone and then fell over.' A few photos of the day emerged, and one of them, to Robert's dismay, turned up on the cover of a Cure **bootleg**. Mary gave Robert a platinum heart as a wedding gift, as well as a silver chain which he always wears. His gift to her, famously, was **'Lovesong'**. Robert always wears his wedding ring, which he has described as his 'most sacred possession'. (Indeed, as far back as 1984, long before he was even engaged, he could be seen wearing a ring on his wedding finger.)

In her twenties, Mary worked in nursing and also did some modelling, but later quit full-time employment so that she could join Robert on tour and in the studio, shifting to voluntary work instead. 'She can't have paid work,' Robert told Suzi Feay of the *Independent* in 1997. 'She'd get the sack, because I'd just keep wanting her with me.'

However, Mary does not live her life as a public figure, and her public appearances are few and far between. In 1982, in a *Flexipop!* article which shed light on their sometimes-bizarre secret life, she is pictured hugging a tree which Robert has climbed. In 1989, she appeared on San Diego radio station 91X talking about her life and introducing her favourite Cure song ('Push', at the time). In 2019, she appeared on camera in the audience as The Cure were inducted into the Rock & Roll Hall of Fame (see **Awards**).

Mary is Smith's muse and his mirror, right down to the voluminous black hair and dramatic red lipstick. She shares his interest in football: she is a Tottenham supporter and, as Robert revealed in *Libération*, they went to see Spurs vs **Queens Park Rangers** in 1985. (The teams were diplomatic enough, on that occasion,

to play out a 1-1 draw.) She even has a similar way of speaking. There's one crucial difference: she has a fondness for dressing all in *white*.

What else do we know of the elusive Mary? We know that she calls him Bob, and he calls her 'M'. He also nicknames her Betty Boop (as the 1930s flapper cartoon character reminds him of Mary), and, he told ITV's *Night Network* in 1987, has worn a Betty Boop T-shirt as a tribute. As he told *Smash Hits*, 'She's fab. My best friend. She's got black hair and very striking looks. In fact she looks like Betty Boop. When I'm with her I just sit back and watch – I don't have to perform any more.'

Oh, and she has an eye for décor: 'In my other life, away from the group,' he said in 2000, 'I am told what to do a lot. At home, you know. I have to help out, and stuff. I don't pick the colour scheme for the curtains. I live in a house that's entirely decorated by someone else so it means I'm not a control freak.'

She has also made sparing cameos in Cure world. The **artwork** for **'Charlotte Sometimes'** in 1981 was a blurred photograph of Mary taken by Robert on holiday in Scotland in 1980. (The same photo, un-blurred, was used on **'Pictures Of You'** in 1989.) Her name appeared daubed on a pull-down screen in the **'Let's Go To Bed'** video in 1982. In 1987 she appeared in the **'Just Like Heaven'** video, dancing with Robert on the clifftop of a facsimile Beachy Head. And this book boldly advances the theory that she is the true identity of mysterious Cure accomplice **Bunny Lake**.

In addition to 'Lovesong' and 'Just Like Heaven', she is – obviously – the subject of 'M' on *Seventeen Seconds*. So, would it be safe to assume that every love song Robert has ever written is about Mary? When asked this in *Cure News*, he gave the curt answer 'No.'

To assume that everything Robert ever writes is from a first-person perspective is to underestimate him as a songwriter. For example, it might be tempting to read far too much into the disenchantment with marriage expressed in several songs on *Wild Mood Swings*. To do so would be to fail to recognise Robert's ability to step outside his everyday reality, and to escape the claustrophobia of constant repetition by describing observed or imagined scenarios. In a 1988 issue of *Cure News* he was asked 'A lot of your lyrics (e.g. **"Boys Don't Cry"**, **"In Between Days"**) seem to be about losing a girlfriend – are you expressing fears about your relationship with Mary, or are they fictitious situations?' He answered 'They are a mixture of fear, fiction and reality. I rarely know calm. In anything.'

The couple never had children of their own, and are happy with that choice. 'I've never regretted not having children,' Robert told the *Guardian* in 2011. 'My mindset in that regard has been constant. I objected to being born, and I refuse to impose life on someone else. Living, it's awful for me. I can't on one hand argue the futility of life and the pointlessness of existence and have a family. It doesn't sit comfortably.' In *Blender* magazine, he elaborated: 'Being a child myself, I kind of know what the two of us have missed, but I think it is more than compensated for by being able to still be the same to her as when we first met. We have absolutely nothing to stop us from saying, "Let's go away for three months," and just walking out the door.' However, they once 'adopted' (in the sense of 'sponsored') a Haitian boy and a Guatemalan girl, paying for their education and receiving progress reports and pictures, and in return sent them 'postcards and photos of England and snow and punks and anything else that will disturb them!' It later emerged, via *Cure News*, that they'd sponsored another child called Aurora in Lima, Peru and that Robert had visited her.

And Robert and Mary are a devoted uncle and aunt to twenty-five nieces and nephews, lavishing presents and treats upon them. 'Every year I hire a coach,' he told *Blender*, 'and we go to EuroDisney and stay at the hotel for a few days. Minnie Mouse coming up to me and asking me for my autograph with all the children looking on in absolute amazement was one of the best and most disturbing moments of my life.'

Mary and Robert's relationship looms large in the hearts of Cure fans, precisely because it is so unusual and so wholesome in the context of rock superstardom. It inspires much fan commentary and creativity. (For example, one YouTuber called Badass Fräulein has uploaded a summary of the Robert and Mary love story, and another called Siouxlita has provided a Mary Poole make-up tutorial.)

'Mary means so incomprehensibly much to me,' Robert told *Pop* magazine. 'I actually don't think she has ever realised how dependant I've been on her during all these years we've been together. She's always been the one that has saved me when I have been the most self-destructive, she's always been the one that has caught me when I have been so very close to falling apart completely, and if she would have disappeared – I am sorry, I know that I'm falling

into my irritating miserable image by saying it – then I would have killed myself.'

When asked in *Cure News* which moment from the past he would go back and repeat, if he could, he answered, 'My first dance with Mary'. (It's OK. You've just got something in your eye.) And, in the *Bloodflowers* tour programme, Robert gave a list of the most important things in his life. The list culminated with one letter.

M.

Meltdown

The Meltdown Festival is a long-running summertime season of concerts across the various venues of London's South Bank Centre, curated each year by a different esteemed artist. Since launching in 1993, curators have included Elvis Costello, Laurie Anderson, **John Peel**, Nick Cave, Scott Walker, **David Bowie**, Lee 'Scratch' Perry, Morrissey, Patti Smith, Jarvis Cocker, Ray Davies, Yoko Ono, David Byrne, Nile Rodgers and Grace Jones.

It has become customary for the line-up to feature artists playing unusual sets, perhaps performing in unique collaborations, or playing a classic album in full (**Siouxsie Sioux**, for example, played the Banshees' *Kaleidoscope* at Yoko Ono's Meltdown in 2013). Robert Smith had attended previous Meltdowns himself: in 2002, he watched David Bowie perform his classic album *Low*. Therefore, when he was approached to curate the 2018 iteration of the festival, he fully understood the premise.

Smith devised a dream line-up, and sent a handwritten letter to every artist on his wishlist. Almost all of them replied in the affirmative. Putting it together, he said in a statement, was not without its challenges. 'As one of my predecessors noted, it is akin to figuring out a giant psychedelic puzzle . . . But as each invitee confirms, as each shimmering piece falls into place, I pinch myself – this is really happening . . . And the complete picture will undoubtedly be out of this world!' His rationale, he told the *Chicago Tribune*, was a simple one. 'It's like a teenage dream, isn't it? I'm trying to achieve – it's very old fashioned, I suppose – a sense of community.'

The line-up he chose, like that of the travelling **Curiosa** festival of 2004, offers a fascinating insight into his tastes. (One band, Smith's particular favourites **Mogwai**, played both Curiosa and Meltdown.) Ninety acts across ten nights were promised, but the reality was more in the region of seventy. Some of them were established names, but many, like the bewitching Icelandic band Kælan Mikla, were new finds, unknown to British audiences. Most of them were **influenced by The Cure**, at least in some way. And some had, themselves, **influenced The Cure**. Artists appearing, in alphabetical order, were:

> 65daysofstatic, A Dead Forest Index, Alcest, The Anchoress, And Also The Trees, Black Moth Super Rainbow, Blue Crime, The Church, Douglas Dare, De Rosa, Death Cab For Cutie, Deftones, Drahla, Eat Static (DJ set), False Advertising, Fear Of Men, God Is An Astronaut, Kristin Hersh, Matt Holubowski, I Like Trains, Indian Queens, Is Bliss, Jambinai Jónsi, Kathryn Joseph, The Joy Formidable, JoyCut, Kælan Mikla, Kagoule, Kiasmos (DJ set), Kidsmoke, Kite Base, The KVB, The Libertines, Loop, Low, Mammoth Weed Wizard Bastard, Manic Street Preachers, Martinez, Maybeshewill, Misas Fall, Mogwai, Mono, Moon Duo, My Bloody Valentine, Nine Inch Nails, The Notwist, The Penelopes, Placebo, Planning For Burial, pg.lost, The Psychedelic Furs, Pumarosa, Jo Quail, Emma Ruth Rundle, Skinny Girl Diet, The Soft Moon, Alex Somers & Paul Corley: 'Liminal', Thought Forms, Tropic of Cancer, The Twilight Sad, Suzanne Vega, Vessels (live and DJ set), Vex Red, James Walsh, Hilary Woods and Yonaka. (Scottish band Frightened Rabbit were also due to appear, but singer Scott Hutchison tragically died by suicide before the show could happen.)

Oh, and The Cure, headlining the final night under the title Curætion-25, as discussed under the entry for the *40 Live* DVD set.

Some of the bands performed Cure cover versions in their sets. Manic Street Preachers did '**In Between Days**', as Robert looked on from the royal box. Placebo, with whom Robert Smith had previously guested at Wembley, did '**Let's Go To Bed**'. The Deftones played 'If Only Tonight We Could Sleep', and The Libertines covered '**Boys Don't Cry**'.

Smith took the idea forward into the following year's Pasadena Daydream Festival, where The Cure were supported by Meltdown acts Deftones, Mogwai (yet again), Kristin Hersh's Throwing Muses, The Joy Formidable, The Twilight Sad, Emma Ruth Rundle and Kælan Mikla (as well as Pixies and Chelsea Wolfe).

Furthermore, The Twilight Sad, Kathryn Joseph, Kælan Mikla and pg.lost all played the Anniversary show a month after Meltdown (see 40 Live), and the Twilight Sad would also support The Cure on their **Lost World Tour** of 2022.

The Meltdown experience inspired Smith to redouble his efforts towards a **fourteenth album**. 'I was offered the chance to curate the Meltdown Festival,' he told the *Chicago Tribune*, 'and I said yes. And then I realised I didn't really listen to very much new music any more. So I threw myself headlong into it and started listening to bands again and meeting kids who were in bands, and something clicked inside my head: I want to do this again. It came as a bit of a shock to me, to be honest. No one really believed me until we started recording . . .'

Mexico

To say that The Cure have a special affinity with Mexico isn't merely a statement of subjective opinion: in many ways it's verifiable objective fact.

Two of The Cure's Top 3 **largest crowds** are from shows in Mexico: No.1 is the audience of up to 70,000 who watched them at Foro Sol on 8 October 2019, and No.3 is the 57,304 who saw them in the same venue six years earlier.

The show on 21 April 2013 nearly didn't happen at all. An earthquake, registering 5.9 on the Richter Scale, struck the region just before showtime and shook the lighting towers, also knocking out mobile phone coverage. (Nobody was injured.) However, it ended up being a special and unique show. On Robert Smith's fifty-fourth birthday, the band attempted to break Bruce Springsteen's longest gig record of four hours and six minutes, but miscalculated and fell three minutes short. 'I was a bit crushed,' he told the *Guardian*'s Dorian Lynskey, 'because we could have honestly kept going for another half an hour.' They did, however, succeed in playing the largest ever number of songs at a Cure concert: fifty (twenty-five in the main set, twenty-five as encores), in front of what was then the largest crowd ever to attend a Cure show.

The fact that Robert chose to celebrate his birthday this way, and in this place, tells us that Mexico is a special place for him. The feeling is clearly reciprocal. Mexico has at least three Cure **tribute bands** (Desintegrados, The Blood Flowers and

Fixion), and their record sales have been enormous there since the eighties. *Kiss Me, Kiss Me, Kiss Me* was Mexico's sixth-biggest selling album of 1987, and *Disintegration* was its biggest-selling album of 1989, ahead of Metallica, **Pink Floyd**, Madonna and **Depeche Mode**. (For comparison, neither album made the equivalent year-end Top 50 in the UK.) On one occasion, while travelling through Mexico, The Cure's tour bus was stopped by guards who wanted the band's autographs (something which happened in one other country: **France**).

It is perhaps impossible to speculate on the exact reasons for The Cure's popularity in Mexico without falling back on clichés, stereotypes and tropes about death, drama and Día de los Muertos. It is, therefore, best not to try. The simple fact is that they are very popular.

They aren't necessarily an outlier or an anomaly. There are analogous cases to be found. It has often been reported that Morrissey is improbably popular among young Mexican men, particularly among ostensibly macho immigrant subcultures in California (though he would struggle to draw a crowd of 70,000 anywhere). More significantly, it's also a fact that emo, a movement massively **influenced by The Cure** and by Morrissey's former band The Smiths, is huge in Mexico.

Mainstream Mexican society, however, has not always been accepting of alternative youth tribes such as emo. In 2008, in Mexico City, Tijuana and Querétaro, there was a wave of violent attacks against followers of the emo subculture, as well as **goths**, and anyone else whose style involved dyed hair, piercings, unconventional clothing, and **make-up** on males. The gangs of attackers, many hundreds strong, included members of other more 'masculine' subcultures such as punk, metal, *cholo* and rockabilly.

The attacks were partly blamed on a Mexican TV personality called Kristoff who launched into an on-air rant in which he described emo as 'fucking bullshit', a worthless movement of pubescent girls who fancied the lead singers of bands. 'It looked like in a way he was inciting this violence,' journalist Ioan Grillo told *NPR*. (Kristoff later backtracked, following the violence, and condemned the attackers for cowardice, claiming his programme was only intended as 'fun'.)

'At the core of this is the homophobic issue', Victor Mendoza, a youth worker from Mexico City, told *Time* magazine. 'The other arguments are just window dressing for that.' Gustavo Arellano, an editor at *OC Weekly* and author of *Ask a Mexican*, argued that

emo's sexual ambiguity was considered provocative by other groups. 'What do you do when you are confronted with a question mark about sexuality in Mexico? You beat it up.'

This argument is borne out by the online activities of the anti-emo factions. On a website called Movimiento Anti Emosexual, attacks were planned and videos were shared. A group called Anti Emo Death Squad on Last.FM, also full of homophobic sentiment, attracted thousands of followers.

(It must be stated that Mexico isn't alone in this anti-emo backlash. In 2008, the Russian Duma banned the 'dangerous teen trend' of emo from schools and government buildings. In Chile, PokEMOns, as emo kids were known there, were attacked by skinheads. In Iraq, fifty-eight emo kids were murdered by Shia militias in 2012.)

Reporting on the backlash for the *Guardian*, Steven Wells drew a direct connection between emo and The Cure. 'Emo in Mexico seems to have become the cultural home for those with an acute need to partake of the following fairly universal teenage activities: dressing like Robert Smith from The Cure, downplaying the positive and accentuating the negative, being sad in public, and exploring one's emotions through bad poetry.'

The wave of violence sparked a number of counter-demonstrations of Emo Pride. When your very identity is under attack, you cling ever-closer to the signifiers of that identity. Being an emo kid in Mexico isn't a casual fashion fling but literally a life-or-death statement. The same, by extension, applies to being a fan of The Cure, the spiritual granddaddies of the whole scene. In Mexico, perhaps more than most places, The Cure *matter*.

Mint Car

The second single from *Wild Mood Swings*, 'Mint Car' was a piece of breezy indie-pop, with a noticeably similar feel and melody to 'Twisterella' by Robert Smith's shoegazing favourites Ride.

'The sun is up, and I'm so happy I could scream', Smith beams after its hurtling, upbeat intro. It was inspired, he told *Cure News*, by 'summer trips', meaning the innocent, non-**drug** variety. The title, he explained, was 'Cure speak for "fast trip"', and the feeling was 'more expectation and happiness, and this time around, no sad ending.'

Speaking to *Blah Blah Blah*, Robert shed a little light on his songwriting process. 'Writing a happy song is a complete different process for me from writing an introspective or melancholic one. I generally write when I'm unhappy or upset. That's when I externalise my fear and try to understand it. When I'm incredibly happy, I just enjoy it. "Mint Car" is about that feeling of expectation when you think: "This is going to be really really good, nothing could be better than what's about to happen". But I wasn't feeling that way when I wrote it. I tried to remember it, manufacture it, get as close as I can on paper.'

The **video** was filmed at Bow Film Studios, and directed by Richard Heslop, who had previously worked with **New Order** and had co-directed The Smiths' short film *The Queen Is Dead* with Derek Jarman. Robert called it 'remarkable for its speed and colour and verve'. He wasn't wrong. It featured Robert and the band in an ever-changing variety of costumes from the golden age of cinema: cowboys, pharaohs, cackling silent movie villains, dashing matinee idols and so forth. It's like something out of the Coen brothers' *Hail, Caesar!*, or the famous scene in *Blazing Saddles* where a Wild West brawl breaks the fourth wall and spills over into a neighbouring studio where a Busby Berkeley musical number is being filmed. Poignantly, in what may be his final appearance on camera, **Associates** singer Billy Mackenzie features in a party scene, his face unmistakeable behind dark glasses, a beatnik beret and a twirled cigarette holder.

Continuing the tin toys theme of *Wild Mood Swings* and '**The 13th**', **Andy Vella's artwork** was a blurred photo of a vintage toy car. Its B-sides were the tongue-tied, lovestruck 'Home' (Robert's explanation: 'How I feel sometimes'), the homesick 'Waiting' ('Being on tour/on a balcony in America'), and the spirited 'A Pink Dream' ('a South American trip/a dream').

Released on 17 June 1996, 'Mint Car' was a minor hit in the UK (No.31) and Finland (No.20), but a major hit in Iceland where it reached No.3 and was the thirteenth biggest-selling single of the year.

In hindsight, Robert felt a sense of injustice at the song's relative failure. Speaking to Pete Wentz of Fall Out Boy, he said 'We did an album in '96 and we had a song on there called "Mint Car" – it was the single, and I thought it was a better song than "**Friday I'm In Love**". But it did absolutely nothing because we weren't *the band* at that time. The zeitgeist wasn't right. It taught me that sometimes there's a tipping point, and if you're the band, you're the band, even if

you don't want to be, and there's nothing you can do about it.'

Musical judgement is subjective, but he's almost *objectively* wrong about that. 'Mint Car' was not as successful as a single because it's not as successful as a piece of songwriting. It doesn't have the massive brain-snagging chorus of 'Friday I'm In Love', something that you can't get unstuck from your head. It's a pleasant three minutes, but it's in one ear and out of the other.

Of course, two things can be true at once. The Cure genuinely weren't *the band* at the time. But even if they were, 'Mint Car' wasn't *the song*.

Mixed Up

'There's always been a dance element to our music.' That's what bands used to say, and everybody laughed at them for saying it. But The Cure, more than most, could point to evidence.

The biggest pop-cultural phenomenon of late-eighties Britain was two-pronged. Firstly, acid house, an underground movement in which thousands swarmed to clubs like Shoom and Future, as well as illegal outdoor raves and warehouse parties, dancing to psych-inflected electronic house music from Chicago and Belgium played by superstar DJs like Danny Rampling, Nicky Holloway, Mike Pickering and Paul Oakenfold, peaking with the Second Summer of Love in 1988. Despite its name, the movement was driven more by ecstasy than LSD. (Anecdotally, football violence decreased around this time because hooligans on the terraces were too E'd up to fight.)

Secondly, baggy (or Madchester). This movement, running parallel to acid house, involved indie bands, many of them from the Manchester area, such as Happy Mondays (who Robert Smith called 'brilliant'), The Stone Roses and The Charlatans playing dance-influenced music, with the Hacienda club (co-owned by **New Order**) as its spiritual hub. Several formerly rock-based bands jumped on the baggy bandwagon, releasing acid or indie-dance tracks in order to jump-start their careers. Some of them, like Primal Scream, were given a free pass, but others, like The Soup Dragons, were mocked for their opportunism.

When The Cure released their remix album *Mixed Up* in 1990, by which time the trend was well-established, Smith was at pains to point out that The Cure had been experimenting with dance music ever since 'The Walk', when only a very few of their peers were doing so (one being New Order, whose Ibiza-influenced 1989 album *Technique* was their response to the ecstasy era).

To some fans, *Mixed Up* felt like an act of appeasement to forces of evil: the baggy and acid crowd were, to a large extent, the sort of lumpen lads who would previously have beaten them up for being a Cure fan. In hindsight, this may seem a ridiculous overreaction. At the time, the battle lines were drawn.

The rationale for the record, Smith explained to *Rapido*, came from trying to figure out a way of re-releasing The Cure's 12-inches in a way that saved Cure fans from having to 'pay through the nose for old records'. Instead, many of those 12-inches did not appear on *Mixed Up* after all, and Smith instead 'farmed our old stuff to new people'.

It was also intended as something of a palate-cleanser after the doom of *Disintegration*. 'After we did the *Pornography* album, we followed it up with three of the most stupid songs we've ever done. Real banal pop. And after doing something like *Disintegration* last year, we'd have been forced, just internally, into doing something pretty superficial. And this has taken care of that side of the group.'

The idea of just remixing the tracks themselves was discussed. 'We talked about it,' Smith told *Vox*, 'but we thought it was probably a bit dull for me to do it cos I sort of know what I'd end up doing. So we talked to **Fiction** and said "What about giving some of the older singles to people who are currently doing remixes, doing stuff we quite like, and see what they do with it, and tell them not to worry about it sounding like us, they can do anything they want."'

Some of the tracks on *Mixed Up* – 'Lullaby', 'Fascination Street', 'Lovesong', 'Hot Hot Hot!!!', 'Why Can't I Be You?' – had indeed already been available on the 12-inch of the original single. Others – 'Close To Me', 'Pictures Of You', 'The Caterpillar', 'In Between Days' – were brand new mixes custom-built for the project. Two – 'The Walk' and 'A Forest' – were completely new recordings, as the original master tapes had been lost. And one – 'Never Enough' – was a brand-new track, released as the album's lead single.

The remixers to which the songs were farmed out were Paul Oakenfold, former hip-hop A&R man turned acid house maestro; William Orbit, an electronic artist who, despite being perceived as part of the new breed, was actually older than Robert Smith; Bryan 'Chuck' New, an experienced producer from Jive

Records who had engineered *Entreat*; and, most prominently of all, Mark Saunders (see **Producers**), who had already worked with The Cure (remixing the singles from *Disintegration*), and whose track record with Bomb The Bass, The Beatmasters, Neneh Cherry and Yazz was his strongest qualification for overseeing this project.

The album began with 'Lullaby (Extended Mix)', remixed by **Chris Parry**, Mark Saunders and Robert Smith – none too radically, with just the subtlest addition of a constant dissonant percussion note and the string motif replaced by a synth.

The second track, 'Close To Me (Closer Mix)' is perhaps the most-heard remix from *Mixed Up*, due both to its release as a single and its **video** which carried on where the original left off. It's perfectly pleasant but a bit Xanaxed out, a remix which sucks the energy out of the original instead of injecting energy in.

'Fascination Street (Extended Mix)', resurrected from the original 12-inch, finds Saunders having fun with the raw materials, adding Morse Code bleeps and plucked harp notes to create an elongated intro which is unrecognisable until, in a superbly thrilling moment, the main guitar riff kicks in.

Saunders is also at the helm for 'The Walk (Everything Mix)', not simply a remix but a remix of a re-recording. As 'The Walk' was a dance track already, the remix is arguably superfluous: a musical tautology. It doesn't fully hit the spot. You're waiting for the big keyboard riff but, for over half its length, that moment doesn't come (and, when it does, once between verses and once near the end, it's fleeting). Instead, the bassline is emphasised. If you'd never heard 'The Walk' before, you could believe it was a Robert Smith guest vocal on an enjoyable **collaboration** with some hipster electroclash track from the early 2000s. But if you know and love 'The Walk', there's something missing.

'Lovesong (Extended Mix)' is another one pulled from its original 12-inch, with Parry, Saunders and Smith pushing the drums far higher in the mix, recontextualising the song, subtracting some of its mournfulness and throwing open a window.

'A Forest (Tree Mix)' is another brand-new entity, not just remixed but re-recorded. While nobody sane would ever claim the remix is better than the original, there's something about its nagging electronic pulse that's a refreshing alternative, once in a while.

Bryan 'Chuck' New's 'Pictures Of You (Extended Dub Mix)', also known as the Strange Mix, gives the song an almost Soul II Soul-ish shuffle. The drum-and-vocal breakdown midway through is a lovely, intimate moment. This remix, according to the Fiction Records website circa *Mixed Up*'s re-release, was a key factor in persuading Robert to take a more adventurous path with the project. 'That mix turned the music on its head, but at the same time left the essential heart of the song intact. As soon as I heard it, I updated the entire *Mixed Up* plan. My revised ambition was to compile an album that was contemporary without being dated, immediate without being obvious, musically inspiring, rhythmically exciting and sonically great!'

The 'Hot Hot Hot!!! (Extended Mix)' from François Kevorkian and Ron Saint Germain, already available on the original 12-inch, is not too dissimilar to the track in its un-remixed form, but lets the guitar chops breathe a little. The French duo had impeccable credentials: Kevorkian had been a frequent guest DJ at Paradise Garage, and created the New York Mix of 'This Charming Man' by The Smiths which Morrissey reputedly loathed (all the more reason to love it). Saint Germain had primarily been associated with pop and soul artists (Diana Ross, Ashford & Simpson, Fatback Band, Aretha Franklin) but had recently been moving in an alternative rock direction via That Petrol Emotion and The Godfathers.

Kevorkian and Saint Germain were also responsible for the eight-minute frenzy of 'Why Can't I Be You? (Extended Remix)', which was also the original 12-inch version, but only appeared on the vinyl version of *Mixed Up*.

'The Caterpillar (Flicker Mix)' by Bryan 'Chuck' New was one of the album's bespoke remixes. The song, so human and so hands-on, doesn't lend itself particularly well to electronica, but when the individual parts from the original are given a chance to shine, it's like one of those satisfying moments in a rock-doc where the producer of a classic song sits at the faders and says 'So, here's the piano in isolation . . .'

Another all-new remix was 'In Between Days (Shiver Mix)' by William Orbit. It's a bit of a dud, but there's some enjoyable choppy crossfader jiggery-pokery with the guitar chords near the end. Robert found it an acquired taste. 'It's the first time ever that I've not been there when Cure stuff has been mixed – ever, right since the very beginning,' he told *Vox*. 'And that's why when the first two mixes – particularly the William Orbit one, it was so out there, so away from the song, that I had to listen to it twice. My initial

reaction was "What the fuck is occurring, what's he done to the song?" but on the third listen, I thought "This is brilliant". He's kept that certain spirit of the song and yet made it sound utterly different.'

The album ended with the only entirely new song, lead single 'Never Enough (Big Mix)', which had already been out for a couple of months on the 12-inch, emphasising the guitars and making it sound even more like The Stooges gone baggy than the 7-inch did.

A few further remixes were completed but didn't make the cut, instead turning up as B-sides. The 'Never Enough' 12-inch featured 'Let's Go To Bed (Milk Mix)'. The 'Close To Me (Closer Mix)' single featured 'Just Like Heaven (Dizzy Mix)' on all formats and 'Primary (Red Mix)' on the 12-inch, CD and cassette.

One remix, however, was so egregious that Robert swore blind that it would never see the light of day: 'The Lovecats'. As he told *Vox*, 'Bill [Chris Parry] took "The Lovecats" to be mixed in New York with two supposedly very contemporary remixers – I won't say who they are, but it was fucking dreadful, it really was – they managed to make it sound like a UB40 B-side, it was that bad. I absolutely refused for it to be released, so unless we die in a crash or something, it will never be heard.'

The artwork – a matte card sleeve with paint swirls of greens, reds and metallic silvers – was, unusually, not by Parched Art but by Maya (who also did 'Lovesong'). A quote by nineteenth-century French novelist, humorist and aphorist Jules Renard on the inner sleeve read: 'Look for the ridiculous in everything and you will find it!' The quote was chosen, Smith told *Cure News*, 'to pre-empt the inevitable criticisms'. (Reviews, however, were generally favourable. In *Melody Maker*, for example, Push reminded readers that The Cure had always been a pop band, so *Mixed Up* was a logical step.)

Mixed Up was released on 5 November 1990. The album reached the Top 10 in the UK and France, and was certified gold in those countries as well as Australia. In the US it reached No.14 and was certified platinum.

Breaking the authorial fourth wall for a moment: seriously, if you haven't listened to *Mixed Up* in a while, listen to it now. It's way better than you remember it being. At least three quarters of it really stands up, shining a different-coloured light on already-loved songs, like seeing familiar friends all dressed up for a party. Maybe you bought it out of b(r)and loyalty, but it barely spent any time on your turntable. Maybe you thought there was something unseemly about The Cure cashing in on the remix craze. Maybe you thought it embodied a craven capitulation to everything The Cure stood against. No matter. It's been sitting there all this time, waiting for you. And it's improved with age.

Robert called it 'a record to listen to on a Saturday night' and 'the perfect party record for drunk Cure fans'. Speaking to *Vox*, he said 'I've listened to it more than any other Cure album we've ever done because it sounds less like us than anything else, and there's no sort of emotional thing tugging at me when I hear any of the songs.' And, on Japanese TV, he conceded that 'It doesn't compare emotionally to some of the stuff that we've done in the past. There isn't that feeling that it's going to engulf you. But as far as dance records go, I think it's up there with Janet Jackson.'

He was sufficiently enamoured with the process to create the sequel *Torn Down* decades later for the third disc on the remastered deluxe CD version of *Mixed Up* in 2018. The second disc of that set, meanwhile, threw in a few more of the band's original 12-inch mixes ('Let's Go To Bed', 'Just One Kiss', 'Close To Me', '**Boys Don't Cry**', 'A Japanese Dream'), as well as those spare *Mixed Up* remixes which had already snuck out on B-sides and . . . jazzy drum roll . . . 'The Lovecats (TC & Benny Mix 1990)'.

This notorious, supposedly never-to-be-heard remix had actually already been briefly available as a free download from The Cure's *Greatest Hits* micro-site in 2001, and here it was again. Robert, clearly, had relented. The guilty party, who Robert declined to name in 1990, was Tony Humphries, a remixer and producer who had worked with The Jungle Brothers, Deee-Lite and Adeva among many others. Listening to his remix now, you can see exactly what Robert meant about 'a UB40 B-side'. In fact, it's more like a cheap karaoke rendering of 10cc's 'Dreadlock Holiday'.

No deaths were necessary in making it public. But it is a bit of a car crash.

Mogwai

'Of all the bands my sister loved,' writes Stuart Braithwaite in his memoir *Spaceships Over Glasgow: Mogwai, Mayhem and Misspent Youth*, 'the one that really got under my skin was The Cure.'

Braithwaite was born in Lanark, Scotland in 1976, and grew up in the small town of Strathaven, twenty miles south of Glasgow. A Cure fan from an early age, he began with his elder sister's copy of *Standing On A Beach* then worked progressively through all the studio albums from *Three Imaginary Boys* to *Kiss Me, Kiss Me, Kiss Me*. In his book, he recalls the anticipation he felt about the upcoming *Disintegration*, and writes vividly about hearing the 'utter grandeur' of 'Plainsong' for the first time.

On 18 July 1989, when Braithwaite was thirteen, an older friend hired a bus to take a mob of fellow fans to see The Cure at Glasgow's SECC. The second chapter of *Spaceships Over Glasgow*, titled **Fascination Street**, is entirely taken up with an eight-page description of that show. 'I'd never heard anything so loud in my life, but it wasn't just volume, there was a clarity to it as well,' he writes. 'I felt transformed.'

Speaking about '**The Caterpillar**' in *Pitchfork*'s 5-10-15-20 feature, he credited The Cure as being the band who introduced him to rock music. 'The Cure, The Jesus And Mary Chain and The Cult were the first bands I became really obsessed with. They were like the alternative to Duran Duran for me.'

Wearing a Cure T-shirt he'd begged his mum to buy him from a local market helped him to bond with other Cure fans at school, and thereby form his first band, called Pregnant Nun. And, when he formed Mogwai in 1995, named after the species of aliens in *Gremlins*, it wasn't long before he was joined by another Cure fan. Guitarist Barry Burns, who joined in 1998, later stated that 'The Cure were one of the first bands I got into as a teenager so I actually know how to play more of their songs than of any other people's songs.'

A mainly instrumental band in the post-shoegaze and post-rock genres, Mogwai's music, typically built from layer upon layer of guitar effects, is audibly informed by the 'utter grandeur' of The Cure, particularly on early material such as the albums *Mogwai Young Team*, *Come On Die Young* and *Rock Action*, and the stand-alone twenty-minute single 'My Father The King'. Braithwaite clearly has more in common with Robert Smith than being a supporter of a hooped football club (Celtic, in his case).

The love is mutual. In 1999 Smith mentioned that he had begun listening to Mogwai, and by 2004 he was telling American radio station 91X 'I have to admit, Mogwai have been my favourite band on the planet for about five years now.'

By that point, Mogwai had already **supported** The Cure for the first time in London's Hyde Park in July 2002. (In his book, Stuart writes about the 'surrealism' of seeing Smith's silhouette watching them from the side of the stage, then the added surrealism of watching The Cure in the company of Gary Numan.) It wouldn't be the last time. In fact, Mogwai hold the unique distinction of having appeared at three separate Robert Smith-curated events: the **Curiosa** tour in 2004, the **Meltdown Festival** in 2018 and the Pasadena Daydream all-dayer in 2019.

Mogwai were one of the bands named by Smith in 2012 as remixers on the proposed *Mixed Up 2*, and were said to be remixing **'Faith'**. This never materialised: when *Mixed Up* successor *Torn Down* finally emerged, it had no input from other artists.

However, in 2023 a nine-minute Lounge Masters mash-up of The Cure's **'Pictures Of You'** with Mogwai's '2 Rights Make 1 Wrong' emerged, for people who can't handle simply hearing Mogwai *before* The Cure, and inexplicably need to hear them both at the same time.

Morgan Studios

Morgan was one of those studios where the gold discs on the wall and the master tapes on the shelves either intimidate you or make you think you've arrived, depending on your mindset.

The studio was founded in 1967 by Barry Morgan, drummer with Blue Mink ('Melting Pot') and CCS ('Whole Lotta Love'), who was running a jazz label and wanted a permanent premises for it. Prior to The Cure's various visits it had been used by Jethro Tull, Lou Reed, **Pink Floyd**, Donovan, Mott The Hoople, Paul McCartney, The Faces, The Kinks, Hawkwind, Alice Cooper, Yes, Paul Simon, The Who, Cockney Rebel, Black Sabbath and any number of venerable beardies and longhairs. Iron Maiden and Thin Lizzy passed through while The Cure were there making their debut album. The carpets were shagpile, **Lol**

Tolhurst later recalled, and smelt of weed and incense. The Cure were only the third act from the punk/new wave generation to darken its doors, after Raped and Squeeze.

Morgan was where, in their **pre-Cure** incarnation Easy Cure, the band auditioned for **Hansa**. It's also where the **'Killing An Arab'** single, the *Three Imaginary Boys* album, the stand-alone singles **'Boys Don't Cry'** and **'Jumping Someone Else's Train'** and the albums *Seventeen Seconds* and *Faith* were recorded, as well as **Cult Hero**'s single 'I'm A Cult Hero', all with Morgan's in-house engineer/producer **Mike Hedges**. For a while, **Chris Parry** was operating **Fiction Records** from an office within Morgan. Essentially, for the first two or three years of their career, Morgan was Cure HQ.

The studio's previous function spooked the band a little during their many sleepovers. 'It was a former church,' said Lol Tolhurst in *Ten Imaginary Years*, 'with a weird roof. With the lights off after we'd gone to bed, you could hear a lot of bizarre noises. Scary. Someone said there were ghosts . . .'

In 1980, Morgan studios 3 and 4 were sold to **Zomba** and renamed Battery Studios; in 1984, studios 1 and 2 were sold to producer Robin Millar and became Power Plant Studios until they closed in 1990.

The Morgan building is now a Savers discount supermarket.

MTV Unplugged

It was Harlan Howard, in the 1950s, who defined country music as 'three chords and the truth'. But when Bono used the phrase on U2's 1988 album *Rattle and Hum*, the trouble really began. That album fixed the idea in the public consciousness that music was somehow at its most 'real' and 'authentic' and 'honest' when at its most pared-down and basic, stripped of studio effects. The success of songs like 'More Than Words' by Extreme and 'What's Up?' by 4 Non Blondes are prime examples of this trend at its early nineties peak.

It's an idea that's still with us to this day, when television ad breaks are routinely filled with breathy troubadours strumming acoustic covers of well-known pop hits of the past to sell anything from cider to cars, and when any heritage act who's run out of creative steam will turn to the cliché of re-recording an album's worth of their classic hits in an acoustic style.

The traction this idea that 'acoustic = authentic' gained in the early nineties can be put down, in part, to a rearguard action from the *Old Grey Whistle Test* generation, who feared the rise of samplers and synths in hip-hop and house music, and wanted to turn back the clock to a time when if you couldn't busk it, it didn't count.

One of the most influential factors in this Boomer backlash was *MTV Unplugged*. Of all the TV channels where an ongoing acoustic session series might reside, MTV was not the most obvious. It had, after all, launched and thrived in the era when the prevalence of synths in pop was at its height, and the artifice of the music video was central to its success. But its founding CEO Robert W. Pittman was from that generation alienated by modernity, and so were television producers Jim Burns and Robert Small, who created the *Unplugged* franchise.

The first episode of *MTV Unplugged* aired on Halloween 1989, featuring Squeeze. The next few episodes featured 10,000 Maniacs, The Smithereens and The Alarm, none of them megastars. However, within twelve months, stars of the magnitude of Elton John, Don Henley, Hall & Oates, Aerosmith and Crosby, Stills & Nash – most of whom didn't exactly need to step outside their comfort zones to go acoustic – were on board.

Recordings initially took place at the National Video Center in New York and, apart from two shows from Los Angeles, remained in that city. The very first episode filmed outside the US was the opener of Season 3 featuring The Cure which aired on Thursday 24 January 1991, recorded at MTV's Limehouse Studios in London. (The second, the very next day, featured Paul McCartney.)

The Cure cannot be accused of playing it safe: the first tune they played that night, '**Let's Go To Bed**', was almost entirely synth-based in its original form. Surrounded by candles and red velvet drapes, the *Wish*-era **line-up** of Smith, **Gallup**, **Thompson**, **Williams** and **Bamonte** sat cross-legged in a crescent, as if gathered around some invisible hippie campfire, reminiscent of their *Top of the Pops* performance of '**The Caterpillar**' (one of the ten songs they performed on the night, complete with violin-scraping from Robert).

The setlist was dominated by hits – '**Lullaby**', '**Just Like Heaven**', '**Boys Don't Cry**' (which Robert introduced as 'the definitive version') – but also

featured a handful of deep cuts in the shape of 'In Your House' from *Seventeen Seconds*, 'The Blood' from *The Head On The Door* and 'If Only Tonight We Could Sleep' from *Kiss Me, Kiss Me, Kiss Me*. There was also a premiere for a song from the upcoming *Wish* album, '**A Letter To Elise**', featuring Perry Bamonte playing a tiny toy piano tuned maybe a semitone sharp (which worked strangely well).

As with many Cure **TV appearances**, their *MTV Unplugged* walked a tightrope between musical magnificence and high comedy. The most enjoyable moment was the finale of '**The Walk**' (as seen being rehearsed in the film *Play Out*), on which Porl Thompson multitasks by strumming his guitar while humming the main riff through a kazoo, assisted by a handful of friends and fans who have also been provided with kazoos. It's ridiculous – you can see Robert and Boris trying and failing to contain their laughter – but also brilliant.

The cultural power of *MTV Unplugged* peaked after The Cure's session. In 1992, the *MTV Unplugged* album by renowned Enoch Powell sympathiser (1976) and anti-mask, anti-lockdown crank (2020) Eric Clapton became the biggest-selling acoustic album of all time. And in 1994, Nirvana's *MTV Unplugged* album became one of the defining moments of that band's short career. BBC2's *Later . . . With Jools Holland*, BBC Radio 1's *Live Lounge* and BBC Radio 2's *Dermot O'Leary's Saturday Sessions* can all be seen, to varying extents, as responses to the success of *MTV Unplugged*.

Simon Gallup, in a September 1994 edition of *Cure News*, carried out some epic hand-that-feeds biting when he described MTV as 'visual McDonalds shit . . . burn it down'. Nevertheless, he and Robert Smith were back on *MTV Unplugged* in 2006 as special guests of Korn, with whom they were now friendly via the **Ross Robinson** connection.

Although The Cure's *MTV Unplugged* performance was never released officially as an album, they did revisit the idea on the *Acoustic Hits* disc of *Greatest Hits* in 2001, with Boris Williams temporarily back in the team. (And Robert has been known to play the odd acoustic number live.)

Even a band as tricksy as The Cure aren't immune to 'three chords and the truth'. It's just that in their hands the chords are likely to be weird ones, and the truth is rarely pure and never simple.

N

N is for . . .

1983 (Robert's Craziest Year)

'I need a holiday. I keep making plans to go every week, but every week I'm in another group . . .'

1983 was Robert Smith's craziest year. And one of the many crazy things about it was that it lasted eighteen months, from November 1982 to May 1984. But we'll come to that.

There exists in Prince fan culture the concept of 'The Flood', coined by Prince scholar and podcaster De Angela Duff. In 1987, six albums were released which Prince either recorded, produced or was heavily involved in. In January, the album *8* by Madhouse, a fictional jazz-funk band that was actually Prince himself with saxophonist Eric Leeds, on his own Paisley Park label. In March, his own masterpiece double album *Sign O' The Times* (originally intended as a triple, and for which enough songs were written and recorded to fill an eventual posthumous eight-disc super-deluxe reissue). In May, the self-titled debut album by protégée and *Purple Rain* star Jill Jones on Paisley Park, co-produced and largely written or co-written by Prince. In July, the self-titled third album by Sheila E., on which Prince co-wrote every track, with the Revolution's David Z. credited as producer, on Paisley Park. In September, Taja Sevelle's self-titled debut on Paisley Park, with the single 'Wouldn't You Love to Love Me' written and played by Prince. In November, a second Madhouse album, *16*, on Paisley Park. (Duff also throws in the debut album by former Revolution members Wendy and Lisa, released in August, on the grounds that many of the songs were about Prince . . .) And that's not to mention the singles he wrote for others: 'Telepathy' by Deborah Allen, 'Baby Go-Go' by Nona Hendryx and 'Eternity' by Sheena Easton. He also played a fifty-one-date world tour. After a year like that, it's no wonder he went mad and thought *Graffiti Bridge* was a good idea.

In 1983 (and the first part of 1984), Robert Smith unleashed a 'Flood' of his own that would make Lady Fuchsia Groan, tragic heroine of *Gormenghast* and The Cure's *Faith*, bash her head in astonishment and tumble off the window ledge. The trouble all began in late 1983 when **Steve Severin**, Smith's closest conspirator outside The Cure, convinced him to rejoin **Siouxsie And The Banshees** for a second stint, while keeping The Cure as a going concern. To make matters worse, Smith and Severin were simultaneously cooking up their own psychedelic side-project, **The Glove**. The chronology of the ensuing year-plus of multitasking and spinning plates runs something like this . . .

November 1982: The first Glove sessions. Siouxsie And The Banshees appear on the *Old Grey Whistle Test*, and begin a UK tour.

December 1982: Siouxsie And The Banshees tour Europe, and appear on the BBC's *Oxford Road Show* and French show *Les Enfants Du Rock*.

January 1983: Smith and Severin co-write the song 'Torment' with Marc Almond for the Marc And The Mambas album *Torment And Toreros*.

February 1983: Siouxsie And The Banshees tour Japan and **Australia**.

Robert Smith enters discussions with Nicolas Dixon of the Royal Ballet, and makes preliminary plans for a **ballet** project.

March 1983: The Cure, with Severin and **The Venomettes**, perform *Pornography* track 'Siamese Twins' on BBC's *Riverside* with ballet dancers. The Glove resume recording.

April 1983: The Glove continue to record their album, *Blue Sunshine*.

May 1983: The Cure record '**The Walk**'.

June 1983: The Cure film 'The Walk' video. Siouxsie And The Banshees begin work on *Hyæna*. Meanwhile, The Cure are working on *The Top*.

July 1983: The Cure release 'The Walk', and perform it on *Top of the Pops*, twice. Siouxsie And The Banshees play the Roskilde **festival** and Stockholm. Work on '**Dear Prudence**' begins in Stockholm and ends in Islington. The Cure play Bournemouth, Bath and the Elephant Fayre festival.

August 1983: The Cure's *Boys Don't Cry* compilation is released in the UK. The Cure tour the **US**. The Glove release '**Like An Animal**'. The Cure play the Musicomanie festival in **France**, and record '**The Lovecats**' in Paris.

September 1983: Siouxsie And The Banshees tour Europe and Israel, and shoot the 'Dear Prudence' video in Venice. The Glove's *Blue Sunshine* is released, and promoted with music press interviews. The Cure play a Richard Skinner session. Siouxsie And The Banshees release 'Dear Prudence', film their *Play At Home* special for Channel 4, and play two nights at the Royal Albert Hall, filmed and recorded for *Nocturne*.

October 1983: The Cure film video for 'The Lovecats'. The Glove perform '**Punish Me With Kisses**' on BBC's *Riverside*. The Cure release 'The Lovecats' and promote it on *Top of the Pops*.

November 1983: The Glove release 'Punish Me With Kisses'. Siouxsie And The Banshees release *Nocturne* (and the *File* EP).

December 1983: The Cure release *Japanese Whispers*. The Cure perform 'The Lovecats' on Christmas *Top of the Pops*, and the Banshees perform 'Dear Prudence' on the same episode.

January 1984: Work on *The Top* and *Hyæna* continues. The Cure play in Munich.

February 1984: The Cure play in Zurich. Siouxsie And The Banshees perform on Channel 4's *The Tube*, and film the '**Swimming Horses**' video.

March 1984: The Cure film the video for '**The Caterpillar**'. Siouxsie And The Banshees release 'Swimming Horses', and tour France and Italy. The Cure release 'The Caterpillar'. Robert plays his final Banshees show in Bologna.

April 1984: The Cure perform 'The Caterpillar' on *Top of the Pops*. Robert works on **Tim Pope**'s 'I Want To Be A Tree'. The Cure perform on BBC's *Riverside* and Channel 4's *The Tube*. The Cure's UK tour begins.

May 1984: The Cure release *The Top*. The Cure's UK tour concludes, with two of the shows recorded for *Concert*, and a European tour begins. Siouxsie And The Banshees release '**Dazzle**', with a video which doesn't feature Robert. Exhausted on tour with The Cure, Robert phones Steve Severin from Hamburg to resign from the Banshees.

June 1984: The Banshees release *Hyæna*, and play their first gig at Brixton Academy with John Valentine Carruthers.

Over the period in question, Robert was a member of three different bands, and involved in the recording and/or release of three studio albums, two compilations, two live albums, eight singles and one EP, and two stand-alone collaborations. He took part in the filming of five music videos, one TV special,

one live film, and at least fourteen TV performances including one mini-ballet. He toured Japan, Australia, Europe (four times) and the UK, as well as playing three festivals and a handful of stand-alone gigs, coming to a grand total of seventy-one performances. He was interviewed countless times. Oh, and he recorded a radio session. (Eat that, Prince.)

Fiction feared that Robert was being pulled in too many directions. Rightly so. Inevitably, this workload took its toll on Robert's health, both mental and physical. As he told Banshees biographer Mark Paytress, 'That period was a high and a low point, it was my best and worst year. The Glove album, The Cure's *The Top*, *Hyæna* – I don't really remember making any of them.' During the simultaneous recordings of *Hyæna* and *The Top*, he told *Uncut* in 2000, he became disoriented and confused about which guitar part was for which group. 'When *The Top* came out,' he recalled, 'I suffered my only serious breakdown. I went on tour with The Cure and realised that the day it finished I had to go off with the Banshees. I just thought, "Fuck, I can't do this." I was shaking all the time – and couldn't feel my legs when I went onstage.'

He presented himself to the family doctor who was shocked at the state of him, advising him that if he didn't stop he would die. 'I was physically exhausted,' he told Paytress. 'It was like the vengeance of God. I had all these boils, and my skin started to fall off. It was like my body was saying "If you refuse to stop, I will stop you." I had everything you can imagine go wrong. My system simply couldn't cope.'

Never Enough

'Never Enough' has the double distinction of being The Cure's first new music with no involvement (even nominally) from **Lol Tolhurst**, and the only new song on *Mixed Up* (for which it served as the lead single).

In order to record the song, The Cure – with the new **line-up** of Robert Smith, **Simon Gallup**, **Porl Thompson**, **Boris Williams** and, making his Cure recording debut, **Perry Bamonte** – set up a temporary studio in an unusual location: an eighteenth-century manor called Beel House in Little Chalfont, Buckinghamshire, former home to matinee idol Dirk Bogarde, star of films such as *The Servant*, *Darling*, *Death in Venice* and *The Night Porter* and, during his wartime service, one of the first Allied officers present at the liberation of Bergen-Belsen concentration camp. Bogarde lived at Beel House for many years with his partner Anthony Forwood, at a time when same-sex relationships were illegal. By the time of 'Never Enough', Bogarde and Forwood had long since emigrated to France, leaving Beel House in new hands and available for hire by people such as The Cure.

Like the album *Mixed Up* itself, 'Never Enough' was The Cure's concession to the then-fashionable indie-dance movement variously nicknamed 'Madchester' or 'baggy', and producer **Mark Saunders**, who had a track record in dance music, was the obvious choice for the project. Consisting primarily of a 'Funky Drummer'-esque backbeat and three descending chords delivered with squalls of distortion and wah-wah, it's a track with a sense of gleeful abandon, as if a pressure valve has been released and all the frustrations of the Tolhurst era have come spurting out. Explaining its lyrics to *Cure News*, Robert admitted that despite The Cure's recent successes – which included winning BRIT **Awards** – he felt an 'overwhelming dissatisfaction' with life.

The video was filmed by **Tim Pope** in his own studio, using a mock-up of Hastings Pier, which in real life is just twenty miles east of Beachy Head, scene of both the '**Close To Me**' videos. As well as (theoretically) taking place in a vertiginous whirl above the waters of the Sussex coast, it shared with 'Close To Me' a sense of claustrophobia, especially in the scenes where the band appear as 'giants' crammed onto a tiny stage, much as they were crammed into a wardrobe previously.

The central conceit of the video is that The Cure are stars of an end-of-the-pier freakshow. At the door, Pope plays the head of a mechanical fortune teller, similar to the 'Zoltar' machine from the Tom Hanks film *Big* (which was released just a couple of years earlier), an example of which can be found on Brighton Pier. This isn't the only cinematic reference. There are numerous nods to Tod Browning's controversial 1932 classic *Freaks*: Simon and Robert play conjoined twins (in a manner which seems calculated to launch a million sordid fanfic fantasies), Porl is a bearded lady, and Robert also plays a human duck.

The video was partly inspired, Robert revealed many years later, by a strange gift from a fan. 'The most scary present we ever got,' he told *Humo*, 'was a scale model of a room or cellar that a fan had made for us. It looked amazing, very detailed, but my hair was standing on end. The creator had made miniature models of all band members made of wood and cardboard. It was as if he was some kind of Hannibal Lecter who wanted to lock us in that little room. When I unpacked it, backstage after a gig, I wanted to leave straight away, I was worried that guy would be waiting for us. But that room had a very bizarre false perspective that we very opportunistically stole as an idea for the video for "Never Enough".' (One can't help wondering what the model-making fan thought of the video, when he saw it.).

Another story Robert told about the 'Never Enough' video was a case of mischievous misdirection. 'Shortly afterwards,' he told *Cure News* in 1998, 'the man playing "the booth man" was arrested for fraud, using a stolen credit card and impersonating **Chris Parry**'. This was an in-joke: the booth man was none other than Chris Parry himself.

Released on 10 September 1990, 'Never Enough' was joined on the B-side by another new song, 'Harold And Joe' (who were, Robert later revealed, 'creatures in Simon Gallup's mind', although it has also been suggested that it refers to the characters Harold Bishop and Joe Mangel from the Australian soap *Neighbours*, which Simon watched). Smith sang it in an unusually deep voice which was compared by one fanzine to Lloyd Cole (though Robert claimed he was trying to sound like Frank Sinatra). The 12-inch also featured 'Let's Go To Bed (Milk Mix)', a remix which didn't make it onto *Mixed Up*. The single sleeve was uncharacteristically straightforward, consisting mainly of a photo of the band distorted as if through a rain-streaked window pane, with Robert wearing the floral shirt he wore often at that time (including in the video).

'Never Enough' was a moderate hit in Britain, reaching No.13, but barely scraped into the **US** Billboard Top 75 (though it went Top 10 in Ireland, and did top Billboard's Modern Rock chart). Its significance, however, was far greater than its sales figures: it proved to the world, as if proof were ever needed, that there was life after Lol.

New Order (and Joy Division)

A tale of two bands. One from the South, one from the North.

The Cure and Joy Division first intersected on 4 March 1979, in a storm of fists and phlegm, when the latter **supported** the former at a dangerously oversold Marquee Club. Speaking to Paraguay's Radio Urbana in 2013, Robert Smith looked back on that show. 'We picked the four bands we wanted to play with us, and Joy Division were one of those bands . . . I heard *Unknown Pleasures* on the radio on **John Peel**, and they were just fantastic . . . They were the best thing I'd seen – not ever, because I'd seen **Bowie** and the Stones – but they were of that generation of bands which is *my* generation of bands. They were so powerful . . . That was our best show that year, I think. We went on after them, and we had to really try hard to match what they did.'

From then on their paths diverged, but remained parallel, like the tines of a tuning fork. Both emerged from the wreckage of punk at the same time. The **Crawley** band and the Macclesfield band both shifted from traumatised, angst-ridden, doom-infused music towards bright, shiny alternative pop, making all their major moves at approximately the same time, sometimes with suspicious synchronicity.

Their debut albums dropped just weeks apart: The Cure's *Three Imaginary Boys* on 11 May 1979, and Joy Division's *Unknown Pleasures* on 15 June 1979. Their follow-ups, too, were closely bunched: The Cure's *Seventeen Seconds* on 18 April 1980 and Joy Division's *Closer* on 18 July 1980. However, Joy Division's records charted much higher than The Cure's: No.5 and No.6, respectively, compared to The Cure's No.44 and No.20.

The same pattern – The Cure getting in there first, but Joy Division surpassing their success – applied to singles. The Cure broke into the Top 40 first, with their career-defining 'A Forest' reaching No.31 in March 1980. That same month, Joy Division recorded their own iconic breakthrough hit, 'Love Will Tear Us Apart', which outdid The Cure, reaching No.13 in June, albeit in tragic circumstances (of which more later).

Joy Division achieved all this despite being on an indie **label**, Anthony H. Wilson's pioneering Manchester imprint Factory, while The Cure had the **Polydor** machine behind them. The difference, perhaps, is that Joy Division arrived fully formed: *Unknown Pleasures* is regarded as an all-time classic, whereas *Three Imaginary Boys* is seen as a shaky, uncertain start.

That gig at the Marquee wasn't quite the last time the two bands shared a stage. On 3 and 4 April 1980,

two Stranglers shows were held at the Rainbow Theatre in Finsbury Park, London in support of their singer Hugh Cornwell, who had been imprisoned on a **drugs** charge. In Cornwell's absence, Robert Smith and **Matthieu Hartley** were part of an all-star supergroup which included Toyah, Hazel O'Connor, Phil Daniels, Jake Burns of Stiff Little Fingers, Ian Dury, Richard Jobson from Skids, Wilko Johnson of Dr Feelgood, and assorted members of Steel Pulse, The Blockheads and Hawkwind, playing The Stranglers' set. The support band were Joy Division. However, they did not stick around to watch Robert and Matthieu in action, as they were obliged to rush away to the Moonlight Club in West Hampstead to make unannounced appearances at a Factory Records residency. On the second night at the Rainbow, strobe lights caused Ian Curtis to suffer an epileptic seizure during Joy Division's final song, 'Atrocity Exhibition'. On a **bootleg** recording, he can be heard shouting 'Turn the lights off!' Curtis collapsed backwards into Stephen Morris' drum kit, which audience members initially believed to be part of the finale, and had to be carried off. (He recovered in time to play the later set at the Moonlight.)

Although they were exact contemporaries, Robert Smith didn't just view Joy Division as peers and rivals. He was a fan. He once stated that 'Joy Division are still my favourite group and always will be', and has on occasion named *Closer* as his favourite-ever album. On the film version of *Show*, shot at a Detroit gig in 1992, Robert plays a bit of Joy Division's 'She's Lost Control' at the end of 'A Forest'.

If Smith loved Joy Division, Peter Hook didn't notice. 'I don't think The Cure liked us,' he wrote in his memoir *Unknown Pleasures: Inside Joy Division*. 'I think they resented us in some way, because we'd managed to stay cool, credible, and independent and they'd, well, sort of sold out a bit . . . I think they thought, "*Wish we were Joy Division*."'

In addition to his epilepsy, Curtis suffered from depression exacerbated by issues in his personal life. He had begun an affair with Belgian journalist and promoter Annik Honoré, and his wife Deborah had initiated divorce proceedings. On 18 May 1980, six weeks after that Stranglers support gig and on the eve of an American tour, Ian Curtis died by suicide, aged just twenty-three. (Famously, Anthony H. Wilson took *NME*'s Paul Morley to a funeral home to show him the dead body of Curtis – see **Desperate Journalist**.)

In the aftermath of Curtis' death, 'Love Will Tear

Us Apart' became a bona fide hit single, and *Closer* followed *Unknown Pleasures* into the Top 10. Joy Division left behind a small but immaculate body of work which, along with the early works of The Cure and Siouxsie And The Banshees, laid the foundations of goth.

The death of Curtis affected Robert Smith both on a personal level and an artistic one. 'It's a shame about Ian Curtis,' he told Radio Urbana. 'It's like Jimi Hendrix or Kurt Cobain . . . People that good come around far too infrequently.' Reflecting on the making of *Faith* to *Uncut* magazine in 2000, he recalled 'The whole thing was reinforced by the fact that Ian Curtis had killed himself. I knew that The Cure were considered fake in comparison, and it suddenly dawned on me that to make this album convincing I would have to kill myself. If I wanted people to accept what we were doing, I was going to have to take the ultimate step . . .' 'Joy Division is still my favourite group and always will be,' Robert said on Fréquence Mutine in 1989 '. . . but I'm nothing like Ian Curtis at all. He was really unhappy about things I really enjoy . . . If you haven't got something you can really enjoy, then there's nothing else. People wanted me to be a new Ian Curtis because people like the idea of someone pushing himself down until he dies, and then they look for someone else. Ian Curtis didn't die for anyone but himself.'

The remaining three members of Joy Division – guitarist Bernard Sumner, bassist Peter Hook and drummer Stephen Morris – regrouped and, with the addition of keyboardist Gillian Gilbert and with Sumner taking on lead vocals, forged ahead under the name New Order.

At the beginning, New Order appeared to be a continuation of Joy Division: their first single, 'Ceremony', released in January 1981, was a leftover Joy Division song. As they found their feet, however, they began emphasising the electronic elements – drum machines, Syndrums (already used on *Unknown Pleasures*), synthesisers – of their sound, and moved in the direction of the dancefloor on singles like 'Everything's Gone Green' and 'Temptation'.

On 7 March 1983 New Order released their groundbreaking 'Blue Monday', a seven-and-a-half-minute single created using an Oberheim DMX drum machine and a Moog Source synth. On 1 July 1983, The Cure released 'The Walk' which, as many observers mentioned, bore a certain resemblance to 'Blue Monday'. The full saga of whether 'The Walk' was or was not a 'Blue Monday' rip-off is detailed in

the *Curepedia* entry for that single. One thing which cannot be disputed is that New Order's single fared better. Both 'Blue Monday' and 'The Walk' were the respective bands' biggest hit to date, but 'Blue Monday' reached No.9 whereas 'The Walk' got no higher than 12. However, in one of the most legendary poor decisions in music history, 'Blue Monday' came in a cut-out 12-inch sleeve, designed by Peter Saville to resemble a computer floppy disk, which was so expensive to manufacture that every copy sold actually lost them money. 'Blue Monday' became the biggest-selling 12-inch single of all time, with over 700,000 copies of the original pressing sold. The Cure, if only by default, therefore probably did better financially out of *their* 'Blue Monday'-esque single than New Order did from actual 'Blue Monday'. (Robert Smith cheekily referenced the rival hit on 'Friday I'm In Love' in 1992: 'I don't care if Monday's blue . . .')

That decade continued the pattern of 'anything Cure can do, New Order can do better' (or, at least, bigger, and sooner). New Order's 'True Faith' reached No.4 in the UK in 1987 and a remixed 'Blue Monday' No.3 in 1988, chart positions The Cure would never reach. In the summer of 1990, they did two more things The Cure had never done: released a football song ('World In Motion', credited to EnglandNewOrder), and scored a No.1 single. They also beat The Cure to No.1 in the album charts with 1989's *Technique* (a feat they repeated with 1993's *Republic*). The Cure would have to wait till 1992's *Wish* to achieve that. It must be acknowledged, however, that this imbalance only applies in the UK. Globally, and especially in the US, The Cure have been far more successful.

Despite this apparent rivalry, The Cure lavished almost as much praise upon New Order as they had upon Joy Division. In 1987, Robert Smith said he only had time for two new albums, and one of them was New Order's *Brotherhood*. The same year, Simon Gallup listed New Order as one of his favourite bands. In 1992, they mentioned they had been listening to New Order on their tour bus in the US, and Robert told MTV's Ray Cokes that 'One of my favourite groups, all through the years, has been New Order.'

He wasn't above the occasional barbed remark, though: in a 1993 *Cure News* he called New Order 'overrated'. And New Order's Peter Hook isn't shy about taking a swipe at The Cure, either. On Radio Urbana, Smith speculated as to the reasons. 'Although The Cure and New Order . . . We come from the same age and everything, but Peter Hook always had a real big problem with us because our bassist Simon Gallup was so much better-looking and the better bass player . . . I think Peter was so jealous he could never get over it, and he stopped the rest of them from being friendly.'

Peter Hook and New Order parted company in 2007, and relations between the bands thawed. 'We've bumped into them over the years,' Smith told Radio Urbana, 'and since he's left, we've played with New Order a few times in the last summer and it's so nice to be able to chat with them, you know, to talk with them because I've always loved New Order. I think they're one of the best bands. They also have a fantastic back-catalogue and they like us, it's so nice to say to Bernard "I like your band" and he says "I like yours as well", and . . . It's taken an awful long time to say "Hello" again to them. They're a good example of a band that gets better as they get older.'

Perhaps the source of Hook's beef is musical. 'The Walk'/'Blue Monday' isn't the only time The Cure have been accused of ripping off New Order. Peter Hook has argued, at various times, that '**In Between Days**' is a steal from either 'Dreams Never End' or 'Love Vigilantes' by New Order. As 'Love Vigilantes' came out on 13 May 1985 (on the album *Low-Life*) and 'In Between Days' came out just two months later on 19 July (and would already have been in the can for some time), it's unlikely that The Cure copied it. However, with 'Dreams Never End', the opening track of New Order's 1981 debut album *Movement*, the case for having influenced The Cure seems more compelling. (A further similarity has been noted between 'Elegia', also from *Low-Life*, and the sound of the whole *Disintegration* album.)

New Order arguably took their revenge on the track 'All the Way' from *Technique*, which has a strong flavour of '**Just Like Heaven**' to it. (A YouTuber called William Power has uploaded a couple of mischievous mash-ups: one of 'In Between Days' with 'Dreams Never End', and another of 'Just Like Heaven' with 'All the Way').

Leaving aside specific songs, the primary comparison between New Order and The Cure is in the bass players. While one may (as Robert noted above) be better-looking than the other, they both hold their instrument in a similar low-slung style, and both have a fondness for the high notes on a six-string. 'The whole *Faith* album has six-string bass,' Robert told *Guitar Player*. 'I think when people talk about the "Cure sound", they mean songs based on

six-string bass, acoustic guitar and my voice, plus the string sound from [string synthesiser] the Solina. Joy Division/New Order and The Cure both got into the sound at the same time.'

Peter Hook, though, isn't having it. 'Plenty of people have ripped us off,' he once said. 'But The Cure really take the piss sometimes . . .'

Nocturnalism

'I very rarely get up before midday', Robert Smith told ITV's *Night Network* in 1987, 'but then I don't go to bed till 5. I live sort of the wrong way round. I just prefer it. I like being able to walk outside when there's not many people around . . .'

Robert Smith has been a creature of the night for most of his adult existence, a situation to which he has become accustomed both as a way of life and a *modus operandi* in the studio. Anyone who has joined The Cure, or worked with them on an album, has had to adapt to his nocturnalism.

In the aftermath of the **Fourteen Explicit Moments** tour, he began sleeping till 1 p.m. then staying up till 5 a.m., a pattern he has more or less maintained ever since. In *Cure News* he once stated that he typically sleeps for anywhere between five and ten hours, usually between 3 a.m. and 3 p.m. All eyewitness accounts of The Cure in the studio refer to this idiosyncratic approach to timekeeping.

Living the 'wrong way round' evidently works for him creatively, assisting his ability as an artist to look at the world through the other end of the telescope. In the diary he wrote about a week in his life for *Flexipop!* in 1982, Robert thought it worth a mention that he had risen at 10.30 a.m. on a particular day. Hilariously, he described this as 'very early'.

Nocturne

If releasing a double album in the post-punk era seemed like a hippie indulgence (see **Kiss Me, Kiss Me, Kiss Me**), and if releasing a live album in the post-punk era seemed like something that only rock dinosaurs were meant to do (see **Concert**), then what does *Nocturne* – a double live album recorded during Robert Smith's second stint – tell us about **Siouxsie And The Banshees**? Well, for one thing, it tells us that they cared about as much for the punk rulebook as The Cure did.

The Banshees weren't the first band of their generation to cross the line – *The Name Of This Band Is Talking Heads* was released a year earlier – but the idea still didn't sit well with many **critics**. In *Sounds*, Robin Gibson wrote that 'the majority [of live albums] are transparently unnecessary. Their sole purpose, seemingly, is the self-gratification of the artist concerned.' *Record Mirror*'s reviewer, meanwhile, sneered, 'They're probably working on a "concept" LP right now. I always presumed the whole point of the new wave had been to sweep away the portentous, self-indulgent flatulence of a cosseted rock "elite" – but what do we find? Siouxsie & co regressing to that very "advanced" stage of development that must surely herald The End.'

Siouxsie's stated rationale was that 'We wanted to document all the old songs which would be relegated once *Hyæna* came out', and also that 'It's something we released as a snub to the bootlegs' (a justification Robert Smith also made for The Cure's *Concert* the following year).

The show, or shows, that the Banshees decided to record were no ordinary ones. On 30 September and 1 October **1983**, they played the Royal Albert Hall in London, arguably London's most prestigious and hallowed venue, for the first and second time. According to Paul Morley (of '**Desperate Journalist**' fame) in the sleeve notes of the 2009 *Nocturne* reissue, they seemed completely at ease in those surroundings. 'They took their place inside the dreamy, historical hall as though it was both an everyday occurrence and also a kind of fairy tale', Morley wrote, and they did so 'with a temporary guitarist in the dazed, agitated, near celebrity form of The Cure's Robert Smith'. In Morley's view, the Banshees 'took the opportunity to treat the venue like a castle – their own opulent private space where they could speak with some authority about invented creatures, spiritual experiences, insane tenderness, psychological woes, whimsical impulses, solitary sexual dreaming, twilight realms, genes and keepsakes and the futile lurchings of the human heart – and got on with their business.'

As their walk-on music, the band used two minutes of Igor Stravinsky's *The Rite of Spring*, a piece commissioned for a paganism-themed **ballet** choreographed by Vaslav Nijinsky which is said to have caused riots upon its premiere in Paris in 1913. Seventy years later there was no such commotion

at the Albert Hall as the classical overture segued seamlessly into 'Israel', the Banshees' 1980 single. This set the tone for a setlist which favoured the hits and the relatively recent past. There were just two songs from their debut *The Scream*, none at all from *Join Hands* (an album with which Robert, having performed it extensively during his first stint as an emergency Banshee in 1979, was very familiar), and the rest from *Kaleidoscope*, *Juju* and *A Kiss In The Dreamhouse* with a couple of B-sides thrown in. The lack of early punk material displeased some hecklers, one of whom repeatedly requested 'Love In A Void' (a song they hadn't played for years), prompting Siouxsie to retort 'What time tunnel did you crawl out of?'

Across the two nights, there were just three songs in which Smith had a hand (or four, if you count the cover of The Beatles' '**Dear Prudence**'). These, all from the work-in-progress album *Hyæna*, were 'We Hunger', 'Blow The House Down' and 'Running Town' (a live recording of which, from these shows, made it onto the fanclub-only *File* EP). However, none of these were included on *Nocturne*, to avoid stealing *Hyæna*'s thunder.

The rest of the time Robert was obliged, as he had been since rejoining the Banshees in late 1982, to reinterpret the work of another guitarist, mainly John McGeoch. For Paul Morley, this was a positive. 'One of the pleasures of hearing the group at the Albert Hall in late 1983 – sending a postcard to themselves and whoever else happens to be passing by – is hearing Smith play with uneasy, intimate precision and a certain tumbling melancholy the role of faithful guitarist in a group that was not his, that was possibly better than his, or certainly more impregnated with traumatised intensity.'

Smith executes a perfect balancing act, bringing something of his own style to familiar songs like 'Happy House', 'Slowdive' and 'Melt!' without trampling all over them with his own personality. Steve Mason of The Beta Band later praised Smith's guitar work on 'Painted Bird', and **sampled** 'a huge chunk' of it for The Beta Band's 'Liquid Bird'. The ultimate example of Smith improving a Banshees classic is 'Spellbound', perhaps the most iconic of all Banshees songs, on which he adds metallic walls of sheet-metal guitar to complement Budgie's thunderclap drumming, making it somehow even more powerful than the studio original.

Banshees bassist **Steve Severin** and producer **Mike Hedges** mixed the album in a week at Pete

Townshend's Eel Pie Studios, while the Banshees were working on *Hyæna*. One night they stayed up till 8 a.m. drinking wine, inserting that 'Love In A Void' heckle between every track. (It can be heard after 'Dear Prudence', and also before 'Melt!') One thing they didn't do, however, was add any overdubs. And they wanted the world to know it: the *Nocturne* sleeve proudly proclaimed 'No overdubs' in much the same way that early Queen albums proclaimed 'No synthesisers were used on this record'. That sleeve, designed by Da Gama (who also did *Hyæna*), was a gatefold. The **artwork** on the front featured a collection of stars and other geometric shapes against a dark blue shatter pattern resembling glass or ice, with a selection of live and studio photos inside.

The double **vinyl** LP came out on 25 November 1983 as the first album released by the Banshees' own Wonderland label. In 1986, a truncated hour-long video version, filmed by the TV crew who made *Play At Home*, was released on VHS. A 2006 version on DVD also included *Play At Home* itself, the 'Dear Prudence' promo video, and *Old Grey Whistle Test* performances of 'Melt!' and 'Painted Bird'.

Reviewers typically went in studs-first on the Banshees for even making a record like *Nocturne*, but grudgingly relented long enough to sprinkle a little praise too. *NME*'s Mat Snow compared Siouxsie And The Banshees to Yes and, repeatedly, Led Zeppelin: 'Heavy, colourful, and varied – the Banshees have inherited LZ's epic mantle'. However, this wasn't entirely intended as a compliment, Snow noting that 'their ideas about stagecraft, even down to the dry ice [were] just the sort of empty spectacle punk was supposed to be reacting against in '76.' He also took issue, as so many did, with the very format of the record. 'Double live albums often appear to conceal creative constipation – could *Nocturne* be a sign of decline?' In *Sounds*, despite attacking them for making *Nocturne* at all, Robin Gibson added the strangely caveated compliment, 'For what it's worth (i.e. little or nothing), the music here is faultless'. In *Melody Maker*, Lynden Barber wrote that *Nocturne* contained 'a host of divine pleasures', but argued that 'like all double albums it should have been a single platter', going on to criticise the flatness of Siouxsie's voice but conceding that the Banshees 'give themselves up to their music with a single-mindedness and dedication that is magnificent to behold' and 'care about every second that is passing by; they play their instruments like they are making love'. (Blimey.)

Nocturne only just snuck into the UK Top 30 and was the Banshees' lowest-selling album to that point, though it was eventually certified silver. There can be little doubt that the existence of their singles compilation *Once Upon A Time* (as much of an essential item in the collection of any self-respecting alternative teen as *Standing On A Beach*) harmed demand for a Banshees live record.

In hindsight, Siouxsie expressed regret that the Banshees' first commercially available concert recording was not one which captured the John McGeoch era. Even when viewed from an entirely pro-Robert Smith standpoint, her logic is hard to challenge. *Nocturne* is neither full McGeoch nor full Smith, but something in between. It documents a show by a band in transition. But what a band, and what a show.

Noko

Noko is the nom-de-bass of Norman Fisher-Jones, whose brief stint in The Cure, stepping in as a substitute for the unavailable **Phil Thornalley**, lasted just a few weeks in early 1984. The Bootle-born musician's duties included a gig on 30 January 1984 in Munich's Alabama-Halle, a BBC Radio 1 session (see **Peel Sessions**) recorded on 15 February (broadcast a week later) featuring 'Bananafishbones', 'Piggy In The Mirror', 'Give Me It' and 'The Empty World', and a live television appearance (see **TV, The Cure appear on**) on the BBC's *Oxford Road Show* on 24 February playing 'Shake Dog Shake' and 'Give Me It'. Visually, Noko slotted into the role perfectly, with his big backcombed hair, bandana, dark glasses and entirely black outfit.

Fisher-Jones, whose blatantly self-penned Discogs biography describes him as a 'sonic visionary', was a member of The Umbrella, who released the EP *Make Hell (For The Beautiful People)* in 1985, but found his greatest success as a member of the electronic group Apollo 440 (whose credits include several remixes for Manic Street Preachers). One of his Apollo 440 bandmates was his schoolfriend **Howard Gray**, who engineered *The Top* and co-produced 'Kyoto Song' from *The Head On The Door*, thereby placing Noko at only one degree of separation from The Cure, well within their orbit, and making him an easy choice when they needed a bassist in a hurry.

He features prominently in the tangled family tree

of Buzzcocks and their diaspora (including Luxuria, Magazine and Pete Shelley's band), and his long list of collaborations also includes work with The Heart Throbs, Billy Mackenzie and Pop Will Eat Itself. He eventually followed in Robert Smith's footsteps by working on two tracks with **Siouxsie** on her 2007 album *Mantaray*.

Nye, Steve

'I learned a lot of technical things just from watching Steve Nye work', said Robert Smith in *Ten Imaginary Years*.

Nye, a producer and engineer as well as a founding member of avant-pop ensemble Penguin Cafe Orchestra, was certainly someone with a wealth of experience to learn from. The Englishman's first job was as a tape op at George Martin's AIR Studios in 1971 where he was discovered and mentored by producer Rupert Hine. One of Nye's early jobs was on the self-titled debut album by Hine's own band Quantum Jump, which spawned a hit single with faux-Native American funk-rock track 'The Lone Ranger', which suggested a gay relationship between the titular character and Tonto. 'The Lone Ranger' holds the distinction of including in its lyrics what *The Guinness Book of Records* believed to be the longest word in the world: Taumatawhakatangihangakoaua uotamateaturipukakapikimaungahoronuku pokaiwhenuakitanatahu (the Maori name for a particular hill in New Zealand). Nye's work would have involved helping Hines to chop that word into manageable rhythmic chunks. If you can do that, you can do anything.

His early years as an engineer involved working with several heavyweights of modern music: Bryan Ferry, Osibisa, Stevie Wonder, Stockhausen, Joe Cocker, King Crimson, Mott The Hoople, Pete Townshend and Frank Zappa. He was also beginning to dip his toe into the new wave when The Cure came calling, having worked with 999, Rezillos, Lene Lovich and, most importantly, Japan.

The art-pop quartet, who shared with The Cure a history with **Hansa**, hired Nye because they were fans of his work with Yellow Magic Orchestra (with whose Ryuichi Sakamoto their leader David Sylvian would go on to collaborate). He produced their classic album *Tin Drum*, which included the singles 'The Art of Parties', 'Ghosts', 'Visions of China' and 'Cantonese Boy'. It was

Nye's work with Japan, specifically the fact that he had extensively used Oberheim gear (of which **Lol Tolhurst** had acquired several pieces) and made electronics sound human, which convinced The Cure to bring him in to Jam Studios to record '**The Walk**' and its B-sides in the spring of 1983.

Nye, known for his obsession with detail (as well as his habit of smoking sixty unfiltered Gitanes a day), went on to produce for XTC and Clannad, as well as continuing to work with Bryan Ferry and Japan's David Sylvian.

Not all artists have been entirely complimentary. 'He was extremely slow and painstaking,' XTC's Andy Partridge once told an interviewer, 'and it tended to kill the spontaneity. We might get to the studio and say, "Hey, let's use some platypus ducks on this." Steve would go, "Now hold on, where are we gonna get them from and what size are they gonna be?"

If he was *that* pedantic, he would have told them that a platypus isn't a duck.

O is for …

Obtainers, The

One July day in 1979, two ten-year-old boys from **Horley** turned up at the house of Robert Smith's parents, clutching in their hands a cassette tape. The boys, both pupils at Hazelwick School in **Crawley**, gave their names as 'Robin Banks' and 'Nick Loot', and the tape contained homemade recordings of their punk band, The Obtainers, featuring Tupperware boxes and spoons instead of a drum kit.

Smith was immediately smitten with this DIY enterprise. 'It was so excellent,' he told *Cure News* a decade later, 'I took them to the studio with me and recorded them, in between takes of "**Cult Hero**".' (The Obtainers also provided backing vocals on the Cult Hero record itself.)

The two tracks Smith produced, if 'produced' is the word for something so resolutely lo-fi, are essentially *a cappella* (with pots and pans for percussion). 'Yeh Yeh Yeh' features the gleefully insulting verse 'You look so flippin' ugly/You are so bloody ugly'. Meanwhile, on 'Pussy Wussy', Robert can be heard warning the duo 'Bloody use that kazoo, it cost 15p!', only to receive some backchat from Loot and Banks: 'We lost it. Bought a new one on Saturday.' The chorus goes 'Pussy Wussy, come to bed/Or I'll kick you in the head' and genuinely doesn't seem to be a double entendre – it's about a cat. It's joyously funny, in a way that you can only achieve when you're that young. It's an English suburban counterpart to American savants The Shaggs, and arguably qualifies as outsider music.

'Yeh Yeh Yeh' and 'Pussy Wussy' were pressed up on 7-inch **vinyl** as the first release on Robert and **Ric Gallup**'s newly formed label **Dance Fools Dance**, with two songs from **Simon Gallup**'s **Mag/Spys** on the other side.

John Peel played it several times on BBC Radio 1, and all copies – estimates of the print run vary between one hundred and five hundred – sold out. ('Pussy Wussy', along with another track called 'Black-Haired Drag', which isn't about Robert, eventually appeared on a compilation of obscure punk called *Bored Teenagers Vol. 8* in 2015.)

The Obtainers never recorded again, and their two members faded quietly back into Sussex life. Robin Banks (Rob Goodey) still lives in Crawley. Nick Loot (Paul Wilson) works at Gatwick Airport. Meanwhile, copies of 'Yeh Yeh Yeh'/'Pussy Wussy' now sell for over £1,700 on Discogs – more money than all but five of The Cure's own **rarities**.

O'Donnell, Roger

Roger O'Donnell is the third longest-serving member of The Cure, with twenty-five years across three separate stints – only Robert Smith and **Simon Gallup** have racked up more years of service. The keyboardist also holds the record for the most separate turns in The Cure (unless **Porl Thompson**'s Easy Cure days count as one, and unless Gallup's health-related hiatus in 1992 and social media flounce in 2021 count as full departures).

O'Donnell was born on 29 October in East London. As he tweeted once, 'Yes strange as it may seem in 2020 I was born at home in the dining room where the family piano sat. As soon as I could stand I would play it and when my Mum played I would sit under it and press the keys from underneath. There's a DH Lawrence poem called "Piano" that talks of this.'

On his first day at art school in 1975, Roger befriended fellow student Ian Wright, the illustrator whose many credits include **artwork** for Ramones, The Beat, **Depeche Mode** and **Pink Floyd**, and who has designed most of O'Donnell's solo album covers. O'Donnell did not complete his course, however, and quit to become a professional musician. His first paid gig was at Oxford Town Hall in 1976 backing warpaint-wearing, flame-helmeted psychedelic madman Arthur Brown of 'Fire' fame (providing ample training for his life with The Cure).

With his friend **Boris Williams** he began playing jazz fusion in pubs, inspired by Weather Report (Williams' favourites) and Herbie Hancock (O'Donnell's). They also both worked as despatch riders.

In 1983 Roger O'Donnell joined the Thompson Twins as a live keyboardist, when Boris Williams was their drummer, and stayed with them for three tours.

His first appearance in a music **video** was in the Thompson Twins' 'Nothing In Common', from the film of the same name starring Tom Hanks and Jackie Gleason, even though he'd left them by that point. He also had spells as a live keyboardist for Berlin and the Psychedelic Furs.

In the late eighties, while still with The Furs, O'Donnell was living in Toronto in an apartment with a view over Lake Ontario from which, on a clear day, he could see the **United States**. It was here that he received the call to join The Cure, who needed a competent keyboardist to augment the decreasingly useful **Lol Tolhurst**.

'All I knew about The Cure,' O'Donnell recalled on his **website**, 'was that one of my best friends was the drummer Boris Williams. When there was talk of adding a keyboard player, he asked me if I was interested, and initially I wasn't until I heard *Kiss Me, Kiss Me, Kiss Me* and realised what an amazing band this was, aside from all the weird **hair** and **make-up**! After about a week of the tour in a hotel room sitting on the floor next to Robert he said to me "I want you to be a part of the group, I want you to play on the next record and be a member of The Cure."'

Roger's first public appearance with The Cure was on the last ever episode of Channel 4's *The Tube* on 24 April 1987, the day after the Marble Arch film premiere for *The Cure In Orange*. His first proper gig was the opening night of the Kissing Tour on 9 July 1987 at the Expo Theater in Vancouver. He subsequently appeared in the '**Just Like Heaven**' and '**Hot Hot Hot!!!**' videos, although he didn't play on them. (He is credited on the deluxe edition of their parent album *Kiss Me, Kiss Me, Kiss Me*, but only for live tracks from the tour.)

In an interview at the 'Just Like Heaven' video shoot, Robert explained the rationale for hiring Roger, detailing a domino effect of delegation. 'It was purely a practical thing,' he said. 'I didn't want to be obliged to play as much guitar as I'd been playing onstage, so I had to delegate my guitar parts to Porl, so Porl had to delegate his keyboard parts to Lol and Lol can't play keyboards. [Ouch.] So we had to get Roger in to play Porl's keyboard parts. Lol just plays Lol's keyboard parts, which are very simple. But we had to have the right person. Roger's fitted in really well. He's in the group now. He's not like a session musician.' He later said of Roger 'He's the first person we've had in The Cure who's a good keyboard player [Ouch again].'

As well as diligently figuring out the necessary sounds for Cure tracks from the time before he joined, O'Donnell has become the *de facto* archivist of all The Cure's instrumentation and effects on any particular track since. He also quickly began contributing to The Cure musically, bringing his technical know-how into play. 'I was living in Toronto at the time,' he later recalled, 'and had bought my first Mac computer and set up a recording studio in my apartment so in early 1988 I started writing songs with The Cure in mind.' When the band reconvened for the *Disintegration* sessions, O'Donnell brought an hour's worth of music for what turned out to be a keyboard-heavy album. During the making of it, he bought a house fifteen mins from Boris Williams' home in Devon, committing fully to The Cure by moving back to Britain.

However, his first tenure as The Cure's keyboardist would be short-lived. He left in 1990, the BRIT **Awards** (where '**Lullaby**' had won best video) being his last public appearance with them for five years. It has been suggested that O'Donnell's first departure was the result of him becoming the scapegoat in the band, following Lol Tolhurst's exit (see **bullying**). 'Simon and Boris didn't really get on with him,' came the official explanation from Robert in *Cure News*. 'No real reasons, just a simmering unease . . . Someone had to leave. It ended up being Roger.' He was replaced by former guitar tech **Perry Bamonte**.

In the interim before rejoining, Roger designed clothes and recorded his first solo album, *Grey Clouds Red Sky*, self-released in November 1994 while living back in Toronto, with three of the songs later made available via The Cure's website. He also played on an album by Icelandic band Maus.

After Porl Thompson's departure in 1993 forced Perry Bamonte to prioritise guitar, leaving The Cure with no dedicated keyboardist, they approached O'Donnell to rejoin. In February 1995 it was announced that he was back in the band.

As well as contributing to their next album *Wild Mood Swings*, O'Donnell and Bamonte collaborated on setting up The Cure's online Information Service, and launching the band's first official website. At the same time, he began uploading music of his own that wasn't right for The Cure, via his own website www.rogerodonnell.com (a site which sometimes tells you everything, and sometimes tells you nothing).

He remained with The Cure through the *Bloodflowers* and *The Cure* cycles but was dismissed in 2005, allegedly via email, followed by a phone call. 'I am no longer a member of The Cure,' he wrote on his website. 'It was sad to find out, after nearly 20 years, the way I did, but then I should have expected no less or more.'

Over the next five years, he concentrated on his own music. In 2006 he released the album *The Truth in Me* with Erin Lang, his then-partner and former member of Canadian band Tuuli. This was followed in 2009 by solo album *Songs from the Silver Box* and in 2010 by *Piano Formations*.

In 2011 he had another call from Robert Smith. 'We had a conversation,' O'Donnell later recalled, 'which was like, "Look. At this age, if we can't get on now and be together to make music and enjoy what and who we are, then we shouldn't even bother trying."' Roger rejoined the band for the **Reflections** concerts, performing the band's first three albums with cameos from Lol Tolhurst, and stayed to become a full member for the third time.

He is still with them. However, his solo output has continued, usually consisting of instrumental albums. In 2011 he released *Quieter Trees* (composed for an orchestra and inspired by the paintings of David Hockney), in 2012 *Requiem*, in 2013 *The Bernhard Suite*, in 2015 *Love And Other Tragedies* (written for a **ballet** adaptation of *Tristan and Isolde*), and in 2020 he released *2 Ravens*. In 2022 he signed a publishing deal with **Daryl Bamonte**'s Archangel Music, and the same year his website featured just one scrawled phrase, 'Seven Different Words for Love', hinting that another O'Donnell album may be on the way.

What else is known of Roger O'Donnell? He is now married to Mimi Supernova, who directs music videos and works as digital visual merchandising manager and art director in the fashion world. He supports West Ham. He is a fan of Devo, Prince, Tortoise and Philip Glass, and once told *Cure News* he was inspired by **Brazilian** music (making it likely that the Latin flavour of several *Wild Mood Swings* tracks was his doing). In 1995, when The Cure did MTV's Most Wanted with Ray Cokes, Roger got Björk's autograph. By 1997 he wasn't a fanboy any more – he was invited to Björk's New Year's Eve party in Iceland.

He follows motor racing. His racing hero was Ayrton Senna, and in 1996 he met Senna's sister Viviane in Brazil. He then wore a Senna shirt onstage with The Cure and wrote 'Senna Forever' in Portuguese on his amp.

He 'talks constantly' (according to Robert in 1990). He once bought a hot air balloon (according to Perry in 1995). Cars he has driven include an AMC Jeep

and a MG Midget. His keyboard of choice, or one of them at least, is a Kurzweil PC3K8. He is also a fan of the Mini-Moog. He once set the record for having the most Sequential Circuits synthesisers onstage at one time.

His likes include tennis and flying.

His dislikes include Tories.

One Hundred Years

'It doesn't matter if we all die.'

Has there ever been a more *Cure* opening line than that? Certainly no Cure song has cut through the usual miasma of mystique and misdirection and headed straight to the point in such a brutally bleak manner.

The opening track from 1982's ***Pornography***, 'One Hundred Years' is **goth** Cure *in excelsis*, with lyrics alluding to revolution, slaughter and civil war, and almost seven minutes of sustained sonic thunder. It's the ultimate expression of existential dread and nihilism, from the band's most dread-filled and nihilistic period.

Nihilism, the philosophical position that nothing has meaning or moral worth, was first given a name by Ivan Turgenev in *Fathers and Sons* (1862), and popularised by Friedrich Nietzsche, whose famous statement that 'God is dead' first appeared in *The Gay Science* (1882) and was further developed in *Thus Spake Zarathustra* (1885). The knowledge that God is dead, or indeed never existed in the first place, can send the mind of the young reader along one of two paths. The first, in the spirit of Aleister Crowley's famous axiom 'Do what thou wilt shall be the whole of the law', is to view the absence of a deity as a licence to pursue absolute carnal abandon and pleasure-seeking. (If God isn't watching, therefore God isn't judging, and there can be no consequences.) The other, taken by those of a gloomier mindset, is to view life as merely a meaningless interlude before dying, and to live it in the shadow of the executioner's axe, 'waiting for the death blow', a line Robert Smith repeats three times in 'One Hundred Years'.

With a masterly economy of words, Smith evokes the futility of forming a romantic relationship when faced with the inevitability of death:

Please love me

Meet my mother
But the fear takes hold
Creeping up the stairs in the dark
Waiting for the death blow . . .

Indeed, love isn't just futile but actively callous in the wider context of human suffering:

Stroking your hair as the patriots are shot
Fighting for freedom on the television
Sharing the world with slaughtered pigs . . .

(This verse, in particular, supports the argument that 'One Hundred Years' is a rare example of a political Cure song – see **Politics**.) It's a lyric which, as *Record Collector*'s Pat Gilbert put it in a 1993 Cure retrospective, 'evoked an internal landscape of complete and utter desolation.'

Musically it is a monster, built around a pitiless drum pattern (made using a Boss DR-55 'Dr Rhythm' drum machine fed through bass and guitar amps) and an abrasive guitar motif which is queasy, uneasy, wavering but unceasing. Through sheer relentlessness, it reaches an unprecedented (and, arguably, unsurpassed) peak of intensity. Playing it live, Cure drummers from **Lol Tolhurst** to **Jason Cooper** have needed to employ backing tracks to replicate the recording. (Incidentally, 'One Hundred Years' is the first Cure track on which Tolhurst is credited with keyboards as well as drums, foreshadowing his imminent full-time shift to keys.)

In the grand pantheon of Cure songs, it occupies a special status. Though never a single, 'One Hundred Years' – like '**A Night Like This**' and '**All Cats Are Grey**' – enjoys a privileged position among album tracks. An early demo version was included on the cassette *Annual Report*, the December edition of **Australian** cassette magazine *Fast Forward*, in 1981 to show what the band were up to in the studio, along with an audio interview. The finished version was sent out to radio stations as a promotional single (catalogue no. CURE 1, now worth approximately £73) to represent the album, with *Pornography*'s actual lead single '**The Hanging Garden**' relegated to the flipside. (It would also appear on the B-side of the gatefold double 'A Single' version of 'The Hanging Garden' itself.) It, along with 'The Figurehead', was one of the two songs The Cure opted to play on BBC **television**'s *Oxford Road Show* on 19 March 1983 instead of their latest single '**Let's Go To Bed**' or their next one, '**The Walk**'. And it has appeared on no fewer than four Cure live albums: *Concert*,

Paris, *Trilogy* and *Festival 2005*, demonstrating its longevity as a Cure live staple.

'One Hundred Years' has been **covered** only a handful of times, most notably by the American art-pop band Xiu Xiu with goth singer Chelsea Wolfe on the 2021 album *Oh No*, but most artists, however inspired by *Pornography*-era Cure they may be, recognise that it's wiser to leave such an unimprovable recording well alone.

As Robert Smith himself wrote in *Cure News* in 1990, '"100 Years" is pure self-loathing and worthlessness, and contains probably the key line – the line that underpinned this period of writing: "It doesn't matter if we all die" . . . Everything is empty. This song is despair.'

In terms of the great spectrum of Cure songs, if '**Friday I'm In Love**' is at one end, then 'One Hundred Years' is at the other. In sound and spirit, it represents an extreme pole of The Cure's oeuvre. And it is nothing less than perfect.

Only One, The

The Cure were not the first band to come up with the idea of a rapid-fire release schedule.

In 1992 The Wedding Present released a single every month for a whole year (and pulled the same stunt in 2022). In 1980 the Clash told CBS they wanted to release an album every month (eventually they compromised by released the triple album *Sandinista!*). In 2020, pub rock veteran Clive Gregson actually did it.

Nevertheless, the news that The Cure were planning to herald the arrival of their thirteenth album, *4:13 Dream*, by releasing a single on the thirteenth of every month for four months was a neat conceptual gimmick, and one that raised a few headlines in the music media and kept the band in the minds of radio and television programmers in the run-up to the album's release.

The first instalment of The Cure quadruple was 'The Only One'. The song had been around for some time, having been debuted live at a show in Mountain View, California, on 7 October 2007, originally under the title 'Please Present' (and also played in **Mexico** City the following week). A likeable, catchy piece of mid-tempo indie pop, it is one of The Cure's most overtly **sexual** songs, with barely ambiguous lines like 'Oh I love, oh I love, oh I love what you do to my head/When you pull me upstairs, and you push me to bed'.

Although the phrase 'Oh I love, oh I love' is far more prominent, it was eventually given the title 'The Only One', from a chorus which is actually less memorable than the verses. (Incidentally, new wave band The Only Ones were a minor influence on The Cure, notably 'Just Like Heaven'.)

A live performance of the song on MTV, filmed in silver-tinged black and white, edited with a busy hand with much use of sudden zooms and fast cuts, functioned as the song's *de facto* video, and was shown often on that station as well as its sister station VH-1.

'The Only One' was released on 13 May 2008 in a Parched Art sleeve with no artwork as such, other than big blurry lettering. The B-side, 'NY Trip', is a love song to a girl with a 'New York Disney smile', which sounds a lot more positive about America than many Cure songs ('Club America' from *Wild Mood Swings*, for example). 'The Only One' also appeared in remixed form on the *Hypnagogic States* EP.

Canadian magazine *Exclaim!* wrote that Smith was sounding 'happier than ever', and the *Observer* noted that it featured 'lovely spiralling guitars, glowing bass and Robert Smith at his giddiest'.

The single reached No.48 in the UK, No.28 in France, No.13 in Poland and, remarkably, No.1 in Spain (the first of three in a row). For information on the other three monthly singles from 2008, see 'Freakshow', 'Sleep When I'm Dead' and 'The Perfect Boy'.

Orange, The Cure in

The previous time that hordes of goths descended upon the Théâtre Antique d'Orange, the year was 412 and the invaders were the Visigoths, hell-bent on sacking the already ancient Roman structure under the orders of Alaric I. A millennium and a half later, the goths entering these majestic ruins were merely a few thousand harmless French fans of The Cure, hell-bent on nothing more than a few outbreaks of light slamdancing under the leadership of Robert Smith.

The Cure In Orange, for the uninitiated, is not a borderline-tasteless photo shoot of the band in Guantanamo prison fatigues, but a 114-minute Tim Pope film of the final date of the band's Beach Party

Tour on Saturday 9 August 1986, a concert otherwise chiefly significant as the day Simon Gallup ripped off Robert Smith's wig.

Using cinema-standard 35mm film rather than video tape, Pope and his crew immortalised The Cure in perhaps the most picturesque venue they have ever played: a UNESCO World Heritage Site in the Provence-Alpes-Côte d'Azur region, in the south-eastern corner of France.

The modern revival of the Théâtre Antique as a music venue had begun over a century earlier in 1869, with an annual festival of opera and drama now known as the Chorégies d'Orange, which has involved such renowned performers as Sarah Bernhardt in 1903 and, in more recent years, Plácido Domingo and Montserrat Caballe.

As a rock venue, however, its history begins with the Orange Festival of 1975, whose prog-heavy line-up featured Procol Harum, Baker Gurvitz Army, Tangerine Dream, John Martin, Nico, Bad Company, Caravan, Wishbone Ash, Soft Machine, Mahavishnu Orchestra and Dr Feelgood. This opened the doors for subsequent shows by Muddy Waters in 1976 and 1977, Frank Zappa, Elvis Costello, XTC and The Police in 1980, Trust and Iron Maiden in 1981, Dire Straits twice (1981 and 1985), and Elton John and Mike Oldfield in 1984.

The town of Orange is not alone in repurposing an ancient Roman amphitheatre for contemporary music performances, even within France. Lyon, 200km due north, has two: the Théâtre Antique de Fourvière (where The Cure played in 1998, see Lowest Point) and the Odéon Antique de Lyon, where concerts have happened since 1952. (Both are in a rather more tumbledown condition than Orange.) And then there's Pompeii, where Pink Floyd famously filmed an audience-less concert in 1972. *Melody Maker* noted a similarity between *The Cure In Orange* and Floyd's *Live at Pompeii*, a comparison tacitly acknowledged by The Cure themselves when they played an immaculate 'Set The Controls For The Heart Of The Sun' during their soundcheck.

This show, then, was not unique. The Cure were far from the first to play the venue, nor was Orange the only Roman ruin staging rock gigs. Nor was *The Cure In Orange* the first time a Cure live show had been made commercially available (it was preceded by the album *Concert* in 1984 and the Japanese-only VHS *Live in Japan* in 1986). Nor would it be the last (it would be followed by *Show* in 1993 and *Festival 2005* in 2006). Nor was it even the only Cure video product fans could get their hands on in the eighties (*Staring At The Sea – The Images*, released in 1986, was only the first of several video compilations).

Nevertheless, the combination of The Cure in their late eighties pomp (the classic **line-up** of Robert Smith, Simon Gallup, **Porl Thompson**, **Boris Williams** and **Lol Tolhurst**), the visual splendour of the location and Tim Pope's direction alchemised into something special, making *Orange* the definitive Cure live film. To any alternative music lover who remembers its release, The Cure are inseparable from the venue and the venue is inseparable from The Cure.

The making of the film entailed plenty of potential pitfalls, both financial and practical, as Tim Pope told *Melody Maker*. 'The risks, of course, are many. Because of the limited budget, all the live filming had to be done on Saturday, at the concert, with close-ups following during Sunday's mock up. Rain on one or both days would have scuppered the whole thing – £150,000 literally down the drain.' Fortunately the Tempestates, the Roman gods of weather, were smiling on The Cure: it didn't rain until the Monday. However, the second day of shooting didn't run entirely smoothly. Lol sprained his ankle walking on the beach the morning after the Orange gig, and had to perform the second, audience-less show with the aid of bandages, injections and pain-killing cream.

In the *Melody Maker* article, Smith explained the rationale for making the movie at all. 'We wanted to film it . . . because every concert we do now reaches a point that has seemed unattainable in the past and I wanted it captured for ever, before we move on or give up.'

Smith also explained the reason for choosing their long-time video collaborator Tim Pope to direct. 'I don't think it's a risk working with Pap [Pope's nickname] because he isn't really a director. We could have got in some proper director to make a film of any old concert but he wouldn't know what the band was about and I want this to be a Cure film about The Cure.' Speaking to MTV in 1990, Pope confirmed this: 'He thought, and these are his words, "Should he get a real film director or should he get me?" And he thought he should get me, right or wrong.'

Pope himself initially had misgivings, worried the film might be 'dreary' because 'they don't do much onstage', but then realised there are 'lots of little looks' between members that he could catch. 'If you're a Cure fan, it's brilliant, it's the best film ever made. If you're not a Cure fan, it's the worst film ever made.'

Orange captures a phase when the length of The Cure's live show was beginning to billow out and expand, like the fog emanating from their smoke machines. The running time, while relatively brief by latterday Cure standards, was already pushing two hours at this point, and '**A Forest**' alone had reached the nine minutes sixteen seconds mark.

The setlist that night, naturally, was *Head On The Door* heavy, with seven songs from the band's most recent album, and three from its predecessor *The Top*. The remainder consisted of two each from *Faith*, *Pornography*, *Seventeen Seconds* and *Three Imaginary Boys*, and five songs originally released as stand-alone singles.

Elsewhere on the tour they had previewed material from their upcoming *Kiss Me, Kiss Me, Kiss Me* album (including, the previous night in Fréjus, its lead single '**Why Can't I Be You?**') but, perhaps not wishing any sneak previews to enter the public domain just yet, the set in Orange was restricted to songs already available.

The film opens with a shock reveal: during the walk-on through clouds of smoke, Simon Gallup grabs Smith's iconic barnet and pulls it from his head, the snatched-away syrup revealing a newly cropped shortish **hairdo** underneath. (Most fans, however, wouldn't see the singer's new 'do until he and Simon Gallup appeared on the 30 August issue of *Melody Maker*.)

The show began in the thirty-degree August heat of le Midi, and for the first seven songs the auditorium was still in blazing sunlight, but by '**In Between Days**' the sun had set behind its western curve. On that song in particular the additional 'cheat' footage, shot by Pope the following day, is obvious: we're shown a fretboard view of Smith strumming the strings (almost identical, in fact, to a recurring shot in the video Pope made for the single) which would have required a camera mounted on the guitar's headstock, but in wider shots such a camera is nowhere to be seen.

In the main, Pope and his crew maintain a discreetly low profile until the encores, but during '**Close To Me**' Smith is seen pursued by the director with a cine camera so massive it takes two men to carry it. 'Give Me It' is the most dynamic and chaotic of all, both musically and visually, with Porl Thompson delivering Roxy-style sax squalls while Pope scampers around the stage amid berserk strobes and smoke, his lens drifting in and out of focus, while his crew swing their big boom camera over a heaving moshpit. Moments like these justify

Pope's description of the film as 'absolute psychedelic madness'.

At other moments, however, Pope exercises restraint, with slow panoramic views emphasising the grandeur of the auditorium. During 'Faith' a long shot of the theatre's enormous back wall shows the band utterly dwarfed, overlooked by a statue of Emperor Augustus in an alcove high above their heads. Another distant shot, taken when 'A Forest' kicks in, captures a firework display, the sole pyrotechnic gimmick in an otherwise typically low-key Cure stage show.

The main focus of attention, of course, is the short-cropped but still charismatic Smith. He doesn't do much, rarely deviating from his trademark stance, radiating infantile **cuteness** with his feet turned inwards and his limbs never fully extended. During the first few songs of the encores, however, liberated from guitar duties, he's able to go into dancing overdrive. There is a minimal amount of between-song chatter, much of it lost on a non-Anglophone audience. Introducing 'Push', for example, he announces: 'This one's about when I used to wear a dress and travel on the train . . .'

After a closing '**Killing An Arab**', a song whose already controversial lyric is especially pregnant with meaning in the South of France, the band disappear into the smoke whence they came, only to reappear up in Augustus' alcove seconds later, waving like royalty. Smith, as if bidding an era farewell, tosses his wig into the Provence night. Porl Thompson is the last to leave, but Robert – not wanting to be upstaged – runs out again for one last shimmy as the credits roll.

The film didn't meet with universal praise from reviewers. 'An astonishingly lavish production number for one of the world's less dynamic live bands,' wrote *Time Out*, 'rendered noteworthy by its setting against the magnificent backdrop of an ancient amphitheatre . . . Smith, in a non-stop run through their best-known numbers, proves that he is not one of the world's great frontmen, but for Cure fans this is as perfect and cinematographically compelling a record of a gig as could be asked for. For the rest of us, it's a bit of a yawn.' (One has to wonder what the reviewer was expecting. To paraphrase Basil Fawlty, David Lee Roth doing star jumps, perhaps? Prince doing the splits? Herds of wildebeest sweeping majestically across the plain?)

The Cure In Orange was screened in selected UK cinemas. Recorded by long-time Cure producer **David M. Allen**, and already augmented by the amphitheatre's fantastic acoustics (those Romans knew a thing or two), the film's audio quality rewarded experiencing it via the big PA system of a cinema rather than the tinny speakers of a 1980s TV set.

With its premiere, held on 23 April at Odeon Marble Arch, the promotional cycle for *The Cure In Orange* and *The Head On The Door* was officially over. The following day the band travelled up to Newcastle to play three new songs from the forthcoming *Kiss Me, Kiss Me, Kiss Me* – '**Catch**', 'Why Can't I Be You?' and '**Hot Hot Hot!!!**' – on the last-ever episode of Channel 4's *The Tube* (see **TV, The Cure appear on**). Channel 4 would later assist the impact of *The Cure In Orange* by broadcasting it, as they had previously done with U2's *Live at Red Rocks* and Talking Heads' *Stop Making Sense* (both of which significantly boosted those bands' popularity).

As well as its London residency, *The Cure In Orange* toured various cinemas around the country, including Irvine, Jersey, Portsmouth, Salisbury, Reading and Preston. Seven years later, in August 1994, it would be re-screened at the National Film Theatre as part of *NME*'s Punk Before and Beyond series.

On 12 November 1987 the film came out on VHS (see **Videos, long form**) and, for the super-rich, Laserdisc, and sold well, going platinum in the **US**. The film's status has slipped in recent years, as it has – for reasons as yet unexplained – never been made officially available on DVD or Blu-Ray. (It was released on VCD and CD in Hong Kong and Malaysia in 2001.)

For the average Cure fan back in 1987, however, its existence was enough to flip your wig.

O'Toole, Peter

Peter O'Toole – no, not that one – was the last lead singer of Easy Cure, the band's final **pre-Cure** incarnation before losing the 'Easy' and installing Robert Smith as vocalist. In *Ten Imaginary Years*, Smith remembers him as 'a demon footballer and **Bowie** fan who'd never sung before'.

O'Toole's reign as frontman stretched from April to September 1977. His debut gig was on 22 April, Robert's belated birthday party at St Edward the Confessor's Church Hall in **Crawley** with a **line-up** of O'Toole, Smith, **Michael Dempsey, Lol Tolhurst** and **Porl Thompson**. ('I remember nothing at all,' said Smith later, 'so it must have been good . . .')

He is the singer on the earliest known footage of any version of The Cure, at the Peace Concert on the bandstand at Queen's Square, Crawley on 3 July (see **Politics**). On the footage, filmed by Robert's father and later included on *Staring At The Sea*, the open-shirted O'Toole sings a thrashy punk number called 'I Wish I Was Your Mother' in front of the local Rumbelows and Halfords, watched by a few curious hippies and teenagers, some of them pogoing. Smith, in a cap-sleeved T-shirt, plays guitar, though he is known to have taken the lead vocal on a **cover** of **Jimi Hendrix**'s 'Foxy Lady' that day, O'Toole stepping aside.

After a run of further gigs at Crawley venues The Rocket and The Lakeside Inn, The Railway Inn in Redhill and a return to St Edward the Confessor's Church Hall, O'Toole decided the rock 'n' roll life wasn't for him. His final gig was at the Rocket on 11 September 1977. The very next day, he left to live on a kibbutz in Israel. A month later, Easy Cure – minus O'Toole – entered the studios with **Hansa**, and the rest is history.

P

P is for ...

Parched Art

Parched Art are to Cure record sleeves what **Tim Pope** is to Cure videos: most of the classics are theirs.

The design duo of **Andy 'Undy' Vella** and **Porl (now Pearl) Thompson** first met when they both studied at Worthing Art College. A chance meeting on a train through Sussex led to getting The Cure commission. Porl told Robert Smith, his old Malice bandmate from **pre-Cure** days, that he didn't like The Cure's sleeves and that he and his friend 'Undy' could do much better. Robert said yes, Porl quit college, and Parched Art was born.

The duo's first jobs were the sleeve of **'Primary'** and a redesign of the **Fiction** logo (replacing the angular original with the now-definitive irregular blobby one), followed by *Faith*. Not that the duo traded under that name at first: on 'Primary' and *Faith* it's just 'Porl and Undy'. The first to be actually credited to Parched Art was **'The Walk'** in 1983.

Parched Art subsequently designed the **artwork** for almost all The Cure's covers from 1984 to 1992 (an exception being 1990's *Mixed Up*, which had uncredited design by Vella and painting by Maya, but no involvement from Thompson). Several Cure sleeves from the nineties onwards have been Vella's work only, without Thompson.

Parched Art's *modus operandi* was immersive: Porl would typically go to The Cure's recording sessions and rehearsals 'to impregnate myself with a piece', he revealed in *Ten Imaginary Years*, instead of working blind. (This is how he was lured into joining the band, having been asked to play some saxophone on *The Top* while observing them for artwork purposes.)

The duo have cited one of their influences as Hipgnosis, the design team of Storm Thorgerson, Aubrey Powell and Peter Christopherson, known for their work with seventies hard rock and prog acts like **Pink Floyd**, Led Zeppelin and Black Sabbath (records which would have been on heavy rotation on the turntable, their sleeves propped against the wall, in the Smith living room during those early proto-Cure get-togethers).

On some Parched Art-designed Cure releases, like 'The Caterpillar', 'In Between Days', *The Head On The Door* and *Kiss Me, Kiss Me, Kiss Me*, the credit is just their logo, a drawing of a cup and saucer. On others, like *The Top*, they take the belt-and-braces approach of the name Parched Art next to the teacup. (Many singles had no artwork credits at all, but are known to be theirs.)

With all Cure albums, the rule is this: if you see 'Parched Art' or a teacup or both, it's Thompson and Vella. If you don't, it isn't.

Paris

Paris is the fourth Cure live album, following *Concert*, *Entreat* and, just six weeks earlier, *Show* (to which it is a twin album of sorts).

France in general has played an important role in the history of The Cure, providing among other things a home for the *Kiss Me Kiss Me Miss Me* sessions, the backdrop for their first-ever feature film *The Cure In Orange*, the **literary** inspiration for 'Killing An Arab', and the scene of troublesome escapades involving **Andy Anderson** and **Matthieu Hartley**. The French capital, specifically, is an important city for The Cure. **Lol Tolhurst** lived there for a while. **'The Lovecats'** was recorded there in 1983. Jules Renard, the author quoted on the inner sleeve of *Mixed Up*, died there in 1910. And in October 1992, on the *Wish* tour at Parisian arena **Le Zénith**, The Cure played the two shows that were recorded for this album.

Positives? It sounds a lot more 'live' than *Entreat* (the crowd noise is higher in the mix, for one thing). And there's a particularly epic version of **'One Hundred Years'** (ending with a snatch of their 'Foxy Lady' **cover**). Negatives? The track listing is skewed towards deep cuts rather than hits, though for some this may be viewed as another positive. And it was hinted in *Cure News* that **Boris Williams** messes up the intro to **'Catch'**. The drummer does indeed seem to trip himself up a little, but it only adds to the song's woozy charm. (It was also suggested, in the same publication, that there was an incident where Boris was playing the drums from **'The Walk'** while **Simon**

Gallup played the bassline from '**Let's Go To Bed**', but if so, it never made the final cut.)

The album was released on 25 October 1993, in **artwork** comprising a blue-tinted close-up of Robert's mouth at the microphone that looks like it was made by an eleven-year-old on MS Paint. Fifty per cent of the royalties went to **charity**, namely the Red Cross and Red Crescent.

It received mixed reviews. *Vox* praised its 'good editing' and 'top-shelf sound engineers', opining that 'there's nothing here that doesn't work' and scoring it 8/10. *Mojo*, however, described *Paris* and *Show* as being part of a 'process of treading water' by the band.

Chart-wise, it fared less well than its close predecessor, reaching 56 and 118 in the UK and **US** respectively (to *Show*'s 29 and 42), and selling only 95,000 copies in the US (to *Show*'s 213,000), its thunder stolen by *Show*'s head start and hits-packed track listing.

Nevertheless, anyone who would cherish a souvenir of *Wish*-era Cure playing their less obvious material can be glad that they'll always have *Paris*.

Parry, Chris

'In a business full of parasites, fools and all other species of human inadequacy going under the handle of the middle-man,' wrote the legendary journalist Nick Kent in *NME*, 'Parry is the proverbial good guy . . .' In *Sounds*, Dave McCullough called him 'the undoubted epicentre of The Cure, the Onassis, Merlin, and only sometimes the Banquo's ghost'.

Why were these writers talking about a manager at all? There are, of course, exceptions, but music business managers are typically shadowy, behind-the-scenes figures. Kiwi import Chris Parry, though, cut an unusually high profile in the punk and new wave era, third only behind Malcolm McLaren and Bernie Rhodes. But perhaps it shouldn't be so surprising: Parry was used to the spotlight long before he moved into management.

John Christopher Parry was born on 7 January 1949 in Lower Hutt, ten miles north of Wellington, to a British father and New Zealander mother, in a family of eleven siblings (five sisters, six brothers). They were, like the families of Robert Smith, **Michael Dempsey** and **Lol Tolhurst**, Catholics, and in his late teens Parry studied at Silverstream College, run by the Marist Fathers sect, and took a traineeship in management at Philips Electrical.

This neatly laid-out path in life came to an abrupt end in 1967, however, when he auditioned as a drummer for local band called Sine Waves. 'I got the job because I had a truck driver's licence', he later said. Sine Waves changed their name to the Fourmyula, and the Fourmyula became New Zealand's biggest homegrown band of the sixties. They had ten Top 20 hits in their homeland between 1967 and 1971. Their 1969 single 'Nature', a piece of mellow, autumnal psychedelic guitar pop, reached No.1 in New Zealand, and was later voted the best song to come out of that country. (Which is a bit harsh on Crowded House, but it's pleasant enough.)

In 1969 the Fourmyula moved to London for the first of two extended stays, hoping to parlay their domestic success into international stardom, but it didn't work out. However, when the band broke up in 1971, Parry returned to the UK, took exams in Marketing at the College of Distributive Trades, and joined Phonogram Records, initially in the International Department, under fellow New Zealander John McCready.

Parry hadn't completely given up on making music himself. He recorded a 'reggae' single under the name Chris Parie in 1972, and somehow got the iconic reggae label Trojan Records to release it. It's not really reggae, however, but a bouncy offbeat-pop earworm in the vein of 'Co-Co' by Sweet or 'Figaro' by The Brotherhood of Man. In terms of reggae authenticity it makes Paul Nicholas sound like Augustus Pablo.

In 1974, executive Wayne Bickerton made Parry an A&R man at **Polydor**, and in the coming years Parry became increasingly interested in the punk movement, befriending punk-embedded journalist Caroline Coon. In 1976 he watched Sex Pistols at Birmingham Barbarella's and became 'pretty pissed off' at Polydor for ignoring his suggestion that the label should sign them. However, after seeing the Jam at the Marquee in February 1977 (on a tip-off from Shane MacGowan of The Nipple Erectors and later The Pogues), he succeeded in signing them to Polydor, producing or co-producing all their singles up to and including 'David Watts', and all their albums up to and including *All Mod Cons*. Parry went on to sign **Siouxsie And The Banshees** and Sham 69 to Polydor. By 1978, however, he had become disillusioned, and began planning his own label.

Meanwhile, in his **Crawley** bedroom, Robert Smith

was going into letter-writing overdrive, sending demo tapes of the band still called Easy Cure (see **pre-Cure bands**) to any major label he could think of, with a teabag and a digestive biscuit enclosed. All of them came back with rejection letters, except one.

One Sunday afternoon in July 1978, Chris Parry listened to a pile of tapes he had grabbed from his desk and taken home with him. The Easy Cure tape, which included '**10.15 Saturday Night**' and '**Boys Don't Cry**', impressed him. 'The idea of a three-piece excited me too', Parry later said, 'the fact that they were a little bit spacey and that this little cassette had come from the backwoods and no one else had touched it.'

When Parry's advice to sign Easy Cure fell on deaf ears at Polydor, just as it had with the Pistols, he decided it was time to launch his own label. His first move was to contact Smith. As he later told RNZ (Radio New Zealand), 'I heard this tape and I really loved it so I called Robert. He'd written his telephone number on the tape. And he walked into my office and I said to him I really liked your music. He was kind of lanky, but I liked his look . . .'

This meeting was on 10 August 1978. The band and Parry spent the afternoon in the Lamb & Flag pub in Mayfair, Parry selling the idea of his new label to a band who were, initially, disappointed that they weren't being chatted up by Polydor proper. Lol Tolhurst, in *Ten Imaginary Years*, recalled 'He looked Italian, very suave, a bit like a bank manager.' Michael Dempsey thought 'He looked very much like he was related to Colonel Gaddafi – same sort of army bouffant hairstyle and craggy jowl.' And Robert Smith remembered 'We just got very drunk on Directors bitter. He had bird shit on his shoulder.'

Parry went to see them live for the first time on 27 August 1978 at Lakers Hotel, Redhill (now a Toby Carvery) where they had been gigging frequently, sometimes supporting new wave bands like 'Turning Japanese' hitmakers The Vapors or local jazz-funk-reggae fusion band The Hotpoints. They decamped afterwards to the Home Cottage pub which, Robert recalls, sold 'horribly strong bitter'.

By now, Parry had seen enough, and in September 1978 a contract was signed between the band now known as The Cure and the label now known, after some wrangling and negotiation, as **Fiction**. Parry paid for and produced their debut single '**Killing An Arab**', farming it out to **Small Wonder** for the initial run because Polydor – through whom Fiction would be distributed – wouldn't put it out before Christmas.

Meanwhile, Fiction, which Parry was operating out of a small office in **Morgan Studios** with fellow Polydor escapee Ita Martin, signed other bands – Purple Hearts, **The Passions, Associates** – and the first of those, a Mod group, beat The Cure to the punch for the first release on Fiction (see '**Jumping Someone Else's Train**'). Those bands, especially the Dundee-based Associates, would often crash at Parry's Watford home to cut down on hotel bills.

Chris Parry – nicknamed Bill ('long story', says Lol) – filled three overlapping roles in The Cure's early career: label boss, producer and manager. He put up enough money to allow them to quit their jobs and studies, taking £25 a week to live on (which represented a 50% pay cut for Lol), and turn fully pro. He immediately began booking them gigs around London to 'toughen them up'.

As a manager, he would always go out to bat for his young charges, turning his first **film** cameo into a bit of promotion for The Cure. In 1978, he was approached to appear in Julian Temple's Sex Pistols exploitation movie *The Great Rock 'n' roll Swindle*, playing himself as an A&R man pissed off at being unable to sign the band. As Cure **fan** Debora Parr remembers, 'He only agreed to do it if he could get a plug in somehow for his new signing. So at about 35 minutes in, Paul Cook (I think) is walking along through a subway and walks past a huge bank of Cure posters, with the old school dropped-C font. I really hope I haven't just imagined all that . . .' (I've checked, and this actually happens. Except it's Steve Jones.)

Parry brought The Cure into Morgan to record their debut album, *Three Imaginary Boys*, which he personally produced. Though Fiction had other bands, The Cure were clearly Parry's priority, and as early as the summer of 1980, he proudly brought them back to his native **Australasia** for a lengthy tour.

Robert Smith was never entirely happy with the sound of *Three Imaginary Boys*, so he determinedly edged Parry out of the **producers**' booth on the follow-up, *Seventeen Seconds* (co-producing with **Mike Hedges** instead). Smith and Parry arrived at a *modus operandi* whereby Smith was the auteur but Parry was the advisor. 'It's got to the point where we can trade insults freely, which is the sign of a healthy relationship,' said Smith in an Australian radio interview in 1981. 'If we were left totally to our own devices, it'd probably become self-indulgent. Even though I don't recognise self-indulgence. He's there as an outside influence . . .'

Parry exercised that influence in ways which often proved prescient. For example, in the aftermath of *Pornography*, it was 'Bill' who persuaded Robert to try some lighter, more frivolous material. 'I convinced him,' Parry later recalled, 'that there was a place for The Cure which was in pop, forget all the **goth**, forget all that stuff, just have fun, let's just write a few pop songs, you write the pop songs, produce them, and we'll see what happens. And if it doesn't work, you can walk away from the contract.' The Cure did not walk away from Fiction. Decades later, Fiction essentially walked away from The Cure.

Parry's other grand project, aside from The Cure, was the radio station **Xfm** (now rebranded Radio X), which he helped steer from its earliest days as a London pirate, allowing it to operate from Fiction's offices on Charlotte Street in the early nineties, tirelessly lobbying for an official licence and raising funds via benefit albums and concerts, through to the station's eventual granting of a licence in 1996.

His stewardship of The Cure, however, began to disintegrate at the end of the century. 'The relationship went sour in around 1999/2000,' **Roger O'Donnell** wrote on his website, 'when Bill sold Fiction and informed Robert by fax telling him if he had any problems he should contact his lawyer.' The Cure moved on to other **labels**, and by the early 2000s Robert Smith was describing Parry as 'a fraud', which he later backtracked from.

Parry, meanwhile, had more or less retired from music at the age of fifty-two to run a dairy farm in Coromandel on New Zealand's North Island. In 2010 the Fourmyula reunited for a couple of shows to promote the box set *The Complete Fourmyula*, and were inducted into the New Zealand Music Hall of Fame.

A happier postscript to this: it was let slip, by someone who would know, that in more recent years Robert Smith and Chris Parry met up for dinner in a spirit of water-under-the-bridge, bygones-be-bygones, life's-too-short. (No lawyers present.)

Passions, The

There would have been no reason to believe, for **Chris Parry** in 1978, that it wouldn't be The Passions, instead of The Cure, who would provide **Fiction** with its big breakthrough. So, the former were afforded the same personnel and resources – **Morgan Studios**, Parry producing with **Mike Hedges** engineering, **Bill Smith** artwork – as Purple Hearts (see '**Jumping Someone Else's Train**'), **Associates** and The Cure themselves. And they did provide that breakthrough in a sense: their 1981 single 'I'm in Love with a German Film Star' reached No.25, a record for a Fiction-signed band which stood until The Cure surpassed it with '**The Walk**' reaching No.7 two years later (although the Passions had actually been folded into parent company **Polydor** by the time of their one hit).

The Shepherds Bush-based new wave band, centred around singer Barbara Gogan and guitarist Clive Timperley, actually released the first record on Fiction: their debut single 'Hunted' in 1979. Their debut album *Michael & Miranda* was also a Fiction release, and they toured with The Cure and Associates on Fiction's fifteen-date Future Pastimes package tour of November and December 1979. Furthermore, it was at the third night of the Passions' month-of-Sundays residency at the Marquee in March 1980 that **Cult Hero** played their only gig.

The Passions released three albums before disbanding in August 1983, but it is for 'I'm in Love with a German Film Star' that they will be remembered. Written about Steve 'Roadent' Connelly, a Clash and Sex Pistols roadie who had appeared in 1979 German miniseries *Das Ding* as the character Joker (and went on to play a vagrant in 2003 comedy-horror *Penetration Angst*), it was atmospheric, poised and mysterious. 'It really moved me', Gogan sang, sounding completely unmoved.

Peel Sessions

DJ John Peel, born John Ravenscroft in Heswall, Cheshire in 1939, was a revered figure in UK alternative culture. British radio's leading advocate of challenging and cutting-edge music, he championed the hippie underground on his Radio London show *The Perfumed Garden* in the sixties, played punk bands before anyone else on his BBC Radio 1 show in the seventies, and spun anything from reggae to thrash metal along with the usual scratchy indie-rock fare during the eighties. His show ran from 10 p.m. to midnight on weeknights, forcing successive generations of teenage music fans to stay up late with a transistor under their covers to catch the latest single by The Revolutionary Army of the Infant Jesus or Stitched-Back Foot Airman.

Robert Smith once stated that John Peel was his biggest influence. From the age of fifteen Smith was one of those sleepless teenagers, tuning in every night. 'I heard "White Riot" and cut off all my hair,' he said in *Ten Imaginary Years*. 'I used to dream of making a record that John Peel would play.'

Specially recorded sessions were a regular feature of Peel's show, overseen by producers John Walters and Dale 'Buffin' Griffin at the BBC's Maida Vale studios using, in many cases, the best equipment the artist had ever used (or ever would). Similar sessions were also recorded for other DJs, including David 'Kid' Jensen and Richard Skinner. The Cure graced Peel, Jensen and Skinner with no fewer than eleven sessions from the late seventies through to the mid-eighties.

The first, recorded on 4 December 1978 by Robert Smith, **Michael Dempsey** (credited as Mick) and **Lol Tolhurst**, was broadcast on 11 December and featured '**Killing An Arab**', '**10.15 Saturday Night**', 'Fire in Cairo', and '**Boys Don't Cry**'. Sessions were almost always broadcast one week after recording. The session proved so popular with listeners that it was broadcast three times, the third being 7 March 1979.

Peel Sessions were often used by bands to test out new ideas ahead of recording an album. The Cure were no exception, and treated Maida Vale as a kind of musical sandpit in their early years, making the most of the opportunity to muck about and/or make a point. In their second Peel Session on 16 May 1979, as well as 'Subway Song', 'Plastic Passion' and 'Accuracy' they recorded the anti-Paul Morley smackdown '**Desperate Journalist** in Ongoing Meaningful Review Situation'. In a Kid Jensen session broadcast on 29 August that year, in addition to 'Boys Don't Cry' (again) and 'Three Imaginary Boys', they recorded the daft satirical dance tune 'Do The **Hansa**'.

Further BBC sessions followed throughout the early eighties. On 3 March 1980, a Cure session by the four-piece **line-up** of Smith, **Hartley**, **Gallup** and Dempsey on the John Peel Show previewed *Seventeen Seconds* with '**A Forest**', 'Seventeen Seconds', 'Play for Today' and 'M'. On 7 January 1981, the Smith, Gallup, Tolhurst trio recorded 'The Holy Hour', 'Forever', '**Primary**' and '**All Cats Are Grey**' for Peel. On 26 February 1981 They recorded 'The Funeral Party', 'The Drowning Man' and 'Faith' for Richard Skinner (meaning that six of the eight

songs on the *Faith* album had been previewed via Radio 1 sessions).

This pattern of previewing the next album continued in the *Pornography* era. On 21 December 1981 They recorded 'The Figurehead', '**One Hundred Years**' and 'Siamese Twins' for broadcast on 4 January 1982. (They also recorded an unfinished version of '**The Hanging Garden**' which was never broadcast.)

As The Cure's popularity grew, they made the time-honoured transition from Peel to becoming Jensen and Skinner regulars, those shows being scheduled earlier in the evening with a larger listenership. On 24 October 1982 Smith, Tolhurst and **Steve Goulding** recorded '**Let's Go To Bed**', 'Just One Kiss', 'One Hundred Years' and much sought-after **rarity** 'Ariel' (eventually released in home-demo form on the 2006 reissue of *The Top*) for Jensen. On 26 August 1983 they were back in Maida Vale for Jensen, this time with the line-up of Smith, Tolhurst, **Anderson** and **Thornalley**, to record 'Speak My Language', 'Mr Pink Eyes' and '**The Lovecats**'. On 22 February 1984 Richard Skinner broadcast a session by Smith, Thompson, Fisher-Jones (see **Noko**) and Thornalley featuring 'Bananafishbones', 'Piggy In The Mirror', 'Give Me It' and 'The Empty World'.

John Peel continued to support The Cure long after they'd become chart stars and no longer needed his endorsement. On 30 July 1985 *The Head On The Door* line-up of Smith, Tolhurst, **Thompson**, Gallup and **Williams** recorded 'The Exploding Boy', 'Six Different Ways', 'Screw' and 'Sinking' for what turned out to be their final Peel Session.

Their first Peel Session from 1978 was released in May 1988 on **vinyl** by Strange Fruit records (catalogue number SFPD050), with a lovely shaped picture disc available in **France**.

Once upon a time, Robert Smith had dreamt about making a record that John Peel would play. Now he'd gone one better, by making something that John Peel played into a record.

Perfect Boy, The

As the publicity stunt of releasing a single on the thirteenth of every month for four months in the lead-up to *4:13 Dream* drew to a close, The Cure put out one of their weakest singles.

'The Perfect Boy', unrelated to the similarly titled

'The Perfect Girl' from *Kiss Me, Kiss Me, Kiss Me*, is a piece of uneventful hazy guitar pop, its two or three chords meandering lazily over a mid-tempo beat, forever in search of a big Cure melody but never quite managing to find one.

The lyrics are a dialogue between a 'Happy Ever After girl' who tells the titular boy that 'You and me are the world', only for him to reply in the second half of the song that 'You and me are *a* world', that pointed use of the indefinite article making it clear, along with 'but not the only one I need', that he's only interested in a quick fling rather than a forever thing. In this respect, it is a mirror image of The Human League's 1981 classic 'Don't You Want Me'. With a vocal effect making his exclamation of 'Oh girl!' all the more dramatic, Robert Smith wishes her luck in one day finding her 'perfect boy'.

As with all the *4:13 Dream* singles, there was no **video** as such, other than some black and white MTV footage. It was released on 13 August 2008 in a **Parched Art** sleeve with a blackened watercolour heart as **artwork**. The extra track was 'Without You', a ramshackle acoustic break-up song in waltz-time, and sadly not a cover of the Badfinger/Harry Nilsson/Mariah Carey lungbuster, which in a Robert Smith voice would be quite special. It made No.37 in Cure-mad **France**, and No.2 in Cure-even-madder Spain. It was later remixed, like the other *4:13 Dream* singles, for the *Hypnagogic States* EP.

At the time of writing, 'The Perfect Boy' remains The Cure's most recent single.

Picture Show

Picture Show was 'an improbable collection' (it said on the box) of Cure music **videos** comprising the next ten videos since *Standing On A Beach/Staring At The Sea*, namely '**Why Can't I Be You?**', '**Catch**', '**Hot Hot Hot!!!**', '**Just Like Heaven**', '**Lullaby**', '**Fascination Street**', '**Lovesong**', '**Pictures Of You**', '**Never Enough**' and '**Close To Me** (Closer Mix)' The first and third of those were represented in their 12-inch form.

The **artwork**, for once, was not by **Parched Art** but by the elusive 'V'. It consisted of a cardboard black and white sleeve with a blurry photo of a girl using a 'planchette' (for automatic writing), from a book Robert was reading called *The Encyclopaedia of the Unexplained* (see **Supernatural, The**). The title

and track listing were printed in a font that looked uncomfortably close to the Caslon Antique famously favoured by fellow **goth** icons The Sisters Of Mercy.

Picture Show was released on 8 July 1991 on VHS for normal people, and Laserdisc for people whose home was like that of a Bond villain. (And, later, DVD.) It reached No.1 in the UK chart and No.3 in the **US**, despite the fact that a lot had changed in the five years between 1986 and 1991 and you could now just switch on MTV, even in Europe, and expect to see a Cure video.

The selling point, of course, was the assortment of 'Other Bits compiled by Robert Smith and **Tim Pope**' (similar to the inter-song snippets on *Staring At The Sea*) which bulked it up to a seventy-seven-minute running time. It's the usual selection of candid hand-held footage of the band doing mundane things like soundchecking, eating, larking about on the tour bus, plus the clip of them wearing dresses on TV in **France** overlaid with 'Hey You!!!' (to which they also lipsynch outdoors in some European city), Robert being interviewed,
and making-of clips from the video shoots themselves.

The most telling moment is Robert leaning over and gobbing on the top of **Lol Tolhurst**'s head in the 'Hot Hot Hot!!!' shoot. Twice.

Pictures Of You

'I think it's overlooked . . . but it's one of the best songs that we've ever done. It's very understated.'

This, in 1990, was Robert Smith's appraisal of 'Pictures Of You' when speaking to MTV, and it's an understandable one. In terms of the singles from *Disintegration*, this 'understated' song is certainly overshadowed by the pantomime fun of '**Lullaby**', the conventional appeal of '**Lovesong**' and the bass-driven might of '**Fascination Street**'. For Smith, however, it had particular personal significance.

As is so often the case with The Cure, there are competing narratives regarding its origin, some candid and some mischievous, made up by Robert because he gets bored in interviews. The version he spun to *Cure News* in 1998 was that it was loosely based on an essay by Myra Poleo entitled *The Dark Power of Ritual Pictures*, and that after reading this essay he destroyed all his old personal photos and most of his home cine and video collection to try and wipe away his past, but then felt huge regret within days. This account is to be treated with extreme wariness, as there is no essay of that name, nor any writer called Myra Poleo – it's an anagram of **Mary** Poole.

Rather more credible is the version recounted in *Rolling Stone*. Supposedly, shortly before the *Disintegration* sessions, a small fire broke out at Robert's house. As he sifted through the wreckage, he found a wallet containing photos of Mary, which sent his mind spinning into the nostalgic reverie which inspired the lyrics.

Whatever the truth may be, it's self-evidently a song about the emotional power of pictures, and the capacity of old photographs to torment you, to highlight your past failings. 'If only I'd thought of the right words, I could have held on to your heart', he sings in the regret-wracked bridge. 'If only I'd thought of the right words, I wouldn't be breaking apart all my Pictures Of You . . .'

A couple of other interesting points about the lyrics: Robert chooses to deliver the penultimate verse in a semi-spoken, intimate voice, like a Barry White record or an old rock 'n' roll ballad. And the line 'You were bigger and brighter and wider than snow' is a callback to three of the adjectives used in the first verse of '**The Lovecats**'.

The song proceeds with an unhurried stately elegance for an extraordinary seven and a half minutes (even the single is nearly five), and two and a half have elapsed before Robert even sings. This duration was always going to hinder its radio play, perhaps explaining its mediocre chart performance.

Nevertheless, the band went to gruelling and traumatic lengths to promote it, with a **video** shot in a blizzard. The chosen location was the village of Glencoe in Scotland, infamous as the site of the 1692 Glencoe Massacre when thirty-eight men, women and children from the MacDonald clan were slaughtered by soldiers on the orders of William of Orange. With the shoot scheduled for February, it was assumed that snow would be on the ground. However, when director **Tim Pope** and his team first scouted the location it was snowless, but they loved the vista enough to commit to it regardless. The band caught the train north, and stayed in the Ballachulish Hotel on the banks of Loch Linnhe, a body of water said in **Scottish folklore** to be home to an *each-uisge*, or 'water horse', on whose back local children would ride, only for the *each-uisge* to gallop into the loch, drown them and eat them. As if by magic, on

their very early start the next morning (due to short daylight hours at that time of year in the Highlands), the band awoke to snow. In fact, the snowstorm didn't relent all day, coupled with gale-force winds which meant that the fake palm trees – the video shoot's main props – needed to be nailed down.

A making-of video of candid footage shows them playing pool, rehearsing their **cover** of 'Hello, I Love You' for Elektra's forthcoming *Rubaiyat* album, pushing their van out of the snow, playing pool, putting on lipstick and throwing snowballs. These high spirits soon evaporated when faced with the reality of a long, miserable and wet day exposed to the sub-Arctic elements, and the dour atmosphere was only partly alleviated by drams of brandy between takes.

The backdrop of the video was the famous, pyramid-shaped mountain Buachaille Etive Mòr which, at 3,351ft, counts as a Munro. It was later used in the James Bond film *Skyfall*, and had previously featured in the video for Nick Heyward's 'Whistle Down The Wind'. On the day of The Cure shoot, the conditions were so poor that one person actually died on the mountain.

Using a Super 8 home cine camera, Pope filmed the shivering, frostbitten band performing the song in front of the palm trees, plugged into battery-powered amps. A polar bear scuttles around, played by crew member Bruno, the only person able to remain relatively warm in his furry suit. At one point, the skeleton of a large animal is briefly visible on the ground – perhaps a stag, or perhaps the *each-uisge*.

The idea of juxtaposing the arctic and the tropical had a recent precedent in The Cure's 1987 song 'Snow in Summer' (a B-side of '**Just Like Heaven**'), with lyrics about being 'high up on this mountain'. However, the likely inspiration was the fact that one of the photos Robert found in his wallet was of Mary on holiday in a castle in Scotland in 1980. In this sense, Smith and Tim Pope were taking a very literal approach to the lyrics by filming the video there. Plus, of course, 'Pictures Of You' itself contains that reference to snow. 'I wanted a sunny feel,' Smith explained in *Select*, 'but it mentions snow in the words. Snow looks like sand in black-and-white, so I thought, "Let's start as if it's in the sun, then pull away and you'll see a blizzard." The old adage "The camera doesn't lie" isn't true . . .'

This was wishful thinking on Smith's part, because the 'sand' effect doesn't actually work in the jittery, grainy finished video: you can see it's a snowy landscape straight away. And the entire UK was a snowy landscape by the time shooting wrapped, meaning that it took the band two days to get back to London, incorporating an unscheduled stop in Birmingham.

The **artwork**, by **Parched Art**, also tied into the lyrics and the photographs. The aforementioned photo of Mary in the Scottish castle was used on the sleeve. It wasn't the first time this photo had been used: a deliberately blurred version was previously seen on the front of '**Charlotte Sometimes**'.

'Pictures Of You' hit the shops on 19 March 1990 and, this being the early nineties, the release was multi-format mayhem. There were two 7-inches (one of which was on green vinyl), two 12-inches and two CDs, with live versions of 'Prayers For Rain', 'Fascination Street', 'Last Dance' and 'Disintegration' scattered across them in various combinations.

In the UK charts it reached a disappointing 24, the lowest position of the three *Disintegration* singles there ('Fascination Street' being a **US**-only release), and 71 in the US, a massive drop from the giddy heights of 'Love Song' which had reached No.2.

In time, though, its status grew. It was given a remix by Bryan 'Chuck' New for *Mixed Up*, which Robert considered one of the standout mixes from that album. It has been **covered** by Lit and by Angie Hart from Frente whose version was used for a road-safety ad campaign in Australia. In 2004, The Cure's version was used in a commercial for HP cameras (a rare example of Cure music being legitimately used in what Robert considered the 'tawdry context' of **advertising**). In the twenty-first century it featured on **television** in episodes of *Gilmore Girls*, *Cold Case*, *One Tree Hill*, *Vampire Diaries*, *Misfits*, *Mr Robot*, *The Politician*, *The Goldbergs*, *Doom Patrol* and *Little Fires Everywhere*, and on films including *One Perfect Day*, *Starter For 10*, *Café de Flore*, *The Vow*, *White Bird in a Blizzard* and *Me You Madness*. And, despite its poor showing in the American charts upon its release, it topped a 2004 fan poll among the overwhelmingly American readership of *Rolling Stone*, and was placed at 278th in that magazine's list of the five hundred greatest songs of all time.

If it was overlooked once, now it's a different picture.

Pink Floyd

'I HATE PINK FLOYD'.

That's what it said on Johnny Rotten's defaced DIY T-shirt and, during the punk era and its immediate aftermath, that sentiment was law. But Pink Floyd weren't just one band. They were (at least) two, and their first incarnation never really stopped being hip.

Formed in London in 1965, the original Pink Floyd were leading lights of the psychedelic underground, building a following by gigging at Middle Earth and the UFO Club in dimly lit basements, their faces illuminated by oil wheels. Their original singer was troubled genius Syd Barrett, who completed just one album with them, 1967's *Piper At The Gates Of Dawn* (and contributed in a much-reduced way to the follow-up *A Saucerful Of Secrets*) as well as a handful of singles including transvestite knicker-thief narrative 'Arnold Layne' and LSD fever dream 'See Emily Play'.

Having developed mental health problems exacerbated by **drug** use, resulting in wild mood swings, lost weekends and increasingly erratic behaviour, Barrett was edged out of the group in 1968 and, after a fitful attempt at a solo career, lived out his days as a recluse in his mother's home in Cambridge.

The version of Pink Floyd which carried on without him, comprising David Gilmour, Roger Waters, Rick Wright and Nick Mason, is the one which attracted the ire of Rotten and the punk generation. As they mutated gradually from psychedelia to prog rock, they came to embody everything punk stood against: mellowness, musical virtuosity and obscene wealth. Their 1973 album *The Dark Side Of The Moon*, which sold forty-five million copies worldwide and was certified fifteen times platinum in the UK and US, was a stoner behemoth, the soundtrack to countless late-night sessions in smoke-filled bedrooms with Persian rugs on the wall, the listeners slumped on beanbags letting the waves of Waters, Gilmour, Wright and Mason's music wash over them.

The first **critic** to cotton on to the connection between The Cure and Pink Floyd was Mike Nicholls of *Record Mirror*. Reviewing a show at the London Lyceum on 1 July 1979 on the ***Three Imaginary Boys*** tour, Nicholls called The Cure 'the Pink Floyd of the new wave'. The Cure were supported that night by the far punkier The Ruts and energetic mod band Purple Hearts, and to Nicholls seemed sluggish and lethargic in comparison. The similarity was heightened by The Cure's comparatively elaborate and very un-punk light show (involving blue gels, white strobes, smoke and dry ice), intended to add some dynamism to compensate for the band's static stage presence. The Floyd comparison was too tempting to resist, and there is no question that Nicholls intended it as an insult.

The comparison gained traction. Backstage at one festival, an Italian interviewer asked Robert, 'Are you the Pink Floyd of the eighties?' Smith spotted the curveball from a mile away, and batted it out of the park. 'We're not at all. We're The Cure of the eighties.'

It wasn't always meant pejoratively. A review of the *Happily Ever After* album in the *Virginian Pilot* noted that 'Sometimes they sound like Gang of Four meets Pink Floyd, acid rock for the Industrial Age' (a fairly accurate description, in fact). Simon Reynolds, a broadly Cure-positive writer, wrote not-disapprovingly that 'The Cure are the post-punk generation's equivalent to seventies dinosaur bands like Genesis and Pink Floyd that Punk aimed to exterminate.'

As the decade wore on, The Cure's penchant for very long, atmospheric songs and very long, atmospheric concerts set off reviewers' Floyd alarms with increasing frequency (*The Cure In Orange* was routinely compared to *Pink Floyd: Live at Pompeii*). And that's without mentioning their audacious decision to release a double album (see *Kiss Me, Kiss Me, Kiss Me*).

If you weren't meant to do this sort of thing, then Robert hadn't read the rule book. He openly spoke of the influence of Pink Floyd's *Ummagumma* on *Faith*, and cited their epic song 'Set The Controls For The Heart Of The Sun' (from *A Saucerful Of Secrets*) as an influence on The Cure in general.

Even their own official biography, *Ten Imaginary Years*, made nerdy Cure–Floyd connections, noting that when The Cure played Chesterfield's Fusion Hall on 5 April 1979 they were the first rock band to play there since Pink Floyd in 1968. (The book also reported that they got busted for smoking weed that night, and you can't get much more Floyd than that.)

There were even crossovers in personnel terms. The Cure headhunted **crew** member Mick Kluczynski, their production manager for most of the eighties, from Pink Floyd's production company Britannia Row. And, via Kluczynski, they hired Pink Floyd's PA, projection equipment and lighting rig for the Picture Tour (to promote *Faith*). 'After we hired the PA we had a day at Shepperton to see how it would look

all set up,' Robert told *NME*. 'It was really absurd seeing it all, ten times bigger than the equipment we usually use.' The huge expense of using Floyd's gear, combined with the relatively modest fees they were receiving for playing small-ish venues, meant that profit margins were low and they were compelled to play almost every night in order to break even.

The stress this caused, ironically, almost sent Robert the same way as Syd Barrett.

Pissing

Normally, when a young rock band out on the road can't control their penises, it means they can't stop having sex with groupies. With The Cure the problem, more often, was pissing. And it usually involved **Lol**.

The first time it happened, somebody else was indulging in the more traditional activity when they were rudely interrupted by Tolhurst's yellow river. On 3 December 1978, when The Cure supported **Generation X** at the Bristol Locarno, Lol burst into a toilet cubicle and, urgently needing a wee and unable to stop the flow, let loose all over their singer Billy Idol, who was busy having sex with a female fan. The bleach-blond heartthrob later immortalised by *Smash Hits* magazine as 'Sir Billiam of Idol' did not see the funny side and, after one further date in Dunstable, The Cure were kicked off the tour, only six dates into a fourteen-date run. This meant missing out on the prestigious pre-Christmas show at London's Electric Ballroom on 20 December (where their place was taken by punk also-rans Chelsea), and having instead to play their own show two miles away at the modestly sized Moonlight Club in West Hampstead, a venue they had already played only a month earlier supporting UK Subs, while Generation X rocked Camden Town. All because Lol couldn't tie a knot in it.

Less than a year later, Tolhurst's todger almost caused an even more serious incident. On the infamous night of 7 September 1979, when the Banshees fell apart in Aberdeen and The Cure had to headline, Lol found himself peeing behind a hedge next to the band's hotel and, as he later told *Curious Creatures* listeners, was alarmed when two red laser dots appeared on the foliage. The British Prime Minister Margaret Thatcher was in town to open the Shell UK Exploration Centre, and her security detail were uneasy about the intentions of the dark, shifty figure they'd spotted lurking among the leaves. One twitchy trigger finger from a Specialist Protection officer and The Cure could have lost a lot more that night than a few support dates with **Siouxsie**.

On the *Three Imaginary Boys* tour, an entire Cure audience caught an eyeful of Tolhurst's private parts in action. The drummer often found himself needing a mid-show toilet break, so the crew had provided him with a bucket hidden behind the backdrop. On one occasion, Lol signalled to Robert to extend the intro to 'Grinding Halt' so that he could avail himself of these ad-hoc facilities. Unfortunately for him, at that exact moment, the lighting technician accidentally backlit him in such a way that his penis was silhouetted on the screen for all to see, leading to a gale of laughter.

Robert Smith, meanwhile, was once **arrested** in Germany for pissing against the side of a Mexican bar. But, more often than not, it was Lol Tolhurst who had the ungovernable urethra. In his autobiography *Cured*, Lol recounts another bladder-based incident. On 25 May 1980, after a show at De Lantaarn in Rotterdam, the band embarked on a serious session at afterhours drinking bar the Heavy Club during which Lol urinated in a phone booth thinking it was a toilet. The Cure were thrown out, and went to the beach instead, Lol's rogue pissing therefore setting in motion a chain of events which culminated in the band getting arrested and having to bribe their way out of trouble.

This wasn't even the first time that a Cure visit to the Netherlands involved some misplaced micturition. On 10 December 1979, during a day off between Dutch dates, the band drank thirteen bottles of red wine between four people. In due course, Lol reached such a peak of drunkenness that he started screaming and freaking out, running up and down the hotel corridors vomiting and trying door handles until Robert let him into his room. Lol locked himself in Robert's bathroom and turned the shower on, shouting 'Let me die!' through the door before passing out. At 5 a.m., Tolhurst woke up slumped in Smith's shower, with the water still running, and went to bed.

Robert's retaliation for this rampage, considering Tolhurst's track record, was perfect. He pissed in Lol's suitcase.

Play At Home

Play At Home was an innovative strand of music programming from the early days of British **television** station Channel 4 in which bands were given forty-five minutes (sixty including ad breaks) to fill as they pleased, and encouraged to perform in unusual and creative ways. Artists featured in the series included Angelic Upstarts, Big Country, Echo & The Bunnymen, **New Order**, The Special AKA and XTC.

In September 1983 **Siouxsie And The Banshees** were offered the opportunity to make an episode of *Play At Home*, shortly before their two concerts at the Royal Albert Hall (the shows immortalised on *Nocturne*). They agreed to do so, in order to take advantage of chance to have the concerts filmed at someone else's expense, as well as to plug their offshoot bands The Creatures and **The Glove**.

Robert Smith, by now in his second stint as a Banshee, had previously suggested to **Steve Severin** that 'the Banshees shouldn't be doing tours, they should be doing something really ambitious like *The Wizard of Oz* on stage'. Severin adapted this idea for their *Play At Home*, switching *The Wizard of Oz* for *Alice in Wonderland* (as a nod to the Banshees' label, Wonderland).

The recurring thread through the Banshees' exceptionally surreal episode was a re-enactment of the Mad Hatter's Tea Party, with all four Banshees dressed as a blonde-wigged Alice, some more convincingly than others. **Make-up** artist Carol Barnes certainly had her work cut out. As Severin told Banshees biographer Mark Paytress, 'Robert is hugely hairy, even after he's just shaved. So both of us looked like something out of *The Dick Emery Show* as we sat there smoking fags in our ill-fitting dresses.' As Siouxsie added, 'Steve and Robert looked hilarious but, scarily, Budgie looked quite normal . . .'

The rest of the cast comprised Don Ash (a fan from Wolverhampton) as Tweedledum, Billy 'Chainsaw' Houlston (who ran the Banshees' fanclub) as Tweedledee, Anni Hogan (Marc and the Mambas' pianist) playing the Dormouse, **Mike Hedges** as the Queen of Hearts, Tim Collins (the Banshees' tour manager) as the March Hare, Jos Grain (the Banshees' drum technician) as the Mad Hatter, and Dave Woods, the Banshees' manager, playing the White Rabbit.

Each individual Banshee was given their own self-scripted slot. Robert Smith is first, giving a five-minute acting performance as the suspect in a police interview room being interrogated by officers in clown masks who communicate only in strange scraping and buzzing sounds, as he does battle with his own faltering memory. Stylistically it's reminiscent of Terry Gilliam's *Brazil*, although that film did not yet exist. A likely inspiration is Franz Kafka's novel *The Trial*.

A low-budget video for The Creatures' 'Weathercade' is next, followed by Budgie mucking about in Soho, Regents Park and London Zoo, reciting a poem about a peccary called Gregory. (Siouxsie had actually adopted a peccary in the zoo and named it Gregory.)

The Glove perform 'A Blues in Drag', providing a pleasantly tranquil Eno-esque interlude, with Severin on upright bass and Smith in dark glasses at the piano, almost certainly both miming. Siouxsie then recites a cannibalistic fairy story, and Severin a fractured assassination narrative.

Finally, the four of them perform 'Circle' from *A Kiss In The Dreamhouse* as a band, with Robert miming John McGeoch's electric piano part (with questionable attention paid to believability or accuracy).

The film ends with live footage of the Royal Albert Hall gigs, which the Banshees convinced production company RPM to shoot in full for the film version of *Nocturne*, thereby killing two painted birds with one stone. The songs shown on Channel 4 were 'Eve White/Eve Black', 'Voodoo Dolly', and 'Helter Skelter' (missing from the *Nocturne* LP but present on the eventual DVD, on which the full *Play At Home* episode is included as an extra). The end credits roll, with thanks to '**Lol** and **Paul** [sic]'.

Play At Home was aired in September 1984, by which time Robert was long gone from the Banshees' ranks and The Glove no longer existed.

Play Out

The Cure Play Out is a fly-on-the-wall documentary which follows a month in the life of The Cure in January and February 1991, when they were unquestionably the biggest band in Britain and one of the biggest in the world. It was made by Peter Fowler, a director for BBC2's *Snub TV* who also created live videos for Pulp and Stereophonics.

It begins with The Cure playing an intimate secret gig at the T&C2 (aka The Garage) at Highbury Corner under the not exactly cryptic name Five Imaginary Boys (the five, at that time, being Robert Smith, **Simon Gallup**, **Porl Thompson**, **Perry Bamonte** and **Boris Williams**) as a warm-up for the Great British Music Weekend. There's something quite emotional about seeing hopeful fans queuing up along Holloway Road for spare tickets as Robert is interviewed inside through the box office window about his reasons for playing such a tiny show.

Five songs from the gig itself appear in the film, including two previously unreleased songs – 'Wendy Time' and 'Away' (later renamed 'Cut') – which would appear on *Wish*. We then see the band larking about backstage with **Chris Parry**, and Porl with a tea towel wrapped around his head while 'Step On' by Happy Mondays plays at the aftershow indie disco, somehow perfectly capturing the mundanity behind the glamour of rock star life.

For much of its duration, *The Cure Play Out* is the anti-*Cure In Orange*: claustrophobic corners versus wide open spaces; the January drizzle of North London versus the July sunshine of the South of France.

We then see the thing they were warming themselves up for: the Great British Music Weekend, a BRIT **Awards** and BBC Radio 1-sponsored event at Wembley Arena where they were supported by The Wedding Present, New Model Army, Jesus Jones, Carter USM and Ride. (Other shows across the weekend were headlined by Ozzy Osbourne and Happy Mondays.) Backstage beforehand, we see Simon teaching Perry a song on guitar: 'No, *jing-ja-jing, jing-ja-jing* . . .' It's supremely *Spinal Tap*. And, in a very meta moment, we see another film crew coming in while Robert calmly sprays his hair and applies his kohl. He's wearing *that* floral shirt: the same one he wore on the '**Never Enough**' sleeve, on the 1990 tour, and would wear through all the events covered by *Play Out*.

A very compact and curt forty-five-minute set of thirteen songs is reduced to just four here, including a ten-minute '**A Forest**'. Backstage afterwards, we see Mary making fun of Robert for wearing a 'mouldy old jumper' that he slept in. We see Simon with his eight-month-old baby **Eden**. And we hear Gallup and Bamonte complaining amiably about the intrusive onstage cameraman, with Gallup admitting 'I made a cunt of meself' after flicking the Vs at him. Do these super-corporate events threaten to swallow The Cure up? 'There's that extraneous pop world', says Robert thoughtfully, 'and we sometimes go for a swim in it.

As long as we can get out and not drown . . .'

The action then turns to the E-Zee Hire rehearsal studio, where the band sit in a circle rehearsing '**The Blood**' acoustically in preparation for *MTV Unplugged*, with Boris on castanets and Perry on xylophone. There's a rehearsal of *that* comical version of '**The Walk**', replacing the synth with kazoos, which Porl almost can't play because he's laughing so much. Boris puts the rest of them off by making Clangers noises with his. 'Are we seriously gonna do that?!' asks Robert. Yes, they were seriously gonna do that.

After a short excerpt from *MTV Unplugged* itself, we find the band at the Dominion Theatre rehearsing for the BRIT Awards. There's a coy discussion about whether it's worth them turning up. (It was: they won Best British Group.) Again, a lot of it is mundanity: Robert grimacing at the taste of a badly poured pint during a soundcheck, the band watching themselves back on a TV monitor in a production van, and so on. But that mundanity is precious, in its way. Simon giving Robert a bottle of Poire Williams schnapps as a gift, for example. Nobody knows what to do with that, but its meaninglessness is precisely the point.

Over at the **Fiction** offices, Simon is mischievously tearing up Chris Parry's post when he's not around, and building an actual snowman on Parry's office chair. Backstage at the BRITs, Porl is crooning Frankie Vaughan's 'Give Me The Moonlight, Give Me The Girl'. Then they're on, performing 'Never Enough' under a massive swinging lampshade (perhaps referencing *Three Imaginary Boys*). When Roger Daltrey presents them with their award, Robert meticulously mentions everyone who's ever been in The Cure, but leaves out **Lol Tolhurst**.

The Cure Play Out was released by Fiction Films via Elektra Video in December 1991 on now long-deleted VHS and Laserdisc formats, with **artwork** depicting a chimps' tea party. In December 2022 the film was remastered in HD and expanded from its original ninety-six-minute running time to two hours fifteen minutes. It is available to watch for free on The Cure's YouTube channel.

Podcasts

A band as popular as The Cure, with such a tangled history and such an enormous body of work, will inevitably be the subject of analysis in all forms of media. There are Cure fanzines, Cure **websites**, Cure **books**, Cure **documentaries**, and of course, that most modern of formats, Cure podcasts.

Prime among them is the fan-made *The Holy Hour: The All Cure Podcast*. This bi-weekly American production is hundreds of episodes deep (sample title: *Episode 142 'The Mythical Robert Smith Solo Album'*), with regulars Gavin, Donald and Chaz conducting a fun chat among friends about their favourite band while also demonstrating a solid command of detail.

A newer arrival is *Close To Me: The Songs Of The Cure*, an album-by-album guide by Ben Shirai which began in September 2022 and is available on Audible.

The nearest thing to an 'official' podcast, of course, is **Lol Tolhurst** and Budgie's *Curious Creatures*, in which the former Cure and **Siouxsie And The Banshees** drummers tell their old war stories with special guests (including, on one occasion, **Michael Dempsey**).

The Cure are often the subject of one-off episodes of existing podcast series. For example, BBC Radio 4's *Soul Music* strand, about the power of songs in people's lives, ran an episode about '**Boys Don't Cry**', with contributions from Tolhurst.

The arts and culture website *Slate* hosts a podcast called *Hit Parade* by chart analyst Chris Molanphy, which has run at least two very interesting episodes dealing with The Cure's impact on American culture in the late eighties, titled *The Lost and Lonely Edition* and *The Bridge: Genre vs Generation*, with music journalist Ned Raggett. (For those who still don't 'do' pods, these two even come with transcripts.)

Poetry

'I've always admired Dylan Thomas,' Robert Smith told *Record Mirror* in 1984. 'I'd like to be able to write good prose, but I know I can't. He died with a whisky bottle in his stomach – not a bad way to go.'

Smith's admiration of, and identification with, the famously dipsomaniac Welsh poet was no fleeting fancy. As someone steeped in literature, Robert was as much inspired by poetry as he was by prose, and Dylan Thomas was evidently a hero of his. He once told *Cure News* that Thomas' 'Do Not Go Gentle Into That Good Night' was his favourite poem, and 'Birdmad Girl', from *The Top*, was inspired by Thomas' 'Love in the Asylum'. The phrase 'bird mad girl' recurred in 1994 on 'Burn', from *The Crow* soundtrack (see **Films, The Cure's music in**).

Smith also felt the lure of tragic heroine Sylvia Plath not once but twice. 'Ariel', a demo from *The Top* sessions, was inspired by Sylvia Plath's poem of the same name (a problematic one, since it casually uses the N-word to describe the colour of some berries). And 'Open', from *Wish*, alludes to Plath with the lines 'And the way the rain comes down hard/That's the way I feel inside', which strongly resemble Plath's words from *Letters Home*: 'I am glad the rain is coming down hard. It's the way I feel inside.'

Charles Baudelaire, whose *Les Fleurs du Mal* ought to be a set text for any **goth** kid, is another influence, and his prose piece 'The Eyes of the Poor' inspired 'How Beautiful You Are' on *Kiss Me, Kiss Me, Kiss Me* (as discussed under that album's *Curepedia* entry).

Pornography, Robert once revealed, was inspired by John Milton's *Paradise Lost*. He described it as 'pure poetry, fabulous, a must for an English grammar school pupil and very influential on the Romantic writers. The style is strong, incredible.'

The title of *Bloodflowers* was inspired by a First World War poem, as discussed under that album's entry. 'The Lovecats', as discussed under that song's entry, bears strong echoes of William Blake and T. S. Eliot among others.

'Treasure' on *Wild Mood Swings* was inspired by Christina Rossetti's 'Remember', a poem often read at funerals. The song begins 'She whispers "Please remember me when I am gone from here",' echoing Rossetti's opening line, 'Remember me when I am gone away'. It ends 'Remember me and smile/For it's better to forget/Than to remember me and cry', echoing Rossetti's 'Better by far you should forget and smile/Than that you should remember and be sad.'

Once you know Robert Smith is such a lover of verse, it's easy to start spotting poetry references everywhere in The Cure's work, even, perhaps, where none exists. It has been suggested, for example, that 'A Foolish Arrangement', from the '**A Letter To Elise**' 12-inch, was inspired by Samuel Taylor Coleridge's 'Christabel', but the evidence for that seems slender, with few similarities beyond the fact that Christabel is the name of the girl in the song.

We're on firmer ground when Smith himself has confirmed the poetic provenance of a song. 'Adonais', one of the extra tracks on '**The 13th**', was written, he has said, with Brandon Lee from *The Crow* in mind (see **Films, The Cure's music in**) but was based on Percy Bysshe Shelley's poem 'Adonais', written upon the death of John Keats. And Keats himself is quoted on an interstitial frame at the start of the *Trilogy* DVD: 'Ay, in the very temple of delight veil'd melancholy has her sovran shrine' (from 'Ode on Melancholy'). The Romantic poets in general loom large in The Cure's work. The *Five Swing Live* EP, for example, was dedicated to the memory of **Associates** singer Billy Mackenzie (the subject of '**Cut Here**'), with a Wordsworth quotation on the sleeve: 'The music in my heart I bore, long after it was heard no more'.

Sometimes, however, poetry can serve as an *anti*-inspiration. During the making of *Wish*, Smith was seen carrying a dog-eared Emily Dickinson anthology and had pinned quotes from her works to the studio wall, but he confessed to *Select*'s Miranda Sawyer that he hated 'nearly all of them. Any I found remotely interesting I put on the wall to justify my having wasted all that energy on her . . .'

Politics

In the late seventies and early eighties, an era defined by the economic recession that followed the election victory of Margaret Thatcher's Conservative government in 1979, and the heightened fears that the sabre-rattling of Republican Ronald Reagan, elected as US President in 1980, would escalate the Cold War to a hot one, bands who refrained from taking a political stance were the exception rather than the rule. Almost every significant figure in the world of alternative-facing post-punk pop had an opinion they wanted to express: The Clash, Gang of Four, The Specials, The Beat, The Jam, The Style Council, Billy Bragg, Bronski Beat, Fine Young Cannibals, The Communards, The Smiths, The Blow Monkeys, Redskins, The Housemartins, Big Audio Dynamite, the list goes on.

In this respect, as in so many others, The Cure were an anomaly. 'The reason for our non-image,' Robert Smith told David Hepworth in *Sounds* in September 1979, just two months after Thatcher's victory, 'was that, as a group, we weren't particularly affiliated with anything. There was no Left Wing, no Right Wing, no nothing.'

He later expressed scepticism that it was possible for bands like The Clash or Gang Of Four to profoundly alter people's thinking through music, despite mass unemployment and the looming threat of atomic annihilation. 'We don't get involved in rock and roll as propaganda. I just cannot think in such pragmatic ways. We refuse to align ourselves with CND or Right to Work, not that we're callous or insensitive . . .'

And, speaking to Paul 'Desperate Journalist' Morley, the emperor of NME critics, in November 1981, he outlined his concerns about what taking a political stance would do to The Cure. 'I do think it's preferable to maintain an independence from identifiable group activity, set ourselves apart from that kind of mainstream agitprop. It'd smother our identity and render any energy comparatively useless.'

So, The Cure are an apolitical band, and it's as simple as that. Isn't it? Well, not quite. As long ago as their pre-Cure days, they were nailing their colours to the mast. One of their earliest shows, and the first captured on film, was a Peace Concert in Queen's Square, Crawley on 3 July 1977, one of a series of gigs arranged by James and Consuelo Duggan to promote peace in Northern Ireland. In 1977 (as Easy Cure) and 1979 (as The Cure) they played two benefit concerts in Crawley in defence of their schoolteacher Dr Anthony Weaver, who had been dismissed from two posts on a homophobic pretext of 'gross indecency'. Both shows were the scene of violence caused by members of the fascist National Front. It wouldn't be the last time that The Cure raised money for what they perceived to be a good cause.

Is fundraising 'political' per se? Many charities are essentially apolitical, except in the fundamental sense that all charities are political, since their existence highlights the government's failure to cope with the issue that charity addresses. (For a selection of apolitical charities supported by The Cure, see Charity.)

Other charities, though, are political by their very nature. One example is the human rights pressure group Amnesty International, which The Cure supported by providing a cover of John Lennon's 'Love' for the 2005 album Make Some Noise. Another is Greenpeace, the radical environmentalist group, which The Cure supported by playing the Sound Waves for Greenpeace concert at the Royal Albert Hall on 25 April 1986. This concern for green issues

is borne out by other gestures and clues, such as a backstage caterer revealing on MTV in 1990 that the band were mainly vegetarian, and the fact that one of the beneficiaries of live album Entreat was anti-animal testing charity the Dr Hadwen Trust (now renamed Animal Free Research UK). And, despite Smith's earlier disclaimer, The Cure did effectively align themselves with CND (the Campaign for Nuclear Disarmament) by headlining the Glastonbury Festival of 1986, which raised funds for the movement.

The first time Smith did align himself with a political party was when Smash Hits asked a selection of pop stars who they would vote for in the forthcoming General Election. 'I'm going to vote SDP,' he said, referring to the centrist party formed in 1981 when a handful of Labour and Conservative MPs jumped ship. 'It's a dreadful thing, but I like Dr David Owen – I think he's the best politician in Britain. I would vote for a centrist government because it's been such a long time since Britain's had one. It's dreadful that Margaret Thatcher's been in power for so long – it's such an inhuman government. Obviously I would prefer a Labour government, but really I think they're both dreadful.'

Only a year later, however, in Cure News, he clarified his position, which turned out to be a lot more solidly left-wing than the Smash Hits interview may have suggested. 'I am a humanitarian socialist,' he said, 'but too inactive. I consider firstly myself, secondly my nephews and nieces, and thirdly everyone else when I vote.' Asked what he would do if he were Prime Minister, he answered that he would 'massively re-allocate a restructured tax-system, mainly from defence to education and health.' And, on the specific issues of nuclear weapons and nuclear power, he replied 'They are both obviously unnecessary and harmful; unfortunately the knowledge and fear that give birth to nuclear defence are too deeply ingrained, and the hidden vested financial interests in nuclear power have more weight than the ecologically and socially more acceptable tidal/solar/wind/fossil fuel alternative.'

If Smith stopped short of telling fans which party to vote for, he didn't mind telling them which party not to vote for. 'Support the anti-roads movement,' he urged readers of Cure News in 1994, 'and don't ever vote Conservative.'

Looking back on the state of Britain (and America) over the course of The Cure's career, it's clear he was in no doubt as to who the villains of the story were.

'There's a certain tone to this country that's really changed for the worse,' he told Dorian Lynskey of the *Guardian* in 2018. 'It's weird how the seventies is often referred to as a period of great unrest and the three-day week, blah, blah. It's bollocks. The period from the Second World War to the seventies, we were on a great trajectory for equality and so forth. It's only since the end of the seventies, Maggie [Thatcher] and Ronnie [Reagan], that things have inexorably gone wrong. It's insane, people's lust for technology and new things.'

He was also disappointed by New Labour. 'The top 1% is hundreds of times richer than the bottom 30,' he said to Louis Pattison of the *Guardian* in 2011, 'and it's got worse – it's got worse under Labour, and why is nothing being done about it? In the West, we see people being rewarded for doing nothing; they create nothing, it wouldn't matter if they died, but we see them being rewarded massive sums of money. . . even I get angry.' (In the same interview he described himself as 'a liberal kind of guy', but that's starting to feel like a classic Robert Smith understatement.)

It's rare, however, for any political content to appear in The Cure's music. 'Us Or Them' from 2004's *The Cure* is one example. A piece of impassioned invective against terrorism, it can also be read as a diatribe of disgust against bigotry in general. 'There is no terror in my heart,' it begins, 'Death is with us all/We suck him down with our first breath/And spit him out as we fall.' Later, it critiques 'the doleful cant of a bigot, blinded by fear and hate'. ('Us Or Them' has been retro-explained in some quarters as being inspired by the 7/7 attacks in London, but this is impossible – they happened a year later.)

There's also a case to be made for **'One Hundred Years'** being a political song. It's impressionistic and imprecise, but lines like 'Stroking your hair as the patriots are shot/Fighting for freedom on the television/Sharing the world with slaughtered pigs' paint a dystopian picture of the world, while 'The soldiers close in under a yellow moon/All shadows and deliverance/Under a black flag/A hundred years of blood' raise the spectres of fascism and warfare.

Have The Cure's live shows been vehicles for political messages? Well, a little. On their 1996 tour, a disfigured image of ultra-conservative American politician Pat Buchanan appeared on a backdrop during **'Lullaby'**. At a gig in **France**, Robert had written 'CHIRAC DIE', a reference to the recently elected French president Jacques Chirac, on his amp. And, at the Reading Festival in 2012, Robert had the

slogan 'CITIZENS NOT SUBJECTS' painted on his guitar. This was consistent with anti-Royalist views he had expressed many years earlier. 'They are dullards,' he said of the British Royal Family in *Cure News* in 1989. 'A waste of time and money – but no more so than a million other things.' In 1990, in the same publication, he added 'The notion of "royalty" is totally ridiculous.'

When asked by France's *Télérama* to elaborate on the 'CITIZENS NOT SUBJECTS' slogan in 2012, he answered 'It's about the dumbing-down of my country, my culture. With how you're supposed to think it's really great that William marries Kate. And that the Queen's been on the throne for, you know. I was part of a punk revolution that celebrated [Sex Pistols'] "God Save The Queen" and thought that the whole thing was going to come tumbling down any time soon. In 1977, the Silver Jubilee, we did a show. That was one of our very first concerts. I fucking hate royalty. I hate the idea of any kind of hereditary privilege. It's wrong. It's not just anti-democracy, it's inherently wrong. What upsets me is that some people I've very much admired over the years get offered a reward by the Royal Family, by hereditary monarchy, and they take it. And they become "Lord" or "Sir". Honestly, I'm never gonna get one but I would cut off my own hands before I accepted that. Because how dare they presume that they could give me an honour? I'm much better than them. They've never done anything. They're fucking idiots.' At this point he raised two fingers at the camera, before adding 'I should be king . . .'

Of course, the elephant in the room when discussing The Cure and politics is the song **'Killing An Arab'**. That's a subject discussed elsewhere in the book, but suffice to say that Robert has made it abundantly clear, on countless occasions, that it was never intended to be a racist or Far Right statement.

Since January 2009, we've all had access to Robert Smith's political leanings via his Twitter account. While rarely making explicitly political statements himself, his retweets speak volumes. For example, he has shared tweets that are damning towards Donald Trump and Boris Johnson, that are critical of the UK government's response to Covid-19, and that attack the activities of multinational tax-dodging corporations and profiteering energy companies. Meanwhile, he has retweeted content that is pro-EU, pro-Freedom of Movement, pro-Amnesty and pro-Antifa. He has retweeted Green Party MP Caroline

Lucas, Greta Thunberg and Extinction Rebellion, rail union leader Mick Lynch and, several times, Labour's left-wing Deputy Leader Angela Rayner. And he has used his account to raise awareness of homelessness and Britain's cost of living crisis.

And, in 2019, speaking to *Rolling Stone*, he said that 'from a young age, I've always held what could be considered a socialist viewpoint on the world. That's why I rail against inequality. What's wrong with the world is essentially inequality.' In the same interview, he explained his reluctance to be overtly political in the band. 'Behind the scenes, The Cure has always been politically active but usually pretty anonymously. It suits the way the band works, and everyone is much more comfortable with that rather than me being overt. They despair sometimes when I've had a few beers and I've done shows and I start spouting off. They're like, "Please, don't start." Because once I start, it's very hard to stop.' And he reaffirmed his location on the political spectrum: 'I don't see how anybody can be on the Right and be right. I think right of centre is always wrong, and that's as political as I get in public.'

He isn't the only Cure member who feels this way. In 2022, in response to the Conservative government's tax-cutting mini-budget, Roger O'Donnell tweeted 'I'm a top rate tax payer and I accuse this govt of vandalism. What's the point of having all the money in the world to live in an unjust cruel morally bankrupt society? Spread the wealth make everyone happy and healthy. Money doesn't trickle down it gets to the top and evaporates.'

So, apart from taking a stand against homophobia, recording a song for a human rights pressure group, playing a concert for Greenpeace and headlining a festival for CND, giving royalties to an anti-vivisection charity, denouncing the Conservatives and Republicans, calling for the redistribution of wealth, criticising Thatcher, Reagan, Johnson and Trump, berating bigots, demolishing the concept of monarchy, shaming profiteering multinationals, opposing Brexit and supporting trade unionists, anti-fascists and environmentalists, The Cure aren't a political band at all.

Polydor

Polydor Records is the big bad major **label** behemoth hiding behind the faux-indie facade of **Fiction**. Formed in Leipzig in 1913, it released classical and big band jazz recordings in its earlier years, before shifting focus to pop and rock. In 1972 it merged with Phonogram to create the mega-corporation PolyGram, of which Polydor then became a subsidiary imprint. The same year, Polydor UK was launched, with its iconic black rainbow logo set against a red background, and became a significant player in the British market via new bands such as Slade and acquisitions such as the Who. In the late 1970s, Polydor was one of the more forward-thinking majors in terms of signing new wave bands such as The Jam and **Siouxsie And The Banshees**, largely as a result of A&R man **Chris Parry**, who started his subsidiary label Fiction in 1978, just in time to snap up The Cure. For all Fiction's renegade capers, it was the conventional market might of Polydor, lurking in the background, which helped establish The Cure as global superstars.

Pornography

'I wanted to make a horrible record,' Robert Smith once said of The Cure's fourth album. He did not fail.

It was a beacon, a bleak 'un, a black sun, radiating darkness and despair like Albrecht Dürer's *Melencolia* from a place in the corner, just out of view. You didn't need to have heard the album *Pornography* by The Cure to experience it: its gravitational pull drew you in. While it may not be indisputably the finest example of their early work (there's a case to be made for *Faith*), nor their most accessible album (*The Head On The Door*), nor their most complete (*Kiss Me, Kiss Me, Kiss Me*), nor their most unified and consistent (*Disintegration*), *Pornography* was to become their most revered, talismanic release. Eventually.

In order to understand *Pornography*, it's instructive to examine the immediate background to it. The exhaustion of the world tour to promote *Faith*, their grief at the recent deaths of **Lol Tolhurst**'s mother and Robert Smith's grandmother, and a general sense of things falling apart all fed into the aggression and nihilism of *Pornography*. Smith was entering a 'manic stage', he recalled in *Ten Imaginary Years*. 'I was due for a break. Too much of everything, no respite. I had no control whatsoever over what I was doing.' Added to this was a frustration with The Cure's reputation in some quarters as mere fashionable bedroom miserabilists. 'A lot of people were calling us a long raincoat band,' said **Simon Gallup** later, 'and I wanted to go out and prove them wrong.'

The writing process began in September 1981, during a month's break between the North American and European legs of the gruelling, hundred-and-nineteen-date Picture Tour. Robert borrowed a drum machine from Lol, and began experimenting at home for six days, working on the music to what would become 'The Figurehead' and 'Cold'. He then decamped to **Steve Severin**'s house in London for a **druggy** sojourn which unlocked the lyrical part of his brain. 'The songs on *Pornography*,' he recalled in **Cure News**, 'were written either stream of consciousness (streams of extreme drunkenness!!) on an old typewriter in my bedroom at home in **Crawley**, or on scraps of yellow paper on hallucinating early mornings walking through and around horrible bits of London in cold December 1981. They range from acutely personal observations on my immediate surroundings and friends to general rants against the futility of everything and everyone, back to the horrors going on inside . . .' (In the same piece, Smith concedes that it's very difficult for him to explain the songs, 'as even within any verse of any one, there are several layers of logically unconnected ideas . . .')

On 3 December the year's touring commitments ended with a show at Hammersmith Palais, by which time '**One Hundred Years**' and 'The Figurehead' had become established parts of the band's live set. They immediately began working full band demos at the Windmill in Surbiton. Robert was first, then Lol joined him, then Simon. Later they decamped to Rhino Studios at Pippbrook Mill in Dorking, a listed building which had stood for nine hundred years, where they were filmed performing 'The Figurehead' by French **television** show Megahertz.

Having recorded all three of their previous albums at **Morgan Studios**, it was time for a change of scenery. For the sessions proper, in January 1982, **Chris Parry** booked them for four weeks in RAK Studios, built in 1976 by legendary RAK Records supremo Mickie Most inside a former Victorian schoolhouse in St John's Wood, and previously associated mainly with pop acts like Kim Wilde and Hot Chocolate. (Most observed proceedings from the safety of his glass-walled office, sipping a drink from

his globe-shaped cabinet, and at one point loaned them the guitar Jimmy Page used on Led Zeppelin's 'Stairway To Heaven'.)

As well as a change of scenery, it was time for a change of **producer**. The relationship between Smith and **Mike Hedges** during *Faith* had been strained, and Hedges was busy with **Siouxsie And The Banshees**' *A Kiss In The Dreamhouse*, so the parties amicably split. The band's original choice to replace him was Kraftwerk and Neu! producer Conny Plank, who they met, but that plan fell through. (In a twist of fate, subsequent long-term Cure producer **David M. Allen** would later acquire Plank's mixing desk for his own studio.) Parry took them to meet several other producers, his own preference being Colin Thurston who had engineered **David Bowie**'s '*Heroes*' and Iggy Pop's *Lust For Life*, produced Magazine's *Secondhand Daylight* and The Human League's *Reproduction*, and had just scored a major hit with Duran Duran's debut.

Smith, however, preferred a younger candidate: twenty-two-year-old **Phil Thornalley**, who had engineered *All Mod Cons* by Chris Parry's **Polydor** signings The Jam, as well as the first two Psychedelic Furs albums (a major plus for Robert, who had become obsessed with The Furs' drum sound). Thornalley was unfamiliar with The Cure's work, having only heard '**Killing An Arab**' (which, he admitted in *Ten Imaginary Years*, he deemed 'a good song but too tricksy for my taste'). However, he accepted the offer, and *Pornography* was to be his first album-length production job, assisted by American-born engineer Mike Nocito, later a member of the very awful (Thornalley-produced) pop group Johnny Hates Jazz.

The relationship between Thornalley and Smith was fractious. To begin with, by Smith's own admission, Thornalley was nicer and more polite than he needed to be, 'because I was anything but'. However, Thornalley was not a yes-man, and dared to challenge Smith, for example by telling him he didn't like Smith's guitar sound. 'His guitar style was his pride and joy,' Thornalley later recalled, 'and perhaps I shocked him, I don't know . . . When you're used to being flattered, it's always a good idea to have someone tell you what they really think.' Furthermore, Thornalley wouldn't put up with Smith's lack of punctuality. They clashed, too, over the album's sound. 'I thought he was making it too nice,' Smith told *Uncut* in 2000. 'I wanted it to be completely unlistenable. I thought it was the culmination of everything I'd done since I left school. I thought it was my grand moment and in the course of making it I was going to die.'

Smith did everything within his power to fulfil the prophecy of an early death. The excessive consumption of alcohol and drugs during the *Pornography* sessions is the stuff of legend. 'I must confess that I don't remember making a lot of *Pornography*,' Smith told Joe Gore of *Guitar Player* in 1992. 'We probably drank and took more drugs than we should have – an interesting process, but one that would kill me now . . . I went a bit weird for a while.' As he recalled in *Cure News* in 1998, 'I discovered the notion of massive quantities of very serious drugs . . . Me and Simon egged each other on to lower and lower depths.'

They ran up a huge tab with the local off-licence, and didn't throw away any of their empties, resulting in a 'can mountain' or 'beer sculpture' in the corner of the room, like an alcoholic art installation. (A photo kept by Lol shows the beginnings of the mountain, consisting mainly of Watney's, Guinness, and Carling Black Label.)

The drinkers weren't only the band and their entourage. There were frequent visitors, including their old keyboardist Matthieu Hartley, Associates including former Cure bassist Michael Dempsey, and the Banshees, with whose bassist Steve Severin The Cure frontman was very close. This closeness led to resentment on the part of Simon Gallup, who considered himself Smith's best friend and closest confidant, contributing to tension between Smith and Gallup throughout the sessions. As Tolhurst recalled in *Record Collector*, 'I think at the time, which was just before Simon left, there was a little bit of antagonism between Simon and Robert. But that's not always a bad thing, because it helped make a good record. Some of the best records are not made under the best circumstances.' Not that Robert cared who he was alienating. 'At the time, I lost every friend I had, everyone, without exception,' he later told *Mojo*. 'I was incredibly obnoxious, appalling, self-centred.' He wasn't the only one. 'Around the time of *Pornography*,' Gallup later told Johnny Black, 'I think we were an evil bunch of bastards'.

To save on hotel bills, the band were staying at Fiction HQ, a half-hour Tube ride across North West London. Robert slept in a 'nest' behind the sofa created by attaching a blanket to the wall with drawing pins to form a makeshift tent, and became annoyed by the drunken antics of Lol, Simon and

friend Gary Biddles (soon to become a fully-fledged member of The Cure's crew).

In classic Cure style, work was mainly nocturnal. A typical day would begin with the band waking up, taking acid, going to the local pub for a few drinks until the hallucinations were manageable, then heading to the studio to record. 'It was a pretty intense time,' Lol told *Record Collector*. 'We did a lot of recording at night. There wasn't much daylight, and I think that contributed to the atmosphere.' On some nights, Smith was in too much of a 'strange place' to function, leaving Tolhurst to tell Thornalley, 'Maybe we won't record today, we'll go home and see you in a day or two . . .'

Somehow, from amid this mayhem, an album emerged. For Thornalley it was, as he posted on Instagram on the album's fortieth anniversary, 'my first chance to show my own sonic influences like Todd Rundgren's *A Wizard, A True Star* album', and to experiment with 'studio techniques like squashing the drums with compression and using microphones at an unprescribed distance to the source, cranking the tone controls to create harshness, hyper clarity or mud'. The band, too, were venturing outside their comfort zones. For the first time, all three members are credited with at least some keyboards. Robert played cello on one track. Lol had special drumsticks made, thicker in the middle, for added power, and borrowed a ten-inch military snare from John Bradbury of The Specials. He also bought finger cymbals and a very loud Chinese cymbal which was used extensively. Smith and Gallup introduced bigger, more powerful Peavey amps.

And they made use of other techniques whose impact was more psychological than acoustic. 'I know for a fact that we recorded some of the songs in the toilets,' Robert later told *Rolling Stone*, 'to get a really horrible feeling, because the toilets were dirty and grim. Simon doesn't remember any of that, but I have a photo of me sitting on a toilet, in my clothes, trying to patch up some of the lyrics. It's a tragic photo.'

They also deliberately deluged their minds with the horrors they would pour out onto the record. 'We immersed ourselves in the more sordid side of life, and it did have a very detrimental effect on everyone in the group. We got hold of some very disturbing films and imagery to kind of put us in the mood. Afterwards, I thought, "Was it really worth it?" We were only in our really early twenties, and it shocked us more than I realised – how base people could be, how evil people could be.'

Although it contained only eight songs – the same number as *Faith* – it was The Cure's longest album to date, at forty-three minutes and thirty seconds. The first track, at six minutes forty-three seconds, was the longest. 'One Hundred Years', a song so significant that it merits its own entry in this book, begins with a line so cartoonishly depressing that it's almost camp: 'It doesn't matter if we all die . . .'

The album doesn't cheer up much from there on in.

It's followed by the echo-overloaded 'A Short-Term Effect', described by Tolhurst on Tim's Twitter Listening Party as 'swirling psychedelia, hallucinatory in its quality'. It had two main influences. One, as Robert confirmed in *Cure News*, was 'a drug and its effect – short term, I thought.' The other was a book he'd read (see **Madness** for full details) in which a mental patient drew charcoal illustrations of strange figures who come to life in his nightmares, hence the line 'a charcoal face bites my hand'.

Track three is the clattering lead single '**The Hanging Garden**' (which has its own entry), and Side 1 is rounded off by a track almost as breathtaking as 'One Hundred Years'. Driven by a slow, steady drum tattoo from Tolhurst, 'Siamese Twins' is The Cure at their most sombre. The imagery is nightmarish ('push a blade into my hands', 'worms eat my skin'), and is intended to evoke, Robert said in *Ten Imaginary Years*, 'the ugliness of love'. Its depiction of human codependency is entirely negative and pessimistic. In *Cure News*, Smith connected it to the song directly before it. '"The Hanging Garden" is something like about the purity and hate of animals fucking, and I think "Siamese Twins" is about the hate and purity of people fucking too.' On Tim's Twitter Listening Party, Tolhurst spoke of his own contribution to the song. 'I admire Sylvia Plath's work. To me, she is among the greatest American writers and poets. My lyrical contributions to "Siamese Twins" reflect that admiration.' Another intriguing reading of 'Siamese Twins' is the theory that it is about losing your virginity to a prostitute. This, if true, makes it a companion song to 'Next' by Jacques Brel (subsequently Scott Walker and, later still, Alex Harvey), with the anguished cry 'Is it always like this?' – a line Lol claims as one of his own – in place of 'NEXT!'

'The Figurehead' is heralded by another punishing drum pattern, a doom-laden descending chord structure and a pain-wracked vocal. The song was inspired by the 'grotesque skull sculpture' Smith had found in the disused asylum they'd used for the '**Charlotte Sometimes**' video shoot. 'I took it home to talk to – to confess to?' he told *Cure News*. 'And this song is about guilt.' The precise nature of that guilt is open to speculation. Is it about groupies and rock-star cheating? 'I can lose myself in Chinese art and American girls' would seem to point that way. In any case, whatever is gnawing away at him, it is causing him insomnia, and the guilt is evident in 'Too many secrets, too many lies' and the repeated 'I will never be clean again'. It ends, brilliantly, with just the drums. Smith has twice named 'The Figurehead' as one of his favourite Cure songs, and it was the opening song of their live set for nearly two years until it was usurped by 'Shake Dog Shake'. They performed it on BBC's *Oxford Road Show* along with 'One Hundred Years' (instead of their current singles).

'A Strange Day' begins with a low, ominous drone, recorded by Thornalley on several different channels then blended together, giving way to another solid, mechanical Tolhurst rhythm (*Pornography* is undeniably Lol's finest three quarters of an hour). The drummer later said he was aiming from Dennis Davis' sound on Bowie's *Low*, and that 'A Strange Day' was the closest he got. The lyric imagined The End Of The World, 1982 being peak Cold War nuclear paranoia: we all *knew* we were going to die in an atomic apocalypse, it was just a question of when, not if. Chris Parry, who considered the album 'a mess', said it was the only track that didn't bore him.

By the time of penultimate track 'Cold', with its looming cello intro (played by Smith) and Numanesque synths, it's hard to believe that anybody, let alone The Cure's own management team, saw *Pornography* as anything other than a masterpiece. 'Cold' was, Smith said, 'another song about another drug and its grip', and with its lines about crawling across a mirror, it's easy to make an educated guess as to which.

The title track, which ends the album, begins with a lengthy interlude of 'found sounds' (inspired by Brian Eno and David Byrne's *My Life In The Bush Of Ghosts*). Smith and Thornalley were flicking through television channels and found, serendipitously, a debate on pornography, involving Australian feminist writer Germaine Greer and *Monty Python*'s Graham Chapman. Their voices were distorted and partially spooled backwards, making their words sound more Russian than English. The song itself is almost anti-music, never quite settling into a set melodic pattern, and finally disintegrating into the entropy which had been incipient throughout the album. By the record's final lines, you realise that, for Smith, the jollity of the upcoming 'Lovecats' era wasn't just a luxury but a necessity: 'I must fight this sickness/ Find a cure/I must fight this sickness.' It was, Smith told *Cure News*, the last song he wrote for a while, and was 'fuelled by the same self-mockery, self-hate that burned in "One Hundred Years", but it is, if only very slightly, a little more hopeful than the others . . . I am escaping (I escaped) by blaming someone else. A murder or suicide? "I must fight this sickness" . . .'

The subsequent **Fourteen Explicit Moments** tour saw this incarnation of The Cure literally fall apart. Robert had had enough of being in a band, and of seeing more of Simon and Lol than he saw of **Mary**. 'We should have met in the middle but it had all gone too far and I knew this album would be the end. It was too violent.'

The album *Pornography* is aptly named: Smith had never been more naked before, and hasn't since. While his words may appear pretentious to some, there's precious little artifice: these are emotions laid bare. 'I thought of it as the way people are treated who don't conform to certain ideas and standards,' Smith later explained. 'To some people, someone obese in a newspaper with no clothes on is pornographic but, for me, it's the way people open the paper and laugh. It's not the subject which is pornographic but the discussion of it.' He elaborated, using an analogy from extreme porn. 'Seeing someone fucking a monkey doesn't particularly shock me. I get much more shocked by someone attacking someone else for doing it. For a lot of people, pornography is tied to old morals and tired values . . . But, after all this discussion, Simon still wanted to call it *Sex*!' Lol Tolhurst, on Tim's Twitter Listening Party, gave a slightly different take: 'To us, what was pornographic was war and destruction of lives by subjugation, power, and greed.'

The **artwork**, unlike that of *Faith*, was not designed by the yet-to-be-named **Parched Art** team of **Porl Thompson** and **Andy Vella**. Instead, it was designed by Ben Kelly using a blurred Michael Kostiff photo of the band's faces, the mauve filter making it look as though the members are burning in Hell. This blurring also continued the deliberate anonymity of the *Seventeen Seconds*, *Faith* and *Three Imaginary Boys* sleeves.

Released on 4 May 1982, *Pornography* broke The Cure into the UK Top 10 for the first time, reaching No.8 and staying on the chart for nine weeks, but was not an immediate hit with **critics**. One wrote that 'The title is appalling, the music inside is terribly icy the whole way', another that it 'plummets like a leaking submarine into depths unfathomable by man'. *Sounds*' Dave McCullough believed that 'Robert Smith seems locked in himself, a spiralling nightmare that leaves The Cure making a pompous-sounding music that is, when all's said and done, dryly meaningless.' In *Melody Maker*, Adam Sweeting wrote 'It's downhill all the way, into ever-darkening shadows . . . passing through chilly marbled archways to the final rendezvous with the cold comfort of the slab.' In *NME*, Richard Cook described it as 'devoid of any rhythmic impetus, chained to drumbeats and guitar lines of spiritless presence', and added that 'it was The Cure smashing into the buffers of a dead stop, almost terrifying in its emptiness, impenetrable and virtually unlistenable'; the same paper's Dave Hill called Smith's lyrics 'tiresomely self-analytical'. Three years later, *NME*'s David Quantick called it a 'Wall of Doom', singling out 'One Hundred Years' for the oft-repeated description 'Phil Spector in Hell'.

Rolling Stone's J. D. Considine argued that *Pornography* seemed 'stuck in the terminal malaise of adolescent existentialism' and 'comes off as the aural equivalent of a bad toothache', adding that 'It isn't the pain that irks, it's the persistent dullness.' In fellow American magazine *Trouser Press*, however, Charles McCardell hailed it as an 'uncompromising and challenging' album.

Unlistenability, of course, was Robert Smith's perverse intention, so it's no surprise that the album was received as such. Hindsight has been far kinder. *The Quietus* has described it, not disapprovingly, as 'a vision of hell', though pop historian Bob Stanley called it 'harrowing to the point of tedium'. *Ultimate Classic Rock* ranked it the second-best Cure album, *Far Out* magazine the third. Most serious Cure-ologists now place it there or thereabouts.

'A lot of the myth that surrounds *Pornography* came afterwards,' Lol Tolhurst later told *Record Collector*, 'when people had listened to it for a few years. I don't think at the time it was regarded as a milestone. For me, it's the LP which actually has the most feeling about what The Cure were. I think it was the best thing we did.'

With posterity, it is possible to view *Pornography* in its proper historical context: post-**Joy Division**, pre-**Sisters Of Mercy**, contemporaneous with the heydays of Bauhaus and Siouxsie, and easily the equal of any of those. It's generally viewed as a sacred text of **gothic** rock. A hugely influential record, its slow, mechanised drums, heavily treated guitars and sombre synths anticipated The Sisters' *Reptile House* EP, the darker works of **Depeche Mode** and the more reflective moments of Nine Inch Nails and Marilyn Manson. Its lyrical themes found echoes in the work of Nirvana's Kurt Cobain and, even more noticeably, Richey Edwards of Manic Street Preachers, whose singer and guitarist James Dean Bradfield has named *Pornography* as one of his favourite records. Its influence is easily audible on the Manics' own masterpiece *The Holy Bible*. (Interestingly, Smith repaid the compliment by choosing the Manics to play his **Meltdown Festival**.)

The album's reputation was enhanced in 2005 when a deluxe edition was released, prompting a slew of reappraisals. It came with an extra disc of demo versions, live tracks and rejected offcuts, mostly fumbling, rudimentary instrumentals of which only 'Temptation' might have become something more, of which 'All Mine', an improvised live track from Hammersmith, is the most interesting to Cure nerds, and of which 'Airlock: The Soundtrack' is the most perplexing, sounding like a bunch of children messing around in a sound-effects department and improvising on a broken piano for thirteen minutes. The album proper, however, had dated very well indeed, and was given another timely reissue on heavyweight **vinyl** in 2016.

The major players on the album itself have tended to look back upon it with mixed feelings. Reflecting on the mythology surrounding it in 2022, Phil Thornalley wrote 'The beer can mountain, days lost to LSD, a bag of Colombia's finest, a well-rehearsed band, an artist in peak focus – some, or all, of these things may be true . . .' Lol Tolhurst has argued that this 'big, monolithic slab of sound' was The Cure's apex as a three-piece.

Robert Smith delivered a beautiful piece of English understatement when explaining the album to MTV in 1990. 'Everyone gets a bit miserable in their early twenties. And that culminated in one of the most miserable albums ever made, which was the *Pornography* album.' The same year, in *Cure News*, he described it as an album 'that almost chokes on itself' and which 'remains a diary of one of my blackest times. But it's one of my favourites!!!' And, in the same publication eight years later, he called

it 'an incredible upswirl of mindless violence and aggression, mixed in with a complete disregard for everything and everyone else'.

Speaking to *Guitar Player* in 1992, he gave an interesting insight into the trauma the album could still trigger, ten years on. '*Pornography* reminds me of things I'd rather not be reminded of. I was quite out of sync, a bit disturbed. I knew then that Mary was the girl for me, because she had stuck by me. But everyone I know reaches a point where they throw out their arms and go berserk for a while; otherwise you never know what your limits are. I was just trying to find mine.'

Smith's best description of *Pornography*, however, is as blunt and to-the-point as the album's opening words. It was, he said, meant to be 'the ultimate "fuck off" record'.

Pope, Tim

The other genius in this story.

Timothy Michael Pope was born on 12 February 1956 to an affluent middle-class family (his parents were bankers) and grew up in Enfield, North London. He attended St Andrew's Primary School, followed by St Michael's Preparatory School, followed by Latymer Grammar School. While at Latymer, he studied the first-ever Film Studies O-Level and was profiled in the *Evening Standard* as 'Tim Pope, aged 17, who wants to be a film director'.

On Saturday mornings he attended the famed Hornsey College of Art, a hotbed of radical creativity where full-time students at around the same time included Adam Ant, Viv Albertine of The Slits, Gina Birch and Ana da Silva of The Raincoats, magazine designer Neville Brody and rock photographer Eric Watson.

Aged eighteen, Pope shot his first short film, *Voyage* (1973) on a 16mm Bolex camera. 'It cost about £20, and was surrealistic, a bit like Buñuel' he told the *Standard* at the time. He also followed a dog around various bombsites in Seven Sisters waiting for it to defecate, for another short film called *Canine Excrement*.

After leaving school he attended the even more famous Ravensbourne College of Art & Design in Bromley, where **David Bowie** had previously studied. It was here that he first put images to music, making a film for an old Frank Zappa track, 'I'm The Slime'.

He had a short spell as a bank clerk after Ravensbourne, but got his first job behind the camera working for HyVision, a company who media-trained politicians such as Chancellor of the Exchequer Denis Healey for television appearances, and would often visit 10 Downing Street. At the end of the working day, Pope would often illicitly borrow HyVision's equipment to film bands like The Specials and The Psychedelic Furs live in concert. In 1979, while still at HyVision, he met Alex McDowell, later a successful Hollywood production designer, and the two formed a strong creative partnership.

Pope's first major commission for making pop **videos** – though he prefers to call them 'films' – was with Soft Cell, shooting over a dozen promos for songs including 'Tainted Love', 'Bedsitter' and 'Say Hello, Wave Goodbye', most of which were laced together with footage which captured the now-vanished sleazy side of Soho to make the hugely entertaining full-length VHS *Non-Stop Exotic Video Show*, including the original banned version of 'Sex Dwarf' which featured chainsaws, meat, blood and actual people with dwarfism.

Pope's intention, he once said, was to do the very opposite of 'running down the corridors in suspenders' videos. His early efforts included Altered Images' 'I Could Be Happy', Bad Manners' 'Samson And Delilah', The Psychedelic Furs' 'Love My Way' and Wham!'s 'Young Guns (Go For It)', but it was his work with Soft Cell which caught the attention of The Cure, who were in the market for a decent director after getting their fingers burned with the clips for '**Charlotte Sometimes**' and '**The Hanging Garden**'.

As Pope told Ned Raggett in the *Quietus*, 'I think that my rather evil wit came in at the point when they were ready for an evil wit. Anyway, [Robert] was stripping the band down and we went for a more clinical approach. I do remember my first meeting with him, which was in Soho, and oh my God, if only I could see film footage from this meeting. He was quite shy and very thin and he had a pair of big trousers on with glinting, golden stripes. I remember this very clearly. I used to have an eye which was a bit off-centre. And he said [in later interviews] he met this director who had an eye off-centre, with a mad shirt and his fly was undone, and he thought, "This is the guy I want to work with."'

Pope's initial impression of Smith, he said in another interview, was of surprise. 'When I first met Robert I thought "This can't be the geezer who makes all these doomed-out records", because he was such a funny little chappy with that hair all stood up.'

The first of Pope's thirty-seven videos with The Cure was '**Let's Go To Bed**'. Filled with high symbolism and low comedy, it was shot at Pope's St John's Wood studios, loosely using a storyboard of The Cure's own making. Pope pushed Smith to *perform* for the first time in a video: 'I saw him as a clown – funny but also tragic.' (For a full description of that video, and all Tim Pope's Cure videos, see the individual *Curepedia* entry for each song.)

Tim Pope, and his company Glo, usually with production designer Alex McDowell, art director Richard Earl and assistants like Jamie Reid, formed a collaborative alliance with The Cure which was unprecedented and remains unsurpassed in pop. No video director and musical artist have created such a sustained run of excellence.

Highlights of his oeuvre with The Cure include the feline houseparty of '**The Lovecats**', the swinging-camera sock explosion of '**In Between Days**', the watery wardrobe shenanigans of '**Close To Me**', the poignant shadowplay of '**Boys Don't Cry**', the dizzy clifftop romanticism of '**Just Like Heaven**', the animal-suited choreography capers of '**Why Can't I Be You?**' and the (BRIT **Award**-winning) arachnid creepshow of '**Lullaby**', as well as his first longform live film, *The Cure In Orange*. 'Tim Pope always did something that was more arty, more clever, and much more original,' said Janice Long on the *Out of the Woods* documentary. 'You knew if a Cure single was coming out, you couldn't wait to see the video.'

In his interview with Ned Raggett, Pope said, 'People in the world of pop videos are not notoriously loyal. I mean, particularly these days when there's so much choice, which is why I don't really do them. But I had a fantastic rapport with the band and they were phenomenally loyal to me.'

Pope brought an element of surrealist strangeness as well as slapstick humour to the then-formulaic world of the pop video, changing the game forever with his inventive ideas. Although Pope didn't consider them as such. 'I wouldn't call them *ideas*', he told TV reporter Gaz Top, 'more a way of life. If people think I'm a nutter when I'm doing a shoot . . . that means it's a good shoot.'

During his first run as The Cure's favoured director (1982–1992), Pope continued to work with other artists. His most notable videos in this period include 'Safety Dance' by Men Without Hats (1983), 'Miss The Girl' and 'Right Now' by The Creatures (1983), '**Dear Prudence**', '**Swimming Horses**' and '**Dazzle**' by **Siouxsie And The Banshees** (1983–84), The Style Council's first eight videos including the homoerotic ear-stroking clip for 'Long Hot Summer' (1983) and a venture behind the Iron Curtain for 'Walls Come Tumbling Down' (1985), Queen's 'It's A Hard Life' (1984), Strawberry Switchblade's 'Since Yesterday' (1984), six videos for Talk Talk including 'It's My Life' (1984), ten for The The starting in 1987, two for **David Bowie** in 1988 and a third in 1990, The Bangles' 'Eternal Flame' (1988), 'Singing In The Shower' by Sparks & Les Rita Mitsouko (1988), Paul McCartney's 'This One' (1989) and two for Tin Machine in 1991, making Pope the first person from The Cure camp to work with both David Bowie and **Reeves Gabrels**.

Pope was a rakish, slender, elegantly dressed, almost aristocratic figure, and it was only a matter of time before he stepped round the other side of the camera and tried his hand at music. His reputation as an eccentric was cemented by his **Fiction**-released single 'I Want To Be A Tree', a piece of knowingly naïve, Anthony Newley/Syd Barrett-influenced outsider-pop whimsy. Its very literal video featured a naked Pope growing out of a tree trunk, sprouting bark and leaves. However, he also cobbled together an alternate version featuring guest appearances from many of his clients, including The Cure, The Style Council, Soft Cell, The Creatures and Paul Young.

By 1987 Pope's status as a director was such that he was being hired for lucrative commercial work such as the Magritte-inspired Tuborg 'Human Train' ad, while still being allowed free rein to express himself artistically. (However, he also made a perfectly sensible ad for Quality Solicitors – it wasn't *all* flying socks and bear suits in Pope-world.) His first television series, Jools Holland and Rowland Rivron's *Groovy Fellers*, followed in 1989.

Smith and Pope had nicknames for each other – Smiffy and Pap – and shared a certain off-kilter worldview. Smith considered Pope 'the most inventive director around', not at all unreasonably. 'He's similarly deranged, which helps', Smith told MTV's Nina Blackwood in 1983. On ITV's *Night Network*, Smith reflected on their early experiences of working together. 'He was much more wayward than people we were used to dealing with . . . He had a slightly more demented side to him. Which was good. He didn't treat us very seriously, which I liked as well.'

In *Ten Imaginary Years*, Pope said that Smith's imagery-rich **songwriting** style made The Cure the ideal band to work with. 'I liked Robert's lyrics

because they're like a spider's web. They're made up of clues. They never present things in an obvious way. It's perfect for film-making, because every phrase has a corresponding emphasis.' He also described them as 'willing fools' at video shoots. 'They're not proud at all,' he told MTV. 'They'll do anything.'

The sheer number of videos Pope made with The Cure allowed him to insert callbacks, little Easter eggs for attentive fans. 'Because I work with people time and time again,' he told Ned Raggett, 'you can get different feelings, different flows, between the videos . . . With The Cure we've done that a lot: we start with an idea, then we restate that later on in another video. For example, doing a 360-degree spin around a band member: **Porl Thompson** in "In Between Days", Robert in "The Lovecats".'

In the nineties, Pope began making Hitchcockian cameos in his own videos, such as '**Never Enough**' and '**Friday I'm In Love**'. The latter proved to be his last Cure video for many years. The director made his move towards the movie world. In 1993 he made a thirty-one-minute short film called *Phone*, about a prank call. In 1996 his first full-length feature **film**, *The Crow: City of Angels* (featuring a song by The Cure), was released and became a No.1 box-office hit in the US. However, it is not a time upon which Pope looks back fondly. 'I had pissed off to Hollywood and had a horrendous experience with a certain Mr Weinstein,' he told Ned Raggett, 'making a movie I wasn't too pleased about.'

His return to The Cure fold came in 1997. 'I'd been away for a few years,' he told Raggett, 'and then they invited me back to do this video, and I remember the band all saying, "Thank God you're back."' Pope's comeback Cure video, for '**Wrong Number**', proved to be a one-off.

Following this reunion, he continued to work on music videos including The Darkness' 'One Way Ticket To Hell And Back' (2005), Kaiser Chiefs' 'Every Day I Love You Less And Less' (2005) and Amanda Palmer's 'The Killing Type' (2012). He also directed *Coming Home*, an ITV documentary about the actress Sheridan Smith.

In 2018 he worked with The Cure once again on the concert film *Anniversary*, capturing their Hyde Park concert from that summer, which was shown in over 1,500 cinemas as well as being included in the **40 Live** box.

After that, Pope's various projects – some of them interrupted by Covid lockdown – have included proposed documentaries about The The and Tim

Burgess, as well as a self-written feature film called *Drone* with *Crow* star Vincent Perez.

Most tantalising of all is a planned documentary on The Cure, covering their entire career. 'Robert Smith is giving me access to 50 boxes of film,' Pope told *Variety*, 'which have never been seen before, of the early Cure days. I want to make a film like *Goodfellas* where Robert is narrating the film in a first-person way, and it is like crazy, and we are on this journey.'

If there's one Cure documentary you would bet on not being canine excrement, this is the one.

Pre-Cure bands

Of all the creatures that were made, man is the most detestable. Of the entire brood he is the only one – the solitary one – that possesses malice. That is the basest of all instincts, passions, vices – the most hateful. He is the only creature that has pain for sport, knowing it to be pain.
– Mark Twain

In 1983, explaining The Cure's origins to MTV, Robert Smith claimed 'There were fifteen of us at one point, then we settled on three.' It sounds like a wild exaggeration. They weren't Dexys Midnight Runners. They weren't The Polyphonic Spree. However, if you add together each recorded individual member of each pre-Cure configuration, it comes to at least fourteen, so it's not far off the truth.

Robert's first attempt at playing in a band in his **youth** happened in the Smith family home in **Crawley** circa 1969, when he was just ten years old. His younger sister Janet was learning to play the piano. His older brother Richard could play **guitar**. Robert had been learning piano, but had switched to guitar. Together with a few of Richard's friends, they formed an ensemble called The Crawley Goat Band playing, as Robert recalled during the MTV Icons special, 'weird jug-band music'.

By the time he was thirteen, he had combined with friends from Notre Dame Middle School to form a band under the absolutely classic 'we are serious' seventies band name of The Obelisk, with the **line-up** of Marc Ceccagno (lead guitar), **Michael Dempsey** (guitar), Robert Smith (piano), Alan Hill (bass) and **Laurence Tolhurst** (percussion). Towards the end of their time there, in April 1972, the Obelisk played their one and only gig at a school function, performing

what Tolhurst remembers as a 'very strange' piece of music. The nucleus of the **Three Imaginary Boys** line-up of The Cure was in place.

In the autumn of 1972, Dempsey, Smith and Tolhurst moved on to secondary school at St Wilfrid's Comprehensive, where they were simply known as The Group ('because it was the only one at school so we didn't need a name'), although they toyed with the idea of calling themselves The Brats' Club (a reference to the Evelyn Waugh novel *A Handful of Dust*).

By early 1976, they were starting to take things a little more seriously. On 23 January 1976 a reconfigured line-up of Ceccagno, Smith, Dempsey, a drummer called Graham and a singer known to history only as 'Graham's brother' held the first of many regular jamming sessions, usually on a Thursday, at St Edward the Confessor's Church Hall in Crawley. 'We had no aims . . . It was just something to do, something to talk about,' said Dempsey in *Ten Imaginary Years*. 'I think it all came about because Marc Ceccagno wanted to be a guitar hero,' Smith later said. 'Michael had a bass, I had got hold of a guitar and our first drummer, Graham, had a drum kit. His brother had an amp and a mic, so he sang.'

After a few weeks their old friend Lol Tolhurst began showing up to watch, and managed to gently evict Graham from the drum stool. It helped that Graham's brother was no good at singing. 'One evening we decided he couldn't stay,' Robert remembered. 'He just couldn't sing.' His replacement was Martin Creasy, a journalist for the *Crawley Observer* who had previously worked at L&H Cloake, the local record shop, and who they hired partly because they thought he might be able to get them a review in the paper, and partly because he could do a decent David Cassidy impression. 'And the same night,' Robert recalled, 'around the end of April, Lol arrived and convinced us he could be the drummer. The problem was, he didn't have a drum kit! But we took him on anyway . . .'

According to Michael Dempsey, the band had to teach Lol to play. On the *Curious Creatures* podcast, Dempsey remembers asking Lol to join the band on Three Bridges station, with the intention of taking him to Keyboard Harmony in Redhill to set him up with a kit. At first, Lol wasn't sure about committing to a band, as he didn't want to fail his Chemistry A-level, but he took a chance. The band, who Robert later remembered as 'sort of a sub-metal punk group, with Michael Dempsey, Laurence and two other blokes', settled on the punkier name of Malice, though a photo from the time shows five not very punk-looking longhairs in checked shirts and flared jeans.

As well as using St Edward's, the band would rehearse *chez* Smith. In the long hot summer of 1976, Robert's parents went away on holiday, leaving Robert in charge of the house. He immediately held a week-long 'band camp'. Mr and Mrs Smith had built an extension onto the home as a party room for family get-togethers, but instead – as Lol Tolhurst told BBC Radio 4 – the band moved in for three years and didn't leave.

The family owned a Hammond organ with a tape recorder built in, which proved useful for the band's rehearsals in that summer of '76. When they weren't rehearsing, Lol remembered on *Curious Creatures*, they would drink, eat fish and chips, raid the record collection of Robert's older brother Richard (whom they nicknamed 'The Guru') including the Mahavishnu Orchestra, Nils Lofgren, The Beatles, The Rolling Stones, **Pink Floyd** and Ray Charles to play on a portable record player, go down to The Fox Revived pub in Three Bridges for a few pints, return to Robert's to play for another few hours, then crash out. (Lol recalls sleeping naked under a Persian rug.)

By October 1976, Malice were practising three nights a week, but without Marc Ceccagno, whose musical interests lay in the direction of jazz-rock complexity, leading him to depart and form his own band Amulet, another absolutely classic 'we are serious' seventies band name.

Ceccagno's replacement was local hot-shot guitarist **Porl Thompson**. Thompson had also worked at L&H Cloake, like singer Martin Creasy, but was known to the band because Lol Tolhurst was dating Thompson's sister, Carol, and Porl had started turning up to rehearsals. 'He was working at Gatwick Airport,' Robert remembered in *Ten Imaginary Years*, 'and he used to turn up in his waiter's uniform.'

The five-piece Malice line-up of Smith, Dempsey, Tolhurst, Thompson and Creasy – described by Dempsey as 'The Cure's early provocative incarnation', began writing their own material, in addition to the cover versions at which Thompson, who had played in cabaret bands, was already adept. Their first public appearance was at (Robert's father's employers) Upjohn Pharmaceuticals' Christmas Party on 18 December 1976 in the minstrel's gallery at Worth Abbey, Crawley. However, for one night only, the name Malice was suspended. 'It was an acoustic set,' Robert later explained, 'and we sat on the floor and

played bongos. We weren't called Malice for this one actually because, in order to get the booking, we had to pretend we were a folk band!'

The second Malice gig is far better-documented. On 20 December 1976 they played an infamous concert at St Wilfrid's Comprehensive School. As a flyer on Michael Dempsey's **website** shows, it was billed as a 'Special Christmas Bumper Bundle Party', featuring Malice, another band called Bootleg (who no one remembers actually playing) and 'speshul guest stars' Amulet, Marc Ceccagno's band, with an admission fee of 30p. Next to a cartoon of a guitarist, drawn by Porl, is the brilliant caption 'No Smooths Please', a vain attempt to pre-emptively weed out townies/normals and avert any trouble.

The booking only happened because the band had told the headmaster they were a pop group, but omitted to mention that Robert Smith was a member 'because he hated me!' By the end of the night, the headmaster would have plenty of reasons to hate the whole lot of them.

Most of the band had dressed up for the occasion. Lol, for example, wore a full-length black studded catsuit and black eye **make-up**, inspired by Alice Cooper. However, Martin Creasy, for reasons best known to himself, turned up in a brown three-piece suit, a Manchester United scarf and a motorbike helmet.

In a famously shambolic show, which began with Thin Lizzy's 'Jailbreak', they performed **covers** of **David Bowie**'s 'Suffragette City', **Jimi Hendrix**'s 'Foxy Lady', as well as two 'triptychs' of their own songs, including '**A Night Like This**'. Eyewitness Vincent Rees, on The Cure Concerts website, is particularly scathing about Creasy, describing him as 'the monotone vocalist'. Creasy, in his defence, says 'I was attempting to sing through a crash helmet, and I'm sure we were all rather the worse for wear . . .' He also admits, 'We only knew about four songs when I sang there, and I didn't know the songs that well. It couldn't have been very good.'

There were mixed reactions from the crowd: some of them left, and others rioted. As Michael Dempsey puts it, '300 people came, 200 left, and the rest got up on stage!' It all escalated further when Lol started singing 'Wild Thing' by The Troggs. 'Porl felt so humiliated he hit him,' recalled Dempsey in *Ten Imaginary Years*, 'and Martin fled with the words "This is shit!" No one's seen him since . . . We immediately broke up the group!'

For Lol, there are some positive memories of the St

Wilfrid's show. He considers it the first real gig (as the previous one was unplugged and acoustic). 'The Cure sound was started!', he tweeted on its anniversary. For Robert, however, the aftermath was worse: he was temporarily thrown out of school. And for Martin Creasy it was worse still: 'I remember it being a rather humiliating experience,' he said on Cure Concerts, 'as just about every musician I'd ever worked with in Crawley was in the audience that night. I woke up the next day thinking "That's it, I'll have to leave town." I did, within a month. I moved to join a band in Hampshire, returning only to pick up my little 60-watt Traynor PA which Robert and the boys had completely blown out at the famous Crawley bandstand gig.' (Of which more later.)

With the temporarily slimmed-down four-piece line-up of Smith, Dempsey, Tolhurst and Thompson, the band spent January 1977 rehearsing and sitting around in Robert's parents' kitchen – the one with the drip-drip-drip tap from '**10.15 Saturday Night**' – trying to come up with a new name in order to distance themselves from the Malice/St Wilfrid's debacle. Using William Burroughs' cut-up technique, they pulled fragments of their own lyrics from a hat, and came up with Easy Cure (from a song written by Lol).

For a short while, they tried out a singer called **Gary X**, but didn't play a gig with him. Next, in April 1977 came the cinematically named Peter O'Toole, whom Robert remembers in *Ten Imaginary Years* as 'a demon footballer and Bowie fan who'd never sung before'. With this new line-up, Easy Cure continued to rehearse in the Smith family home.

The first Easy Cure gig took place as Robert's belated eighteenth birthday party at St Edward's. It was the first gig at which Robert could legally drink **alcohol**, and he evidently made the most of it. 'I remember nothing at all,' he later said, 'so it must have been good . . .'

On 6 May 1977 Easy Cure played the Rocket in Crawley when Amulet pulled out. Their set, a mix of their own material and covers (including 'Locomotive Breath' by Jethro Tull) clearly hit the spot, as it proved to be the first of thirteen shows at that pub. Before long they were attracting crowds of three hundred people 'because there was no one in Crawley who'd ever done anything like what we were doing.' Robert later theorised that Easy Cure had 'a really drunken following, and we were really just a focal point, an excuse for people to go out, get really drunk and

smash the place up.' Another factor behind their pulling power, he believes, was the star on guitar. 'Whenever we played, we all thought it was awful – there was loads of feedback and you could never hear anything except Porl's guitar. That's the only reason we kept getting rebooked, because he became the local guitar hero.'

After further gigs at the Railway Inn, Redhill and the Rocket again (which is now, confusingly, known as the Railway), Easy Cure were booked to play a Peace Concert (see **Politics**) on the bandstand in Crawley shopping centre on 3 July 1977. The concert, organised by activists James and Consuelo Duggan, was intended to promote peace in Northern Ireland. 'We just wanted people to come along, listen to the music and think about peace. Not just in Northern Ireland but everywhere.' Whether they thought about peace will never be known, but about three hundred people turned up on a hot Sunday afternoon to see Easy Cure and a few other bands. Robert's father Alex filmed the show, thus bequeathing to history the earliest existing footage of any incarnation of The Cure. An excerpt, showing them playing a thrashy punk number called 'I Wish I Was Your Mother', with an open-shirted O'Toole on vocals and a cap-sleeved Smith on guitar, while a few curious hippies and teenagers loiter in front of the local Rumbelows and Halfords, some of them pogoing, can be seen at the start of the *Staring At The Sea: The Images VHS*.

There was also, according to *Curious Creatures*, another open-air show that summer at 'Nobstock', held on a golf course next to a pub in Earlswood to coincide with the Queen's Silver Jubilee, where they played to '10 or 20 people'. A silent twenty-second clip from that day shows them loading their gear into a van that Michael Dempsey had bought from a pig farmer.

What Robert, Michael and Lol should have been doing in the summer of '77, Tolhurst later reflected, was getting ready to go to university, like their older brothers. But punk had hit them hard, and they turned down their uni places (Robert, for example, was lined up to go to the University of Sussex), sticking around instead in the annex behind the Smiths' house to carry on rehearsing.

Next-door neighbour Wendy Paton remembers them thrashing away. On the Crawley Museum website, she writes: 'Robert's father had a studio built in his garden so that Robert and his friends could practise their music. They were trying to form a band and his father gave him a year to succeed. The studio was right under our bedroom window so we were frequently woken by their music well into the night . . . [including] strains of what turned out to be their first hit, "**Boys Don't Cry**" coming from the studio.'

Peter O'Toole played another run of gigs at the Rocket, St Edward's and the Lakeside Inn, playing his final Cure show on 11 September 1977 before flying out the next day to live in a kibbutz in Israel.

Robert, who had already handled a few lead vocals such as 'Foxy Lady' at the Peace Concert, took over as Easy Cure's singer, on the basis that they'd already had about four 'useless frontmen' and he couldn't be any worse. As he later told *Musician* magazine, 'When we started, and were playing in pubs, I wasn't the singer . . . I was the drunk rhythm guitarist who wrote all these weird songs. We went through about five different singers – they were fucking useless, basically. I always ended up thinking, "I could do better than this." I mean, I hated my voice, but I didn't hate it more than I hated everyone else's voice. So I thought, "If I can get away with that, I can be the singer." I've worked on that basis ever since.'

Another Peace Concert, which couldn't decide whether it was called Peace Party or Peace Jam, took place on the same bandstand on 9 October 1977 (it must have been freezing), with The Cure headlining. The poster, archived at Michael Dempsey's website, is covered in swirling hippie symbols, moons and stars and sponsored by Pick'N'Save Cash'N'Carry – 'an early example', he says, 'of absence of creative control in poster art.' (Dempsey believes *this* is the concert shown on *Staring At The Sea*, but almost all other sources disagree.)

Earlier that year, Robert Smith had replied to an advert in the music press from the record label **Hansa** looking for new bands. Easy Cure were one of the winners, and travelled to London twice on 11 October and 15 November to record sessions at **Morgan Studios**. (The details of that ultimately dissatisfying relationship are detailed under the entry for Hansa.)

Meanwhile, they carried on gigging. On 16 October 1977 they played a **charity** show at Felbridge Village Hall in aid of the Arthritis and Rheumatism Council. The flyer, designed by Robert, features a Porl Thompson illustration of a monkey-like being dressed as a school lollipop man who Dempsey believes is 'almost certainly Lol Tolhurst'. The support act is Mr Wrong's Rock Disco, actually a schoolfriend with a turntable and a limited collection of Led Zeppelin and Lynyrd Skynyrd records. Admission is 'a mere 30p' and there is 'malheureusement no bar!' For Dempsey,

this was 'a clear indicator that you came with you own supply', adding that Robert recalls, predictably, 'the police intervened'.

Easy Cure were back at St Edward's Church Hall on 28 October 1977, again in aid of the Arthritis and Rheumatism Council. In a bit of Surrey–Sussex rivalry, the **artwork** poked fun at punk band Sham 69 with the warning 'DON'T BE HYPED' and, underneath, an *NME* cutting which claimed that 'Before becoming Sham 69 . . . the boys in the band were known as Jimmy and the Ferrets when they'd mime to Bay City Rollers hits'. An alternate version of the poster promised 'Good music all night', signing off 'Rockingly yours'. There were free badges for the first fifty people, featuring a picture of a man vomiting on a fishing trip who was either Frank Bell of **Cult Hero** fame or **crew** member Brian Adsett, depending whether you believe Michael Dempsey or **John Taw**. By now they were charging 40p – a 33% hike from the Felbridge and St Wilfrid's gigs. But at least **Ticketmaster** weren't sticking a fee on top of that.

The band rounded off 1977 with shows at Effingham Park Hotel, Lakers Hotel in Redhill, another Upjohn Christmas Party, and another notoriously chaotic show on New Year's Eve which summoned unwelcome memories of Malice a year earlier. Michael Dempsey's brother-in-law Richard, who had unilaterally appointed himself manager and printed up business cards reading 'Easy Cure for all occasions', had booked them a gig at Orpington General Hospital's staff New Year's Eve party for a fee of £20. Their set now included original material such as '10.15 Saturday Night' and '**Killing An Arab**', but that wasn't what a restless crowd of NHS workers in their forties and fifties wanted to hear at their big festive bash. In the interval, the band quickly learned cheesy pop standard 'Tie A Yellow Ribbon' by Dawn, which Porl used to play in his cabaret days, in the hope that it would placate the crowd in the second half. The tactic didn't work, and bottles were thrown. Robert got into a fight with disgruntled patrons, and someone attacked them in the car park wanting a refund. Michael's brother-in-law destroyed the rest of his five hundred Easy Cure cards after that, and stepped down.

On 19 February 1978 Easy Cure played a show with local punk band **Lockjaw** at the Rocket. Lockjaw's audience trashed the venue, but the bands bonded. A couple of months later, Lockjaw and Easy Cure met up for drinks, and carried on from 5 p.m. until 2 a.m., becoming good friends. One member of

Lockjaw in particular would play an enormous role in the other band's future: bassist **Simon Gallup**.

On 29 March 1978 Easy Cure severed all ties with Hansa after the label refused to release 'Killing An Arab' as a single, sending them back to square one, until Simon's older brother **Ric Gallup** gave them £50 to record some more demos.

Easy Cure played their final show on 22 April 1978 at Montefiore Institute Hall, Crawley (a set which included 'Subway Song', which would survive onto *Three Imaginary Boys*). After that show, Porl Thompson left for the first time. He'd been dating Robert's sister Janet, and often disappeared during rehearsals to be with her. Furthermore, Porl's ornate guitar style didn't suit the direction the other three wanted to take. 'The songs were getting starker, more minimal, and I was beginning to loathe Porl's lead guitar,' Robert explained in *Ten Imaginary Years*. 'The music was in the process of changing,' recalled Porl, 'and, as I was known as the fast guitar player, when punk came along I became obsolete.'

And then there were three. Sending out the demo tapes to every major label in London, Robert wrote 'We are The Cure. We have no commitments. We would like a recording contract. Listen to the tape.'

The thinking behind the name change was that Easy Cure sounded 'a bit hippyish, a bit American-sounding, a bit West Coast', and The Cure sounded sharper, more punk. There was another reason. 'We arrived in an era of negatively named bands,' Robert told Ted Mico of *Spin* in 1989, 'and the name The Cure was a positive statement. We wanted to provide some hope for people by seeing our name in the charts.'

And that they did.

Presence

Presence was the band **Lol Tolhurst** formed in 1990 in the wake of his acrimonious ejection from The Cure, with the assistance of assorted Cure personnel and associates past and future.

Old **Crawley** friend **Gary Biddles**, a former Cure **crew** member and singer with **Fools Dance**, was lead vocalist. **Michael Dempsey** was an early member, co-writing some of the songs and playing on early demos, but left before any records were released. Dempsey's replacement on bass was **Roberto Soave**, who had played with **Associates** and **Shelleyan Orphan** and would later stand in for **Simon Gallup** on a Cure tour, and later still, join **Babacar** with Caroline Crawley from Shelleyan Orphan and **Boris Williams**. Even **Porl Thompson** played some guitar for Presence at one point, although he did not know, according to *Cure News*, that Tolhurst was about to launch a **lawsuit** against The Cure. To rescue Presence from being a supergroup entirely comprised of people who have their own entries in this book, their shifting line-up also included keyboardist Chris Youdell, formerly of shoulderpad rockers Then Jerico, drummer Alan Burgess, formerly of The Complaints, and guitarist Rob Steen, another future Babacar member, who also looked after the **artwork** and later illustrated Ricky Gervais's *Flanimals* books.

The first sighting that the wider public got of Presence was a report on BBC music programme *Rapido* in March 1991, on which presenter Antoine de Caunes described Lol Tolhurst as a 'chubby little music mischief-maker' when introducing an item from Lol's studio-cum-farm base in Devon where he and his bandmates were filmed miming in the open air, rehearsing in a barn and walking around carrying a chainsaw.

In the interview, Lol was asked about the inevitable Cure comparisons. 'We're all strong enough to go through that,' he said, 'and what we do is strong enough to wipe that out of the way.' It didn't help matters, though, that they literally released a single called 'Act Of Faith'.

The debut single from Presence, showcased on *Rapido*, was 'In Wonder', and it was typical of their material: a technopop undercarriage with busy beats, indie-pop guitars, and strained, high-pitched vocals. It sounded somewhat dated, like something you might have heard on the Janice Long show eight or nine years earlier.

Presence released two albums. The first, *Inside*, was recorded in London and released on their own Reality label. The second, *Closer*, released by Reality in 1994, was recorded at Sound City in Los Angeles with former Smiths producer John Porter, who had once played in Roxy Music on the *For Your Pleasure* album and the subsequent tour. (Porter wasn't the only person connected with Presence to have played with Roxy Music: Michael Dempsey also had a spell as Roxy tour bassist in the eighties.)

In the **US** the first Presence album was released by Chicago-based label Smash via Island, but Smash declined to release the second. Perhaps because they'd noticed, unlike Presence, that *Closer* was already a **Joy Division** album title.

Presence were neither a commercial nor a critical success. *Melody Maker*'s Andrew Mueller, who interviewed The Cure on a US tour in 1992, reported that Robert Smith gleefully recited extracts from appalling reviews received by Presence. (He also reported that The Cure had a Lol Tolhurst dart board on the tour bus, given to them by a friend.) By the mid-nineties, Presence became an absence, and Lol Tolhurst went on to form **Levinhurst**.

In February 2013, a Facebook post announced that Presence were writing new songs. The revival, however, was not to be, as Gary Biddles passed away that April.

Presence's problem, Tolhurst said in hindsight, was 'too much baggage – we were either too much like The Cure, or not enough . . .'

Primary

Chk-chk-chk-chk . . .

'Primary' is the lead single from *Faith*, and a straight-up Cure classic. No guitars. No keyboards. Just Robert Smith and **Simon Gallup** playing duelling basses through various effects pedals, with **Lol Tolhurst** driving it relentlessly onwards with a mechanical simplicity and **Mike Hedges** keeping tight control of it all. The idea of using a bass as a lead instrument was not unique to The Cure – Peter Hook of **New Order** was doing it too in the same period, albeit in a very different style – but there was something attractively brittle, arid and airless about 'Primary', with its lack of treble to sugar the pill.

The band made their first abortive attempt to capture the song on tape, along with '**All Cats Are Grey**', with Mike Hedges at **Morgan Studios** on 27 September 1980. 'They were slow, plodding and sounded very dead,' Robert later said of the recordings. 'We wanted to get something that sounded funereal but they just sounded dull.' Six days later it made its live debut in Gothenburg on 2 October 1980, and has remained a live staple ever since. They finally nailed the recorded version during the album sessions proper, between 2 and 11 February 1981, and funereal was the last thing it sounded. It's arguably The Cure's most urgent single.

It's a song in which Smith, in a traumatised tone, seems to mourn the loss of the openness of childhood, and the arrival of guarded diffidence during adolescence:

> The further we go
> And older we grow
> The more we know
> The less we show

He envies, it seems, the ability of infants to sleep soundly, unhindered by adult concerns:

> Dressed in red and yellow
> Innocent forever
> Sleeping children in their blue soft rooms
> Still dream

(He later stated, however, that the song was inspired by the idea of dying very young.)

The **video**, a straightforward performance clip with added spectral Victorian girls scrabbling through a pile of old clothes and playing dress-up, was directed by Bob Rickerd. Though he'd had experience in film and television before, Rickerd was a novice to directing and, apart from The Cure's 'Other Voices', never directed again. It's worth noting that even at this early stage Robert is wearing lipstick and eyeliner (as is Lol), putting paid to the idea that his **make-up** style was copied from **Siouxsie**.

'Primary' was the first Cure single with artwork from **Porl Thompson** and **Andy Vella** (who had yet to adopt the **Parched Art** name), after a chance meeting on a train during which Porl told Robert The Cure's sleeves were no good and that he and his mate could do better. The 'Primary' cover was a modified photo of three primary-age girls in yellow dresses with the faces of old men highlighted in red, taking the lyrics very literally. One of the pillars of classic Cure visual style was now in place (the other being **Tim Pope**'s videos).

The B-side, 'Descent', was a *Faith* outtake and, like 'Primary', involved duelling basses, though much slower than the A-side. It was an instrumental because, Smith said, 'I'd written all I needed for the *Faith* album and really had nothing more to say.'

Upon its release on 20 March 1981, 'Primary' received mixed reviews from **critics**. In *Smash Hits*, David Hepworth wobbled his head in disapproval: 'I do wonder how long The Cure can continue to prop their songs against the same chord progression, with its clambering bass and deadpan drums. At the moment their fast song (this one) sounds just like their slow one speeded up.' In *NME*, Chris Bohn wrote that 'Smith's dry lost vocal tells of an unsettled individual listening out for a strange guiding voice while the band play an attractively doomy tune'. In *Record Mirror*, Simon Tebbutt noted that they sounded 'incredibly bored'. In *Melody Maker*, however, Adam Sweeting called it a 'triumphant return' after the 'limpid wanderings of **Seventeen Seconds**' and praised it for 'matching a new-found sense of space with a brilliantly focused precision'. (A strange compliment, because the one thing 'Primary' *doesn't* have is space. It's intensely claustrophobic.)

The single entered the UK charts at 43 then dropped like a stone. It was enough, however, to earn a spot on *Top of the Pops*. It has become part of Cure folklore, thanks to *Ten Imaginary Years*, that the presenter forgot the band's name, and that they subverted the miming format of the show by dressing up their instruments in clothes. (This has since been repeated in other Cure books.) This is, sadly, nonsense. The footage is available for all to see, and presenter Peter Powell gets their name right (as well as plugging their album and tour at the end). And there is no subversion, just an uneventful pretend performance.

The story is, like so many things about The Cure, **fiction**.

Producers

'I understand enough,' replied **Porl Thompson** when asked by *Cure News* how *au fait* he was with studio technology, 'to know that most producers are prats.'

This blunt appraisal from The Cure's on-again, off-again multi-instrumentalist ties in with a certain belief among artists that producers are an unwanted intermediary filter between the purity of the musician's expression and the ears of the listener. It also, in the case of The Cure, speaks of a residual DIY punk ethic: once you've figured out how to work the faders, why would you get someone else to do it?

It's notable that ever since **Chris Parry** received sole credit for producing The Cure's debut *Three Imaginary Boys*, all producers who have worked on a Cure album are credited, at best, as co-producers with Robert Smith.

Some of these producers – **Hedges**, **Thornalley**, **Allen**, **Robinson**, **Uddin**, **Nye** – are so integral to The Cure story, and/or enough of a big deal in the business, and/or have a surname beginning with a usefully under-represented letter, that they merit

their own entries in *Curepedia*. But the contribution of others, who have made cameo appearances in The Cure's discography then bid them adieu, should also be acknowledged.

Born on 20 March 1959, Mark Saunders' first professional job in music was as a drummer for country star Carlene Carter, daughter of June Carter and Johnny Cash. Fascinated by the production process, he landed a job working as an assistant for legendary duo Clive Langer and Alan Winstanley, engineering albums for acts including Lloyd Cole and the Commotions, Madness, Gary Moore and Mighty Lemon Drops, as well as **David Bowie** and Mick Jagger's chart-topping charity cover of 'Dancing in the Street'. It was as a dance music producer, however, that he began to make a name for himself, working with the likes of The Beatmasters and Yazz, and co-producing one of the greatest singles of all time, Neneh Cherry's 'Buffalo Stance', with Tim Simenon of Bomb The Bass. This brought him to the attention of The Cure, who hired him to mix the single versions of all the singles from *Disintegration*, including '**Lullaby**', a UK No.5, and '**Lovesong**', a US No.2. 'When we met Mark,' Robert Smith told *Vox* in 1990, 'he was a really nice, affable bloke and the way he did "Lullaby" was brilliant, it was really sympathetic to the song.' His services were retained for *Mixed Up*. 'The difference between him and any of the other remixers on the album', said Robert, 'is that he tends to remix things more musically than anyone else, that's probably why I like him, he's more concerned with tunes and melodies than he is with beats. He played along in the studio – you could tell he was itching to play as well as mix, which I think is healthy.' Saunders is also credited with mixing on *Wish* and *Wild Mood Swings*, and his work with The Cure led directly to being hired by Tricky for his 1995 trip-hop masterpiece *Maxinquaye*. He now operates out of Stroud in the Cotswolds.

Steve Lyon is the Twickenham-born producer who worked for several years at George Martin's Air Studios in the late eighties and whose pre-Cure CV includes working with The Wedding Present, Prefab Sprout, **Depeche Mode**, and **Siouxsie** side project the Creatures. It was his work with Depeche Mode which gained the attention of Robert Smith. His first jobs with The Cure were 'Dredd Song' on the **film soundtrack** to *Judge Dredd* and their **cover** of Bowie's 'Young Americans' for *104.9 – An Xfm Compilation Album* in 1995, which led to a co-production job on *Wild Mood Swings* the following year. However, Smith did not have as many kind words for Lyon as he did for Saunders. 'He is credited as co-producer because I am generous', Smith said, ungenerously. Lyon, who now works out of his own PanicButton Studios, went on to specialise in industrial and electronic music, and has carved out a niche as the producer of many Italian pop acts.

Mark Plati is the New York-based producer whose career began in 1987 under the tutelage of electro legend Arthur Baker, and who went on to work with names as big as Talking Heads, Fleetwood Mac, Lou Reed, the Bee Gees, Roger Waters, Janet Jackson and Rush. It was his work with David Bowie, however, which brought him into The Cure's orbit. After working on remixes from Bowie's *Earthling* album, their paths first crossed at Bowie's fiftieth birthday celebration where, with **Reeves Gabrels**, Plati approached Robert Smith and **Tim Pope** and drunkenly bent their collective ear about the 'Lullaby' video. When Smith needed someone to remix '**Wrong Number**', Plati was summoned to London, and brought Gabrels, who happened to be in the UK with Bowie's band, with him to add guitar parts (which Plati suspected was Smith's plan all along). The sound of Smith's voice coming out of the vocal booth was too much for Plati, already a big Cure fan. 'I started jumping up and down, beaming – saying "It's Robert Smith! It's Robert Smith!" to nobody in particular. Robert actually asked me what the problem was! I had to tell him how fantastic the whole thing was for me. His reply was something along the lines of "Really? Nobody ever gets excited when I sing . . ."'

Plati's remix of 'Wrong Number' became the single. Plati later produced the new songs '**Cut Here**' and '**Just Say Yes**' for their *Greatest Hits* album, as well as 'Believe', a track written and sung by Robert Smith for Bowie alumnus Earl Slick's solo album *Zig Zag*. In 1999 Mark crossed to the other side of the glass and began a three-year stint as MD and guitarist/bassist with Bowie's live band. He has since been operating his own studio, Alice's Restaurant, in New York. However fleeting his dealings with The Cure may have been, Plati's main contribution – bringing Reeves Gabrels into their world – has proven invaluable.

The final example is British producer Paul Corkett, who began working as Jacobs Studios' in-house engineer, on albums including ABC's *How To Be A Zillionaire*, then going freelance, his big break being Tori Amos' *Little Earthquakes*. Midway through the nineties, a decade in which he became very busy

in big-name alternative pop, either engineering or producing Julian Cope, Sleeper, Björk, Nick Cave and Placebo, Corkett was called in to help out on *Wild Mood Swings* in 1996. This led, two years later, to working on the **COGASM** project and, two years after that, co-producing *Bloodflowers*.

If producers like Corkett, Plati, Lyon and Saunders were really so pointless, Robert Smith wouldn't keep hiring them. Mark Plati was once asked what he thought Robert Smith looks for in a producer. 'I think Robert looks for somebody to help him keep the project moving forward,' he replied. 'After all, he knows how to make records, he knows his own voice, and he has a vision of what he wants in the end. He just needs a sounding board along the way, a person who can help him try things out but also keep the project in focus, and be honest with him when something isn't working. He also seems to look for people with their own sonic imprint or sensibility, who can add what they do to what The Cure does, and take it someplace a little different.'

In short, someone who isn't a prat.

Punish Me With Kisses

The second single by **The Glove**, the **1983** project comprising Robert Smith, **Steve Severin** of **Siouxsie And The Banshees** and **Zoo** dancer Jeanette Landray, 'Punish Me With Kisses' was actually the first song written by them, originally demoed in November 1982.

A sunny synthpop tune with another high-looming **New Order**-ish bassline, it told a tale of damaged, dysfunctional love:

Your morning smile of torture
Holds me in its grip
You trace the taste of yesterday
The bruise upon my lip

On the B-side was the instrumental 'Tightrope', which had a nightmarish quality, like Open University between-programmes music heard half-awake through a fever.

Release on the Banshees' Wonderland label on 18 November 1983, its **artwork** by Da Gama was a montage of photos of Landray which echoed the spiral design of '**Like An Animal**'. The run-out groove on the **vinyl** bore the inscriptions 'Please don't interrupt while I'm soliloquizing' and 'Laughter? There was never laughter', both lines spoken by Vincent Price and Christopher Lee in *The House of the Long Shadows*, further evidence of Smith and Severin's all-consuming horror habit.

No music video was filmed for 'Punish Me With Kisses', though they did mime to it on the BBC's *Riverside* (where Smith and Severin had previously staged a **ballet** performance of The Cure's 'Siamese Twins'), Robert and Steve in white dinner jackets and Jeanette in a black PVC catsuit.

Reviewing the single for *Record Mirror*, Eleanor Levy wrote '"Like An Animal" was a disappointing single from Severin and Smith but this is much more like it. Jeanette Landray's vocals don't sound like she's in pain this time and the whole thing has a delicious pulse about it. Soothing guitar, rippling keyboards, dreamy singing. Very nice indeed.'

The record-buying public begged to differ. The single was not a hit anywhere, at all. All those Cure and Banshees fans did not rally round to raise The Glove. Instead, they punished them with misses.

Q

Q is for ...

Quadpus

Quadpus and *Half An Octopuss* (sic) are the names of two EPs with overlapping track listings released primarily to the North American market by Elektra in 1986.

Quadpus was a 12-inch single that played at 33rpm, and featured '**A Night Like This**', 'New Day' (only available on this EP at the time), '**Close To Me**' (12-inch mix) and 'A Man Inside My Mouth' (from the B-side of 'Close To Me'). *Half An Octopuss* was a 10-inch single that played at 45rpm, featured 'Close To Me' (7-inch version), 'A Man Inside My Mouth', 'New Day' and 'Stop Dead' (from the Australian 12-inch of 'Close To Me'). A limited-edition version of *Half An Octopuss* had been put out in the UK by **Fiction** in 1985, but isn't particularly rare: it averages at £14.99 on Discogs.

Despite the EPs' mollusc-mutilating names, the **Parched Art artwork** – identical on all versions – features a happy-looking blue octopus with a full set of tentacles.

Queens Park Rangers

'On the one hand,' wrote **Lol Tolhurst** in *Cured*, 'Robert is the dark, brooding, creative, melancholic sort. It's obvious from the way he carries himself that his head is somewhere in the clouds . . . [He's] the tortured artist, the all-seeing poet, the messenger with news from the other side. He's also quite normal, someone who enjoys sitting down with a pint and watching football.'

The dichotomy between these two sides of Robert Smith's personality is sometimes too much for fans to take. Many were bewildered, even horrified, in 1986 when Robert Smith appeared on the front of *Melody Maker* in full England football kit, leaping for a ball with Big Country's Stuart Adamson in Scotland kit, in the run-up to the Mexico World Cup. But that photo, taken by **Tom Sheehan**, merely told the truth – or, at least, *a* truth – about who Robert Smith is, and what he loves.

Football in general, but Queens Park Rangers in particular, captivated the young Robert Smith almost as much as music. Even though he had no connections to West London, where they are based, QPR were always his team. 'It's a family thing,' he told *FourFourTwo*. 'My dad supported them and so did my brother.' His earliest memories of Queens Park Rangers will have been a team of romantic underdogs. In 1967, around the time Robert was turning eight years old, QPR won the Division Three championship under manager Alec Stock and also won the League Cup – the first and only Third Division club to win that competition, and the first and only major trophy QPR have won – overturning a two-goal deficit to beat West Bromwich Albion 3–2 in the final, courtesy of a memorable winning goal from the young Robert Smith's hero, Rodney Marsh. It was during Marsh's reign at the Rangers that Robert began going to matches, and he never forgot the impression Marsh made: asked by *Cure News* to reveal his childhood idols, Smith named Jimi Hendrix, Spike Milligan, Alex Harvey, and Rodney Marsh. (Lol Tolhurst has revealed that Robert's first lyric, in Notre Dame Middle School, was not a piece of Existentialist verse inspired by **Camus** or a **gothic** horror narrative influenced by Poe, but an ode to Marsh.)

'The Rs' were on the rise, and were promoted to the top flight in 1968, before being relegated after just one season. 'It taught me that there's more to life than winning, anyway,' said Robert of the highs and lows of following the team. Their spell in Division Two brought new heroes: Terry Venables, Phil Parkes, Don Givens, Dave Thomas, Dave Clement, Ian Gillard, Mick Leach, Gerry Francis and above all Rodney Marsh's replacement, long-haired maverick Stan Bowles. Bowles was the archetypal seventies rock 'n' roll footballer (playing while drunk, turning up late to the stadium via a detour to the betting shop, etc.), and absolutely mesmerising to young kids. (There's a photo of me in an oversized QPR shirt aged eight, having fully caught the bug.) Manager Dave Sexton led this swashbuckling iteration of the team to second place in the First Division in 1976, beaten by Liverpool by just one point. This achievement led to a European adventure, making it all the way to the quarter-finals of the UEFA Cup where they lost to AEK Athens on penalties. The seventies version of the 'Super Hoops' – so nicknamed because of their ultra-cool blue and white hooped shirts – had captured the public's imagination.

In 1979 they were relegated again, but even this catastrophe was catnip to kids. There was never a dull moment as a QPR fan: they were either going up or down, a classic English 'yo-yo club'. (Other football cultures also have the concept of a yo-yo club: in German it's *Fahrstuhlmannschaft*, in Greek it's ομάδα ασανσέρ, in Spanish it's *equipo ascensor*, in Danish it's *elevatorhold*, in Russian команда-лифт and in Chinese 升降机, all of which mean 'lift team' or 'elevator team'. In Dutch it's *heen-en-weer club* meaning 'to-and-fro club', in Romanian it's *ABBA* in reference to Divizia A and Divizia B and, most brilliantly of all, in Polish it's *wańka-wstańka*, which translates to 'roly-poly toy'.)

While still on the downstroke of the yo-yo, languishing in the Second Division, QPR made it to the FA Cup Final of 1982, repeating their 1967 feat of reaching Wembley as a lower-division team, now managed by former playing star Terry Venables, but this time they were beaten by Tottenham Hotspur after a replay.

After another promotion to the top flight, assisted by their controversial Astroturf pitch, and a fifth-place finish in 1983–84, there was another brief European adventure for QPR, but Robert was unable to attend the home games against Iceland's Knattspyrnufélag Reykjavíkur and Yugoslavia's Partizan Belgrade due to Cure gigs in Auckland and San Francisco respectively. In 1986, QPR again reached the League Cup Final (knocking out champions Liverpool along the way), where they faced Oxford United. Robert had no reason not to attend this time, there being no Cure gigs to get in the way. They lost.

Queens Park Rangers have always been a glamour club, despite never being hugely successful. Part of the appeal is the intimacy of Loftus Road, their small, tightly packed ground. So, for some, was its proximity to BBC Television Centre between 1960–2013, which made the club attractive to celebrities wanting to catch a match. Stars who have been claimed (to varying degrees of verifiability) as QPR supporters include musicians Peter Doherty of The Libertines, Mick Jones of The Clash, Glen Matlock of Sex Pistols, Alan Wilder of Depeche Mode, Ian Gillan of Deep Purple, Nick Cave, composer Michael Nyman, DJs Fearne Cotton and David 'Kid' Jensen (host of more than one Cure session), cricketer Ashley Giles,

comedian Bill Bailey, actors Martin Clunes and Adrian Edmondson, and politicians Alan Johnson and Michael Gove. Debbie Harry of Blondie was photographed attending at least one game in the seventies, and Snoop Dogg once wore a Hoops shirt onstage. And one QPR player made moves in the opposite direction: nineties forward Daniele Dichio had a side-hustle as a club DJ during his time at Loftus Road.

At some point in the nineties, however, Robert stopped going to see QPR. 'They just toy with your emotions,' he told *Q* magazine. 'I've got two brothers-in-law and a nephew who are season ticket holders, and the anguish they go through . . .' This presumably means he missed Trevor Sinclair's Goal of the Season against Barnsley in the FA Cup in 1997, an outrageous overhead kick from the edge of the penalty area and the very definition of what Ruud Gullit termed 'sexy football'. The following year, however, Smith was back: as he told *Cure News*, he saw QPR thump Middlesbrough 5–0 then 'went on a bender'.

The football allegiances of certain other Cure members are also documented. Lol Tolhurst supports Chelsea, and **Roger O'Donnell** supports West Ham. **Simon Gallup**, however, appears to have switched. In the eighties he listed Arsenal's Alan Smith and Paul Merson as his favourite sportspersons, and occasionally attended games at Highbury in the nineties, but by the 2000s he seems to have switched to Reading, whose flag has been seen draped over his bass amp at many festivals.

One thing on which they all agree is the England team. In that *Melody Maker* piece in 1986, Robert did not mince his words when appraising the team's chances. 'Perhaps if England get taken apart,' he said, '[manager] Bobby Robson will hang himself which will probably be a lot more exciting than anything England do on the pitch.' Smith's main beef with Robson, and sidekick Don Howe, was their perceived caution. (He later made similar points about Sven-Göran Eriksson.) 'The thing that's forgotten', he elaborated, 'is that it's supposed to be entertaining, and watching the England team right now is like suffering a Test Dept concert because you wanna be seen there.' For Smith, flair is worth more than workrate: tellingly, he once nominated the mercurial genius George Best as his favourite sportsperson. (He also once said the best player ever was Jairzinho, but he was talking to a Brazilian publication at the time . . .) In the *Maker* article he also spoke highly of Peter Shilton, which didn't age so well after Diego Maradona made him a global laughing-stock. Smith ended, though, with a flourish: 'The England team should be a combination of real bastards at the back and almost like effeminate gods at the front. Sadly it isn't.'

The 1986 tournament itself coincided with the **Glastonbury Festival**, at which The Cure arrived in a rainstorm to find a demoralised crowd covered in mud. To make matters worse, The Cure delayed their headline set so they could watch the quarter-final between France and Brazil, which ran to extra time and penalties. They never made that mistake again: 'It's not obvious from what we do musically,' Robert told *FourFourTwo*, 'but we plan our tours around European Championships and World Cups.'

Somewhat amazingly, for the next World Cup, Italia '90, The Cure actually submitted an England World Cup song. 'We didn't get anywhere', he told *FourFourTwo*. 'It was too gloomy. Surprisingly . . .' (The job was given, instead, to The Cure's compadres/nemeses **New Order**.) Despite the snub, Robert told *Cure News* that they were sufficiently invested in England's run to the semi-final that he and Simon 'ran riot' in a bar in Austria the night Germany 'stole' England's win 'and yes, Gazza made me cry'. And, despite England's abject failure to reach the next World Cup in the US, Robert still went along to a match (Ireland vs Italy, a game anecdotally said to be the largest gathering of Catholics on American soil since the visit of Pope John Paul II).

Robert isn't just an armchair fan. 'I played football (at school),' he told *Cure News*, 'but in strange clothes.' He was a winger in the school team, but when he was dropped, he concentrated on music instead. In later years he would have **TeamCure** shirts (in QPR white and blue, of course) made for the band and **crew** to play five-a-side matches, and enjoyed having a kickabout with his younger nephews. 'I like playing football because it was a way of being able to express myself non-verbally. And music was another way of being able to do that . . .'

He takes an interest in other sports too. He plays tennis 'infrequently and badly', and once went to watch Ivan Lendl vs Boris Becker (of whom he was a fan) in the final of the Benson & Hedges tournament at Wembley Arena in 1985. He also went through a phase of watching American Football, his favourite NFL team being Dallas Cowboys. But football – soccer – is his game.

If The Cure are unlikely football fans, are any footballers unlikely Cure fans? At least one is certain: Stuart 'Psycho' Pearce, who played in that 1990 semi-final, is a big Cure fan and turned up at a show where he was spotted by the band. 'He was wearing a shellsuit,' said Robert, 'but at least it was black. And, anyways, who's going to tell him it's anything less than attractive?'

Smith finds the idea that artistic types shouldn't like football a ridiculous one. 'I don't think it's two sides of my character'; he told Simon Reynolds in 1992, 'it's all me. In the group, we have quite intense, emotional conversations about things. At the same time, we can go to the pub and get so drunk that I can't remember how I got home, but I don't feel bad about it later; I don't think it doesn't fit with how I'm supposed to be. Equally, I wouldn't feel embarrassed if someone asked me what I'm reading at the studio, and I said *Love* by Stendhal. I never feel guilty about either end of the spectrum. I object to people who revel in either end of the spectrum and the other aspect. People who only exist to go down to the pub, or people who think, "Ooh no, you can't watch football, it's just a pack of men kicking a ball around a field." I would feel weird excluding one aspect cos I felt it wasn't appropriate. It's all me.'

Quietly Torn

Quietly Torn was a late nineties rock quartet formed by **Porl Thompson** during his twelve-year break from The Cure, after he had moved to Zennor in Cornwall. Their membership was completed by sixteen-year-old vocalist Martin Jackson, double bassist Tom Rickman (who had played cello on PJ Harvey's debut album), and drummer Nick McLeod, who went on to play in a number of projects, beginning with And the Native Hipsters. The young Jackson was brought in to replace Quietly Torn's original singer, Mimi Goese of New York experimental rock act Hugo Largo, who was returning home to the US.

In promotional photographs they look impeccably of-their-time, with Porl sporting a soul patch micro-beard and a comb-forward, and Martin with a 'curtains' cut that made him look a lot like Brian Molko from Placebo.

Their live debut was in the spectacular surroundings of the open-air Minack Theatre, carved into the clifftops at Porthcurno near Land's End. They also played the WOMAD Festival (where they shared a bill with **Boris Williams**' band **Babacar**), Guilfest, and the University of Surrey Students' Union among others. At these digs, Quietly Torn's sole recording, a five-track promotional cassette called *Red C Sessions* manufactured by **Fiction** with all songs written by Thompson, was given out free.

After Porl left the band, the other members continued under the name The Ascension Plan and collaborated with, of all people, Mimi Goese, playing a gig at, of all places, the Minack.

R

R is for . . .

Rarities

As well as being one of the most **bootlegged** bands on earth, The Cure are one of the most collectable. (The two often go hand in hand.) And, just as The Cure's generous number of official live albums and concert films hasn't entirely destroyed the bootleg market, nor has the existence of compilations like *Join The Dots*, or the increasing appearance of hard-to-find tracks on deluxe reissues of classic albums, completely killed off The Cure collectors' market. If anything, the further we get in time from their most celebrated releases, the more desirable original copies of those releases become, especially limited-edition ones. A *Record Collector* list of the rarest Cure records from 1988 seems quaint now. Top of the chart was a 12-inch **vinyl** promo of *Kiss Me, Kiss Me, Kiss Me* in a First Aid box, in a limited run of 100, valued at £100. Even allowing for inflation, that would be a mere £257 in today's money. Its real price now? An average of £575. Things have really escalated.

The following examples are a mere snapshot of the items available, and the prices asked, at the time of writing.

The most expensive Cure record on Discogs is a white test pressing of *Disintegration*, of which only twenty-five are believed to exist. The seller is asking ten thousand Canadian dollars.

Next, at €3,000, is an unopened promo box of *Wish*, containing the album on CD and cassette and an 'EPK' (Electronic Press Kit, i.e. a promotional VHS tape including interviews).

Third, at £1,200, is a French promotional single of '**10.15 Saturday Night**' with their **cover** of 'Foxy Lady' on the B-side. (The official French release, with 'Accuracy' on the B-side, goes for a mere £500.)

Fourth, at £1,000, is a near-mint 1982 copy of *Pornography* still in its shrink-wrap but slit open to access the record. That seller, frankly, is having a laugh . . . but you still wouldn't bet against some wealthy Cure completist, somewhere, forking out the cash.

Some of the most expensive items aren't actually records. On eBay, a 1979 flyer for Manchester venue the Factory, featuring upcoming gigs including The Cure, Joy Division, Echo & The Bunnymen and Adam & The Ants is listed at the eye-watering price of £765.

Various full band autographs from the mid-eighties sell for around the same price.

Also on eBay, a **Fiction** 12-inch promo of 'Grinding Halt'/'Meathook', sent out to radio stations as the band's intended new single but withdrawn after **Chris Parry** had a change of heart due to poor reactions from DJs, is going for £465, and that actually seems about right.

An **Australian** pressing of '**A Forest**', on 7 Records in a cheesy picture sleeve with Christmas trees and the title spelled out in a tacky 1930s Gillies Gothic font that makes it look like an advert for an ice rink, is £460. (The same record, but a New Zealand pressing, is $237.) However, for roughly double that amount, there's a far more interesting version of 'A Forest' from the same label: a promo copy with tracks by the Tourists and Midnight Oil on the flipside.

The ultimate authority on Cure rarities is Daren Butler, whose **book** *The Cure on Record* was written with the help of Robert Smith, Fiction and **Tim Pope**. His own most-prized rarity is a test pressing of 'Lament' (see *Flexipop!*), one of only six in existence, which had previously belonged to BBC Radio 1 DJ Janice Long. It is, literally, priceless: no copies are on sale anywhere, so its value is impossible to report.

Down at the more attainable end, in the £50–£100 bracket, there are endless items. The *Five Swing Live* EP, for example, limited to five thousand copies, is now worth an average of £67. And, to illustrate that The Cure's diligent reissues programme does little to dent the value of original artefacts, the *Lost Wishes* cassette, whose songs have now been released on the 2023 deluxe version of *Wish*, is still worth £106.

Cure rarities don't even need to be particularly old, or the music therein particularly scarce, to fetch top dollar. Even relatively recent items are considered desirable, purely because they're by The Cure. *Blue Top Head Kiss*, a 2006 **The Glove**/The Cure promotional CD sampler featuring three tracks each from *Blue Sunshine*, *The Top*, *The Head On The Door* and *Kiss Me, Kiss Me, Kiss Me*, goes for an average of £56, even though it doesn't include anything that's not available elsewhere, doesn't have notable **artwork** and lacks historicity.

These Cure fans are crazy.

Red Light District

> Have you noticed that Amsterdam's concentric canals resemble the circles of Hell?
>
> *La Chute* (*The Fall*), **Albert Camus**

The most recent Cure live album is from one of their least recent gigs. In 1979 The Cure travelled to the Netherlands for a seven-date Dutch tour, followed by further shows in **France** and Belgium. They played Utrecht on the 10 December, Eindhoven on the 11th and – the show captured on *Red Light District* – Amsterdam on the 12th. These were The Cure's first shows abroad as a four-piece, having played a few as a three-piece, also mainly in the Netherlands, in the summer before keyboardist **Matthieu Hartley** joined. (This was the tour when **Lol Tolhurst** went on a drunken rampage that culminated in Robert **pissing** in his suitcase.)

The venue was Melkweg (Milky Way), an entertainment complex so named because it is a former dairy, on Lijnbaansgracht, a partly filled-in canal near the popular nightlife square Leidseplein. The Cure played Melkweg's Oude Zaal (Old Hall) with a capacity of seven hundred.

The gig was a pretty standard forty-seven-minute, sixteen-song Cure set for that era, starting with '**Seventeen Seconds**' and ending with '**Killing An Arab**', by way of a very high-speed '**A Forest**' (which they played twice, reprising it for the final encore). In his few moments of crowd interaction, Robert announced '**Jumping Someone Else's Train**' as 'our new single', even though it had been out for six weeks, and pretend-grumpily acceded to requests for '**Boys Don't Cry**' in the encores with 'This one is for everyone that's been shouting it out all night'.

As the show was recorded for broadcast on Dutch FM radio, the sound quality is reasonable. Recordings have been easily available as **bootlegs** for four decades, but *Red Light District* is the first time it's been released commercially.

In *La Chute* (*The Fall*) by Albert Camus, the author who inspired 'Killing An Arab', the concentric canals of Amsterdam represent Dante's circles of Hell, with the final ring being the city's red light district. The title of *Red Light District*, however, is misleading – Melkweg is a mile and a half, and four canals, away from the main sex workers' district, De Wallen. (The location of The Cure's hotel that night, however, is another matter.)

The **artwork** is a disappointingly plain effort: a photo of the Tolhurst, Hartley, Smith, **Gallup line-up** from that tour, standing in a **Crawley** street, with the band's name and the album title above in red. The album was released on 7 October 2022 as a double LP on red **vinyl** (as well as normal black vinyl and CD) by Wicker Man, a **label** with a track record for putting out live recordings whose status is unofficial but not illegal by the likes of Kraftwerk, Frank Zappa and Black Sabbath. (It was sold, for example, by Rough Trade shops in England.)

In this respect, perhaps the title makes some kind of sense. Selling Cure gigs for money is a trade almost as old as sex work itself.

Reflections

In 2011, The Cure went back to where it all began by travelling to the furthest point away. For just two shows (initially, at least), the band revisited their first three albums – *Three Imaginary Boys*, *Seventeen Seconds* and *Faith* – at the Sydney Opera House, under the banner of Reflections. And the biggest surprise was the presence of the ex-Cure member who came up with the idea: **Lol Tolhurst**.

A bridge between the two having been rebuilt, and the **lawsuit** now water under it, Lol contacted Robert Smith to suggest celebrating the thirtieth anniversary of *Faith*. Robert replied with the suggestion of performing the first three albums in **Australia** (an echo of the *Trilogy* concerts from 2002, but with different records).

In May 2011, Lol Tolhurst walked into a live room at Brighton Electric (one of The Cure's habitual rehearsal spaces) and rejoined a much-changed version of the band he co-founded for the first time in twenty-two years. A dress rehearsal followed at the Gaumont in Southampton, a venue they first played in September 1979 as support to **Siouxsie And The Banshees** when *Three Imaginary Boys* was still fresh, and flew to Australia.

The cameo appearance by Tolhurst wasn't the only change to the band's line-up. **Porl Thompson**, whose Cure farewell was their previous gig at Coachella in April 2009, had left for the third time, and would never rejoin. Meanwhile, **Roger O'Donnell** had rejoined for the third time, and is still with them.

From this head-spinning revolving-door membership, the Reflections shows featured a line-up which shifted shape according to the album. For the first section of the show, The Cure Trio of Robert Smith, **Simon Gallup** and **Jason Cooper** played *Three Imaginary Boys*. For the second, The Cure Quartet of Smith, Gallup, Cooper and O'Donnell played *Seventeen Seconds*. For the third, The Cure Quintet of Smith,

Gallup, Cooper, O'Donnell and Tolhurst (standing to the left of Cooper's drum riser, adding percussion and keys) played *Faith*. For the encores, the quartet version, with further cameos from Tolhurst, played a selection of early B-sides and stand-alone singles.

Although the experience was emotionally draining, especially when revisiting the dark days of *Faith* (after the title track of which Simon was seen to check on Robert to see if he was alright), Smith considered Reflections enough of a success to parlay the two-date Sydney residency into a mini-tour.

After a normal, Tolhurst-free festival appearance at the Isle of Wight in September, Reflections resumed in November at London's Royal Albert Hall. Though Reflections has never been released officially in any format, a split-screen, fan-sourced **bootleg** version of relatively high quality exists on YouTube. 'Hello,' Robert began. 'Thank you for coming to these Reflections shows. I'll talk some more later. This is 1979 . . .' And talk some more he did, going into a long rambling speech in the encores about, paradoxically, how he 'cannot do patter'. Later, after '**The Hanging Garden**', he joked, 'As I said earlier in the year, this time I am off to drop some acid.' (At least, one assumes it was a joke, though he does disappear from view for around a minute.) 'Right, hurry before it kicks in,' he continues, before introducing '**Let's Go To Bed**' with '. . . and this is why you shouldn't take **drugs**.'

The solitary London show was followed with a further three at the Pantages Theatre in Los Angeles, and three at the Beacon Theatre in New York. When Lol Tolhurst walked off at the end of the final night on 27 November 2011, it would be the final time he ever set foot on stage with The Cure.

Religion

Robert Smith wasn't touched by the hand of God. But he was touched by the hand of God's alleged representative on Earth. 'I met the Pope,' he told *The Face* in 1985. 'Not the present one, about three Popes ago. I was quite young, and I was in St Peter's and there was a mass and he was carried in on a chair and I grabbed hold of his hand . . .'

This would almost certainly have been Pope Paul VI, aka Giovanni Montini, who previously, when working as the Vatican's foreign affairs representative, had assisted Nazis in fleeing along the 'ratlines' to Spain, and had attempted to work with Nazis to organise a mercenary army in Africa (as letters released in 2011 revealed).

Robert Smith was raised in a Catholic family. His schools were all Catholic ones: St Francis' Primary and Junior Schools, Notre Dame Middle School and St Wilfrid's Comprehensive School. **Lol Tolhurst** went to the same strictly religious schools, and **Michael Dempsey** also went to the latter two.

Not that the future Cure members were the most diligent or devout students of Scripture. They would frequently bunk off from Religious Education and go to the school's music room instead, messing around with kettle drums, vibraphones, Spanish guitars, etc. 'We learned to play weird versions of various contemporary songs,' Robert recalled in *Ten Imaginary Years*, 'and by throwing some semi-religious words on top, we created a uniquely awful new form of music.'

This humorously heretical spirit continued into The Cure proper. On 9 July 1978, at the Rocket in **Crawley**, they performed a special show called Mourning the Departed (the 'departed' being **Porl Thompson**, this being only their third gig without him). In *Ten Imaginary Years* Robert described it as 'a 40-minute mock religious ceremony . . . a séance in the pub'. Smith nailed some wood to his guitar to make it into the shape of a crucifix, and wore a priest's costume. They made up for the lack of Porl's guitars with a backing tape of organ and drum machine sounds. At the end, Porl himself turned up in disguise, and poured a pint of beer over Lol's head.

Shaking off the indoctrination of the Church, however, can be hard. As late as 1980, according to a 1989 article in *Q* magazine, Smith could still be seen attending Sunday services in the Friary, Crawley, with **Mary**.

What Smith was doing, in truth, was struggling to get his head around the futility of religious belief. These questions fed into the album *Faith*, which is almost a concept album on that topic. 'I was 20 years old,' Robert told **France**'s *Télérama* in 2012, 'and I was coming to terms with it. I was brought up in a religious family, a Catholic family. But I knew at 8 years old that it was shit. And it took me a long time to escape the mindset of Hell. Of angels and devils and stuff.'

Faith wasn't the end of The Cure's interest in religion. Themes of the divine crop up frequently. '**The Blood**', the Spain-only single from *The Head On The Door*, has the chorus 'I am paralysed by the blood of Christ' (though it's actually about **alcohol**). The **COGASM** song 'A Sign From God', from the Mormon-mocking **film** *Orgazmo*, has the lyric 'No, not religion, I'm talking serious OOBE' (Out Of Body Experience). 'Your God Is Fear', a B-side from 2004, can certainly be read as anti-religious, though it could just as easily be about shedding inhibitions. And **unreleased song**

'Step Into The Light', intended for the aborted *4:14 Scream* (see **fourteenth album**) and performed live in 2016, is a song which, like Tim Minchin's 'Storm', expresses the frustration of trying to reason with someone who believes reason is trumped by belief: 'It really is insane, all this crazy desperate need/For unknowable magic, strange supernatural power . . .'

Are any Cure songs favourable towards religion? Not really, though 'Wailing Wall' on *The Top* celebrates the irrationalism of the believer, from a detached distance. 'The Wailing Wall itself [in Jerusalem],' said Smith in *Ten Imaginary Years*, 'was brilliant: the most beautiful noise I've ever heard, total religious insanity.'

Ultimately, Robert Smith's rational mind will not allow it. 'I don't believe in God or any spiritual force,' he told *Oor* in 1989, 'and in the worst cases, I believe in nothing at all. I think everything is as it seems to be. I believe in myself and in others, but I don't believe in life after death. The bleakness of many of our songs is due to that. It gives you this empty feeling you can't seem to get rid of. People hang on to religion, because they are afraid and can't accept their own finiteness. I don't know. If you believe in something, then that's true for you. I always face that confrontation, just as each time I step into a plane, I face my own mortality.'

When The Cure became huge in the **US**, it was reported in *Cure News*, some Christians accused them of being Satanic. 'I believe in neither the Devil nor God,' railed Robert. 'So it's bollocks!' When French television asked Robert what he would tell Bob Dylan if he met him backstage at a festival, he mischievously replied 'I'd tell him God doesn't exist.'

Lol Tolhurst has an interesting take on having a religious upbringing. On *Curious Creatures* he has advanced the view that the culture of British Catholicism led to great art, from The Beatles onwards, as young people indoctrinated into that faith grew up fighting against its strictures.

But is Cure fandom itself a faith? 'If The Cure is a religion,' Smith told *Télérama*, 'I wouldn't do it. I hate religion. I hate all religion. I think that religion is at the heart of so much discontent and idiocy in the world. I think that all faith is terror.'

Robinson, Ross

Nu metal is possibly the most inglorious musical genre of all time. A style of boisterous, aggressive rap-metal adopted by backwards baseball-hatted frat boys with beer cans where their brain cells ought to be,

not for nothing was it also known as 'sports metal'. Characterised by bands such as Limp Bizkit, Papa Roach, Slipknot, Linkin Park and Korn, it became the vehicle in the late nineties for a nightmare cocktail of adolescent entitlement and ugly male rage, culminating in the horrific, dystopian hellscape of rape, sexual assault and arson that was Woodstock '99.

It's probably unfair to point the finger of blame at any one of those bands for the boneheaded, knuckledragging mentality of the nu metal subculture. (Well, maybe at Limp Bizkit.) Take Korn, for example, whose 1994 debut album is often credited with creating the genre. That album contained the song 'Faget', inspired by singer Jonathan Davis's experience of being bullied at school by jocks for wearing frilly shirts and eyeliner and being into alternative new wave bands like The Cure. (Davis would later reaffirm his love of The Cure by inviting Robert Smith and **Simon Gallup** to join Korn on their *MTV Unplugged* appearance.) There's a bleak irony in the fact that those bullies Davis sang about on 'Faget' became the prime market for bands like his.

That album was produced by Ross Robinson. If Ross Robinson didn't create the genre of nu metal, he certainly played midwife to it. Born in Angleton, Texas in 1967, the son of Byron Katie, an author of inspirational self-help books, Robinson played in various bands as a thrash metal guitarist before getting his first break as a producer on Fear Factory's 1991 album *Concrete*. After his big breakthrough with *Korn*, he produced Limp Bizkit, Machine Head, Slipknot, Deftones (another band with whom The Cure have a bit of a mutual appreciation society; see **covers**), Sepultura and Amen, establishing himself as the go-to nu metal producer.

Robert Smith and Ross Robinson met backstage at a **festival** in the summer of 2002. This has sometimes been reported as Coachella and sometimes as a festival in Switzerland. The latter is more likely, as The Cure did not play Coachella until 2004, but did play Ministry of Rock in Frauenfeld in July 2002, where Robinson's friends Soulfly were also on the bill. In any case, during the conversation, Robinson persuaded Smith to let him produce The Cure's next album, and even to sign to his **label**, the **Geffen** subsidiary I Am. 'I was on the point of making the album I had been waiting to make for about fifteen years', Robert told *Rolling Stone*. 'I knew after the first day of sitting and talking to him that I wanted to work with him. He reawakened all the old passion for The Cure that was dormant in me; he reminded me why people love what we do so much.'

And work with him he did – see *The Cure (2004 album)*.

S

S is for . . .

Samples (of The Cure)

The website WhoSampled.com, the oracle of sample culture, lists one hundred and twenty instances of The Cure's music being sampled by other artists.

The song that's been raided the most often is **'Lullaby'**, with a total of twenty-six samples. Something about the solid thwack of **Boris Williams'** drums and **Porl Thompson'**s spidery guitar lines has proven irresistible. For example, the 2003 single 'Snowflakes' by English rapper Just Jack was built entirely on the backing track of 'Lullaby', as was Akala's 'I Don't Know' in 2007. 'Spiders, Crocodiles & Kryptonite' by Faithless from their 2006 album *To All New Arrivals* is entirely built on 'Lullaby' and features Robert Smith reprising his vocal (see **Collaborations**). 'It's All About Me', a 2005 album track by Rachel Stevens, features a slowed-down 'Lullaby' loop. And Motionless in White's 2012 album *Infamous* opens with a track called 'Black Damask (The Fog)' which allegedly features the borrowed lyrics 'His arms are around me, and his tongue in my eyes' and 'The spider man is having me for dinner tonight', but if you can hear that among all the guitar-shredding and death-screaming, congratulations, you have the ears of a bat.

Their second most-sampled track is **'Close To Me'**, with twenty-one instances. These range from the 2022 single 'Tissues' by Yungblud, which only uses the drums, to Afroman's 2000 single 'There's a Price 2 Pay' which interpolates the whole song. UK rapper Lady Sovereign's 2009 single 'So Human' not only samples the song but features Sov singing the first verse ('I waited hours for this . . .'). In the video her hair was crimped and backcombed like a stereotypical Cure fan.

'The Lovecats' has also proven tempting for light-fingered bands, with 'Tornado' by Mindless Self Indulgence lifting some of the lyrics in 1999 and 'Cops and Robbers' by The Hoosiers interpolating huge chunks of the music in 2007. **'Lovesong'** is also popular, a notable example being Wiz Khalifa who rapped over it on his 2008 mixtape *Low Riding Freestyle*.

The earliest high-profile sample of a Cure track came in 1998 when Massive Attack sampled **'10.15 Saturday Night'** on their cover of The Paragons' reggae single 'Man Next Door' on the album *Mezzanine*. (The 'drip-drip-drip' part appears about three minutes in, laid over the drums from a sample of Led Zeppelin's 'When the Levee Breaks', then reappears near the end.)

The biggest-selling example, however, is almost certainly Rihanna's Billboard chart-topping, multiple platinum-selling 2011 single 'S&M', which interpolates the keyboard riff from **'Let's Go To Bed'** about halfway through.

Some artists just can't leave The Cure alone. French band Rinôçérôse have sampled The Cure at least three times, always from one specific album, *Seventeen Seconds*. In 1997 they sampled 'In Your House' on 'Machine Pour Les Oreilles', in 1999 'Three' on 'La Guitaristic House Organisation' and in 2002 'M' on 'Lost Love'.

The Cure's hits provided plentiful source material for the bootleg mash-up craze of the early 2000s. One very popular example was 'Is There A Cure For The One Minute Man?' (also known as 'One Minute Cat'), a mash-up of Missy 'Misdemeanor' Elliott's 'One Minute Man' with 'The Lovecats' created in 2002 by Kurtis Rush, the alter ego of DJ producer Erol Alkan (the man behind London's hugely influential Trash club). Another remixer, DJ Tripp, put exactly the same artists, but different songs, together on **'Jumping Someone Else's** Freak', while A Plus D combined those artists on 'I'm Really **Hot Hot Hot'**. A Plus D also juxtaposed The Cure with Robyn on 'Close To Konichiwa Bitches'. Perhaps the most inventive repurposing of The Cure's music, however, is Digitalism's 2007 track 'Digitalism In Cairo', which chopped up **'Fire In Cairo'** to superb effect.

The Cure themselves have been very sparing in their use of other people's music. There are only five Cure tracks which have used samples. 'Accuracy' sampled 'The Magic Mirror' from *Snow White and the Seven Dwarfs*. 'Hot Hot Hot!!!' interpolated 'She' by Charles Aznavour. Their 1993 **cover** of Jimi Hendrix's 'Purple Haze' sampled 'Feel Good, Party Time' by J. R. Funk and the Love Machine and 'Take Me to the Mardi Gras' by Bob James. And, unsurprisingly, the *Mixed Up* project featured a couple of tracks which utilised samples: 'A Forest (Tree Mix)' sampled Johnny Jenkins' 1970 cover of Dr John's voodoo blues classic 'I Walk On Gilded Splinters' while 'Close To Me (Closer Mix)' sampled 'N.T.' by Kool & the Gang. That track, in turn, was sampled in 1995 by the Bloodhound Gang on their dumbass disability-mocking 'She Ain't Got No Legs'.

If pop is eating itself, The Cure are clearly one of its favourite flavours.

Seventeen Seconds

Is Seventeen Seconds the great forgotten Cure album?

Every fan of a certain age wants to claim they were there at the very beginning for Three Imaginary Boys. And every scholar of pop history knows that Faith and Pornography were founding texts of goth. Seventeen Seconds tends to slip through the gap, under-loved and, 'A Forest' apart, under-discussed.

The background to the album was bleak, even by Cure standards. On 3 October 1979, while in Newcastle on the Join Hands tour with Siouxsie And The Banshees (for a gig which was actually cancelled because Sioux was ill), Robert Smith was jumped by three businessmen in a hotel lift. The fight spilled over into the corridor. As he recalled in Ten Imaginary Years, 'I put this bloke's head through a glass door and his mates really did me over.' With his head and hands badly bruised and bleeding, Smith stayed up for seven or eight hours and wrote 'virtually three quarters' of what would become The Cure's second album. While it's not always obvious that the songs themselves are about the events in Newcastle, what's clear is that those events unlocked something in Smith. In Lol Tolhurst's words, Robert 'used the energy and pain' of the incident and channelled those feelings into his songwriting.

Another factor in the mood of the album was the ticking of the clock. 'I was twenty when I made it,' said Robert later, 'and we were all realising that we were no longer young.' (If you think Robert's obsession with reaching the ripe old age of thirty circa Disintegration was insanely premature, it pales into insignificance next to his absurd despondency a decade younger circa Seventeen Seconds.)

On a more positive note, the relative failure of the debut album they'd made as teenagers gave Robert a new sense of artistic freedom. 'The fact that people hadn't gone for Three Imaginary Boys pleased me in a strange way, because it set me up to do something different.' He homed in on an eclectic selection of influences, listening intently to Nick Drake's Five Leaves Left, Jimi Hendrix's Live at the Isle of Wight, Van Morrison's Astral Weeks, and what he called 'the clear, finished sound' of David Bowie's Low. 'I wanted The Cure to become some weird hybrid of the four,' he later told journalist Simon Reynolds. In another interview, with Joe Gore of Guitar Player, he was even more specific. 'When we were recording Seventeen Seconds, I would listen over and over to a tape with four songs: Jimi Hendrix's 'All Along The Watchtower' from Live at the Isle of Wight, Nick Drake's 'Fruit Tree', Van Morrison's 'Madame George' from Astral Weeks, and the Khachaturian ballet piece that's on the 2001 soundtrack. I was trying to get a combination of all the things I liked about those four things, even though there were so completely disparate.' Furthermore, he had been listening to cello music, and wanted it to sound 'rather acoustic'. He remembered that 'I thought it would be good to have drums, bass and a guitar with a huge hole in the middle.' (It has also been suggested, many times, that the sound of Seventeen Seconds was inspired by the Banshees and Wire.)

After the Banshees tour ended, Smith began writing demos on his sister's Hammond organ using the preset swing and bossa nova rhythms, and his lyrics from that night in Newcastle. Not everybody who heard the demos was impressed by Robert's new direction. 'I remember him saying he wanted to make the next album really boring,' said bassist Michael Dempsey in Ten Imaginary Years, 'and I couldn't quite grasp that concept.' Smith was unimpressed with Dempsey being unimpressed, and thought 'fuck it' and went round Simon Gallup's house. Dempsey was fired, Gallup was hired, along with his Mag/Spys bandmate Matthieu Hartley on keyboards, and the rest is history.

On 17 December 1979, barely six months after Robert's Tyneside beating, on the Future Pastimes tour with their Fiction labelmates Associates and The Passions, The Cure debuted eight of the new songs at the London School of Economics. They continued to play these still-unreleased tunes through the rest of the tour and, on 3 January 1980, with the new four-piece line-up in place, rehearsals for Seventeen Seconds began at Robert's house. Between 13 and 20 January all eleven tracks were recorded at **Morgan Studios**, with mixing completed between 4 and 10 February.

Producer **Mike Hedges** was retained from the *Three Imaginary Boys* sessions, and **Chris Parry**, at Robert's request, became more hands-off, letting the band get on with it. One problem was that Parry was no keener on the new demos than Dempsey had been. Another was that he was still obsessively micromanaging Lol Tolhurst's drum kit. He was told his input wasn't needed while fiddling with a snare. 'I don't think I'll come in tomorrow', Parry said. 'If you do,' Smith threatened, 'you'll be bleeding . . .'

Hedges, conversely, was a fan of the demos. 'I really appreciated the musical direction – morose, atmospheric, very different to *Three Imaginary Boys*'. Furthermore, he was willing to facilitate Robert taking the reins. 'By the time of *Seventeen Seconds*,' Smith told *Guitar Player*, 'I decided that I wanted to produce because I knew how it ought to sound, and I didn't want anyone else involved in the chain. I had to know how everything worked, because there's an awful lot of bullshit flying about when you're in the studio. I know the entire process of what we do. I learned how to operate the desk, what mikes are being used, the whole technical side. It's really a very simple process if you know what you want and have the capacity to learn.' Lol Tolhurst, recalling the sessions for Tim's Twitter Listening Party in 2021, agreed that Hedges engendered a sense of autonomy: 'We felt free to be ourselves with this album and for the first time, we had a say in everything about the album.'

In an in-depth interview about lead single 'A Forest' for *Sound on Sound*, Hedges, who didn't drink when working, remembers *Seventeen Seconds* being one big party. Literally, at one point: Lol's birthday fell in the middle of it (he has tweeted a photo of himself at Morgan with streamers and a birthday balloon). Smith, however, was always professional. 'Robert knew his limit and he stuck to it, and it was within his limit to be able to work and actually do a really good job of it. The others, meanwhile, would finish their parts and get so off their faces that they'd sort of fade out of the way because they couldn't stand up.' The band slept under newspapers in the studio to get an 'us against the world' feeling (as Robert later told *Cure News*), usually working till the early hours then being woken by the cleaners hoovering in the morning.

Hedges described the band's willingness to experiment with emerging techniques and technologies, such as tape delay. 'There'd be a big rush, a big build-up of sound on top of itself, getting really messy, and that was great, kind of like a reggae thing. Reggae used that quite a lot.'

In less than a fortnight, they ended up with an album which, as *Uncut*'s James Oldham put it in 2000, 'dismantled The Cure's punk sound and replaced it with something far more introspective, blank and bleak.'

The opening track, 'A Reflection', is an instrumental which begins with contemplative piano – a brand new sound for The Cure. It could have been the incidental music for a documentary about the melting of the polar icecaps. It set the mood for the whole record, and reflected Smith's love of Bowie's *Low* in more than one sense. On this track, the band experimented with swapping their instruments, as Tony Visconti had asked Bowie's band to do during the *Low* sessions. However, The Cure were unhappy with the results, and the only sound that survives is the background wailing on this track (which Lol believes is a violin that Robert 'played').

'Play For Today', however, was not such a radical departure and could easily have slotted onto *Three Imaginary Boys*. There's a simple reason for that: it was already written before *Three Imaginary Boys* came out, and Michael Dempsey remembers recording an early version before leaving the band. The song is named for the strand of BBC dramas which ran between 1970 and 1984 with plays from writers including Alan Bleasdale and Dennis Potter and directors including Ken Loach and Mike Leigh. The lyric, however, bears no relation to the series and is, Robert told *Cure News*, about 'the fraudulent aspects of an insincere relationship'. 'Play for Today' enjoys a special status among Cure album tracks: it was included on the CD release of the singles collection ***Standing On A Beach***, despite not being a single (but was omitted from the cassette). It is also their fourth most-played song, and a tradition has arisen of fans singing along with Matthieu Hartley's keyboard line. 'You should know it was a beautiful moment of spiritual connection for me,' Tolhurst tweeted, 'every time I heard that!'

The wonderful and oddly Fleetwood Mac-like 'Secrets' is the third track. Smith, singing a lyric about 'hopelessly wishing to have the courage to seize missed opportunities' (*Cure News*) provides his own backing vocals, narrating the words in an up-close-and-personal monotone, while simultaneously singing them in a distant, heartbroken refrain.

'In Your House', like '**10.15 Saturday Night**' before

it, is another song about time passing slowly. It's also one of many Cure songs which refers to **drowning**: 'I drown at night in your house, pretending to swim' (Lol Tolhurst has cited this as one of his favourite Cure lyrics). The lyric is, Robert later explained, about 'feeling uncomfortable in someone else's presence but still always returning'. Tolhurst's drum track was created using tape loops, with an arpeggiated guitar riff that Tolhurst considers 'a Cure trademark' laid over the top. Lol considers the overall effect 'hypnotically beautiful', and he's not wrong.

The almost-instrumental 'Three', a skeletal piece made from reverb-drenched pianos and dubby guitars which had its origins in onstage improvisation, has no official lyrics but in the background one can hear Robert narrating a conversation with someone who is berating him to stand up straight. In *Cure News* he cryptically explained it as being about 'the eternal triangle'. Whether anyone involved likes it or not, it's definitely a bit gothic.

The same could be said for 'The Final Sound', which opens Side 2 with more reverberating piano. A sinister, atmospheric interlude, like the incidental music from an old horror film, it was originally intended to be longer but, due to financial constraints, the tape literally ran out. Robert described it simply as 'Matthieu's elegy'.

It is often said that The Cure took a while to find their feet. But 'A Forest' (which has its own entry) is right there on their second album: a career-defining song that is almost always in their live set. The album version begins with Matthieu's synth, then the iconic riff, then some arpeggiating, before the drums start and the song kicks in. It's gothic as hell, horror-adjacent, but in this elongated format also strangely warming and welcoming.

'You'll fall in love with somebody else again tonight', sings Smith on 'M', over chords reminiscent of Patti Smith's 'Dancing Barefoot'. 'M', which – like 'Play For Today' – was already written before *Three Imaginary Boys* had even come out, doesn't require too much deciphering. It's 'about a girl', Robert told *Cure News*, and that girl is obviously **Mary**. (In the *Bloodflowers* tour programme, the last thing on Robert's list of the most important things in his life is 'M'.) However, as Lol Tolhurst confirmed on Tim's Twitter Listening Party, 'It has an obvious connotation . . . and a **literary** one as well.' Its opening words, 'Hello image', are a direct reference to an English translation of **Albert Camus'** *A Happy Death* (an originally unpublished precursor to *The Outsider*,

which inspired '**Killing An Arab**'). 'After making love, at that moment when the heart drowses in the released body, filled only with the tender affection he might have felt for a winsome puppy, Mersault would smile at her and say, "Hello, image."' (It's also notable that the novel's protagonist, Meursault, and his love interest, Marthe, both have names beginning with 'M'.)

The utterly superb 'At Night', its pummelling, brutal, minimal, dirty bassline reminiscent of 'Dead Souls' by **Joy Division**, was inspired, said Smith, by the Franz Kafka short story of the same name, yet another literary reference in The Cure's work.

The closing 'Seventeen Seconds' mentions 'the girl' again – one cannot help but wonder whether it's the same one from 'A Forest' – in a song which Tohurst believes 'sums up the whole Cure ethos'. Interestingly, a barefoot Smith played that song during a lockdown gig from his home in December 2020 to raise money for mental health **charities**. As for the title *Seventeen Seconds*, Robert told *Cure News* it was 'an arbitrary measure of time – one that seemed to be suddenly everywhere once the song was written.'

Reviews of *Seventeen Seconds* were often less than glowing. *NME*'s legendary **critic** Nick Kent characterised its mood as one of 'limpid suspense', writing that 'this mode of musical arrangement and construction finds its fullest realisation in the single 'The Forest' [sic] – yet the scenario, once created, soon sounds limp, devoid of tension or any compelling sense of mystery. It's neither agreeably trancelike – in the mode of Can, an easily definable influence – nor is it effectively "whole" in its conceit. One keeps waiting for a sudden lift-off, yet the song just lies there twitching occasionally.' Kent concluded that the album 'occupies a midway land where much is insinuated but nothing truly delivered. The music and the listener seem caught in that very sense of "distance" that Smith seems so obsessive about keeping up.' He concluded by describing it as 'depressingly regressive', though admitted that he awaited their next move with interest.

In *Record Mirror*, Chris Westwood agreed. He saw it as 'a sidewards step' rather than a progression; and found the material 'biteless, a bit distant', showcasing a 'reclusive, disturbed Cure, sitting in cold, dark, empty rooms, watching clocks.' (To which one could easily reply, 'That's the point . . .')

Posterity, however, has been kinder to *Seventeen Seconds*. In his post-punk history *Rip It Up and Start*

Again, Simon Reynolds praises it as 'translucent-sounding', with 'shades of *Another Green World* Eno, Durutti Column and Young Marble Giants'.

The **artwork** on the front of the album sleeve, by **Bill Smith**, consisted of a scratched, distorted photograph of some trees (evoking 'A Forest'), and the reverse bore four deliberately blurred images of the band members from photographer Andrew Douglas (who later became a filmmaker best known for his poorly received remake of *The Amityville Horror*). The imprecise images were Robert's idea, encouraging people to focus on the music instead. 'Showing ourselves clearly would have made things too obvious,' he later explained. 'With us, the record's always been more important than our appearance so what's the difference if we're elegant or filthy?'

Released on 18 April 1980, the album took them into the Top 20 in the UK and Netherlands and Top 10 in New Zealand, an improvement on *Three Imaginary Boys*, but Robert wasn't happy. 'The only time I've been disappointed,' he said in 2000, 'is *Seventeen Seconds*. I was really sad, for about a week, that we'd made what I thought was a really great album, at the time the best I could do, and no one wanted to listen to it. It sold 15,000 around the world, or something stupid. I remember sitting down with Simon and thinking "Why doesn't anyone like us?"'

A mood of gloom pervaded the ensuing tour, on which Smith and Gallup would habitually sit in silence, listening to Walkmans and not sleeping. On stage, the songs grew longer and longer, with the same chords repeated over and over. As Smith later told Simon Reynolds, 'I was twenty-one, but I felt really old. I actually felt older than I do now. I had absolutely no hope for the future. I felt life was pointless. I had no faith in anything. I just didn't see there was much point in continuing with life . . . In the next two years, I genuinely felt that I wasn't going to be alive for much longer. I tried particularly hard to make sure I wasn't.'

Despite its miserable immediate aftermath, *Seventeen Seconds* itself has had a significant legacy, and has often been **sampled** or referenced by modern acts. 'Lost Love' by French band Rinôçérôse incorporates elements of 'M', 'At Night' was **covered** by Iva Davies & Icehouse on *The Berlin Tapes*, and John Frusciante of Red Hot Chili Peppers once cited *Seventeen Seconds* (and *Faith*) as major influences, though it is hard to hear anything of The Cure in RHCP's belligerent cock-funk.

Increasingly, along with the more-fêted *Faith* and *Pornography*, it is taking its rightful place as one of the albums which set the tone for the entire goth movement and, in The Cure's own pantheon, it was ranked fourth by *Ultimate Classic Rock* and fifth by *Far Out* magazine.

'I think on *Seventeen Seconds* we truly became The Cure,' Lol Tolhurst told Tim's Twitter Listening Party. 'It wasn't goth, it wasn't punk, it was The Cure.' Producer Mike Hedges found it to be a useful calling card: 'The album turned out to be crucial to my career because a lot of musicians liked it, and after that, no one ever took me for a pop producer.' And Robert Smith once called it 'The most important record we ever made' because 'it decided the way the public thought of us for at least three years'.

Never has taking a beating proven so productive.

Severin, Steve

It could have been 'S is for . . . Spunker'.

Steven John Bailey was born in Highgate, London on 25 September 1955 and spent his early years in Archway before moving to Bromley aged eleven. His formative musical experiences were in his mid-teens: in 1970 he saw Captain Beefheart's Magic Band, which he remembers as a life-changing experience, and in 1971 he discovered the Krautrock band Can via a friend's older brother who was stationed in an army base in Germany. His early influences as a bassist were Can's Holger Czukay and Cream's Jack Bruce.

In 1975, at a Roxy Music concert, he met Susan Ballion from Chislehurst, soon to be known as **Siouxsie Sioux**. He, with his short peroxide-blond hair, and she, with her jet-black crop, became recognised faces on the punk scene the following year, and were considered – along with the likes of Soo Catwoman and Billy Idol – to be part of the so-called 'Bromley Contingent' who followed Sex Pistols around.

On 20 September 1976 the duo made their first live performance at the 100 Club Punk Special when another act had pulled out, performing a chaotic, atonal twenty-minute version of the Lord's Prayer, assisted by future Ant, Marco Pirroni and future Pistol, Sid Vicious. **Siouxsie And The Banshees** were born, and Bailey – now rechristened Steve Severin, after the character from Leopold Von Sacher-Masoch's short story 'Venus in Furs' (as mentioned in The Velvet

Underground song of that name – became their only continuous member apart from Sioux herself. He had briefly dabbled with the name Steven Havoc, and at one point considered Steve Spunker. It's rock 'n' roll's loss.

Severin's first exposure to the wider public was obscured by a blizzard of swear words. When Sex Pistols appeared on Thames Television's *Today* programme on 1 December 1976, the Bromley Contingent came along. And, while drunken presenter Bill Grundy attempted to flirt with Siouxsie, and Steve Jones called him 'a fucking rotter', Severin looked on silently.

The notoriety that the Bill Grundy incident won Siouxsie didn't immediately translate into a career for the Banshees. It took two years for them to settle on a steady line-up and release their first single, 1978's 'Hong Kong Garden'. But Siouxsie And The Banshees wasted no time in setting the musical agenda for the post-punk era with the dark, abrasive albums *The Scream* and *Join Hands*. Regular audience members at their London and Croydon shows included the three members of The Cure.

Robert Smith first met Steve Severin at a Throbbing Gristle gig at the YMCA in London on 3 August 1979, introduced by **Chris Parry** (who had signed the Banshees to **Polydor**), and the pair instantly became friends. Later that month, The Cure supported Siouxsie And The Banshees on the *Join Hands* tour, an eventful couple of months which took a sudden swerve when two members of the Banshees quit in Aberdeen and Robert Smith was recruited as a stand-in guitarist, playing two sets a night, with Budgie from The Slits as their new drummer.

After the tour ended, Smith and Severin kept in touch, and when The Cure toured the UK in November and December 1981, Severin supported them as part of 13.13, the band fronted by American singer Lydia Lunch. Smith enjoyed bonding with Severin, even though he thought 13.13's music was 'atrocious'. In the run-up to Christmas, Smith stayed with Severin in London. Severin was, by now, Smith's closest lieutenant outside the band, leading to strained relations with **Simon Gallup** who was convinced that Smith would go off with Severin (which, in a manner of speaking, he eventually did). 'I'd always prided myself on being his confidant,' said Gallup, 'and I wanted it to stay that way.'

Smith's drug-fuelled lost weekends at Severin's London pad fed into the creative process behind their 1982 album *Pornography*. Severin was almost

as much of a serial collaborator as Smith: he had produced Banshees support act Altered Images as well as Lydia Lunch, and would later produce The Flowerpot Men. It was almost inevitable that he and Smith, another musician with wanderlust, would collaborate.

When The Cure temporarily fell apart at the end of the **Fourteen Explicit Moments** tour, with Simon Gallup having quit, Smith and Severin began recording together for the first time. Severin played bass on an early version of The Cure's 'Lament', given away with *Flexipop!* magazine, when there essentially wasn't a Cure to be part of. The two then continued to work together on demos for what would become their psychedelic supergroup **The Glove**'s album *Blue Sunshine*.

When guitarist John McGeoch quit the Banshees in October 1982, Severin again headhunted Smith to step in, this time as a full member, thus precipitating the mayhem of **1983, Robert's craziest year**. As well as recording and touring together as Banshees through 1983 and early 1984, including the singles '**Dear Prudence**', '**Swimming Horses**' and '**Dazzle**', the album *Hyæna*, the film *Play At Home* and the live album *Nocturne*, the inseparable Smith and Severin collaborated in other ways. On 7 March 1983 Severin played bass on The Cure's 'Siamese Twins' for their experimental **ballet** performance on the BBC's *Riverside*. (This, combined with 'Lament', makes him not only a one-song wonder but a one-gig wonder, in Cure terms.) The pair also co-wrote the song 'Torment' for Marc And The Mambas.

Siouxsie perceived an element of hero-worship in Robert and Steve's friendship, with Smith becoming Severin's Mini-Me. 'Robert started to act like Severin's little brother,' she told Mark Paytress in Siouxsie And The Banshees' authorised biography. 'He started to wear the same clothes as Steven: shades, crucifixes and beads. And he nicked loads of clothes off me, too.'

'I think I was seen as this elemental on his shoulder, telling him not to be in The Cure,' Severin later said. By the time of *Hyæna*, Severin admits he really was trying to get Smith to leave The Cure. Instead, the Banshees was the plate that Robert stopped spinning, and he focused entirely on The Cure. In fact, Smith's reason for remaining in the Banshees for as long as he did, despite its toll on his health, was that he wanted to remain friends with Severin.

Siouxsie, Severin and Budgie continued with an

ever-shifting cast of guitarists until the Banshees split in 1996. Severin went on to create his own label RE, and has released seventeen albums and five EPs, often for films. These include the score for 1989's *Visions of Ecstasy*, the only film ever banned by the British Board of Film Certification for reasons of blasphemy (for its sexual depictions of St Theresa), the music for a theatrical production of Lautréamont's *Les Chants de Maldoror* (coincidentally one of Robert Smith's favourite pieces of **literature**), the soundtrack for horror film *London Voodoo* (in collaboration with his wife Arban Severin), and a live performance of his original score for the classic German Expressionist silent horror, *Vampyr* (Severin's longest composition of this kind). He has also been supervising the reissues of Siouxsie And The Banshees' back catalogue.

In the early nineties Smith and Severin had a falling out, and didn't speak to each other for a decade, until they broke the ice when Severin visited Smith backstage at The Cure's Hyde Park show in 2002.

'Robert has a tendency to edit people out of his life when he has tired of "draining" them,' Severin once said. 'I have the impression that he lives in a rock star hermetic cocoon surrounded by sycophants. If so, he's welcome to it. I doubt we would have much in common any more.'

Sex

Just as The Cure are not outwardly a boozy band – they aren't The Pogues (see **Alcohol**) – they aren't an outwardly sexy band either. They aren't Prince.

The boyish aspect of Robert Smith's persona would suggest the exact opposite, in fact (see **Cuteness**), but he does have a surprisingly sexual side to him once you start looking. And **Simon Gallup**, with his low-slung bass and moody expressions, exudes unadulterated sexiness.

The pair of them gave an interesting though comedic insight into their views on sex in June 1992 when they co-hosted KROQ's *Loveline*. In a radio phone-in which felt like America's revenge for the 'Big Tits Across America' broadcast immortalised on Sex Pistols' *Some Product* album, callers' topics included a bisexual *ménage à quatre*, a step-parent incest scenario, any number of young women whose relationships are being ruined by their obsession with Robert Smith, and a (hopefully) prank caller who

claimed to be having sex with his Golden Retriever. 'It's a shame Laurence isn't still in the band,' said Robert, 'because he was the expert on that kind of thing.' (**Lol Tolhurst** had previously been on KROQ as a love doctor.)

A dozen years earlier, all this saucy talk would have been frowned upon. The punk generation sometimes seemed like the Junior Anti-Sex League from Orwell's *Nineteen Eighty-Four*. Even kissing was seen as decadent, and writing about sex was something that the corrupt, discredited older generation did. For example, until 'Slowdive' (1982), **Siouxsie And The Banshees** had avoided sexuality altogether, and their most famous song about sex, 'Peek-A-Boo' (1988) expressed revulsion at the customers of the Soho sex industry.

If you did write about it, you had to strike just the right note of cynicism. The idea that sex was merely a transaction, a meaningless exchange of body fluids, was prevalent in punk and post-punk thinking. In their earliest days, The Cure obeyed the rules. On *Three Imaginary Boys*, 'Object' was suitably cynical:

> But don't try to hold me
> Because I don't want any ties
> You're just an object in my eyes

And so was 'It's Not You':

> Dress to inflame
> But douse any ideas of passion

On *Pornography* – that least erotic of albums – 'Siamese Twins' is seemingly about sex, but in the most traumatised way, radiating fear of the flesh:

> She glows and grows
> With arms outstretched
> Her legs around me
> In the morning I cried

'**Let's Go To Bed**', in 1982, was full of nihilism, reluctantly acceding to an offer of meaningless sex, the lines 'Another girl, another name / Stay alive, but stay the same / It's a stupid game, stupid game' channelling the transactional coldness of the institutional sex described in The Sensational Alex Harvey Band's cover of Jacques Brel's 'Next'.

In 1983, **The Glove**'s surreal 'Sex Eye Make-Up' navigated the **goth** nexus between sex and mortality:

> Someone coughing took away my breath
> Inches of glass all shiny and new
> Screaming laughing – fucks me to death

On the same album, *Blue Sunshine*, 'Orgy' ('a tongue explodes in my mouth') is about a spree of killing, not sex.

Somewhere around the halfway point of the eighties, however, there was a shift. 'Stop Dead', the American B-side of '**In Between Days**', seems to describe fellatio:

> You said I tasted right
> And swallowed me alive

And this time Robert doesn't want it to stop – the song ends:

> Stay there until day
> Stay there until morn
> Stay there until light

On *Kiss Me, Kiss Me, Kiss Me* – an album with an almost unsettlingly sexual close-up of Robert's lips on the front – you didn't need a particularly filthy mind to read sexual subtext in the lines 'And even though it felt soft at the time, I always used to wake up sore' ('**Catch**') or 'Show me how you do that trick, the one that makes me scream' ('**Just Like Heaven**'), and Robert confirmed to *Cure News* that 'All I Want' was about sex. Not that it really needed confirming: 'Tonight I'm feeling like an animal, tonight I'm going wild', he sang, Iggy-like, 'all I want is to hold you like a dog.'

He cooled down on *Disintegration*, but there was nevertheless something strangely sensual about '**Lullaby**', with its breathy, whispered lines about 'a tongue in my eyes'. By the time of *Wish*, he was back at it again. 'Doing The Unstuck' was Smith's most blatantly sexual moment yet:

> It's a perfect day for kiss and swell
> For rip-zipping button-popping kiss and, well
> There's loads of other stuff can make you yell

On the other hand, 'Wendy Time' seemed to recount the offer of a one-night stand – 'You know that you could do with a friend, she said / You know that you could use a word like feel or follow or fuck, she said' – but it's an offer he rejects.

Wild Mood Swings has so many rampantly sexual songs it's bordering on a one-track mind. Lead single '**The 13th**' seemed to be about giving in to lust:

> As she slides towards me smooth as a snake
> I can't swallow I just start to shake
> And I just know this is a big mistake

Opening track 'Want' is all about his desire for

> More drink more dreams more bed more drugs
> More lust more lies more head more love.

On 'Round And Round And Round', pondering what it is that draws bands back to the **touring** ritual, he answers, 'Maybe it's the sex with the drugs and the fools'. And on 'Club America' he's looking for 'some trigger-happy intercourse'. It's The Cure's randiest album.

On *Bloodflowers*, 'Watching Me Fall' describes a bleak sexual scenario which, Smith revealed, came from an article he had read about Rohypnol, a drug which had become synonymous with date-rape, but this bleakness was a fitting throwback to the mood of the *Pornography* era (as was the album as a whole).

On *4:13 Dream*, 'The Real Snow White' is another transparently lust-crazed number ('It was a tricky gun to load, and I didn't get to fire'), and single '**The Only One**' is entirely about how much he loves 'what you do to my head', 'my hips' and 'my bones'.

If you were to knock up a playlist of all the songs above, you could be forgiven for believing that The Cure make Prince look as chaste as a nun. Working title: *The Cure: Sexier Than You Think They Are*.

And if you feel like you need a cold shower after all that, maybe so does Robert Smith.

Sheehan, Tom

Tom Sheehan is a legendary rock photographer, given to speaking in baffling Cockney rhyming slang, who first shot The Cure for *Melody Maker* in November 1982, and struck up such a rapport that when Robert Smith married **Mary** Poole in May 1988, they chose Sheehan to take the wedding photos. He estimates that he has snapped The Cure more than any other band, and it's likely that The Cure have been snapped by him more often than any other photographer. His own **book**, *In Between Days: The Cure In Photographs 1982–2005*, comes with a foreword from Robert Smith himself.

The list of classic Cure photos taken by Tom is almost endless, but here are a few: Sheehan took the Robert Smith and Stuart Adamson football photo (see **Queens Park Rangers**) in 1986. Sheehan was in **Orange**, snapping away. Sheehan photographed the Elephant Fayre **festival** set which marked the watershed between Gloom Cure and Pop Cure. Sheehan brought Smith together with J. Mascis of Dinosaur Jr, who had just **covered** The Cure's '**Just Like Heaven**', for a photo shoot at Bray Studios in Berkshire, home of the Hammer Horror movies and scene of *The Rocky Horror Picture Show*.

And, perhaps most historic of all, Sheehan brought **Siouxsie** and Robert together at the Floral Hall in Covent Garden. In the pictures, extraordinarily, both Smith and Sioux are smiling. As anyone who's worked with him will surmise, Tommy had almost certainly just said something completely mystifying in Cockney rhyming slang and set them off.

Shelleyan Orphan

'Mother of this unfathomable world! Favour my solemn song . . .'

The words 'solemn song' are repeated twice in Percy Bysshe Shelley's 1816 poem 'Alastor, or The Spirit of Solitude'. Shelleyan Orphan, whose name was inspired by 'Alastor', knew a thing or two about solemn songs. (And also blissful, carefree ones.)

Formed in Bournemouth by Caroline Crawley and Jemaur Tayle via a mutual appreciation of Shelley's **poetry**, Shelleyan Orphan moved to London in 1984, landed a Richard Skinner session on BBC Radio 1, and were signed by Rough Trade in 1986. In time they, like **And Also The Trees** and **Cranes** in different eras, would become one of The Cure's 'pet bands'.

Their bucolic, sun-dappled debut *Helleborine*, recorded at Abbey Road and released on Rough Trade in 1987, combined chamber music and ethereal dream pop in the vein of Les Disques du Crépuscule acts like Virginia Astley and Louis Philippe and 4AD bands like the Cocteau Twins, Dead Can Dance and This Mortal Coil (with whom Crawley would later sing). Their second album, *Century Flower*, featuring such un-rock instruments as cellos, oboes and clarinets, was produced by **David M. Allen** in 1989 and came to the attention of Robert Smith, who invited them to support The Cure on the Prayer Tour. During this tour, Crawley began a relationship with Cure drummer **Boris Williams**.

Shelleyan Orphan's third album, *Humroot* (1992), was almost a Cure side project, as their line-up had swollen to include Williams, **Porl Thompson**, and **Roberto Soave** (of **Presence** and, briefly, The Cure).

Returning the compliment, Caroline Crawley sang backing vocals on The Cure's 'Halo' (B-side of '**Friday I'm In Love**'). On 22 July 1993, Porl, Boris, Caroline and Roberto performed onstage as part of 4AD's 13 Year Itch shows, the only non-4AD band on a bill which also featured The Breeders, Insides and Red House Painters. Shelleyan Orphan broke up shortly afterwards, and Crawley, Williams and Soave went on to form **Babacar**.

Shelleyan Orphan reunited fleetingly to record a cover of 'Buzzin' Fly' for Tim Buckley tribute album *Sing a Song for You* in 2000, then reunited again (without Tayle or Soave) for one final album *We Have Everything We Need* in 2008.

Caroline Crawley passed away on 1 October 2016.

Shoes

There exists a photo, first published in *Smash Hits* magazine in May 1986, of Robert Smith circa his fifth birthday wearing outsized shoes, big enough to be his father's. Some habits last a lifetime.

From roughly halfway through the eighties till the present day, the bottom end of Robert Smith's body has been almost as iconic as the top. Ever since the picture sleeve of the 1986 version of '**Boys Don't Cry**', those giant puffy high-top trainers, making his legs look like two pipecleaners jammed into marshmallows, have been nearly as recognisable as his hairstyle. (He is, as Andrew Mueller once wrote in *Melody Maker*, 'the only rock star with a famous silhouette.')

Sneaker geeks have sometimes attempted, through the detective work of zooming in on archive photos and freeze-framing Cure videos, to nail down THE definitive Robert Smith high-top trainer model. It has been proposed, for example, that LA Gear Brats are what he wears on 'Boys Don't Cry', while others will insist they're Reeboks. Why is it even in doubt? We'll come to that . . .

It wasn't always like this. In The Cure's earliest days, Robert Smith was usually pictured wearing sensible, nondescript black work shoes in keeping with the band's anti-image image, or sometimes creepers. Then, from a fleeting period in which The Cure emerged as figureheads of the **goth** movement, photos exist which prove that Smith and his bandmates wore the pointy pixie boots typical of that scene.

Midway through the decade, however, Smith took the then-heretical decision to wear enormous white trainers. It's almost impossible now, in the era of sneaker ubiquity, to convey how shocking this seemed at a time when any type of sporting footwear was seen as anathema to alternative culture. The eighties were a period of brand obsession, from the designer labels of haute couture to the overpriced sportswear favoured by football casuals and hip-hop artists. (Prime example: Run DMC's hook-up with Adidas.) It was the era of conspicuous consumption, the impulse to demonstrate one's worth and status by ostentatiously buying the most expensive products, preferably with a massive logo on display. What on earth was Robert Smith doing, aligning himself with all that?

Clue: he wasn't. This was not conspicuous consumption. And The Cure had not sold out their anti-sponsorship principles (see **A is for … Advertising**) by hooking up with a shoe manufacturer. In fact, they did the opposite. In a quiet act of rebellion, Robert Smith unpicked the stitching which held the shoes' logo in place, and threw it away. Look at any picture of his feet from that era, and the big padded tongue poking out at the top of his shoe is almost always plain white.

This is one reason why the sneaker geeks are wasting their time. Another is that even if they could pinpoint the style he wears in a particular photo, there is no one definitive Robert Smith shoe. Over the years, he has migrated back and forth between various brands.

Hi-Tec is one that can be named with confidence: in a photo from 29 November 1985, backstage at the Philipshalle in Düsseldorf, he's sitting cross-legged with his feet to the fore, and the brand label is visible. (Clearly he hadn't yet got around to picking it off.) He also told *Cure News* in 1990 that he owned three pairs of Hi-Tecs: two black, one white. (In a previous issue he also mentioned owning Reeboks, purchased from Lillywhites, the sportswear shop near Piccadilly Circus.) Interestingly, Hi-Tecs were considered somewhat downmarket and not particularly cool. Being seen in Hi-Tecs was, therefore, almost an anti-fashion statement in itself. In his footwear choices, Robert was opting for comfort, not for style. (Paradoxically, more by accident than design, he made comfort *into* style.)

Smith and the whole band wore the more retro-styled Converse Chuck Taylor All-Stars at the video shoot for '**Hot Hot Hot!!!**' in early 1988: they're visible on screen, and also in the photos **Andy Vella** took the same day. (Robert had previously been seen wearing white All-Stars in the early eighties.)

If anything changed in the nineties, it was the colour. The shoes Smith wore in the '**Friday I'm In Love**' video were typical in every way, except for one: they were black. This trend continued with his penchant in the early nineties for chunky black industrial boots by companies such as Ridge. A photo of Robert also appeared in the book *Dr Martens* by Martin Roach wearing DMs onstage. But it was still the white marshmallows of the '**Boys Don't Cry**' sleeve that were fixed in the public imagination.

So much so, in fact, that the poster for the 1990 Roskilde Festival – headlined by The Cure – was built around an artist's impression of Robert Smith's trainers, Converse-style, laces half-undone, toes turned inwards. At a glance, any Danish music lover would instantly have known who it was, just as easily as they would if the poster artist had used the outline of Robert's **hair**. To this day, the association between The Cure and trainers is such that several online retailers and Etsy sellers offer canvas sneakers with Robert's face or the band's logo printed on them.

A Denver punk band called Despair Jordan got their name from the joke – Q: 'What kind of shoes does Robert Smith wear?' A: 'Despair Jordans'. Their Nike-parodying logo is a silhouette of Robert Smith – not Michael Jordan – slam-dunking the ball. The irony is that while Nike may be the world's most popular brand of sportswear, Robert Smith has never been seen wearing it.

In this sense, as in so many others, he is determined to walk his own path. In comfortable shoes.

Show

Show, the first of two live albums from the *Wish* tour (the second, *Paris*, arriving just six weeks later) was recorded on 18 July 1992 at the Palace of Auburn Hills, Michigan. Built in 1988 in the northern hinterland of Detroit (and demolished in 2020), the Palace had previously hosted gigs by the likes of Sting, **Pink Floyd**, Michael Jackson, Janet Jackson, Aerosmith, Van Halen and U2. It was a cavernous indoor multi-purpose sports arena, built to accommodate basketball, ice hockey, indoor soccer and indoor football.

And, in all honesty, that's how it sounds. The audio version of *Show* sounds hollow, as if recorded in a high-ceilinged steel shed. Which it was. The intention, Robert Smith told *Cure News* in 1999, was to document 'that group at the height of its powers', that group being the Smith, **Gallup**, **Thompson**, **Williams**, **Bamonte** line-up. And document them it does, for all its aural shortcomings.

Released on 13 September 1993, in **artwork** depicting a celluloid slide attached by tape to a black card, *Show* included many of The Cure's most famous songs, such as **'Pictures Of You'**, **'The Walk'**, **'Fascination Street'**, **'Friday I'm In Love'**, **'In Between Days'** and **'Let's Go To Bed'**. Points of interest include the oddly hurried version of **'Lullaby'** they were playing on that tour, with Robert interpolating a couple of lines of Mary Howitt's children's poem 'The Spider and the Fly' near the end, and the way that in **'Just Like Heaven'** Robert opts, on the line 'Why are you so far away, she said', to use the lower melody sung by J Mascis on Dinosaur Jr's **cover** version.

In most territories, *Show* was a double CD with eighteen tracks. In the **US** it was a single disc of fourteen tracks, but an EP titled *Sideshow*, containing the four missing songs plus a bonus 'Just Like Heaven' (which was also on the single disc) was available too. 'Just Like Heaven' and 'Doing the Unstuck' were sent out to radio stations as a two-song promotional CD called *Showpro*, and there were plans to release 'Doing The Unstuck' as a live single, but these were scrapped.

The album sold reasonably well, reaching the Top 30 in the UK and going silver, reaching the Top 20 in Austria and **Australia**, selling 213,000 in the US. It was significantly more successful than its sister album *Paris*, no doubt due to having a six-week advantage and a more hit-packed track listing.

A review by Christian Wright in *Rolling Stone* touched upon the paradoxical nature of a band whose audience is a tribe of loners. 'A curious thing happens on *Show* . . . Waves of applause swell between songs, which interrupts the solitary nature of being an individual, alienated Cure fan but underscores Smith's power to unite such fans collectively. The Cure play stadiums now.'

There was also a film version, directed by Aubrey Powell of album cover designers Hipgnosis (an influence on **Parched Art**), whose directorial credits include Paul McCartney's Get Back concert film (not to be confused with the nine-hour Beatles documentary). While working on *Show*, Powell also shot the **'A Letter To Elise'** video during a soundcheck. The film begins with four minutes of sepia-tinted footage, shot by local film students, of death rock/dark wave kids milling around outside and inside the arena, and probably missing the superb support band, **Cranes**. Suddenly, as The Cure walk on to a stage that looks like the tide-rippled sand from the *Standing On A Beach* sleeve, it all switches to colour. In an interview with Susan Compo of *Spin*, Smith confirmed her suggestion that this switch to colour was inspired by *The Wizard of Oz*. 'The whole idea for the colour was portraying that sort of magical world that was almost unreal, like hyper-real, and I thought of introducing us as characters because, despite ourselves, it's very difficult not to ham when there's a camera around.' One further notable moment: at the end of **'A Forest'** (which appears in the film version only), Robert plays a bit of Joy Division's 'She's Lost Control' (see **New Order**).

'Show is there for posterity really,' Smith told Compo. 'I think it'll be watched more in the future. I suppose in a way a film of people who have either died or given up is interesting. That's why this film will be more interesting in about five or ten years, in a funny way. My only reluctance about making the film was that it was another period of looking back, a retrospective. And I just sort of worry because that's what record companies do to groups when they've run out of ideas.'

Siouxsie And The Banshees

Sometimes the best things happen by accident. Siouxsie And The Banshees sprang into existence spontaneously, and changed popular culture for ever.

Siouxsie Sioux (born Susan Ballion on 27 May 1957 in London, and raised in suburban Chislehurst) and **Steve Severin** (born Steven John Bailey in London on 25 September 1955) met by chance at a Roxy Music concert in 1975. In early 1976 they and a group of friends, which included future **Generation X** singer Billy Idol and punk icon Soo Catwoman, began following Sex Pistols, and were nicknamed the Bromley Contingent by *Melody Maker*'s Caroline

Coon. Sioux, with her black fetish attire, spiked hair, dramatic Cleopatra eyeliner make-up and scarlet lipstick, became one of the best-known faces around the London punk scene.

Sioux and Severin made their move from follower to performer at the 100 Club Punk Special on 20 September 1976. One of the bands had pulled out, and the pair persuaded Pistols manager Malcolm McLaren to let them go on stage, despite the fact that they had no band and no songs. With Sioux on vocals and Severin on bass, assisted by future Adam & the Ants guitarist Marco Pirroni and future Sex Pistol Sid Vicious on drums, Siouxsie And The Banshees delivered a twenty-minute improvised version of the Lord's Prayer, embodying the anyone-can-do-it ethic better than anyone else on the bill.

Later that year, Siouxsie went from localised punk celebrity to national notoriety. On 1 December 1976, Thames Television's early evening magazine programme *Today* had a sudden vacancy when Queen pulled out. At the last minute, their EMI labelmates Sex Pistols were sent in to replace them by McLaren, with the Bromley Contingent in tow. Presenter Bill Grundy, visibly drunk, began goading the Pistols with deliberately disrespectful questions about their musical seriousness, their attitude to money and their supposed outrageousness. Singer Johnny Rotten said the word 'shit', unheard by Grundy but already shocking enough in the context of 1976 to cause uproar. Then the presenter turned his attention to Siouxsie Sioux, who was standing behind the band, and made her the object of some horribly ill-judged flirting, ending with the creepy promise, 'We'll meet after the show, shall we?' This prompted Pistols guitarist Steve Jones to unleash a heroically sustained barrage of swearing, live on television. 'You dirty sod. You dirty bastard. You dirty fucker. What a fucking rotter.'

Before the credits had even rolled (bringing an end to Grundy's career), Fleet Street journalists were already typing their shock-horror headlines (the *Daily Mirror*'s 'The Filth and the Fury' being the most enduring), catapulting Sex Pistols to national, rather than niche, fame. The coverage ran for days, and a photo of Sioux took up a quarter of the *Mirror*'s front cover the day after 'The Filth and the Fury', with the headline 'Siouxsie's A Punk Shocker!'

In the coming months, Siouxsie And The Banshees morphed into a real band, with John McKay becoming their permanent guitarist and Kenny Morris their drummer. Despite their growing profile, no record deal was forthcoming, and 'Sign the Banshees!' graffiti

sprang up around London. Eventually it was **Polydor** who took a chance on them, signing them on 8 June 1978.

Their debut single, a bright, brash punk-pop banger called 'Hong Kong Garden', became a huge hit, and their albums *The Scream* (1978) and *Join Hands* (1979), with their abrasive textures, inventive structures and challenging subject matter, charted a new course for post-punk, away from three-chord thrash and towards more avant-garde territory. As the decade came to a close, Siouxsie Sioux was well on her way to becoming an icon of alternative culture, and the Banshees were well on their way to accidentally inventing **goth** (whether they welcomed that or not).

The Banshees and The Cure's paths crossed, inevitably, via **Chris Parry** and his Polydor contacts. Parry had given Severin a copy of '**Killing An Arab**', and the Banshees bassist was impressed. Severin and Robert Smith met for the first time at a Throbbing Gristle gig at the YMCA in central London on 3 August 1979, with Smith wearing a strange green checked 'Charlie Cairoli' (famous clown) suit remembered by both parties. The pair got on well. By the end of the month they would be touring together.

After rehearsing at an empty Hammersmith Odeon, the *Join Hands* tour – Siouxsie And The Banshees supported by The Cure – began on 29 August 1979 at Stateside Center [sic] in Bournemouth. From almost the very start, it would be an eventful tour. The PA broke down in Bournemouth and there was audience **violence** the following night in Aylesbury. The bands then took the ferry to Belfast on 5 September where **Lol Tolhurst** was held at gunpoint by police outside the Europa Hotel (famously the most-bombed hotel .in Europe). To make matters worse, the road crew had fallen asleep in Liverpool with the upshot that the Banshees' gear hadn't arrived, forcing them to borrow kit from Belfast band The Outcasts (in a deal facilitated by local legend Terry Hooley of Good Vibrations records). And then came Aberdeen.

In Cure folklore, the *Join Hands* date at the Capitol Theatre in Aberdeen on 7 September 1979 could simply have been the night Lol Tolhurst was nearly shot by Margaret Thatcher's security men for urinating in the bushes (see **Pissing**). But two members of the Banshees made it into something far more significant.

At 4 p.m. on the afternoon of the show, Siouxsie And The Banshees were booked in for a meet-and-greet at the Other Record Shop on Union Street. It did not run smoothly. Polydor had only sent fifty copies of *Join Hands* to the shop, instead of the two hundred and fifty promised, so tour manager Nils Stevenson sold thirty promotional copies to the owner. This meant fans were paying money for product with 'Not for Sale' stickers on, which wasn't a great look. John McKay and Kenny Morris were particularly unhappy, and started giving copies away for free, and replaced the Banshees with *Cut* by The Slits on the shop's turntable (in an ironic foreshadowing of Morris' eventual replacement). Tensions and creative differences had been simmering for some time, and the signing mix-up proved the final straw. An altercation ensued between, on one side, Morris and McKay and on the other, Sioux and Stevenson (with an angry shop owner also involved). There was pushing and shoving, and the drummer and guitarist stormed out.

The Banshees camp assumed Morris and McKay would cool down and turn up to the soundcheck. Instead, they'd gone back to the hotel, made dummies of themselves in the beds with pillows, pinned their tour passes to their pillows and fled town. Nils Stevenson actually caught up with them as they were leaving in a car, but they wound the window up on his hand, telling him 'We can't take the pressure'.

As doors opened, there were still hopes that the two fugitives would make an appearance, but by then they were many miles away. (There are varying versions as to where they went, but according to Dorothy 'Max' Prior, of Siouxsie And The Banshees' previous support band Rema Rema, 'John and Kenny had run away to a safe house with Rema Rema's manager Linda.')

After opening band The Scars, The Cure went onstage and played an extended set in the vain hope Kenny and John would return. When they failed to show, Siouxsie went onstage to tell the audience, 'Two original members of the band are here tonight. Two art college students fucked off out of it. All I can say is, we'll be back here with some friends who have got some roots. If you've got one per cent of the aggression we feel towards them, you have my blessings to beat the shit out of them. Next time you see them . . . *Pow!*' (Sioux and Severin later spotted Kenny at a Blondie party at Notre Dame Hall and confronted him themselves.) The Aberdeen audience were offered their money back.

Banshees manager Dave Woods panicked, and asked The Cure to go back out and play an encore to pacify the crowd. They played two still-unfinished numbers, '**Seventeen Seconds**' and 'M', then announced two special guests: Siouxsie Sioux and Steve Severin for the Lord's Prayer, a reprise of their debut performance at the 100 Club. Sioux gave McKay's guitar to an audience member. Filling McKay's place in the band on a longer-term basis wasn't so easy.

That night, Smith got drunk with Sioux and Severin in the hotel and, semi-joking, semi-serious, offered his services as a replacement guitarist. After all, he knew all the songs and he was a fan. But the tour, it appeared, was off. 'I think he was more annoyed by it than we were,' Severin said later, 'because it was their first big tour and these two people were pulling the rug out from under his feet immediately.'

Rancour flowed from both factions in the music press for weeks afterwards, with official statements followed by retorts from the absconders. In the meantime, the remaining Banshees looked at their options. Cancelling the entire tour would have cost the Banshees about £50,000 in lost venue deposits and other costs. In that era, this would have been enough to end a band's career. Recruiting two replacements and soldiering on was the least bad option.

Auditions were held, and **John Peel** gave a shout-out for help every night on his Radio 1 show. Rumours abounded – Marco Pirroni from the Ants, Steve Jones and Paul Cook from the Pistols – but nobody was quite right, until Cook suggested drummer Budgie (real name Peter Clarke) from The Slits. He was a natural fit, and now they only needed a guitarist. Sioux and Severin remembered Robert Smith's drunken offer in Aberdeen. 'The more we thought about it,' remembers Severin, 'the better the idea sounded.'

The two Banshees turned up to **Morgan Studios**, where The Cure were recording '**Jumping Someone Else's Train**', and persuaded Smith to join. Six days of intensive rehearsals followed. Budgie, on the *Curious Creatures* podcast, later recalled Robert putting scrawled A4 notes on paper on a lectern, but Budgie's electric fan blowing them everywhere. Instead of collecting them up, whenever he lost his place in a song, Robert staggered over the stage to where the relevant piece of paper had landed, and carried on from there.

Amazingly, only five dates needed to be cancelled, and the *Join Hands* tour resumed at Leicester De Montfort Hall on 18 September, with Robert playing a full Cure set then, after an interval, a full Banshees set. He even underwent a modest costume change: Smith would wear a mac when onstage with The Cure, then take it off the Banshees set.

'On stage that first night,' he would later tell *NME*, 'I was blown away by how powerful I felt playing that kind of music. It was so different to what we were doing with The Cure. Before that, I'd wanted us to be like the Buzzcocks or Elvis Costello, the punk Beatles. Being a Banshee for the rest of the tour really changed my attitude to what I was doing.'

The two newcomers, Robert and Budgie, inevitably made a few errors, but audiences were forgiving, grateful just to have the Banshees back on the road. 'I got through it OK,' Smith said later, 'though it was the first time I'd ever tried to copy a guitarist. I found that peculiar.'

The main visual document we have of the Banshees with Budgie and Smith in 1979 is an episode of the BBC2 youth programme *Something Else*, filmed in Manchester on 20 September on a day off, performing 'Love In A Void'. They made no errors that time.

The newcomers bonded quickly with the band using a time-honoured social lubricant. 'Robert was fond of his booze,' Siouxsie told Banshees biographer Mark Paytress, 'as we were, and bringing him on board just accelerated the rate of our consumption ... **Alcohol** was a great short cut to the immediate deep friendships that we felt we had to make with Budgie and Robert.'

According to Severin on the *Out of the Woods* **documentary**, 'In some strange way, the fact that he was playing with the Banshees as well was divorcing him from his own band.' Robert would travel in the Banshees bus while the rest of The Cure went in Robert's **car**, a green Maxi, and had his head turned by the relatively luxurious food in their dressing room and the fact they were driven everywhere.

Smith played seventeen shows in 1979 as a Banshee, culminating at Hammersmith Odeon on 15 October, which was The Cure's biggest indoor show to date. Along the way, however, there were further cancellations when Siouxsie fell ill with laryngitis and, later, hepatitis, and was hospitalised. One of them was the show in Newcastle on 3 October, the night Robert was badly beaten up by drunken businessmen in his hotel (see *Seventeen Seconds*).

After Hammersmith, Robert returned to focus on The Cure and embark on **Fiction**'s Future Pastimes tour.

'There had always been an understanding that Robert would go straight back to The Cure as soon as the tour was over,' Siouxsie told Mark Paytress. 'They were on the verge of breaking through themselves, so obviously he wanted to concentrate on that.' Budgie stayed on as a Banshee, and Smith was replaced by John McGeoch, a genius of post-punk guitar, previously of Magazine and Visage, and later of Public Image Ltd.

Smith was relieved that his life as a touring member of two bands was over. 'Towards the end of the Banshees tour,' he told *Sounds*, 'The Cure was like a circus on stage. A horrid grind. No emotion. We had reached a new level – jolly bleak.'

Nevertheless, without any doubt, The Cure took something forward from their Banshees experience and incorporated it into their own approach. Lol Tolhurst calls The Cure 'nice, polite middle-class boys', and believes they learned assertiveness from the Banshees. Smith has cited Siouxsie And The Banshees as 'a massive influence on me,' acknowledging that 'they were the group who led me towards doing *Pornography*. They drew something out of me.' Speaking to *Uncut* in 2000, he admitted, 'The two groups that I aspired to be like were the Banshees and the Buzzcocks,' he recalls. 'I really liked the Buzzcocks' melodies, while the great thing about the Banshees was that they had this great wall of noise which I'd never heard before. My ambition was to try to marry the two.'

Severin, in *Out of the Woods*, ventured the theory that what Smith took from the Banshees wasn't purely musical. 'I think he learnt how to be a frontperson just from standing next to Siouxsie every night for a couple of months. He completely changed his persona after that. He came out of his shell.' Severin believes Smith learned how to be a bit more flamboyant, how to use stagecraft, and how to manipulate an audience. 'And of course his whole look changes as well. He borrowed Siouxsie's lipstick, went to the toilet, and came back with his trademark look.'

During the interim between Smith's two stints with them, Siouxsie And The Banshees, with McGeoch in scintillating form, released the classic albums *Kaleidoscope*, *Juju* and *A Kiss In The Dreamhouse*, and a phenomenal run of singles – 'Happy House', 'Christine', 'Israel', 'Spellbound', 'Arabian Knights', 'Fireworks', 'Slowdive' and 'Melt!' – which established them as probably Britain's foremost alternative rock band. The Cure, meanwhile, released *Seventeen Seconds*, *Faith* and *Pornography*, and the singles 'A Forest', 'Primary', 'Charlotte Sometimes' and 'The Hanging Garden'. The two bands would often hang out together, the Banshees visiting Morgan during the *Pornography* sessions and Smith visiting Abbey Road when the Banshees, with Mike Hedges, were putting the final touches to *A Kiss In The Dreamhouse*.

Siouxsie And The Banshees are a band who have had the same kind of luck with guitarists as Spinal Tap had with drummers. In October 1982, John McGeoch suffered a nervous breakdown, brought on by the stress of touring and exacerbated by clinical depression and problems with alcohol and, after an erratic show in Madrid at the end of a European tour, was forced to leave the Banshees.

Steve Severin was by now a close friend of Robert's, and had played bass on The Cure's demo version of 'Lament' for a free *Flexipop!* flexidisc that summer when they were short of a bassist. Smith owed him a favour, and Severin asked him to rejoin. (Smith claims Severin's idea was to have McGeoch and Smith both in the band, and make them more guitarry, when McGeoch had sorted his head out. It never worked out that way.) And so, with The Cure just about to relaunch themselves as a duo with 'Let's Go To Bed', Robert found himself in two bands again.

The timing, in other ways, was fortuitous. Being someone else's sideman allowed him to escape the burden of being the frontman of The Cure for a while. 'I wanted to step back from being just Robert Smith of The Cure,' he told Richard Skinner on the *Old Grey Whistle Test* in 1984. 'It becomes a bit wearisome after a while because you start to think of yourself as that . . . I thought playing with the Banshees would allow me to move off and be forgotten. Obviously standing behind Sioux, you're standing behind *Sioux* . . .' Speaking to MTV in 1990, he added 'I was fed up with people expecting me to *know* things.' And 'providence smiled on me because Siouxsie needed a guitarist.' Musically, too, it gave him a different sort of outlet. 'It allowed me to play serious music,' he told Mark Paytress, 'big chords and, crucially, I was no longer the focal point. I was just the guitarist. They brought a lot of *Join Hands* stuff back into the set to make it easier for me. Playing with the Banshees was different to playing with The Cure. It was big music, dead loud on stage.'

By this time, Robert and Siouxsie's images had merged: both had increasingly big hair, heavy eyeliner,

pale faces and bright red lips. In the early-to-mid 1980s Smith and Sioux were perceived as evil twins, he a male version of her, and she a female version of him. (A superb Tom Sheehan photo shoot from that time captures the two of them with mischievous, conspiratorial grins.) Paul 'Desperate Journalist' Morley, in *Out of the Woods*, notes that Robert had begun dressing like a Banshee, with crucifixes around his neck. 'He took it very seriously: I'm in a group, this is their uniform, I will wear their uniform.'

Smith's first job as an official Banshee, rather than a temporary substitute, was a television appearance on the *Old Grey Whistle Test* on 12 November 1982, performing 'Melt!' and 'Painted Birds' from *A Kiss In The Dreamhouse*, which had been released just a week earlier, between McGeoch's sacking and Smith's unveiling. Once again, he was having to learn and tour someone else's guitar parts.

The next day, on 13 November at Birmingham Odeon, the Banshees began an eleven-date UK tour, backed by string section The Venomettes, who had played on the album. The tour was not a particularly successful tour – one show, at the Futurist Theatre in Scarborough, was called off due to poor ticket sales – but Smith was fully embedded as a Banshee. Further television appearances included the *Oxford Road Show* on 3 December, playing 'Overground' and 'Melt!', and later that month in France, during a European tour, a *Les Enfants du Rock* special entitled *L'Embûche de Noël '82* (The Christmas Ambush '82) in which they performed French carol 'Il Est Né Le Divin Enfant', with Smith dolefully crashing cymbals together in a mocked-up mediaeval square.

Then began Robert Smith's craziest year. For most of 1983, Smith was juggling the responsibilities of being in *three* different bands. The other Banshees' schedules were almost as packed, being members of merely two bands (or, in Severin's case, two and a half). The full minutiae of Robert's insane itinerary are detailed in N is for . . . 1983, but in broader terms, chiefly through a Banshees looking-glass, this is how it unfolded.

Firstly, it wasn't enough for Robert just to quietly ease himself into the Banshees. He and Severin had already begun working on their psychedelic side project The Glove in November 1982. Meanwhile the other two Banshees, Sioux and Budgie, had reactivated their own side project the Creatures, originally launched in 1981. Both these acts were very busy through 1983, both releasing their debut albums and two singles each. Very successfully, in the Creatures' case: their singles 'Miss The Girl' (the first release on the Banshees' own Wonderland label) and 'Right Now', at No.21 and No.15 respectively, were bigger hits than any Banshees releases in the previous three years, and the latter charted higher than anything since 'Hong Kong Garden' way back in 1978. In the week their album, *Feast*, was released, they made the front cover of both *Melody Maker* and *NME*. The Cure, meanwhile, recorded and released 'Let's Go To Bed', '**The Walk**' and '**The Lovecats**', played a **US** tour as well as festivals in Britain and France and a couple of small UK shows, performed a ballet for the BBC, recorded a Radio 1 session, and began work on *The Top*. (And Robert wrote a song for Marc And The Mambas.) All these singles and albums had to be promoted, with videos shot, interviews conducted, television appearances and so on.

For mere mortals, that would be plenty. But Sioux, Severin, Smith and Budgie also had a jam-packed calendar of Banshees activity. Once Siouxsie and Budgie had returned from recording *Feast* in Hawaii in January, the Banshees headed to Japan in February. Already, the pressure on everyone was beginning to show: in Osaka, Siouxsie smashed her suicide-locked hotel room window with the phone to let fresh air in, then Robert did the same with his. On 14 February they moved on to **Australasia** for ten days, during which time Banshees manager Dave Woods put pressure on Robert to leave The Cure and commit fully to the Banshees, which irritated him.

Between March and June the various factions – Cure, Glove, Creatures – worked on their own projects, but the Banshees reconvened in July for the Roskilde Festival in Denmark, followed by a show in Stockholm on 9 July. Robert had been insisting that his second spell with the Banshees be documented with an actual record, so work on '**Dear Prudence**' began in Stockholm. However, to everyone else's annoyance, he had to leave the session to promote 'The Walk'. ('Dear Prudence' was finished later in Islington.) The same month, work started on the Banshees' sixth studio album, *Hyæna*.

Smith concentrated on The Cure in July and August, with shows in the UK, US and France, and the recording of 'The Lovecats'. During this period, the *Boys Don't Cry* compilation was made available in the UK. Meanwhile, the Glove's debut single, '**Like An Animal**', came out.

September 1983 was devoted mostly to the Banshees. They toured Europe and then Israel, of

which Robert said, 'It was very peculiar there. I sort of liked it and hated it. I remember hiring a big old American car and driving the Banshees to the Dead Sea. I lost my shoes there – I think I was drunk. All I remember is this shoal of flying fish . . .' They also shot the 'Dear Prudence' video, released the single, made the *Play At Home* film, and played the Royal Albert Hall on 30 September and 1 October (recorded and filmed for *Nocturne*). Still, the Glove's album *Blue Sunshine* came out on 9 September, and The Cure found time to play a Richard Skinner session on 21 September.

In October, the Glove performed on BBC's *Riverside*, and The Cure released 'The Lovecats'. That month, Robert was asked about his ambiguous role in the Banshees. 'A lot of the time,' he replied, 'I'm still trying to play John McGeoch's guitar parts and failing. If I went on like this, I'd be the next one to have a breakdown. It's a balancing act, and as long as I don't fall over, I'll be alright.' Prophetic words.

The Glove released their second single on 18 November, and a week later, the Banshees' live album *Nocturne* was released (with a live EP, *File*, available exclusively to fan club members), creating further clashes of priorities, and leading to further pressure on Robert to commit to just one band. In December, The Cure's compilation *Japanese Whispers* came out, and on the Christmas *Top of the Pops*, both The Cure and the Banshees appeared (doing 'The Lovecats' and 'Dear Prudence' respectively).

During the tail-end of 1983 and the first part of 1984, the clash of interests reached breaking point when Robert was recording The Cure's *The Top* and the Banshees' *Hyæna* albums concurrently, getting taxis between London and Reading between shifts. 'I'm as much of a member as I could be,' he said of the Banshees, 'but I don't have as much say as them. That's why it's always good when I go back to The Cure. I am The Cure.' Meanwhile, Smith's understandably catatonic state was beginning to bother the boss. 'Robert's whole demeanour used to irritate the fuck out of me,' said Sioux. 'I thought he was quite sweet to start with, but I was getting tired of his shuffling and mumbling.'

The Cure played a couple of dates in Germany and Switzerland at the end of January and start of February 1984, but most of February was taken up with Banshees activity, such as performing new tracks 'Running Town', 'Bring Me The Head Of The Preacher Man' and 'Blow The House Down' on Channel 4's *The Tube*.

Siouxsie And The Banshees' '**Swimming Horses**' came out on 16 March, then they embarked on a French tour (during which The Cure's '**The Caterpillar**' came out), then did some Italian dates. An exhausted Robert became notorious for sleeping in too long, unplugging his hotel room phone and barricading the door. At one hotel in Italy, Sioux climbed out of her window from the room next door and crawled across into his, picked up his boots from the floor and hit him with them, screaming 'Get up you bastard!' To add to tensions, one gig promoter in Italy had tactlessly billed them as 'Siouxsie And The Banshees with Robert Smith'. The show at Teatro Tenda in Bologna on 31 March 1984 would be his last with the Banshees, though nobody knew that yet.

'Literally the day I arrived back in England,' Smith told Mark Paytress, 'I thought "If I do the Banshees tour, something serious is going to happen to me." So, for the first time since I was a child, I went to my family doctor. I walked in, and it was one of those moments where someone's face just falls. He didn't have to say anything. Then he told me, "Whatever it is you're doing, you have to stop."' The doctor gave him a note, which Smith subsequently showed to the Banshees' insurer, that essentially read 'This man can't walk, let alone tour.'

The Cure began their own UK tour at the end of April and through early May, during which *The Top* was released. On 13 May *The Top* tour moved to Europe. The Banshees' '**Dazzle**', co-written by and featuring Robert, came out on 25 May. A day later, his tenure as a Banshee officially ended. Smith phoned Severin from Hamburg to tell him he couldn't do the upcoming Banshees tour of the UK and North America, as it would be too exhausting. One of The Cure's own shows, scheduled for 29 May in Utrecht, was postponed by two days.

'It was almost a repeat of when John McGeoch left,' Severin told Paytress. 'We had major tours of Britain and America just two weeks away and we were being left in the lurch. There had always been a gentleman's agreement that Robert could leave the band when it conflicted with his role in The Cure, but it was such short notice. I was personally upset because he was my mate.'

Siouxsie and Budgie, at the time of Smith's bombshell, were on holiday in Bali and uncontactable. When they arrived home and heard the news, it was ten days before the Banshees' opening night at Brixton Academy. 'I wasn't sad to see him go,' said Sioux, 'but his timing was atrocious . . . Budgie

was greeted by all these angry "Hope you fucking enjoyed yourselves!" messages from Severin on his answerphone.'

A press release went out citing 'nervous strain and exhaustion' as the reason for the departure of Smith, who was replaced at very short notice by John Valentine Carruthers (formerly of Clock DVA), who stayed with the Banshees for the next three years. *Hyæna*, Smith's one and only Banshees studio album, was released on 8 June 1984, and they played their first gig without him at Brixton the following day.

'It was an insane period for us,' Siouxsie recalled in *Classic Rock*, 'extremely busy. We were just being totally hyperactive. I think it took its toll maybe a year or so later. John [McGeoch] had been hospitalised for stress and overworking, so he was suffering a bit. Robert stepped in, for the second time, as he did in '79, so the show was still going on, and the touring was all pretty intense and crazy. We went on to record *Hyæna* together, and then he imploded as well. He just couldn't cope with it.'

Speaking to ITV's *Night Network* in 1987, Smith drew some positives from his spell as a Banshee. 'I used to get criticised for being immobile. Right up until 1982, when the group broke up and I went and joined the Banshees for a while. That brought me out of my shell. Before that, I thought that even moving my right hand to play guitar was pretty demonstrative.'

He also reflected on that time in *The Hit* magazine. 'I look back on the Banshees period with mixed feelings. I enjoyed it, but it got a bit messy towards the end. The reason why I joined them for a while was because I got fed up with being the singer in The Cure and nothing else. But eventually I became frustrated because I couldn't have the same control over what they were doing. Being a naturally disordered person, I didn't find it hard to cross over between the two bands. But I don't think I was the right guitarist for them. My involvement was mostly based on my friendship with Steve Severin, although I'd always been a fan of theirs.'

By the time of Mark Paytress' Banshees biography in 2003, Sioux had hardened in her views. 'I never trusted Robert. I always thought he had another agenda, that he was using the situation. Look at the facts. In October, "Dear Prudence" made it to No.3, thanks in part to the Creatures keeping the band's profile high. The Cure's first hit, 'The Lovecats', came out just as 'Dear Prudence' was peaking. When he left, it felt a bit like "Thanks for the ride, I'm off."

All that bollocks about a sick note. That wounded sparrow act doesn't wash with me . . .' (Siouxsie's accusation doesn't really stand up, as 'The Lovecats' was not The Cure's first hit, and 'The Walk' was already a significant hit before 'Dear Prudence' even came out.)

Speaking to Suzy Feay of the *Independent* in 1997, Robert acknowledged that relative chart positions and sales figures caused some disharmony. 'It caused quite a bit of friction at the time, because The Cure were actually selling more records than the Banshees. We did 'The Lovecats' and it was a big hit! When I was with the Banshees, I refused any payment. It meant they couldn't make me do anything. Sioux found it difficult; she's unused to males saying no to her.'

The Banshees continued for another eleven years, releasing five more albums: *Tinderbox* (1986), *Through The Looking Glass* (1987), *Peepshow* (1988), *Superstition* (1991) and *The Rapture* (1995). They split up in 1996, reuniting briefly for the *Seven Year Itch* tour in 2003.

The Creatures reactivated intermittently, with the albums *Boomerang* (1989), *Anima Animus* (1999) and *Hai* (2003). In 1998 they toured America with John Cale, during which Budgie, in an echo of Smith's first stint with the Banshees, also drummed with Cale, therefore playing two shows a night.

Severin became a prolific composer of film scores in the post-Banshees era, while Budgie became a lecturer at BIMM in Berlin, a co-host (with Lol Tolhurst) of the *Curious Creatures* podcast, and a percussionist with John Grant, also collaborating with artists including Efterklang, Talvin Singh and Peaches.

Siouxsie released an acclaimed solo album, *Mantaray*, in 2007, and toured it. In 2013 she performed the Banshees' *Kaleidoscope* at Yoko Ono's **Meltdown Festival**, followed by a run of hits including 'Dear Prudence'. She announced another return to action in 2023.

The Banshees' later material left Robert Smith unimpressed. When asked about *Peepshow* in *Cure News*, he replied that there were four good songs on it but 'It is a bit samey – maybe I've grown away.'

Sleep When I'm Dead

The third of the four singles released on the thirteenth day of each month in the lead-up to *4:13 Dream*, 'Sleep When I'm Dead' had the embarrassing misfortune of sharing its title – albeit minus the word 'I'll' – with an abysmal 1993 hit from New Jersey poodle rockers Bon Jovi. In fairness, that perhaps could not be helped: the song had been around since 1985, having been written during the sessions for *The Head On The Door* (originally under the working title 'Kat 8', taken from its repeated chorus). That said, *I'll Sleep When I'm Dead* had already been the name of a Warren Zevon song and compilation, and a crime drama from *Get Carter* director Mike Hodges. This sort of association-by-accident is the inevitable hazard when you use a common aphorism as a song title.

The almost quarter-century delay benefited the song. Its YOLO, live-fast-die-old sentiments had matured with time, and felt more fitting from someone who was nearly fifty than someone who was still only twenty-six. Musically it's a fairly standard piece of urgent, wah-wah and distortion-driven alternative rock, notable for having a keyboard part at a time when The Cure didn't have an official keyboardist.

A black and white performance clip, taken from the same MTV session as 'The Only One', functioned as the song's video. The band also performed it on NBC's *Last Call with Carson Daly* among other **television** appearances.

Released on 13 July 2008 and (also later that year in a remixed form on the *Hypnagogic States* EP), it came with **artwork** depicting a wavy watercolour of a big charcoal-grey hand, designed by **Parched Art** whose **Porl Thompson** figures prominently in the video, his remarkable head tattoos on full display. Its B-side 'Down Under', a breezy mid-paced number with **Jason Cooper**'s drums mixed unusually high by **Keith Uddin**, was a cryptic allusion to sirens and **drowning** rather than a homage to **Australasia**. However, as it shared its title with 1983 Aussie-reggae hit by Men At Work, one started to wonder if they were carrying out some sort of conceptual prank by naming both sides after famous songs from the past.

Though it failed to chart in the **US** and crept to a lowly 68 in the UK, 'Sleep When I'm Dead' was a Top 10 hit in Poland and actually reached No.1 in Spain, as did the previous two singles – a remarkable burst

---

of **success**, especially in an era when their popularity had faltered elsewhere, and the only times The Cure have reached No.1 in the singles chart of any major market.

'Sleep When I'm Dead' is, if not an all-time Cure classic, a creditable advertisement for the album on whose track listing it was about to occupy eleventh place.

Small Wonder

Small Wonder is the independent record label which released the original 1978 single of '**Killing An Arab**'/'**10.15 Saturday Night**'.

Pete and Mari Stennett ran the label out of their record shop at 162 Hoe Street, Walthamstow between 1975 and 1983. The shop's paper bags proclaimed that the shop sold 'BLACK MUSIC – WHITE MUSIC – GREEN MUSIC'. The label's logo was a Victorian photograph of a white mother, black father and their mixed-race baby, with their priest. It is ironic, then, that Small Wonder's eleventh single release would be a song which stirred up controversy due to its perceived racist intent.

By the time of The Cure collaboration, the label had grown a reputation for being eclectic and uncompromising, having previously released records by bands including The Zeros, The Cravats, Angelic Upstarts, Leyton Buzzards, Punishment of Luxury and Crass. It would later be namechecked in 'Hitsville UK' by The Clash.

Chris Parry of **Fiction** decided to sub-let The Cure to Small Wonder because Fiction's parent company, **Polydor**, didn't want to release any Cure product before Christmas. The deal was that Small Wonder would put out the first fifteen thousand copies, then Fiction would take over. Those fifteen thousand copies, with the catalogue number SMALL11, are now collectors' items, typically selling for upwards of £50.

Small Wonder would go on to release 'Bela Lugosi's Dead' by Bauhaus, considered by many to be the first true **goth** record. 162 Hoe Street is now an Eastern European grocery called Arbat. A blue plaque on the wall marks its musical heritage.

Smith, Bill

Bill Smith – no relation – was already a well-established designer and photographer before working with The Cure. He'd been art director at Octopus Books and **Polydor Records** before going solo in 1978 with Bill Smith Studios, and designed dozens of jazz albums in the seventies. The **artwork** for *Boys Don't Cry*, *Three Imaginary Boys* and *Seventeen Seconds* were all his. His enormous body of work also includes Kate Bush's *Hounds Of Love* and every single by The Jam from 'In The City' through to 'The Bitterest Pill (I Ever Had To Swallow)'.

Perhaps most importantly, he designed the '**Killing An Arab**' single sleeve with the dropped capital 'C', thereby creating The Cure's first iconic logo.

If you've ever tried to copy *that* Cure logo onto your exercise book or leather jacket, thank Bill Smith.

Smith, Robert

'You're a disease,' mumbles Sylvester Stallone's character Lieutenant Marion Cobretti to a deranged hostage-taker in the atrocious 1986 film *Cobra*, throwing a knife with ninja accuracy at the baddie's abdomen. 'And I'm the cure.'

Robert Smith is The Cure. With immense respect to the dozen-or-so other musicians who have passed through The Cure, and the half-dozen temporary players, Robert is the band's only permanent member throughout their nearly half a century of existence. Without him, there *is* no Cure. This book is essentially *about* Robert Smith, so even having an entry under his name is arguably redundant. (It was tempting just to say 'See rest of book'.) For his youth, see **youth**. For his hair, see **hair**. For his politics, see **politics**. For his make-up, see **make-up**. For his relationship, see **Mary**. For his shoes, see **shoes**. For his voice, see **voice**. For his love of football, see **Queens Park Rangers**. And so on. Therefore, this entry shall be a relatively brief repository of anything that didn't fit neatly into another section, but which may or may not shed some light on his personality. For example . . .

He is 5ft 10ins tall, and has blue eyes (though they're sometimes considered grey). Those eyes aren't working as well as they used to, and he wears glasses when not on stage. 'I'd had really good eyesight before it suddenly started to deteriorate,' he told *Q* in 2000. 'I thought, "Fuck, I'm going to be blind at this rate". It was around when I turned thirty, so it was probably stress-induced.' His nickname, circa *The Top*, was Robin, after 'Hush! Hush! Whisper who dares! Christopher Robin is saying his prayers' from A. A. Milne's 'Vespers'. But he hates anything with 'Bob' in it.

'The Robert Smith on TV or **video**,' he once told *Spin*, 'isn't the real Robert Smith.' But even if it is, he's not afraid to break character (just look for the photo of him cuddling up to Santa Claus). Asked in *Cure News* to describe his personality in two words, he chose 'bemused' and 'clear'. He believes his sense of the absurd has saved him.

In terms of hobbies outside music, he once claimed he wanted to give it all up and pursue pottery and sculpture. Circa 1990 he began to paint. 'I bought some oil paints. I even went for an afternoon of golf last month. I decided I'd try all the things I never thought I'd do – clay pigeon shooting I liked, but it brought out the bad side of me. I'm not sure I should pursue that – it might be my downfall.' And, he told *Spin*, if he had enough time off he would love to spend it on an archaeological dig as an observer ('Like a medieval one in Northern England'), taking piano lessons and buying a grand ('They influence you mentally, make you feel more inspired'), and reading.

Robert has listed his non-musical heroes as Spike Milligan, Albert Einstein, Richard Burton, Martin Luther King, Sylvia Plath, Marie Curie and Joan of Arc, and has said that philosophically his biggest influences are **Albert Camus**, Jean-Paul Sartre, Franz Kafka and his dad. He once told KROQ that he and Mary had photographs in their home of Marilyn Monroe, Rudolf Nureyev, George Best and (this one dates it) Béatrice Dalle. And when he wrote to Spike Milligan at the age of ten, that's what he received in return: a photograph.

His watching habits? Leaving aside cinema that has directly influenced his music (see **The Glove** for plenty of examples of that), films he has named as his favourites include: *Eraserhead*, *2001 – A Space Odyssey*, *Mary Poppins*, *My Life as a Dog*, *Re-Animator*, *Who's Afraid of Virginia Woolf*, *Star Wars*, *A Streetcar Named Desire*, *Apocalypse Now*, *The Purple Rose of Cairo*, *Taxi Driver* and *One Flew Over the Cuckoo's Nest*. Film directors he admires include Stanley Kubrick, Nicolas Roeg, Werner Herzog, Ridley Scott, Terry Gilliam, David Lynch, Steven Spielberg, and Tim Pope. His favourite actors include Jack Nicholson, Malcolm McDowell, Klaus Kinski, Audrey Hepburn, Nastassja Kinski and Isabella Rossellini. And, like most people, he loves *The Simpsons*.

He once named his favourite places to go as **Paris**, the Lake District, Kyoto, Hamleys, and bed. It's notable that only one of them needs to be reached by plane. Robert's fear of flying is well-documented. The idea that The Cure cross the Atlantic by ship always sounds like a lie, especially given that the journey takes six to eight days, but there's footage of them actually doing it in the nineties, filmed by TV-am (see **TV, The Cure appear on**).

He has listed his favourite foods as Indian, Vietnamese, lemons, Twiglets, Hula Hoops and Juicy Fruit chewing gum. In 1989 he cooked Christmas dinner for thirteen people. In 1992 he became hooked on playing *Tetris* on the GameBoy. His preferred scents are rose musk or vanilla. He has never worn a watch.

But do all these disparate, fragmentary shards of information actually coalesce into any sort of picture of the man? Before we descend any further into a spiral of unprocessable trivia, let's circle back around to the notion that this grey-blue-eyed, Kyoto-loving, Lynch-watching, Twiglet-munching guy is The Cure. Is it an unfair statement?

'Within the group,' Robert said in a television interview in 1988, 'there's this unspoken term that what I want happens.' In The Cure's official biography, *Ten Imaginary Years*, he says 'At the beginning, we were supposed to be a democracy but it was often me who took the decisions. Democracy existed in that everyone got the same amount of money and everyone was credited for the songs but that's all. I wanted it to be like that to avoid the possibility of someone in the band coming up with a bad song and me having to accept it.'

And, speaking to *Pulse* in 1996, he put it this way: 'It is a group, but they'll all tell you if there's a stand-off and the four of them want to do something and I disagree, it won't happen. It's terrible, I know, but this is my life. From the age of 15, The Cure has been the way I've expressed myself, but it is a lot looser than it was. I do actually listen to what other members of my group say now, whereas 10 years ago I didn't care what anyone else thought. If people disagreed they had the option to leave . . .'

Is Robert Smith The Cure, then? That sounds a lot like a 'Yes'.

Soave, Roberto

With a CV like his, it was only ever a matter of time before Roberto Soave joined The Cure.

The bassist had already played with three different bands in The Cure's orbit: **Associates**, **Shelleyan Orphan**, and **Lol Tolhurst's Presence**. (He would later be in yet another: Cure/Shelleyan Orphan supergroup **Babacar**.) The Cure's gravitational pull was dragging him inexorably inwards. His association with Cure outcast Lol Tolhurst proving no obstacle, Soave's opportunity to actually play with the band arose in November 1992 when **Simon Gallup**, who had contracted a debilitating case of pleurisy, was forced to leave the *Wish* tour. Soave made his debut in Marseille, not looking very Cure in his turned-up blue jeans and long hair but sounding just fine. He deputised at a dozen dates in total, as the tour rolled on through Barcelona, Madrid, San Sebastian, Toulouse, Bordeaux, Rennes, Lievin, and two nights each in Birmingham and Edinburgh. Robert Smith was appreciative of his efforts. 'Roberto Soave, who used to play in a band called the Associates, stepped in with a day's notice and filled in remarkably well', he told MTV's Ray Cokes afterwards.

Once Gallup had recovered, Soave faded back into the shadows and currently creates music in the trio Dogtablet, making dark electronica and soundtracks with Martin King from Pigface.

Solo Album

The smart question isn't 'Will a Robert Smith solo album ever happen?' The smart question is 'Has it happened already?'

The Cure's **songwriting** process, after all, varies from album to album: some are genuinely collaborative efforts, and others are essentially Robert bringing his latest songs to the table and getting the rest of the band to play them. There are, arguably, Cure albums which are Robert Smith solo albums in all but name.

As long ago as 1983, **Siouxsie** and **Steve Severin** told Kris Needs of *Flexipop!* that the Banshees' new Wonderland label would be putting out a solo album by Robert Smith. The previous year, on a Richard Skinner session (see **Peel Sessions**), The Cure had recorded the song 'Ariel' which, *Cure News* would

later reveal, was intended for Smith's solo project. (It eventually surfaced in demo form on a deluxe edition of *The Top*.) It wasn't all just hot air, then: material existed. The plan hasn't gone away since. It's an itch he has, for one reason or another, yet to scratch.

The idea stayed with him. In January 1988, while announcing that there would be a new Cure album recorded that summer (which turned out to be *Disintegration*), he promised 'I will be doing something on my own sometime soon too . . .'

In January 1989 he floated the idea that the solo album might be a semi-**collaborative** effort, involving him and 'maybe a couple of guests'. That year, the rumour peaked in intensity. 'Perhaps now I'll finally do my solo album,' he told Ted Mico in *Spin*. 'I've got all these songs that never seemed quite right for The Cure to do. Before this album, I was joking that The Cure would make an instrumental album, but now I definitely think that if we do make another record, it'll be instrumental. It would be a more filmic way of writing, which I think would be really good fun.' (This instrumental idea would re-emerge a few years later, as a proposed companion disc to *Wish*.)

Speaking to Michael Azerrad of *St Louis Post Dispatch* that year, he described the proposed solo venture differently, stating that it would be a folk-style album in the Nick Drake vein. In an interview with *Oor*, he spoke of the appeal of a more stripped-down way of recording. 'A few years ago I got worried that The Cure would become too big and I wanted to make small songs. You don't need a six-member band if a piano and cello are sufficient.' However, when it came to the crunch, Smith's solo ideas were shelved in favour of *Disintegration*. That record became a Cure album, he told Simon Witter of *Sky* magazine, mainly because he missed his friends.

By April 1990 Smith was admitting that the solo material may creep into a Cure project (if it hadn't already). One working title was *Music for Dreams*, a name attached to several projects over the years. However, in March 1992, at a press conference for *Wish*, he claimed the solo album had already been secretly recorded pre-*Disintegration*. 'It's really miserable', he said, to zero gasps from the audience. In September 1994's *Cure News*, he again touted the name *Music for Dreams* as the title for a solo album. Then it all went quiet.

At the turn of the new millennium, it turned out that Robert Smith had been working on The Cure album that was the closest yet to a solo effort: *Bloodflowers*. In a 2000 interview he said:

I was very difficult to work with on this album, as I was on *Disintegration*, for that reason: I insisted that everything was done exactly as I wanted. So it's kind of unpleasant for the others, really. Cos they don't feel that they're of any value, I suppose, when we're making a record. Although I try and impress upon them the fact that without the group it wouldn't sound like The Cure. To me that's really important: who's in the group defines the sound . . . But as soon as we met up for *Bloodflowers*, I said 'I hate to tell you this, but you haven't got any say for the next three months.'

Nevertheless, in the same interview, he doubled down on the solo plan: 'I really want to try something on my own, to see what it's like. If I don't like it on my own, I'll go back to The Cure again.' And, in *Uncut*, he insisted that whatever the success or failure of *Bloodflowers*, the next album he released would be a solo one.

Speaking to *X-Press*, however, he admitted that there was a very fine margin between a Smith-dictated Cure album like *Bloodflowers* and a Smith solo album. 'Either way I'd probably get the others to play on it anyway,' he said. 'I'm getting on with them so well I can't really see any point in asking anyone else to do it. In some ways it's really whether I want to think "is now the time I want to be a solo artiste or do The Cure make another record?" To me it's more important what it sounds like. I don't really worry about what it's going to be called until I've done something else.'

And, speaking to Swiss television in 2002, he once again made the claim that he'd already recorded a solo album, but that it wouldn't be released for a while.

There's a case to be made that the vast array of extra-Cure-icular collaborations in which he was involved in the twenty-first century went some way to scratching that itch, perhaps explaining the non-arrival of the mythical Robert Smith album.

However, as recently as 2022, speaking to *Rolling Stone*, he revealed that he was once again toying with a solo release which, he said, wouldn't come out till 2023. 'I have to keep revisiting it,' he explained. 'It's a thing I've wanted to do for so many years. I realise I've only got one shot at doing it, so I've now started to add real instruments and acoustic instruments, whereas this time two years ago it was literally just feedback – but I've kind of grown a bit disenchanted with it. I've listened to it like three times, and I think it's rubbish.'

Songwriting

Robert Smith's approach to songwriting varies from album to album. Often – perhaps most often – Robert has written demos alone, then gathered the band together to flesh them out. This was the case on *The Head On The Door*, for example, and *Bloodflowers*. On other occasions, such as *Disintegration*, the entire band have been asked to bring ideas to the table. Much more rarely, the self-titled *The Cure* apparently being an example, songs were worked up collectively in the studio.

One thing which rarely changes, Robert told *Cure News* in 1988, is that ninety per cent of the time the music comes first. 'The words are always scribbled and hidden away; I come back to them months later (usually when I don't understand them any more!)'.

Even though Smith's lyrics are often impenetrably arcane, he always aims for universality on at least some level. 'Our best songs', he told *Cure News*, 'are the ones that musically you don't even need to understand what I'm singing. You *get* what I'm singing, from the combination of the sound of how I'm singing it and the music. That's when you know you've written a good song. When you know that someone who can't speak your language is gonna know what that song means . . .'

Splitting Up

If it was going to happen, it would have happened already. Robert Smith has announced the imminent demise of The Cure so often now that there's an element of *The Boy Who Cried Wolf* to it.

When *Melody Maker* asked 'Do The Cure even exist any more?' in November 1982, it was a valid question. Depleted to a duo in the messy aftermath of the **Fourteen Explicit Moments** tour, they came as close as they've ever come to ceasing. But Robert and **Lol Tolhurst** soldiered on, gathered new recruits around them, and The Cure have survived ever since, in one incarnation or another. If The Cure *were* going to split up, it seemed, it would be on Robert Smith's terms.

One of those terms, he once stated, was too much **success**. 'If we ever have a No.1 record,' he said in 1985, 'I'd disband the band immediately.' (When *Wish* went to No.1 in 1992, he had quietly forgotten that vow.)

Robert appeared to have mixed feelings on the idea of artistic longevity. 'I never adhered to the philosophy of the "dinosaur",' he told *NME*'s Mat Snow in 1984. 'I never accepted the fact that a group or a person could only have a limited lifespan. It only happens in music, it doesn't happen in any of the other creative arts. People aren't dismissed because of age, which is all it boils down to. You can work for years, whether it's on the periphery or in the heart of contemporary music and still do things. The obvious case would be of **Bowie**.' However, he told another music press interviewer, 'The time I stop working in contemporary music is getting close', and explained to the *Old Grey Whistle Test*'s Richard Skinner that it was 'because I'm getting too old.' (At the grand age of twenty-five.) 'I've been in a group for nine years,' he said. 'I shouldn't think I'll be in a group for another nine years. So it's sooner rather than later . . .'

A major danger point was the *Disintegration* campaign. The album itself was riddled with Robert's discomfort at turning thirty, and Robert announced in *Cure News* in September 1989 that the Prayer Tour would be their last ever, 'but that doesn't mean we will never play another concert.' He had already said goodbye to British crowds at the end of '**Killing An Arab**' at Wembley Arena on 24 July 1989 with the words 'Goodnight. We'll hopefully see you again, but we probably won't. Thank you very much for being there all through the years.' His farewell at the end of their **American** tour at the Great Woods Center for the Performing Arts in Mansfield, Massachusetts on 24 September 1989 shared an air of finality with Johnny Rotten's 'Ever get the feeling you've been cheated?' (Winterland, San Francisco, 1978) and David Bowie's 'This is the last show we'll ever do' (Hammersmith Odeon, London, 1973). 'You'll never see me again', said Smith. But, as with Sex Pistols and as with Bowie, it wasn't final, and we would see him again. In less than twelve months he'd be back on a stage (Place de la République, **Paris**). And The Cure would play that very venue in Mansfield, MA no fewer than four further times in 1996, 2000, 2004 and 2023.

Circa *Wild Mood Swings* in 1996, the danger bubbled back to the surface. There was even a song on that album, 'Round and Round and Round', about splitting up which acknowledged that Smith is ultimately unable to do it: 'But however many times that we've said it before, once more is never the end . . .' Of the accompanying tour, in *Cure News*, he said 'I hope you enjoy the concerts – it could be the last time.' (It wasn't.)

As the Millennium loomed, the chronological goalposts shifted, and another life landmark presented itself as an excuse to call it quits. 'My long-term plan has always been to stop the group when I'm 40,' he said, 'which is in 1999. I hope I have the courage to stick to it.' And he later told Swiss television that he had planned to split The Cure after the release of *Galore* in 1997, when his disenchantment was at its peak, as the band's second singles compilation would provide a neat and tidy ending.

'I always intended giving up in 1999,' he told Sylvie Simmons of *Rolling Stone*. 'When *Standing On A Beach* was released and we re-signed a 10-year contract, I thought "Right, now it's all falling into place." I will be 40 years old in April '99 and I think it will be awful to enter a new millennium still in a band called The Cure. I just can't see myself doing it. I would be *horrified*. And, as our contract will be running out, I realise I can do the last record exactly how I wanted. The next album will be the last . . .'

He did do The Cure's next record – *Bloodflowers* in 2000 – exactly how he wanted, but it was not to be their last. At the time, *X-Press* magazine asked him if it really was the end for The Cure. 'Well . . . I really struggle to imagine this band playing any more shows after this year,' he said. 'I really don't think we will. I think the others know that, they've taken me seriously. Certainly the way that everyone's played this year and the general mood of the tour has been such that I'm led to believe that everyone is kind of convinced that this is going to be it.' He then added the caveat that it would be 'pretty stupid to decide to knock it on the head' when his band were sounding so good, and left the door open for further recordings, but he'd be happy if it didn't work out 'because I think *Bloodflowers* is a fantastic way to end.'

By 2019, Robert was self-aware enough to know that the credibility of the constant wolf-crying was wearing thin. Speaking to the *Chicago Tribune* on the subject of the rumoured **fourteenth album**, he said 'Being the contrarian that I am, I'd be very unhappy if it was the last one. We'll be onstage tomorrow and I'll be saying to them [the band], "This is the last time in Paris," and they'll look at me and shrug their shoulders. At some point, I will be proved right.' (He was not right, on this occasion: they were back in Paris in November 2022 on the **Lost World Tour**.)

One problem with splitting up The Cure is . . . well, *how*? When journalist John Robb said 'Robert Smith is The Cure and The Cure is Robert Smith' in the *Out of the Woods* **documentary**, he was only making a point that Smith himself had made in 1983 when he told *Melody Maker* 'I *am* The Cure'. It's a statement reminiscent of Robert's post-punk peer Mark E. Smith, who famously once told *NME* 'If it's me and your granny on bongos, it's The Fall.' If it's Robert Smith and your granny on bongos – and, circa *The Top*, it almost was – it's The Cure. In 1996, Smith had shifted in that view. 'The Cure isn't Robert Smith and whoever-else-happens-to-be-there . . . It is a group in the sense that it wouldn't exist without the others. I wouldn't do it as just me and a bunch of anonymous people.' But the question remained: how do you split *yourself* up?

One way of doing it would be to quietly fade from view. 'When we stop,' he said while hosting MTV's *120 Minutes* in November 1990, 'we won't announce that we've stopped. We just won't have done anything for such a long period of time that it'll be obvious that we'll have stopped.' But that isn't Robert's style. He's an over-announcer, not an under-announcer.

He has, on occasion, conceded that these dire warnings are often deployed tactically. In 1988 he admitted that the previous year's rumours that *Kiss Me, Kiss Me, Kiss Me* would be the last Cure album and the Kissing Tour the last tour were lies 'spread to create atmosphere'. And, speaking to *X-Press* in 2000, he mused that 'I suppose part of me says things to motivate the others. I think if we just approached this as another tour and another album it would have been dismal, really, because I knew that that's what was wrong with the band. There was a complete lack of passion. I think that telling everyone "This is it, you can believe it or not," that they have believed it, and I actually believe it as well.'

Maybe, in the heat of the moment, every time Robert Smith announces that The Cure are splitting up, he means what he says: in his mind, they really *have* split up. Until they un-split, and phone calls are made, and rehearsals are had, and tour dates are booked, once again.

The question isn't so much 'Will The Cure ever split up?' The question is 'Will they ever *stop* splitting up?'

Standing On A Beach

Everybody had it. *Everybody*.

If you were a teenage fan of alternative and indie music in the 1980s, there were a small handful of compilation albums which were absolutely essential to own. Getting hold of the early singles by your favourite alt-rock icons was expensive and, if you didn't live anywhere near an independent specialist shop, all but impossible. That's why, when these best-ofs came along, you jumped upon them eagerly.

These were as follows: *Once Upon A Time: The Singles* (1981) by **Siouxsie And The Banshees**, *Hatful Of Hollow* (1984) and *The World Won't Listen* (1987) by The Smiths, *The Singles 81–85* (1985) by **Depeche Mode**, *Songs To Learn And Sing* (1985) by Echo & The Bunnymen, *Substance* (1987) by **New Order**, *Substance* (1988) by Joy Division, and *Standing On A Beach: The Singles* (1986) by The Cure. These, perhaps along with *Flogging A Dead Horse* by Sex Pistols, *Singles Going Steady* by Buzzcocks and *ChangesOneBowie* by **David Bowie**, and whichever studio albums you could afford (Lou Reed's *Transformer* on the budget Fame label, perhaps) were your crash course in the cool stuff. Your induction, your indoctrination.

Standing On A Beach: The Singles was one of the most satisfying of all. It did exactly what it said on the tin. All killer no filler. Its thirteen tracks were The Cure's UK singles to that point, in chronological order. Nothing more, nothing less. ('**10.15 Saturday Night**', a single in **France** only, was omitted, though it did make the CD version, as well as the VHS, *Staring at the Sea*.) If you were drawn in by hits like '**The Lovecats**' or '**Close To Me**' and wanted to hear more, this LP filled a lot of gaps.

The version of '**A Forest**' was a special edit somewhere between the 7-inch and 12-inch (aka album) versions, and '**Boys Don't Cry**' was included in its original form despite the 'New Voice – New Mix' version being released specifically to drum up interest in the compilation. A double cassette version included an 'Unavailable B-Sides' tape (an early predecessor of *Join The Dots*). Essentially, though, those thirteen tracks were the definitive deal, played to death on constant rotation in the bedroom of every adolescent dreamer and trainee goth. It wasn't a perfect representation of The Cure's oeuvre so far, as most albums only had one single (and some had none at all), but it was enough to pique the interest and inspire The Cure-curious owner to investigate the band's back catalogue.

The rationale for releasing it was an ominous foreshadowing of the rationale for releasing *Greatest Hits* more than a decade later. 'We've come to the end of our **Polydor** contract,' Robert told *Record Mirror* in 1986, 'and if we don't release it with our blessing, they'll release it anyway. And if we have any more singles it would have to be a double album, which would be rather tedious.'

The face on the front of the album was not that of a member of The Cure, but that of sixty-six-year-old John Button, a fisherman from Rye in Sussex. He was discovered by **Tim Pope**, who cast him in the video for '**Killing An Arab**' that was made specially for *Staring At The Sea*. Button was a Second World War veteran who served in Egypt and was captured by the Nazis as a prisoner of war. According to local chronicler Elaine Peprell, 'He was the first Rye prisoner of war repatriated and a dance was held in the town, which he attended as the guest of honour.' In December 1966 he met the Queen, representing all Rye's fishermen. By the time of *Standing On A Beach*, he had been a fisherman for four decades. Every wind-lashed week of that life was etched into his craggy, weatherbeaten features, which were faintly reminiscent of Samuel Beckett, and which perfectly matched the aesthetic The Cure were aiming for with the **artwork**. He is, along with the Nirvana baby Spencer Elden, one of the most famous non-famous people to appear on a major album sleeve.

'If I can help these youngsters break through, after all, why not . . .', Button was quoted as saying by French magazine *Rock & Folk*. He had never heard The Cure's music, but promised he would buy a new cassette player to listen to *The Head On The Door*, out of curiosity.

Meanwhile, millions were buying the record with Button's face on it. *Standing On A Beach* went gold in the UK, double-gold in France, double-platinum (two million) in the **USA**, platinum in New Zealand and triple-platinum in Australia. In the UK it reached No.4, making it The Cure's highest-charting album until it was surpassed by *Disintegration*.

More importantly, from a Cure point of view, every owner was hungry to hear what The Cure would do next. '*Standing On A Beach* was a huge commercial success', Smith told *Uncut* in 2000. 'Suddenly we were being sold in garages. Everything I'd ever dreamed of doing was coming to fruition. I suddenly realised that there was an infinite amount of things I could do with the band.'

Staring At The Sea

When Robert Smith wants to be alone, he told *Cure News* in 1990, 'I go to the sea and just stare'.

Released on VHS in 1986, *Staring At The Sea: The Images* was the video companion to *Standing On A Beach: The Singles*. (Confusingly, *Staring at the Sea* was the name of the CD version of the singles compilation in the **US**. Even more confusingly, *Staring At The Sea: The B-Sides* was the title of Side 2 of the cassette version.) Like *Standing On A Beach*, *Staring At The Sea* took its title from a line in The Cure's debut single, '**Killing An Arab**'.

Eighty-two minutes long, it contained **videos** for all the songs from *Standing On A Beach* in chronological order of release, as well as '**10.15 Saturday Night**', 'Play For Today', 'Other Voices' and '**A Night Like This**'. The majority of the clips, from '**Let's Go To Bed**' onwards (and including the retrospectively-made videos for '**Boys Don't Cry**', in its 'New Voice – New Mix '86' version, and 'Killing An Arab') were directed by **Tim Pope**, and the reverse of the box read 'All extra bits by The Cure put together by Timothy Pope and Robert Smith.'

Those extra bits include the footage of **pre-Cure** outfit Easy Cure playing 'I Wish I Was Your Mother' on the bandstand in **Crawley** shot by Robert's father, poor-quality cine of The Cure at the Reading **Festival** in 1979 with the audio from an 'It's Not You' demo laid over the top, sped-up footage of the inside of the tour bus and the band larking about in Central Park to the sound of 'Another Journey By Train', Robert and **Simon Gallup** pushing **Lol Tolhurst** around in a wheelchair at the '**Charlotte Sometimes**' shoot, **Phil Thornalley** figuring out his upright bass part, Robert posing for photos, Lol playing 'Jumping Someone Else's Train' on a xylophone and **Andy Anderson** laying down his brushed snare part at the '**Lovecats**' sessions in **Paris**, and various other shots of inconsequential loitering at studios or soundchecks.

The **artwork**, by **Parched Art**, is of the back of a man's head, intended to resemble John Button (the retired fisherman whose face adorns *Standing On A Beach*), staring at a painting of some blue fish. The American version came with a big yellow sticker saying 'Includes all Cure videos ever made', and a black sticker clarifying that 'Killing An Arab' had no racist intent.

For the American viewer who didn't want to wait all day for a Cure video to appear, or the British viewer who couldn't even get MTV, an hour and a half staring at *Staring at the Sea* was time well spent.

But then, so is staring at the sea.

Strange Attraction

Chaos Theory was a popular science buzzphrase in the early 1990s. The fractal geometry of the Mandelbrot Set, with its constantly recurring and unfurling shapes, was used by countless raves for their visual projections or flyer graphics (becoming to the acid house generation what paisley and oil wheels were to the acid rock generation). And every pub bullshitter worth the price of a pint could tell you the basics of Edward Norton Lorenz's *Does a Butterfly Flapping Its Wings in Brazil Cause a Tornado in Texas?*, or at least recite the title, leaning back and waiting for you to say a long, slow 'wow . . .'

Robert Smith, like any stoner, was not immune to this admittedly fascinating topic. In a *Cure News* run-through of the tracks on *Wild Mood Swings*, he summarised the meaning behind 'Strange Attraction' as 'chaos theory / true life / a dream', and was more forthcoming in another issue, explaining that he was using the language of Chaos Theory to tell a story of miscommunication. 'I have often endured whole correspondences as a non-participant,' he wrote, somewhat cryptically. 'My answers are often, unknowingly, contained in my songwords . . .'

Those songwords recount a long-distance flirtation with a certain 'Blossom' conducted via messages written in books, poetry and greetings cards, and set against a soft-rock backing with a lightweight Latin feel. Butterflies are mentioned in the first verse, making 'Strange Attraction' the second lepidoptera-based Cure single (after '*The Caterpillar*'), and the chorus runs, 'Strange attraction spreads its wings/It alters but the smallest things'.

Unusually, no **video** was made for 'Strange Attraction'. Reportedly, the reason for this was that the previous time they'd released a **US** single, '**Fascination Street**', Smith was unhappy with the video. Consequently, it is the only Cure single (other than the original '**Boys Don't Cry**' without one). They did, however, perform it live on *Late Night with Conan O'Brien*, fresh from a gig at Radio City Music Hall, with **Perry Bamonte** playing auxiliary synths on the opposite side of the stage to **Roger O'Donnell** to replicate the keyboards-heavy sound of the single,

and **Simon Gallup** wearing a pair of Adidas tracksuit bottoms as though interrupted on his way to go jogging in Central Park. (They stuck around to play out the show with the more crowd-pleasing 'Boys Don't Cry'.)

The song was remixed by celebrated dub producer Adrian Sherwood for single release, and came with remixes of '**The 13th**', '**Gone!**' and album track 'This Is A Lie' as additional tracks, in a CD sleeve featuring a tin toy of a bird-like creature riding a horse, in keeping with the **artwork** style of *Wild Mood Swings* and its associated singles.

'Strange Attraction was released on 8 October 1996 as a single from *Wild Mood Swings* in **Australia** and the United States only, reaching No.145 in the former and failing to chart in altogether in the latter, making it the first Cure single released in America to miss out on the Billboard Hot 100 in over a decade. They would never chart there again. How the mighty were fallen.

In a review of *Galore* for *NME*, Johnny Cigarettes retrospectively accused 'Strange Attraction' (along with 'Gone!') of trying 'to be vaguely spicy and strange-sounding in a "*Kiss Me* . . ." stylee, but comprehensively fail to engage on any level.' Harsh but fair. And, given that they've never performed it live since the *Wild Mood Swings* campaign ended in 1996, The Cure probably agree.

Stylorouge

Stylorouge is the design house founded in 1981 by Rob O'Connor. He had studied Graphic Design in Brighton and Coventry before joining **Polydor**, to which he had been attracted by the new wave bands it was signing including **Siouxsie And The Banshees** (for whom he created **artwork** on several occasions) and The Cure.

When O'Connor broke away from Polydor, he adopted the French for 'red pen' as his artistic alias; the redness to reflect his 'comfortably left-of-centre' politics and the Frenchness as a nod to the aesthetics of the New Romantic movement. Stylorouge quickly became established as one of those names that seemed ubiquitous on record sleeves, along with Hipgnosis, Assorted iMaGes, Designers Republic, Peter Savile and Simon Halfon. Significant Stylorouge clients include Alison Moyet, Tina Turner, George Michael, Morrissey and Squeeze. It was O'Connor who designed Blur's lowercase logo and, it is said, added the exclamation mark to Wham!

Rectangular panels of colour are a typical Stylorouge trait, as seen on the Banshees best-of *Once Upon a Time*, the works of the Britpop band Menswear and, most iconically, the poster for the film *Trainspotting*.

Stylorouge's association with The Cure began early. In the words of their own website, 'Stylorouge have had the pleasure of working with the band on sleeve designs on a number of occasions, creative director Rob O'Connor having been working in-house at Polydor Records when the band's Small Wonder debut single '**Killing An Arab**' b/w '**10.15 Saturday Night**' was re-released on **Chris Parry**'s seminal **Fiction Records**. O'Connor acted as label liaison when the band ventured into the studio to shoot the video for the single '**Primary**', and later on put together a sleeve for the band's 12-inch EP *Japanese Whispers*.'

Stylorouge would, however, need to wait a long time for their next Cure commission, following the long reign of **Parched Art** partners **Porl Thompson** and **Andy Vella**. Latterly O'Connor and his team worked on the album *Bloodflowers* in 2000, the single '**Cut Here**' in 2001, the *Greatest Hits* album the same year, and the self-titled *The Cure* in 2004. And not a coloured rectangle in sight.

Success

'It was like dropping coloured ink in water,' Robert Smith told *Uncut* in 2000, in a beautiful metaphor for his sudden fame circa *Kiss Me, Kiss Me, Kiss Me*. 'I became public property and I wasn't prepared for the level that we'd reached. It was fanatical. Suddenly I was recognised everywhere I went in America, and when I got back to London, there would be 30 or 40 people camped outside my flat. By the end of that tour, my personality had changed a lot, I'd become really conceited, not just pretending to be a pop star, but living in it, and I realised that things couldn't go on like that.'

Just ten years before that album's release, a career advisor at St Wilfrid's Catholic School in **Crawley** asked Robert what he wanted to be. He said 'pop star'. Be careful what you wish for . . .

In 1981, speaking to *Sound International*, Robert confidently predicted 'We're not mainstream and we never will be, unless the mainstream changes to us.' After a handful of early hits, the mainstream did start changing to The Cure, circa *The Head On The Door* in 1985. This success, he told *Cure News*, made him feel vindicated 'after watching all these other people who were really shit sell bucketloads of records', and 'everything we'd done up to that point was re-evaluated. Suddenly, we were an important group.' Already, though, he was feeling some discomfort with the looming prospect of pop stardom. 'If I found myself in the Top 10,' he told *The Hit*, 'I'd stop doing interviews and disappear for a while. I'd never allow us to be a 'big group' – I'd break us up if that ever happened.'

Of course, **splitting up** was never really on the cards, despite his intermittent threats. But the trigger for doing so – Top 10 success – did happen. There was a spell circa *Disintegration* in 1989 when The Cure could legitimately be said to be the biggest band in the world. The European leg of the Prayer Tour that year ended with three nights at Wembley Arena. I was there for one of them, and a gauge of just how mainstream The Cure had become is that very straight-looking members of the audience laughed at me for wearing make-up and having big hair. (I pointed to the stage and said, 'Um, have you seen that guy?') Meanwhile, in the **US**, they were No.2 in the Billboard charts with '**Lovesong**', held off the top only by Janet Jackson, and able to fill New York's 44,000-capacity Giants Stadium (the first 30,000 tickets having been sold in one day, a remarkable feat in the pre-internet era), with the *Disintegration* album selling four million copies worldwide. Smith later said 'It was never our intention to become as big as this . . .'

If anything, they only got bigger on the *Wish* cycle three years later, as a live draw. That album reached No.1 in the UK and No.2 in the US, selling three million worldwide, and the accompanying tour was the longest and largest of their career. **Porl Thompson** and Robert Smith were both troubled by this. The former told *Cure News* he preferred small gigs, and the latter preferred them 'larger but not too large (10,000 people feels good)'. He was worried, he told a press conference, that huge live shows just become 'a spectacle rather than an experience.'

And it's not as if they became any less of a crowd-pulling attraction in later years. The biggest (70,000) and third-biggest (57,000) crowds of their career – at a Cure show as opposed to a **festival** headline – both happened in **Mexico** in 2019 and 2013 respectively, with Hyde Park, London's 65,000 from 2018 (see *40 Live*) in second place.

With all this success comes financial reward. Robert had always been very sensible with money – in the early days, every time **Fiction** gave The Cure an album advance, he put it in the bank and they paid themselves a set wage from it. He has never been a showy, extravagant spender, and the fanciest luxury The Cure have ever allowed themselves is probably the time they travelled on separate buses, one for smokers and the other smoke-free (Porl went on the smoke-free one).

When Smith's wealth has been publicised, he has found it extremely difficult. 'Because I've been in the Top 20 of wealthiest pop stars,' he told *Humo*, 'and that's obscene. That kind of info overshadows the music. It also irritates me that the really rich, who've made their money in a lot less elegant ways, never end up in a Top 20 like that. Where are the weapons traders?'

Just after *Kiss Me, Kiss Me, Kiss Me* – that ink drop moment – Smith once said he was convinced The Cure weren't *famous* famous because taxi drivers never recognise them. If that was true then, it isn't now: I was once driven by a taxi driver in **Bognor Regis** who told me, 'I had that Robert Smith from The Cure in the back of my cab the other day.'

Things had already escalated, recognition-wise, by the time *Disintegration* was sweeping the world. 'It reached the stage in Europe,' he told *LA Times*, 'where I was unable to go out for a walk. We were in some of the most beautiful cities in Europe, and I couldn't go out without having an entourage . . . I tried a disguise and it didn't work. I had no **make-up** and my **hair** flat and a hat on, but people recognised me, and when I asked them how they knew it was me they said it was my **shoes**, so the second time I did it I changed my shoes, and I was still recognised.'

In 2000, Robert told an interviewer 'The Cure have had far more commercial success than I ever imagined. Or ever wanted, in some ways. It's been quite difficult at times. Particularly in America. The level of success has been something that just as an individual I've found awkward sometimes, to be as famous as I've been, through the years.'

It's too late now. That inky water will never be clear again.

Supernatural, The

Given Robert Smith's love of gothic **literature**, and the existence of Cure songs with titles such as 'The Hungry Ghost' and 'Fear Of Ghosts', should one assume that he is a believer in the supernatural?

It's a complex question. In *Cure News*, he often discussed such matters, in answer to fan queries or in relation to The Cure's work. In 1988, for example, he stated that while he did believe in telepathy and clairvoyance, and took an interest in John Dee, the sixteenth-century occultist, ghosts were a step too far for someone who had disavowed **religion**. 'Ghosts require life after death, and I am denied this comforting faith.' The following year, his answer on ghosts had shifted to 'sometimes', a response he also gave to the question of UFOs.

In 1992 Robert revealed that the artwork for *Picture Show*, depicting a girl using a planchette (for automatic writing), came from a book he was reading called *The Encyclopaedia of the Unexplained*, hinting at an interest (if not necessarily belief) in matters Fortean.

Other members of The Cure have been forthright in their supernatural experiences. When **Simon Gallup** was four, he told *Cure News* in 1994, he saw a hand coming out of a wardrobe trying to do a puppet show. And, in 1998, **Roger O'Donnell** claimed he had been 'haunted' while making *Wild Mood Swings* at St Catherine's Court in Bath.

As for Robert, his last word on the matter, in *Cure News* at least, was that he has had out-of-body experiences but 'nothing that's made me believe in an afterlife'.

The answer to the question, then, is no. But with just the ghost of a maybe.

Support Bands

The industry norm, for major touring bands, is for the support act to 'buy on' to the tour: that is, to pay a flat fee for the privilege of exposure to the bigger act's fanbase. While the support act will almost always be within broadly the same genre as the headliner, the pairing of the two acts is often purely a commercial transaction, or one facilitated by corporate factors such as a shared management company or record label.

The Cure, in this regard as in so many others, do things slightly differently. One always senses that The Cure's support acts are genuinely hand-picked by Robert Smith on their musical merits, according to his own **tastes**.

Some of them are picked frequently enough to be perceived as The Cure's 'pet bands': **And Also The Trees**, **Shelleyan Orphan**, **Cranes** and **Mogwai**. These are the bands whose connection with The Cure typically goes beyond sharing a stage on multiple occasions and also involves **collaboration** in various forms. One might also add to this category current title-holders the Twilight Sad, the Scottish quintet who were The Cure's support band in 2016, 2018, 2022 and 2023, who have credited The Cure with 'saving' them, and whose song 'There's A Girl On The Corner' was **covered** by Robert Smith on a 7-inch single in 2015. Robert praised them effusively in *NME*: 'I asked The Twilight Sad to join us on The Cure Tour 2016 because they are the best band playing the best songs – consistently brilliant, emotional, intense, inspiring, entertaining.' (When they first received the request via email, guitarist Andy MacFarlane initially suspected it was Barry Burns from Mogwai playing a joke on them.)

Some support bands have an impact on Cure history: see **Zerra 1** for that band's involvement in the **Fourteen Explicit Moments** tour. Others go on to make history themselves. When The Cure played a residency at the Marquee in London in 1979, the opening act on the first night was Joy Division (see **New Order**).

In an August 1992 edition of *Cure News*, members other than Robert were asked to name their ideal support bands. **Simon Gallup** chose Ride and Cranes, **Boris Williams** chose PJ Harvey, and **Porl Thompson** chose God Machine (who were signed to **Fiction**), Nirvana and Dinosaur Jr. The last of these had just happened: Dinosaur Jr, noted for their inspired **cover** of '**Just Like Heaven**', supported The Cure in Pasadena that year.

An insight into Robert's favourites at various moments can be gained by examining the support acts at larger events he Cure-ated, such as **Curiosa** and **Meltdown**, each of which has a *Curepedia* entry. Other examples are the Garden Party all-dayer at Crystal Palace Bowl in 1990, at which they were supported by All About Eve, James and Lush, and the Pasadena Daydream of 2019 which featured Chelsea Wolfe, Deftones, Emma Ruth Rundle, Kaelan Mikla, Pixies and The Joy Formidable, several of whom were serial Cure-supporters.

Most Cure support acts went on to achieve at least a modicum of success, or were already doing just fine without a Robert Smith endorsement. Others vanished without trace, despite the platform of a Cure tour. For example, Lefaye, a prog-goth band from Hookwood near **Horley** whose membership included keyboardist William D. Drake of Cardiacs. Lefaye supported The Cure on eleven UK dates in 1992, but broke up in 1993 without ever releasing a record.

Some support bands cannot be saved.

Swimming Horses

The fourteenth single by **Siouxsie And The Banshees**, and the second from Robert Smith's stint as a recording member of the band, had a gestation almost as unusual as that of the sea creatures it references.

As Siouxsie explained to *Melody Maker*'s Cathi Unsworth, she had seen a documentary about a Middle East-based charity called Les Sentinelles who rescued women in cultures where pre-marital sex is punishable by death, carried out either by the eldest brother in the family, or by public stoning. 'There was this instance of a woman whose daughter had developed a tumour,' Sioux told Unsworth, 'and, of course, gossip abounded that she was pregnant. The doctor who removed the tumour allowed her to take it back to the village to prove that, no, it wasn't a baby – but they wouldn't believe her. The woman knew her daughter would have to be stoned to death, so she poisoned her, out of kindness, to save her from a worse fate. Now, this organisation has all these escape routes for women like her, mainly through the elder brother who pretends to have killed them. But once they've been saved, they can never go back. So the song starts, "Kinder than with poison".'

The imagery of the chorus, 'He gives birth to swimming horses', she explained, derived from the peculiar **zoological** fact that it is male seahorses who give birth, 'so they're the only species that have a maternal feel for the young.' Siouxsie drew a connection between the situation in the documentary and this quirk of aquatic biology. 'It was, I suppose, an abstract way of linking it all together without being sensationalist. I remember just being really moved by that programme, and wanting to get the sorrow out of me.'

This powerful subject matter was given a suitably potent musical backing by the Banshees and producer **Mike Hedges**, a hesitant, stop-start piano motif interlaced with spindly, reverberating guitars from Smith.

In the video, directed by **Tim Pope** (retained by the Banshees after '**Dear Prudence**'), Robert literally plays a background role. Smith, in a white tunic, is shown alternately wearing what appears to be a white papier mâché replica of a Renaissance plague doctor's beak-like mask, and standing alongside the other male Banshees observing Siouxsie without moving. They were intended to be human projection screens, but the effect didn't quite work.

Siouxsie hated the video, and never allowed it to be shown on TV. It was, she later said, 'a fiasco'. First of all, an intended abstract blurry background effect didn't come off, secondly a make-up artist made Siouxsie look orange, and thirdly there were problems with the swimming horses themselves. They were filmed in a pool where convalescent horses go for physio, but the best shots of the actual swimming horses couldn't be used: 'When the cameraman came back,' she told biographer Mark Paytress, 'he said he hadn't realised that each time a horse enters the water it spontaneously pisses. These were the only shots I liked.'

The main B-side was the similarly piano-based 'Let Go', which imagines an astronaut on a space walk contemplating detaching and floating away to their death. The 12-inch also featured the more experimental 'The Humming Wires', which could be about breaking news of the death of a motor racing driver, but could also be about no such thing.

Released on Wonderland, the Banshees' own label (via **Polydor**) on 16 March 1984, 'Swimming Horses' got no higher than No.28 in the UK singles chart. However, it had an afterlife of sorts. The piano motif was re-employed by Robert Smith only a year later on *The Head On The Door* track 'Six Different Ways'. Later still, the single's production was specifically cited by James Dean Bradfield of Manic Street Preachers as one of the reasons for hiring Hedges to produce their career-defining *Everything Must Go* album.

T

T is for ...

10.15 Saturday Night

No '10.15 Saturday Night', no deal. That might sound like an exaggerated claim, but according to interviews in the booklet of the deluxe reissue of *Three Imaginary Boys*, it was the demo of '10.15 Saturday Night' which first snagged the attention of **Chris Parry**, ultimately leading to the **Fiction** founder signing The Cure to his newly created label.

The song, co-credited to Robert Smith, **Lol Tolhurst** and **Michael Dempsey**, was written when Smith was just sixteen and performed in the **pre-Cure** days in gigs around the **Crawley** area. '"10.15 Saturday Night" was written at the table in our kitchen,' wrote Smith in the booklet. 'Watching the tap dripping, feeling utterly morose, drinking my dad's homemade beer . . . My evening had fallen apart, and I was back at home feeling very sorry for myself!'

As well as being the opening track of the *Three Imaginary Boys* album, it was the first song of their live set during their residency at London's Marquee in 1979 and the whole Three Imaginary Boys tour. It was a composition of which they were evidently proud.

Rightly so. It's a masterpiece of minimalism. Two verses, four items (a strip light, a dripping tap, a sink, a telephone), and one situation. There's no mystery, nothing cryptic, just the bare bones of a simple scenario. He's in the kitchen, waiting for the object of his affections to phone, and wondering what she's doing. And he begins to cry.

The music is onomatopoeic, mirroring the 'drip drip drip drip' of the tap with its nagging, insistent, low-key notes, ramping up the tension before the sudden detonations. (The Cure were using a QUIET-loud-QUIET-loud dynamic years before Pixies, never mind Nirvana.) It operates in a comparable way to what is wrongly known as 'Chinese water torture' (the use of dripping water as a torture method was first described by Italian lawyer Hippolytus de Marsiliis circa 1500).

The Cure's first-ever **video** was made, interestingly, not for '**Killing An Arab**' but for '10.15 Saturday Night', despite the latter being the B-side of the former. It was directed by Piers Bedford, who went on to direct **Siouxsie And The Banshees**' 'Happy

House' and the 2003 documentary *Punk: The Early Years*. It's a simple performance clip, documenting their **hairstyles** at a formative moment: Lol with a curly mop, Robert a bowl cut, Michael a shaggy new wave cut. It's characterised by the band's expressions of concentration and diligence, and their reluctance to show off or 'rock out', Lol gently and impassively tapping the hi-hat till it's time to explode.

The clip was never shown, nor even seen by the band, till the time came to assemble **Staring at the Sea** in 1986, when Robert remembered it had happened, and someone at **Polydor** found it gathering dust in a cupboard. 'What it looks like,' Robert said to an interviewer in 1988, 'is the kind of po-facedness that we used to adopt when we thought something was incredibly stupid.'

'10.15 Saturday Night' is a B-side that is straining for A-side status. 'I always wanted "Arab" and "10.15" to be a double A-side,' wrote Robert in the *Join The Dots* liner notes. '"Arab" was a great rabble-rouser when we played it live, but it was almost a novelty song, whereas "10.15" was more representative of what we were trying to do.' In **Australia**, it was also a B-side in 1980, but with '**Boys Don't Cry**' on the A-side. However, it was released the same year in **France** as a single in its own right, with 'Accuracy' on the flipside and a sleeve with the same image as *Three Imaginary Boys*. Copies of the French single are **rarities**, worth something in the region of £500. A French promotional version with 'Foxy Lady' on the B-side, combining the virtues of Frenchness and promo-ness, is on sale at the time of writing for £1,200.

'Killing An Arab' was singled out for mention by reviewers. In *Sounds*, reviewing the single, Dave McCullough wrote that 'It hits upon the value of sparseness in rock 'n' roll like no other record has in, oh, as far as I can think back.' In *NME*, Nick Kent called it 'Something of an isolated vignette, hopefully portraying a whole mood of rejection'.

'10.15 Saturday Night' has had a long afterlife. It has been performed live during most of The Cure's full-length shows since its release. It is their sixth most-played song, and is a regular feature of their extended encores to this day. No fewer than four different versions were included on the expanded

Three Imaginary Boys. Its cultural reach extends beyond The Cure: the Newcastle-based artists Aly & Mick Smith have painted a diptych in oils – a driptych? – inspired by the song, and it was **sampled** by Massive Attack on their cover of John Holt's 'Man Next Door' from their 1998 album *Mezzanine*.

Its impact at the time, however, is perhaps best summarised by one anecdote from *Ten Imaginary Years*. On 8 December 1978 The Cure played the Corn Dolly in Oxford. Only about twenty people turned up, but the band ended up playing '10.15 Saturday Night' about eight times because one guy kept shouting for 'that drip drip drip one'.

13th, The

. . . or 'The Cure go Bossa Nova'. Or is it?

The lead single from *Wild Mood Swings* was a heady cocktail of disparate Latin elements. Something about The Cure chimes with Latin America, and something about Latin America chimes with The Cure. That much is well-documented (see **Mexico**, see **Argentina**, see **Brazil**, see **South America**).

After an intro which sounds like a New Orleans jazz funeral tuning up, 'The 13th' is a delirious, demented, almost nightmarish whirl of Mariachi horns and Samba-derived percussion. Interestingly, **Perry Bamonte**, speaking to Susan Masters of *Pulse* circa *Wild Mood Swings*, spoke of the band being impressed by local musicians when touring in Brazil, home of samba and bossa nova. 'These beggars used to come round to this café outside the hotel,' he recalled, 'and play music on really fucked guitars and drums made out of oil cans. They were excellent, but you can't emulate that sound; it's in the blood.' Nevertheless, emulate that sound is exactly what The Cure did. Producer **Steve Lyon**, on the *Out of the Woods* documentary, described 'The 13th' as 'almost Brazilian-esque . . . a Western European's eye on what South American music can sound like.' Peter Parrish of *Stylus* described it as 'a pseudo-Latin number with a not-especially-hidden message about giving in to your lust.'

Is that what it's about? In *Cure News*, Robert Smith revealed that the song was originally called 'Two Chord Cool', and that its inspiration was 'a club in Italy/a book about vipers and "the buzz"'. The song's main storyline seems to be a hymn to a seductive nightclub jazz diva, not dissimilar to Soft Cell's 'Torch'. But Peter Parrish had a point: with its repeated and unsubtle yelps of 'Do it to me!', this one is about **sex**. Robert Smith's vocal is split between his outer and inner thoughts, between a strange croon and *sotto voce* commentary, as though duetting with himself.

> 'If you want I can take you on another kind of ride'
> 'Believe me I would, but . . .'
> Deep inside the 'But' is 'Please'
> I am yearning for another taste
> And my shaking is 'Yes' . . .

He finishes on a sudden 'It feels good-ah!'

The **video** was filmed at Bow Film Studios in East London by Sophie Muller (who had previously made videos for Annie Lennox and Shakespears Sister), making it only the second official Cure video since 1982 not to be directed by **Tim Pope**. A couple of years later, *Cure News* summarised the inspiration: 'On a night off in Rio in 1995, they decided they should enter a local nightclub talent show, R. S. drew the short straw and sang "Copacabana". The winner, a woman called Angelica, sang "The 13th" even though he hadn't finished writing it. Sophie Muller tried to capture the mood of that night and the next morning.'

It's one of The Cure's strangest videos, and it is not without strong competition on that front. Its bizarre narrative begins with a battered and bruised Robert, wearing a turquoise dress shirt and apparently the victim of a kidnap situation, holed up in a hotel room with a ghostly bride, watching a news item about hotel slayings. The TV switches channels to a brightly coloured variety show whose guests include a Madonna impersonator who turns out to be a drag act, and The Cure dressed as a Latin showband. (**Roger O'Donnell** was less than thrilled at being obliged to wear these Mariachi costumes on *Top of the Pops* shortly afterwards.) As the fourth wall between the TV show and the hotel-dwellers becomes increasingly permeable, the viewer is left uncertain. Who is the real Robert? Who is the real *anyone*?

The chaotic TV show's beleaguered host is Sean Hughes, the comedian with whom the band had become friends after appearing on his programme *Sean's Show* in 1993 performing 'High' (see **TV appearances**). Hughes' 2015 live show *Mumbo Jumbo*, just two years before his death, included an anecdote about hanging out with musical heroes The Cure, but being too shitfaced to enjoy it. (He did remember being serenaded at the break of dawn by Robert Smith at Jane Seymour's house in Bath.)

The sleeve, designed by **Andy Vella** alone (in **Parched Art** partner **Porl Thompson**'s absence), is a photo of a tin toy panda playing a drum, in the style of the tin clown on its parent album. Its B-sides, across various release formats, were 'It Used to Be Me' (inspiration: 'the group's history . . . one of my parts'), 'Ocean' ('how I feel sometimes') and 'Adonais' ('a poem/a dream/sort of written with brandon lee, the crow in mind'). The third of these was based on the poem 'Adonais', written by Percy Bysshe Shelley upon the death of Keats (see **Poetry**).

Released on 22 April 1996, just ahead of *Wild Mood Swings*, 'The 13th' was a modest hit (15 in the UK, 44 in America), though it did reach No.2 in Hungary and No.5 in Italy. It remains a divisive track – many fans hate it – and has seldom been played live, although this is partly due to the logistics of hiring a horn section.

However incongruous 'The 13th' may seem among The Cure's singles – a mash-up of Mexican, Brazilian, Spanish and Italian influences – it's worth remembering that 'bossa nova' literally means new wave. Whatever The Cure became for the space of this song, it was only a minor adjustment.

Taking Off

As might have been signalled by the fact that their current album was named after themselves, the second single from 2004's *The Cure* saw The Cure in self-referential mode.

'Taking Off' was, like the rest of the album, produced by Ross Robinson and recorded in London's Olympic Studios. This sweet, mid-paced three-minute and nineteen-second pop song was described by Andy Greenwald of *Blender* as 'a strummy echo of 1992's chart-topping *Wish*' in contrast with the 'abyss' of the remainder of *The Cure*, and that's about the size of it.

Its lyric is about fleetingly escaping the repetitive Groundhog Day of living by spending time with your loved one – 'But tonight I climb with you/Tonight, so high with you . . .' – before the grim grind starts again. The word '**high**' is where the self-referentiality begins, as the song echoes the feel of the 1992 single of that name. The song was later reworked as 'The Dragon Hunters Song', the theme for the French

fantasy anime series *Dragon Hunters* (see **TV, The Cure appear on**).

The **video** was directed by the Saline Project (the name used by the trio of Adam Toht, Ben Toht and Jesse Roff), who had previously only made one video for Keane but were retained for The Cure's next video '**alt.end**', and went on to direct for Eminem, Black Eyed Peas and Gwen Stefani among others. It begins with Robert doing the very opposite of taking off: wearing big black bird wings, he falls to earth where he and the band, mostly in shadow, perform the song among giant blades of grass. He does eventually take off again, soaring above the ground in a callback to his kite ride in the video for the aforementioned 'High'.

Its B-sides were the lugubrious, dense and arguably anti-**religion** 'Your God Is Fear', and 'Why Can't I Be Me?', a self-critical riposte to their 1987 single '**Why Can't I Be You?**' Far slower and more contemplative than the hectic eighties hit, it ends with a whispered, 'Simply inelegant', an echo of 'You're simply elegant' on the original.

The **artwork**, by Robert's niece Gabrielle (as per the album sleeve which was drawn by his nieces and nephews) is a crayon drawing of a dinosaur, or possibly a giraffe, eating cherries from a tree.

Released on 18 October 2004 on the I Am **label**, 'Taking Off' marked the last time a Cure single made the UK Top 40, sneaking in at No.39.

After that, Cure singles never quite took off.

Tastes (of Robert Smith)

Robert Smith's musical taste is, helpfully, a matter of public record. Numerous outlets, often *Cure News*, have repeatedly canvassed Robert about his favourite music, leaving us with a body of evidence which offers a shifting timeline of his tastes over the years. There is a massive crossover, of course, between this and The Cure's influences, but it isn't complete: some of it is purely music for pleasure. (It's hard, for example, to discern Paula Abdul's influence on *Wish*.)

In the first category are what we might call the classic rock artists which predate The Cure and were around in Robert's **youth**. The top three, predictably, are the 'rogue characters' who were his formative heroes: **Jimi Hendrix** (thirteen mentions for the first artist he ever saw live), **David Bowie** (eight mentions for the artist whose Ziggy Stardust album was the first he ever bought) and The Sensational Alex Harvey Band (seven mentions). There are also three mentions for Captain Beefheart, two each for **Pink Floyd** and Van Morrison, and one each for Bad Company, The Beatles, Be Bop Deluxe, Black Sabbath, Nick Drake, Dr John, Brian Eno's ambient music, John Mayall, T. Rex and The Velvet Underground.

The next category contains The Cure's punk, post-punk and eighties contemporaries. Of these, Kate Bush is winning the war with six mentions, though **New Order** get five and Joy Division four, which – as they are essentially the same band – puts them in the lead. There are also three mentions each for Echo & The Bunnymen and Tom Waits, two each for Cocteau Twins and The Psychedelic Furs, and one each for 10,000 Maniacs, Elvis Costello, The Human League, Public Image Ltd, **Siouxsie And The Banshees** and The Stranglers. The most obscure selection from that era is Corpses For Bedmates, namechecked by Robert on Australian radio in 1984. (They actually existed. German-American act. Unsettling experimental industrial **goth** in a Death In June vein. Actually pretty good.) It can also be assumed that **And Also The Trees** and **Shelleyan Orphan**, both frequent Cure **support bands**, are artists Robert liked, along with **Associates** and Marc And The Mambas, with whom he **collaborated**. At the end of the decade, he said the Bunnymen were his favourite band of the eighties, but that 'Joy Division is still my favourite group of all time and always will be.'

However, his tastes in that era could be surprisingly poptastic. He once gave his twelve-track Christmas Party playlist to a magazine, and most of it was soul, funk and disco: Heatwave, the Commodores, the Gap Band, Mary Wells, the Jackson Five, Sister Sledge and Evelyn 'Champagne' King. There was also room for some glam rock from Alice Cooper, T. Rex and Gary Glitter, some sixties pop from Sandie Shaw and just one piece of edgy art-rock from Yoko Ono. And in 1989, speaking to *Oor*, he said 'I've got a tape with ten songs who get me out of any down mood. That's my get-up-and-go-tape when I can't really get out of my bed. Kate Bush is on it with "Running Up That Hill" and New Order with "Dreams Never End" from their first album. Also "Don't Get Me Wrong" by The Pretenders and "Out of Touch" by Hall & Oates. The last track is "Straight Up" by Paula Abdul, with that brilliant tap-dance-beat . . .'

Then came the Next Generation Along: bands who emerged in The Cure's wake in the late eighties and into the nineties. There's a noticeable slant towards shoegaze in Robert's tastes at this time. Ride are mentioned three times, My Bloody Valentine, **Mogwai** (who he once named as his 'favourite band on the planet'), Curve and Eat Static twice each, there's been endless praise for Dinosaur Jr and their **cover of The Cure's** 'Just Like Heaven', and there are also favourable mentions for Banco de Gaia, The Breeders, Chapterhouse (whose 'Mesmerize' he once listened to twenty times in a row), **Cranes** (another regular Cure support band), Death in Vegas, Deftones, Ani DiFranco, God Machine, PJ Harvey, Kid Loco, Lush, Madder Rose, Nirvana, Pixies, Portishead, Sneaker Pimps, The Sugarcubes and Supergrass. In 1990, when asked which of the groups of the day he would most like to be in, he chose My Bloody Valentine. On the tour bus, however, the band tended to fall back on old favourites like T. Rex, Gary Glitter and Middle Of The Road, and the *Easy Rider* soundtrack.

Into the twenty-first century, a whole wealth of information about Robert's tastes can be inferred from the bands he chose as support acts (e.g. The Twilight Sad), the bands who played events he curated such as **Curiosa**, **Meltdown** and Pasadena Daydream (Interpol, The Rapture, Manic Street Preachers, Death Cab For Cutie, Kaelan Mikla and dozens of others), and those with whom he has collaborated (such as Republica, Placebo, Orbital, Crystal Castles, Korn, 65daysofstatic, Billy Corgan, Faithless, Gorillaz and Chvrches.). He has also praised Godspeed You! Black Emperor, the catalogue of Danish ambient label Relax With Nature, and one act this author needed to look up: Aerial Love Feed (New York post-shoegaze band from the early 2000s. Also pretty good).

It doesn't necessarily follow that Robert likes a band just because they have been **covered by The Cure** – the seventies pop hits performed at the Marquee by **Cult Hero**, for example, were surely done mainly for a laugh – but, for the record, artists to receive that honour include Black Sabbath, The Beatles, the Bee Gees, David Bowie, **Depeche Mode**, The Doors, Gary Glitter, The Sensational Alex Harvey Band, Jimi Hendrix, The Kinks, John Lennon, John Martyn, Frank Sinatra, Slade, Thin Lizzy, The Troggs, The Twilight Sad, Wendy Waldman and Wings.

Robert is also a lover of classical music. Erik Satie gets three mentions, and there are also mentions of Beethoven, Chopin, Debussy, Sibelius, Gregorian chants, and John Williams' theme from *The Mission*. The works of Bach, Schumann and Schubert were all used in 1990 as pre-show music. And Robert once said that for his funeral he would like Barber's *Adagio for Strings*, Khachaturian's *Gayaneh* (as used in *2001: A Space Odyssey*), Elgar's *Variation No.9 (Nimrod)*, Tchaikovsky's *Symphony No.6 Finale*, Mahler's *Symphony No.5 Part 3*, Mahler's *Adagietto*, and Mozart's *Requiem* to be played, along with some Hendrix, Bowie, Nick Drake, Alex Harvey and Joy Division 'and a couple of Cure songs'.

There are also nods towards jazz, with Louis Armstrong, Billie Holiday (The Cure's walk-off music on the *Wish* tour), Django Reinhardt and Frank Sinatra receiving mentions, and towards what we might broadly call 'World Music' with Flamenco artist Camarón, 'a load of Russian folk', and 'Eastern music'.

The answer Robert gives will depend on how the question is framed. When asked to choose his favourite albums of all time, he has, at various times, named the following: *Hounds of Love* by Kate Bush (three times), *Five Leaves Left* by Nick Drake (three times), *Next . . .* by The Sensational Alex Harvey Band (twice), *Astral Weeks* by Van Morrison (twice), *Low* and *David Live* by David Bowie, *Are You Experienced?* and *Axis: Bold as Love* by the Jimi Hendrix Experience, *Treasure* by Cocteau Twins, *This Year's Model* by Elvis Costello and the Attractions, *Closer* by Joy Division, *Mirror Moves* by The Psychedelic Furs, *Kaleidoscope* by Siouxsie And The Banshees and *Rattus Norvegicus* by The Stranglers.

When asked to name his favourite song or single, he has chosen 'Life On Mars?' by David Bowie no fewer than four times, 'just because it reminds me of the first time I danced with **Mary**'. The Jimi Hendrix Experience's 'Purple Haze' gets mentioned twice, and 'Are You Experienced?' once. Three different Joy Division songs are named: 'Decades', 'Love Will Tear Us Apart' and 'The Eternal', along with 'Everything's Gone Green' by New Order. The Sensational Alex Harvey band get one each for 'Give My Compliments To The Chef' and 'Next'. And there's one mention each for Kate Bush's 'Running Up That Hill', The Chiffons' 'Sweet Talking Guy', Hall & Oates' 'Out Of Touch', Pink Floyd's 'Set The Controls For The Heart Of The Sun', The Pretenders' 'Don't Get Me Wrong', Frank Sinatra's 'I've Got You Under My Skin', The Velvet Underground's 'Venus In Furs' and Tom Waits' 'Tom Traubert's Blues'.

'And . . .', Robert once added, 'Hmmm . . . "**Faith**" by us.'

Taw, John

Without John Taw, we might know what the early Cure sounded like, but we'd have a far fainter idea of what they looked like.

A local photographer who studied at Reigate School of Art and Design, Taw was there when it mattered to document the band's beginnings.

Sometimes this meant live shots, like the **Cult Hero** gig at the Marquee, or an early Cure gig at which the logo with the dropped 'C' is already visible on an amp. Sometimes it meant candid snaps, like the shot of **Lol Tolhurst** and Robert Smith in a twin-bed hotel room, the former drinking whisky and the latter messing around with a tape recorder, or his shot of **Michael Dempsey** in the passenger seat of a British Leyland hatchback, reading a map.

Most importantly, he was behind the lens for their first real photo sessions, all of them outdoors. These included black and white shots of the trio in a cemetery lifting the lid of a grave from which a guitar neck is poking out, sitting halfway up an electricity pylon next to the *Danger – 132,000 Volts* sign, standing next to the fence of Gatwick Airport as a twin-prop plane takes off over Lol's head, manhandling a fashion mannequin, and trespassing on the tracks of the London–Brighton mainline just north of **Horley** (a stretch which is fleetingly seen from the driver's cab in the video for '**Jumping Someone Else's Train**'), while Robert holds his Woolworths Top 20 **guitar**. When the band started sending demo tapes to record companies, they used a John Taw session shot on the cover.

He also became involved in the band's merchandise, making their first badges for Easy Cure (see **Pre-Cure bands**), given away free when they played St Edwards's Church Hall in Pound Hill on Friday 28 October 1977. This badge, which Robert wore onstage, depicted a man being sick on a long-distance fishing trip. According to Taw, that vomiting man was Brian Adsett (later Robert's security guard – see **Crew**), though according to Michael Dempsey it was Frank Bell of **Cult Hero**. In addition, his photos were often used in early Cure fanzine, *The Clinic*.

Taw, who also happens to be Robert Smith's brother-in-law, moved away from music photography, pursuing a career in construction management, while maintaining an interest in wildlife photography as a side hobby. His place in Cure history, however, is indelible.

Thompson, Derek

Only the second-most important Thompson in The Cure, Derek Thompson was born in London and raised on traditional Irish music reflecting his family's County Mayo heritage. He first came to prominence via a relatively brief spell as a member of SPK, the Australian industrial band whose name was sometimes believed to stand for Sozialistisches Patienten Kollektiv, but was also given a variety of backronyms including Selective Pornography Kontrol and Surgical Penis Klinik. The only SPK release on which Derek Thompson appears is the 1983 single 'Metal Dance'/'Will to Power' (a Nietzschean reference that wouldn't be Thompson's last), contributing percussion, trumpet and keyboards. He left SPK after founder Graeme Revell took them in what Thompson deemed too commercial a direction.

His departure from SPK came at just the right moment for The Cure, who needed two musicians to fill out the **line-up** for a live appearance on the BBC's **TV** music programme *The Oxford Road Show* on 18 March 1983. One of them was drummer **Andy Anderson**, the other was Derek Thompson, hired, he once claimed, after meeting Robert Smith in a bar. Smith asked him what colour his bass was, and Thompson replied 'black'. Thompson is known for his mischievous interview answers, but that's his story, and he's sticking to it.

Watching the *ORS* footage now, he doesn't look out of place. A long-limbed, lugubrious presence in black clothes who does indeed play a black bass, he looks like a standard-issue Curebloke. He dutifully plays the right notes in the right order on '**One Hundred Years**', then capably takes the lead on the intro to 'The Figurehead'. After just two songs, his spell in The Cure was over.

He later gained a degree of notoriety in 1990 under the name Hoodlum Priest, an industrial hip-hop project he formed with Christian rapper Paul Sevier, whose debut album on the ZTT label made heavy use of film samples. Hoodlum Priest rarely played live, but their appearance at the Surfers Against Sewage festival in Newquay featured a line-up which became the nucleus of Apollo 440, a band whose members include **Noko**, whose stint in The Cure was almost as short as Thompson's, and which also included *The Oxford Road Show*.

Outside Hoodlum Priest, who released three albums in the nineties, he has recorded under the names Surfers for Satan, Technietzsche (there it is) and Komuso, remixed the likes of Pop Will Eat Itself and the aforementioned Apollo 440, and worked as a composer on obscure films including *Pete and Deadly*, *The King Is Alive* and *Groove: Requiem in the Key of Ski*. He also created music to accompany a book called *Leafscape*, featuring the nature paintings of Britain-based artist Ursula Romero.

His most talked-about recording, however, was never released at all. In 1990 Hoodlum Priest recorded a single called 'Cop Killer' (not to be confused with the track by Ice-T's Body Count) which featured the voices of several film characters plotting to murder police officers. Despite having thrived on provocation and controversy just five years earlier in the heyday of Frankie Goes To Hollywood, it was all too much for ZTT, who refused to release it.

Interviewed later by Jon Bains, Thompson doubled down: 'It wasn't supposed to be a great piece of music or art, just 100% "Kill cops". If you don't do anything with your life . . . go and kill pigs.'

A statement which is to be taken as literally as anything else Derek Thompson says.

Thompson, Porl / Pearl

If you're in a group whose lead singer is Robert Smith, but somehow, without even seeming to try especially hard, *you're* the strangest and most enigmatic member, you must be doing something right. The Cure's lead singer may understandably have pulled focus, but guitarist Porl – now Pearl – Thompson was always the real deal, an effortlessly fascinating and genuinely eccentric man.

The multi-instrumentalist was born in Surrey as Paul Thompson on 8 November 1957. And, before we go any further, some clarity about nomenclature. Thompson legally changed his name to Pearl – his nickname within the band for a long time – in 2012 after turning his back on music. (And those pronouns are still correct: he/him.) The intention was to draw a line under that part of his life. 'It's really all about starting afresh,' he told *ContactMusic* in 2015. 'Friends have always called me Pearl and it really seemed to fit with my new path. I'm legally Pearl now. I think it's good for your mind to say, "Right, that was then, this is now".' For the purposes of *Curepedia*, he shall be referred to as 'Porl' when discussing his early life and his tenure as a member of The Cure, but

'Pearl' in anything that happens post-2012 when he legally changed his name. As a child, he was Paul. As a musician, he was Porl. As an artist, he is Pearl. It is not the intention of this book to deadname anyone, but, as much as possible, to remain era-appropriate.

Paul Thompson grew up in the Merton/Wimbledon area of South West London. His favourite childhood memory, he once told *Cure News*, was seeing the world through orange glasses in his father's sidecar (he would become a motorcyclist himself in later life). The first record the teenage Porl owned was the Jimi Hendrix album *What D'I Say*, a compilation of early live recordings released in 1972 on the budget MFP label, bought in Woolworths for 75p. Though he left school with no qualifications, he later credited his teachers Ms Thornborough, Mrs Pegram and Mrs Saunders with inspiring his love of art.

After moving to **Crawley**, his life began to intersect with those of the future members of The Cure. It was in 1976, while working at record shop L&H Cloake in Queen's Square, that he first met Robert Smith. Robert had come in to buy the Roger Payne whalesong album *Songs of the Humpback Whale*, and the pair bonded over a shared love of The Sensational Alex Harvey Band.

Thompson first met **Lol Tolhurst** via Porl's sister Carol, whom Lol was dating. Meanwhile, Porl himself was dating Robert's sister Janet, bringing him ever further into the proto-Cure's orbit. He started coming along to Malice rehearsals, as Robert recalled in *Ten Imaginary Years*. 'He was working at Gatwick Airport . . . and he used to turn up in his waiter's uniform.'

This was one of several short-lived jobs Porl had as a young man. In the summer of 1976 Lol got him and **Michael Dempsey** summer jobs at electrical manufacturers Hellermann's. (That summer, he and Porl were at the Notting Hill riot immortalised on The Clash's first album.) Also, he told *Cure News*, he once had a job 'trying to build a jetty, up to my knees in mud, with the tide coming in'.

It was only a matter of time before Porl, who was already known around town as a skilled guitarist who owned a black Les Paul copy, joined Malice. He played their very first public show, at Worth Abbey in Crawley on 18 December 1976, and stayed with the **pre-Cure** incarnation of the band through the name change to Easy Cure, up to and including the **Hansa** sessions.

His final gig with them, first time around, was on 22 April 1978 at Montefiore Institute Hall, Crawley, their last show as Easy Cure. He'd been disappearing

from rehearsals to be with Janet, and meanwhile Robert was beginning to dislike the elaborate flourishes of Porl's guitar style. 'The songs were getting starker, more minimal, and I was beginning to loathe Porl's lead guitar,' Robert explained in *Ten Imaginary Years*. Porl confirmed this: 'The music was in the process of changing and, as I was known as the fast guitar player, when punk came along I became obsolete.'

Porl left the band to attend art college in Worthing. While studying, he played in two 'Roxy Music-ish' bands, The Exotic Pandas and A Lifetime Of Trials. He also rejoined his Crawley mates to play on the **Cult Hero** record and their one gig at the Marquee on 18 March 1980, and for a one-off Cure gig at the Lakeside in Crawley, where he joined them for an 'I'm A Cult Hero' encore.

It was as an artist, though, that he made his biggest contribution to the early years of The Cure. After a chance meeting on a train during which Thompson convinced Smith that The Cure's sleeves were rubbish and that he and his art school friend **Andy Vella** could do better, he was commissioned to design the artwork for '**Primary**' and, soon afterwards, *Faith*, the album it came from, and the new **Fiction** logo. Thus began Thompson and Vella's company, **Parched Art**, who designed almost all The Cure's record sleeves between 1984 and 1992. Thompson was a frequent presence at Cure rehearsals and recording sessions thereafter, aiming to 'impregnate myself with a piece' instead of working blind.

Thompson collaborated with Smith by performing with **The Glove** on their television appearances, and his first musical involvement with The Cure also involved miming to records on which he didn't actually play. In July 1983 he mimed bass on '**The Walk**' for the first of its two appearances on *Top of the Pops* (see **TV**), and in October he stood in for **Phil Thornalley** on the same show miming double bass on '**The Lovecats**'.

His first contribution to an actual Cure record was during *The Top* sessions. 'I was going into the studio,' he recalled in *Ten Imaginary Years*, 'showing them how the cover was coming along, and one evening Robert asked me to play sax on 'Give Me It'. Then he asked me to stay for the tour. No one ever said to me "Come back", but little by little our relationship became more open and I stayed.' Robert realised that the fuller sound of *The Top* required additional personnel to reproduce live, and that Porl, who could help out on synth as well as guitar, was the perfect fit. He joined the tour, and by the time of the next album, 1985's *The Head On The Door*, he was a full member and what many consider the 'classic' Cure **line-up** was in place.

In so many ways Porl Thompson was a misfit even within a band of misfits like The Cure. He did not have the typical alternative eighties look. There was something quietly rebellious about his decision not to wear his hair in standard-issue spikes and instead in tumbling Pre-Raphaelite curls, sometimes tied back into a Bonnie Prince Charlie ribboned ponytail. Porl Thompson ran his own race.

By this time, he had moved on from his Les Paul copy and was playing, among other **guitars**, a cherry-red Epiphone and a Gibson 345 semi-acoustic. And playing them loud. 'Porl always plays everything as loud as possible', Robert once told *Cure News*. In an interview in *Guitar Player*, Smith and Thompson discussed their contrasting styles. 'Porl prefers to play things that aren't very tied down', said Robert. Porl said this stemmed from his love of Jimmy Page. 'In the past, that type of playing was always frowned upon in the group. It was a joke – **Boris [Williams]** and I would be doing Zeppelin covers at soundcheck, and we'd stop when everyone else showed up.' Robert also spoke of Porl's love of feedback. 'I'd wake up in the morning hearing feedback coming from his room above the studio,' he said. 'Feedback lets you add sound without adding on a whole new part,' explained Porl.

As well as Page/Zeppelin, musical influences Thompson has acknowledged include Gustav Mahler, chamber music, Brian Eno, Captain Beefheart, The Rolling Stones, The Incredible String Band and John Williams. He appears to have no 'off' switch, musically: for evidence, just look at him singing Frankie Vaughan backstage at the BRIT **Awards** on the *Play Out* documentary, or picking out *The Third Man* theme between takes at the '**In Between Days**' video shoot. As well as being a 'shit-hot guitarist', Lol Tolhurst acknowledges him as the most versatile musician in The Cure.

Although a very private man, his status as a member of The Cure during their glory years meant that we've inevitably learned plenty of trivia about him, especially via questionnaires in *Cure News*, beyond the basic stuff about height (5ft 7in) and eye colour (green). He enjoyed watching old black and white films, or anything involving Dirk Bogarde, Gregory Peck or Malcolm McDowell. His reading matter of choice included the novels of D. M. Thomas and *Journal of a Sad Hermaphrodite* by Michael de Larrabeiti. His listening habits included 'trippy hippy stuff' like The Orb and Ozric Tentacles. The best live show he'd seen, as of 1987, was by the Demon Drummers of Kodo.

Thompson drove a Land Rover 90 V8 and, a biker like Boris Williams, rode a Harley Davidson 883 Sportster which he once fell off and dislocated an elbow, obliging him to play some of the *Wish* tour in a plaster cast. He was also, like **Simon Gallup**, a cyclist and, completing the full set of wheeled modes of transport, a skateboarder. His other hobbies included camping and, unusually for a vegetarian, fishing.

In 1987 he lived on a farm with Janet where he kept seven pigs with names like Ping, Poppy, Wes, and Herb, fish called Shirley and Plop, and a rabbit called Mus. As Robert told ITV's *Night Network*, 'Porl has a Vietnamese pig called Desmond which he claims is extremely intelligent and can read and write. He lives in a totally inaccessible place so nobody can ever prove him right or wrong . . .'

In March 1988, Porl Thompson and Janet Smith married, formally making him Robert's brother-in-law. They had four children, Tod, Noosha, Bodhi, and Darcie, before the marriage ended circa 2000.

Porl left The Cure for the second time in 1993 after the *Wish* tour, having made his decision during it. He wanted to spend more time with his family, and work on his art and other musical projects. 'I admire his decision to concentrate on his painting and his own music,' Robert told *Cure News*. 'I like courage and conviction.'

During the ensuing break from The Cure, Porl considered opening a tattoo parlour in Cornwall (a plan which was abandoned), but instead learned to play the banjo, and continued to paint. His influences as an artist include Man Ray and Joan Miró. His first exhibition was held in Cornwall in May 1999, and in 2002 he held another, called *100% Sky*, coinciding with the publication of Sarah Brittain's book of the same name.

He was sporadically active in music while not a Cure member. He played on a **Presence** single, without realising that Lol Tolhurst was about to launch a **lawsuit** against The Cure. He also guested on the album by **Babacar**, the band Boris Williams formed with his partner Caroline Crawley of **Shelleyan Orphan**, having previously contributed to Shelleyan

Orphan's *Humroot* in 1992. He formed his own band, **Quietly Torn**. And he was also, as of 1999, reportedly working on solo music to be released online, under the name Wild Flower.

The biggest call-up he received, however, came from his heroes. In 1994, Led Zeppelin alumni Robert Plant and Jimmy Page headhunted Porl to join their touring band, as immortalised on the Page and Plant live album *No Quarter*. During the tour, Page and Plant paid a respectful nod to Porl's past by covering '**Lullaby**'.

Whether a member of The Cure or not, Porl Thompson was always a part of the extended Cure family, both figuratively and literally. In 2005, shortly after **Perry Bamonte** and **Roger O'Donnell**'s departure, he was once again drafted into the band. His image by this point had changed dramatically, his hair shaven into tram-lines and his body covered in many floral and tribal tattoos, including ones on his scalp which were mirrored by a design on one of his guitars. (The video for 2008 single '**The Only One**' offers a clear look at the all-new Porl.) He appeared on the 2008 album *4:13 Dream*, and the *Festival 2005* DVD.

Circa 2009, Porl was said to be working outside The Cure on a new band called Swanson's Daughter, with a track called 'Butter Knife' shared on SoundCloud via his website, but the website and the SoundCloud link have since vanished.

In 2011, he finally left The Cure for (probably) the final time. In 2012 he officially changed his name to Pearl (which had been his nickname for a long time, as well as 'Poz'). Although there has been speculation that this name change, along with his increasingly feminine way of dressing, implies that Pearl is transgender, he has never publicly identified as such, and articles about him still use male pronouns.

Although he'd sold off most of his musical equipment after leaving The Cure, Pearl could occasionally be lured out of retirement. In 2013 he played the World Forgiveness Concert in Bethlehem with Finbar O'Hanlon, performing a quite Cure-ish instrumental track. In 2016 and 2017 he contributed to the studio album *Callus* and the remix album *Mandela Effect* by the American vocalist, producer, DJ and yogi Gonjasufi (real name Sumach Ecks), both in a psychedelic hip-hop style, both on Warp Records. 'I'd had enough of music in 2012,' he told *ContactMusic*, 'but I thought he was cool and so we jammed for a few days, but I won't be going out on the road or committing to any music ventures. I'm not

really in that area right now.' He added, 'I doubt if I would go back to music in a full-time way unless Iggy Pop calls . . . If he was looking for somebody, I'd be intrigued – just for a period.'

Pearl married his second wife Dali'esque on 13 November 2014 and told interviewers they were living on a houseboat in England. His main artistic passion by now was painting, and he launched his first major exhibition, *Looking Through the Eyes of Birds*, at Mr Musichead Gallery in Hollywood in March 2015. Inspired by his Animist beliefs, and with titles like *Falling Moon*, *Silent Cactus Poem* and *Pyramid Cloud*, the paintings were abstract images of wildlife and nature which were drawn from many hours Pearl spent in the canyons of Topanga and Malibu. Speaking to *Hollywood Reporter*, he compared the act of painting to the act of playing music. 'The physicality of painting, you have that rhythm. Once you find the medium and size you want to work with, it's very physically like hitting a guitar.'

Though Pearl Thompson has never rejoined The Cure, he was inducted with them into the Rock & Roll Hall of Fame in 2019, looking resplendent in a gold dress, fishnets, high heels and sparkling make-up, his head partly shaven with a topknot. He did not, however, take part in the band's performance that night.

But, asked *Hollywood Reporter*, could he ever imagine doing so again? 'I can never say "No",' he replied. 'Because how many times have I left The Cure and rejoined them?'

Thornalley, Phil

Philip Carden Thornalley, sometime Cure producer and for eighteen months their bassist, was born on 5 January 1960 in Worlington in Suffolk. His best friend, Mike Nocito, was the Italian-American son of a high school principal on the USAF air base at nearby Mildenhall. 'These Air Force bases were incredible,' Thornalley later recalled. 'It was a real culture shock going into those places. That's where I got my first bass guitar, a fancy Fender Precision, from the PX.'

Inspired by The Beatles but also the American records he was hearing via Nocito and Mildenhall – Burt Bacharach, Jimmy Webb, Steely Dan and, above all, his lifelong obsession Todd Rundgren – the two friends began making music. Thornalley had a piano and drum kit in his bedroom, and learned guitar, messing around with phaser pedals and tape recorders, as well as forming a band playing Eagles covers.

Thornalley's first recorded work, however, was with two other friends, Chris and Jem Murrell. The First Steps, a punk trio whose repertoire included Ramones and Sex Pistols covers, released two singles in 1979 and 1980, 'The Beat Is Back' and 'Anywhere Else But Here', receiving airplay from David 'Kid' Jensen, Mike Read and **John Peel** on BBC Radio 1 as well as positive reviews from *NME* and *Sounds*. As well as The First Steps, Thornalley played in a nine-piece soul band who gigged at the American Air Force bases around Suffolk.

By this point, however, Thornalley was already moving into the technical side of things. Aged eighteen, he began an apprenticeship with RAK Studios, founded by legendary pop impresario Mickie Most, and followed the time-honoured trajectory from tea boy to tape operator to engineer to producer, working under the likes of Steve Lillywhite, Alex Sadkin and Most himself, and lurking around RAK after hours to work on his own 'shitty demos', improving his craft as a producer and songwriter.

Looking back at his apprenticeship four decades later on Instagram, he offered a pro-tip for tea people: 'If you want to "get ahead" make bad tea; the producer will send someone else to do it and you'll spend more time watching how records are made.' The first session he witnessed was one which produced Hot Chocolate's chart-topping 'Every 1's A Winner', and his early years at RAK included working on **Siouxsie And The Banshees'** 'Hong Kong Garden', the album *All Mod Cons* by fellow **Chris Parry** signings The Jam, Racey's smash 'Some Girls', Barry Manilow live at the Royal Albert Hall and, crucially in terms of bringing him to The Cure's attention, the first two Psychedelic Furs albums (including the original 'Pretty in Pink').

After **Chris Parry**'s original choice (Colin Thurston) and Robert Smith's (Conny Plank) to produce *Pornography* fell through, Thornalley ticked a lot of boxes. He was the same age as the band, and he'd worked on *those* Furs records. Alongside his pal Mike Nocito, who engineered it, Thornalley navigated a somewhat tricky creative friction with Robert Smith to oversee the creation of a classic Cure album. Once recording had wrapped, however, Thornalley went back to his regular job as an engineer for hire, impressing Alex Sadkin in December 1982 with his work on Duran Duran's 'Is There Something I Should Know?', which became a UK No.1 the following March and a Top 10 hit in several countries including the US.

Even before being lured into The Cure's ranks, Phil Thornalley's **1983** was almost as mad as Robert Smith's, with almost as many competing priorities and almost as many plates being spun. As well as working on acts as varied as Ricky Gervais' synth duo Seona Dancing to reggae legends Clint Eastwood & General Saint, he was making the first of several attempts to launch a solo career with the synthpop single 'So This Is Love'. Then, in June, he received the call to fill the vacant bassist's position in The Cure following the rancorous departure of **Simon Gallup** the previous summer. The band were filming the **video** for **'The Walk'** at **Tim Pope**'s studio, not far from RAK, and visited Thornalley to invite him to play bass with them at the Elephant Fayre festival in Cornwall. Thornalley looked the part, he could play, and he knew the band's latest album inside-out. He was a logical choice. His first gig was a warm-up in Bournemouth on 27 July 1983, alongside fellow newcomer **Andy Anderson** on drums, and he held onto the role until the following November.

Thornalley's decision amazed his peers. 'When I told [fellow producer] Sandy Roberton that I was going on the road with The Cure,' Thornalley later recalled, 'he was like, "You're nuts! You've just established yourself as a producer. You're making good money." But the life experience was good.' As he told *Music Week*, 'I'd had quite a few hits at that point, [and] producing *Pornography* by The Cure was an amazing calling card. But much to the chagrin of various managers, I'd gone on tour with The Cure – I'd established myself as a producer, and then said, "No, I want to go out on the road . . . "'

He was also recruited to play on **'The Lovecats'** as well as producing it, delivering what *Bass Player* magazine ranked as the twenty-third best bass part of all time on an upright bass, on his very first attempt at playing one. However, his other studio commitments made him unavailable for the recording of *The Top*. Thornalley spent the autumn of 1983 juggling Duran Duran's sessions in Montserrat for *Seven And The Ragged Tiger* with the Thompson Twins' sessions in London for *Into the Gap*, for which he would be nominated for a Grammy. 'I was parachuted in to finish off Duran,' he remembered in *TapeOp*, 'got on a plane, went back to England, and went straight from the airport to the studio and mixed [Thompson Twins hit] "Hold Me Now". I was so hot!'

Thornalley's duties included a number of **television** shows, including a *Top of the Pops* appearance miming to 'The Walk' (a record on which he didn't actually play), though he was unavailable for the episode featuring 'The Lovecats' (his place taken by Porl Thompson), thus earning Thornalley the strange and perhaps unique dual distinction of appearing on *Top of the Pops* to perform a song on which he didn't play, but failing to appear for a song on which he *did*. He also appeared on the BBC's *Oxford Road Show* in early 1984, by which time he had gone 'full Cure' in his appearance: bandana, lipstick, dark glasses and spiky hair. And, of course, there was the endless touring. Not only festivals but tours of the UK, North America, Europe, Australasia and (again) North America dates, his final show being the Beacon Theatre in New York on 17 November 1984. On that **US** tour, it was Thornalley, through his contacts with The Psychedelic Furs and the Thompson Twins, who provided The Cure with a temporary drummer (**Vince Ely**) and a permanent one (**Boris Williams**).

There are competing did-he-jump-or-was-he-pushed narratives around how Phil Thornalley ceased to be a member of The Cure. In terms of personality, he never quite fit in with the rest of the band, being far less of a heavy drinker. Also, as the *Pornography* sessions had shown, he wasn't afraid of standing up to Smith (when asked by *Cure News* to describe Thornalley in one word, Smith chose 'difficult'). Explaining away his departure to David 'Kid' Jensen, Smith said that Thornalley had never officially joined The Cure, and 'just did a stint'. (Thornalley says he declined the offer to be permanent bassist.)

Whatever the truth, Phil Thornalley threw himself straight back into production, delivering an all-time classic single in Prefab Sprout's 'When Love Breaks Down' and a Spanish No.1 in soft rock supergroup Wax's 'Right Between The Eyes', as well as playing on recordings by Orange Juice, Strawberry Switchblade and Hollywood Beyond. He also, in 1988, made another attempt to launch himself as a solo star with his debut album *Swamp*, which he later described as 'an honest effort that flopped'.

And then there's Johnny Hates Jazz, the insipid late eighties pop group, formed by Calvin Hayes (Mickie Most's son) with Mike Nocito (Thornalley's childhood friend and engineer on *Pornography*) and, originally, Thornalley himself. Under the pseudonym L. Da Vinci, he wrote their debut single 'Me And My Foolish Heart' and recorded the original vocal, only to bail out due to production commitments with Robbie Nevil (whose 'C'Est La Vie' became an international hit), leaving JHJ in the lurch without a singer. Clark Datchler took Thornalley's place and the single failed to chart, but not without an almighty underhand effort from Most, who was investigated by UK chart compiler Gallup (no relation) for trying to bump the record into the charts by buying six copies at a time from assorted record shops.

Legitimate hits followed, like 'Shattered Dreams' and 'Turn Back The Clock', encouraging Datchler to believe he could make it as a solo star. Once again, Johnny Hates Jazz were without a singer and Thornalley, believing he owed them something, stepped up. 'I dumped them right in it the first time,' he told the *Newcastle Evening Chronicle*, 'and I was not expecting to be invited back, but it's like coming full circle. I'm doing something I should have been doing five years ago.' (*Cure News* reported that Thornalley said he'd rather tour with Johnny Hates Jazz than The Cure.)

However, he was inheriting a sinking ship. The first Thornalley-fronted single, 'Turn The Tide', stalled at No.84 in the UK in late 1989, and the band's second album, *Tall Stories*, received brutal reviews. Phil Bryant of the *Crawley News* damned it with faint praise: 'The ten songs are all pleasant enough, but maybe there's the rub! Pleasant it may be, but it isn't original.' Jon Selzer of *Melody Maker* wrote that it 'sounds like the kind of music they play to illustrate trysts in soap operas, where a lovelorn character wanders by a lake to get a free blow-dry, or the touching moment in those human-dramas-on-Bognor-Pier the Beeb are so good at.' And *NME*'s Andrew Collins wrote that the introduction of Thornalley '[does] not make a sod of difference to the Johnnys' spiritless, dreary coffee-table adultsoulpopdirge'.

The album completely failed to chart (a dramatic fall from grace for an artist whose previous album, only three years earlier, was a No.1), and any hope of turning things around had already been ended on the eve of its release when Thornalley and Hayes were involved in a serious car crash which left Hayes in hospital for two years.

The failure of *Swamp* and *Tall Stories* made Thornalley realise that he was 'a studio person' and that 'my passion was for writing songs [and] not performing them'. Once again bandless, he returned to the studio, his nineties work including engineering Blur's abortive Andy Partridge-produced sessions for

Modern Life Is Rubbish. Finally, in 1997, he achieved a breakthrough of sorts when a song he'd written *and* produced, 'Today's The Day' by soap star Sean Maguire, cracked the Top 30. However, his really big break came with a song he'd written way back in 1991, when still technically a member of Johnny Hates Jazz.

'**Torn**' was co-written with Scott Cutler and Anne Preven of Ednaswap, but first recorded in 1993 by Lis Sørensen in Danish (renamed 'Brændt', meaning 'Burnt'), and in 1996 by American-Norwegian singer Trine Rein, reaching the Danish and Norwegian Top 10s respectively, with Ednaswap recording their own version in 1994. However, it wasn't until the song reached former *Neighbours* actor Natalie Imbruglia that the song really took off. Imbruglia's version of 'Torn' reached No.2 in the UK in November 1997, broke records for radio airplay, and became the UK's 85th biggest selling single of all time. Imbruglia's album, *Left Of The Middle*, which featured a total of five Phil Thornalley songs, was an Australia No.1 and reached the Top 5 in Belgium, the Netherlands, Germany, Italy, Sweden, Switzerland and the UK. 'Torn' is considered one of the defining pop songs of the nineties, and was covered by One Direction on their DVD *Up All Night: The Live Tour*, making Phil Thornalley a very rich man. 'The making of "Torn" was phenomenal and its effect on my life has been phenomenal,' he told *Music Week*. 'That's not overstating it. It really turned my career around.'

Since 'Torn', operating from his Swamp home studio in West Hampstead, Thornalley has gone on to further successes. He wrote Top Ten hit 'Back Here' for British pop trio BBMak, Top 10 hit 'The Way You Make Me Feel' for Ronan Keating, and Australian No.1 'Drive' for Shannon Noll, and co-wrote and co-produced two back-to-back No.1s for Pixie Lott, 'Mama Do' and 'Boys And Girls'. His most enduring collaboration has been with Bryan Adams, spanning twenty years and several albums. Thornalley was even lured back on the road, playing bass for Adams on two world tours.

In 2018, Thornalley released an eponymous album under the name Astral Drive (named for the Los Angeles street where his hero Todd Rundgren recorded much of his classic album *Something/Anything?),* followed by an EP in 2019 called *Love Is Real* (featuring a cover of Rundgren's 'A Dream Goes On Forever') and a further Astral Drive album called *Orange* in 2021 (featuring a cover of 'Open My Eyes' by Rundgren's band Nazz). In 2022, under his own name, Thornalley released a solo album called *Now That I Have Your Attention*.

Whether or not these releases reach many ears, there's something heartwarming about the fact that, due to his post-Cure successes, Phil Thornalley – a nice man and a talented man, if not an especially *Cure* man – can now afford as many musical love letters to Todd Rundgren, and as many 'honest efforts that flopped', as he likes.

Three Imaginary Boys

Three actual boys. That's what The Cure were when they walked into **Morgan Studios** in Willesden, North London on 20 September 1978. None of the band's three members – Robert Smith, **Lol Tolhurst**, **Michael Dempsey** – had even turned twenty yet when the sessions began for their debut album.

This wasn't The Cure's first visit to Morgan: they'd already been there for the ill-fated **Hansa** sessions. Furthermore, **Chris Parry** was running **Fiction** out of a small office in the Morgan building. It was beginning to feel like home.

That first September session didn't finish till 5.30 a.m. the next day. Lol had to phone in sick to his job, claiming to have boils on his backside. Sessions resumed between 8–10 January 1979, with the band recording late at night to save money and sleeping in Parry's spare room. It was, paradoxically, 'big budget and bare bones', as Lol put it in his memoir *Cured*.

One problem with doing things on the cheap was that The Cure's equipment simply wasn't up to the task. Getting Lol, and his kit, in a fit state to perform was a dual challenge. 'Lol was a very temperamental drummer', recalled Parry in *Ten Imaginary Years*, 'and could only play well if he felt well.' Dempsey felt that Parry, a former drummer, spent too long getting Lol's kit sounding perfect and not enough on the other instruments. A solution was found by borrowing a brand-new black Yamaha kit from Rick Buckler of The Jam, fellow Parry signings to **Polydor**, who were recording in the room next door. (Years later, **Boris Williams** would use a similar kit.)

Then there was Robert's **guitar**, the cheap Woolworths Top 20 model, made in Japan by Tiesco, that he'd had for years. Parry persuaded a reluctant Smith to invest in an expensive Fender Jazzmaster but, to Parry's dismay, he installed the pick-up from the Woolworths on the Fender. He wouldn't change his amp, either, until it fell apart after recording the guitar solo on 'Three Imaginary Boys' and Parry bought him a Roland JC160 amp.

Parry was funding the whole enterprise, so Smith felt that the manager had them 'over a barrel' when disputes arose. However, The Cure had an unlikely ally in the shape of **Mike Hedges**. Although Chris Parry is credited with having produced the album himself with Hedges (hired 'because he wanted someone young with no preconceptions') on tape-op and engineering duty, in reality Hedges did most of the production, and in arguments over the record's sound he tended to side with Smith. In three nights the band somehow recorded twenty-six songs, twelve of which made it on to *Three Imaginary Boys*.

The album opens with '**10.15 Saturday Night**', which has its own section here due to being a single, but which laid the band's sonic cards firmly on the table with its counterintuitive approach to which parts should be loud and which should be quiet.

'Accuracy' has a certain tapered new wave charm, with its rolling 6/8 rhythm and its succinct two-line verses which Robert later explained as expressing 'the ease and desire of hunting someone you sometimes love' ('hunting' being presumably a typo for 'hurting'). Its minimalism was a conscious aim, and made it one of Robert's favourites. 'The most perfect of songs: few words, little music.'

'Grinding Halt' was almost as pared down, lyrically. Lol had written the words, but Robert edited them so that only the start of each sentence was sung. Its message was one of 'entropy and apathy', Robert later said, running counter to its fairly cheery power-pop melody. At the end, the tape slowed down to – literally – a grinding halt. (This literal-mindedness carried through on to the Future Pastimes tour, on which the song became the main set-closer.) 'Grinding Halt' was slated to be a single, with white label promos sent out (Dave McCullough in *Sounds* called it 'the new single' in his album review, and *Record Mirror* even reviewed it), but it was pulled after negative reactions from radio stations.

'Another Day', at three minutes forty-four seconds the longest song on this terse LP, feels as though it's occupying the space that the other songs shun, taking all the time in the world by comparison. Robert described it as being 'purely about boredom and repetition', 'another entropy and apathy song', and 'how I sometimes (often) felt on waking'.

The next track, 'Object', was Robert's least **favourite** Cure song as late as 1988. He later

described it as 'A dismissive sneer hiding a sour desire', and 'a pastiche of a sexist song', claiming that they were pretending to be 'unwholesome'. Its title is both a noun ('you're just an object') and a verb ('I don't object if you touch me there'). Taking a nihilistic, de-romanticised view of **sex** as a meaningless physical transaction was a very punk thing to do, devaluing and demystifying the act at a time when artists like Prince and, later, Madonna were singing of sex as the ultimate purpose of human existence.

The side ends with 'Subway Song', built on a descending jazzy bassline reminiscent of 'Blank Generation' by Richard Hell and the Voidoids with added hi-hats, fingerclicks and harmonica. It's a grisly narrative of a woman being stalked through a subway and murdered. It ends, just before the run-out groove, with the woman letting out a monstrous horror-movie scream, giving the listener a jump-scare on a par with the post-credits sequence of *Carrie* (which came out two years earlier). According to Lol on *Curious Creatures*, the subway they had in mind was a specific one in **Horley** through which the band would run, after last orders at the Kings Head pub, to an Indian restaurant which had a licence till midnight. (He also says there is a blue plaque there, but this may have been a joke.) For some time, Robert would claim that the song's narrative was based on a true story, but in *Ten Imaginary Years* he confessed 'I had this habit of telling people I know someone who'd been murdered in a subway. It wasn't true at all.'

Side 2 begins, after a little studio chatter to whip away the wizard's curtain and break the fourth wall, with a throwaway tin-pot **cover version** of **Jimi Hendrix**'s 'Foxy Lady' (which had been part of Easy Cure's live repertoire in the **pre-Cure** days). It's sung by Michael Dempsey, putting on a bizarre American accent through a distorted, telephone-like mic. At no point does he, or anyone else, sing the actual words 'foxy lady'. Robert later explained 'Michael wanted to sing a song, and I didn't like the idea of him singing my words, so we picked a cover version, and this one was chosen because it was so unlikely at the time!'

'Meathook' also dated back to Easy Cure days. One of the first songs they ever wrote, it had been recorded at the Hansa sessions. In defiance of the producer who told them they had 'no hooklines', it was about as hooky as the album got: if it weren't for the scratchy production it could have been a slick American new wave group like The J. Geils Band or The Cars. Robert explained the lyric as being 'a strained comparison' between catchy chart pop songs and 'revolting dead meat'. Even if he was labouring the point, 'Pass me some of that stuff, that slaughterhouse art . . .' was a great line.

Most of the songs were already written before sessions began, but 'So What' is an exception, partially coming together in the studio. With Robert's punky semi-Cockney vocal (it's 'me drunk!!!', he later wrote) and its muddy production, it was very of-its-time, but it had an inventiveness beyond the capabilities of The Cure's peers. According to a contemporary article by Chris Westwood in *Record Mirror*, the song was originally called 'Cheap Sex', with completely different lyrics, but when Robert was tiring of recording one day, he 'strutted into the studio, clutching a sugar bag in one hand, and proceeded to verbalize straight from the ingredients thereon.' But it wasn't quite as simple as that. Half of each verse consisted of Robert reciting words from a bag of icing sugar offering £1.52 off a cake-decorating set ('Order now, allow 21 days for delivery/Offer closes 31st December 1979', a date then a year into the future), the other half someone's innermost emotional monologue ('nobody's taken your place', 'if you were sane your heart wouldn't ache', 'forget all the lies, forgive me the wounds . . .'). The juxtaposition of the mundane and the heartfelt does the same trick as Glen Campbell's 'Wichita Lineman', a song which it otherwise resembles in no sense whatsoever. Smith contrasts the emptiness of consumerism, and the false desires created by **advertising**, with real human desires and needs.

'Fire In Cairo' is one of the album's triumphs, a high point of The Cure's early works. Robert later described the song simply as 'an eastern fantasy', while Lol on *Curious Creatures* claimed that he wanted a phrase that had a similar meaning to 'coals to Newcastle', and the one thing he knew about Cairo was that it was 'bloody hot'. In any case, Robert's forlorn delivery, the mournful melody and its tongue-twisting refrain ('F-I-R-E-I-N-C-A-I-R-O!) made it a standout track, and an enduring fan favourite. It, perhaps more than any other *Three Imaginary Boys* track, pointed the way forward for The Cure.

'It's Not You', described by Robert as 'another hateful song', once again expresses Smith's cynicism and disillusionment with love and sex. 'You wear your smile like it was going out of fashion', he spits, 'Dress to inflame but douse any ideas of passion/You carry your love in a trinket hanging 'round your throat.'

The title track has a slower-paced, would-be epic feel, describing a crepuscular walk through a mysterious garden of shadows and statues and staircases, with the pervading feeling that something is not right. It is arguably The Cure's first proto-**gothic** song, and the first of countless songs inspired by Robert's **dreams**.

The album tails off with a track unofficially known as 'The Weedy Burton', a silly retro rock 'n' roll instrumental which was the lowest-ranked album track in *Slicing Up Eyeballs'* poll of all Cure songs (coming in at 221). The inclusion of this type of goofing around (see also 'Foxy Lady') is inexplicable, given that fourteen of the twenty-six songs recorded had to be left out. Furthermore, opting to include neither their first single, **'Killing An Arab'**, nor their next single, **'Boys Don't Cry'** (released just a month later) was a brave, ballsy move, and one that may have undermined the album's prospects: anyone lured into The Cure by either song would be disappointed that they weren't present.

In general, it's the production on *Three Imaginary Boys* that is a little . . . *off*. As was the case on 'Killing An Arab', the drums crash too loudly compared to everything else. But that sort of 'mistake' ends up being creative. Everyone, audibly, is figuring out how to make a record. Some of it sounds in hindsight like a neatly tailored little new wave/power-pop band like The Jags or The Vapors, but in other places it's bursting with ideas – a willingness to do things you're not meant to do.

The most striking aspect of its sound is minimalism. Parry, in *Ten Imaginary Years*, stated that he encouraged that stripped-down side. 'I was convinced, after the punk thrash, that people would want something more mysterious.' Being a trio, Smith told *Melody Maker*'s Ian Birch in March 1979, 'broadens rather than limits us. You can do much more with less instruments.' Two decades later, that's still how Smith saw things. "People picked up on it', he told *Uncut* in 2000, 'because it sounded very different to from anything else at the time. The whole LP did. Because Lol couldn't drum very well, we had to keep everything very, very simple. Our sound was forced on us to a certain extent.'

Smith also made a case that by playing lead melodies on the bass, they were entering a 'relatively unexplored' area for rock (something they would explore more fully a couple of years later with **'Primary'**). Interestingly, in this regard, journalist John Robb (speaking on the *Out of the Woods* documentary) detected 'a dub reggae influence, the way it's mixed almost back-to-front'.

The most divisive aspect of *Three Imaginary Boys* was the **artwork**. The album cover depicted three household objects – a vacuum cleaner, a standard lamp and a refrigerator – against a pink background. The words 'Three Imaginary Boys' did not appear anywhere on the front (though The Cure's logo did). According to Tolhurst in *Cured*, they would always make up stories to journalists about who was the fridge, who was the standard lamp and who was the vacuum cleaner. (Nobody wanted to be the fridge.) In 1987, Tolhurst told Steve Sutherland 'I'm the Hoover, Robert's the lampstand and Michael's the fridge'. At the time, however, Paul '**Desperate Journalist**' Morley wrote 'Lol Tolhurst (drums) is a fridge. Michael Dempsey (bass, voice) is an upright Hoover. Robert Smith (guitar, voice) is a standard lamp.' **Bill Smith**, who actually designed it, later explained that it was meant to look like an Ideal Homes Exhibition catalogue, and suggested that Robert was the lamp. If anyone agrees on anything, it's that Robert is the lamp.

On the back, there were no song titles, just visual and graphic clues provided in the form of additional photography by Martyn Goddard (a meat hook, a Polaroid of **Mary**) and illustrations by Dave Dragon and Connie Jude. (These cryptic images were echoed in the advertising campaign, with a white chalk outline of a body on the floor of a subway, and two bags of Tate & Lyle sugar, hinting at some of the songs.) The Cure's only input was a list of names on the inner sleeve (people who had been part of their history) as a thank you – for example, the mysterious Vernon, Lol revealed in *Cured*, was a dandily dressed venue promoter from Wolverhampton's Lafayette Club.

As with 'Killing An Arab', The Cure had nothing to do with the look of *Three Imaginary Boys*. The sleeve was presented to the band at a gig at the West Runton Pavilion on 30 March 1979 as a fait accompli, and Robert immediately hated it. In retrospect, Michael Dempsey liked it because 'it created a mystique', but he was in the minority. Parry later claimed credit (or accepted responsibility). 'I thought, let's make it completely dispassionate, let's pick the three most mundane things we can possibly find. People might be upset and think it pretentious but that was a risk I was prepared to take.' As well as pretentious, it was plain confusing: *Melody Maker*'s Ian Birch didn't realise the album had a title at all, and just called it *The Cure*.

Three Imaginary Boys was released by Fiction on 11 May 1979 to broadly positive reviews. Ian Birch called The Cure a 'no image' band playing 'practical pop', and described the record as 'the missing link between the Kinks 1966-style and the Banshees 1978-style'. Chris Westwood of *Record Mirror* wrote 'the drums, particularly, are dominant, hard, driving and surprising, characterised by a glorious cheap-cymbal tish.' (Anyone who's heard The Cure's 1978–79 material knows what he meant.)

The most famous, or notorious, review came from Paul Morley in *NME*, who wrote that the album 'does a lot less than please, and a lot more than irritate', that 'they make things much worse than they could be by packaging this insubstantial froth as if it had some social validity', that 'the lads go rampant on insignificant symbolism and compound this with rude, soulless obliqueness' and that 'The Cure are absolute conformists to vaguely defined non-convention'. (It was this review, described by Smith as 'word salad', which inspired the song 'Desperate Journalist'.)

'I thought there was a concentration on trying to market mystery,' Morley later explained in the *Out of the Woods* documentary, 'and at the time that got up my nose.' He also admitted that he reviewed it on the same night that Margaret Thatcher had won the General Election – he was in a bad mood, and took it out on the album.

The album reached No.44 in the UK charts and 37 in Parry's native New Zealand – not hugely successful, but respectable enough. The Cure had made an album, and were on the map.

In retrospect, The Cure camp have expressed generally negative views of *Three Imaginary Boys*. Chris Parry has called it 'highly flawed', while Robert Smith complained that 'a lot of people said they liked it for its diversity but that's the exact thing I didn't like about it. It sounded like a compilation album or something.' Smith often all but disowns it, and has never stopped being sore about the sleeve. 'I thought the artwork was a bag of shite, too,' he told *Uncut* in 2000. 'It was all Parry's idea, he had this vision of the group that I reluctantly went along with. He even chose which songs should go on the LP. By the time it came out, I'd already written 'M' and 'Play for Today' [later to appear on *Seventeen Seconds*], so I'd mentally divorced myself from it anyway. I thought what we were doing was soulless.' In *Cured*, Tolhurst suggests that Smith doesn't rate *Three Imaginary Boys* highly because he had insufficient input in the production. Nevertheless, Smith oversaw a vinyl remaster of *Three Imaginary Boys* in 2018.

Hindsight is more generous to the album than The Cure themselves are. It was ranked fifth in a list of Cure albums by *Ultimate Classic Rock* and sixth by *Far Out* magazine – surprisingly high placings.

Three Imaginary Boys unquestionably has charm, but try to imagine a parallel universe where this was the only album The Cure made. They wouldn't be remembered by anyone other than real post-punk obsessives.

Two things, at least, are for sure. The best was yet to come. And Robert is the lamp.

Ticketmaster

Not all heroes wear capes.

Anyone who has tried to attend live shows by a major act in the twenty-first century will know that it has become prohibitively expensive. This is the result of three separate but interrelated forces. Firstly, the greed of artists and promoters in setting eye-wateringly high ticket prices in the first place. Secondly, the fact that those ticket prices are nominal and theoretical, as it is almost impossible to purchase at that price and one must instead pay an official agency disproportionately large 'administration fees' on top. And thirdly, the existence of secondary sellers (online touts, essentially) who mysteriously manage to snap up most or all of the best seats within zero seconds of the tickets going on sale.

In 2012, Channel 4's *Dispatches* won the right to screen a documentary exposing the activities of reselling platform Viagogo, despite a High Court injunction from that company. The programme exposed the nefarious practices of venues which sell whole blocks of the best seats to secondary sellers, and that it was routine for artists and their management to receive financial kickbacks. It made the claim that the majority of tickets on Viagogo were not being offered by individual **fans**, but by professional ticket resellers or via deals signed with promoters. Examples given were the claims that Viagogo had been allocated nine thousand tickets from SJM Concerts and Metropolis Music for Coldplay's upcoming stadium tour, and more than three thousand tickets for Westlife's final tour promoted by LiveNation.

Despite a public outcry, there was little **political** will to tackle the problem in the UK, where the ruling Conservative Party was ideologically opposed to any restraint of free trade (even though there is little 'free' about the practices exposed by *Dispatches*). When Sajid Javid was appointed Culture Secretary in 2014, it became known that he had previously described touts as 'classic entrepreneurs' who were 'providing a service that deserves to be rewarded' and dismissed critics as 'chattering middle classes and champagne socialists'. The Consumer Rights Act of 2015 included some measures designed to ameliorate the problem, such as the requirement that anyone who resells an event ticket via a secondary market website should provide details of the block, row and crucially the seat number, as well as the face value and information about any restrictions. However, the lived experience of music fans attests to the fact that enforcement is weak and loopholes are many.

Robert Smith is not the first artist to challenge these practices. In 2015 the comedian and *Guardian* columnist Stewart Lee took Viagogo and its American parent company StubHub to task for reselling his concert tickets at prices inflated by up to 400%. The same year, Prince tweeted a photo of a vulture, captioned 'A. Scavenger, B. Vulture, C. Tout, D. All of the above', followed by a link to a Which? report on the 'ticket resale rip-off'.

In 2017 primary ticket agency Ticketmaster made a show of tackling the secondary market by launching its Verified Fan program, which uses an algorithm to collect user data and determine whether that user is a scalper, bot or a genuine fan. However, this system was open to abuse and exploitation by major artists and corporations (suspiciously so, one might say), as it allowed them to turn fans of artists such as Taylor Swift into an unpaid army of publicists by incentivising tweets, and rewarded multiple purchases of albums with a slightly better chance of being able to buy concert tickets. As *Consequence of Sound* reported, 'Something that's especially troubling in all of this is the fact that you can purchase Swift's new album up to *13 times* to receive further boosts to your spot in line. There is even a 'progress bar' showing how your purchases are advancing your place in the virtual line.

In the UK, the weakness of the regulations became clear in 2021 when '**Lovesong**' singer Adele announced shows at London's Hyde Park the following summer with tickets ranging from £90 to £600. These prices were jaw-droppingly high already, but within ninety minutes of going on sale the basic £90 tickets were going for £400 on secondary ticketing sites. There was further controversy when tickets to her Las Vegas residency, originally priced as low as $85, were seen on sale on StubHub for between $1,000 and $37,000.

Robert Smith already had a track record as a forward-thinking artist where ticketing matters were concerned. The Cure's 2018 *Anniversary* show in London's Hyde Park (see **F is for . . . 40 Live**), part of the BST season, declassified ticketing so that anyone could enter BST's barriered 'Golden Circle' at the front. In 2023, he once again set an example to others.

On 9 March 2023, The Cure announced a thirty-date US leg of the **Lost World Tour**. An official statement, originally tweeted in Smith's familiar all-caps style (removed here to spare your eyes), read:

> We want the tour to be affordable for all fans, and we have a very wide (and we think very fair) range of pricing at every show. Our ticketing partners have agreed to help us stop scalpers from getting in the way; to help minimise resale and keep prices at face value, tickets for this tour will not be transferable. If something comes up that prevents a fan from being able to use a ticket they have purchased, they will be able to resell it on a face value ticket exchange. Unfortunately, despite our desire to protect our low ticket prices for fans, the states of NY, IL and CO make this very difficult – they actually have laws in place that protect scalpers! For shows in these states we urge fans to buy or sell tickets to one another on face value exchanges like Twickets.Live and CashOrTrade.org. Fans should avoid buying tickets that are being resold at inflated prices by scalpers, and the sites that host these scalpers should refrain from reselling tickets for our shows.

A statement on an advert for the tour read: 'The Cure have agreed all ticket prices, and apart from a few Hollywood Bowl charity seats, there will be no "Platinum" or "dynamically priced" tickets on this tour.' Their website also announced 'We have priced tickets to benefit fans and our efforts to block scalpers and limit inflated resale prices are being supported by our ticketing partners.'

However, this statement of intent in itself wasn't quite enough. As the BBC reported, 'when fans went to Ticketmaster on Wednesday, they were charged additional fees that, in some cases, doubled the price the band had set. Frontman Robert Smith said

he was "sickened" by the outcome. Addressing the added fees, he wrote: "To be very clear, the artist has no way to limit them. I have been asking how they are justified. If I get anything coherent by way of an answer, I will let you know."' One example given in the BBC article was a pair of $20 tickets in Phoenix going for $75.25 because of fees.

Rather than back away and wash his hands of responsibility, Smith dived deeper into the mechanisms of the industry, unleashing a series of tweets calling out Ticketmaster's 'dynamic pricing' (where prices fluctuate according to demand) as 'a greedy scam', and secondary ticketing sites as 'a con', offering fans advice on how and where to buy.

Behind the scenes, it emerged, he had been in negotiation with Ticketmaster. On 13 March, he was able to tweet some good news. 'After further conversation, Ticketmaster have agreed with us that many of the fees being charged are unduly high, and as a gesture of goodwill have offered $10 per ticket refund to all verified fan accounts for the lowest ticket price ("LTP") transactions . . . and a $5 per ticket refund to all verified fan accounts for all other ticket price transactions, for all Cure shows at all venues; if you already bought a ticket you will get an automatic refund; all tickets on sale tomorrow will incur lower fees.'

Smith's intervention implicitly shamed all other major artists who ignore the issue and shrug about 'market forces', and scored an extraordinary victory, one which made headlines across the world. The best of all came from American entertainment website Vulture: 'Ticketmaster Pissed Off The Wrong Goth'.

Tolhurst, Lol

Laurence Andrew Tolhurst was born on the Day the Music Died. On 3 February 1959, when a plane crashed at Clear Lake, Iowa, killing Buddy Holly, Ritchie Valens and the Big Bopper, Lol Tolhurst came into the world in **Horley**, West Sussex.

The fifth of six siblings, with three brothers (Roger, Nigel and John) and two sisters (Jane and Barbara), he was, like Robert Smith, raised a Catholic. His father was an atheist, but his mother a Catholic convert. Lol's parents were relatively old, both in their forties when he was born, and his three oldest siblings had already left home.

Lol was close to his mother, Daphne, but his father,

William, was a remote figure. An engineer on a British Navy gunboat from the age of eighteen, he had, according to Lol's autobiography *Cured*, witnessed the horrors of the Nanjing Massacre (the incident once known as the Rape of Nanking), and was traumatised by memories of severed heads and body parts floating in the River Qinhuai. William Tolhurst returned from the Second World War a changed man. 'He was either a miserable recluse who barely spoke to me,' writes Lol, 'or an angry **alcoholic** who was prone to loud bouts of shouting.' The fatal combination of post-traumatic stress disorder with a stoic stiff upper lip, so common among Englishmen of that generation, drove many to drink. 'Sailor Bill', as he was nicknamed in the local pub, was subject to wild mood swings, his only moments of levity coming when he would drunkenly bash out sea shanties on the piano at home. Lol never bonded with his father, and recalls 'my whole life was bleak'. They only went on one family holiday, to Hayling Island when Lol was eight or nine, and it was not idyllic.

Lol's grandmother lived next door to Robert Smith's family on Vicarage Lane, and Lol lived three streets away on Southlands Avenue. Lol and Robert first met in September 1964 when they were five years old, on their first day at St Francis of Assisi Primary School, five miles away. Their mothers put them on the bus together at Hevers Avenue, telling them to hold hands and look after each other. The two became friends. (When Robert was seven, by which time the Smiths had moved to **Crawley**, his parents held a jelly-and-ice-cream birthday party for him, and Lol was invited.)

Between the ages of seven and fourteen, Lol was an altar boy in the local church, singing at funerals and weddings wearing a cassock, cotta and alb, accompanied by Franciscan monks with acoustic guitars. Saturdays, when weddings usually happened, were the best, because altar boys would receive tips. This **religious** schooling, like a spiritual version of the scouts, wasn't too gruelling. 'It was a straitjacket, but a cotton wool straitjacket. It wasn't outwardly brutal, but it was enough to make you toe the line, the whole time.'

In the autumn of 1970, when Lol was eleven, he attended Notre Dame Middle School, a radically liberal establishment founded by Lord Longford, despite the daily commuting distance of five miles, 'because my mum thought that Catholic school would be better than any of the other schools on offer'. At Notre Dame he befriended **Michael Dempsey**, and reconnected with his former neighbour Robert Smith over their shared love of **Jimi Hendrix** (Lol had bought a copy of *Are You Experienced?* from Radio Rental, and Robert had borrowed a copy from his brother.) Once a week, children were allowed to use the instruments in the school music room, and Robert plugged a guitar into the stereo, jamming with Lol and Michael. Tolhurst remembers the regime of headmistress Sister Kathleen Bulley as an unusually progressive one, with four different classes going on in the same room, with no dividers.

At the age of thirteen, he remembers in *Cured*, Lol painted his bedroom bright orange and lit it with a single red bulb, and would sit inside listening to records. His teenage jobs, delivering newspapers and later working at Woolworth's, funded his **vinyl** habit and also allowed him to read the music papers (*NME*, *Sounds*, *Melody Maker*) for free. If he couldn't find the discs he wanted in the shops, he'd borrow them from the local library. He, like Smith, had his mind blown by the **David Bowie** 'Starman moment' on *Top of the Pops* in July 1972, but Tolhurst's tastes leant more in the direction of American hard rock and psychedelia. For example, he bought *It Crawled Into My Hand, Honest* by The Fugs from a bargain bin in the local tobacconists, and also explored the likes of Steppenwolf as well as Hendrix's back catalogue.

On the *Curious Creatures* podcast, he remembered his fashion *faux pas*. He had a pudding-bowl **haircut**, making him look like 'some sort of strange monk', before it grew out into the 'halfway afro' for which he was later known. He once bought a pair of stack-heeled shoes in Brighton, but fell down the stairs as soon as he put them on.

At the age of fifteen, Lol, Robert and Michael all wore white (instead of black) to stand out, like the Droogs from *A Clockwork Orange* (but Robert accessorised it with a long fur coat and scarf). Later, when punk hit, Lol wore an orange jacket with porn stars' faces on, and 'No Change' stencilled on the back, as well as safety pins, drainpipe jeans (formerly flared Levis that his mum had taken in for him) and winklepicker shoes. They were, as he puts it, 'the first punks in Crawley'. But they weren't the only flamboyant dressers in town: **Porl Thompson**, a couple of years older, could be seen in a satin jacket and a pair of strappy multicoloured boots called 'rooster boosters'.

Aged sixteen, Lol left school to work for Hellermann Deutsch in East Grinstead, manufacturers of electrical connectors and (unbeknownst to Lol at the time) parts for missiles, while also attending Crawley Technical

College as a trainee chemist – 'a blend of personal and professional interests', he drily notes.

The older they got, the more Tolhurst and Smith obsessed over music, swapping the details of punk songs they'd heard on the **John Peel** show, hanging around record shops, and going to see bands like The Jam, The Clash, The Stranglers, Thin Lizzy, Can, **Siouxsie And The Banshees**, U2, XTC and Buzzcocks (see **early gigs (attended)**). Lol got into the habit of sneaking 200%-proof alcohol, stolen from the laboratory at Hellermann's, into these gigs to pour into his pint.

Tolhurst, Smith and Dempsey, with Porl Thompson, also played together in various **pre-Cure bands** throughout their teens (The Obelisk, The Band/Brats Club, Malice, Easy Cure). Lol's only qualification for this was that he had learned a little classical piano. 'My sister is a music teacher,' he later said, 'and I used to get her to teach me some basic theory on the piano, but she'd lose patience and whack me round the head.' He soon switched to drums. (Ironically, ten years later, he would switch in the other direction.) In 1976, when Smith and Dempsey needed a drummer for their name-shifting outfit, Tolhurst lied that he could play, and quickly swotted up on drumming from a Buddy Rich book in the library. He also took lessons from a local cruise ship drummer called Andy who played big band jazz. (This, at least, is *his* story. Michael Dempsey says they had to teach Lol how to play.)

All he needed was a kit. His brother John had left behind some drumsticks, and Lol stole a cymbal from the school drum kit which he later used on **'Killing An Arab'**. This was a start. But he managed to persuade his mother to buy him a flimsy four-piece Pearl Maxwin kit with a 'hideous brownish-gold sparkly finish', the cheapest in the range. Later, when he'd made some money, he traded it in for a Premier kit (first an orange one, then a dark blue one with added toms), but this still wasn't of a high enough quality for recording purposes: he later had to borrow a kit from Rick Buckler of The Jam when making The Cure's debut album *Three Imaginary Boys*.

The group all spoke of a determination not to be 'wage slaves', and to do something extraordinary with their lives. 'We didn't grow up in a big city where we could follow the example of others,' Lol writes in *Cured*. 'We were on our own. This proved to be a blessing. We were allowed to flower on our own with fewer outside influences than most bands of our time.'

The first time Lol Tolhurst drank alcohol, he writes in *Cured*, was at the age of thirteen at a going-away party for his brother John, who was emigrating to Australia, and he drank himself unconscious. 'From the very beginning,' he admits, 'I was a blackout drinker.'

Lol's heavy drinking continued through into the early days of The Cure. After a gig in Hull in October 1979, he went missing. Robert Smith and **Steve Severin** of tour mates Siouxsie And The Banshees searched the Humber riverbank with cigarette lighters, following a trail of empty bottles, and eventually found him asleep in the bulrushes. He refused to move, so they left him there to sleep it off. In December that year, after a night of heavy drinking in Eindhoven, he went on a rampage through the band's hotel, eventually locking himself in the bathroom with the shower running, shouting 'Let me die.' And his **pissing** exploits – urinating on Billy Idol of **Generation X**, for example, were also at least partly booze-related.

Stories like these – and there are many – make Lol Tolhurst sound like some sort of sad clown figure. Chris Bohn, in *NME*, called him 'The Cure fall guy and comic'. But he undoubtedly made a significant contribution to The Cure's music and direction in the early days. Such key early songs as 'Grinding Halt', 'Fire In Cairo' and 'So What' on *Three Imaginary Boys*, **'All Cats Are Grey'** on *Faith* and 'Siamese Twins' on *Pornography* were all, he claims, his work to some extent.

Was he ever any good at drumming? In **Chris Parry**'s opinion in *Ten Imaginary Years*, 'Lol was a very temperamental drummer and could only play well if he felt well.' But the truth is that, while no **Boris Williams**, Lol was as good as he needed to be. His shuffling, behind-the-beat performance on **'A Forest'** is superb, and the *Pornography* album is his finest hour.

At the end of May 1981, just before heading out on the European leg of the Picture Tour, Lol visited his mother Daphne. It would be the last time he saw her alive. On 24 June, at a gig in Sittard in the Netherlands, Lol was told between the main set and the encores to phone home. He received the news that Daphne Tolhurst had died from lung cancer. He returned to the stage, managed about a minute of 'Faith', then sat there immobile, unable to play. Michael Dempsey flew out to the Netherlands to see Lol, even though he had been sacked from the band

and replaced by **Simon Gallup**. After the funeral, Robert, Simon and Lol played an acoustic show just for themselves at Daphne's graveside. Incredibly, the tour resumed. Lol had decided that if they didn't carry on, he'd go mad.

The death of his mother affected Lol profoundly, and was one of the factors which fed into the dark atmosphere of the *Pornography* album and the **Fourteen Explicit Moments** tour, at the end of which the Smith-Tolhurst-Gallup **line-up** of The Cure imploded. At that point, they had played 377 gigs in three years, approximately one every three days for a thousand days. Lol needed a break. He'd met a French girl called Anne, and went to live in **Paris** for a while, on Rue Cadet in the 9ème, then travelled around **France** and Catalonia on something of a Salvador Dalí pilgrimage through Montpellier, Figueres, Cadaqués and Port Lligat before returning to London.

With The Cure slimmed down to a duo of just Smith and Tolhurst, Lol switched from drums to keyboards. First, he took up piano lessons. 'I went to see a little old lady in Maida Vale who looked like Miss Havisham,' he told *Record Collector*. 'She was three-and-a-half feet high. She had two baby grands in her basement flat, and she'd slap me on the back of my hands if I got anything wrong.'

More importantly, he got into synthesisers. He phoned the local Musicians' Union for advice, and found an instructor. He began learning on a Sequential Prophet-5, then bought his first synth, a Roland Juno-60. He also acquired an Oberheim OB-8, DSX sequencer and DMX drum machine (as heard on '**The Walk**'), and a Boss Dr Rhythm. Lol was captivated by the first wave of drum machines, as he told *Keyboard* magazine in 1987. 'I was fascinated by the fact that you could actually play all the ideas you had in your head by just pushing some buttons. I thought, "This kind of thing is the future," and I wanted to be involved in it.' He was equally enraptured by the Yamaha CX5M computer. 'The idea of being able to program eight different tracks of music into it, and being taught to read music as I was writing into it, was very emotional. Especially for everybody else who lived around me at the time. I didn't have a monitor, so I had to use the only available television. They had to come in and say, "Haven't you finished yet?!" "No, I've just gotta get this finished, and then you can watch television . . ."'

So, again, was Lol any good at keyboards? Simon Gallup, speaking to Johnny Black in 1995, was sceptical. 'He was never a very good drummer, which is why he went onto keyboards . . .' But again, while no **Roger O'Donnell**, he was as good as he needed to be, and was especially adept at finding ways of mimicking real-world sounds on Cure records. The 'sitar' on 'If Only Tonight We Could Sleep' is an Ensoniq Mirage, as is the koto on 'Kyoto Song'. The reversed guitar sound on 'Snake Pit' was sampled by Lol on an Emulator, and the 'violin' on '**Catch**' is an Emulator too. And the 'trumpet' on '**Why Can't I Be You?**' was – deep breath – 'a combination of a patch on the Roland JX-8P called 'Stab Brass,' MIDIed to a trumpet sample on the Mirage, together with an Emulator brass sound.

This new-found technological ability enabled Lol to **collaborate** outside The Cure. In 1983 he produced the debut album by **And Also The Trees**, a Cure **support band**. In 1984 he produced the *Today* EP by French new wave band Baroque Bordello. He also worked with a band called Bonaparte, and on a never-released project with Paul Bell from **Zerra One**.

There were some within The Cure who believed Lol wasn't earning his keep. When Simon Gallup rejoined the band in 1985, he was upset to discover that he, Boris and Porl were on a wage of about £80 a week, while Lol was on a percentage, and therefore able to swan around in nightclubs, flashing his money, ostentatiously getting a £50 note out instead of a £5 to buy a packet of cigarettes. As Gallup told Johnny Black, 'Lol liked the fame side of it, not the creative side of it'. According to Gallup, 'the only reason he was in the group was the dosh,' and 'Lol loved limos and bollocks like that.' As Simon told *Oor*, 'He seemed unable to exist without the group. When he ordered a pint, he immediately told them he was member of The Cure.' And, said Smith in the same interview, 'He was the only one who used the group's name when booking a table in a restaurant. It's the small things, but they do shine a light on one's personality.' In fairness, Lol himself has admitted he enjoyed the high life. 'Is fame and fortune and recognition all that it's cracked up to be?' he asked rhetorically on *Curious Creatures*. 'I will go back to David Bowie's quote about this matter. He said the only reason fame is any good is to get a better table at a restaurant. And he's got a very good point . . .'

The financial imbalance between the members whose surname wasn't Smith, however, was soon rectified in 1986 when The Cure's deal with **Fiction** was renegotiated and Lol was, as he saw it, demoted from partner to employee (leading, eventually, to the disastrous 1994 **lawsuit**).

In the second half of the eighties, Tolhurst's musical contribution to The Cure decreased as his drinking increased, and he became a disruptive influence. At one recording during the *Kiss Me, Kiss Me, Kiss Me* sessions, Gallup told Johnny Black, Lol came in 'bollocksed' while Simon and Roger were working on a track, stumbled over the microphone and ruined the track, then told them 'It doesn't matter cos it was shit anyway.' He became belligerent towards his bandmates. During the recording of the soundtrack for the opening film of the Kissing Tour in 1987, Lol told Simon 'Fight me, you're a wimp.' **Perry Bamonte**, then a **crew** member, told Lol to leave it. But when Perry left, Lol and Simon had a fight anyway.

The rest of The Cure were starting to make disparaging comments about Lol in public. 'I think he gives heart to everyone who can't play an instrument that they can still be in a group,' said Robert in 1987.

At the start of the South American leg of the Kissing Tour, Lol writes in *Cured*, he went into a vicious circle of anxiety and self-medication. When the tour reached North America, Gallup later recalled, Lol had taken to walking around shouting through a megaphone to get attention, and passed out on the tour's opening night, obliging the crew to get him into the hotel on a baggage trolley. Back in London, he went to his friend Pete's wine bar in Queens Park one night, and drank so much that he ended up unconscious on the street, and was picked up by a police van and dumped in a cell for the night. The Kissing Tour ended with three nights at Wembley Arena in December 1987, the final night closing with a cover of Slade's 'Merry Xmas Everybody'. It would be Lol's final Cure gig for nearly a quarter of a century.

Tolhurst was, Gallup believed, in a very fortunate position: 'Because he'd known Robert since school, Robert felt an obligation towards him.' Smith more or less confirmed as much in a 1988 TV interview. 'I think Lol's like an old blanket, really, that gets very threadbare and dirty,' Robert said, 'and you don't really think about why you're carrying it about, until someone says "Why are you carrying around this old threadbare blanket?", and you suddenly realise you couldn't throw it away and get a new one because you've got emotionally attached to it, due to mutual experience.'

A year later, he would throw away the blanket.

Tolhurst had, at least, begun to acknowledge that he needed help. He had already occasionally visited health farms, and in 1988 he checked into a detox unit for the chemically dependent in the private Lister Hospital on Chelsea Bridge Road, London, where he was seen by a psychiatrist, informed that he was suffering from delirium tremens, and prescribed Librium and vitamin shots. The following day he was visited by two men from Alcoholics Anonymous who told him he had two choices: give up drinking, or end up dead or in prison. He discharged himself after a week, stayed sober for a fortnight, then fell off the wagon and back into 'the abyss'.

Matters reached an ugly climax during the recording of *Disintegration*. Lol was drinking brandy for breakfast, and bringing almost nothing to the table creatively. 'He'd be pissed at breakfast,' Gallup later remembered, 'Go to bed at 7 p.m., get up at 2 a.m., and tell us what we were doing was shit.' Lol later acknowledged that only 'an idea or two' of his made it on to *Disintegration*, but his 'mental fog' prevented him from contributing more.

Lol was making himself an easy scapegoat within the band (see **bullying**), and a target for the frustrations of others. For example, Simon recalled, they put balloons down his toilet for 'jolly japes'. But he didn't exactly help himself.

When the band gathered at RAK for a listening party to hear the final mixes of *Disintegration*, Lol stood up after several beers and announced 'Half of it is good but half of it is shit', arguing that some songs sounded like The Cure but others did not. (He now considers it 'quite a wonderful album'.)

He was told of his sacking via the Royal Mail. As Roger O'Donnell later remembered, 'We both received the same letter from Robert, which was addressed to Lol and basically said that we would be **touring** the album that year but as a five-piece, and Lol was no longer in the band. So, two shocks in one, no more Lol and a world tour to support the record. I think it was absolutely the right thing to do for Lol, and it was for his own good. He would probably have killed himself or worse with drink if he'd have stayed in the band.'

Explaining the decision in *Cure News* in September 1989, Robert said 'He lost touch with the rest of us; mentally, spiritually and socially . . . I haven't spoken to him (I hadn't spoken to him for several years anyway – that was part of the problem).'

If he'd stayed in the band, Smith later said, he'd

either have died from drinking or 'Simon would have thrown him off a balcony. And then my best friend would be in jail and Lol would be dead. It was much easier for him not to be in the band.' Speaking to *Rapido*, Robert said 'I think the rest of the group were surprised that I actually went ahead and told him that he wasn't in the group. Because he'd become such a fixture. But he'd just changed too much. The only one of us suffering, that had been changed by the group in an adverse way. And obviously we all change but mentally and physically he's really suffering. And it's in his own interests not to be in the group at the moment. As much as it is ours.'

In the aftermath of his sacking, Tolhurst married his girlfriend Lydia while The Cure were on tour without him. He continued to drink heavily, until – after making a disgrace of himself on a visit to Michael Dempsey's house and on the train home – he went back to the Lister and later checked into private mental health hospital the Priory in a bid to fix himself.

In 1990, with Dempsey and former Cure crew member **Gary Biddles**, Lol formed a new band, **Presence**, who were active until 1993 when Lol and Lydia relocated to Southern California. Tragically, Lydia and Lol lost a child, Camille India, at only two weeks old due to birth complications caused by lack of oxygen. A few months later Lydia fell pregnant again, leading to the birth of a son, Gray.

Tolhurst found himself in the news again for all the wrong reasons in 1994 when he launched, and lost, a lawsuit against his former band. And, to round off one of the worst years of his life, Lol and Lydia's marriage disintegrated shortly afterwards in November 1994 when Lydia informed Lol that she wanted a divorce on the day he arrived at their new place in West Hollywood, obliging him to stay with friends instead.

However, he was on the road to recovery. Literally. Lol had become interested in spirituality (*Cured* opens with a quote from Hindu guru Nisargadatta Maharaj), and decided to go on a road trip to Zabriskie Point in Death Valley in search of a sense of clarity and positivity.

The following day, he met Cindy Levinson through a mutual friend, and went on a date. Lol and Cindy soon married, moved into a house in West LA, and brought up Gray there after a custody struggle with Lydia, with Lol as a stay-at-home dad. (Gray Tolhurst is now living in San Francisco and plays in a band called Topographies, who have released music on a label called, fittingly, Funeral Party.)

In the late nineties, Lol became able to make peace with his Cure past. In 1997 he appeared at a Cure convention with his new band, Orpheus, and took questions from the crowd. (Robert, in *Cure News*, found this 'laughable', adding 'I thought conventions were for fans?') In 1999, *Cure News* reported, Lol was doing shows where he remixed Cure songs live onstage. And in 2002, with Cindy, he formed the group **Levinhurst**, whose setlist was more than half made up of early Cure songs.

In 1999, Lol wrote a letter to Robert Smith admitting guilt for what had gone wrong, and expressing a wish to make things right. (This is a classic element of the Twelve Step programme: the eighth step is 'Made a list of all persons we had harmed, and became willing to make amends to them all.') Robert replied, asking Lol to come and meet him when The Cure played the Palace in Hollywood in February 2000. During the show, 'The Figurehead' was dedicated to Lol. They hugged backstage, and Robert told Lol he was forgiven. The band, with Lol, all went to a club afterwards, and carried on talking long into the night back at Robert's hotel.

In 2011, the unimaginable happened: Lol Tolhurst returned to the stage with The Cure. Robert had decided to stage another **trilogy** show, called **Reflections**, performing The Cure's first three albums. (Lol had suggested doing something to celebrate the thirtieth anniversary of *Faith*.) Tolhurst performed during the third part of the show – *Faith* itself – at the Sydney Opera House and again in London, Los Angeles and New York. His redemption was complete.

In more recent years, Tolhurst has rediscovered his creativity in a number of ways. He has rekindled his love of drumming. 'I love to play drums now I'm older,' he told Tim's Twitter Listening Party. 'It's really become a beautiful experience. The drums have become a mantra for me . . .' He has launched the excellent **Curious Creatures** podcast with former Banshees drummer Budgie, and has launched the supergroup Lol Tolhurst x Budgie x Jacknife Lee. And he has written **books**, most recently *Goth: A History*.

The most cathartic endeavour, however, is his memoir, *Cured: The Tale of Two Imaginary Boys*. It is, he told *Vice* in 2016, 'the most creative thing I've done since I left The Cure'. In it, as many of the extracts above demonstrate, he completely owns his imperfect past, including his history of addiction. 'I read Pete Townshend's book, and I thought, "Well, Pete was a heroin addict and he never once cops to it in the book." But why not? Because it's part of your life . . .'

Top, The

The unloved Ugly Duckling of The Cure's oeuvre in their eighties pomp, *The Top* is not without its charms. And that, in itself, is a miracle.

There's probably no worse place you could have put The Cure in the eighties, and expect them to get anything done, than a flat above a pub with unlimited access to **alcohol**. In 1983–84, The Cure put themselves in a flat above a pub with unlimited access to alcohol. During the sessions for *The Top*, they resided at the John Barleycorn, an 1810-built coach house in the Berkshire village of Goring-on-Thames, near Reading. The pub allowed them to help themselves to the bar's stock after hours, resulting in all-night drinking sessions, during which the band would write down what they'd consumed on an honesty pad. And when they weren't drinking booze, they were imbibing something even more psychoactive. As Robert Smith told the *Guardian*'s Dorian Lynskey, recently recruited drummer **Andy Anderson** 'used to make a huge pot of magic mushroom tea at the start of every day and it just went on from there.' (This psilocybin potion directly inspired 'Throw Your Foot', a song which didn't make the album but ended up on the 12-inch of '**The Caterpillar**'.)

The hostelry was chosen for its proximity to Genetic Studios in Streatley, Berkshire. Genetic had been open since 1980, established by legendary producers Martin Rushent and Alan Winstanley in a barn at the bottom of Rushent's garden. It had already given the world *Dare* by The Human League and *Homosapien* by Pete Shelley before *The Top* sessions.

After the punch-up with **Simon Gallup** in Strasbourg on the **Fourteen Explicit Moments** tour and the subsequent onstage break-up in Brussels of the **line-up** that made *Faith* and *Pornography*, it was a surprise that there was even a Cure to be having any such sessions (whether drinking or recording). But Smith and **Lol Tolhurst** had regrouped, recorded '**Let's Go To Bed**' and '**The Walk**' as a duo then hired Anderson and bassist **Phil Thornalley** for '**The Lovecats**'.

Thornalley, however, was out of the country helping to produce a Duran Duran album, so Smith had to play the bass parts on *The Top* himself, with a little help from engineer **Howard Gray**. In fact, Smith played all the instruments apart from drums and saxophone. Given that work on *The Top* began in the middle of **1983, Robert's craziest year**, and ran concurrently to the making of **Siouxsie And The Banshees**' album *Hyæna*, obliging him to take taxis from London to Reading and back with almost zero sleep, this added musical responsibility was a pressure he didn't need.

In fact, far from being a diminished half-presence on *The Top*, it was the nearest Robert Smith had yet come to a **solo album**. Songs were demoed at Eden Studios before moving to Genetic, where Robert, though running on empty, nevertheless ran the show, with the assistance of producer **David M. Allen** (making his Cure debut), **Chris Parry** and Howard Gray. Smith and Tolhurst weren't getting on particularly well, a situation exacerbated when Tolhurst slipped on some ice outside Genetic and broke Robert's prized Vox Teardrop **guitar** which had only just been repaired (after Lol broke it the first time). Robert wrote most of the lyrics during Banshees downtime, while Siouxsie and **Steve Severin** were doing interviews. Lol, who had few other demands on his time, contributed only a couple of songs. 'I couldn't really complain that the creative responsibilities were becoming more one-sided,' he wrote in *Cured*, 'because I didn't feel well enough to take on more.' Smith himself, though, wasn't finding it easy to come up with ideas. He would sit in the dark for hours, surrounded by toys and instruments, waiting for inspiration to strike while Allen looked on patiently.

In the long term, the most important assistance The Cure received on *The Top* came from an old friend. **Porl Thompson** had visited Genetic to show them the **artwork** he and **Andy Vella** had created for the album. While he was there, they lured him into contributing a bit of saxophone to 'Give Me It', continuing his gradual reintroduction to the fold (already having appeared on *Top of the Pops* as Phil Thornalley's stunt double) six years after being edged out of Easy Cure for being too good at guitar. Getting Thompson back on board was vital: the album was far too musically complex for the current line-up to tour with, but the versatile Porl was the missing jigsaw piece.

Opening track 'Shake Dog Shake', a big frazzled, mangled mess of psychedelic open-tuned guitars, begins with a madman's laugh, and was written, Smith later revealed, 'about me during the Banshees tour'. Its first verse encapsulates the frustration and self-loathing he felt as an inmate on someone else's tour:

> Wake up in the dark
> The after-taste of anger in the back of my mouth
> Spit it on the wall
> And cough some more and scrape my skin with razor blades

It's a song which has a certain special status among tracks from *The Top*. It was sent out as a promo disc to radio in **France** (copies are a **rarity**, currently worth £171), and it became their gig-starter for years. It is still often their go-to opener. To this day, when Cure fans hear that song, muscle memory has them anxiously edging towards a non-existent stage barrier.

'Birdmad Girl', written about a 'mentally ill girl', combined two long-running Cure tropes: **madness** and **zoology**. It was inspired, Tolhurst confirmed at the time, by a Dylan Thomas **poem**, 'Love in the Asylum', which mentions 'a girl mad as birds'. With its open-ended acoustic strums and its tinkling pianos, it's a song with an exquisite lightness of touch, closer to 'Tinseltown in the Rain' by The Blue Nile than to anything The Cure had previously done. The song repeatedly mentions polar bears, explained by Robert in *Cure News* thus: 'the polar bear was the symbol (zoo-wise) for me, insensible savagery caged to be stared at'.

The consciously Middle Eastern-sounding 'Wailing Wall' was inspired by Smith's visit to Jerusalem with the Banshees, and reprises *Faith*'s scepticism regarding religion:

> The holy city breathed
> Like a dying man
> It moved with hopeful tears
> With the tears of the blind

It also references an actual incident where he somehow lost his shoes:

> Through broken streets that sucked me in
> My feet were bare and cut with stones

As he told Steve Sutherland, 'The roads were dirty, it was revolting. But the Wailing Wall itself was brilliant: the most beautiful noise I've ever heard, total religious insanity.'

'Give Me It' gave no quarter, a maximalist maelstrom of pummelling Andy Anderson drums and skronking, atonal no-wave sax from Porl Thompson that's half early Roxy Music, half James White and the

Contortions. The song was originally intended for **The Glove**, inspired in part by Nicolas Roeg's *Bad Timing* (one of the films Robert watched with Severin during the making of **Blue Sunshine**).

Rounding off Side 1 in far more relaxed mode, 'Dressing Up', with its floaty recorders and sparkling keys, was written about Robert's feelings before going onstage, putting on his **make-up**.

Side 2 began with the album's one hit single, 'The Caterpillar', famously featuring the sound of Andy Anderson slapping his leather-trousered thighs to suggest butterfly wings. The fourth pop-facing Cure single in a row, it doubtless lured many purchasers in to buying *The Top* unawares, ill-prepared for some of the craziness within.

'Piggy In The Mirror' has an unhurried soft-rock grandeur to it, with Smith adopting a strange, slurred, baritone croon, creeping half-heartedly upwards at the end of each verse into an enfeebled falsetto. With lyrics about someone, or something, with 'sixteen white legs and a row of teeth', it initially appears to be a surreal acid-trip narrative, but Smith revealed in *Cure News* that it's a song of self-loathing, mocking his *Pornography*-era self, with a side order of cinematic allusions. 'Me hating myself again – references I recognise to the Nic Roeg film *Bad Timing* which Severin and I watched one night in slow motion . . . too many **drugs** . . . blah blah blah'. It wasn't the first time Smith had berated the state of himself in the mirror: 'Mr Pink Eyes', B-side to 'The Lovecats', had pursued a similarly pitiless line of self-appraisal.

'The Empty World', another song inspired by the novel *Charlotte Sometimes*, has marching band percussion and flutes, matching its lyrics about armies. It's beyond bad, and actively irritating. As the *Guardian*'s Dorian Lynskey wrote in a review of the 2006 reissue of *The Top*, 'Only "The Empty World" is misjudged, as songs employing cod-military drum tattoos usually are.' In its favour, it is only two minutes thirty-six seconds long.

'Bananafishbones', like 'The Empty World', had a **literary** origin. With harmonicas and sixties garage-rock keyboards zig-zagging around him, Smith spits angry lines like 'Or leave it senseless like a suck on a gun? "Put a piece of metal in your head", you said, "Make you dead" . . .' This, like its title, is a reference to the J. D. Salinger short story 'A Perfect Day for Bananafish', in which a Second World War veteran, suffering from what we would now call post-traumatic stress disorder, sits on a hotel bed next to his wife and calmly shoots himself. It was also, Smith told *Cure News*, another song about 'me hating myself'.

The Top ends, like *Pornography*, *Faith* and **Seventeen Seconds** before it (and even **Three Imaginary Boys**, if we discount the daft instrumental 'The Weedy Burton'), with the title track. The track is topped (literally) and tailed by the whirring of a spinning top toy, a sound effect which took over twelve hours to get just right. In between, Smith sings what he deemed 'something of a milestone lyric' about 'finally coming to my senses', which has been interpreted by many fans as a lament for the departure of Simon Gallup:

> Every day I lie here and know that it's true
> All I really want is you
> Please come back

The Top is every bit as disjointed as you would expect from a record whose main cited influences were as disparate as Billie Holiday's 'Getting Some Fun Out Of Life' and **Pink Floyd**'s 'Interstellar Overdrive'. However, only three years later, on *Kiss Me, Kiss Me, Kiss Me*, such musical variety would be viewed as a positive. Taken as a whole, *The Top* is like listening in on a stoned Sunday session: it feels like you're *privy* to something. (An unkind wag would point out that 'privy' is an archaic word for 'toilet'.)

The Top was release on 4 May 1984, in the **Parched Art** sleeve that Porl Thompson had been carrying under his arm when he visited Genetic and became a sax-tooting Cure member. It comprised smudgy washes of blue, yellow and pink, with green and gold quasi-mediaeval lettering, and some sort of golden circular sigil involving a snake, a bird and a pyramid. It looked great on T-shirts.

'*The Top* will test the patience of all but the most resilient Curist,' wrote Danny Kelly in *NME*. 'If it has any value it's only as a vivid illustration that the cleansing turmoil of the late Seventies can slide into the same miasma of self-indulgence that nurtured the sickness we thought had been purged forever.' (The sickness being the excesses of psychedelia and prog rock.) *Melody Maker*'s Steve Sutherland had no such problems with its acid rock leanings, calling it 'psychedelia that can't be dated'. Jack Barron of *Sounds* agreed: 'In 20 years' time, when the next generation blush with excitement at the word "Psychedelic", it'll be regarded as a classic'.

It was promoted with live performances on the BBC's *Oxford Road Show* ('Shake Dog Shake'

and 'Give Me It') and Channel 4's *The Tube* ('Bananafishbones' and 'Piggy in the Mirror'). *The Top* subsequently entered the UK charts at No.10, their second Top 10 album in a row, and went silver. It also reached the Top 20 in **France** and the Netherlands. If it didn't dramatically ramp up The Cure's trajectory of success, it at least kept them in a level holding pattern before the breakthrough of **The Head On The Door**.

The Top tour set out with a new line-up of Smith, Tolhurst, Thompson, Anderson and a returning Thornalley, though the latter would leave at the end of it, and Anderson would leave midway through, making 1984 The Cure's Year of Three Drummers (analogous to Britain's Year of Three Prime Ministers in 2022).

The album was re-released in 2006 in a deluxe CD edition, with an extra disc containing Robert's demo versions of songs from (and rejected from) the album. The most noteworthy of these was 'Ariel', a Sylvia Plath-inspired song, co-written with Lol in the aftermath of the Fourteen Explicit Moments tour, which had been tried out on a Kid Jensen session on BBC Radio 1 and which Robert had suggested might appear on a solo record. In 2012, *The Top* was reissued again on limited-edition gold vinyl as part of the Back to Black series.

These reissues have done little to rehabilitate *The Top*. It has a fairly poor reputation among fans, and was ranked twelfth of thirteen Cure albums by *Ultimate Classic Rock* and eleventh by *Far Out* magazine.

Robert himself has been disparaging, once claiming that it had been mastered at the wrong speed. He also called it 'the most difficult to talk / write about – a lot of it is me working things out of myself that were very unpleasant and old . . .'

The most diplomatic reappraisals of *The Top* describe it as a 'transitional' record, midway between The Cure's darkest phase and their reinvention as pop-**goth** superstars. Smith gives that interpretation a qualified endorsement, calling it 'A really self-indulgent album – a reaction against "The Lovecats" in a way. I had to get it out of my system, but there are songs on there that were really pointing the way to what I wanted to do.'

Torn Down

Torn Down (Mixed Up Extras) was another album of Cure remixes, released in 2018, this time executed entirely by Robert Smith rather than outsiders.

That wasn't always the plan. In a press conference in **France** in 2012, he announced there would be a *Mixed Up 2* 'this side of Christmas', on which 'The Cure's favourite bands remix The Cure'. He named **Mogwai** and **Cranes** as two examples, saying Mogwai would be remixing 'Faith'. The album never happened.

When it did arrive, some six years later, it was created chiefly by Robert with assistance from **Keith Uddin**, Tim Young and the ever-mysterious **Bunny Lake**. Premiering it on Shaun Keaveny's show on BBC 6 Music with an exclusive play of the 'Time' remix of 'Want', he explained that he 'just fancied doing some remixes' and that he had consciously chosen to 'remix Cure songs that wouldn't normally be chosen for remixing, songs like "The **Drowning** Man", the more sort of esoteric Cure songs.'

Torn Down did indeed focus on deep cuts and non-obvious choices: only two tracks had been singles, and only one of them a recognised hit. Each track represented a different Cure album, sequenced in chronological order. They were as follows: 'Three Imaginary Boys' (*Three Imaginary Boys*), 'M' (*Seventeen Seconds*), 'The Drowning Man' (*Faith*), 'A Strange Day' (*Pornography*), 'Just One Kiss' (*Japanese Whispers*), 'Shake Dog Shake' (*The Top*), 'A Night Like This' (*The Head On The Door*), 'Like Cockatoos' (*Kiss Me, Kiss Me, Kiss Me*), 'Plainsong' (*Disintegration*), 'Never Enough' (*Mixed Up*), 'From The Edge Of The Deep Green Sea' (*Wish*), 'Want' (*Wild Mood Swings*), 'The Last Day of Summer' (*Bloodflowers*), 'Cut Here' (*Greatest Hits*), 'Lost' (*The Cure*) and 'It's Over' (*4:13 Dream*).

The mixes tended to be more spacious than *Mixed Up*, and – as might be expected – more vocal-centred. Highlights included a superbly abrasive 'A Strange Day', a looser, dirtier 'Never Enough' and a radically different, almost House-like 'A Night Like This'.

With **artwork** by **Andy Vella** featuring an image of Robert's face in the same quasi-Fauvist style as *Mixed Up*, it was released on 21 April 2018 as a stand-alone **vinyl** LP on Record Store Day in a limited edition of 7,750 copies, and also as the third disc in the deluxe reissue of *Mixed Up*. The individual *Torn Down* did not chart, having been pressed in such restricted quantities, but as part of the new *Mixed Up* it reached the Top 20 in the UK and Germany.

Touring

When is a tour not a tour, and just a series of dates? What distinguishes a proper Tour with a capital 'T' from a mere run of live shows is a sense of unity and identity. Typically this includes specially made **artwork**, a bespoke light show, perhaps some projections, a sustained period on the road with no gaps, and ideally a name. The Cure have played forty-three Tours with a capital T. They are, in chronological order:

Supporting *Generation X* – UK, November-December 1978

Unnamed UK tour – February-April 1979

Three Imaginary Boys Tour – UK, May-July 1979

Join Hands Tour (supporting *Siouxsie And The Banshees*) – UK, August-October 1979

Future Pastimes Tour – UK, November 1979

Unnamed European tour – December 1979

Unnamed **US** tour – April 1980

Seventeen Seconds Tour – UK and Europe, April-June 1980

Get a Dose of The Cure Tour – **Australasia**, July-August 1980

Unnamed European tour – October-November 1980

The **Primary** Tour – UK, November 1980

The Picture Tour – UK, Europe, Australasia and North America, April-October 1981

Eight Appearances Tour – UK, November-December 1981

Fourteen Explicit Moments aka **Pornography** Tour – UK and Europe, April-June 1982

Unnamed US tour – August **1983**

The Top Tour – UK, Europe, Australasia, North America and Japan, April-November 1984

Unnamed European tour – June-August 1985

The Head Tour – UK, North America and Europe, September-December 1985

The Beach Party Tour – North America and Europe, July-August 1986

Unnamed South American tour – March-April 1987

The Kissing Tour – North America, July-August 1987

The Honeymoon Tour – Europe and UK, October-November 1987

The Prayer Tour – Europe, UK and North America, May-September 1989

The Pleasure Trips – Europe and UK, June-August 1990

The Wish Tour – UK, North America, Australasia and Europe, April-December 1992

The Team Tour – Europe, June-July 1995

The Swing Tour – Europe, UK and North America, May-December 1996

The Radio Festivals Tour – North America, November-December 1997

The Summer Festivals Tour – Europe, July-August 1998

The Bloodflowers Album Launch Tour – UK and North America, February 2000

The Dream Tour – Europe, North America and Australasia, March-October 2000

The Summer Festivals Tour (again) – Europe, July-August 2002

Euro Festivals Summer '04 Tour – Europe, June-July 2003

The Curiosa Festival Tour – North America, July-August 2004

Unnamed European tour – July-September 2005

4Tour World Tour – Asia, Australasia and North America, July-October 2007, and Europe and North America, February-June 2008

The Trilogy Tour – Australia, UK and North America, May-November 2011

Summercure 2012 Tour – Europe, May-September 2012

LatAm2013 Tour – Latin America, April 2013

The Great Circle – Korea, Japan and North America, July-August 2013

The Cure Tour 2016 – North America, Australasia, Europe and UK, May-December 2016

Summer Festivals 2019 – Europe, Japan and North America, June-September 2019

The Lost World Tour – Europe and North America, November 2022-July 2023

Some of these tours are more eventful and notable than others. The Generation X tour was cut short when The Cure were thrown off for urinating on Billy Idol. Join Hands was the tour on which *Lol Tolhurst* was almost shot by Thatcher's goons while **pissing**, Robert joined the Banshees on guitar, and was beaten up in a Newcastle hotel room. Future Pastimes was the **Fiction** package tour featuring **The Passions** and **Associates** (with whose singer Billy Mackenzie Robert struck up a friendship). The

Picture Tour, promoting *Faith*, featured the *Carnage Visors* film as the support act, and took place in 2,000-capacity circus tents for some of the European stretch. Fourteen Explicit Moments (in the UK) or the Pornography Tour (in Europe) was the calamitous tour on which Robert and **Simon Gallup** had a bar fight, and the band broke up live on stage in chaotic scenes involving **Gary Biddles** and **Zerra One**. The Top Tour featured several scenes of drama surrounding **Andy Anderson** who departed midway, and starred not one but two new drummers in **Vince Ely** and **Boris Williams**. The Beach Party Tour culminated with *The Cure In Orange*. The South American tour of 1986 saw carnage in **Argentina** and hysteria in **Brazil**. The Honeymoon Tour was so named because Smith and Gallup, both recently married, brought their wives along in lieu of a real honeymoon. The seventy-six-date Prayer Tour would have been seventy-seven but, Robert told a TV interviewer, '[Bulgaria] wouldn't let us in, because we were ideologically unsound.' The Wish Tour, with 111 dates, remains The Cure's biggest ever (Simon Gallup was forced to leave near the end, having contracted pleurisy, temporarily replaced by **Roberto Soave**). The Swing Tour was particularly ill-starred, with a lighting problem causing the rescheduling of the first three dates, and Robert falling ill with ear, eye and throat issues after the American leg, causing a whole section of the tour to be postponed, and fell ill again in Japan. The Summer Festivals tour of 1998 is generally considered The Cure's **lowest point**. The Trilogy shows were significant because of the temporary reunion with Lol Tolhurst. And the Lost World Tour was notable for the sudden reintroduction of **Perry Bamonte** and the gradual unveiling of the core of a **fourteenth album**.

Some number-crunching: The Cure have played an estimated 1,377 concerts under that name, with an additional twenty-seven by Easy Cure and three by Malice (see **Pre-Cure bands**). Their busiest calendar years were 1981 (119 shows), 1992 (111 shows) and 1996 (ninety-eight shows). There have been seven calendar years with no Cure gigs at all: 1988, 1994, 2010, 2015, 2017, 2020 (Covid lockdown) and 2021 (Covid lockdown). Other quiet years include 1993, 1999 and 2006 (one show each), 2003 and 2018 (two shows each), 1991 and 2001 (three shows each), and 2009 (four shows).

One thing that The Cure's relentless touring has done is to broaden their horizons and prevent them from becoming a parochial **English** concern. Their first gig outside England came on the Three Imaginary Boys tour, when they played Newport's Stowaway Club on 21 March 1979, but it was their early European excursions which formed their mindset as an international band. 'It means we can keep going and we can still experiment,' Robert told Paul '**Desperate Journalist**' Morley of *NME* in 1981. 'If we had stayed in England we wouldn't be going any more because you get derided by so many people you just think "What's the point?"'

The Cure typically travel by bus and boat, because Robert and Simon don't like flying (and nor, in his time, did **Porl Thompson**). The items Robert was never without on the bus, he told *Cure News* in 1997, were: a drink, aspirins, sunglasses, his own pillow, at least a thousand CDs, chewing gum, pen and paper, two stuffed cats, a phone, a camera, earplugs and milk.

Oh, and the lamb. This is probably the place to clarify that the lamb The Cure allegedly took on tour (see **Zoology**) wasn't a real one, but a gift from Robert's girlfriend. (Insert your own '**Mary** had a little lamb' joke here.) 'I took a lamb on tour,' he told *The Face* in 1985, 'but it was a stuffed one; it was full of strawberry-scented soap and I used it as a pillow. I used to rest my head on it in the van. It wasn't a real dead one. It was like a pyjama case.'

For a band with well over a thousand shows under their belt, The Cure have sometimes seemed to loathe the touring process. 'A lot of groups try to drum up enthusiasm and support by playing live concerts,' Robert told *Chicago Tribune* in 1989. 'With us, it's really tended to be the other way around: we always play reluctantly.' The following year, on MTV, he reflected on their most recent jaunt: 'Too many people have too long a face. That's how I remember touring.'

For all those long faces in the past, The Cure must enjoy touring on some level nowadays. After all, their most recent adventure, the Lost World Tour, was their longest since 1992, and the famously epic shows aren't getting any shorter. As **Roger O'Donnell** said of the 2016 tour, 'We rehearsed over 120 songs for that tour. Of course, if we're going to pull number 117 out the bag for the next show, then we'll play it in the soundcheck the day before. I remember that I was complaining once about trying to remember so many songs and Robert was like, "Yeah, every night I go on stage, I basically have to remember the words from an entire book . . . and sing them." So I was like, "Yeah, OK, whatever. I'll stop complaining." I keep telling him to get a teleprompter, but he doesn't want

to. I don't know how he does it. I mean, his **voice** is better now than it's ever been . . .'

Which is why each Cure show is a type of tour in itself. A *tour de force*.

Tribute Bands

After The Beatles, The Rolling Stones and Elvis Presley, there's a strong possibility that The Cure are the most-tributed band on earth.

Forming a tribute band to artists who are still very much alive and active may seem like a futile pursuit. And nothing can compete with the experience of seeing the actual Cure. But there is reason in the madness.

Firstly, committed road-warriors as they may be, Robert Smith and his band cannot be omnipresent and cannot cover all the corners of the planet where there is demand for Cure concerts. In some places, there may be years, even decades between a real, first-hand Cure experience. Secondly, The Cure tend to play huge fields, enormo-domes or, at best, large theatres, so a tribute band can offer an intimate experience to which the real band said goodbye in the early eighties. Thirdly, ticket prices are considerably cheaper. And fourthly, tribute concerts provide real-life gathering points for isolated Cure **fans** (does any other kind exist?) in a way that social media groups simply cannot.

The names of these acts, as is typical of tribute bands, fall into three main categories: puns (which range from the ingenious to the atrocious), song titles, and Ronseal ('does exactly what it says on the tin'). Imagine a name for a Cure tribute band, and it's 99% certain you'll find that name somewhere in the (incomplete) inventory below.

The foremost Cure tribute band, certainly in the UK (and arguably the rest of the world), are The Cureheads, who have been active since 1990. They began when Cure superfan Gary Clarke, also a member of **goth** band Nosferatu, was busking his way around Europe to raise money for his travel to cities on the Pleasure Trips tour, and they played their first show in Stockholm that year. They originally performed as Fat Bob & The Cureheads, until it was suggested to them by Ita Martin of **Fiction** Records that Robert Smith might find this a little offensive.

The Cureheads' live set often includes obscurities

as well as the obvious hits. They often function as their own support band, bringing in singer Sally Holliday or, later, *Torchwood* and *Emmerdale* actress Ceri Ann Gregory to front **Siouxsie** and the Budgiees on a double-headline show entitled *The Story of Goth*. They have performed extensively in Europe and **South America** to audiences as large as ten thousand (in a stadium in Chile), and they estimate that they have played to combined audiences of over half a million.

The Cureheads hold the distinction, though not a unique one, of having once had a former Cure member in their ranks: drummer **Andy Anderson**, with whom they parted company after only four months in 2012 when he failed to turn up to the airport for a South American tour. **Ron Howe**, saxophonist on *The Head On The Door*, has also performed with The Cureheads. (Their line-up has included alumni of Killing Joke and Queen Adreena.)

The Cureheads, however, aren't even the only tribute band to have featured an actual Cure member: Irish Cure tribute Fire In Cairo played a few shows with **Lol Tolhurst**, the man whom Anderson replaced on drums, in 2017 as part of Lol's book tour for *Cured* (see **Books**). Nor are The Cureheads the only Cure tribute band in Britain: to name but one, Norwich-based Liqueur have been active since 2006.

And the UK isn't the country with the highest number of Cure covers bands. The **USA** has at least a dozen, active or dormant. These include Disintegration (New York), PriMary (Chicago) and Cover The Tracks (Bellingham, WA). California alone has more than one: The Curse (El Monte) and The Cured (San Diego). So does Oregon: theXplodingboys (Portland) and a black metal Cure tribute band called Curezum (also Portland). So does Texas: Boys Don't Cry (Houston) who, like The Cureheads, sometimes tour with a Siouxsie impersonator as support, and Le Cure (Dallas), opting for essentially the same pun as Norwich's Liqueur.

Le Cure, however, aren't even the only Le Cure. There's also a LeCure in Auckland, New Zealand and another Le Cure in **France**.

Le Cure, however, aren't even the only Cure tribute band in France. There's also Thérapie (Lille), Pictures Of You aka Other Voices (Saint-Laurent-de-Neste), and The Figureheads (Haute-Savoie).

The Figureheads, however, aren't even the only Figureheads tribute band in existence. Italy also has a Figureheads (Palermo).

The Figureheads of Palermo, however, aren't

even the only Cure tribute band in Italy. There's also Seventeen Seconds (Tolentina), Easy Cure (Florence) and Concura (Turin), the latter another band who moonlight as a Siouxsie tribute act.

. . . And so it continues. There's a band called The Obscure in the Los Angeles area. The Obscure, however, aren't even the only Cure tribute band with that name. There's also ObsCure (Barcelona) and The obsCURE (Antwerp).

The obsCURE, however, aren't even the only Cure tribute band in Belgium. There's also The Lovecats (La Louviere).

The Lovecats, however, aren't even the only Cure tribute band with that name. There's a Lovecats in Australia. There's also The Love Cats (New Jersey), featuring Frank Iero of My Chemical Romance as well as members of noted punk/emo bands The Bouncing Souls and Thursday. And in 2009, Peruvian singer Pelo Madueño formed a side project called The Lovecats who recreated rock classics in a jazz style.

Rewinding a little, ObsCure aren't even the only Cure tribute band in Spain, nor are theXplodingboys of Portland the only band with that name. Both are ticked off by the award-winning The Exploding Boys (Madrid).

And that's without mentioning Accureacy (Greece), Four Imaginary Boys (Germany), The Disease (Dublin), The Ordinary (Czech Republic), and the very literal-minded The Cure Tribute Bulgaria (Bulgaria) and The Cure Cover Brasil (Brazil).

The Cure Cover Brasil (Brazil), however, aren't even the only Cure tribute band in Latin America. In November 2020, an Argentinian-organised online event called The Cure International Tribute Day featured The Cure Cover Brasil along with, among others, Bananafishbones (Argentina), Three Imaginary Boys (Colombia), Six Different Ways (Bolivia), Desintegrados (Mexico), The Blood Flowers (Mexico), The Push (Peru), Venezuela – Curetaje (Venezuela), 4:13 Dream (Puerto Rico) and Fiction (Chile), not to be confused with Fixion (Mexico), all attesting to the enormous interest in The Cure in the Hispanic world.

All of the above either exist, or existed at one point. It's difficult to ascertain, however, whether there has really been a Cure tribute band called Prevention, because it's used so frequently as the set-up for a bad joke. (The same applies to The Vaccine, especially in the era of Covid.)

There's evidently a place for these bands. If you go to see your local Love Cats, Figureheads, Exploding Boys, Fiction, Obscured or Le Cure, try to defocus your eyes as you peer at them through the smoke. Maybe you can kid yourself, for a second or seventeen, that it's the real thing.

Trilogy

When *Bloodflowers* came out in 2000, Robert Smith never missed an opportunity to state that he saw it as part of an 'invented trilogy' with *Pornography* and *Disintegration*. It was a smart line of attack: it implicitly placed *Bloodflowers* on a par, quality-wise, with those two (thus making it a must-buy item), and also forewarned listeners that it was going to be *that* kind of Cure album.

'Yeah, it was slightly disingenuous of me saying that,' Robert admitted in an interview with *Xpress*. 'I was doing it just to let Cure fans know in advance that what we were working on was something in that kind of area. The *Pornography*/*Disintegration* side rather than another *Wild Mood Swings* or a *Japanese Whispers* style . . . or a *Mixed Up* album, God forbid. That it was just gonna be the more introspective side of The Cure. It was also the best way to describe to the others [Cure members] that what I wanted was this imaginary trilogy of *Pornography* and *Disintegration*, with *Bloodflowers* as the third part.'

For anyone who didn't take the bait, however, Smith had one more trick up his sleeve. In 2002, The Cure played that 'invented trilogy' live. If you wanted to see The Cure play *Pornography* and *Disintegration*, you also had to hear *Bloodflowers*. Each night, he would have a captive audience of people who were, by definition, open to *that* kind of Cure album. And any fairweather fans, just going along to check out a Cure gig, were going to hear *Bloodflowers* whether they liked it or not.

The idea of playing classic albums in full alongside the most recent one was inspired by the experience of seeing **David Bowie** play his then-new *Heathen* with 1977's *Low* at the **Meltdown Festival** he curated in 2002. 'It worked perfectly,' said Robert on the *Trilogy* DVD. 'I've seen Bowie a few times and it was the best I'd ever seen him on stage for years and years. And I thought if we could do that with three albums, that would be a big undertaking.'

The other band members were 'a bit incredulous at first' when Robert told them of his plan, but he had faith in their ability to carry it off. 'I think this line-up is the most dynamic we've ever had,' he said. 'It can be the most subtle line-up and also the most powerful.' He admitted that when he listened back to *Pornography*-era trio playing that album, 'we weren't that good', and believed the 2002 Cure, by contrast, could do it justice.

Tapping into the emotions that created *Pornography*, and by extension the toxic atmosphere of the **Fourteen Explicit Moments** tour (after which Robert and **Simon Gallup** didn't speak for nearly a year) was a concern. 'I worried about how we would respond, looking across at each other', Robert said. Simon agreed. 'Hopefully you can touch upon those feelings without getting showered in it. It would bloody kill you if you acted like a 20-year-old again.'

The first *Trilogy* concert, unfilmed, was in the Vorst Nationaal, Brussels on 7 November 2002. The Cure then played a normal, non-*Trilogy* gig on 9 November before moving on to Berlin for the two shows captured on film on 11 and 12 November. The choice to play in Berlin was arrived at carefully. The Cure's previous live film, *Show*, had been made in America but, Robert said on the *Trilogy* DVD, 'I felt this trilogy had a Northern European feel, and the city in which we did it would have an effect on how we did it.' Moscow and Prague were also considered. And it wasn't as simple as picking Robert's favourite city. 'Barcelona – one of my favourite cities – wouldn't be right for this. Maybe Barcelona would be the place for *Kiss Me, Kiss Me, Kiss Me* . . . It was important that when we stepped onstage to do *Pornography* we hadn't just been in a tapas bar. We needed to have that heavy atmosphere around us. The sense of history in Berlin, and all that's gone on.'

The concerts took place at the Tempodrom, a giant pagoda-shaped circus tent originally built in 1980 during the Cold War on the west side of Potsdamer Platz, the historic square bisected by the Wall. The Tempodrom was relocated a number of times, and by 2002 permanently sited on the former site of Anhalter Bahnhof, a railway terminus which had been used during the Second World War to deport Jewish people to concentration camps, and which was later destroyed by Allied bombing. If Robert wanted a heavy atmosphere with a sense of history, few other cities could compete with that.

The *Pornography* section of the concert did indeed pack an emotional gut-punch. 'The initial feeling, when we went on and did **"One Hundred Years"**,' said Robert, 'was like AAARGH! It really was. It's the first time in years we've gone onstage and started with something that's like, BANG! And that makes me feel young. It's like being in a really young band.' **Roger O'Donnell**, although not a Cure member when the album was made, was overwhelmed by the intensity. 'You can't go onstage and laugh your way through a song like 'One Hundred Years'. When I first joined the group, and we first started to play 'One Hundred Years', I was almost in tears, playing that song.' Between albums, said **Jason Cooper**, they had civilised and relaxed 'tea breaks' to decompress before going out for the next one.

Some songs, like 'A Short Term Effect', hadn't been played live since 1982, and several hadn't been filmed live before, like 'The Same Deep Water As You', which they had only played, Robert estimated, 'about five times in ten years'. The first encore each night was a pair of *Kiss Me, Kiss Me, Kiss Me* songs, 'If Only Tonight We Could Sleep' and 'The Kiss', and the second featured three *Seventeen Seconds* songs, 'M', 'Play for Today' and '**A Forest**', with 'Grinding Halt' and '**Boys Don't Cry**' added on the final night.

The film of *Trilogy* or, to give its full DVD title, *Trilogy: Live in the Tempodrom Berlin November 2002*, featured footage from both the Berlin shows and was directed by Nick Wickham, who would also direct both halves of *40 Live* (*Anniversary* and *Curætion*) with **Tim Pope** in 2018. A quote from Keats, 'Ay, in the very temple of delight veil'd melancholy has her sovran shrine', appeared on the screen at the start, showing once again Robert's love of **poetry**.

The encores included on the DVD were the two *Kiss Me, Kiss Me, Kiss Me* songs, 'If Only Tonight We Could Sleep' and 'The Kiss'. Writing in the *Quietus*, Ned Raggett had particular praise for the latter. '"The Kiss", the brutal, glowering opening song for [*Kiss Me, Kiss Me, Kiss Me*], was already extreme enough in its slow-burn guitar build and portrayal of an utter love-hate situation; the *Trilogy* version has Smith going even more crazy on guitar, the band creating a steadily more oppressive-yet-beautiful backing build. By the time Smith's vocals finally kick in – and especially later when he adds a wholly new wail to finish off the lyric – the concert really IS over, because where else could one go?'

On the reverse of the DVD's **artwork**, the front of which involved a simple live photo of Robert, there was a quote from the singer stating that 'the realisation of this *Trilogy* show is one of the highlights of my time in The Cure.' So, would they do it again? 'We've been talking about doing another trilogy', said Robert in the interview on the DVD, 'but I don't think

it's a good idea.' Simon Gallup concurred. 'I think we've done the in-the-pasting now.' **Perry Bamonte** worried about the danger of a band 'putting off death by repetition – there should be chapters and endings.' Roger O'Donnell added, 'I think the reflection period is over.'

An interesting choice of words from the keyboardist, as The Cure would indeed play another *Trilogy*-style series of concerts in 2011, under the name *Reflections*. In 2014 it was announced by *Pitchfork* that The Cure would perform a third trilogy of *The Top*, *The Head On The Door* and *Kiss Me, Kiss Me, Kiss Me*, but this never transpired. (They did, however, mark the thirtieth anniversary of *The Top* by playing all the songs from it at three Hammersmith Apollo shows, albeit non-consecutively.)

Probably the wisest call. A trilogy of trilogies would have been too much 'in-the-pasting' for everyone.

TV (The Cure appear on)

'Time has convinced me of one thing,' said Noel Coward. 'Television is for appearing on, not looking at.'

The first time The Cure were appearing on television, not just looking at it, happened in **France**. On 16 December 1979 a concert they'd played the previous week at Théâtre de l'Empire in **Paris** was broadcast by the TV show *Chorus*, presented by Antoine de Caunes, on the channel Antenne 2. As well as being The Cure's TV debut, it is notable for featuring an early version of '**A Forest**', then titled 'At Night'.

The Cure's first UK television appearance also involved that song, but this time they were miming it. On 24 April 1980 the band appeared on the BBC's primetime pop programme *Top of the Pops* because 'A Forest', as it was now known, had crept into the Top 40. They had flown back from the **USA** to do it, on the same flight as The Specials, whom they had befriended while over there. Robert Smith still had a bandaged thumb left over from an injury sustained during some drug-induced horseplay in America while trying to fix a hubcap.

By being there at all, The Cure were gatecrashing the pop party, and enforcing an interlude of sombre seriousness amid the show's usual frivolity. There were, however, a number of punk, new wave and ska acts on that episode (Cockney Rejects, The Undertones, Elvis Costello, Bad Manners and, at No.1, Dexys Midnight Runners). The punk taboo about appearing on such a cheerfully commercial show as *Top of the Pops* (The Clash, famously had refused to do it) had been abandoned by most bands. Robert, however, still had reservations.

'I didn't want to do it,' he later recalled in a TV interview. 'I distinctly remember at the time saying I thought it was a bad idea. We were trying to succeed without doing programmes like *Top of the Pops*.' His bassist **Simon Gallup**, however, talked some sense into him. 'Simon said "If we don't do it, someone else is going to do it. And you can't change things if no one knows who you are." And he was right, really. And I came to see that. We had to get some level of exposure. And you can't present a choice if people don't know the choice exists. We had to let people know we were there. And if we didn't do it, there were ten other groups behind us queuing up to do it.' (He described the experience, in hindsight, as 'horribly disappointing'.)

And so presenter Steve Wright, sporting a stripy blazer, seventies sunglasses and a Fu Manchu moustache, brightly beamed 'Right, here comes a good band, called The Cure!' and there they were, sandwiched between videos for Paul McCartney and Elvis Costello. Robert, wearing a tightly buttoned-up black shirt with his **hair** in a brushy close crop, was not the main focus of the camera crew. Instead, drummer **Lol Tolhurst** was pushed to the front – a strange directorial decision (but one that *TOTP* intermittently made – The Jam's 'Beat Surrender' and Slade's 'My Friend Stan' being two other notable examples). Footage from that performance was later cut together by director Dave Hiller with footage of actual forests to create the song's official video.

Top of the Pops was watched by over fifteen million people, and was the most direct way for any band to reach a young audience: see the entry on **David Bowie** for the 'Starman moment'. The Cure would create many 'Starman moments' of their own over the coming years, their sheer out-of-context *otherness* blowing teenagers' minds.

Further notable *TOTP* appearances include '**The Caterpillar**', with the band sat cross-legged on the floor like hippies, '**The Walk**', before which presenter and serial paedophile rapist Jimmy Savile snuck up behind them and leered 'Oh, sons of Dracula! You are looking ten thousand per cent', the Christmas 1993 episode when Robert appeared twice (once doing '**The Lovecats**' with The Cure and once doing '**Dear Prudence**' with **Siouxsie And The Banshees**), and '**Lullaby**', a performance in which a drunk (he later admitted in *Cure News*) Robert had even fewer close-ups than on his debut, due to the terrifying facepaint which the producer feared would frighten viewers.

Smith's double appearance in 1983 was a rarity at the time, incidentally, having been achieved by just four other men: session singer Tony Burrows in 1970 (with Edison Lighthouse, Brotherhood of Man and White Plains) and footballers Glenn Hoddle and Ray Clemence (Tottenham Hotspur and the England World Cup Squad) and Steve Archibald (Tottenham Hotspur and the Scotland World Cup Squad) on the same episode in 1982. This record was blown out of the water in 1984, however, by the appearance of Band Aid on the same episode as several of the individual stars who sang on 'Do They Know It's Christmas?'.

The Cure also appeared on ITV's *The Roxy*, a shonky, short-lived knock-off rival to *Top of the Pops*, in June 1987 performing 'Catch' live. And live performance was much more The Cure's comfort zone, despite their many memorable mimed appearances. Their first non-mimed Cure appearance was an extraordinary one-off: the **ballet** performance of 'Siamese Twins' on BBC's *Riverside* on 7 March 1983, featuring **Steve Severin** on bass, making his only appearance as a Cure member. *Riverside* invited Smith and Severin back for a performance by **The Glove**.

One show on which The Cure were repeat guests was the BBC's Manchester-based *Oxford Road Show* (or *ORS*), filmed in front of a live audience. Their first appearance, on 18 March 1983, was the first-ever live (as opposed to mimed) performance by a full-strength Cure on British television. At the last minute, they perversely opted to play '**One Hundred Years**' and 'The Figurehead' from *Pornography* instead of their recent single '**Let's Go To Bed**'. They closed out the show, with an 'invigorated' (Lol's words) Robert playing the Vox Teardrop guitar which Lol would later break (twice, see *The Top*), and wearing a lipstick beauty spot on his cheek (as was Lol). They were joined by stand-in bassist **Derek Thompson**, making his only appearance with The Cure. Robert credits *ORS* with reviving the band, in a sense. When the **Fiction** office told him that *ORS* were interested, he said yes in order to force himself to put a band together and do something. 'Part of it was to prove to Simon [Gallup had quit in 1982] that the band could carry on without him,' he later admitted. 'There was pride involved.' The Cure would return to *ORS* in February 1984, this time with **Phil Thornalley** on bass, to perform 'Shake Dog Shake' and 'Give Me It' from *The Top*, again avoiding any of their hit singles.

Another show on which they were regulars was *Whistle Test* (which had lost *The Old Grey* from its name by the eighties), whether being interviewed on the Orient Express on the way to Verona or performing '**In Between Days**' and '**Close To Me**' in front of an audience. (Sometimes they didn't mind doing the hits.)

The Cure also appeared more than once on Channel 4's groundbreaking, alternative-slanted music show *The Tube*, filmed in Newcastle and broadcast live on Friday evenings. On 6 April 1984 they showcased *The Top* tracks 'Bananafishbones' and 'Piggy in the Mirror'. And on 24 April 1987, *The Tube*'s last ever show (and **Roger O'Donnell**'s first ever Cure performance), they played '**Catch**', '**Why Can't I Be You?**' and '**Hot Hot Hot!!!**'

Some of Robert Smith's most interesting television appearances, however, came as a member of the Banshees. These include the bizarre, experimental, *Alice in Wonderland*-inspired episode of Channel 4's *Play At Home* and a performance of French Christmas carol 'Il est né, le divin Enfant' for *Les Enfants du Rock* (another show presented by Antoine de Caunes).

The Cure's connection with France often created memorable television performances, such as the *Pornography*-era live set they played for *L'Echo des Bananes* on 11 April 1982, and a 1987 performance on *Les Enfants du Rock* where they made the **drug**-assisted decision to wear dresses (which had been sewn by **Boris Williams**' girlfriend Cynde at Miraval during the *Kiss Me, Kiss Me, Kiss Me* sessions). This appearance was screened in **Brazil**, and boosted their already-significant popularity there.

The funniest foreign TV performance of all, however, came when they travelled to the Netherlands to mime 'Close To Me' on *Countdown*. As Robert explained to *The Face*, 'Well, we did this Dutch TV show and Bananarama pretended to mime playing the instruments because the boys were too pissed and they just danced. I mimed the song because otherwise we would have to do the song over and over again. I fell over when we finished . . . Bananarama are the first people I've met who've managed to keep up with us drinking.' Footage survives, showing Siobhan Fahey dancing

an improvised pseudo-tango with Lol Tolhurst, Keren Woodward plucking randomly at Simon Gallup's bass strings, Sarah Dallin lurking pointlessly behind the amps, Robert Smith pretending to play the trumpet with dubious credibility, and Boris Williams looking more like a member of Bananarama than anyone. It's truly life-affirming.

Of course, a massive percentage of The Cure's presence on television, especially in America, consisted of those impactful, unforgettable videos by **Tim Pope**. But even in the UK, where MTV didn't yet exist, those videos were important. When you caught sight of one – on *Top of the Pops*, on the *Chart Show*, on *Whistle Test*, on *Earsay*, on TV-am – it only needed to be seen once. And Robert comprehended their importance, happy to discuss them at length on French television or on ITV's *Night Network*, thus guaranteeing another few showings.

On 17 January 1991 The Cure played a semi-secret show at London's Town & Country Club 2 under the name Five Imaginary Boys, clips of which were shown on BBC2's *Snub TV*. The Five Imaginary Boys gig, along with their appearance at the Great British Music Weekend and at the BRIT **Awards**, also formed part of the documentary *The Cure Play Out*. As the nineties wore on, and The Cure's elder statesmen status became solidified, Cure **documentaries** (which have their own *Curepedia* entry) became an increasing feature of their television coverage.

If documentaries imply seriousness, then it's worth noting that a flavour of *fun* crept into The Cure's television appearances in the nineties. No longer the scary **goth** weirdos whose motives were mistrusted, they were embraced as national treasures. For example, in October 1990, in a then-rare example of Robert appearing as a personality rather than promoting The Cure, he reviewed the latest singles on the classic show *Juke Box Jury* (revived under former Tube presenter Jools Holland) on a panel which included the yet-to-be-megafamous Craig Ferguson. In January 1991 The Cure were the house band on the *Jonathan Ross Show*, where they played B-side 'Harold and Joe' and a **cover** of The Doors' 'Hello, I Love You'. In 1992 TV-am filmed them sailing to America on the *QE2* where Robert broke the ear off a giraffe toy in the play room, and **Perry Bamonte** sweetly showed an interest in the ship captain's explanation of North Atlantic iceberg fields.

They were increasingly invited onto comedy shows. In 1993 they performed '**High**' on *Sean's*

Show, a vehicle for Irish comedian Sean Hughes, who subsequently appeared in the video for 'The 13th'. Robert also made a number of appearances with Rob Newman & David Baddiel, as discussed under **TV, The Cure referenced on** (a category which also includes *Mastermind*, *South Park*, *The Mighty Boosh* and *Springwatch*).

They appeared twice each on *Later . . . With Jools Holland*, *TFI Friday* and the *Jack Docherty Show*, recorded an episode of *VH-1's Hard Rock Live*, and perhaps most importantly, an episode of *MTV Unplugged*. The Cure's relationship with that channel proved highly beneficial. They also filmed an episode of *MTV's Most Wanted* in December 1995 with presenter Ray Cokes (at whose St Tropez wedding they played live in 1999), and MTV shot the live videos for all four singles from *4:13 Dream*. 'The Only One', 'Freakshow', 'Sleep When I'm Dead' and 'The Perfect Boy'.

As well as becoming a familiar sight on British screens, The Cure moved into the American talk-show circuit in 1996 with a guest spot on *Late Night with Conan O'Brien* followed by the *Jay Leno Show* in 1997. And, though their television presence decreased drastically in the new century, in 2008 they scored the treble of Leno, Carson Daly and Jimmy Kimmel.

Perhaps The Cure's most random televisual credit, however, is one where their faces are not seen. In 2006 they recorded 'The Dragon Hunters Song' (actually 'Taking Off' with different lyrics) for the French fantasy anime series *Dragon Hunters* – a show which they appear on, but almost certainly never watch.

If Noel Coward got it right, The Cure are living correctly.

TV (The Cure referenced on)

1) The Cure's first UK Top 40 single which begins with the lines 'Come closer and see, see into the trees' has what title?

2) In the band's early days, which member of the band married Janet, the sister of the frontman Robert Smith?

3) For most of the 1981 Picture Tour to promote the album *Faith*, the band chose not to have a support act and instead showed a twenty-seven-minute animated film, with what two-word title?

4) Under what band name did the group, who were later to become Malice, then Easy Cure and finally The Cure, first play together in public in a one-off performance at their school in **Crawley**?

5) The title of the song 'Bananafishbones' was inspired by the short story 'A Perfect Day for Bananafish', written by which American author?

6) In which American city, the final date of the band's first **US** tour, did Robert Smith injure his thumb resulting in the large bandage he wore on their *Top of the Pops* debut?

7) After **Andy Anderson** was fired as the band's drummer but before **Boris Williams** was recruited to replace him, which former member of The Psychedelic Furs joined The Cure on a temporary basis during their 1984 world tour for *The Top*?

8) What's the title of the track that opens the album *Disintegration*, and whose lyrics begin '"I think it's dark and it looks like rain," you said, "and the wind is blowing like it's The End Of The World," you said . . . '?

9) What was the name of the fisherman whose photograph became the cover image on the 1986 **compilation** album *Standing On A Beach*?

10) When recording their debut album *Three Imaginary Boys*, The Cure shared studio time with which other band, who had the same manager, **Chris Parry**, and were recording an album at the same time?

11) Long before he joined the band in 2012, the guitarist **Reeves Gabrels** had played as a guest on which 1997 Cure single?

12) The 2008 remix EP *Hypnagogic States* was a fundraising release in aid of which charity?

If you got more than seven of those correct (no cheating by looking up the answers in *Curepedia*), you did better than Christopher McBride, an accountant from Northern Ireland who chose The Cure as his specialist subject on the long-running British TV quiz show *Mastermind* in November 2022, coming second in his heat. (Bonus points if you were screaming at the screen 'But Chris Parry never actually managed The Jam – he was only the A&R man who signed them to **Polydor**!')

To be deemed suitable as a specialist subject on the august and austere *Mastermind* is, itself, a sign that you are now a fixture in the mainstream of popular culture. But The Cure needed no such validation – they have been referenced in television programmes even more often than in films, over a period of many decades.

As soon as The Cure came to *mean something*, television writers couldn't resist using them as visual shorthand to *mean* that *thing*. Here's Andrew Mueller in his book *Rock and Hard Places*, about his working trip to follow The Cure on their American tour of 1992:

> When I come back and turn on the television, there's one of those uncountable, indistinguishable, sub-*90210* teen-angst soap operas on. This particular episode revolves around an outwardly normal, obviously beautiful, and tiresomely over-achieving young woman who takes a stack of pills in an effort to kill herself. On her bedroom wall, looming above her as she belts back the downers, is what the show's producers doubtless imagined was a definitive signifier of tormented youth: a poster of The Cure.

Back in the UK, stand-up comedy was being described as 'the new rock and roll', the primary evidence being the success of Rob Newman and David Baddiel, a duo who were at one stage popular enough to headline Wembley Arena (an unthinkably large venue for comedy at the time). On their breakthrough TV show *The Mary Whitehouse Experience* in 1992, The Cure were the subject of a running joke in which Newman, dressed as Smith, would sing jolly children's songs such as 'The Laughing Policeman' (or, on their *History Today* live video, 'Heads, Shoulders, Knees and Toes') in a doom-laden, depressed voice over Cure-esque backing music.

In 1993, the real Robert even made a couple of appearances on the duo's next show, *Newman & Baddiel in Pieces*. In one of them, Robert stands next to television presenter Mariella Frostrup and former footballer Garth Crooks as graveside mourners at Baddiel's imagined funeral. Each adds their own tribute. 'I've never been this miserable,' says Robert (the joke being that Smith is known for being ultra-miserable). 'I always preferred him to the other one . . .' He then leads a celebratory conga line through the cemetery with a paper hat on his head and a party blower in his mouth. In another, Newman's character Ray, afflicted with a permanently sarcastic tone of voice, is given a copy of *Disintegration* by a friend. The skit ends with Ray meeting his hero Robert, who is walking past cheerfully singing 'The Sun Has Got His Hat On', but Ray sounds sarcastic when greeting him. Robert breaks the fourth wall,

says 'Oh no, what a personal disaster' to camera, then punches Newman/Ray to the floor.

There was clearly a mutual affinity between Newman & Baddiel and The Cure: the comedians were Cure fans, and Robert found their parodies funny. That wasn't the case with all programmes which sought to reference The Cure, however. Smith once refused permission for a contestant on *Stars in Their Eyes*, ITV's Saturday evening dress-up karaoke contest, to impersonate him. 'To me,' he explained, '*Stars in Their Eyes* represents a side of British culture I abhor. I don't just pay lip service to the notion that we're doing this to be rich and famous, because we're not. We turned down *The National Lottery*, and *Stars in Their Eyes* represents something similar to me, which is shit.'

The Cure were referenced twice in Series 2 of surreal noughties cult comedy series *The Mighty Boosh*. In one episode, the Moon sang '**The Lovecats**'. In another, reference is made to a super-strong goth-friendly **hair** product called Goth Juice, described as 'the most powerful hairspray known to man. Made from the tears of Robert Smith. It can hold a satsuma in mid-air with one spray.'

The use of Cure tropes in comedy isn't restricted to their home country. In **Australia**, comedian and chat show host Shaun Micallef, who was formerly in a Cure **tribute band**, once presented a whole episode dressed as Robert Smith. In America, Santa Rosa-based stand-up comedian Oliver Graves became one of the unlikeliest stars of the 2018 series of *America's Got Talent* with a persona and image heavily based on Robert Smith. And MTV once ran a parody of home improvement show *This Old House* in which a comedian playing Robert Smith interrupts a workman who is trying to fix up his apartment to tell him, in a terrible region-shifting English accent, that actually he'd *prefer* decaying walls, blacked-out windows, dripping ceilings and broken floor tiles, because 'I like being depressed in the bath'.

Some of the most satisfying Cure references in television are those which are inserted by stealth. During the 2010 series of the BBC nature programme *Springwatch*, presenter Chris Packham – a known fan of new wave and post-punk music – managed to namecheck as many as thirty-four songs into twelve episodes, even cajoling co-presenter Kate Humble into joining in with a couple. Some ('**A Forest**', 'Birdmad Girl', '**The Caterpillar**') were easier to crowbar into a **zoological** show than others ('Fire in Cairo', '**Boys Don't Cry**', 'Plastic Passion'). Packham had form for this kind of fun: the year before he had done The Smiths, and the year after he did Manic Street Preachers.

The big one, of course, is *South Park*. Robert Smith, **Jason Cooper** and **Reeves Gabrels** had already, under the name **COGASM**, collaborated with Trey Parker and Matt Stone by providing them with a specially written song for their 1997 film *Orgazmo*. It was only a matter of time before Robert – already a human cartoon character (see **Butcher Billy**) – made it onto Parker & Stone's gleefully scatological animated series. In fact, it happened in the very first season. Parker, a Cure fan, sent Robert a video tape of the first two episodes of *South Park* ahead of broadcast, which he watched backstage. 'I saw the episode with George Clooney as a gay dog,' Robert later recalled, and 'pissed myself laughing'. He wrote to tell them he thought it was excellent. 'And they wrote back asking if I'd do a part. I assumed they'd want me to be a gay cat or something.' Instead, they wanted him to play himself in the episode 'Mecha-Streisand', saving the town by doing battle Godzilla-style with a giant mechanical Barbra Streisand. 'I stayed up all night,' he told *X-Press* in 2000, 'and went into this radio station and recorded my words down a phone line. I had no idea what it was all about. I had one of them on the other end of the line directing me, saying "Please sound more like Robert Smith. Come on!" About six months later I saw it, and I was completely thrown by what they had done with it. It was great. When I'm walking off and Stan's saying "*Disintegration* is the best album ever", it's one of my greatest moments in life.' The episode, the show's twelfth, gained the highest ratings of any *South Park* episode so far at the time. It also left an impression on Smith's family members. 'It's strange existing in the same world as Cartman. My younger nephews and nieces think that's what I do, what my job is. They look round my back to look where my wings are . . . That's actually what clued most of them, well the middle lot, into who I was. Up until that point they thought I was just some disturbed individual that turned up every now and again . . .'

The simple use of The Cure's music in soundtracks is almost as prevalent on television as it is in film. British royalty drama *The Crown*, for example, used 'Boys Don't Cry', as did shows including *My Mad Fat Diary* and *Deutschland '83*. *My Mad Fat Diary* and (sequel series) *Deutschland '86* couldn't get enough of The Cure, both using '**Close To Me**' (a song which was also used in shows including HBO's *Entourage*).

And '**Lullaby**' was used on the trailer to the TV show The Secret Circle and was featured in *Misfits*, *Fresh Meat* and *Being Human*, as well as Episode 7 of *American Horror Story: Hotel*. (The Cure's music has frequently been used in *AHS*, with 'Faith' and 'Siamese Twins' also getting an airing.)

But 'Lullaby' isn't even the most frequently used Cure song on TV. 'Pictures Of You' has featured on episodes of *Gilmore Girls*, *Cold Case*, *Misfits*, *Vampire Diaries*, *Mr. Robot*, *The Politician*, *The Goldbergs*, *Picture Perfect*, *Doom Patrol* and *One Tree Hill*.

One Tree Hill, incidentally, is a repeat customer for Cure tunes. Season 3 Episode 10 of the teen drama series featured two: 'To Wish Impossible Things' and 'Disintegration'. *One Tree Hill* also had a habit of using Cure songs as episode titles, such as 'To Wish Impossible Things' (S1E18), 'From The Edge Of The Deep Green Sea' (S3E47), 'The Same Deep Water As You' (S4E68) and 'Pictures Of You' (S4E80).

Surprisingly, one show never to feature The Cure's music is *Stranger Things*. The music of many of their peers – **New Order**, The Clash, **Siouxsie And The Banshees**, Kate Bush, The Psychedelic Furs, Dead or Alive, Talking Heads – has appeared on the soundtrack, and The Cure would seem an obvious fit for a spooky, eighties-set drama, but for whatever reason, it hasn't happened. Yet.

u

U is for …

Uddin, Keith

There can't be many men who are as comfortable working with the likes of Atomic Kitten, Westlife and Blazin' Squad as they are with The Cure, but Keith Uddin is just such a man.

Born on 24 February 1979, Uddin, who sometimes operates under the name K.U., is a **producer**, engineer and songwriter whose CV includes work with Nick Cave, Paul McCartney, Madonna, No Doubt, Björk, Oasis and Spice Girls. In 2010 he was nominated for Producer of the Year at the Music Producers' Guild Awards.

His first credit with The Cure came as engineer of the *Acoustic Hits* disc of their *Greatest Hits* in 2001. He has also worked on a variety of issues and reissues in the 2000s and 2010s, including *Disintegration*, *Entreat Plus*, *Mixed Up*, *Bestival*, *Anniversary* (see *40 Live*), *Trilogy* and *Torn Down*, often simply credited with 'tape transfers'.

In 2008, however, he was elevated to the role of co-producer of the *4:13 Dream* album. He therefore also presided over the preceding singles '**The Only One**', '**Freakshow**', '**Sleep When I'm Dead**' and '**The Perfect Boy**', as well as the remix EP *Hypnagogic States*.

Outside of The Cure, the biggest job of Uddin's career is one that never actually happened. In 2009 it was reported in *Keyboard* magazine that Uddin had been hired by Michael Jackson to work on his *This Is It* residency at the O2 Arena in London. Jackson's team were said to have been specifically impressed by his work with The Cure, and Jackson supposedly requested that Uddin should build and operate a recording studio for him within the mansion he was inhabiting in England during the *This Is It* concerts, with a view to Uddin producing Jackson's next record. Michael Jackson died before the concerts, or the next record, could happen. However, on the posthumous documentary DVD of *This Is It*, largely consisting of rehearsal footage, Keith Uddin is credited as Keyboard Technician and Backline Crew Chief.

Unreleased Songs

The Cure are not misers with their music. There is no Prince-like vault of thousands of unreleased songs. Almost everything they record ends up released in one form or another, and almost all **rarities** and obscurities eventually surface somewhere easier to find.

However, the waters are muddied by the existence – or, rather, non-existence – of a **fourteenth album**. And that album – Schrodinger's Record – is actually at least *three* albums which we might broadly break down into three categories: those from the abortive *4:14 Scream* (i.e. songs originally intended for the sister album to *4:13 Dream*, or its planned double disc version *4:26 Dream*), those from the abandoned *Live From The Moon* sessions, and those from the more recently touted *Songs Of A Lost World* (see **Lost World Tour**).

The first of these categories includes songs Robert Smith described in interviews, but which never made the cut, such as 'Lusting Here in Your Mind' ('It sounds suspiciously like heavy rock to me') and 'Christmas Without You' ('That's not a very happy song'). But it also includes two songs that we *have* actually heard, albeit only in live form: 'It Can Never Be The Same' and 'Step Into The Light', both premiered in 2016 and both captured on film in 2018 at the Curætion concert (see **40 Live**) which closed Robert Smith's **Meltdown Festival**. These, therefore, are arguably no longer 'unreleased'.

The second of these categories is the most mysterious: the album with the working title *Live from the Moon*. In 2019 Robert Smith told *NME* that eight songs had been written for this album, and four weeks of recording at Rockfield Studios had already happened. Smith apparently later went cold on the project, and the fate of those eight songs, or even their titles, remains unclear.

The third category, *Songs Of A Lost World*, includes the songs 'Alone', 'Endsong', 'And Nothing Is Forever', 'I Can Never Say Goodbye' and 'A Fragile Thing'. As these were played live, and even uploaded to The Cure's Vevo with lyric videos, they are also arguably no longer 'unreleased'.

Delving further back into the past, some unreleased songs develop a cult and a mythology around themselves. One of them is 'A Boy I Never Knew', written for the self-titled *The Cure* in 2004 but not included on the album. Demo versions leaked, and the song was performed live circa 2007–2008. Lines like 'I'd love to see him sleep, I'd love to know his dreams / To hold his hand in mine and listen to him breathe' caused some fans to speculate that it is a song about Smith's feelings about not being a father. Speaking to the *Guardian*'s Louis Pattison in 2015, he revealed that it was partly inspired by friends who had lost children, but initially by the story of Turkana Boy, a fossil discovered by the paleoanthropologist Richard Leakey.

> He was a million years old, so he was not quite one of us, but close enough. I read a very moving article that pieced together his last day: he fell in mud by a riverbank, died, and was fossilised. The bond between parent and child is something I'll only experience one way, and it seems to transcend pretty much everything. Every animal would rather die themselves than lose their offspring. But it's just genes, isn't it? All of our existence is spent worrying about the next generation, but we don't actually seem to get anywhere. It's me worrying about that, really.

Speaking about the same song to Italian magazine *Rockstar* prior to the album's release in 2004, Robert said 'I wrote many sad songs for this album and **Ross Robinson** is sorry I did not include them. He believes they're the best of them all. One is the saddest I've ever written. It's called 'The Boy I Never Knew'. I played it to everyone who came to the studio, and everyone broke into tears. Too much for me. I didn't feel like releasing it now, but someday I will.' Further songs from *The Cure* sessions are known to exist, including 'Please Come Home' and 'Strum', but it is 'The Boy I Never Knew' which has made the biggest impact.

Another song which had a cult following was the Sylvia Plath-inspired 'Ariel' (see **Poetry**), recorded for a Kid Jensen session on Radio 1 in 1982. It, along with the similarly obsessed-over 'Forever', originally recorded for **John Peel** in 1981, surfaced on *The Top*'s deluxe reissue in 2006.

Sometimes the unreleased songs from album sessions have almost amounted to a whole separate album. For example, no fewer than eight 'new' tracks – 'Fear Of Ghosts', 'Noheart', '2 Late', 'Esten',

'Delirious Night', 'Pirate Ships', 'Out of Mind', 'Babble' – surfaced when *Disintegration* was given its multi-disc reissue in 2010 (and were all performed as the encore in 2019 when that album was performed in Sydney). Some of these, however, had already been included in the 2004 odds-and-ends box set *Join The Dots*.

To confuse matters somewhat, many Cure songs which appear to be 'unreleased' are actually well-known songs under an earlier alias. 'Cats Like Cheese' became 'Give Me It', 'Two Chord Cool' became '**The 13th**', and 'Cold Colours' became '**Primary**' (albeit with different lyrics).

Many songs, however, remain stubbornly unreleased. These include 'Faded Smiles' (a demo from the *Seventeen Seconds* era), 'Slvvy' (sic) and 'Old England' (both from the *Wish* sessions), and 'You're So Happy', 'Heavy World' and 'Everything Forever' (all *Bloodflowers* outtakes). And that's before we even consider **pre-Cure** tracks like Easy Cure's 'I Just Need Myself', 'I Want To Be Old' and the notorious 'See The Children' (also recorded by **Cult Hero**).

Until Robert gets round to compiling *Join The Dots Part 2*, that's probably how they'll stay – officially, at least.

USA

'Everything's so big and so impersonal,' Robert Smith once said of America, 'that you can never really know who's being friendly and who isn't, because everyone's so nice all the time. They're either nice or they'll shoot you.'

A certain distrust of America, and Americans, was endemic among the post-punk generation in Britain. The rise to power of President Ronald Reagan, an ally of the hated Prime Minister Margaret Thatcher, combined with the stationing of cruise missiles at RAF Greenham Common in the 1980s, and the proposed stationing of Pershing missiles at RAF Lakenheath, led to a fear that Britain was being prepared for use as a launchpad for the nuclear annihilation of the Soviet Union, in turn making Britain a nuclear target. The UK was, to quote the single by New Model Army, the '51st State' of America. Or, to quote Orwell's *Nineteen Eighty-Four*, Airstrip One. Added to this was the fact that most of the American culture fed to the British public was of the most glitzy and superficial kind. The oil millionaires soap *Dallas* began airing on the BBC in 1978, and the copycat show *Dynasty* followed in 1981.

Over the years, Robert Smith's own instinctive distrust of America softened to acceptance and, eventually, genuine affection. However, The Cure's first visit to the USA didn't begin well: upon arrival on 10 April 1980 they were called 'a faggot band' by an immigration official for wearing earrings. The first photograph of The Cure on American soil, taken on 11 April by Allan Tannenbaum (the rock photographer who had previously taken the famous shot of John Lennon and Yoko Ono in bed, and the one of Sid Vicious being led away in handcuffs), shows the quartet leaning against a wall on Columbus Avenue, Robert in a pleated checked suit and **Simon Gallup** in a biker jacket bedecked with badges, looking uncomfortable in their new surroundings while a group of police officers eye them with suspicion.

The Cure's first American concert took place at a venue called Emerald City in Cherry Hill, New Jersey on 12 April 1980, supported by Los Angeles punk jokers The Dickies. Emerald City was a venue of reasonable status: the previous show there was by disco legend Sylvester, the following one was by fellow British new wavers 999. Reviewer Frank Chmielewski, however, was baffled by 'The unknown Cure', confused as to why they didn't sound like Talking Heads, and described their music as 'brain-stroking'. The first brain-stroking song The Cure played in America was '**Seventeen Seconds**'. As it ends, on a **bootleg** recording, a dazzled Robert can be heard complaining 'Can we not bother with the spotlight, please?' Later in the decade he would have to get used to America's spotlight.

Their first gig in New York itself was at Hurrah at 36 West 62nd Street on 15 April, the opening date of a sold-out three-night residency. Attendees included Blondie's Debbie Harry and Chris Stein, and New York Dolls' David Johansen. (*Sounds* journalist Phil Sutcliffe, along for the ride, reported that Robert did everything possible to avoid having his photo taken with Debbie.) The band were, much to Robert's bewilderment, heckled with calls of 'Take a piss on Portobello Road!'

The sheer surrealism that most British people feel on their first visit to New York City – like walking onto a film set – was overwhelming. They wanted to soak in every second. 'It was like a holiday,' said Robert in *Ten Imaginary Years*. 'Even at this point, everything we did, we didn't think we'd be doing again so we

used to go to bed at about 5.00 in the morning and get up again at 8.00 just to go out and see New York.'

New York was followed by further shows in Philadelphia, Washington and, on the eve of Robert turning twenty-one, Boston. The Boston show which was filmed by a videographer. As the clock tripped over into Robert's birthday, the band had taken enough **drugs** for it to seem like a great idea to car-surf on the bonnet of the videographer's Volkswagen Beetle the wrong way round a roundabout.

After returning to the UK, Robert told *Record Mirror* that America meant 'being bombarded by people who all ask the same questions and all want to shake your hand . . . You just find yourself getting sucked into the whole rock 'n' roll trip which we're trying so hard to get away from.'

A year later, though, they were back. And this time, narcotically speaking, they misjudged their limit. After the first of two nights at New York's Ritz, Robert and Simon were given Quaaludes (a brand name for the sedative Methaqualone, popular as a recreational drug in the 1970s) in a nightclub. Although they were advised only to have half a pill each, they each took two, and passed out on their feet, walking around in a state of dissociative unconsciousness. (Simon Gallup stated, in *Ten Imaginary Years*, that he believes they 'nearly died' that night.)

The following morning they were due to meet the press. They kept writers waiting for two hours, and several of them went home. As Quaaludes stay in the system for between twenty and sixty hours, it's unsurprising that **Chris Parry** considered The Cure's second Ritz gig the worst he'd ever seen from them.

By 1983, something had changed. '**Let's Go To Bed**' had become a radio hit, especially on the West Coast, and during a six-date American tour in August that year they had their first taste of being treated like pop stars. According to **Lol Tolhurst**, they suddenly had girls screaming at them, having previously attracted a very male audience. In typically perverse Cure style, 'Let's Go To Bed' was the one song they declined to play, concentrating instead on the utterly anti-pop *Pornography* album. 'We could play things like "**One Hundred Years**" to an audience that was quite young and expected pop', Robert later recalled.

Three years later, their pop-star status was becoming impossible to dodge. The *Standing On A Beach* compilation of 1986 had gone gold within a year of release, despite never breaking the Top 40. 'They represented something to Americans,' said Paul '**Desperate Journalist**' Morley in the *Out of the*

Woods documentary, 'that they couldn't get from their homegrown people.' In one particularly horrific incident of hysteria, *Cure News* reported, a fan jumped onstage at a Los Angeles gig and repeatedly stabbed himself, in front of a crowd of eighteen thousand who thought it was part of the act.

Robert's attitude towards the US was beginning to thaw, a little. 'I used to really hate America. But I've grown to like it now. I used to be really scared of America. It was so big, and threatening. I felt that what we were doing as a group meant nothing. It was a lost cause, it was hopeless, the first five or six years of going there . . .'

In the second half of the eighties, a cultural shift took place in America regarding British music. The hugely popular teen movies of John Hughes such as *Pretty in Pink*, *Sixteen Candles*, *The Breakfast Club* and *Ferris Bueller's Day Off* typically featured several alternative or new wave bands from the UK on the soundtrack (though, oddly, never The Cure), and bands including Simple Minds, Wang Chung, The Psychedelic Furs and The (English) Beat were able to use it as a springboard to Stateside success.

The rise of college radio brought with it the coining of a new genre – 'modern rock' – and alternative artists who were already well-established in the UK, such as The Cure, New Order, Depeche Mode, Echo & The Bunnymen and Morrissey, were able to gain some traction, as did bands who weren't even a big deal at home, like Love & Rockets, a band formed by ex-members of goth heroes Bauhaus. (When Billboard's Modern Rock chart launched in March 1988, its first chart-toppers were Smith's old friends Siouxsie And The Banshees with 'Peek-A-Boo'.) On television, MTV's alternative-leaning shows *The Cutting Edge* (which ran from 1983 to 1987) and *120 Minutes* (1986–2000) helped give exposure to all those videos by Tim Pope, placing The Cure at the front of the Brit Pack.

In this increasingly favourable climate, 1987's *Kiss Me, Kiss Me, Kiss Me* broke into the Billboard Top 40 for the first time in The Cure's career, ending the year as America's hundredth biggest-selling album, and was eventually certified platinum. It meant that they were now playing what Tom Popson of the *Chicago Tribune* called 'cow-palace-size venues'. Robert, in hindsight, felt that they milked the cow too much on the Kissing Tour. 'We went to places we shouldn't have gone. Like Arizona, which was boring.' (They had played Mesa Amphitheatre, Arizona in July 1987.)

Robert found himself concerned by the 'cultural atmosphere' in America. At one show he sent crew member Perry Bamonte out into the crowd with a video camera, and didn't like what he saw. 'It's quite horrifying the people that were coming to see us . . .' Instead of enjoying the sight of sold-out arenas, he found himself worrying that they'd lost sight of the point of being in a band. There was little he could do, however, to stop the runaway train of his pop stardom. At the end of 1987, the Readers' Poll in *Star Hits* (America's sister magazine to *Smash Hits*) placed The Cure in the Top 3 in almost every category.

'We'll never go back there,' Robert vowed that autumn. 'We'll never play a concert in America again. I told everyone I met that we'd never go back. Because we've become too popular there. We'd become another Simple Minds if we carried on playing there. So we should stop. I didn't like some of the audience we were attracting because they're too stupid. That's the difficulty of becoming too well-known . . .'

Robert's growing fear of fame was accompanied by a fear of flying. At least, that's what he told Fiction. 'For about three years,' he later admitted, '1989 to 1992, I kept the pretence that I had this phobia. We did two American tours sailing over on the *QE2*, which was very civilised.'

When The Cure stepped off the *QE2* in August 1989 for the American leg of the Prayer Tour, they weren't greeted by homophobic officials but by a frenzied pack of reporters. The *Disintegration* album, released that May, was already well on the way to selling four million copies, another platinum disc, and by the tour's end 'Lovesong' had reached No.2, an extraordinary achievement for a British alternative act. They were now one of the biggest bands in the world, and those 'cow-palaces' were only getting bigger, with crowds of seventy thousand not atypical. The Cure's audience increased not only in size but in intensity. 'In the States,' Robert later told *Humo*, 'our fans suddenly thought it was trendy to throw test tubes with blood on stage like some sort of sacrifice.'

On the plus side, they enjoyed Disneyland.

'I don't really like a lot of America,' Robert told *Cure News* in 1990, 'only due to the people in lifts and foyers, garages and bars, and driving past sweating in cars, etc. etc.' However, his opinion was now becoming nuanced: 'But I do like the Americans who talk without shouting, smile without saying "Have a nice day", and don't stare like we're men from Mars . . . Americans [who are] like us? It's just a question of scale . . . My dislike of the glossy and brash has been stretched out of context. I don't hate Americans – there!' Speaking to BBC2's *Rapido*, he made a similar concession. 'We met a lot of nice Americans on the last tour. Far more nice Americans than I thought there were, in the whole world . . .'

1992's **Wish** sold slightly less but charted higher, partly due to improved Soundscan technology for counting sales. When the *Wish* tour reached the US for twenty-eight dates, Robert couldn't walk unrecognised in the streets. Sometimes the tour bus would depart from the hotel empty, while The Cure were quietly snuck out in unmarked windowless minibuses. The events were becoming ever more extravagant: a show at Nassau Coliseum in 1992 ended with a twenty-minute firework display. And, in an act of pathetic fallacy, a show at the Pasadena Rosebowl in 1993 was followed by a major earthquake, 7.3 on the Richter Scale. On the plus side, they enjoyed Universal Studios.

The Cure's rare lyrics about America reflect this ongoing love–hate dichotomy in Smith's view of the place: on 'Club America' (1996) it's closer to hate, and on 'NY Trip' (2008) it's closer to love. By the mid-nineties, however, he seemed to be making his peace with it. In 1997, for example, The Cure played that mainstream behemoth, *The Jay Leno Show*, a sure sign that he was no longer running scared from celebrity. And, the same year, in the video to 'Gone', he wore a LA Kings hockey shirt – a garment one could never imagine him wearing even four years earlier.

America, meanwhile, never stopped loving The Cure, even if their record sales have never again reached the *Disintegration* heights. When they were inducted into the Rock and Roll Hall of Fame in 2019 (see **Awards**), the red carpet clip which went viral (Carrie Keagan: 'Are you as excited as I am?' Robert Smith: 'Um, by the sounds of it, no . . .') was widely cited as the perfect example of the clash between American exuberance and British reserve. But the wry smile on Robert's face, and the fact The Cure were there at all, speaks of a very real affection for the people of the United States.

'America hasn't changed,' Smith once told *MTV*. 'It's me, and my attitude towards it.'

V

V is for ...

Vella, Andy

Born and raised in Southampton, photographer Andy Vella was given his first proper camera, a Yashica Mat twin-lens reflex, by a tutor called Dick. After experimenting by taking photos of driftwood on Southsea beach and developing the picture, he fell in love with the process of photography. In his Cure photography book *Obscure* (see **Books**) he writes, 'It's beautiful. It's magical, it's alchemy. It's a metamorphosis, the capture of a fleeting moment, an idea becoming an image.'

Andy has been capturing fleeting moments of The Cure's career and turning them into an image for four decades. His relationship with the band began while he was still a student at the Royal College of Art, and he once used the college's facilities for a Cure photo shoot under the pretence that he was working on a project towards his Masters. Having graduated in 1985 with an MA in Graphic Design, he was taken under the wing of **Chris Parry** and put in charge of the art design side of **Fiction Records**. He later worked with Chicago-based acid house label Desire, and names the 1988 compilation *In The Key Of E* as his favourite from his tenure there. (The acclaimed prog rock sleeve designer Roger Dean also named this as a favourite.)

Some of the most famous photos of The Cure were taken by Andy Vella, including the picture of the band wearing lurid fluorescent **make-up** at the '**In Between Days**' video shoot which was used on a poster to promote *The Head On The Door*. The iconic photo of Robert with his back to the camera, from the sleeve of the 1986 version of '**Boys Don't Cry**' (re-used on the *Join The Dots* box set), is also one of his. He was often present at Cure **video** shoots, documenting them during downtime when **Tim Pope** wasn't filming.

He is also one half of the design team **Parched Art** with **Pearl Thompson**, whom he first met when both were students at Worthing Art College, and has designed several Cure record sleeves, either solo or in collaboration with Thompson, sometimes under the humorous handle 'Undy Vella'. Their work features in the permanent collection of MOMA NY.

In the mid-1990s a commission to create six covers for Bloomsbury Publishing launched Andy's career as a leading book designer. Under the name Vella Design, he has since created eye-catching covers for the likes of John Berger, Tobias Wolff, Susan Irvine, Nadine Gordimer, Stieg Larsson and Margaret Atwood, working for many major publishers, including Harvill, MacLehose Press, Penguin, Abacus, Flamingo, John Murray, Quercus and music-based imprint Foruli, for whom he is art director. His work with Foruli includes the bespoke editions of Peter Hook's *The Hacienda: How Not to Run a Club* and Glenn Hughes' *Deep Purple And Beyond*, as well as books by Sex Pistols' Glen Matlock and The Adverts' TV Smith, and special lyric prints with Iggy Pop and Mick Rock. He also created the unique A-Z illustrations for *Curepedia*.

His work with The Cure led to commissions from, and collaborations with, other bands including Spiritualized, Swervedriver, Gene, Pavement, The Warm Jets, The God Machine, Jeff Buckley, Atari Teenage Riot, Arthur Baker, Altocamet, Fairground Attraction, Carter USM and Vincent Gallo.

In his own words, in *Obscure*, he spent the time during The Cure's albumless hiatus 'shooting fashion and playing with my banjo'. These fashion shoots have included supervising and commissioning the work of other photographers including Rankin and Perou. He has also helped to create branding for the likes of **Xfm** (now Radio X) and Planet Rock.

Vella has also worked in academia. He is currently a Senior Lecturer at Arts University Bournemouth, and has toured the world lecturing on creative thinking and the power of 'the happy accident' (which he considers a major part of his creative process).

When The Cure gave a globally-livestreamed performance of *Disintegration* from the Sydney Opera House in 2019, Vella brought the visuals of that album to life with a series of vast projections onto the building's iconic sails. His work with The Cure is ongoing: Andy continues to collaborate with Robert Smith on covers and merchandise. 'Andy's best record cover is his next rather than the past,' says **Simon Gallup**, self-deprecatingly adding '(or maybe that's wank).'

He has acknowledged the influence of painters such as Pablo Picasso, Joan Miro and Saul Steinberg on his work, 'from the colours, from the textures and obviously the composition', and is particularly drawn to 'the beautiful anger' of Georges Grosz. He has also cited designers such as Saul Bass and Storm Thorgerson, photographers such as Man Ray, Georges Hugnet, Brassaï, André Kertész and Germaine Krull, and filmmakers such as Jean Cocteau as key inspirations.

He believes, he says, in finding inspiration in the unlikeliest places. 'Go out and experience the world, and you never know. You might just see the way that two bits of metal have been joined on the quayside somewhere, and the way they're rusting, and you're looking at that thinking, "There's a bit of type play", and this often inspires me in how to use it. I do really think it's all around you.'

Venomettes, The

In Cure terms, The Venomettes are – like **Noko** and **Derek Thompson** – one-gig wonders. As, indeed, is **Steven Severin**, who was part of the same performance. They, or a subdivision of them, were the string section when The Cure performed '**Siamese Twins**' as a **ballet** on the BBC's *Riverside* programme on 17 March 1983.

Virginia 'Gini' Hewes was a graduate of the Royal College of Music who formed a 'punk classical' group called Humoresque with Anne Stephenson. Hewes and Stephenson were subsequently hired by producer **Mike Hedges** for **Siouxsie And The Banshees**' *A Kiss In The Dreamhouse* album. This led to the pair contributing to **The Glove's** *Blue Sunshine*, and subsequently becoming integral members of Marc Almond's post-Soft Cell project Marc and the Mambas, beginning with the album *Torment And Toreros*. It was for Mambas purposes that they rebranded themselves The Venomettes, in keeping with the main band's serpentine name.

By the time of their sole Cure performance, they had already recorded with Mari Wilson, The The, Sex Gang Children and The Undertones, as well as the other half of the recently disintegrated Soft Cell, Dave Ball, who coincidentally comes from Robert Smith's native **Blackpool**, and whom Gini would later marry. (On many releases she is credited as Virginia Ball.)

Gini went on to work with Psychic TV as well as continuing to collaborate with both Dave Ball and Marc Almond. Anne became a familiar sight on British television due to her spectacular shock of backcombed hair, appearing with bands including The Style Council, The Communards and S'Xpress. Her son, Pete Bennett, briefly became more famous than her by winning the British series of *Big Brother* in 2006. The duo

later reunited in an ensemble called Brilliant Strings, recorded with the likes of McAlmont & Butler, Natalie Imbruglia and The Magic Numbers.

But what of the other Venomettes, absent from the *Riverside* ballet? One was cellist Martin McCarrick, who had plenty of brushes with Robert Smith over the years: he, along with Anne and Gini, was on *Blue Sunshine*, and the Banshees' '**Dazzle**', written by Robert. He went on to join the Banshees full time (long after Robert's stint).

The forgotten Venomette is double bass player Bill McGee, who had a couple of near misses. He played on the Banshees' *Thorn* EP in 1984 – the first record after Robert left. And he, along with McCarrick, Hewes and Stephenson, even played on a Smith-penned tune: Robert wrote the song 'Torment' with Severin for the *Torment And Toreros* album (although on the record sleeve, for contractual reasons, it's credited to 'Almond/Severin').

To further entangle the Mambas/Venomettes/Cure connections, on Marc Almond's next release (*Bite Black + Blue*, released under the name Raoul & the Ruined), Anne and Gini's place was taken by Audrey Riley, who later appeared on The Cure's *Wild Mood Swings*, as well as performing with Anne and Gini on Manic Street Preachers' *Everything Must Go*, on which they were reunited with **Mike Hedges**.

If this is starting to feel more like a spider's web than a rock family tree, you can be forgiven. It sometimes seems as though there are only about eight classical strings players performing with alternative musicians in the whole of London, and they've all been working together in various confusing configurations since about 1982. But it's The Venomettes – or, at least, half of them – who were, for one wondrous gig, part of The Cure.

Videos

ACTION.

Robert Smith hates making videos. At least, that's what he told *The Hit* magazine in 1985. His main gripe seemed to be the long hours. 'That's what I hate about videos – having to be on call from first thing in the morning. If I had to go to heaven at nine in the morning I think I'd be quite unhappy. You also have to put so much into them so it looks like you're having a good time, when really you're in a semi-coma wishing you were home in bed . . .'

Six years later, in an interview on Japanese TV, he

doubled down: 'I don't think we really enjoy making videos. They always end up looking good. And I suppose the bits that take place behind the camera, away from the camera are quite fun. I find them quite trying. Because it's all acting. And it becomes a bit of a strain. And I always have to worry how fat I'm looking. It's a very vain occupation. But we always try to make our videos look ridiculous rather than flattering or glamorous.'

Though he may loathe the process, there can be no arguing with the quality of the results. As makers of great pop videos, The Cure are almost unrivalled. (Of their generation, only Madness can come close.)

Much of the credit for that, of course, goes to Tim Pope (as discussed under his *Curepedia* entry), director of all The Cure's official videos between 1982 and 1992 (and another in 1997), making twenty-three videos in total as well as several long-form video projects. 'We didn't think about videos until we met Tim Pope,' Smith once said. 'He fired an enthusiasm that was latent in us for ways we could present the group that would be complementary to what we did musically.' (Before Pope, he said, Fiction called the shots: 'There was no input from us.')

Of the non-Pope videos, four directors have two to their name: David Hillier, Bob Rickerd, Richard Anthony and The Saline Project. Nine have directed just one each: Piers Bedford, Mick Mansfield, Chris Gabrin, Gerard de Thame (unofficial video for 'The Blood'), Aubrey Powell, Sophie Muller, Richard Heslop, Steve Hanft and Floria Sigismondi. A further four, made in the run-up to *4:13 Dream*, were filmed live by MTV.

MTV is the elephant in the room here: The Cure, having observed the power of the music video during the British Invasion of the early eighties (Culture Club, Duran Duran, Spandau Ballet, ABC, et al), realised that there was no more powerful method of being everywhere at once, and keeping your music in the minds of faraway audiences in the US or Japan without having to physically be in those places. Those peak Tim Pope videos were crucial in breaking the band in America.

Circa 2000, Robert said that he'd decided that 99% of videos he was seeing were banal (except those made by Beastie Boys), so he didn't want to contribute to that banality. It didn't stop him making videos, though. In fact, the only proper Cure single to have no video at all, unless you count remixes like 'A Forest (Tree Mix)' and 'Want (Time Mix 2018)' or the original releases of 'Boys Don't Cry', 'Killing An Arab' and 'Jumping Someone Else's Train' (all given after-the-fact videos by Tim Pope in 1986), was 'Strange Attraction' in 1996.

In fact, The Cure have gone above and beyond the call of duty when it comes to making videos, filming several clips for songs that weren't even A-sides, such as 'A Night Like This', 'Other Voices' and '10.15 Saturday Night'.

The best Cure video? Easy. 'Close To Me' (original). The worst? Also easy. 'Charlotte Sometimes'. But arguing the toss over which other videos are glorious or atrocious is all part of the fun of whiling away an afternoon with *Staring At The Sea* or *Greatest Hits* in the DVD player.

For a band who hate making videos, The Cure have selflessly provided the world with a rich treasure chest of videos to watch and enjoy, Robert Smith valiantly putting himself through all those early morning calls and unflattering camera angles for the sake of the common good.

CUT.

Videos (long-form)

Nobody loved them. Nobody misses them.

When vinyl was superseded by CD, many music-lovers remained faithful to the old format, and could point at legitimate reasons for its superiority. There's even been a vinyl revival, fuelled by more than mere nostalgia. When VHS was replaced by DVD, nobody lamented its passing. And, despite the existence of films such as *Be Kind, Rewind* and *Son of Rambow*, there doesn't seem to be much genuine nostalgia for them.

It's not surprising. The plastic boxes were ugly, brick-like things with cellophane covers of poor opacity, and they took up far more real estate on your shelves than the ninety-minute pleasures contained within could possibly justify. The cassettes were always getting chewed up by the machine, and would deteriorate after a few years anyway. The only thing they had going for them was that you could keep your place when you pressed eject, and carry on where you left off next time you put it in. DVDs were more slimline and elegant, less perishable, and allowed the inclusion of a much greater amount of content.

Nevertheless, for the first half of The Cure's career, video tapes were the only game in town if you wanted to own a physical copy of their long-form films, or compilations of their music videos. VHS releases, many of which have their own *Curepedia* entries, are detailed here.

The first, *Live in Japan*, was released in Japan only on VHS and Betamax (the rival format which many considered superior, but which fell by the wayside). Filmed in Tokyo in 1984, it captures the Smith, **Tolhurst**, **Thornalley**, **Anderson** Cure **line-up**. A decision was made not to release it elsewhere, for two reasons. 'I hate it – I was sick and I look it!', Robert explained (it's true, he does, a knotted headband failing to staunch his cold sweats), adding that 'the line-up changed just after it was shot so it's out of date.' A further Japan-only release, *Tea Party*, came out in December 1985.

Then came the big one. Well, the big two. *Staring at the Sea: The Images* was released worldwide in May 1986 on VHS and Betamax as well as Laserdisc and VCD (even though nobody's ever met anyone who owned the equipment on which to play those two non-tape formats). If it isn't *quite* true to say every alternative kid in the world bought it, then every alternative kid knew someone whose house you could go round and watch it. The same applies to *The Cure In Orange*, released in November 1987.

One planned long-form video never happened. A compilation of all the tracks on *Kiss Me, Kiss Me, Kiss Me*, plus a day-in-the-life film of The Cure on tour, was mooted with the working title *When You Never Come Home* (as announced in the May 1988 issue of *Cure News*), but curiously didn't materialise.

Orange and *Staring* were followed by four long-form videos in the nineties: *Picture Show* (VHS/Laserdisc/VCD, July 1991), *Play Out* (VHS/Laserdisc, November 1991), *Show* (VHS/CD-i/Laserdisc, September 1993) and *Galore: The Videos 1987-1997* (VHS/VCD, November 1997).

Then, over the horizon on silver wheels, DVD came to the rescue. The Cure's first DVD release was *Greatest Hits* (VHS/DVD, November 2001), then they grew increasingly ambitious with the format, releasing *Trilogy* (DVD/VHS/Blu-Ray, June 2003), *Festival 2005* (DVD only, November 2006) and, biggest of all, *40 Live: Curætion 25 + Anniversary* (DVD/CD box set, October 2019).

DVD itself has begun to feel a somewhat outdated format since the advent of downloading and streaming, but there will always be fans who prefer to hang on to physical media in case streamers close down or withdraw content.

But what of those old VHS tapes? Even **charity** shops won't take them. Without doubt, the majority of those once-tolerated (if not exactly cherished) relics are currently either gathering dust in attics, or buried in landfill sites, slowly poisoning the British countryside.

Vinyl

Vinyl is the ultimate fabric of pop.

The physical act of placing a needle into a plastic microgroove and listening to the vibrations transmitted through the speakers is an act of holy communion with the music, and can never be superseded by putting a cassette into a deck, putting a CD into a drawer, or pulling up an album on Spotify. And, when The Cure began recording, vinyl was the only game in town.

The canvas of a 7- or 12-inch square record sleeve lent itself to **artwork** far more readily than a 4.724-inch square CD jewel case or, worse, a 300-by-300-pixel jpg. The Cure, especially once **Parched Art** took over, embraced the possibilities of that canvas beautifully.

Some vinyl wasn't meant to last. Flexidiscs, such as The Cure's 'Lament' (as given away with *Flexipop!*), were only meant as promotional tools, and could only be played a handful of times before degrading. But well-made vinyl records in the eighties were remarkably durable, much to the chagrin of a music industry which desperately wanted to move everyone on to its next big format, the compact disc.

In the 1990s, record labels successfully weaned consumers off vinyl and on to CD (which had a bigger mark-up) by deliberately issuing poor-quality vinyl. However, the myth of compact discs' indestructibility soon became clear. The slightest scratch and a CD is unplayable, whereas a scuffed vinyl record will still play, give or take a few crackles and pops. (There's a reason why original vinyl copies of *Pornography* currently go for £22.50, and CDs for £8.50, and it isn't just scarcity.) There's also the problem that with anything recorded before the mid-eighties, every choice made in the studio by the producer, engineer and musicians will have been calibrated to make the record sound good on a cheap home record player, or a cheap transistor radio, so the alleged pin-sharp 'clarity' of CD remasters is revisionism: the record was never meant to be heard that way.

Since approximately 2007, a vinyl revival, to some extent hipster-led and to some extent audiophile-led – with a side helping of nostalgists – has been underway. New albums released on vinyl, now perceived as a luxury format, are invariably more expensive than on CD. It is, however, still a niche interest, with vinyl making up less than 6% of all music sales.

The Cure have embraced this trend, steadily reissuing their back catalogue on heavyweight 180g vinyl, often coloured (once a lower grade of vinyl for listening purposes, but times have changed). *Kiss Me, Kiss Me, Kiss Me*: lipstick red. *Wish*: blue (not, strangely, deep green). *Wild Mood Swings*: yellow. *Faith*: grey (of course). *Pornography*: red. *Seventeen Seconds*: white. *Three Imaginary Boys*: pink (what else?).

There's at least one instance of a vinyl-only Cure release. On 21 April 2018 – Record Store Day – The Cure released *Torn Down*, a further album of Cure remixes intended as a companion to *Mixed Up*, as a stand-alone double vinyl LP picture disc in a limited edition of 7,750 copies. (It was also available as the third disc on the deluxe reissue of *Mixed Up*, but if you wanted it as a discrete entity, it had to be vinyl.)

The Cure understand. To most of the world, vinyl obsession may be baffling. But to the blessed 6% (and growing), that plastic passion will never die.

Violence

'Girl Bites Off Boyfriend's Ear at Punk Show' – *Bournemouth Daily Echo*, March 1979.

You're thinking Sham 69. You're thinking Angelic Upstarts. You're thinking Cockney Rejects. You're wrong. It was The Cure.

Eruptions of violence and bloodshed at gigs in the punk and post-punk era were almost as common as eruptions of violence and bloodshed at football matches. And it wasn't always the most obvious acts who attracted trouble: The Specials, a pacifist and anti-racist band, regularly had their gigs disrupted by skinheads from the National Front (the leading far-right party of the time). The Cure, similarly, don't seem a predictable focus of what people at the time would have termed 'aggro'. Nevertheless, aggro seems to have followed The Cure around. Disproportionately so, even taking into account the fact that boneheaded racists took the song '**Killing An Arab**' as a rallying call.

The Cure themselves were not shy about getting involved. **Lol Tolhurst** remembers pint glasses flying at early gigs, and the band jumping into the crowd to sort it out. Robert Smith had aggressive tendencies which he actively chose to curb – 'I've got a really violent temper, but it's not physical, because I don't think I should vent my frustrations and depressions onto anyone else,' he told Paul '**Desperate Journalist**' Morley in 1979 – but when a crowd got out of hand, he didn't mind unleashing the physical side.

The violence at Cure shows began early, and close to home. The second-ever gig by **pre-Cure**

configuration Malice, at St Wilfrid's Comprehensive School on 20 December 1976, degenerated into a stage invasion, with **Porl Thompson** punching Lol Tolhurst onstage. On New Year's Eve 1977 Easy Cure, as they were now known, played a show at Orpington General Hospital which culminated with Robert fighting disgruntled audience members and the band being attacked in the car park. On 16 October 1977 their benefit concert for teacher **Dr Anthony Weaver** at Felbridge Village Hall was targeted by the local National Front, prompting them to assemble an 'Easy Cure Wrecking Crew' to see off any future assaults.

But the Wrecking Crew couldn't protect them on the road. On one date of the **Generation X** tour in November 1978 The Cure were attacked by skinheads. In February 1979, a Cure show at the Nashville Rooms in London attracted a contingent of skinheads who had taken 'Killing An Arab' too literally. However, their bare-chested, eagle-tattooed leader took a liking to band, somehow pacified by '**Boys Don't Cry**', and became their *de facto* protector at several subsequent gigs.

In the space of one week in 1979, three unsavoury incidents took place. On 4 March The Cure played the first night of a residency of four consecutive Sundays at the Marquee in London, where they were supported by Joy Division (see **New Order**). Nine hundred people were let into an 800-capacity venue, the resulting aggressive atmosphere leading to regular stage invasions and endless gobbing. Robert gave a gruesome description of the results in *Ten Imaginary Years*. 'I held my hand out and it was like it was covered in elastic bands'. On 7 March the Bournemouth ear-ripping incident took place. And on 8 March at Hounslow Borough College a battle broke out between security and skinheads who didn't like the **support act**, a reggae band called Samaritans.

On 6 April that same year there was a battle between skins and police with dogs when The Cure played Watford College. On 29 April, during another benefit for Dr Weaver at **Crawley** College, the NF showed up again, intent on burning the place down, but were easily faced down by a combination of the local Anti-Nazi League and a Cure Wrecking Crew which included Frank '**Cult Hero**' Bell and Brian Adsett who went on to run The Cure's security. However, at another Crawley College show on 7 December, the fascists got the upper hand and trashed the venue.

In general, though, troublemakers were advised not to venture too close to The Cure. If they weren't swinging punches, they were losing lunches. On the second night of **Fiction**'s Future Pastimes tour, at the London School of Economics on 17 November 1979, Robert vomited all over a punk in the front row, his stomach disturbed by a dodgy sausage from a motorway services on the way down from Liverpool.

Aggro continued to stalk The Cure into the eighties. At Newcastle University on 3 May 1980, the band had to chase someone out of the hall who had been throwing stuff at them. On 31 May, on **Simon Gallup**'s birthday (see **Bootlegs**), The Cure played a gig at the Scala in Herford, Germany, a town which was home to the 1st (United Kingdom) Armoured Division at Westfalen Garrison. The audience was full of flag-waving, football-chanting squaddies who spat so much beer at **Matthieu Hartley** that, in a scenario reminiscent of Spinal Tap's Nigel Tufnel smashing his guitar at a US Air Base, he threw his synth at them. In **France**, there was further violence when a riot broke out during The Cure's set at the Rettel **Festival** on 14 June and police tear-gassed the crowd, causing headliners Roxy Music to pull out.

Through 1981 violence continued to be a regular feature of Cure gigs, with Smith and Gallup frequently leaping into the crowd to silence disruptive fans, then getting back on stage to carry on. Some of the worst crowds were those in the Antipodes: 'If a Fosters can hits you,' Robert told Paul Morley, 'then you know that you're in **Australia**.'

Thereafter, The Cure began playing larger venues with better security, and the trouble died down. However, foreign festivals were still fraught with danger, as the rioting in Greece in 1985 (see **Depeche Mode**) and **Argentina** in 1987 demonstrated.

The Cure were also the victims of violence when off duty. On 3 October 1979, during downtime on the **Siouxsie And The Banshees** Join Hands tour, Robert was badly beaten up by businessmen in a Newcastle hotel, an experience which caused him to write many of the songs on *Seventeen Seconds*. On 23 December 1979 at an end-of-tour party in Ghent, Lol Tolhurst was glassed by a local. The glass missed his eye by one centimetre, and the wound required fifteen stitches. (Robert punched out the assailant.)

Cure-on-Cure violence was also an occasional feature, such as the incident in Strasbourg on 27 May 1982 when Robert and Simon had a fight in a bar (see **Fourteen Explicit Moments**), and the final date of that tour in 11 June when the band disintegrated onstage and Lol threw his sticks at **crew** member **Gary Biddles**' head.

When Robert told *The Hit* magazine 'We throw each other out of the hotel windows rather than the furniture', he wasn't entirely joking.

Voice (of Robert Smith)

'I remember,' **Roger O'Donnell** once said, 'during a recording session, Robert explaining that it didn't really matter what genre of music or style we played, because as soon as he sang on it, it became The Cure.' There's no denying that. As **Steve Severin** put it in The Cure documentary *Out of the Woods*, 'He has a very distinctive voice. You know it's him, immediately.' Distinctive, for sure. But anyone can do 'distinctive'.

On the face of it, Robert Smith may seem like just another *anti-singer*, an archetype which proliferated during the new wave and post-punk years. In truth, there's far more to his vocals than that. Where many of his post-punk contemporaries had one shtick, vocally, Smith has far more variety to his voice.

'It's very emotive', Severin correctly states, but that emotion is rarely one-dimensional. 'There are so many emotions in his voice,' said legendary DJ Janice Long. 'It can sound vulnerable, paranoid, manic . . .' The trademark Robert Smith tone that Simon Reynolds, in *Rip It Up and Start Again*, described as 'forlornly withdrawn' is only part of his armoury. He can switch into a kittenish yelp, a leonine roar, a doleful moan, a heartbroken sob or a harrowed howl, expressing fear, disgust, euphoria, desolation, petulance, longing, love and madness in the space of a few short syllables.

We live, of course, in an era when the definition of a 'good' singer – codified first by Whitney Houston and Mariah Carey and solidified by *The X Factor* and other television talent shows – has been reduced to technical ability in the narrowest of senses: the capacity for vocal acrobatics and melodic accuracy. Smith, by those standards, fails. But those standards are worthless. He wouldn't make it past the first round of auditions on one of those shows, but nor would almost anybody worth listening to in the last fifty years.

It's not as if Smith lacks technique, in any case. His wayward relationship with his own melodies, bending the note, and riding roughshod over the rhythms of his own songs, takes skill in itself (not dissimilar to the tricks of a great improvisational jazz singer). He simply doesn't abide by the established tropes and codes of rock or soul singing, nor will he alter the **Englishness** of his accent to meet America halfway.

So, no, Robert Smith is not a 'good' singer. He's better than that.

W

W is for . . .

Walk, The

Soft Cell. Yazoo. Tears For Fears. Blancmange. Eurythmics. Pet Shop Boys. Erasure.

The synth duo was one of the defining musical formats of the 1980s. All these groups, taking their lead from the example of Sparks (and to a lesser extent Suicide) in the late seventies, typically featured a colourful, charismatic singer and a quieter, more enigmatic keyboardist. For a very fleeting time, The Cure – in instrumentation, if not necessarily personality – were one of them.

The genesis of 'The Walk' was the challenge laid down by **Chris Parry** for The Cure to write a pop hit. They'd tried, and failed, with '**Let's Go To Bed**', the first of what Robert termed their three 'fantasy singles' (the third being '**The Lovecats**'), which reached No.44. That single had featured drummer **Steve Goulding**, but this time they entered Jam Studios near Finsbury Park as a bona fide synth duo. With the exception of a strange bit of stray guitar at the end of the video version, 'The Walk' is entirely a synthesiser record.

Its incredibly memorable earworm of a main riff was written by **Lol Tolhurst**, who had begun collecting synthesisers and associated gadgets after getting hold of a Synclavier and getting synth lessions prior to 'Let's Go To Bed'. This time, in order to make sure he was getting the most from the machinery, a producer was enlisted: **Steve Nye**, Penguin Cafe Orchestra co-founder and a keyboardist himself, who had impressed The Cure with his work on *Tin Drum* by fellow **Hansa** escapees Japan. 'It was the first time we had worked with a "proper" producer,' wrote Lol in *Cured* (a little harshly on **Mike Hedges**), 'as opposed to doing production with an engineer that we really liked.'

Three pieces of machinery were used on 'The Walk', all made by Oberheim (whose equipment Nye had used extensively on *Tin Drum*). The synthesiser was an OB-8, which was already a familiar sound as an integral part of **Depeche Mode**'s music. The sequencer, a DSX, had been released in 1981, a year before MIDI existed, and getting different machines

to 'talk' to each other was still a tough task. Martin Rushent had managed it pre-MIDI on The Human League's *Dare*, but sometimes, even in the hands of an expert like Rushent, mistakes would be left in, such as the out-of-time 'miaow' sounds at the start of 'Love Action (I Believe in Love)'. A similar thing happened with 'The Walk': the big dirty bass note at the start was an accident, because Nye and Tolhurst couldn't get the sequencer to fire up in time with the drum machine. And that drum machine was . . .

. . . a DMX. And thereon hangs a tale. The DMX, a cornerstone of eighties synthpop and early hip hop, was an expensive item: $2,890 then, which is $9,174 (£6,504) now. It was most famously used by The Cure's peers and rivals **New Order** on their world-changing 12-inch single 'Blue Monday'. Many people noted close similarities between 'The Walk' and 'Blue Monday', not least New Order themselves. 'Plenty of people have ripped us off,' said bassist Peter Hook, 'but The Cure really take the piss sometimes . . .' Robert Smith later argued that if 'The Walk' was stealing from anyone it was Japan, not New Order, although in 1985 he did choose 'Blue Monday' in No.1 as his favourite single of that magazine's two-year lifespan. Lol Tolhurst, in *Cured*, also says the similarities are coincidental, due to both bands using electronic instruments, synths, sequencers and drum machines at a time when the range available was limited.

This is where the plot thickens. The Cure's own official biography, *Ten Imaginary Years*, states that Robert decided to record a follow-up to 'Let's Go To Bed' in May 1983. However, that book also makes the claim that 'The Walk' was recorded prior to 'Blue Monday' (a claim also made by Tolhurst). 'Just after we'd finished it,' says Smith, 'New Order released "Blue Monday", which had exactly the same overdub set-up, and it was so similar in sound, we actually debated whether or not to release it. But we decided it was different enough although, of course, people accused us of plagiarism!'

The problem here is that 'Blue Monday' actually came out on 7 March 1983. Therefore, one of those two claims in *Ten Imaginary Years* must be false. Either The Cure recorded 'The Walk' *before* May 1983 (before *March* 1983, in fact), or they were perfectly aware of 'Blue Monday' while recording it. Either way, the world is a better place for having both of them in it. 'The Walk' is one of The Cure's very finest singles: a pulsating electro-rock monster, striking the perfect balance between their traditional darkness and the state-of-the-art sounds of eighties pop.

The lyrics are a cryptic **dream**-like narrative not dissimilar to Robert's accounts of his and **Mary**'s nocturnal walks in the famous *Flexipop!* diary. There's a howling woman, a rainy lake, and someone who looks 'like a Japanese baby'. It all gave **Tim Pope** plenty to work with when he made the **video**. The Pope/Cure partnership was hitting its stride. The video featured Robert in a child's paddling pool, Lol in a frock dancing with a baby doll which had a Japanese mask on it and doing tricks with cards and fire, a variety of pedagogical tools (an abacus, a ball-and-stick molecular model, an inflatable globe, some coloured building bricks) and a random tumbling cheese grater, and an older woman – a sign language teacher – mouthing and interpreting the words. Not that the video was seen much: 'The BBC didn't want to show it,' said Lol later, 'because we had make-up on, and they thought we were gay!'

Released on 1 July 1983 with a **Parched Art** sleeve featuring a close-up of a housefly, 'The Walk' came with 'The Dream' on the 7-inch B-side, and 'The Upstairs Room' (written while kipping on **Steve Severin**'s floor) and a re-recorded version of 'Lament' (see *Flexipop!*) added on the 12-inch. In North America and continental Europe, though not the UK, it was also released on a mini-LP entitled *The Walk* featuring 'The Upstairs Room', 'Just One Kiss', 'The Dream', 'The Walk', 'Lament' and 'Let's Go To Bed', thereby combining the entire contents of The Cure's last two singles. (Incidentally, the version of 'The Walk' which appeared on *Mixed Up* was a re-recording as, like '**A Forest**', the original master tapes had been lost.)

'The Walk' was, with all due respect to 'A Forest', The Cure's first proper hit single. It soared to No.12 in the UK charts, their first appearance in the Top 20. 'It's nice that it's got in the charts,' said Robert to *Sounds*, 'for the sole reason that it'll be heard on the radio. I'm not being big-headed but I think it's better than 90% of what you hear on the radio now.' Speaking to *International Musician*, he said 'I didn't expect it to get so high, but I suspected something was up when my mum liked it. She normally hates any Cure stuff I play her.' He added that 'It occurs to me that a lot of idiots must be buying "The Walk" . . .'

Chris Parry heard the good news about the song's chart position while yachting off Jersey, and celebrated by eating and drinking himself 'into a stupor' with a seafood platter. Smith, meanwhile, was called back from touring with **Siouxsie And The Banshees** in Scandinavia (see **1983**) in order to appear on *Top of the Pops*. The band performed 'The Walk' twice, in fact, on *TOTP*, with **Porl Thompson** miming the bass on the first occasion, and **Phil Thornalley** standing in on the second with **Andy Anderson** miming drums, even though none of them are on the record. Robert wanted to perform with a live snake, but this was forbidden by producers for health and safety reasons.

As well as *Top of the Pops* stars, 'The Walk' had made The Cure into persons of interest to *Smash Hits* magazine (prompting a black and white full-page feature by Dave Rimmer), solidifying them as teen pop idols, but it took a while for the band to adjust to this new status. Perversely, when they headlined the Elephant Fayre festival at stately home Port Eliot in Cornwall on 30 July 1983, with 'The Walk' riding high in the charts, they opted not to play their current and biggest hit (despite having trialled it in Bath two days earlier), instead playing a set heavily based on *Pornography*, *Faith* and *Seventeen Seconds* – the old **gothic** Cure.

They eventually started playing it on their American tour that year, and it's stayed in their set more or less ever since (one of the most enjoyable versions being the run-through on *MTV Unplugged* with Porl Thompson playing the riff on a kazoo).

The Cure soon got bigger – in personnel and in popularity – but never too big for 'The Walk'.

Weaver, Dr Anthony

Dr Anthony Weaver was, **Michael Dempsey** once said, 'probably the first outrageous homosexual we ever met, and a marvellous character.' As well as being an inspirational teacher of languages at their school, Dr Weaver became the impetus for the (Easy) Cure to take a stand against bigotry.

In 1977 Dr Weaver was dismissed from his job for allegedly committing an act of 'gross indecency' with another man in a public place, 'gross indecency' being a term pertaining to the homophobic Victorian legislation which had led to the convictions of Oscar Wilde and, later, Second World War codebreaker Alan Turing.

The Easy Cure (see **Pre-Cure Bands**) played a benefit concert in **Crawley** in Weaver's defence, Robert's reckoning being that 'We didn't think someone's sexual preferences should have any bearing on whether or not they were considered to be a good teacher.' This seems an uncontroversial stance now, but it was a bold step for teenagers in the late seventies, at a time when homosexuality had only been (partially) legalised eight years earlier and gay jokes were a staple of mainstream entertainment. Furthermore, the local headcases weren't happy. Members of fascist party the National Front attended with the intent of causing trouble, and police had to break it up. 'From then on,' said Robert in *Ten Imaginary Years*, 'whenever we played local concerts, there was usually a lot of trouble, so we started gathering together our own Easy Cure Wrecking Crew.'

Two years later, history repeated itself. Dr Weaver once again lost his job, this time at Crawley College, and once again 'gross indecency' was cited as the reason. The band, now renamed The Cure, played another show in his defence. 'We felt he had been run out of Crawley College unfairly,' **Lol Tolhurst** remembered in *Cured*, 'and because we admired his stance as an anti-establishment figure, we had a gig arranged.' The show was at Northgate Community Centre on 29 April 1979, with support from Amulet, the jazz-rock band of former Obelisk/Malice/Easy Cure guitarist Marc Ceccagno. And, as before, the fascists turned up.

The skinheads circled the building, and tried to set it on fire as The Cure played. 'The whole night was a disaster really, pure **violence** from beginning to end,' Robert later recalled. 'It was a shambles, but it made the papers.' This time, however, The Cure camp were prepared for them. The Anti-Nazi League had turned up for a counter-demonstration, and they and the band's Wrecking Crew, including Frank '**Cult Hero**' Bell and Brian 'Headset' Adsett (later of The Cure's actual **crew**), saw off the NF with some ease. According to an eyewitness, one Stephen C. on cure-concerts.de, The Cure ended with a song which had the defiant final chorus 'Weaver Stays OK'.

There's an unexpected coda to this story. The following year, their beneficiary was able to return the favour. The Cure needed a venue for their Christmas Party on 18 December 1980, featuring performances by **Associates**, Scars, Tarzan 5, **Siouxsie And The Banshees** and themselves. They opted for Notre Dame Hall, off Leicester Square.

'And who do you think was in charge of the hall?' asked Robert in *Ten Imaginary Years*. 'Dr Weaver!'

Websites

For almost as long as there has been an internet, The Cure have been on it. Just as they were pioneers in other ways, they were early adopters of the worldwide web.

It all began with The Cure Information Service – an online companion to, or successor to, *Cure News* – which the more technically minded members of the band, **Perry Bamonte** and **Roger O'Donnell**, helped to set up in 1995. (*Cure News* itself is archived at www.curenews.net.) A year later, in 1996, The Cure's official website was launched. It was relaunched on Robert's birthday, 21 April 1997, at www.the-cure.com (a domain name which has since lapsed), and was at one stage formatted like a house, based on St Catherine's in Bath (Jane Seymour's house) where they had recorded *Wild Mood Swings*. (Robert wanted it to be based on Mandelbrot Sets, but this proved impractical.) The Cure's official site, now at www.thecure.com, is the ultimate source of information from the horse's mouth. It's particularly good, for instance, for getting the definitive version of any indistinct or disputed lyrics.

The Cure have used their website in a number of imaginative ways, often involving online exclusives. For example, the *Five Swing Live* EP in 1997 was only available via the website's shop, alongside Cure mouse mats (which really dates it). And they once broadcast something called Curevision from Parkgate Studios on two consecutive Saturdays, featuring Robert writing a song live over the internet and **Jason Cooper** writing messages to the world on his stomach in felt tip. The Cure's official online presence now includes accounts with the handle @thecure on Twitter, Facebook, Instagram and YouTube. Robert Smith's personal Twitter account (@RobertSmith), on which he posts, typically in capital letters, about **politics** and, increasingly, the iniquities of the concert-ticketing trade (see **Ticketmaster**), is superb. And if The Cure's official account sends anything out in capitals, you know who typed it.

Roger O'Donnell is perhaps the most active current member of The Cure. He's @RogerODonnellX on Twitter, @rogerodonnellmusic on Facebook, @rogerxdonnell on Instagram, and @rogerodonnell on Vimeo and SoundCloud. His website www. rogerodonnell.com is minimal, but has in the past hosted fascinating blogs on, for example, the making of *Disintegration*.

Reeves Gabrels is @reevesgabrels on Twitter and Instagram, and @reevesguitar on Facebook, and has a Bandcamp account reevesgabrels.bandcamp.com. Jason Cooper is on Twitter as @jasontoopcooper. **Simon Gallup** was on Twitter (where he announced his temporary resignation in 2021), but has since deleted his account. Perry Bamonte doesn't really do the whole internet thing these days.

Many ex-members of The Cure also have a presence (no pun intended). **Lol Tolhurst**'s website www.loltolhurst.com is well-designed, with information about his books and the *Curious Creatures* podcast. Lol is @loltolhurst on Twitter, @lol.tolhurst on Instagram and @officialloltolhurst on Facebook. *Curious Creatures* is at www. curiouscreaturespodcast.com, and @curecreatures on Twitter and @curiouscreaturesofficial on Facebook and Instagram. His supergroup Lol Tolhurst x Budgie x Jacknife Lee is at @LolBudgieJCKNF on Twitter and @lolxbudgiexjacknifelee on Instagram.

Phil Thornalley's Instagram account is a pleasant, relaxing read, featuring reminiscences about his work with The Cure and clips of his own music. On Facebook he is @philthornalleymusic.

Michael Dempsey's website www.mdmmedia. com includes a small collection of early Cure posters, as well as material on **Levinhurst** and **Associates**.

Eden Gallup is @edvgallup on Twitter and, as a **crew** member, often posts from the frontline (or, rather, backline) of Cure gigging. His band Violet Vendetta are at www.violetvendetta.co.uk and @ violet_vendetta on Twitter. His other band Serpent Ride are @serpent_ride.

Matthieu Hartley is @matthieuhartley on Instagram. The late **Andy Anderson**'s Twitter account @andyandersonkit is still up. **Derek Thompson** is at www.hoodlumpriest.net, @hoodlum23 on Twitter and @Hoodlum-Priest-aka-Derek-Thompson on Facebook. **Vince Ely**, **Noko**, **Roberto Soave** and **Boris Williams** don't have readily discoverable online presences.

Pearl Thompson used to be at www.113percentstrange.com and www.pearl113. com but those sites have vanished, as has Pearl's Instagram account. Pearl's design company **Parched Art** does not have an official online presence.

However, the other half of Parched Art, **Andy Vella**, whose illustrations accompany this book, is at www. velladesign.com, @andyvelladesign on Twitter and @ vella.andy on Instagram.

Moving on to what we might call the para-Cure or Cure-adjacent, **Tim Pope** is at www.timpope.tv, and is @timpopedirector on Twitter and @tim-pope-director on Facebook. **Fiction Records** is fictionrecords. co.uk and @fictionrecords on social media. **David M. Allen**'s Studio 7 is at studio7music.co.uk, and @ studio7london on Facebook and @studio7music on Instagram. **Mike Hedges** doesn't do social media, and nor does **Chris Parry**.

Siouxsie And The Banshees are at www.siouxsieandthebanshees.co.uk, @ siouxsieandthebanshees on Instagram and Facebook, and @siouxsieandtheb on Twitter. Siouxsie herself is at www.siouxsie.com and @siouxsiehq on all social media. **Steve Severin** is at www.stevenseverin.com, @severin.steven on Facebook and @stevenseverin on Twitter and SoundCloud. Budgie is @budgie646 on Instagram, @tuwhit2whoo on Twitter and @ budgieofficial on Facebook.

There are dozens of unofficial Cure **fan** sites, some of them extremely active and up-to-date, others disused but still out there sending back ghostly signals, like abandoned satellites. (Ones which have vanished entirely include Stiff as Toys, Scott's Concert Page, Club America, Bloodflowers, Close to Cure, and Cult Hero Simon which was 'all about the most drunken bassist in the world'.) The longest-running is Chain of Flowers at www.craigjparker.blogspot.com, run by Craig Parker from New Orleans, an authority on the band. It's been active since 1997 and was once named by Roger O'Donnell as his favourite ('Craig often knows things before we do'). Craig is also on Twitter as @CraigAtCoF.

Cure Concerts at www.cure-concerts.de is an impressively thorough repository of all knowledge about, as the name suggests, Cure Concerts, updated regularly. (A fan called Craig Hogan had previously uploaded a Complete Cure Show List at www. deepgreensea.com, and was mentioned in *Cure News*, but that has since bitten the dust.)

The Cure Etc, at www.thecuretc.wordpress.com, is a site on which Tonino Cagnucci has painstakingly transcribed a large number of Cure interviews from the printed press. A Foolish Arrangement www. afoolisharrangement.com/Cure/cure.asp hasn't been updated since 2009, but nevertheless includes a vast array of Cure press cuttings. Pictures Of You www.

pictquresofyou.us has not been updated since 2010, but is also rich with material. Flowers of Love aka www.thecure.cz is also superb for this, and includes scans of **The Further Adventures Of TeamCure**. And The Cure Muse www.curemuse.wordpress.com is another good source of archive interviews.

Curiosity at www.curiosity.de hasn't been updated since 2005, but contains, among other things, downloadable fonts mimicking several classic Cure logos and **artwork**. The Cure Database on YouTube, @TCDB, has almost two hundred Cure **video** clips. The Cure Fan Page Argentina, on Facebook as @thecurecomunidadargentina, has sixteen thousand followers and is regularly updated.

CureFans www.curefans.com hosts a thriving forum for Cure discussion. An archive of fans' old newsgroup discussions exists at www.alt.music.thecure.narkive.com (once upon a time, newsgroups and MSN or Yahoo communities were the only game in town).

Some Cure websites are wonderfully niche and specific. Cureious at www.cureious.co.uk examines the **literary** influences behind Cure songs. The Cure in Scene at www.charlottesometimes.webs.com/thecureinscene.html collects information on Cure video locations.

The music website www.post-punk.com has plenty of good Cure content, as do Louder Than War www.louderthanwar.com and the Quietus www.thequietus.com.

A few links related to *Curepedia* itself. White Rabbit Books is at www.whiterabbitbooks.co.uk and @whiterabbitbks on Twitter, Instagram and Facebook. Photographer Richard Bellia is at @richardbellia and has a website www.richardbellia.com which includes pictures of The Cure, including the original of the image used on the front of this book. Oh, and I'm @simon_price01 everywhere, and my Brighton alternative eighties night Spellbound, where you'll always hear plenty of Cure, is @spellboundclub. My personal website www.simonprice.dj is currently dormant but I may have rebooted it by the time you read this.

All of The Cure-related websites above have been very useful in researching *Curepedia*. My thanks go out to their creators – without them, this book literally wouldn't exist.

And if there are any I've missed, please don't give me a bad review.

Why Can't I Be You?

'Why Can't I Be You?' is *too much*. A sugar rush of a song, hopped up on Haribo and Sunny Delight, it comes haring out of the traps like a one-year-old husky that's been cooped up in a bedsit for a week and finally allowed a run out in the local park. Its sheer musical maximalism contains more musical whizzbangs in its three minutes fourteen seconds than an entire Cure album from their earlier days.

The lead single from *Kiss Me, Kiss Me, Kiss Me*, and in hindsight an odd choice (when '**Just Like Heaven**' was ready and waiting), it cannot be accused of shirking its responsibility of grabbing your attention. On its first radio appearances, it blasted all rivals out of the way and seized the listener by the lapels, screaming into their face: 'The Cure are back!'

The song, Robert Smith revealed in *Cure News*, was written during a trip to Peru to visit a child he was sponsoring. It arose out of a conversation in a bar with someone who said the phrase 'Why can't I be you?' to Robert, to which Robert replied that they should never think that, and should always try to be themselves. 'It got very convoluted, but I went away thinking that in there somewhere there's a really good idea for a pop song.' Smith took the phrase and ran with it. The lyric is one of desire tripping into overload: when it's no longer enough merely to *have* that person, and you're driven across the boundary into cannibalism ('I'll eat you all up', 'You make me hungry for you') as if, through some arcane act of transubstantiation, you can *become* them.

For the second album in a row, they'd led with a single on which **Boris Williams** bashed out a Motown backbeat, in this case specifically the one from 'You Can't Hurry Love' (Supremes) and 'I'm Ready For Love' (Vandellas), as previously pilfered by The Jam for 'Town Called Malice'. Williams hits the drums so hard you almost picture him using his sticks the wrong way around. It sets the tone for a production into which **David M. Allen** and Robert Smith throw everything, including the kitchen sink. The berserk blasting horns (actually played on a synth) carry the tune, which is just as well, because Smith's vocal is one of his most wayward ever, staying attached to the melody only by a very long bungee cord as he spills out made-up words like 'angelicate' in the manner of Cole Porter, Noel Coward or Gilbert & Sullivan. There were many who found it annoying. But there were none who found it forgettable.

The song was premiered to **French** fans at a show in Fréjus, but omitted from the filmed gig in **Orange**. The main initial exposure it received was, instead, via the literally all-singing, all-dancing **video**. And what a video it was: as Robert described it on MTV, 'the night The Cure discovered sequenced dancing'.

Between rehearsals for their upcoming South American tour, the band and director **Tim Pope** decamped to Dublin where, in a room at the Westbury Hotel during a night of beer and cigarettes, they worked out their dance routine. Their ideas were brought to life by a professional choreographer who had worked with 1970s television dance troupe the Second Generation, whose members included Debbie McGee and who performed on *Sunday Night at the London Palladium*, *Morecambe and Wise* and *The Two Ronnies*, and toured with James Last and Chris de Burgh, thereby bringing to the video a flavour of mainstream variety entertainment which The Cure were able to disrupt and subvert.

The following day, they travelled twelve miles south to Mary Tyler Moore Studios (now known as Ardmore Studios) in Bray, County Wicklow, where films including *The Lion in Winter*, *Excalibur*, *My Left Foot* and *Braveheart* were made. And, when they got there, they dived straight into the dressing-up box.

The video's multitude of costumes were 'an attempt to catalogue the menagerie of imaginary characters I had invented during my stay', Smith later explained. Robert played a schoolgirl, an explorer in a pith helmet, but mostly a polar bear. He spent fourteen hours in a furry suit and reckoned he lost a stone and a half, only for **Simon Gallup** – himself dressed variously as a crow or a Morris dancer – to tell him that he looked more like 'a gay Viking'. **Porl Thompson**, meanwhile, is in traditional Scottish dress, **Boris Williams** is a vampire, there's a disembodied walking mouth, and **Lol Tolhurst** does the really heavy lifting as a red and white striped bumblebee dangling from wires, and a flashing Humpty Dumpty. 'He had a strobe light strapped to him inside the Humpty Dumpty outfit,' Robert told ITV's *Night Network*, 'and it sent him completely berserk. It was good.'

The disconnect between The Cure's natural rock 'n' roll shambolicism and their instructor's professionalism was the root of the comedy. 'There was this fantastic Irish choreographer,' Pope told the *Quietus* in 2019, 'and she was counting them in, going "One, and two, and three, and four." And so for the first ten minutes all of them, and Simon in

particular who'd had a pint of beer and a cigarette, were being quite cocky about it. Cut to them ten minutes later, and in their minds, they were serious dancers. I have never laughed so much.'

The sight of this once-cool goth band having to knuckle down and learn dance steps was the cause of much hilarity for Pope. 'I literally wet myself that night,' he later said. *Melody Maker* were on hand to report on the shoot, and Pope was beside himself with glee. 'This is it! The video I've always wanted to make. The Cure dancing. I can't believe I'm seeing this. They're *finished*!' Smith, too, was only too aware of the rapid and irreversible demystification that the video entailed. 'I always thought I was destined for great things but look at me. I'm in the scruffiest, laziest group in the world dressed up in a fucking animal suit!', he told the *Maker*. 'Any vestiges of reality that surround the group, any accusations of musicianship that might be levelled at us on the release of the album, will be shattered . . .'

The concept, he said, was inspired by The Monkees (of whom all, except Porl, were fans), Pan's People (seventies *Top of the Pops* dance troupe) and familial pop quintet Five Star. 'We wanted to be Five Star in this video. And this is what we thought Five Star looked like . . .' Speaking to ITV's *Night Network*, Smith bullishly claimed 'I think we look tight', but also admitted that 'Boris definitely runs away with that video. He's the only one of us that doesn't look like they're on strings.'

The elephant in the room is what happens in the first two seconds. Almost the first thing you see is Lol Tolhurst in a tuxedo and bow tie, wearing blackface. (One band member called him Prince's ugly brother.) Speaking to the *Quietus* thirty-two years later, Pope addressed the issue. 'I think it was a very inappropriate choice. That is now a given. I guess that was probably a reference to (infamous BBC television variety programme) *The Black and White Minstrel Show*. Quite shocking in the more enlightened times we live in. And how insidiously bad was that idea? It's not a thing I feel great about retrospectively. On Lol's part, I think it probably came from a sort of more thoughtless place. I remember the band members were endlessly coming out in different costumes. I didn't specifically know what the costumes would be . . . he said, rubbing the problem away from himself. And I just remember Lol appearing like that and we filmed it. We shouldn't have done it. That was inappropriate and wrong. It was not good.'

Packaged in a sky-blue **Parched Art** sleeve, its

artwork a partially completed squiggle-drawing of a polar bear's face, 'Why Can't I Be You?' was backed by 'A Japanese Dream' (not one of their best, but the B-sides left over from a double album are never going to be), and also available on a double 7-inch with live versions of 'Six Different Ways' and 'Push', a 12-inch with an eight-minute remix by François Kevorkian, and even a CD Video format, with extended remixes of both sides of the single, plus album track 'Hey You!!!' and the 'Why Can't I Be You?' video, which must have been nice for the seven people in the world who had a machine to play it on.

Released on 10 April 1987, it reached a disappointing No.21 in the UK charts (though it did make No.54 in America, their highest placing to date, and No.5 in Spain).

Maybe because, if you'd heard it once, that was already enough. Or *too much*.

Wild Mood Swings

'In the UK, Britpop did kill us.' So said Robert Smith to *Uncut*'s James Oldham in 2000, reflecting on the relative failure of *Wild Mood Swings*, The Cure's tenth studio album, released in the summer of 1996 when the British media's obsession with Blur and Oasis was at its peak and its interest in The Cure was at an all-time low. 'For the first time,' he continued, '*NME* and *Melody Maker* were right in their view of how the public perceived us.'

Paul Morley, Mr '**Desperate Journalist**' himself, agrees with this analysis. 'A lot of bands who were experimental in nature had a problem,' he said in the *Out of the Woods* documentary. 'There was that nostalgic need to go back to the sixties, to normal shapes of pop songs . . . The Cure were one of the bands who would have suffered. Because The Cure were, by nature, experimental. You did get the feeling that bands like The Cure were slipping off the planet, almost.'

There's no doubt that the attention of Britain's music scene had moved on. Four years after *Wish* – the longest gap between Cure albums at that stage – it wasn't so much that a new Cure album was long-awaited; more that people had forgotten The Cure were still going at all, with so many shiny new bands to stare at. But it's a peculiarly Anglocentric view, of course, which holds that a movement as parochial as Britpop could single-handedly thwart

Wild Mood Swings. The Cure could, surely, still have visited any country in Europe, where Britpop was a distant and barely relevant blip, and be welcomed as towering gods.

On a global scale, the hegemony of grunge is more likely to have been a factor. As *Metro Weekly*'s Chris Gerard wrote in 2013, 'By the time *Wild Mood Swings* finally arrived in 1996 alternative rock had changed and The Cure no longer fit comfortably into a radio format that favored heavy guitar-rock bands influenced by the emergence of Nirvana, Pearl Jam, Alice in Chains and others.'

There's no denying that *Wild Mood Swings* is The Cure's most-maligned and least-loved album, but that's true among fans and critics across the world, and across the last quarter-century. Blaming the temporary and localised popularity of Blur and Oasis (or, for that matter, the more widespread popularity of Nirvana and Pearl Jam) doesn't cut it.

Going into the making of the album, Smith was in a positive and optimistic frame of mind. In *Cure News* he said the year leading up to *Wild Mood Swings* was the most enjoyable of his life (equal with the year when he was thirteen), a statement he repeated in interviews. Recording began at Haremere Hall, a Grade I listed Jacobean mansion near Etchingham in Sussex with gilded ceilings and candle-effect light fittings, which was once the residence of James Temple, one of the judges in the trial and execution of King Charles I. Work then moved for a further nine months to St Catherine's Court, an even older Tudor mansion in Bath, said by some (including Thom Yorke of Radiohead, who recorded *OK Computer* there in 1997) to be haunted. It was owned by former Bond actress Jane Seymour (photos of whom, clad in lingerie, smouldered at them from the bedroom walls). Importantly, it had a wine cellar.

Making albums in country houses which had been repurposed, temporarily or permanently, as residential recording studios had become The Cure's modus operandi for some time: Miraval (*Kiss Me, Kiss Me, Kiss Me*), Hook End (*Disintegration*) and the Manor (*Wish*) being the previous three. The Cure were the first to use St Catherine's, but were followed by others including New Order, Robbie Williams and the aforementioned Radiohead. They evidently found it to their liking, as they returned to record *Bloodflowers*. Speaking to Susan Masters of *Pulse* magazine, Robert said 'This album's something that's grown out of us being here [St Catherine's]. In the past we had to get in, record an album, leave and start the whole process over again, but with this record it's seemed inexorably linked with our lives. When we've been playing we've never known whether we've been recording or just having fun.'

And time, when you're having fun, flies. The recording of *Wild Mood Swings* took longer than any Cure album. It was initially promised for the spring of 1995 (in *Cure News* no.15, September 1994) but wouldn't actually appear until another year after that. One reason was out of The Cure's control: the majority of 1994 – from February to September – was taken up, on and off, with fighting the **lawsuit** filed by **Lol Tolhurst**.

Another reason was a seismic shift in the band's **line-up**, which went partly unresolved until deep into the making of the album. **Porl Thompson** had left in 1993, replaced by **Perry Bamonte**, who moved sideways from keyboards to guitar (with **Roger O'Donnell**, absent from *Wish*, persuaded to rejoin on keys). More disruptively, drummer **Boris Williams** left in 1994, after Robert had already demoed approximately twenty songs with him in a 'very acoustic' style, only for that approach to be scrapped following Williams' departure. 'I had a little keyboard at home that played very bad string sounds,' Robert told Susan Masters of *Pulse*, 'but I was imagining a real string quartet – something that sounded incredibly simple but also really beautiful. Originally the whole thrust of the record was going to be strings, piano, acoustic instruments recorded very quickly in one take over one weekend . . . That was the plan anyway, but when Boris left I had a rethink.'

That rethink involved the auditioning of several drummers during the sessions themselves. Some of their work made it to the final edit: Mark Price, formerly of All About Eve (and Nik Kershaw's band) can be heard on '**Mint Car**', 'Trap' and 'Treasure', Ronald Austin of The God Machine is on 'This Is A Lie', and Louis Pavlou of German **goth** band Pink Turns Blue is on 'Club America'. Others who drifted in and out without leaving their mark included Bob Thompson (who had worked with Heather Nova), Martin Gilks (ex-The Wonder Stuff and Mighty Lemon Drops) and, according to *Cure News*, 'someone called Scott'. The one who stuck, however, was **Jason Cooper**, the former My Life Story drummer who played on the majority of *Wild Mood Swings* and who remains with The Cure to this day.

There was also a major change on the production side. *Wild Mood Swings* was the first time The Cure

hadn't worked with long-time collaborator **David M. Allen** since *Pornography* fourteen years earlier. Instead, they brought in **Steve Lyon**, whose work as an engineer with **Depeche Mode** Robert had admired. There were pros and cons to this decision. 'What we lost,' Robert told Susan Masters, 'was Dave's knowledge of our limitations, but in some ways it helped working with someone we didn't know. In the past when I've been singing no one's known what to expect, not even me. I've done it, listened to it and worked on it. This time I've had to think a lot more about what I'm going to do and I've really tried not to make so many mistakes so that it doesn't come out sounding horrendous and embarrass me.' This measured appraisal, however, slipped a little when the album's release was safely six months in his rear-view mirror. 'He is credited as co-producer', Robert told *Cure News* in October 1996, 'because I am generous'.

In the documentary *Out of the Woods*, Lyon gave his own view of the project. 'The brief was to move the band on from where they'd been. Because they'd been one of the biggest bands of the eighties and early nineties. And my impression was that he [Smith] felt a bit stagnated in what they'd been. And now was a whole new evolution of the band, because two of the major members had left. When I started, there was no drummer. And we gradually put the band together over the first recording sessions.'

If the album has a strange, disjointed feel, then the ever-changing roster of drummers must be part of the reason. According to Lyon, he, Robert, Perry and **Simon Gallup** would typically put a basic track together, playing along to a click track, and then each prospective drummer would play to that (a somewhat back-to-front way of recording). 'Robert would be in this huge house with the rest of the band, and popping his head round the corner seeing how things were going.'

Even without the multiple drummers, *Wild Mood Swings* features by far the largest list of personnel to play on any Cure album. The string section was led by Audrey Riley (a hugely experienced player and arranger who had previously worked with The Smiths, The Style Council, Marc Almond and The Go-Betweens) with her regular colleagues Sue Dench, Chris Tombling and Leo Payne, and the brass section, led by Will Gregory (later better known as one half of Goldfrapp) featured Steve Sidwell, Richard Edwards and John Barclay. An array of big-name mixers were also brought in, including Grammy-winning MOR producer Tom Lord-Alge, dub maestro Adrian Sherwood and shoegaze specialist Alan Moulder. It's barely an exaggeration to say that epic blockbuster movies have cost less money, taken less time, and employed fewer people than *Wild Mood Swings* by The Cure.

The album begins in suitably epic style with 'Want', a classic Cure album-opener whose grandiose three-note guitar motif continues for all of two minutes twenty seconds before Robert's vocals even begin. 'I'm always wanting more,' he cries, 'anything I haven't got . . .' He elaborates on what it is that he wants more of: 'more drink, more dreams, more bed, more drugs, more lust, more lies, more head, more love, more fear, more fun, more pain, more flesh, more stars, more smiles, more fame, more sex . . .' It's a song of excess and extreme sensory indulgence, but ultimately of dissatisfaction, evoking a feeling of jaded emptiness that no amount of **sex**, of **drugs** or **alcohol** can satisfy. Whatever he does, it's **never enough**. 'Want' is one of The Cure's most frequently performed album tracks, ranked thirty-first in their most-played songs, ahead of any of the *Wild Mood Swings* singles.

It's followed by 'Club America', the latest instalment in Smith's ongoing love-hate relationship with the **USA**. Built on what sounds like a leftover dance beat from the *Mixed Up* project with some Stooges wah-wah laid over the top, it begins with the words 'I ride into your town on a big black Trojan horse/I'm looking to have some fun/Some kind of trigger-happy intercourse . . .', sung in a strangely sonorous tone, reminiscent of Iggy Pop. 'It's a bit tongue-in-cheek,' Smith explained to *Blah Blah Blah*, 'which is why I sing in a different voice.' It's a satire of superficial hangers-on and starfuckers they'd encountered in the States: 'And it's not too hard to guess from your stick-on stars/And your canary feather dress/Your hair in such a carefully careless mess/That you're really trying very hard to impress . . .' Echoing **Bowie**'s 'Breaking Glass' from *Low*, the chorus taunts 'You're such a wonderful person, living a fabulous life . . .', Smith's delivery dripping in sarcasm. Interestingly, it was the track chosen (in remixed form) to showcase the album in CD magazine *Volume*, and one of the five later chosen for the *Five Swing Live* EP.

'This Is A Lie', recorded in waltz time with Audrey Riley's strings to the fore, is – in Smith's words – 'an argument about "love" / a poem'. The scare-quotes

around 'love' are telling: this is an album on which Robert seems especially cynical about the concept of monogamy, and this song poses the question: 'Why each of us must choose/I've never understood'. It's comparable both to the cold 'I don't care if you don't' callousness of **'Let's Go To Bed'** and Manic Street Preachers' 1994 single 'Life Becoming a Landslide', with its recurring line 'there is no true love, just a finely tuned jealousy . . .'

The next three songs – the bossa nova of **'The 13th'**, the similarly Latin-flavoured **'Strange Attraction'** and the breezy indie pop of 'Mint Car' – were all singles and each have their own entry, but suffice it to say that they constitute a long interlude of light, sunny tunes that would have done little to satisfy doomhounds of the *Disintegration* or *Pornography* tendency.

That tendency will have been sated somewhat, however, by the dolorous and semi-acoustic 'Jupiter Crash', which – like 'Want' – has been a more frequent presence in Cure setlists than any *Wild Mood Swings* single and which, he told *Cure News*, was his favourite track on the album. (*Jupiter Crash* was even considered as the album's title.) It would appear to be a reference to Comet Shoemaker-Levy 9, which broke apart in July 1992 and collided with Jupiter in July 1994, slap bang in the middle of the *Wild Mood Swings* sessions. Shoemaker-Levy 9 provided the first direct observation of an extraterrestrial collision of Solar System objects, highlighting the planet's role as a 'cosmic vacuum cleaner' and, as such, generated much coverage in the popular media. The two protagonists in the song, however, engaged in a fraught conversation on a beach, find it underwhelming: 'Was that it? Was that the Jupiter show? It kinda wasn't quite what I'd hoped for, you know . . .'

The upbeat and curt (two minutes thirty-eight seconds) 'Round and Round and Round' is, Robert said, about 'the group'. Specifically, it's about the repetitiveness of touring and its attendant media circus, and the insincerity which that repetition instils: 'We squeak with idiot fake surprise/Flap our hands and flutter our eyes . . .' He wonders aloud why The Cure even do this anymore: 'Maybe it's the sex with the drugs and the fools . . .' Ultimately, however, he knows **splitting up** is never likely: 'But however many times that we've said it before, once more is never the end . . .'

The album's fourth and final single, **'Gone!'**, which

has a retro sixties feel (and which has its own entry) is followed by 'Numb', which edges the timeframe only slightly further forward into the early seventies with its psychedelic sitar intro (courtesy of B. K. Chandrashekhar) and Led Zeppelin-esque twelve-string guitars. A bleak depiction of someone escaping the pain of real life through narcotics – becoming comfortably numb, to paraphrase **Pink Floyd** – it was inspired, said Robert, by 'Kurt Cobain and other suicides'.

'Return' (inspirations: 'being on tour / true life / a dream') is one of several *Wild Mood Swings* tracks to use Will Gregory's brass section, and carries a flavour, whether intentionally or not, of The Boo Radleys' Britpop smash 'Wake Up, Boo!' (released in February 1995, while the *Wild Mood Swings* project was ongoing). Again, as on 'Club America' and 'Round and Round and Round', Smith sounds disenchanted with the experience of band life, this time focusing on backstage hospitality: 'You've done everything to please!/Stolichnaya! Banco de Gaia! *Bad Timing* on TV!'

'Trap', made distinctive by some Hammond organ from O'Donnell, again seems to be railing against the self-imposed prison of monogamy. 'Any love you once felt for me has turned into this travesty of selfishness and jealousy . . .' Smith howls, 'so why can't you just let me go?' The final time, however, there's a twist: it's 'why can't *I* just let *you* go?'

The stately 'Treasure', with Audrey Riley's strings at their loveliest, is inspired by the poem 'Remember' by the Victorian writer and Pre-Raphaelite associate Christina Rossetti, often read aloud at funerals (see **Poetry**).

The album ends with the epic 'Bare', on which Smith sounds openly disillusioned with marriage, and fatalistic about its seemingly inevitable conclusion. 'We know we've reached the end/We just don't know how/Well, at least we'll still be friends.' An eight-minute acoustic lament, it's brutally candid and emotionally raw, hence its title. It's Roger's favourite song on the album, and one of Robert's. Indeed, *Bare* – along with *Jupiter Crash* – was briefly considered as a title for the album itself, before *Wild Mood Swings* (a title which had been knocking around since the *Disintegration* sessions) was finally chosen.

It's a suitable finale to an album which seems to be about Smith's feelings of frustration with constantly chafing against the chains of two things: firstly, the societal strictures of conventional relationships, and secondly, the expectations and obligations of being in a band. (When bands start writing about life on the road, it's usually a fatal sign. Here, however, Smith carries it off.)

Artwork was created by The Cure with **Andy Vella** (his **Parched Art** partner **Porl Thompson** being unavailable due to his stint playing guitar with Page and Plant), using a clown doll bought from a mail-order catalogue of Russian and Chinese tin toys. If the clown is intended to represent Smith, then it is perhaps significant that its face is fractured down the middle.

The album was given a relatively soft launch. On 23 January 1996 The Cure premiered six of its songs to the Brazilian press in a hotel in Rio de Janeiro, where they had just played a pair of stadium gigs. On 6 May, the eve of its release, the album was launched with a secret show at L'Opéra Bastille in **Paris**, followed by another at Adrenalin Village in Chelsea on release day itself (broadcast live on MTV).

The reviews it received from **critics** were mixed. *Trouser Press* called it 'a potent and sweeping dissertation on melancholy and tentative dreams denied', and 'consistently compelling'. *Rolling Stone*'s Anthony DeCurtis wrote that 'too much of *Wild Mood Swings* recedes into generic Cure styles – brooding meditations on loss and shiny, happy, self-consciously clichéd pop songs. The horns and strings Smith intermittently introduces to freshen his sound . . . fail to make much of a difference.' For all its horns and strings, and all its Latin textures, *NME* described the album as 'quintessentially goth with pop overtones', to Simon Gallup's despair. 'We were listening to a playback the other day,' he told Susan Masters, 'and were wondering just what we have to do not to be thought of as goth.' It was ranked thirteenth out of thirteen Cure albums by *Ultimate Classic Rock*, and tenth by *Far Out* magazine.

The album crept into the UK Top Ten at No.9, and made No.12 in America, though it did reach the Australian and Belgian Top 5s and peaked at No.2 in Sweden. In their home country, it has still not been certified gold.

The Swing Tour, scheduled to promote the album, was ill-starred. Some dates, such as NYNEX arena in Manchester, were poorly attended, and only a dozen shows were booked in the US. The first three gigs had to be rescheduled due to problems with the lighting. Robert was taken ill after returning from New York with, according to Cure News, an infection to his ears, eyes and throat, meaning that a section of the tour had to be rescheduled to later in the year. He also fell ill in Italy.

It was nearly even worse, as Robert told *Alternative Press*. 'On the cover of *Wild Mood Swings* we put a picture of a tin toy puppet that looks innocent and scary at the same time. When we toured with that album, I wanted the same atmosphere in the decor: a defective roller coaster with big dolls dangling out of it, or something like that, Coney Island off-season. I had that stuff built, and when it was finished the band went to look at it. I saw the fear in their eyes: they were scared I was going to like it. Thankfully I thought it looked ridiculous too, so I let us be static. We'll save the kitsch for *The Cure: The Musical*.'

The band's retrospective assessment of *Wild Mood Swings* was bullish at first, when the dust had barely settled. A couple of years after its release, Robert was still holding the line that it's 'One of our best albums', although Roger found it 'difficult to listen to', considering three or four songs 'truly classic' but others 'shall we say, less than classic?'. Both he and Perry told Cure News in 1998 that they thought some of the B-sides were better. In 1999, Robert even called it 'the best and most complete album I've ever made', which he attributed to 'having discarded a methodology that I was over-familiar with.'

However, by 2000 – the year of *Bloodflowers* – he'd changed his tune. Speaking to *Uncut*, he admitted he was disappointed with *Wild Mood Swings* in hindsight, saying that it felt unfocused and incoherent because 'when I was making it, *I* was unfocused and incoherent.' He also regretted taking so long over it: 'In February I was doing "Bare" – by the time of doing "Gone!" in September I was a different person.'

Robert's hope was 'that people would like the album, that it would resonate and that we would re-establish ourselves as a band.' He was accepting, however, about its failure. 'I understand why they didn't like it, although I do think it was unfairly criticised.'

On Record Store Day in 2021 the album was re-released on double yellow vinyl, a small move towards rehabilitating its reputation. But there's one statistic that *Wild Mood Swings* can never shake off: it was the first album in The Cure's history that didn't do better than the one before it.

These things, of course, are relative. '*Wild Mood Swings* was perceived as a failure,' Robert said to *Uncut*, 'even though it sold two million around the world. Any other band would think "We've made it . . . ".'

Williams, Boris

'The only 'new' member to our line-up', Robert Smith told *The Hit* magazine in 1985, 'is Boris, who suffered three years with the Thompson Twins and is now revelling in the freedom of The Cure.' And so, with an enjoyably sly dig at one of their mid-eighties pop rivals, began Boris Peter Bransby Williams' induction into what many still consider The Cure's definitive **line-up**.

Born in Versailles, France on 24 April 1957, one of seven siblings, Boris was the only member of The Cure known to have attended a boarding school. He spent some time in Belgrade before the family moved to Chichester, West Sussex. Though he grew up listening to The Rolling Stones, his first musical involvement was in a jazz fusion band, playing local pubs with future Cure keyboardist **Roger O'Donnell**. 'He was into Herbie Hancock,' he later recalled, 'and I really liked Weather Report. I went down that road for a while, but I got fed up with it. I decided I didn't want to just work on my technique all the time.'

Prior to joining The Cure, he had played cymbals on the album *Quick Step and Sidekick* by the aforementioned Thompson Twins, and the same year joined Kim Wilde's touring band. He toured with Thompson Twins in 1983 and 1984 in a band which also featured his old friend Roger O'Donnell.

Williams happened to be on holiday in Los Angeles with his then-girlfriend Cynde when he got the call from The Cure. The Psychedelic Furs' **Vince Ely** had stepped in at short notice to replace the sacked **Andy Anderson** for the first eleven dates of an American tour, but could not complete the dates. At the suggestion of his friend, Cure bassist **Phil Thornalley**, who had engineered *Quick Step and Sidekick*, Boris was approached. He quickly learned the songs, and – just three days after Vince Ely's last – played his first Cure show at First Avenue in Minneapolis, the club immortalised in Prince's *Purple Rain*. After returning to Britain he was asked to join permanently because, said Robert in *Ten Imaginary Years*, 'he had a Cure sense of humour'. His only qualm, according to an interview in *Record Collector*, was that by leaving the Thompson Twins he would be taking a considerable pay cut. 'But we kept saying, "Boris, Boris, think of your *art*," and he eventually agreed,' Robert later claimed.

The first that Cure fans heard of his style on record, as opposed to in concert, was the crashing intro to '**In Between Days**', lead single from his first Cure album *The Head On The Door*, in July 1985. Though highly technically skilled, his style was unfussy, preferring to let the drumming serve the song, rather than getting in the way of it. 'I suppose most of the time I'm playing underneath my technique', he once said. But restraint is a part of technique in itself. (If you want an example of Williams' technique, however, just listen to the first thirty seconds of 'Push'.) Boris Williams was, and by the reckoning of many fans remains, The Cure's greatest drummer. In a Curefans poll, he was far and away the most popular of the band's four main drummers.

Snippets of information revealed about Boris by *Cure News* include that he rode a Ducati motorbike (having previously worked as a dispatch rider), drove a Land Rover MGB, read Kafka, drank Pabst Blue Ribbon and didn't drink at all. And he took at least five hours to get ready in the morning.

Choosing to live in Brushford Barton, a country house in Devon, he was able to keep a distance from the rock 'n' roll circus – until the rock 'n' roll circus came to him. For several weeks in 1988, his home played host to the *Disintegration* demo sessions, and photos for The Cure's official 1989 calendar were taken in and around his home.

His services as a session drummer were still in demand during his Cure career, and he did his fair share of moonlighting, playing on the only album by **goth**-pop duo Strawberry Switchblade, including their classic single 'Since Yesterday', and *Candleland*, the solo album by Ian McCulloch of Echo & The Bunnymen. He also played on the 1992 album *Humroot* by **Shelleyan Orphan** whose singer, Caroline Crawley, he was dating. In the late nineties he and Caroline resurfaced in a new group called **Babacar**.

Williams' final studio album with The Cure was *Wish*, and his final concert with them was on 13 June 1993 in Finsbury Park at a benefit concert for London's **Xfm** radio station. His departure was confirmed in 1994, with no apparent animosity on either side, and he was replaced by **Jason Cooper**.

He was reunited with them briefly in 2001 when he helped them re-record classic songs for the *Acoustic Hits* disc of their *Greatest Hits* collection, but did not officially rejoin the band. Ever since, having once

enjoyed the freedom of The Cure, Boris Williams has been enjoying freedom *from* The Cure.

Wish

Put the average music fan on the spot and ask them to name the most successful album by The Cure – most of them would say *Disintegration*. In second place, on such a *Family Fortunes* or *Pointless* survey, would be *Kiss Me, Kiss Me, Kiss Me*, perhaps with *The Head On The Door* coming in third. What relatively few of them would say is *Wish*. But *Wish* is the correct answer. (At least in the UK, and also elsewhere by certain metrics and parameters.)

The Cure entered 1991 on something of a high. They won two BRIT **Awards** including Best British Group in February, the *Mixed Up* remix project the previous year had bought them time to recharge the creative batteries for their next studio album, and the prospect of a **lawsuit** from **Lol Tolhurst**, which would begin in in earnest in 1994, was still only a faint rumbling.

The musical climate, too, was favourable. The rise of genres like Madchester and grunge had meant that the line between the alternative and the mainstream was blurred, and The Cure were no longer awkward outliers fighting against the tide. One subgenre in particular had snagged Robert Smith's attention: the so-called shoegaze groups like Ride, Chapterhouse and Slowdive: young southern English middle-class indie bands who used heavily overloaded guitar effects to create quasi-psychedelic walls of noise – 'sonic cathedrals of sound', as the parodic character Pretentious Music Journalist from *Steve Wright in the Afternoon* put it – **influenced** by My Bloody Valentine, The Jesus and Mary Chain, Cocteau Twins and, without any doubt, The Cure themselves.

And the shoegazers were now re-**influencing** The Cure – a positive feedback loop. 'For *Wish*,' he revealed to *Guitar Player*, 'I would listen to "Mesmerise" by Chapterhouse for its feeling of abandon and "Human" [created by state-of-the-art R&B producers Jam & Lewis] by The Human League. One night I must have played "Mesmerise" 20 times, drinking and turning it louder and louder, putting myself into a trance.' (However, the shoegaze influence on *Wish* is overstated. With The Cure, unlike the 'gazers, you can still distinguish all the individual parts.)

The Cure had also undergone one of their not-infrequent personnel reshuffles. The album that became *Wish* (its original working title was *Swell*) was something of a watershed moment in terms of Cure line-ups. First and most obviously, it was their first studio album without Lol Tolhurst involved in any capacity. **Roger O'Donnell** had also gone for the time being, replaced not with another keyboardist but with guitarist **Perry Bamonte**, working on his first Cure album (although he had played on '**Never Enough**' from *Mixed Up*). And, though nobody knew it at the time, it would be **Boris Williams**' last (although he did later rejoin them on percussion for the acoustic disc of *Greatest Hits*).

The first four new songs from this seemingly refreshed, inspired Cure to be namechecked in *Cure News*, midway through 1991, were '**A Letter To Elise**', 'The Big Hand' (the eventual B-side to 'A Letter To Elise'), 'Wendy Time' and 'Away' (which later became 'Cut'), with reports that they were going to constitute an EP. In fact, in September, the band began work on a whole new album.

The sessions took place at the Manor, a Tudor mansion in Shipton-on-Cherwell in Oxfordshire owned by Virgin supremo Richard Branson. The Manor had been a residential studio since 1971, at first specialising in prog-rock acts: Mike Oldfield's *Tubular Bells* had been recorded there, along with albums by Henry Cow, Tangerine Dream, Faust and Gong. In the post-punk era, XTC and Public Image Ltd both recorded there. And, in more recent years, it had been used by **goth**-rock acts like The Cult, The Mission, All About Eve and New Model Army.

A visiting Miranda Sawyer from *Select* magazine described fixtures and fittings that might have come straight out of a Hammer Horror movie set: a heavy studded wooden door, giant antique mirrors, heavy velvet curtains, Persian rugs, a large fireplace and an enormous dining table. There was also a mad mural featuring the faces of stars like Jim Kerr, Boy George, Feargal Sharkey, Mike Oldfield, Bono, Phil Collins (whose likeness Perry vandalised) and, weirdest of all, Branson's children.

When the band weren't recording, they were playing snooker, drinking Sandeman's port, trying fire-eating, and setting off fireworks in the grounds, including ones that Perry had customised or created himself. The stay lasted for six months in all (they could afford that, by now), and Bamonte later remembered it as 'a wonderful time in a beautiful place'.

The approach to recording was maximalist: producer **David M. Allen**, making his final Cure album, had forty-eight channels at his disposal, and used most of them. There was also time for experimentation. As Allen told BBC 6 Music's Andrew Collins in 2010, he and **Simon Gallup** tested out various six-string basses for *Wish*, and found out that the one which sounded best was for some mysterious reason Robert's, only to discover, when they took it apart, that it was wired up incorrectly.

The songwriting methodology varies according to which version of Robert Smith you want to believe. He told MTV's Ray Cokes that *Wish* was the first time The Cure had written songs as a band from the very first idea (as opposed to the previous method of everyone bringing in their own ideas which could be accepted, modified or rejected). But he also told *Rolling Stone* that 'On the *Wish* album I felt much more isolated, like I was making the album on my own, and the others were just playing. Some days it would be really, really great, and other days it would be really, really horrible.' (There have also been suggestions that he had actually written some of the songs over the previous two years.)

The album opened, as would the subsequent tour, with 'Open' (you see what they did there). A brooding alternative rock monster recorded through a sonic dust haze, it featured a regret-wracked Robert paraphrasing Sylvia Plath (the lines 'And the way the rain comes down hard/That's the way I feel inside' echoed her words from *Letters Home*: 'I am glad the rain is coming down hard. It's the way I feel inside.').

By contrast, the sweetly sentimental '**High**', the album's lead single (but far from its most enduring or famous) was next, and has its own *Curepedia* entry. It was followed by the contemplative and unhurried 'Apart', on which Robert witnesses a 'he' and 'she' who are struggling to communicate: two voices, both Robert's, cry 'How did we get this far apart?'

The album's big showpiece number was the first track on Side 2. 'From The Edge Of The Deep Green Sea', an almost eight-minute epic, begins with the clanking of marine chimes then builds and builds – *swells*, you might say – via a persistent guitar motif, the same sort of insistent piano *ostinato* that John Cale added to The Stooges' 'I Wanna Be Your Dog' and The Velvet Underground's 'I'm Waiting For The Man', and Smith guitar solos that keep clambering higher into the sky. Its lyric describes a relationship which lurches inexplicably from beatific declarations of love to utter despair, the most startling couplet being 'And just as I'm breaking free/She hangs herself in front of me'. It is clearly a song close to Smith's heart: though never a single, 'From the Edge of the Deep Green Sea' is The Cure's fourteenth most-played song live (ahead of big hits including 'Friday I'm In Love' from the same album) and was chosen for a remix on the *Torn Down* album.

'Wendy Time', which starts with a trademark crashing Boris Williams drum fill, came from a musical idea by Simon Gallup, and would be the most 'pop' moment on any Cure album which didn't have 'Friday I'm In Love' on it. When Gallup called *Wish* 'lighter', 'brighter' and 'more immediate' than *Disintegration*, he was talking about songs like 'Wendy Time'. It begins with a girl telling Robert 'You look like you need a friend', and pursuing a line of seduction which leaves him cold. 'It doesn't touch me at all' are the words he repeats with a shudder of disgust. Incidentally, in an interview with Simon Reynolds, he noted that 'Wendy Time' was the first time he had used the word 'man' (rather than boy) to describe himself in a song. 'Five years ago, the line in question would have been "the last boy on earth". I've always been worried about doing music past the age of thirty, about how to retain a certain dignity. The vulnerable, "little boy lost" side of my image is gradually disappearing (see **Cuteness**). I'm in the unusual position of having four very close male friends around me in this group, I don't feel the slightest bit of inhibition around them. I've got more intimate as I've got older.'

The free-and-easy 'Doing The Unstuck', said to be the first song written for *Wish*, is blatantly about **sex**, but also, more broadly, about enjoying life. With sentiments like 'Let's get happy!' and 'Kick out the blues/Kick out the gloom', Robert had the song lyrics pinned to the studio door to foster a spirit of *carpe diem* among the troops.

'Doing The Unstuck' is also perhaps the only Cure song to employ a comedic enjambment or 'Miss Susie' (that trick that comedy songwriters play on the listener where your mind is directed by the first half of a rhyming couplet towards expecting a rude word at the end of it, only for it to veer away at the last second into a more innocent word, which may not rhyme at all, thereby drawing attention to the word that *could* have been there). 'It's a perfect day for doing the unstuck/For dancing like you can't hear the beat/And you don't give a . . . further thought.' Very droll. 'Doing the Unstuck' is Simon Gallup's favourite from *Wish*, and

was one of two songs they chose to play on Channel 5's *Jack Docherty Show* many years later.

Side 3 begins with the Marmite-divisive 'Friday I'm In Love', which may not have been the reason *Wish* initially shot into the charts (as its release came later), but was probably the reason for its long tail, picked up at petrol stations by motorists who had just heard the song on daytime radio.

'Trust' is a naked plea for his lover not to desert him:

There is no one left in the world
That I can hold onto
There is really no one left at all
There is only you

It's one of The Cure's least mysterious, most direct lyrics (and also their closest to a Chicago soft-rock ballad). And it's none the worse for that. The two minutes forty seconds of elegant piano and strings which precede Smith's vocal are utterly lovely.

'A Letter To Elise', the album's third single, is sweet but not hugely impactful on the public consciousness, and has its own *Curepedia* entry.

'Cut' (i.e. 'Away' sped up and renamed), with its wayward wah-wah guitars, does a little to justify all the 'Cure go shoegaze' hype around *Wish*, as Smith laments the ugly death of a once-beautiful relationship:

If only you'd never look like that
When I look at you
I see face like stone

On the sepulchral 'To Wish Impossible Things', later named by **Jason Cooper** (not yet a member of The Cure at this point) as his favourite Cure song, Smith's fingers squeak on the frets as Katie Wilkinson (who had previously played with **Shelleyan Orphan**) adds elegant viola. Smith sings from the point of view of someone whose entire will to live has ebbed away because his romantic relationship has curdled.

It was the sweetness of your skin
It was the hope of all we might have been
That filled me with the hope to wish impossible things

In contemporary discussions of this song, Smith came on like Alexander the Great, weeping for there were no worlds left to conquer. 'I do sometimes wonder "What is there left for me to do?",' he said to Simon Reynolds. 'I think maybe I should do something I don't feel confident about, to try to get back that sense of danger. But then I wonder if I really miss that danger. Do I really want to sacrifice my happiness for the chance of experiencing more, when I've already jeopardised my entire life many times just for the sake of experiencing things?' He also added, 'Any desires I have left unfulfilled are so extreme there's almost no chance of them happening.' (He went on to say he'd really love to go to space, and that he wished peace and plenty for all, like a Miss World contestant.)

Wish opens with 'Open' and ends with 'End'. This much-discussed song, Robert's favourite on the album, is another with a detectable shoegaze influence, with its pedalboard-kicking guitar FX and its backwards-echoing vocals. Its lyric is a response to what Reynolds calls 'Smith's harrowing squirm in the spotlight'. The song addresses his status as an icon, even a messiah in the eyes of some, with which he was never entirely comfortable. 'Please stop loving me,' he repeatedly begs the listener, 'I am none of these things'. The final verse is directed at himself, a merciless appraisal of his own repetitiveness:

I think I've reached that point
Where every word that you write
Of every blood dark sea
And every soul black night
And every dream you dream me in
And every perfect free from sin
And burning eyes
And hearts on fire
Are just the same old song

Self-loathing in Cure songs was nothing new – *The Top*, in particular, was marinated in it – but this was a different flavour, abdicating his own worthiness of worship. It's Smith's way of saying that he's not the messiah – he's a very naughty boy. Now, go away.

For *Wish*, **Parched Art** came up with **artwork** depicting a blue planet in a red sky, surrounded by hand-scrawled eyeballs on stalks. Or perhaps a circle of blue sky being watched from a red-hued subterranean hole by many-eyed monsters. Robert interpreted it as meaning 'unfulfilled desire'. Incidentally, for the first time on a Cure album sleeve they were credited solely as 'Cure', without 'The', explained in *Cure News* as 'an aesthetic decision, because it looked better with the *Wish* logo'.

Wish was launched with a press conference at the Randolph Hotel in Oxford (with playback and a Q&A). At the conference, it emerged that they'd originally written thirty-three songs and had planned to release

two albums in 1991: *Wish*, and an instrumental one called *(Music for) Dreams*, but ran out of time, and that the instrumental tracks would probably be released as a twenty-five-minute EP later in 1992. (In the end, those tracks, which sounded a lot more shoegaze than anything on *Wish* itself, were released as the *Lost Wishes* EP in 1994, available to fan club members with proceeds going to charity.)

The album received middling-to-negative reviews. In *Spin* magazine, Jon Young described it as 'Fitting comfortably into the category of Another Cure Album', adding that 'most tracks feel planned to death, sacrificing spirit for detail' and concluding 'Robert Smith isn't lazy, but he's extremely conservative. The boy needs some fresh air. Or a kick in the behind. Whatever it takes to shake him up.' Robert Sandall, in *Q*, echoed the view of a band treading water. 'Any agnostics who haven't joined the ever-growing legion of obsessives must be asking themselves whether they haven't heard all this little-goth-lost stuff a few too many times before', he said, though he did praise 'the overall quality and variety of the song construction'.

Regardless of the disdain of **critics**, it sold extremely well. In the UK, the album shot straight in at No.1 and in the **US** it debuted at No.2 (held off the top by Def Leppard), The Cure's highest positions in those countries to this day. Less of a slow burner than its predecessor, sales-wise, it was bought immediately by *Disintegration* fans, on trust. It was also No.1 in **Australia**, and reached the Top 5 in Switzerland, New Zealand and Germany. It went platinum in America and Australia and gold in the UK. However, worldwide sales were estimated at three million (1.2 million of which were in the US), down from *Disintegration*'s four million, so be careful when phrasing that pub quiz question.

The *Wish* tour began in Bradford at St George's Hall on 21 March 1992 – Robert's thirty-third birthday, and the day of release. (To celebrate, they went out after the show for a curry, a Bradford speciality.) The show opened, like all the *Wish* shows, with a specially recorded instrumental tape, commonly known just as 'Tape', before launching into 'Open' amid frantically flickering blue lights to begin a set which typically wove about eight of the *Wish* songs among the hits.

The venues tended to be theatres rather than arenas: in the UK at least, The Cure had stayed true to Robert's word when it came to wanting to make things smaller again, even though the album's success merely reaffirmed that they were now global superstars who could fill stadiums. That said, the UK leg did culminate with three nights at Kensington Olympia. And, by the time the tour moved on to America, Australasia and Europe, the stadiums and arenas came thick and fast.

The audience response to The Cure seemed to lag one album behind the band's current reality, as it had done on the previous tour. As Robert told *Melody Maker*'s Andrew Mueller, on the *Disintegration* tour people threw flowers and teddy bears at him, 'whereas this time, when we've come out with a more upbeat record, you know, "Friday I'm In Love" and all that, we've been getting a lot of phials of blood and Baudelaire books.'

The **line-up** was the most musically muscular they'd ever toured with, featuring three guitarists. On the decision to replace O'Donnell with a guitarist, Smith told Simon Reynolds, 'Because we didn't have a keyboard player, no one was really bothered about working out keyboard parts. On *Disintegration* there were all these lush synthesiser arrangements, but this time we tried to do it with mostly guitars. We also had in mind the way it feels live, to play as a guitar band; it's so much more exciting.'

This particular iteration of The Cure is captured on two live albums, *Show* and *Paris*. 'The Show concert in Detroit was the band at the peak of its powers,' said Robert. 'We had been together at that point for eight years, and it was so tight, but I set up the film because I knew that after the Wish tour the band would fall apart.'

And fall apart it did. **Porl Thompson** went first, and then Boris Williams. For a short, little-reported period, even Simon Gallup quit. 'Perry and I were sitting in a room talking about doing demos for a new album,' Robert later recalled, 'and we just both burst out laughing because we realised that we didn't have a band anymore.' Speaking to Susan Masters of *Pulse* magazine, he recalled his feelings of fatalism about it all. 'I felt the *Wish* album had a real note of finality – ending with a track called 'The End'. And then when that line-up fell apart . . . I just thought this is how it's going to end, not with a bang but with a whimper.'

Wish was reissued on Record Store Day 2020 on deep blue vinyl, missing an open goal for a 'deep green' visual pun. A 2022 CD deluxe reissue on three discs made the *Lost Wishes* instrumentals available to a wider audience, and also included several other instrumental demos, most of which were clearly intended to have vocals added ('Miss Van Gogh', for

example, is crying out to become an actual song), corroborating the story that they wrote dozens of songs and simply ran out of time.

Looking back on *Wish* in *Rolling Stone* in 2004, Smith had mixed feelings, and acknowledged some of the criticisms of it.

> After *Bloodflowers*, *Wish* is actually my favourite Cure album, but I felt we weren't really doing anything different with it; I just felt we were making an album. I suppose that's what was wrong with it. It was almost like consolidating where we were. We were gonna go back out and we were gonna get more fans and we were gonna play bigger places, and somehow I lost my enthusiasm. There were elements lyrically and the way I was singing that I was almost going through the motions.

That sounds about right. *Wish* is more than just an answer to a quiz question. And less than their best.

Wrong Number

'Wrong Number' began life as one of those token new songs used to entice completist fans into buying a compilation album, but ended up something of rather greater importance.

For one thing, Robert Smith was proud enough of the song to include it on *two* compilations – *Galore* (its first appearance) and *Greatest Hits* – just four years apart, when other seemingly higher-status songs missed out. For another, its creation involved a first appearance for a major future collaborator, and an overdue reappearance for a past one.

Robert Smith first met **Reeves Gabrels** when the latter was musical director for **David Bowie**'s fiftieth birthday concert in January 1997, at which Smith sang, as well as a member of Bowie's band. They became friends, and began a series of **collaborations** which included a vocal cameo from Robert on Gabrels' album *Ulysses (Della Notte)* and the **COGASM** project.

Robert invited Reeves, along with Mark Plati, who had most recently worked on Bowie's *Earthling*, and Mark Saunders (who had worked as a mixer/remixer on *Wish* and *Mixed Up* and Cure drummer **Jason Cooper** to work on 'Wrong Number' at Parkgate Studios in Battle, East Sussex, with backing vocalists Andrea Groves and Angela Murrell (who had both previously sung with Stereo MC's among others). The only musicians playing instruments on the record were Smith, Cooper and Gabrels, though **Simon Gallup** and **Roger O'Donnell** appeared in the video.

The resulting track had a very late nineties sound palette, in a techno-rock style not dissimilar to Nine Inch Nails or The Cure's own '**Never Enough**' (on which Saunders worked). Along with some playful stream-of-consciousness nonsense about 'lime green, tangerine' and so forth, its lyrics were heavily suggestive of **sex**:

> She pulls me down just as I'm trying to hide
> Grabs me by the hair and drags me outside
> And starts digging in the dirt

It ends with Robert, in his natural **Crawley** accent, speaking into a telephone: 'Hello, are you still there? Sorry, wrong number . . .'

The video was directed by **Tim Pope**, with whom Robert had become reacquainted following 'a tearful reunion' at the Bowie show. Filmed at Castle Studios in South London, it used the full six-minute edit of the song, allowing for all manner of extended chaos. As well as a band performance, elements included, but were not limited to, worms, maggots, and other slithering things (a man eating noodles, plasticine forced through a phone receiver) superimposed explosions of lime green and tangerine (taking the lyrics surprisingly literally), miscellaneous zombies, a dancing Ed Sullivan lookalike, a nightmarish wedding scene starring a man with bouffant blond hair and tangerine skin which seems to anticipate the rise of Donald Trump, human-faced, spermatozoa-like comets impacting the moon, and Robert using a live snake as a microphone.

Released as a single on 7 November 1997, it came with **artwork** by Jen Roddie consisting of a photo of a miniature television from a hotel bathroom (showing a blurry image of what looks like hotel porn), and no new songs as B-sides but no fewer than eleven different remixes of 'Wrong Number' across its various formats, all with web and phone related names like 'P2P mix' and 'ISDN mix' which must have seemed very forward-looking at the time.

It peaked at a disappointing No.62 in the British charts. As Robert said in an Italian interview, 'The single "Wrong Number" didn't get the success it deserved, except in the USA; no radio played it in UK. I even wondered if it wasn't a conspiracy! That's what killed the band as a pop band. So I decided to give up this part of the band.'

As it was the first new Cure music since *Wild Mood Swings*, there was a feeling that 'Wrong Number' might have indicated The Cure's next musical direction. Robert never saw it that way. 'It was just like an aberration. I mean it was good fun, but it was a one-off,' he told *X-Press* magazine in 2000. 'It just arose out of a jam, really. It turned into a nice, heavy pop song. In some ways, we did actually start to go down that road. That's when I thought "This isn't really what we do best". It was a weird hybrid of rock, dance and something else. It just wasn't working, because without Reeves it just didn't sound good. I've kind of accepted over the years that there's a certain type of music that The Cure play really well and that's what I wanted to concentrate on. In the past I think we've tended to pretend to be another band from time to time. It's probably when I'm least convinced of what we do.'

Ultimately the importance of 'Wrong Number' was less to do with the musical and more to do with the personal (and the personnel). In its aftermath, Reeves Gabrels appeared onstage with The Cure for several songs on selected nights on their American tour in late 1997, and they kept in touch. Fifteen years later, he would become a full member. Meanwhile, Tim Pope rekindled his friendship with Robert Smith, if not his working relationship. But the future is unwritten . . .

X

X is for . . .

Gary X

The mysterious Gary X was hired and quickly fired as singer with **pre-Cure band** Easy Cure in March 1977, and replaced by **Peter O'Toole**. X's tenure may have been brief, but alphabetically he is a hero.

Xfm

It's hard to believe now, listening to Radio X with its depressingly conservative playlist of wall-to-wall Foo Fighters, Kings Of Leon and Noel Gallagher, but that bloke-centric London-based lad-rock radio franchise has its roots in a far more forward-looking, groundbreaking station, and The Cure were integral to its story.

It all began in 1989 when Londoner Sammy Jacob, a man with a background in dance pirate station Horizon Radio and his own pirate Solar Radio, had the brainwave that there might be an audience out there for a pirate station playing alternative music. Broadcasting illegally from his bedroom in Hackney, Jacob balanced running that station, Q102, with his job as a sound engineer and promoter for the Mean Fiddler organisation. The station gained a significant amount of media coverage, and listening figures were promising.

After a year, Cure manager **Chris Parry** became involved, and the enterprise moved to **Fiction**'s offices at 97 Charlotte Street. On 1 September 1990 a transmitter was set up on the Charlotte Street roof and The Cure made a pirate radio broadcast, Cure FM, from Fiction HQ, playing tracks from *Mixed Up* for first time. They did so in the company of MTV's Lewis Largent, 91X San Diego's Mike Halloran, several music journalists and a crew from MTV, who captured what Robert later called 'very seedy footage of very seedy blokes taking part in what is known as a scam'.

Two weeks later, on 6 October, they did it again, this time with phone lines open to listeners. Members of The Cure answered the phones, and **Porl Thompson** pretended to be the weather man. Guests this time included **Tim Pope**, whose song 'Drive You

Round the Band' was played, as were Cure favourites like 'Another Girl, Another Planet' by The Only Ones. (**Bootleg** tapes of this broadcast exist.)

Meanwhile, Sammy Jacob had been examining the provisions of the UK government's Broadcasting Act 1990, which allowed for RSLs (Restricted Service Licences), permitting a limited-period broadcast over a limited area. In 1991 he operated one of the very first RSLs at the Reading Festival. A *modus operandi* was taking shape.

In 1992, Sammy Jacob and **Chris Parry** officially launched the successor to Q102 (and Cure FM), named Xfm, and began broadcasting sporadically in London using RSLs while lobbying for a permanent licence. The final date of the UK leg of The Cure's *Wish* tour, at Kilburn National on 13 August 1992, was broadcast on Xfm to raise awareness of the station. On 13 July 1993, The Cure's only gig of the year was the Great Xpectations concert at Finsbury Park in London, organised by Parry and Robert Smith to support the station's bid for a Londonwide licence, with guests Carter USM, The Frank And Walters, Belly, Blur, Guy Chadwick, The Family Cat and Kingmaker displaying the level of desire among the alternative rock community to make Xfm a reality. (These shows were fateful ones for The Cure's membership: Kilburn was Porl Thompson's last in the UK for a decade, while Finsbury Park was **Boris Williams**' last.) An album of the Great Xpectations concert, featuring two Cure songs ('**Just Like Heaven**' and '**Disintegration**'), was released by Pinnacle.

Despite the campaign, Xfm's bid for a permanent licence was initially declined, much to Robert's anger. The station then ran into financial problems, and once again The Cure stepped in to help, donating a **cover version** of **David Bowie**'s 'Young Americans' for the Various Artists album *104.9* in 1995, released to raise funds for Xfm's ongoing efforts.

In 1995, Robert Smith appeared on the station with his boyhood hero David Bowie, the two icons interviewing each other. It's an incident upon which Smith looked back with regret. He went into the interview drunk and spoke across Bowie for two hours. 'I think my opening gambit was, "We can both agree you've never done anything good since 1982",' he told the *Guardian*'s Dorian Lynskey in 2018. (Partial transcripts of the conversation don't actually look that bad.)

In 1996, Xfm was finally awarded a permanent licence. The station went on air on 1 September 1997, but The Cure hijacked the airwaves the day beforehand to play their favourite songs and two versions of '**Wrong Number**'. By this point, Smith's stake in Xfm was more than emotional – he was actually a shareholder.

In its earliest days, The Cure kept up their connection with Xfm by playing a live lunchtime acoustic set on 5 November 1997, and an intimate show from Shepherds Bush Empire from December 1997 (of which there were two), broadcast the following February.

Before long, however, the situation began to shift. In 1998, much to Robert's dismay, the station was sold to the Capital Radio group, dropped its wide-ranging alternative music policy in favour of a narrower, more commercial version, moved its premises to the Capital studios on Leicester Square, and incorporated more football (then very much a male pursuit) and male-oriented output into its programming. The spirit of Q102 suddenly seemed a long time ago. With the exception of the Ricky Gervais and Stephen Merchant show, which became a wildly successful podcast, there was precious little worth listening to.

The franchise flourished, however, opening a Manchester branch in 2005, a Scottish one in 2006 and a Cardiff one in 2007. In 2015, Capital itself was bought out by Global, and Xfm was rebranded Radio X with a controversial marketing brochure which openly described it as 'the first truly male-focused, fully national music and entertainment brand for 25-44-year-olds'.

Peter Robinson, in the *Guardian*, brilliantly compared it to Rowntree's Yorkie and KP's McCoys. 'This is the radio equivalent of a chocolate bar, whose pieces must surely be too chunky for the delicate hands and tiny mouth of a lady, or possibly a ridged, beef-flavoured crisp that would be impossible for a woman to consume given that she'd be holding a dainty parasol in one hand while pushing a pram with the other.'

The station retained some small saving graces, such as the excellent Elis James and John Robins show from 2014 to 2019 (which was only listenable in podcast form, which excised the acres of Landfill Indie that punctuated their comedy).

In its Radio X guise, the station survives, still blatantly aimed at a certain kind of man. These days there are some female presenters – Elspeth Pierce, Sarah Gosling – but they are typically restricted to the graveyard shift rather than primetime. Its musical output is overwhelmingly lad rock from the post-Britpop era (Stereophonics, The Verve, Arctic Monkeys, etc.), and at the time of writing, only two of the eleven tracks on its Daytime Playlist were female or female-fronted. (On the X-Posure playlist, relating to a show hosted by John Kennedy, the last survivor of the station's alternative days, it was a bit healthier: seven and a half out of seventeen.) Dipping into X one random afternoon in 2022, only two of the last forty records played were female-fronted.

Occasionally, there'll be an old track from the pre-lad rock era: The Clash, Joy Division, maybe Buzzcocks.

But there's one band you never hear any more. The Cure.

Y

Y is for …

Yesterday's Gone

'Yesterday's Gone' is a song by **Reeves Gabrels**, featuring the vocals and guitar of Robert Smith, from Gabrels' 2000 album *Ulysses (Della Notte)*. This **collaboration** is a bittersweet lament for lost love and vanishing possibilities, performed with a gorgeous lightness of touch. And it is absolutely not being given its own entry in this book purely to fill up the otherwise-threadbare 'Y' section, randomly selected instead of 'Your God Is Fear', 'You're So Happy (You Could Kill Me)', 'You Stayed,' 'You Really Got Me' or 'Young Americans'.

Youth (of Robert Smith)

At thirteen minutes past midnight on 21 April 1959, Robert James Smith was born in the seaside resort of **Blackpool**, Lancashire to mother Rita Mary Smith (née Emmott) and father James Alexander Smith, known as Alex.

The Smiths were a Catholic family, and Robert was the third of four siblings, coming after Richard (born 12 July 1946) and Margaret (Feb 27 1950) and before Janet (13 August 1960). 'My mum wasn't supposed to have me,' he explained in 1989. 'That's why there's such a big age gap between us. And once they got me, they didn't like the idea of having an only child, so they had my sister. Which is great, because I would have hated not having a younger sister.' Robert revelled in the role of older brother, and even discouraged Janet from speaking so that he could act as her interpreter. 'I would say, "Oh, she wants ice cream," when in fact she was desperate to go to the toilet . . .'

Alex Smith owned a Super-8 camera, and he would film his family, especially baby Robert fooling about on the beach. 'There are a lot of films,' Robert told Placebo's Brian Molko in a 2001 interview, 'where I can be seen running like a crazy man, with some donkeys in the background. I remember seeing my

sister eat worms – and to be honest, I dug them up and she ate them. I was about 3 and she was 2. And my mother punished me. It must be one of the few times I was hit. I also remember the smell of the donkeys.'

The smell of the donkeys would soon fade into the distance. Alex Smith, who had previously served in the RAF, completed his training in Canada, was now in the pharmaceuticals industry, and had taken a job with Upjohn Pharmaceuticals, the Michigan-based company which was then engaged in pioneering the mass production of cortisone. Upjohn had opened a plant in 1957 on Fleming Way, **Crawley**, and Alex was to be its head.

In 1962, when Robert was just three years old, the Smiths moved south to Surrey. Robert's earliest memory, he once told *Smash Hits*, is arriving into London on a steam train. 'Steam trains! That dates me, doesn't it?' They settled in Vicarage Lane, **Horley**, a leafy suburban road with a lawn tennis club at one end. Their next-door neighbour was the grandmother of **Laurence Tolhurst** who lived three streets away on Southlands Avenue.

The only Catholic primary school nearby was St Francis of Assisi in Crawley, five miles to the south. Robert Smith and Laurence Tolhurst first met one September morning in 1964 when their mothers walked them to the bus stop on Hevers Avenue to put them on the bus to St Francis of Assisi, and made them hold each other's hand and told them to look after each other. Soon afterwards the Smiths moved again to a cul-de-sac in Crawley itself, a town he has described as 'like a pimple on the side of Croydon'.

The Smith household was a musical one. Robert's mother played trumpet and piano, and his father sang. The first music Robert Smith remembers hearing, he told *Télérama*, was 'Hit The Road, Jack' by Ray Charles. By the time he was four, he had learned all the words to all the songs by The Beatles, a band his older sister Margaret had been to see. He once told *Cure News* that one of the most important events in his life was the first time he heard 'Help'.

Both Robert and younger sister Janet took piano lessons from an early age. '[Janet] was a piano prodigy', he told Joe Gore of *Guitar Player*, 'so sibling rivalry made me take up **guitar** because she couldn't get her fingers around the neck.' (Robert also admitted, in *Cure News*, that his piano teacher advised him to try another instrument.) When Robert was seven, he was taught a few basic chords by his older brother Richard, a mentor figure in Robert's life who, as well as having an impeccable record collection, also kept chickens and grew organic vegetables. A couple of years later, Robert took formal lessons, using a guitar borrowed from his brother. 'I started on classical guitar, actually. I had lessons from age 9 with a student of John Williams, a really excellent guitarist.' (Another more romantic version of the tale, as spun in *Cure News*, is that Smith took guitar lessons from a blues guitarist he met in the street.) The first song he learned to play was 'Jimmy Crack Corn', an American nineteenth-century blackface minstrel song about the death of a slave owner.

After about eighteen months, Smith stopped taking the lessons. He once said the tutor was 'horrified' by his playing, but on another occasion said 'I learned a lot but got to the point where I was losing the sense of fun. I wish I'd stuck with it.' After that, he was self-taught. 'I have been my own teacher struggling with the lazy pupil ever since.'

In around 1969 he formed his very first band, the Crawley Goat Band, mucking around at home with his siblings and their friends. The following year, in the summer of 1970, his brother took him to the Isle of Wight Festival where he saw **Jimi Hendrix**, a formative experience. Another incident in 1970 would have a long-lasting impact: that of Robert's head against the road. He fell off his bike and suffered severe concussion, and would consequently suffer 'fleeting but intense' hallucinations of a girl called 'Bunny' (see '**Catch**', see **Bunny Lake**) for the next two years.

In September 1970, aged eleven, Robert Smith moved to Notre Dame Middle School, 'a very free-thinking establishment' founded by social reformer Lord Longford. A radically liberal school, it employed experimental teaching methods, and allowed children an unusual degree of freedom. 'If you were crafty enough, you could convince the teachers you were special: I did virtually nothing for 3 years,' he remembered in *Ten Imaginary Years*. 'It was the first of the middle-school experiments,' he elaborated in a *Q* interview. 'We did pottery and tie-dyeing, and the school had a camera so everyone got to make a 5-minute film. I suppose you could say we were indulged, but I think that's how school should be.'

At Notre Dame, Robert befriended future Cure bassist **Michael Dempsey**, and reconnected with Lol Tolhurst over their shared love of Jimi Hendrix (whose album *Are You Experienced?* Robert had borrowed from Richard, whom the younger kids nicknamed 'The Guru'.)

Ever the unconventional thinker, he turned up to Notre Dame one day not wearing his school uniform but, instead, his mother's black velvet dress. 'I really don't know why,' he told Johnny Black of the *Times*. 'I thought I looked good. My teachers were so liberal they tried hard not to notice . . .' Such was the liberalism of the school that the staff said nothing. 'I think the teachers in the staff room laughed about it,' he told *Q*, 'but they had to keep a straight face when they were dealing with me.' Speaking to *Smash Hits*, he speculated that 'the teachers just thought "Oh, it's a phase he's going through, he's got some personality crisis, let's help him through it."' On the way home, he was beaten up.

1972 was the year Robert ramped up his interest in the guitar, and 'started to learn and play frenetically' by borrowing Richard's records and trying to learn them. In April that year, his **pre-Cure band** The Obelisk (which also featured Dempsey and Tolhurst) performed at Notre Dame. It was also the year he bought his first album, **David Bowie**'s *The Rise And Fall Of Ziggy Stardust And The Spiders From Mars*. By the end of the year, it was clear to everyone that Robert's obsession with music wasn't going away, so Richard gave him the guitar he'd been borrowing as a Christmas present. 'I'd commandeered it anyway, so whether he was officially giving it to me at Christmas or not, I was going to have it!'

At the age of thirteen, Smith, Dempsey and Tolhurst all moved to the somewhat stricter St Wilfrid's Comprehensive School. At school, he told *Cure News*, he hated maths but loved English, exploring the world of **literature** which would become a key influence on his songwriting. Robert's bedroom, Lol, recalls, was full of **Camus** and Sartre novels, and a collection of tin cans on a shelf, like a 3D Warhol Pop Art installation. However, Robert, Michael and Lol were completely uninterested in the Catholic school's **religious** education, and would dodge those lessons, instead sneaking into the music room, messing around with kettle drums, vibraphones, Spanish guitars, and so on. 'We learned to play weird versions of various contemporary songs,' he recalled, 'and by throwing some semi-religious words on top, we created a uniquely awful new form of music.'

Because Robert's earliest years were spent in the North, and because a Lancashire accent was what he heard at home, the way Robert spoke made him stand out from the Surrey kids. 'When I came down South,' he told *Q* in 2000, 'I actually had quite a broad Northern accent and the piss was taken out of me mercilessly at school. That probably didn't help me integrate.' In 1987, he told *No.1* '[My accent] always stuck out at school, which I never realised at the time – I thought everyone was saying 'grass' incorrectly – but I toned it down on purpose when I got into my teens. By then I think it would have been a bit pretentious to have affected a Northern accent . . .'

This sense of outsiderdom was something he shared with his two closest friends. As well as rehearsing in various configurations as a band, Robert, Lol and Michael bonded through being misfits. 'We weren't academic and studious,' recalled Michael, 'and we weren't tough kids who were always out for a fight.' The one love they shared was music, turning up to school in army surplus greatcoats with LPs inside (T. Rex being a particular touchstone). They were, wrote Lol Tolhurst in *Cured*, 'the first punks in Crawley'. Smith was, at that age, a less ostentatious dresser than Tolhurst, typically wearing creepers and a long raincoat, or 'a great big woman's fur coat which stretched right down to the ground', or sometimes a leather jacket that the band all shared, donated by a local biker called Arthur. Their social life consisted of youth club discos at Horley Methodist Church where the music would be interrupted by prayers, enlivened by Robert bringing his dad's home brew.

It was at this time that Robert began wearing **make-up**. 'I wore lipstick at school,' he told *Q* in 2000. 'I copied the lipstick from my mum, not **Siouxsie**, although there are similarities between the two. I've worn make-up to varying degrees since I was 13 . . .' He'd also grown his **hair** very long.

It was at St Wilfrid's, during a drama class, that Robert met his future wife **Mary**. Pupils were told to choose a partner for an activity, and Smith plucked up the courage to ask her. Other life-changing events during that period include his first David Bowie concert at Earls Court in 1973, one of the many **early gigs attended** by the young Robert.

At Christmas 1976, Robert's band Malice played a show at St Wilfrid's which was so chaotic that he was expelled from the school's sixth form, along with bandmate Marc Ceccagno, for being 'an undesirable influence' (though he was later readmitted). 'I got

taken back [in 1977],' he told *Smash Hits*, 'but they never acknowledged that I was there.' Speaking to Jonh Wilde of *Melody Maker* in 1989, however, he claimed he was suspended because his 'attitude towards religion was considered wrong'.

As Malice mutated into Easy Cure, Robert studied for his exams. 'I did three A-levels – failed Biology miserably, scraped through French and got a 'B' in English.' He once told *Cure News* that leaving school was the most terrible day of his life.

After St Wilfrid's, Smith joined Tolhurst at Crawley Technical College, 'whose dull, unimaginative campus could have been dreamed up by Joseph Stalin' in the words of Tolhurst, but didn't stay long.

Robert became Easy Cure's lead vocalist, and they gigged through the summer of 1977 while he lived at home with his parents. 'I spent 8 or 9 months on Social Security until they stopped my money,' he recalled, 'so I thought "Now's the time to make a demo and see what people think".'

Those Easy Cure demos weren't straightforward: after an abortive attempt to work with German label **Hansa**, they tried again with £50 given to them by friend **Ric Gallup**. In the meantime, Robert worked on his music, with no parental pressure to pursue a more stable career. He occasionally worked part-time – 'I had five weeks as a gardener on an industrial estate in the height of summer and they were five of the happiest weeks of my life,' he told *Sounds* – but he knew the 9-to-5 life was not for him.

'It came to the point,' he told *NME*, 'where I'd rather have killed myself than get a job. I told Social Security to give the jobs to those that want them, that I'd rather stay at home listening to music, but they'd tell me I had to work and I'd just ask "Why?" Which is the point most people don't get to . . .'

The day after his nineteenth birthday, in April 1978, Easy Cure played their last show under that name. That summer, The Cure – as they were now known – played several of their **earliest gigs** in the local area. In August their singer, still a teenager, sent a demo tape to **Chris Parry**. By the end of the year, it was clear Robert Smith would never need to get a job.

Z

Z is for . . .

Zénith, Le

Le Zénith is a six-thousand-capacity arena in **Paris**, on the north-eastern edge of the city, just inside the Boulevard Périphérique, in the nineteenth arrondissement, on the banks of the Canal de l'Ourcq. The Parc de la Villette, in which it is located, is built on the site of a number of enormous slaughterhouses, to a design from architect Bernard Tschumi in consultation with Jacques Derrida, the Algerian-born French philosopher who is not **Albert Camus**. It opened in 1984. Your author went there once, in 1989, to write a live review of Rick Astley. (The things we do to make a living . . .)

Its relevance to The Cure is that their shows at the venue in October 1992, on the *Wish* tour, provided the recordings for the 1993 live album *Paris*. Since those days, 'Zenith' has become a brand in **France**, with seventeen different venues bearing the name. The Cure's Euro 22 tour took in no fewer than three Zeniths (in Toulouse, Nantes and Strasbourg). An astronomer might argue that, by definition, there can only be one zenith. But the astronomer would need to take it up with the Ministry of Culture.

Zerra One

Formed in Dublin in 1982, Zerra One (or Zerra 1) were one of those typical corporate-alternative bands of the mid-1980s, all cockatoo hair, tastefully scuffed leathers, videos with things on fire, 'epic' guitars, and overproduced songs with over-heroic titles like 'The Banner Of Love (How I Run To You)' or 'Ten Thousand Voices, Message From The Peoples'.

Signed to Mercury, they were a perennial bought-on **support act** of the era (along with the likes of Cactus World News and Screaming Blue Messiahs). They supported The Cure in 1982, as well as touring with Echo & The Bunnymen, U2 and Peter Gabriel, but somehow, despite all those support slots and all the money Mercury threw at them, they never once troubled the charts.

After releasing three albums, they split up in 1987.

Their former drummer, Korda Marshall went on to become a music industry bigwig, working as an A&R man, launching the faux-indie labels Anxious, Mushroom and Infectious, working with bands including Psychic TV, The Primitives, Pop Will Eat Itself, Curve and Garbage, as well as serving on the board of the British Phonographic Institute.

Zerra One's main relevance to The Cure is their presence on the **Fourteen Explicit Moments** tour. They took part in the mass jam onstage at the final date in Brussels on 11 June 1982, and their backing vocals can be heard on 'The Cure Are Dead'. Subsequently singer Paul Bell, who had been **Lol Tolhurst**'s drinking partner on the tour, nearly formed a breakaway band with Lol. (A Bell/Tolhurst project was recorded in 1983, but never released.)

And they had the decency to begin with a 'Z'.

Zomba

Zomba was a music company formed in London in 1975 by the South African duo Clive Calder and Ralph Simon. It was an umbrella company with interests in many areas of the music industry. Its **labels** included Jive, Silvertone, LaFace and Music for Nations, and it was instrumental in developing the careers of acts as varied A Tribe Called Quest, The Stone Roses, TLC and Cradle of Filth before it was eventually bought out by BMG/RCA and then Sony/Universal.

Zomba's original headquarters on Willesden High Road were a mere one-minute walk from **Morgan Studios**, where The Cure recorded *Three Imaginary Boys* in 1979. Within a year of The Cure finishing the album, Morgan inevitably fell into the gravitational pull of its powerful neighbour, and owner Barry Morgan sold two of the four studios to Zomba in 1980.

Zomba also had a music publishing wing (any ska fan of the early eighties will have been familiar with the credit 'The Beat/Zomba'), as well as publishing **books**. Zomba Books, in conjunction with **Fiction**, published the official Cure biography *Ten Imaginary Years* in 1987: the 'Z' on the spine is its logo.

Zoo

Zoo were the resident dance troupe on the British music show *Top of the Pops* (see **TV, The Cure appear on**), following in the questionably choreographed footsteps of Pan's People, Ruby Flipper and Legs & Co. The troupe is routinely disparaged by fans of the show for its often inappropriately cheery and facile moves which served to highlight the dancers' egos rather than enhance the song: the popular TOTP-based podcast *Chart Music* routinely refers to its members as 'Zoo wankers', and the collective as 'City Farm' (i.e. not even worthy of being called a zoo). In their handful of *Top of the Pops* appearances during Zoo's reign of terpsichorean terror, between 1981–1983, The Cure mercifully managed to avoid being danced to by the troupe.

Zoo alumni include MTV presenter 'Downtown' Julie Brown, pop-soul singer Haywoode and, most importantly, Jeanette Landray, the dancer with distinctive spiked blonde hair who was recruited to sing lead vocals with **The Glove** due to Robert Smith being contractually forbidden to do so.

Landray and Smith did once appear on the same episode of *Top of the Pops* on 21 July 1983, when Zoo's dance routine to 'The Crown' by Gary Byrd & The GB Experience was directly followed by The Cure performing '**The Walk**'. However, this is not how they met. (They were already well-acquainted, and the Glove's album *Blue Sunshine* would follow only a month later.) Landray was known to **Steven Severin** because she had once been the girlfriend of **Siouxsie And The Banshees** drummer Budgie.

Zoology

Tenuous? You might think so. But an interest in the creaturely runs throughout The Cure's oeuvre. Almost as often as he uses imagery involving dreams and drowning, Robert Smith reaches for metaphors deriving from the animal kingdom in his songs.

Titular examples include (but are probably not limited to) 'Like Cockatoos', 'Bananafishbones', 'Birdmad Girl', '**The Caterpillar**', '**The Lovecats**', 'Piggy in the Mirror', 'Shake Dog Shake', '**All Cats Are Grey**', 'Foxy Lady', 'The Snakepit', 'Where The Birds Always Sing' and 'The Dragon Hunters Song' (hey,

Komodo dragons are real). And that's just with The Cure. With **Siouxsie And The Banshees** he helped create the album *Hyæna*, the single '**Swimming Horses**', and the B-side 'Throw Them To The Lions'. The debut single by Cure/Banshees supergroup **The Glove**, whose singer was a dancer with a troupe called Zoo, was '**Like An Animal**'. Robert's collaboration with Faithless gave rise to 'Spiders, Crocodiles & Kryptonite'. And 'Meathook' is where they end up.

Cats, in particular, are everywhere. 'The Lovecats' goes without saying, but it is joined by feline references such as 'Fires outside in the sky looked as perfect as cats' ('**Let's Go To Bed**') and 'When I see you kitten as cats' ('**High**').

Buried in The Cure's lyrics, you'll also find lines like 'the spider man is having me for dinner tonight' ('**Lullaby**') and 'Oh, I should be a polar bear' ('Birdmad Girl'). Of the latter, Robert said 'The polar bear was a symbol (zoo-wise) for me of insensible savagery, caged to be stared at. Or something like that . . .'

On '**Fascination Street**' B-side 'Out Of Mind' he compares his own mental state to zoochosis:

> I've been up for days
> And I feel like a menagerie
> I'm scratching till I bleed
> And I keep on seeing imaginary lemurs in the street

Later, he sings 'I feel like a laboratory rat inside a maze'. On '**The Only One**' B-side 'NY Trip' he goes into multi-species overdrive, with 'whales swimming down the track, spitting monkey tails' and 'vultures on the line'.

Animal references in videos were not restricted to songs which are about animals. 'The Caterpillar', naturally, featured cocoons, caterpillars and butterflies, and there are further butterflies in the 'Strange Attraction' video. But there's also the recurring (Tim) Papal motif of animal suits, such as the bear in '**Pictures Of You**', the bear and the bumblebee in '**Why Can't I Be You?**', and a whole aquarium's worth of undersea creatures in 'Close To Me (Remix)'.

Want to get really obscure? The run-out groove of *The Head On The Door* had a reference to how often tigers have sex. And a rejected working title for a song on *Disintegration* was 'Tale Of The Lonely Badger'.

Robert once told the press he took a live lamb on tour, telling *Smash Hits* that he once found hotel staff feeding it. In *Sounds* he claimed it was a present from a fan and now lived on his brother's farm in Wales: 'I went to see it recently. It didn't remember me at all.' This tale should be taken with a huge pinch of salt (or mint sauce), and is perhaps a satire of the true story that fellow **Chris Parry/Polydor** signings The Jam (from quite-nearby Woking) had taken an actual lion cub on tour. It's actually **Pearl Thompson** who has the most legitimate claim to animal husbandry, having once lived on a farm with a collection of pigs, fish and rabbits. That said, Robert's fascination with fauna did once extend to climbing into Edinburgh Zoo at midnight.

With all this animalistic content, it wasn't too difficult for Chris Packham, presenter of the BBC's nature series *Springwatch*, to namedrop Cure songs in the show. Once you notice it, it's everywhere. Noah and Doctor Doolittle have got nothing on these guys. If you fed The Cure's lyrics into a random lyric generator and asked it to create an artificial Cure song, the AI would probably churn out something like 'I dreamed of drowning cats in the zoo at midnight' as the opening line.

And zat's all, folks.

Acknowledgements

To my wife Jayney, for her unlimited support and encouragement, and for keeping me cheerful and, frankly, alive during this whole process, I give my undying gratitude and love.

For their help, advice, and patience under sometimes unreasonable duress, very special thanks go out to Lee Brackstone and his colleagues at White Rabbit: Georgia Goodall, Sophie Nevrkla, Ellie Freedman, Tom Noble, Paul Bulos and Krystyna Kujawinska. Thanks also to Carrie Thornton at HarperCollins in New York and all other partner publishers around the world – I hope the end product repays your faith. Thanks to Kasimiira Kontio at Atelier PR for kicking up a storm of publicity. For helping to make this book look as great as it does, thank you to photographer Richard Bellia and illustrator Andy Vella. And thank you to my agent Matthew Hamilton for making it possible in the first place. We got there in the end . . .

Thanks also to June and the Welshes, Rob and the Summerses, Nicola and Mike Fleet, and all the rest of my extended family. I am eternally grateful to my mother Christine, who didn't live to see this book published, but who was always intensely proud of my achievements. And thanks to our friends Jade and Alan, Sharron and Julia, Richey and Sarah, Neil, Tony, and anyone else who kept us sane during lockdown, when much of *Curepedia* was being written.

I owe a significant debt of gratitude to everyone who's gone before me in gathering the world's assembled knowledge about The Cure. This includes websites like A Foolish Arrangement, Chain of Flowers, The Cure Concerts Guide, The Cure Database, Pictures Of You, The Curetc, Stiff As Toys and Tall As Men, The Cure Muse, The Cure News Archive and Curefans. It also includes previous Cure authors like Steve Sutherland, Ian Gittins, Jeff Apter, Daren Butler, Richard Carman and Simon Goddard. And it includes every other journalist who has interviewed, reviewed, photographed or reported on The Cure, especially in their earliest days, when I was still in short (or, at least, flared) trousers. Appreciative nod to the excellent archive Rock's Backpages for hosting many examples thereof. Without your invaluable groundwork, this book would just be me going on about what I reckon for two hundred pages, and nobody's buying that.

For helping in miscellaneous ways big and small, sometimes without knowing it, thanks to Daryl Bamonte, Stuart Braithwaite, Tim Burgess, The Cureheads, John Doran and Luke Turner at the *Quietus*, Carl Gosling, Elis James, Marion Little, Al Needham, Debora Parr, Alexis Petridis, Tim Pope, Ned Raggett, Aileen Regan, Jamie Reid, Cathy Rentzenbrink, Tom Sheehan, Jake Shillingford, the Social, Julian Stockton, Tivoli Vredenburg, Robin Turner, anyone who threw me a bit of work to keep me going (including BIMM, LCCM, *Record Collector* and *Sparks*), and all the regulars at Spellbound in Brighton.

For creating a magnificently rich body of work in which it has been an absolute pleasure to lose myself for a couple of years (and a lifetime), I offer enormous thanks and respect to Robert Smith, Lol Tolhurst, Michael Dempsey, Simon Gallup, Matthieu Hartley, Phil Thornalley, Pearl Thompson, Andy Anderson, Boris Williams, Perry Bamonte, Jason Cooper, Reeves Gabrels, Siouxsie Sioux, Steve Severin, Budgie, Jeanette Landray, Chris Parry, Mike Hedges, David M. Allen, and every other player and producer in this story.

And thank you for reading this book. I hope you enjoy it.

The Cure Songwriting Credits

'A Forest', (The Cure), Lyrics by Robert Smith
'A Letter To Elise', (The Cure), Lyrics by Robert Smith
'A Night Like This', (The Cure), Lyrics by Robert Smith
'Alt.end', (The Cure), Lyrics by Robert Smith
'Out Of This World', (The Cure), Lyrics by Robert Smith
'Where The Birds Always Sing', (The Cure), Lyrics by Robert Smith
'Maybe Someday', (The Cure), Lyrics by Robert Smith
'Coming Up', (The Cure), Lyrics by Robert Smith
'The Last Day Of Summer', (The Cure), Lyrics by Robert Smith
'There Is No If', (The Cure), Lyrics by Robert Smith
'The Loudest Sound', (The Cure), Lyrics by Robert Smith
'Spilt Milk', (The Cure), Lyrics by Robert Smith
'Looking Glass Girl', (The Glove), Lyrics by Steve Severin
'Sex-Eye-Make-Up', (The Glove), Lyrics by Robert Smith
'Mr Alphabet Says', (The Glove), Lyrics by Steve Severin
'Orgy', (The Glove), Lyrics by Steve Severin
'A Perfect Murder', (The Glove), Lyrics by Robert Smith
'The Blood', (The Cure), Lyrics by Robert Smith
'This Twilight Garden', (The Cure), Lyrics by Robert Smith
'Happy Birthday', (The Cure), (*presumed by Robert Smith*)
'I Dig You', (Cult Hero), Lyrics by Robert Smith
'Labyrinth', (The Cure), Lyrics by Robert Smith
'Truth, Goodness and Beauty', (The Cure), Lyrics by Robert Smith
'Anniversary', (The Cure), Lyrics by Robert Smith
'(I Don't Know What's Going) On', (The Cure), Lyrics by Robert Smith
'Fake', (The Cure), Lyrics by Robert Smith
'This Morning', (The Cure), Lyrics by Robert Smith
'Cut Here', (The Cure), Lyrics by Robert Smith
'Dazzle', (Siouxsie And The Banshees), Written by Siouxsie And The Banshees
'Throw Them To The Lions' (Siouxsie And The Banshees), Written By Siouxsie And The Banshees
'Desperate Journalist In Ongoing Meaningful Review Situation', (The Cure), (*presumed Smith*)
'Plainsong', (The Cure), Lyrics by Robert Smith
'Closedown', (The Cure), Lyrics by Robert Smith
'Last Dance', (The Cure), Lyrics by Robert Smith
'Disintegration', (The Cure), Lyrics by Robert Smith
'Close To Me', (The Cure), Lyrics by Robert Smith
'Kyoto Song', (The Cure), Lyrics by Robert Smith
'The Drowning Man', (The Cure), Lyrics by Robert Smith
'Just Like Heaven', (The Cure), Lyrics by Robert Smith
'Pictures Of You', (The Cure), Lyrics by Robert Smith
'NY Trip', (The Cure), Lyrics by Robert Smith
'Down Under', (The Cure), Lyrics by Robert Smith
'How Not To Drown', (Chvrches ft Robert Smith), Written by Cook, Doherty, Mayberry, Smith
'Numb', (The Cure), Lyrics by Robert Smith
'The End Of The World', (The Cure), Lyrics by Robert Smith
'This Morning', (The Cure), Lyrics by Robert Smith
'The Reason Why', (The Cure), Lyrics by Robert Smith
'The Real Snow White', (The Cure), Lyrics by Robert Smith
'The Hungry Ghost', (The Cure), Lyrics by Robert Smith
'This. Here and Now. With You', (The Cure), Lyrics by Robert Smith
'It's Over', (The Cure), Lyrics by Robert Smith
'The Holy Hour', (The Cure), Lyrics by Robert Smith
'Other Voices', (The Cure), Lyrics by Robert Smith
'The Funeral Party', (The Cure), Lyrics by Robert Smith
'Faith', (The Cure), Lyrics by Robert Smith
'Fascination Street', (The Cure), Lyrics by Robert Smith
'Lament', (The Cure), Lyrics by Robert Smith
'Gone!', (The Cure), Lyrics by Robert Smith
'Painted Bird', (Siouxsie And The Banshees), Lyrics by Sioux
'The Hanging Garden', (The Cure), Lyrics by Robert Smith
'High', (The Cure), Lyrics by Robert Smith
'Belladonna', (Siouxsie And The Banshees), Lyrics by Steve Severin
'Pointing Bone', (Siouxsie And The Banshees), Lyrics by Steve Severin
'In Between Days', (The Cure), Lyrics by Robert Smith
'Jumping Someone Else's Train', (The Cure), Lyrics by Robert Smith
'Just Say Yes', (The Cure), Lyrics by Robert Smith
'The Kiss', (The Cure), Lyrics by Robert Smith
'Catch', (The Cure), Lyrics by Robert Smith
'How Beautiful You Are', (The Cure), Lyrics by Robert Smith
'The Snakepit', (The Cure), Lyrics by Robert Smith
'Hey You!!!', (The Cure), Lyrics by Robert Smith
'Shiver And Shake', (The Cure), Lyrics by Robert Smith
'Let's Go To Bed', (The Cure), Lyrics by Robert Smith
'Like An Animal', (The Cure), Written by Severin and Smith
'Alone', (The Cure), (*presumed Robert Smith*)
'Endsong', (The Cure), (*presumed Robert Smith*)
'And Nothing Is Forever', (The Cure), (*presumed Robert Smith*)
'I Can Never Say Goodbye', (The Cure), (*presumed Robert Smith*)
'A Fragile Thing', (The Cure), (*presumed Robert Smith*)
'The Lovecats', (The Cure), Lyrics By Robert Smith
'Let's Go To Bed', (The Cure), Lyrics by Robert Smith
'High', (The Cure), Lyrics by Robert Smith
'Mr Pink Eyes', (The Cure), Lyrics by Robert Smith
'Lovesong', (The Cure), Lyrics by Robert Smith
'Just Like Heaven (Live Version), (The Cure), Lyrics by Robert Smith
'Lullaby', (The Cure), Lyrics by Robert Smith

'The Figurehead', (The Cure), Lyrics by Robert Smith
'A Short Term Effect', (The Cure), Lyrics by Robert Smith
'Bombs', (Mag/Spys), (*presumed written by Mag/Spys*)
'Mint Car', (The Cure), Lyrics by Robert Smith
'Friday I'm In Love', (The Cure), Lyrics by Robert Smith
'Yeh Yeh Yeh', (The Obtainers), (*presumed written by The Obtainers*)
'Pussy Wussy', (The Obtainers), (*presumed written by The Obtainers*)
'One Hundred Years', (The Cure), Lyrics by Robert Smith
'The Only One', (The Cure), Lyrics by Robert Smith
'The Perfect Boy', (The Cure), Lyrics by Robert Smith
'Pictures Of You', (The Cure), Lyrics by Robert Smith
'Snow In Summer', (The Cure), Lyrics by Robert Smith
'Treasure', (The Cure), Lyrics by Robert Smith
'Us Or Them', (The Cure), Lyrics By Robert Smith
'One Hundred Years', (The Cure), Lyrics by Robert Smith
'Siamese Twins', (The Cure), Lyrics by Robert Smith
'The Figurehead', (The Cure), Lyrics by Robert Smith
'Pornography', (The Cure), Lyrics by Robert Smith
'Primary', (The Cure), Lyrics by Robert Smith
'Punish Me With Kisses', (The Glove), Lyrics by Severin/Smith
'Step Into The Light', (The Cure), (*presumed Robert Smith*)
'Close To Me', (The Cure), Lyrics by Robert Smith
'In Your House', (The Cure), Lyrics by Robert Smith
'M', (The Cure), Lyrics by Robert Smith
'Object', (The Cure), Lyrics by Robert Smith
'It's Not You', (The Cure), Lyrics by Robert Smith
'Siamese Twins', (The Cure), Lyrics by Robert Smith
'Let's Go To Bed', (The Cure), Lyrics by Robert Smith
'Sex-Eye-Make-Up', (The Glove), Written by Severin/Smith
'Orgy', (The Glove), Written by Severin/Smith
'Stop Dead', (The Cure), Lyrics by Robert Smith
'Catch', (The Cure), Lyrics by Robert Smith
'Just Like Heaven', (The Cure), Lyrics by Robert Smith
'All I Want', (The Cure), Lyrics by Robert Smith
'Lullaby', (The Cure), Lyrics by Robert Smith
'Doing The Unstuck', (The Cure), Lyrics by Robert Smith
'Wendy Time', (The Cure), Lyrics by Robert Smith
'The 13th', (The Cure), Lyrics by Robert Smith
'Want', (The Cure), Lyrics by Robert Smith
'Round And Round And Round And Round', (The Cure), Lyrics by Robert Smith
'Club America', (The Cure), Lyrics by Robert Smith
'The Real Snow White', (The Cure), Lyrics by Robert Smith
'The Only One', (The Cure), Lyrics by Robert Smith
'Just Like Heaven', (The Cure), Lyrics by Robert Smith
'Strange Attraction', (The Cure), Lyrics by Rober Smith
'Swimming Horses', (Siouxsie And The Banshees), Written by Siouxsie And The Banshees
'The 13th', (The Cure), Lyrics by Robert Smith
'Taking Off', (The Cure), Lyrics by Robert Smith
'Why Can't I Be Me?', (The Cure), Lyrics by Robert Smith
'Object', (The Cure), Lyrics by Robert Smith
'Meathook', (The Cure), Lyrics by Robert Smith
'So What?', (The Cure), Lyrics by Robert Smith
'Fire In Cairo', (The Cure), Lyrics by Robert Smith
'It's Not You', (The Cure), Lyrics by Robert Smith
'Shake Dog Shake', (The Cure), Lyrics by Robert Smith
'Wailing Wall', (The Cure), Lyrics by Robert Smith
'Piggy In The Mirror', (The Cure), Lyrics by Robert Smith
'Bananafishbones', (The Cure), Lyrics by Robert Smith
'The Top', (The Cure), Lyrics by Robert Smith
'Plainsong', (The Cure), Lyrics by Robert Smith
'Why Can't I Be You?', (The Cure), Lyrics by Robert Smith
'Want', (The Cure), Lyrics by Robert Smith
'Club America', (The Cure), Lyrics by Robert Smith
'This Is A Lie', (The Cure), Lyrics by Robert Smith
'Let's Go To Bed', (The Cure), Lyrics by Robert Smith
'Life Becoming A Landslide', (Manic Street Preachers), Lyrics by Nicky Wire and Richey James
'Jupiter Crash', (The Cure), Lyrics by Robert Smith
'Round And Round And Round And Round', (The Cure), Lyrics by Robert Smith
'Return', (The Cure), Lyrics by Robert Smith
'Bare', (The Cure), Lyrics by Robert Smith
'Open', (The Cure), Lyrics by Robert Smith
'From The Edge Of The Deep Green Sea', (The Cure), Lyrics by Robert Smith
'Wendy Time', (The Cure), Lyrics by Robert Smith
'Doing The Unstuck', (The Cure), Lyrics by Robert Smith
'Trust', (The Cure), Lyrics by Robert Smith
'Cut', (The Cure), Lyrics By Robert Smith
'To Wish Impossible Things', (The Cure), Lyrics by Robert Smith
'End', (The Cure), Lyrics by Robert Smith
'Wrong Number', (The Cure), Lyrics by Robert Smith
'Let's Go To Bed', (The Cure), Lyrics by Robert Smith
'High', (The Cure), Lyrics by Robert Smith
'Lullaby', (The Cure), Lyrics by Robert Smith
'Bird Mad Girl', (The Cure), Lyrics by Robert Smith
'Out Of Mind', (The Cure), Lyrics by Robert Smith
'NY Trip', (The Cure), Lyrics by Robert Smith

Author Biography

Simon Price is an award-winning Welsh music journalist who worked for *Melody Maker* for nine years and the *Independent on Sunday* for twelve, and wrote the bestselling rock biography *Everything (A Book About Manic Street Preachers)*. But that was almost a quarter of a century ago, and he didn't want to be a one-hit wonder.

At the age of fourteen, Simon tore out a magazine diary article about one week in Robert Smith's life, folded the page up, put it into his blazer pocket and took it to school every day because he found the sheer strangeness inspiring. When he was sixteen, he persuaded his mother to knit him an oversized baggy black mohair jumper, and bought himself an eyeliner pencil. When he was eighteen and working in a pub, he was wearing his treasured T-shirt of *The Top* when a bar brawl broke out, and it was ruined by blood, booze and broken glass. By the time he was twenty and studying in Paris, he looked like such a stereotypical Cure fan that passers-by would sing 'The Lovecats' and 'Just Like Heaven' at him in the street (even though he was probably more into the Banshees). He coveted Simon Gallup's hair circa *The Head On The Door*, though these days he covets any hair at all. He has seen The Cure a number of times since the eighties, but he can't remember what that number is. His three favourite Cure albums are *Pornography, Faith* and *Kiss Me, Kiss Me, Kiss Me*.

A member of The Cure once told him to 'cheer up'. He thought this was a bit rich, all things considered.